LONGMAN LINGUISTICS LIBRARY

ENGLISH HISTORICAL SYNTAX

LONGMAN LINGUISTICS LIBRARY

General editors
R. H. Robins, University of London
Martin Harris, University of Manchester
Geoffrey Horrocks, University of
Cambridge

A Short History of Linguistics
Third Edition
R. H. ROBINS

Structural Aspects of Language
Change
JAMES M. ANDERSON

Text and Context
Explorations in the Semantics and
Pragmatics of Discourse
TEUN A. VAN DIJK

Introduction to Text Linguistics
ROBERT-ALAIN DE BEAUGRANDE
AND WOLFGANG ULRICH
DRESSLER

Spoken Discourse
A Model for Analysis
WILLIS EDMONDSON

Psycholinguistics
Language, Mind, and World
DANNY D. STEINBERG

Dialectology
W. N. FRANCIS

Principles of Pragmatics
GEOFFREY N. LEECH

Generative Grammar
GEOFFREY HORROCKS

Norms of Language
Theoretical and Practical Aspects
RENATE BARTSCH

The English Verb
Second Edition
F. R. PALMER

A History of American English
J. L. DILLARD

Historical Linguistics
EDITED BY CHARLES JONES

Pidgin and Creole Languages
SUZANNE ROMAINE

General Linguistics
An Introductory Survey
Fourth Edition
R. H. ROBINS

A History of English Phonology
CHARLES JONES

Generative and Non-linear
Phonology
JACQUES DURAND

Modality and the English Modals
Second Edition
F. R. PALMER

Semiotics and Linguistics
YISHAI TOBIN

Multilingualism in the British
Isles I: the Older Mother
Tongues and Europe
EDITED BY SAFDER ALLADINA
AND VIV EDWARDS

Multilingualism in the British
Isles II: Africa, Asia and
the Middle East
EDITED BY SAFDER ALLADINA
AND VIV EDWARDS

Dialects of English
Studies in Grammatical Variation
EDITED BY PETER TRUDGILL AND
J. K. CHAMBERS

Introduction to Bilingualism
CHARLOTTE HOFFMANN

Verb and Noun Number in English:
A functional explanation
WALLIS REID

English in Africa
JOSEF S. SCHMIED

Linguistic Theory
The Discourse of Fundamental Works
ROBERT DE BEAUGRANDE

English Historical Syntax
Verbal Constructions
DAVID DENISON

English Historical Syntax:

Verbal Constructions

David Denison

LONGMAN
LONDON AND NEW YORK

Longman Group UK Limited
Longman House, Burnt Mill,
Harlow, Essex CM20 2JE, England
and Associated Companies throughout the world.

Published in the United States of America
by Longman Publishing, New York

First published 1993

ISBN 0–582–216206 CSD
ISBN 0–582–291399 PPR

British Library Cataloguing-in-Publication Data
A catalogue record for this book is
available from the British Library

Library of Congress Cataloging-in-Publication Data
Denison, David, 1950–
    English historical syntax : verbal constructions / David Denison.
        p. c.m. — (Longman linguistics library)
    Includes bibliographical references and index.
    ISBN 0–582–29139–9 Ppr. 0–582–216206 Csd.
    1. English language—Syntax. 2. English language—Grammar,
Historical. I. Title. II. Series.
PE1361.D46 1993
425—dc20   92–20598
                                                                           CIP

Transferred to digital printing 2004

Set by 8M in 10/11 pt Times
Produced by Longman Singapore Publishers (Pte) Ltd.

Printed and bound by Antony Rowe Ltd, Eastbourne

Contents

Preface   ix
Acknowledgements   xii
Abbreviations   xiii

PART I: GROUNDWORK

   Overview   1
1 Introduction   3
    1.1 Data collection   3
    1.2 Importance of context   4
    1.3 Background knowledge   4
    1.4 Sources of information   5
2 Background   8
    2.1 Prehistory   8
    2.2 Periods of English   8
    2.3 A sketch of Old English   9
    2.4 A sketch of Middle English   10
    2.5 A sketch of Modern English   12
    2.6 Further reading   14
3 Nominal morphology   16
    3.1 Old English   16
    3.2 Middle English   20
    3.3 Modern English   22
    3.4 Question for further research   23

PART II: WORD ORDER

   Overview   25
4 Word order   27
    4.1 Introductory remarks   27
    4.2 The data   30
    4.3 Descriptions and explanations   30
    4.4 Synchronic accounts in non-generative linguistics   31

4.5   Synchronic accounts within generative linguistics   35
4.6   Diachronic, non-generative explanations   39
4.7   Diachronic accounts within generative linguistics   50
4.8   Ramifications   55
4.9   Questions for discussion or further research   55

PART III: SUBJECT AND VERB PHRASE

Overview   59
5   Impersonals   61
    5.1   The problem   61
    5.2   The data   63
    5.3   Explanations   73
    5.4   Explanations involving reanalysis   74
    5.5   An explanation without reanalysis   80
    5.6   Explanations involving semantics-based syntax   83
    5.7   Other syntactic approaches   87
    5.8   Mainly descriptive accounts   91
    5.9   Dummy *it*   97
    5.10 Questions for discussion or further research   99
6   Dative Movement and the indirect passive   103
    6.1   The problem   103
    6.2   The data   104
    6.3   Explanations in non-generative linguistics   112
    6.4   Questions for discussion or further research   119
7   The prepositional passive   124
    7.1   The problem   124
    7.2   The data   125
    7.3   Explanations in non-generative linguistics   134
    7.4   Explanations in generative linguistics   144
    7.5   The complex prepositional passive   153
    7.6   Indirect and prepositional passives   155
    7.7   Questions for discussion or further research   159

PART IV: COMPLEX COMPLEMENTATION

Overview   163
8   VOSI and V+I (Control verbs)   165
    8.1   The problem   165
    8.2   VOSI   166
    8.3   V+I   170
    8.4   The data   172
    8.5   Explanations   192
    8.6   Philological and semantics-based accounts   193
    8.7   Accounts in generative syntax   197
    8.8   Text-based, structural accounts   201
    8.9   Infinitive ± *to*   213

   8.10 Questions for discussion or further research   215
9 Subject raising   218
   9.1   The problem   218
   9.2   Raising   220
   9.3   The data   220
   9.4   Explanations   242
   9.5   Questions for discussion or further research   250

PART V: AUXILIARIES

   Overview   253
10 Origins of periphrastic DO   255
   10.1   The problem   255
   10.2   The data   256
   10.3   Explanations in non-generative linguistics   274
   10.4   Explanations in generative linguistics   285
   10.5   Questions for discussion or further research   287
11 Modals and related auxiliaries   292
   11.1   The problem   292
   11.2   Modals in Present-day English   292
   11.3   The data   295
   11.4   Explanations   325
   11.5   Questions for discussion or further research   337
12 Perfect   340
   12.1   The problem   340
   12.2   The HAVE perfect   340
   12.3   Other HAVE + past participle constructions   341
   12.4   The BE perfect   344
   12.5   Data on the HAVE perfect   346
   12.6   Data on the BE perfect   358
   12.7   Explanations   364
   12.8   Questions for discussion or further research   368
13 Progressive   371
   13.1   The problem   371
   13.2   Progressives versus related constructions   372
   13.3   The data   380
   13.4   Explanations of the origins of the OE progressive   397
   13.5   Explanations for the ME and ModE progressive   400
   13.6   Explanations for the 'passival' progressive   408
   13.7   Questions for discussion or further research   410
14 Passive   413
   14.1   The problem   413
   14.2   The data   416
   14.3   Explanations   437
   14.4   Questions for discussion or further research   443
15 Multiple auxiliaries, regulation of DO   446
   15.1   The problems   446
   15.2   The data   446

15.3 Explanations of history of auxiliary category   452
15.4 Explanations of regulation of DO   457
15.5 Questions for discussion or further research   468
15.6 Envoi   469

PART VI: BIBLIOGRAPHY AND INDEXES
Glossary of technical terms   475
Secondary sources (references) (indexed)   482
Primary sources (texts) (indexed)   502
Index of verbs in examples   519
General index   526

This book is dedicated to the memory of my parents.

Preface

Historical syntax

Historical syntax has attracted increasing attention over the last fifteen years or so. When the modern science of language started to blossom in the nineteenth century the study of historical change – nowadays often called **diachronic** linguistics – was well to the fore, but with phonology, morphology and lexis central to linguistic theory and syntax treated only descriptively if at all. In transformational generative grammar of the 1950s and 1960s, on the other hand, syntax had a central role but now little attention was paid to language change: most theoreticians concentrated on the study of timeless states of a language, **synchronic** linguistics. The renewed interest in historical change is beginning to bring these two traditions together. The explicitness of current linguistic theory should provide better explanations of historical change, while historical facts can play their part in testing and shaping linguistic theory – at least such have been the intentions behind much recent work. In synchronic generative linguistics the predominant source of data for English-speaking linguists has been Modern English, and English is a natural field of study in historical syntax too because of its conveniently long recorded history. Hence this book and the research it presents. It provides materials for the study of some of the central topics in English historical syntax, both data and analysis.

Methodology

For each of the topics discussed there is a critical review of work that has been published on the topic in both the philological and linguistic traditions, with the results of my own research incorporated. I do not attempt to acknowledge and review everything ever written on a given topic. My approach is eclectic, often with a straightforward use of traditional terminology, in order to make the book accessible to people working within any of the formal or informal frameworks current today. Indeed I shall often

compare different approaches to the same material. No linguistic discussion
is ever wholly value- or theory-free, of course, but my choice of an eclectic
approach is deliberate. Linguistic theory is a fickle thing, and close
identification with one version of one theory makes for a monograph with a
great deal of technical, theory-bound argument whose usefulness may be
very short-lived. In any case, no one existing theory gives a satisfactory
account of every aspect of syntactic change.

What about the division of historical syntax into topics? Synchronic syntax
is a seamless whole, and discussion of, say, auxiliary verbs will eventually
have to be integrated with, say, considerations of sentence word order in the
language of a particular epoch: it is artificial to keep them separate.[1] From
complete synchronic grammars of different epochs we might then move on
to diachronic changes linking them. But we have to begin somewhere. Short
of presenting a complete cut-and-dried analysis in a single theoretical
framework, that ideal methodology would have to be compromised in all
sorts of ways, certainly in a book of this size, and I have chosen what I think
is a more useful way in. My procedure in this book is to isolate topics which
seem to form relatively coherent and self-contained fragments of syntax, to
discuss them individually on a historical basis, and to nest the topics in such
a way as to permit – indeed encourage – their integration into larger
domains of English syntax. (For obvious practical reasons the selection of
topics is limited. The majority concern Old and Middle English data since it
is during Middle English that syntax changes most.)

But this diachronic approach raises another problem: is it legitimate to
trace a particular syntactic pattern over a period of time? After all, as
Lightfoot puts it, 'there is no clear basis for saying that a certain sentence of
Old English "corresponds" to some sentence of Middle English' (1979: 8).
Nevertheless, that is what we shall do, and what even the greatest
methodological purists do too. The data *must* be sliced up in various ways in
order to be dealt with at all, and it is standard practice to gather examples of
a given construction from different texts and periods in order to discuss such
matters as the date of first appearance and reason for adoption by the
language. The practice is all right just as long as we bear in mind that at
different periods a construction may have a different relation to the rest of
the grammar.

Using this book

To the extent that the book matches my original intentions for it, it should
serve three purposes. It is a source of data for researchers on the history of
English syntax. It is intended also as a contribution to research. And for
students it is a textbook on what has been found out so far.

How it is used as a teaching text will naturally depend on both teacher
and students. Each chapter is designed to give an overview of some problem
and a presentation of different solutions which encourages comparison and
criticism. Where appropriate it concludes with some open-ended questions
for discussion. The commentaries are intended to help less experienced

students to work through some demanding recent research publications, and to enable more advanced classes to 'cover the ground' more efficiently.

There is more material in this book than can be covered thoroughly in a typical undergraduate course, and students and teachers may well wish to pick and mix a selection of chapters. (Researchers will, of course, home straight in on their own interests.) The division into parts and chapters is intended to make a selective approach practical. Not that the different topics do not have links with one another: of course they do. To some extent this follows merely from the truism that language – and most of all syntax – is a system *où tout se tient*, where everything hangs together. In part, though, it is because topics have been deliberately chosen and arranged to bring out links.

Sections marked with an asterisk deal with more advanced and/or more technical aspects of a topic and can be omitted by undergraduate readers. Technical terms which appear in **bold italics** at their first appearance in a chapter are explained in the Glossary. Students will probably need to have had some prior introduction to Old and/or Middle English, though all examples in the text are fully glossed.

Here is one approach, tested on early versions of the material, which has been used successfully with seminar groups of three to ten students. A topic is selected for a future meeting, and everyone reads the appropriate chapter. Certain members of the group are also assigned individual tasks, perhaps the close reading of one or two important articles, or (in more advanced groups) actual research on some aspect of the topic. These members introduce the discussion with a presentation of their findings. The chapter will have served its purpose if everyone in the group is equipped to contribute usefully to discussion and stimulated to explore the topic further. 'Doing' English historical syntax should be an exploration.

Organisation

The book is laid out as follows. Part I, Groundwork, covers background knowledge and nominal morphology, which are of pervasive importance to the topics of the remainder of the book. So too is Part II, Word Order, where the syntax proper begins. Part III, Subject and Verb Phrase, deals with constructions where the relationship between a verb and its (mostly) nominal **arguments** has altered. Part IV, Complex Complementation, covers constructions in which one argument of a verb itself contains another verb – in other words, structures involving the embedding of one clause within another. Part V, Auxiliaries, comes next because most uses of auxiliaries derive historically from clause embedding constructions. These topics by no means exhaust the subject of English historical syntax – of course not! – but they form a coherent set which includes much of the most interesting material studied to date. And the writing of this book had to stop somewhere.

Part VI gathers together the reference material, including a glossary of technical terms, indexed lists of primary and secondary sources, an index of verbs in citations, and a general index.

Acknowledgements

The writing of this book has taken much longer than intended or expected. I have been given generous help by friends, colleagues and students (non-discrete groups, these), some of it noted at the appropriate places. I must thank above all Wim van der Wurff for detailed comments on an earlier draft of Chapters 1–7 and 9 (part), and Elizabeth Traugott for her reading of the near-final version of the whole book, as well as Fran Colman (1–3), Willem Koopman (4), Cindy Allen (5 and part of 6), and Linda Roberts (7). I have also benefited from points raised by Ans van Kemenade (1–7), Bob Stockwell (4), Pat Poussa (10), Laurel Brinton (12), Mats Rydén (12), Jean Aitchison, and several generations of students from Amsterdam, Manchester and the University of British Columbia (Vancouver), and from the literary expertise of my departmental colleagues. Nigel Vincent at Manchester and Guy Carden and Michael Rochemont at UBC filled me in on so-called empty categories. Martin Harris has given support and good advice throughout. Over the years in the departmental office at Manchester, Shelagh Aston and Maxine Powell have saved me from many an anxiety attack, while Mary Syner has in addition given me generous and invaluable assistance with checking of examples. In the last stages Chris Jordan of Epson Canada came up with the timely loan of a printer, and UBC English Department let me get on with checking and printing out.

None of them are to be held responsible for the book as it now is, but without their help it would have been much the poorer.

And my family have seen far less of me than is right. Biz, Alice and Rosie: Thank you for just about putting up with (and without) me.

David Denison

Note

1. On the other hand, it is also artificial to exclude the time dimension from an account of, say, Present-day English. It ignores age-related differences among speakers (see the work of Labov and followers), as well as 'frozen' features of syntax, semantics, spelling and so on which reflect the productive grammars of various past ages. Few generative linguists seem to question the legitimacy of idealising time away, however.

Abbreviations

/ /	encloses phonemic transcription
[ ]	encloses phonetic transcription
< >	encloses graphemic transcription
' '	encloses gloss (translation, meaning)
−	links items which occur together in the order indicated
+	links items which collocate together but not necessarily in that order
~	links contrasted items
*	(i) (before linguistic forms) ungrammatical or unattested (ii) (after section numbers) more technical and/or advanced material
!	(before linguistic forms) inappropriate meaning or paraphrase
1,2,3	(before SG or PL) first, second, third person
A	adjective
ACC	accusative
aci	accusative cum infinitive
AdvP	adverbial phrase
AmE	American English
AP	adjective phrase
BrE	British English
CLAN	clause and nominal construction
DAT	dative
d.o.b.	date of birth
Du.	Dutch
e	(i) (before language abbreviations) early (ii) (in GB analyses) empty node
EST	Extended Standard Theory
FEM	feminine
Fr	French
GB	Government-Binding
GEN	genitive
I,INFL	(in GB analyses) inflectional constituent
IMP	imperative
INDECL	indeclinable (no variation for case/gender/number)

INF	infinitive
INST	instrumental
l	late
Lat.	Latin
LFG	Lexical-Functional Grammar
MASC	masculine
ME	Middle English
ModE	Modern English
N	noun
NEUT	neuter
NOM	nominative
NP	noun phrase
np	lexically empty NP node
O	object
OBJ	objective
OBL	oblique
OE	Old English
ON	Old Norse
P	preposition
PA	past tense, (before PTCP) past
PDE	Present-day English
PIE	Proto-Indo-European
PL	plural
PP	prepositional phrase
Pred	predicative complement
PRES	present tense, (before PTCP) present
prt	particle
PTCP	participle
REL	relative
S	(i) (in word order) subject
	(ii) (in GB analyses) sentence/clause
	(iii) (in 'S-structure') surface
SG	singular
SUBJ	(i) (in NPs) subjective
	(ii) (in verbs) subjunctive
s.v.	Lat. *sub voce, sub verbo* 'under the/that word'
t	trace
TG	transformational-generative
V	verb
v	finite verb
V-1	verb-first order
V-2	verb-second order
V-3	'verb-third' = SVX order
V-F	verb-final order
V+I	catenative v̲erb + i̲nfinitive
VOSI	catenative v̲erb + o̲bject/s̲ubject NP + i̲nfinitive
VP	verb phrase
X	(in word order) element other than S or V

Part I

GROUNDWORK

Overview

Part I is one part which should not be skipped by the inexperienced reader, as it contains material which has a direct bearing on every single topic discussed in Parts II–V. Chapter 1 is an introduction to the study of the historical syntax of English, with a discussion of methodological issues and a survey of the reference works which are of central importance. Chapter 2, Background, is a brief survey of English linguistic history other than syntactic, intended to give a historical and more general linguistic context to the syntax at the core of the book. Chapter 3, Nominal Morphology, introduces some theoretical issues in the case syntax of the noun phrase and discusses the history of nominal inflection, though the details of paradigms in Old and Middle English are left for the handbooks. It is most important to have some grasp of the changes sketched in §§3.1.1–2, 3.2.1–2, and 3.3. These matters, apparently far removed from verbal syntax, are actually directly relevant.

Chapter 1

Introduction

1.1 Data collection

How should the data for historical syntax be collected? Scholars working on Present-day English syntax have relied on introspection or, increasingly, on data which can be retrieved by computer from a stored corpus. Both methods are convenient. Historical data are less easy to collect. Scholars have tended either to work through a chosen corpus of texts, or simply to borrow their examples from such great repositories of information as the *Oxford English Dictionary* (*OED*) (1933, 1989) or Jespersen's *Modern English Grammar* (1909–49) or Visser's *Historical Syntax* (1963–73), especially the last-named. Now Visser's work is a remarkable and quite indispensable compilation, but – probably inevitably in a one-man work of such encyclopaedic coverage – there are many examples of misquotation and misclassification. One of the aims of this book is to provide a selection of data, taken from good editions, which has been checked carefully and can be relied on as the basis for linguistic argument.[1] For this purpose I have found Visser the best secondary source of material and freely acknowledge my debt. The concordance of Venezky and Healey (1980) is also proving invaluable for research on Old English syntax.[2] In future the materials collected for the Helsinki Corpus of English Texts should provide a useful controlled sample, especially for comparing usage in different periods, genres, registers, and so on. Examples of my own finding do not come from a single systematic reading programme within a defined corpus. Many were noted in texts and linguistic discussions in the course of research on particular topics, others were come across merely by chance. In addition to the better-known texts of Old English and Middle English I have tried to look at non-literary texts, to counter the prevailing emphasis on literary styles of discourse, and at editions only recently published.

For certain approaches to historical syntax it is necessary to make much fuller collections of data than can be attempted in a book of this scope. Especially for Old English it is now possible to aspire to complete collections of instances of a given construction, while for variationist research it is necessary to have statistically valid samples of data. When the data come from different sources it may be desirable to minimise differences of genre, or alternatively such differences may be exploited as a reflection of sociolinguistic differences in a speech community. For these purposes a more systematic measure of text type is useful, on which see Biber and Finegan (1986).

1.2 Importance of context

Historical syntax done in isolation is prone to error. Often it is misleading to confine attention to a single sentence-fragment or even sentence because the syntax is partly determined by the wider discourse context – a point often neglected in formal linguistics. Then the stylistic differences among different kinds of text need to be taken into account. Is the work a translation from French or Latin, and if so, how close does it stick to the original? If it is verse, to what extent is the syntax modified by the verse form? If it is a work preserved in manuscript, how much scribal corruption or modification is there? If it is a work from, say, the nineteenth century, to what extent is the syntax modified by the strictures of prescriptive grammarians, and what is the relation between the written form and speech? We must also know whether a medieval work has been edited with the manuscript punctuation retained or at most slightly adapted, or whether modern ideas of sentence structure have been imposed. These and other such points can be summed up by saying that our data must always be interpreted in context: the context of the discourse, of the form and genre, of the register, of editorial procedures, and so on. That warning places an implicit constraint on all the discussions of historical syntax which follow.

The dating of citations raises another question. If we assume that most features of an author's syntax are fixed before adulthood, or even just that behaviour with respect to linguistic *variables* is always liable to be affected by age-grading within a population, then the birthdate of the author may be more significant than the date of publication. The use of data grouped by authors' birthdates is beginning to appear in historical studies, for example Allen (1984), Rydén and Brorström (1987), in effect taking account of one aspect of the sociolinguistic context. The point is rarely of practical relevance before the Modern English period.

1.3 Background knowledge

Readers of this book unacquainted with the general history of English ought really to use it in conjunction with one of the standard histories (see §2.6 below). In order to make the book just about self-contained, however, the following chapter contains an outline of the history of English which will give some context for the syntactic facts. Readers who know better had better skip it.

1.4   Sources of information

Rydén (1979, 1984) gives a convenient survey of what needs doing in English historical syntax, different approaches to doing it, and major sources of information.

1.4.1   Data and analysis

Apart from editions of the texts themselves, the most important source is Visser (1963–73), already mentioned in §1.1 above, a work focusing on the verb and so having little to say on the syntax of the noun phrase (NP), for example. Nevertheless almost everything else is covered, and with copious exemplification, somewhere or other in this four-volume work, and it is worth spending some time on the contents pages to get a feel for its organisation. For Old English the work of Mitchell (1985) is an essential source book. Like Visser it is essentially descriptive, based on a traditional parts-of-speech terminology, and comprehensive in its survey of secondary material. Unlike Visser it covers nearly everything (only word order is treated less than fully) and is exceptionally accurate in detail. For Middle English there is Mustanoja (1960), a less detailed, traditional work notable for its judiciousness and clarity. Although ostensibly only 'Part I', *Parts of Speech*, it contains much useful information on syntax generally. These reference works will soon be supplemented by the more manageable and modern survey chapters in *The Cambridge History of the English Language* (*CHEL*): Traugott (1992) on Old English and Fischer (1992a) on Middle English, and later Rissanen (in prep.) on early Modern English and Denison (in prep.) on late Modern English. Overall surveys aimed at students include Traugott (1972), a clear account of the main lines of development within a coherent generative framework, and Schibsbye (1972–7), a descriptive treatment of all facets of the history of English, whose syntax sections are generously exemplified but not as overwhelming as Visser's.

Individual grammars and readers give more concise information. For Old English the best on syntax written in English are Mitchell and Robinson (1992) and Quirk and Wrenn (1957). For Middle English Mossé (1952) and Burrow and Turville-Petre (1992) give a simple overview, while Bennett and Smithers (1968) goes into considerable detail on certain specific points. A survey of early Modern English syntax is included in Görlach (1991), and Barber (1976) is very informative.

The great historical dictionaries of English provide a lot of information on aspects of syntax which can be related to particular lexemes. *The Oxford English Dictionary* (*OED*) covers the whole historical period but concentrates on Middle English and later. The search program available with the computer-readable version on CD-ROM should open up new possibilities for research.[3] The Michigan *Middle English Dictionary* (*MED*) has far more detail on Middle English and at the time of writing had covered the letters *A* to *S*. For Old English there will be a very full picture in the Toronto *Dictionary of Old English* (*DOE*), but it has only just begun publication with the letters *D* and *C* and will take some years to work back to *A* and then forwards through the rest of the alphabet. Meanwhile there is

'Bosworth–Toller' (Toller 1898, 1921), where you must turn first to the *Supplement* for the letters *A–G* because of the unreliability of early parts of the *Dictionary*, but first to the *Dictionary* for *H–Y*, and in both cases cross-check afterwards with the other volume. Despite its cumbersomeness and citation from obsolete editions the work remains useful and surprisingly comprehensive. Clark Hall (1960) is handier and also provides a useful index to the Old English material in *OED*, but unlike the other, large dictionaries mentioned so far it has no illustrative quotations.

1.4.2 Bibliography

Visser (1963–73) provides a comprehensive bibliography for each topic that he covers, but given the date of publication these include hardly anything from the generative school apart from some early studies of Present-day English syntax. Reasonably up-to-date bibliographies can be compiled from the classified annual lists in the *Bibliographie Linguistischer Literatur*, the *Bibliographie Linguistique/Linguistic Bibliography*, the *Annual Bibliography of English Language and Literature*, and – with the shortest time-lag – *Old English Newsletter*; from the critical surveys in *Year's Work in English Studies*; or by selective use of the *Arts and Humanities Citation Index* and *Modern Language Association Bibliography*. Of particular interest to students of English historical syntax are the bibliographies of Kennedy (1927), covering all kinds of work on English language up to 1922, and Fisiak (1987), for selective coverage of historical studies to 1983. Two complementary bibliographies provide more specialised coverage: Scheurweghs and Vorlat (1963–79) list Modern English syntax and morphology work up to 1960, while Tajima (1988) covers Old and Middle English language studies up to 1985. To the latter we must now add Mitchell (1990, and planned supplements), whose comprehensive listings of works on Old English syntax are very helpful, as too his clearing away of now-outdated scholarship. The cavalier dismissal of much 'modern linguistic' work may not accord with the interests of readers of this book, however.

1.4.3 Theory and methodology

Syntactic theory is a big industry, and new general introductions are brought out quite frequently. I have found Radford (1988) useful for some of the details of **Government-Binding (GB) theory**, while Sells (1985) provides an accessible introduction to the main features of three major theories: GB, **Lexical-Functional Grammar (LFG)** and **Generalized Phrase Structure Grammar**. Of these, GB and LFG at least have been used in historical research.

Finally there are many theoretically oriented works on historical syntax which could be recommended here. I will confine myself to three books which cover specific aspects of English historical syntax as well as offering a theoretical perspective: Lightfoot (1979), Allen (1980a), and Warner (1982). Each presents a coherent, individual approach within some version of generative grammar, and each has interesting comments on theory and methodology. Another book worth mentioning is Samuels (1972a), whose espousal of multi-factorial, functional explanations is relevant to syntax, even though most of the actual case studies belong to morphology, phonology and lexis.

Notes

1. There are nearly 1200 examples; see the list of primary sources at the end of the book for information on the texts. Word-for-word translations of Old and Middle English examples present the following difficulty:

   Should the modern rendering be the present phonetic counterpart or the old meaning? – should e.g. Old English 'sellan' be rendered 'sell' or 'give'? I am afraid I have not been consistent.

   I share the difficulty with, and borrow the confession from, Schibsbye (1972–7: I, Preface).
2. The high-frequency words concorded in Venezky and Butler (1985) will doubtless play a part in future syntactic research. The complete corpus of Old English is available in machine-readable form, and modern computer software allows sophisticated investigations to be carried out – even more readily when the words have been grammatically tagged with form-class labels, as has been done for some corpora of Modern English.
3. More so with the CD-ROM version of the *second* edition of *OED*, especially with improvements in the accompanying software.

Chapter 2

Background

2.1 Prehistory

English belongs to the Germanic branch of the Indo-European family of languages. The reconstructed language known as Proto-Germanic, spoken somewhere in what is now Scandinavia or North Germany in the last few centuries BC, is the principal ancestor of English, as also of Dutch, German, and the Scandinavian languages (except Finnish). Of Germanic languages which no longer survive the most important is Gothic, represented mainly by a bible translation of the fourth century AD which easily predates the other Germanic remains.[1] The exact relationship between the early Germanic dialects is a matter of dispute, but it can safely be said that the oldest recorded English shows greatest affinity with Frisian (itself close to Dutch), and also some evidence of a close relationship with the Scandinavian subgroup.

2.2 Periods of English

The continental Germanic tribes who settled in Britain, mainly Angles and Saxons, started their large-scale immigration in the fifth century AD. It used to be common to give the name 'Anglo-Saxon' to their language, but the term is now usually reserved for cultural or racial description and 'Old English' is the standard linguistic label for the period from which written records survive. The historical period of English is conventionally divided into three stages, **Old English** (OE), **Middle English** (ME), and **Modern** (or New) **English** (ModE). Sometimes Early Middle English (eME) and Early Modern/New English (eModE) are distinguished.

Old English	700
Middle English (eME up to 1350)	1100
Modern English (eModE up to 1700)	1500
	present

The labels are purely for descriptive convenience and the approximate transition dates (slightly different dates are given by different authorities!) do not imply sharp discontinuities in the history of the language. Note therefore that Modern English includes but is to be distinguished from Present-day English (PDE).

2.3   A sketch of Old English

The first historical, as opposed to reconstructed, stage of the language is Old English, because for the first time writing came into widespread use and was done on a durable material, parchment made from sheep- or calfskin.[2] Christian missionaries from Ireland and subsequently direct from Rome worked out a writing system for (Old) English after the sixth century AD. This system used the Latin alphabet, augmented by the symbols 'ash' <æ> (perhaps influenced by sporadic <ae> in Latin), 'eth' <ð> (a crossed *d* of uncertain origin), and 'thorn' <þ> (borrowed from the runic alphabet).[3] The letter <æ> represented a low-mid front vowel, maybe [æ] or [ɛ], while <ð> and <þ> both represented the dental fricatives [θ, ð] (which were not phonemically distinct). Phonemic vowel length was not systematically represented, but otherwise spellings were more or less phonemic. Modern editions often mark long vowels by a macron as an aid to students, e.g. *stān* 'stone', and sometimes palatalised /k, g/ (i.e. [ʧ, j]) are indicated by a dot, e.g. *ċeap* 'price' (cf. ModE *cheap*), *ġeolu* 'yellow'. Such editorial marks and indeed scribal accents are ignored in this book.

Spelling in Old English is unusually consistent for a medieval vernacular, because of the strong scribal tradition which developed. There is, however, some chronological variation, for example an early use of <th>, replacement by <þ> and <ð> for most of the period, and eventual reappearance of <th> right at the end. There is also a certain amount of dialectal variation, less noticeable in the main literary texts.

Most prose texts survive in the West Saxon dialect, that used in the south-west of England, while the poetry is mostly in a mixed dialect with Anglian (midlands and northern) characteristics – a conventional statement usually associated with phonological, morphological and lexical features. A distinction is often drawn between 'early' and 'late' West Saxon (i.e. c900 and c1000 AD), but the differences are mainly to do with vowel spellings. West Saxon is the dialect used in teaching grammars for the illustration of forms. There is some promising work on stylistic traits which can be associated with particular scriptoria in Anglo-Saxon England, but so far work on OE syntax has largely ignored dialectal variation.

As for date, apart from sporadic OE names cited in Latin texts there is little surviving in original manuscripts from before the eighth century, and major prose works only appear in the Alfredian period (c900) and subsequently. Much OE material survives only in copies made long after the original composition, in some cases well into the eME period.

Old English had a vocabulary inherited almost entirely from Germanic or formed by compounding or derivation from Germanic elements. There were

Latin loan words, mainly to do with philosophy, religion and medicine, and some compounds *calqued* on Latin forms. Word stress regularly fell on the first syllable, except for inseparable verbal prefixes. One such prefix, *ge-*, is so common and sometimes makes so little discernible contribution to the meaning of a verb that many dictionaries and glossaries ignore it in alphabetisation. The inflectional systems showed a great deal of reduction compared with Indo-European and Germanic but were still more varied and important than those of Modern English. Nominal morphology plays a major part in the history of English syntax and will be dealt with separately in the next chapter, so only the inflectional morphology of verbs will be sketched here.

The verbal system showed a clear two-term tense contrast. Let us call the two tenses 'present' and 'past', though the correlation between tense and time was little closer than it is now. For each tense there was an indicative mood (with potentially four distinct endings for 1 SG, 2 SG, 3 SG, and 1/2/3 PL) and a subjunctive (with a simple SG ~ PL distinction). For the majority of verbs the stem(s) of the past tenses were formed in one of two ways:

(A)   by vowel change as compared with the present stem: these are vowel-ablaut, 'strong' verbs
(B)   by the addition of an alveolar suffix, *-(e)-d-* (which might be realised as *-t-* after a voiceless consonant) or *-o-d-*: these are consonantal, 'weak' verbs

Thus the strong verb SINGAN 'sing' has indicative 3 SG PRES *singeð*, 3 SG PA *sang*, 3 PL PA *sungon*, while the weak verb HÆLAN 'heal' has *hælð*, *hælde*, *hældon*. Modern English preserves both of these types, though with fewer distinct stem vowels and fewer endings. OE verbs are conventionally cited by their infinitive form.[4]

2.4   A sketch of Middle English

The ME period is one of great linguistic diversity, partly because of two invasions which had taken place during the OE period but whose linguistic effects took longer to become evident.

Invasion and immigration at various times between the ninth and eleventh centuries resulted in extensive Scandinavian settlements in the north and east of the country. The surviving lexis borrowed from Old Danish and Norwegian amounts to some four hundred words in standard Modern English, perhaps two thousand in dialect. Imported features tended to appear first in the old Danelaw (the area under Scandinavian control in the Anglo-Saxon period) and spread southwards during the course of the ME period. An example is the personal pronouns *they*, *their*, and *them* (to give them their ModE spellings), which first appeared in the east midlands in the twelfth century and worked their way south one after the other over the next two centuries or so. Borrowing of pronouns also shows the intimate nature of contact, since closed-class items like pronouns are in general less readily borrowed than open-class items like nouns. Existing morphosyntactic tendencies in English were certainly reinforced by contact with Scandinavian, but it is doubtful whether any syntactic changes in English were wholly due to Scandinavian influence. It has been suggested that the mixing of two similar languages could have resulted in a kind of creole, and certainly some eME developments – acceleration in the loss of inflections and fixing of word order – are characteristic of creoles. Poussa (1982) makes an interesting case for Anglo-Scandinavian creolisation. Compare the surveys in Görlach (1986) and Thomason and Kaufman (1988: 263–342) (sceptical) and Wallmannsberger (1988) (measured) for summaries, with references, of evidence for alleged creole phases in Middle English, whether Anglo-Scandinavian or Anglo-French.

The Norman Conquest of 1066 also had a profound effect on the language, bringing French-speakers into all positions of authority in England. The Anglo-Saxon aristocracy was more or less wiped out, the cultural, educational and literary traditions were broken except in the south-west midlands, and an enormous transference of lexis took place. At first the influence was from mother-tongue Norman French within the Anglo-Norman kingdom; later it came rather from the acquired and culturally higher-valued Central French of the Paris region. By the end of the ME period, when English had once again become the first language of all classes, perhaps the bulk of OE lexis had become obsolete (measured by type, not token, of course: many of the common OE words are still in daily use), and some ten thousand French words had been 'borrowed' into English, maybe 75 per cent surviving into Modern English (Baugh and Cable 1978: 178). One effect was to make English a language of free stress, with different words accented on different syllables. Another was to make a permanent alteration in the balance between word formation and foreign borrowing in subsequent extensions of vocabulary, in that English has remained particularly open to lexical borrowing ever since.

French supplied a class-based influence with little of the geographical restriction shown by Scandinavian. Changes which had already been taking place in spoken English became increasingly visible in written English once the educational and scribal traditions were disrupted. Furthermore the practices of French-trained scribes changed the appearance of written English greatly in both handwriting and spelling. The OE letters <æ> and <ð> died out during early Middle English, while <þ> became indistinguishable from <y> in many styles and was lost in the fifteenth century (except in the contractions y^e 'the' and y^t 'that'). Meanwhile, the continental <g> was introduced as a separate letter from the insular <ȝ> (which was now called 'yogh'), with typical values [g] and [χ, j], respectively; by the end of the ME period <ȝ> had been supplanted by <gh> or <y>. The letters <q> and <z> were newly adopted; <k> was systematically used and distinguished from <c>; <v> was distinguished from <f>; and all sorts of new spellings were introduced, including digraphs like <ch> and <ou>.

The only significant foreign influence apart from Scandinavian and Norman French was Latin, which continued to provide lexis principally and perhaps some syntactic influence too (see §§8.5–8 and 10.2.2 below). However, for the first time since the Anglo-Saxon settlement there were some large-scale population movements within the country, particularly migration to London from East Anglia in the fourteenth century and then from the central midlands at the end of that century. Linguistic evidence for changes in London speech correlates well with historical evidence of migration patterns (Samuels 1972a: 169). The English of documents originating in the Chancery (court of record) became an important incipient standard in the early fifteenth century (Fisher 1977, etc.).

Middle English is more heterogeneous than either Old English before it or Modern English after it, since by and large scribes spelled as they spoke – and there was as much dialectal variation in speech then as at other times. As a result it has been possible to map ME dialects with a precision not attained for any other period of English (including the present day). Regional differences in orthography, lexis, and inflectional morphology have been found in the corpus used for *The Linguistic Atlas of Late Mediaeval English*, but Benskin and Laing have voiced doubts as to whether the corpus will yield a regional syntax (McIntosh et al. 1986: I,32), even though there is undoubtedly syntactic diversity in Middle English.

The vowels of nearly all unstressed syllabic inflections were reduced to [ə], spelled <e>. The amount of inflectional differentiation was less than in Old English, especially and earlier in the north. (One *post-hoc* justification of the terms Old English, Middle English and Modern English is to call them the periods of full, reduced and zero inflections, respectively.) In verb morphology the main changes were the transfer of many strong verbs to the still productive weak class, reduction in the number of vowel alternations in surviving strong verbs, and reduction in the number of distinctive person-number endings. The 1 SG (singular) *-e* and 2 SG PRES (present tense) *-(e)s(t)* endings remained distinct in most dialects. In the midlands 3 PRES SG *-eþ* was distinguished from PL (plural) *-en*, whereas *-es* in the north and *-eþ* in the south served for both. Past tenses increasingly failed to differentiate singular and plural as the period wore on. Van Kemenade (1987: 204) suggests that the last-named change plus loss of 1 SG PRES and PL PRES endings, which she places in the fourteenth century, was of significance for verbal syntax. By the end of the period inflectional [ə] had disappeared in word-final position and was in process of loss when followed by a consonant.

2.5   A sketch of Modern English

From the fifteenth century the commercial, political and cultural dominance of London began to have an effect on English. In both speech and writing, London dialect provided a standard for the whole of England – though Scotland continued to take Edinburgh as a standard and newer Englishes in America and elsewhere have partly gone their own way too. From the late fifteenth century there is little sign of dialectal diversity in published English. And from that time, of course, publishing increasingly means *printing*, a medium which, at least after the idiosyncrasies of the early printers, massively contributed to homogenisation of spelling and perhaps of other linguistic features too.

Spelling developed more slowly in the eModE period and began to fall behind changes in pronunciation. By the sixteenth century the essentials of modern spelling were present, although with much inconsistency and a great use of superfluous doublings and final <e>. By the eighteenth century, as <i> and <j>, <u> and <v> came to be distinguished as vowel and consonant letters rather than mere positional variants, public spelling had stabilised in almost its present form. (Right up to the nineteenth century, however, private letters even of educated people frequently showed surprising divergence from printers' spellings.)

During the eModE period the language borrowed enormous lexical resources from the classical languages of Latin and Greek. It has been estimated that lexical borrowing from Latin in all periods has brought a good quarter of all Latin vocabulary into English (quoted by Strang 1970: 129). Influence from writings in the classical languages was also responsible for highly elaborate periodic sentence structure in certain styles. As the British Empire expanded, so the range of lexical influence widened to ever more exotic source languages.

As far as texts are concerned, the first relatively informal letters come from the fifteenth century,[5] and the quantity and range of surviving material shoots up from that time on, including more and more that approximates to colloquial registers of speech. Wyld (1936: xi–xiv) lists some sources of colloquial English which date from the fifteenth century – which is really Middle English – to the eighteenth, and Stein (1990) some more. Nearly twenty million words of seventeenth-century writing in a variety of registers (and indeed languages) is currently being compiled in machine-readable form at Sheffield University as the Hartlib Papers Project; see Leslie (1990). For Modern English the Helsinki Corpus of English Texts: Diachronic and Dialectal includes much written material which is speech-based (e.g. records of trials) and/or colloquial in nature (e.g. private letters). Kytö gives useful details of some available early American English data and on the early Modern British English part of the Helsinki Corpus (1991: §3).

Morphological changes in the ModE period tended to have minimal effect on the syntax of lexical verbs and NPs (though cf. §11.4.5.2 below on auxiliaries). In the course of the sixteenth and seventeenth centuries 3 SG PRES -(e)th was replaced by the originally northern ending -(e)s,[6] and 3 PL be(en) was replaced by are. The past tense forms and past participles of strong verbs and irregular weak verbs underwent a great shake-out as the language finished shedding all differences of stem vowel in strong verbs between singular and plural[7] and often past participle too: compare OE INF (infinitive) feohtan 'fight', 3 SG PA feaht, 3 PL PA fuhton, PA PTCP gefohten with ModE INF fight, PA fought, PA PTCP fought. In strong past participles a form with or without final -en was seemingly arbitrarily picked on (compare BrE (British English) got with forgotten). Right up to the nineteenth century there was widespread fluctuation within standard English in irregular past morphology (e.g. past tense drunk ~ drank), as of course still remains in non-standard usage. Loss of the 2 SG form thou and its associated verbal inflection -(e)st (-t with some auxiliaries) meant that most verbs retained only one inflectional distinction in the present tense, 3 SG vs. the rest, and none in the past tense, and that modal verbs had no person-number inflections at all.

From the sixteenth century various aspects of the language became matters of lively intellectual interest. From the seventeenth century grammars of English began to appear in English, and a prescriptive tradition of teaching English grammar grew up, largely based on the grammar of Latin. It is from this time that explicit mention appears of 'rules' of syntactic etiquette. Some of them are reasonable but many now seem entirely arbitrary, such as the condemnation of clauses which end with a preposition or which employ multiple negation or which have as subject of the passive what would be indirect object in the active.

Finally here we must point to two factors which make the external history of late Modern English quite different from all earlier periods of English. One is that up to the seventeenth century the entire English-speaking population amounted at most to a few million people, all within the British Isles, and having limited contact between regions. Since then and particularly in the last hundred years a vast growth has taken place both in population and in means and capacity for travel and communication. Mass communication, especially sound movies and telecommunications, accelerates certain linguistic changes, though it can act as a brake on the differentiation of dialects. The second factor, due originally to the importance of the British Empire and later to the economic might of the United States, is the dominance of English as a world language, with recent estimates of over 300 million mother-tongue speakers, a further 300 million second-language speakers, and altogether about 1500 millions living in countries where English has official status or is one of the native languages (Quirk et al. 1985: 3,5). The most important consequences are for the many languages subject to English influence or threat, but the sheer number and variety of speakers may have consequences for the future development of English too. It is too early to say whether the rate or the nature of syntactic change in recent times differs from earlier periods, but it would be an interesting topic for research.

2.6   Further reading

I would recommend Strang (1970) as the best of the one-volume histories of English, particularly on the internal history, syntax included: Professor Strang always made a strong attempt to *explain* developments. More detail on the external history can be found in Baugh and Cable (1978). A good short survey is Barber (1972, forthcoming). *CHEL* (1992–) should become the standard source as publication proceeds. A readable introductory work on language change in general is Aitchison (1991). The nature and extent of Latin influence on OE prose has been discussed mostly in relation to specific constructions. For an overall discussion and references see Fischer (1992b). Foreign influence on lexis is treated in Serjeantson (1935). For spelling history see Scragg (1974). There is useful material on standardisation in late Middle English in Samuels (1972a). The progress of standardisation in early Modern English is well surveyed by Nevalainen and Raumolin-Brunberg (1989), who also describe the Helsinki Corpus.

Notes

1. Apart from some inscriptions written in the runic 'futharc', an alphabet peculiar to Germanic, though related ultimately to other alphabetic writing systems.
2. What we have of Old English amounts to some three million words in two thousand texts (Healey and Venezky 1980: ix). Healey (1985: 245) gives the figure of *three* thousand texts, though here 'text' refers to items in the *DOE* computer corpus and can range from a fragmentary scribble through a single book of *Or* or *Bede* to the whole of the Canterbury Psalter (p.c. 28 April 1988).
3. The upper case forms corresponding to *æðþ* are *ÆÐÞ*. Other symbols, notably 'wynn', used for the sound [w], and the insular *g* <ȝ> used for [ɤ, j, g], need not concern us here, as they are regularly replaced in modern editions and in this book by the corresponding modern letters <w> and <g>.
4. Notice that I follow the convention of using small capitals for a **lexeme**. The point of citing verbs as lexemes is to indicate that different inflectional forms are subsumed. Whether the infinitive form cited is Old English (e.g. SINGAN), Middle English (SINGEN), or Modern English (SING) depends on context; utter consistency is beyond me. A few non-verbs which exhibit striking variations of form are also cited in small capitals.
5. Poussa (1982: 82) cites Taylor (1956: 132) on the replacement of parchment by paper in the 1420s, and the consequential spread of letter-writing beyond the very rich and powerful.
6. Recent work by Dieter Stein (1985, 1990) has suggested that the choice between *-(e)th* and *-(e)s* was exploited as a discourse marker during the changeover period.
7. The only surviving trace is in *was vs. were*.

Chapter 3

Nominal morphology

3.1 Old English

3.1.1 Surface inflections

Noun phrases carried inflections which potentially at least marked the phrase for number, gender and case. These inflections appeared on the head (pro)noun and on determiners and adjectives associated with it. There was a two-term **number** contrast of singular and plural in the NP, except in first and second person pronouns, which could show a three-term contrast: singular, dual, plural. Number is a fairly straightforward semantic category.

Nouns belonged to one of three **gender** classes: masculine, feminine, neuter. Grammatical gender was largely a morphological matter, fixed for nearly all nouns, though the semantics of natural gender played some part too: most nouns for human males were masculine, for instance. The gender of many nouns was arbitrary and semantically unmotivated, however.

The final inflectional category, a purely syntactic one, was **case**, which helped to show the syntactic function of an NP and its relation to other constituents of the clause. Case form and syntactic function should not be confused, however. Nouns showed a four-term case contrast, for which the Latinate terms nominative, accusative, genitive, dative are conventionally used. A crude summary of the main uses of each case is given in [1], where dotted lines represent less common form-function pairings:

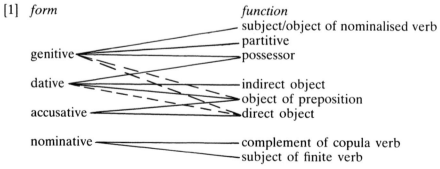

[1] *form*   *function*
                                                     subject/object of nominalised verb
                                                     partitive
         genitive   possessor

         dative   indirect object
                                                     object of preposition
         accusative   direct object

         nominative   complement of copula verb
                                                     subject of finite verb

Some pronouns and adjectives had in addition a fifth case, instrumental, in the masculine and neuter singular, used for inanimates in functions like means, manner, accompaniment or time. Elsewhere the instrumental had coalesced with the dative.[1]

Determiners and adjectives showed agreement for number, gender and case. Few elements of the NP showed the maximum potential inflectional variation implied by the description just given. Nominal inflection was fusional, not agglutinative: usually a single morph realised case, number and (where appropriate) gender. Nowhere in Old English was it possible to distinguish inflectionally between nominative and accusative singular neuter, for instance, or between nominative and accusative plural in any gender (except in first and second person pronouns). Despite this degree of neutralisation the traditional categories (2 numbers × 3 genders × 4 cases) can each be justified on the basis of explicit formal distinctions found somewhere in OE morphology. For details of the forms see for instance Campbell (1959), Keyser and O'Neil (1985).

3.1.2 Prepositions

Prepositional marking of syntactic function is the closest equivalent to surface case marking of an NP, and in languages like Old English using both methods there may be considerable overlap. There were nearly 80 prepositions in Old English,[2] many of them still surviving, e.g. *þurh* 'through', though not always in identical meanings, e.g. OE *of* '(away) from' and *wið* 'against'. For certain functions there was alternation between an oblique case and a prepositional phrase, thus e.g. *þy ilcan geare*(INST) ~ *on þam ilcan geare* '(in) the same year', *lytle werede*(INST) ~ *mid lytlum werode* 'with a small troop'.

3.1.3 Case in linguistic theory

Theories of case in modern linguistics form a vast and complex subject. All I shall attempt here is to identify some general approaches to case which have been applied in recent years to Old English.

3.1.3.1 Case Grammar

Case Grammar is best known from the work of Charles Fillmore and John Anderson.[3] In Case Grammar every NP in a given clause has (usually) one semantic role, its **deep case**: Agent, Experiencer, Instrument, and so on. Deep case – not the same as the surface cases discussed in §3.1.1 – may be expressed on the surface in various ways, thus accounting for alternative realisations of 'the same' clause. One sort of variation used to motivate claims of underlying identity is:

[2] (a) John opened the door with a key.
    (b) John used a key to open the door.
    (c) A key opened the door.
    (d) The door opened.
    (e) The door was opened by John.

The various NPs may appear in different syntactic functions and with or without various prepositions, but with the same underlying semantic role. A typical extension of Case Grammar is to regard deep cases as essentially **localistic** in origin, so that all semantic roles depend on, or are figurative extensions of, spatial notions like Source, Location and so on.

3.1.3.2 Government-Binding theory

Government-Binding theory, the current version of Chomskian transformational generative grammar, consists of a number of autonomous modules. One such is Theta Theory. Semantic case roles are called **thematic relations** or **θ-roles**, and appear to be broadly similar to Fillmorean deep cases.

3.1.3.3*

Another module of the GB framework is Case Theory, within which definitions of abstract case continue to evolve with bewildering rapidity; much of the discussion is wholly theory-internal. Case in GB theory is essentially a syntactic property of NPs; its bearing on semantics is quite indirect; nor is it the same as surface (morphological) case, though they are related. There were at first two main kinds of abstract case in GB theory: 'inherent' case, associated with θ-role and so lexically determined at *D-structure*, and 'structural' case, determined at and by *S-structure* and independent of particular lexical items. The case of object NPs is in recent work either 'oblique', which is inherent, or 'objective', which is structural. 'Nominative' case, which seems to correspond exactly with surface nominative, is assigned structurally through government by INFL (the constituent which dominates tense). Fischer and van der Leek (1987: 95–7) provide references to early work on case in GB theory and trenchant criticism of its vagueness.

3.1.3.4 Deep and surface case

Recent work inside and outside the tradition of generative linguistics has been attempting to find systematic correlations between surface case forms in Old English and some notion of underlying semantic role or deep case or case relation.

Frans Plank has studied verbs which allow a choice of case in object NPs, arguing that in many instances the choice is motivated rather than arbitrary (1981, 1983). He claims that dative marking of object NPs tends to signal a relatively low degree of opposedness between the referents of object and subject NPs, accusative marking relatively high opposedness (correlated with patient function for the object), while genitive marking tends to encode circumstantial roles rather than full participants. His hypothesis is nicely illustrated by the following pair:

[3] *Phoen* 591

    Him   folgiað fuglas scyne
    him(DAT) follow birds brilliant

    'brilliant birds follow him'

[4] *Beo* 2933

    ond ða   folgode feorhgeniðlan
    and then pursued deadly-foes(ACC?)

    'and then he pursued deadly foes'

Whether FOLGIAN means 'follow' or 'pursue' is allegedly signalled by the
case of its object NP. Similarly, GEEFENLÆCAN + ACC is said to mean
'imitate', but + DAT 'resemble':

[5] *BenR* ii 11.16

    . . . and þa unandgytfullan   . . . hine   geefenlæcen.
    . . . and the unintelligent(NOM) . . . him(ACC) imitate(SUBJ)

    '. . . and the unintelligent . . . may imitate him'

[6] *ÆCHom* II, 13.129.71

    Gif he geeuenlæcð gode
    if   he resembles   God(DAT)

Appealing though the hypothesis is, there seems to be some special pleading
going on.[4]

3.1.3.5* Anderson

Anderson has in recent work reduced the number of deep cases in his Case
Grammar framework to four **case relations**:

    ergative (erg):   source of action
    absolutive (abs): thing affected, moved, located
    locative (loc):   location or goal
    ablative (abl):   spatial source

(I quote here from Colman 1988: 40, summarising e.g. Anderson 1985: 4.) Every
clause contains an abs argument. All constituents of a clause apart from verbs
carry one or more of these case labels. Anderson suggests (1985) that the four
main surface cases in Old English should be analysed as 'morphologisations' of
certain case relations and/or grammatical relations. Thus erg is typically
associated with nominative, erg/loc and loc with dative, abs with accusative, abl
with genitive. These typical associations may be overridden by subject-formation
(which in the absence of erg extends erg-hood to the next available argument on a
hierarchy of case relations), genitive-formation (which substitutes abl for another
case relation), or particular lexical specifications attached to prepositions. See also
Anderson's (1988) use of this framework for OE impersonal verbs, discussed in
§5.6.2.2 below.

3.1.3.6 Fischer and van der Leek

These ideas have been taken up by Olga Fischer and Frederike van der
Leek (1987), who build on Plank's observations and on localistic case theory
to suggest that in Old English there is a major difference between
nominative and accusative cases on the one hand and genitive and dative on
the other. A non-argument NP will be more peripheral than an *argument*,
either having no direct relation with the verb at all or else fulfilling a
peripheral semantic role. Thus in the ModE sentence:

[7] Jim painted Joe's bike in the garage.

NPs headed by *Jim*, *bike* are arguments of PAINT, by *Joe*, *garage* not. (A
further refinement is to distinguish between [VP-]**external** arguments like *Jim*

and **internal** arguments like *bike*.) Fischer and van der Leek suggest that in Old English, nominative and accusative mark NPs which are arguments of a verb – their θ-roles are assigned by the verb – whereas genitive and dative mark independent θ-roles, not arguments of a verb. More will be said about their approach in §5.6.3 below, in the chapter on impersonal verbs.

3.2 Middle English

3.2.1 Surface inflections

By the early ME period many OE inflectional distinctions were obsolescent. Dual number in pronouns did not survive beyond the early thirteenth century, grammatical gender survived only in the sporadic use of historically correct determiners – and then only in the south – until the fourteenth century; see here Jones (1988), Markus (1988a). There were major changes in determiners. From a two-term *deictic* system (OE SE 'the, that' ~ ÞES 'this') with enormous person/number/case differentiation, the forms and functions were eventually rearranged into a three-term deictic system (ModE *the* ~ THAT ~ THIS) with limited number differentiation. Adjectival inflections were reduced to a contrast between Ø and -*e* at most, and then mainly on certain monosyllabic stems. Where inflectional -*e* in adjectives had any grammatical significance at all, it could mark plurality or (especially in early Middle English) a *weak* adjective.

As for nouns, case *syncretism* meant that all nominative ~ dative ~ accusative distinctions were lost. Often they would have fallen together by ordinary phonetic change, but where they would have differed the actual ME form comes from the old nominative or accusative. The genitive survived as a formally marked category but no longer served as a case governed by verbs or prepositions. Thus there were two noun cases, which we can call 'common' (the *unmarked* form) and 'genitive'.

In animate personal pronouns it was the old dative form which survived rather than the accusative,[5] and this remained distinct from the old nominative. These surviving cases can be called 'objective' and 'subjective' (or 'nominative'), respectively. An appropriate table for a typical noun, *arm* 'arm', and for the 3 MASC (masculine) personal pronoun would therefore in many dialects show these contrasts in the singular:

[8] genitive *armes*   *his*

common *arm*   { objective *him*
                 { subjective *he*

This particular paradigm has not changed except in phonological detail since Middle English. (For details of the full range of nominal inflection in Middle English see for instance Mossé 1952.)

Recognition of three NP cases is justified for Middle English (and Modern English) by their formal distinctness in personal pronouns, even though determiners, adjectives, and nouns no longer showed an objective ~ subjective distinction. In addition to the changes in the formal case system since Old English there was also a slight redistribution of functions. The formal distinctions are presented in [9] so as to be applicable either to nouns or to personal pronouns:

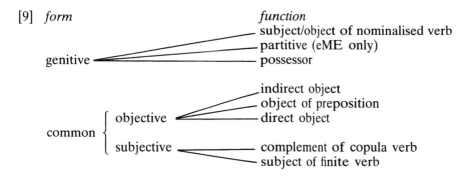

[9] *form*   *function*
                                                subject/object of nominalised verb
                                                partitive (eME only)
genitive   possessor

                                                indirect object
                            objective   object of preposition
                                                direct object
common
                            subjective   complement of copula verb
                                                subject of finite verb

Compare diagram [9] with [1]. The inflectional genitive marking the object of a nominalised verb – **objective genitive** (*John's killing/betrayal* = 'the killing/betrayal of John') – became rarer when there was possibility of confusion with the **subjective genitive** (*John's killing/betrayal* = 'the killing/betrayal by John'), but it has remained in the language.

3.2.2 Prepositions

Prepositional use in Middle English shows enormous expansion over Old English. Mustanoja devotes a long chapter to the subject (1960: 345–427), detailing how a number of new prepositions entered the language from native and foreign sources and how prepositions increased in frequency of occurrence and in range of use. Comparing Middle English with Old English in this respect he writes:

> The syntactical relationships formerly expressed by means of the case-endings now come to be expressed mainly by means of word-order and prepositions. *Of*, for example, becomes a favourite equivalent of the genitive . . . ; *to* and *for* are widely used for the original dative . . . , and *mid*, *with*, *through*, *by*, and *of* for the instrumental. (1960: 348)

Prepositional marking was in part a functional replacement for case marking. New prepositional usages play an important part in the topics discussed in Chapters 6 and 7.

3.2.3 Theories of case

In GB theory the changes in surface case forms sketched above in §3.2.1 can be correlated with changes in syntax; see Chapters 5 and 7 below.

In the framework of Relational Grammar, relations such as Subject and Direct Object and not structural configurations are treated as primary. Paul Bennett (1980) has interpreted the loss of dative case in English in Relational Grammar terms. He identifies the emergence of 'unmarked case' (our common case) with an extension of the scope of the relation Direct

Object, whether underlying or derived. His analysis will be discussed in §7.6.3, in a chapter concerned with the appearance of new passives in Middle English.

3.3 Modern English

There are few surface changes to report in Modern English. The pronunciation of the inflection spelled *-es* in most dialects of Middle English became [ɪz] in the dominant dialect, and such inflections as survived became non-syllabic where vowel loss would not lead to unacceptable consonant clusters, thus for example *-es* [ɪz] > *-s* [s, z]. Adjectives lost all trace of inflectional variation apart perhaps from comparative and superlative formations like *longer, longest*; and even here syntactic comparison with *more* and *most* has spread at the expense of synthetic forms, thus PDE *most ungrateful* rather than eModE *ungratefull'st*.

In the pronoun system the main changes affect second-person forms. The plural form was increasingly used with singular reference, at first with various social implications but increasingly as unmarked replacements of the historically singular forms *thou* and *thee*. By the seventeenth century it was *thou* and *thee* which had become the socially or stylistically marked forms for singular reference; they later became obsolete in most registers of standard English, though not in all dialects. Meanwhile from the end of the sixteenth century there was confusion between (historically) subjective *ye* and objective *you*; eventually *ye* was lost except as an archaism. The second person system has therefore ended up with one form in the standard language, *you*, where first and third persons have up to four.

The main functional change in case usage has been a continued shift towards objective as unmarked form, most noticeable in such patterns as *It's me* and *taller than me* (cf. Harris 1981, Kjellmer 1986), where subjective *I* would have been normal at earlier times. Here is an early example with the copula verb PROVE (compare with [74] in Chapter 12 below):

[10] 1697 Vanbrugh, *Provok'd Wife* IV.iv.7

But if it prove her, all that's woman in me shall be employ'd to destroy her.

The ME table of [9] must therefore be modified slightly as follows for late Modern English:

[11] *form*

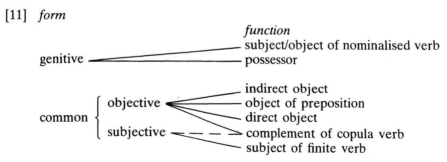

There are grounds for a more substantial modification too, namely to treat the genitive as an *enclitic* word rather than a noun inflection (though what to do with genitive pronouns would be a moot point). This is because *'s*[6] can now be added not just to nouns but to NPs and even coordinated NPs in the so-called **group genitive**:

[12] the player on the inside's control

In [12] it would be inappropriate syntactically or semantically to treat *'s* as an inflection on *inside*. However, the history of the group genitive is essentially a matter of the internal structure of NPs, and if we allow the actual locus of case to remain vague, [11] can stand as a summary of case usage in NPs in Modern English.

3.4 Question for further research

Use the *Concordance* of Venezky and Healey (1980) to gather examples of FOLGIAN 'pursue, follow' and/or (GE)EFENLÆCAN 'imitate, resemble' with a view to testing the semantics of case choice for the object NP (see §3.1.3.4 above). Be prepared for dialectal or diachronic variation within Old English.

Notes

1. For fuller descriptions of OE case usage see Quirk and Wrenn (1957: 59–68) or Mitchell and Robinson (1992: §§188–92). Mitchell (1985: §§1240–1427) is the standard reference.
2. Mitchell lists 78 undoubted OE prepositions (1985: §1178).
3. See Fillmore (1968) for a seminal sketch of the theory, Anderson (1971, 1977, and later papers) for fuller working out.
4. Examples [3]–[6], from Plank (1981: 20; 1983: 247), have been quoted approvingly by Fischer and van der Leek (1987: 92–3) and Traugott (1992: 204). However, a cursory inspection of Venezky and Healey (1980) suggests that in Ælfrician manuscripts at least, GEEFENLÆCAN normally took a dative object even in contexts which suggest the meaning 'imitate' (namely the imperative, or after UTON 'let us', or with the object *his dædum* 'his deeds', etc.); thus also Sweet (1897) s.v. *efenlæcan*. As for *feorhgeniðlan* in [4], it is not unambiguously accusative and is actually listed as dative in Klaeber's glossary of *Beo*.
5. Southern dialects of Middle English maintained a distinction between dative and accusative only in MASC and NEUT (better, inanimate) 3 SG pronouns, with MASC *hine* and inanimate *hit* as direct object forms, MASC (or occasionally inanimate) *him* as indirect object form (Strang 1970: 198). The pronoun of inanimate reference in prepositional object function was most commonly *proclitic þer(e)* in all dialects.
6. Or conceivably just the apostrophe in writing ([Ø] in speech) if the NP happens to end in *-s*:

   (a) ?the leader of the insurgents' voice

Part II

WORD ORDER

Overview

Part II consists of the single Chapter 4, Word Order. This aspect of syntactic organisation is placed here because it is self-evidently of major overall importance in verbal syntax, to be discussed in Parts III to V. Despite the fact that I have relatively little to contribute from my own research, Chapter 4 is a long chapter, and one in which the difficulty of reconciling different theoretical approaches is particularly apparent. Readers who do not wish to work through all the detailed commentaries might like at least to read §4.1.

Chapter 4

Word Order

4.1 Introductory remarks

4.1.1 Relation to (other aspects of) syntax

We can talk about the word order either of a particular utterance or of a language as a whole, in which case we mean the general, typical, **unmarked** order(s) found in the language at a particular time.[1] Word order and syntactic structure are closely interrelated. It could be said that the word order of a language (in the general sense) merely follows from – is the sum of – the orders of all relevant syntactic constructions. Then word order would be a derivative notion. A word order change would simply mean that a number of syntactic constructions had begun to manifest themselves differently. However, since it is usually possible to state rules or tendencies of word order in such a general way that they apply to a wide range of syntactic patterns, it is more common to regard the overall word order rules as having priority over individual constructions. That is the viewpoint we shall adopt in this chapter. We shall make use of the idealisation that word order has an existence independent of the individual syntactic constructions which manifest any given ordering. Later chapters on particular constructions will allow us to look back on word order change from the alternative viewpoint.

4.1.2 SVO, SOV, VSO, etc.

A pioneering cross-linguistic study by Greenberg (1966) listed the basic word order of 30 languages in terms of the relative order of just three elements: subject (S), verb (V) and object (O).[2] This simple classification into potentially six different orders came to be of central importance in the new field of **language typology**. It was shown to correlate significantly with other ordering relationships, and later work – a recent example is Dryer (1991) – tried to establish an **implicational hierarchy**[3] for word order facts. In those terms Modern English is clearly an SVO language, since no unmarked declarative clause deviates from that order. Whether Old English should be labelled SVO or SOV is far less clear, since clauses of both types were common. The answer might well vary with the date or genre of the text(s) analysed. In any case the use of blanket labels like SVO or SOV, however necessary for cross-linguistic comparison, is hardly practicable for Old English. In an OE text sample containing 251 clauses I found a mere handful that were actually suitable for counting as SVO, SOV, OSV or whatever (Denison 1986: §5.1): all the rest had at least one of those elements split or missing altogether, were marked in some way, or were clearly affected by weight ordering (see §4.6.1 below). For a method which is essentially statistical this is a big problem.

Labels like SVO, SOV, VSO can carry a rather different significance. For generative linguists they stand not for the most frequently attested ordering – with or without allowance for deviations due to some kind of marking – but rather for an abstract underlying order from which all attested surface orders can be derived with the greatest economy. This is legitimate within a particular linguistic model, but careless usage might blur the distinction between the unmarked/most frequently attested sense on the one hand and the abstract/underlying sense on the other. Certainly the term **canonical order** is sometimes used with worrying shiftiness.[4]

4.1.3   Verb position

Labelling the position of the (finite) verb has proved useful in dealing with the history of English word order. Four possibilities are usually allowed for in this nomenclature. A language – or perhaps a subset of clause types in a language – may be **verb first** or **V-1** or **V1**. Arguably ModE polar (i.e. yes/no) interrogatives can often be V-1, though of course only if the *finite* verb is counted as 'V':

[1]   (a)   Have you seen Jimmy?
      (b)   Will Fred be coming?
      (c)   Is that so?

It may be **verb second** or **V-2**, in which case one sentence constituent precedes the verb. *Wh*-interrogatives and a very few other constructions in Modern English are V-2:

[2]   (a)   Who gave you that camera?
      (b)   Which delegate did you take a picture of?
      (c)   Never in all my life have I been so embarrassed.

In Modern Dutch and German all declarative main clauses are V-2. A language or subset of clauses may be **verb third** or **V-3**, a somewhat unhappy choice of label for a situation in which the verb follows the subject regardless of whether or not there is any pre-subject element. ModE declaratives are then V-3, both in main and subordinate clauses:[5]

[3]   (a)   Jimmy spoilt his chances.
      (b)   *Last year spoilt Jimmy his chances.

    (c)   Last year Jimmy spoilt his chances.
    (d)   (You must know) that Jimmy spoilt his chances.
    (e)   (the chances) which Jimmy spoilt by his foolish behaviour

Notice that although the order of [3](a) could be due to a V-2 constraint, the non-occurrence of [3](b) and the existence of [3](c–e) show this to be fortuitous: only the V-3-ness of [3](a) is significant, however inappropriate the name. Last on our list is **verb final** or **V-F**. This order is not found systematically in Modern English, but subordinate clauses in Dutch and German are V-F. A variant of V-F is **verb-late** (Vennemann 1984), which is essentially V-F but with some provision for 'afterthought' elements.

4.1.4 Other terminologies

Many other ways of labelling particular word orders will be found in the literature. For Old English Smith (1893: 215) adopted from a grammar of German the terms **normal, inverted** and **transposed** orders, standing for SV, VS, and S. . .V, respectively. The presuppositions of these terms are no longer in favour: to call SV 'normal' and the other orders deviations from normality is to beg the question. Alternative labels within similar systems include **direct** and **neutral** orders (= SV = SVX[6]), **demonstrative** order (= XVS), and **subordinate** and **conjunctive** orders (= S. . .V = SXV), the latter terms embodying assumptions about the clause-types which use that order. Bruce Mitchell uses SV, S. . .V, and VS (1964; 1985: §3900), which seem acceptably neutral until one realises that apparently arbitrary variants (licensed by ModE parallels) are permitted within each category. Thus, for example, a pattern is still SV if 'elements such as adverbs or phrases' intervene between subject and verb, though not if nominals or non-finite verbs intervene (1985: §3901). The choice of S and V as pivotal elements is simply taken for granted. Furthermore V-1 and V-2 are not distinguished. Mitchell's terminology implicitly codes a classification and an analysis.

    Other scholars have drawn on the notion of **topic** (often T) and **comment**, as in the suggestion that one stage of Old English was TVX. The topic of a sentence is the element which is given, usually in the preceding discourse, while the comment is what is new. Typically the topic will be an NP, and often it will coincide with the subject. A largely equivalent terminology is **theme** (for topic) vs. **rheme** (for comment). Sometimes 'theme' is used for the discourse notion of givenness so that **topicalisation** can be reserved for the syntactic property of 'an optional fronting of a constituent from some other, syntactically neutral position' (Kohonen 1978: 69). In that case 'theme' and 'topic' will not be equivalent terms even if in a particular sentence they often coincide.

4.1.5 The problem

Ignoring a large body of exceptions and some evidence of non-homogeneity within Old English, we might claim that Old English was a mixed V-2/V-F language like Dutch or German, with V-2 predominant in main clause declaratives and V-F predominant in subordinate clauses. Modern English, on the other hand, is consistently V-3 or SVO. How and why did word order change? This I take to be the main problem to be investigated.

Subsidiary questions include the following. How should we deal with the Old English exceptions? Are they systematically explicable, and if not, how then should we describe and explain the word order of Old English? What was the role of 'dummy *hit*'? – see §5.9 on this question. What exactly were the word order rules during the transitional period? What is the history of non-finite verbs (infinitives and participles)? Do interrogatives and imperatives, whose largely V-2 or V-1 ordering appears to have changed little over the centuries, constitute independent domains? (The last question is hardly discussed here and is left as an exercise.)

4.2 The data

Word order studies require large numbers of examples in order for statistically significant generalisations to be drawn. To illustrate this point, consider the claim, already stated above, that Modern English is SVO. What then of the following?

[4]   Such problems I avoid.
[5]   (a)   Down it came.
      (b)   Down came the rain.

Example [4] is OSV or XSV, [5](a) is XSV, while [5](b) is XVS. Yet the generalisations can be allowed to stand because [4]–[5] are clearly exceptional: [4] is a marked order with topicalisation of the object NP, while the topicalisation of a directional adverb in [5] is both marked and very limited in application.[7] Analysis of a large ModE corpus would probably reveal the infrequency of patterns [4]–[5] and the special contexts to which they are confined.

For Old English, where both data and intuitive knowledge are more limited, it is harder to discriminate between rules and exceptions, though numerous scholars have had a go undeterred. In Middle English the problem is worse, since the language is messier (more heterogeneous, see §2.4) than Old English and probably for this reason has been less fully studied. And for any period, just what constitutes relevant data, let alone how to assess it, depends very heavily on the theoretical assumptions of the analyst. All of this makes a neutral account of the evidence particularly difficult, and I shall not attempt one. A few examples will appear incidentally in the course of a survey of scholarly investigations. Each study really has to be taken as a whole; I draw comparisons where I can.

4.3 Descriptions and explanations

I have made a rough-and-ready four-way division of the scholarly material: synchronic versus diachronic, and non-generative versus generative. Not all contributions sit happily inside this categorisation, of course, but overall it should help to keep the almost overwhelming variety of material under control. I have also been rather selective in my choice of studies to discuss.

In synchrony most attention has been paid to Old English (apart, of course, from Present-day English, which I neglect entirely). The traditional viewpoint on Old English word order is represented here by Smith and to some extent Mitchell. Bacquet concentrates on the idea of marked and unmarked order, while Reszkiewicz explores weight ordering. Smith goes on to consider the breakdown of the OE system, and Mitchell also compares a very late OE/early ME text with older and later states of the language. Generative accounts of Old English word order are represented by Koopman and by Pintzuk and Kroch.

Diachronic accounts are more in the linguistic than the philological tradition. They include Fourquet, Strang, Vennemann, Stockwell, and Canale, all of whom look for functional explanations of developments which run from the pre-historic period through and beyond Old English. Bean attempts to test some of the theories on offer against an OE corpus, while Kohonen has the most thorough statistical study – his corpus includes Old and early Middle English texts – and discusses the widest range of factors. Gerritsen goes for a bird's-eye view of word order change in the entire Germanic language family, while Danchev and Weerman have independently pointed to Anglo-Scandinavian contact. An important diachronic account which is strictly generative in its approach is that of van Kemenade. Different, semi-formalised approaches are represented by Canale, Colman, and Stockwell and Minkova.

4.4 Synchronic accounts in non-generative linguistics

4.4.1 Smith

C. Alphonso Smith made one of the first serious studies of Old English word order (1893), using the Alfredian *Orosius* and Ælfric's *Homilies* as source material. His avowed aim was 'to find the syntactic norm' (1893: 212), that is, the order dictated by syntactic factors and not by rhetorical considerations or euphonic ones (the latter applying in any case only to poetry).

Smith deals with his main order types one by one: SV, VS, SXV. The positions of other sentence elements in the SV type are described systematically, though the explanations are somewhat impressionistic, and the same relative orders of minor elements are to be presumed for the VS and S. . .V types – apart from the order of auxiliary and main verb, which is discussed once in relation to SV order and again for dependent clauses generally. A detailed table of contents ('index') is given at the end of the article.

As has already been noted, Smith takes SV order to be normal. Datives, he says, usually preceded direct objects if both were full NPs – this is not confirmed by Koopman (1990d) – and direct objects normally preceded other verbal modifiers. If pronominal, however, both datives and direct objects normally preceded V. The position of a non-finite verb was not yet determined by a syntactic norm: it could follow the finite immediately, go to the end of the clause, or appear somewhere between those two positions, but with a tendency to final position if there were few other elements in the VP.

(X)VS order is taken to be a marked order and is discussed under two heads: the initial element, if present, which 'caused' inversion (giving XVS, a kind of V-2 pattern), and the clause-types which could be signalled by inversion (i.e. VSX or V-1 order), namely conditional, concessive, interrogative, and 'command'.

SXV order is characteristic of subordinate clauses in his texts, though occasional examples in main clauses are considered briefly (1893: 231–2). Smith also discusses the reasons for individual instances of VS or SVX in dependent clauses, where rhetorical principles have overridden syntactic ones, for example the non-final position of *gemunde* in [6]:

[6] *Or* 33.6

for þon ðe se cyning ne gemunde   þara monigra teonena þe
because   the king not remembered the many   wrongs which

hiora   ægðer oþrum   on ærdagum   gedyde
them(GEN) each the-other(DAT) in former-days did

'because the king did not remember the many wrongs which each of them had formerly done to the other'

Smith explains the order of [6] as allowing an antecedent (*þara monigra teonena*) to be adjacent to its relative clause (*þe . . . gedyde*).

Smith gives detailed figures for compound tenses in dependent clauses, which I summarise now with the abbreviations v = finite verb and V = non-finite verb. The most common order by far in *Orosius* is SVv (no object) at 43 per cent, while the orders SvOV 11 per cent, SvV (no object) 15 per cent, and SOVv 17 per cent account for most of the rest. In the Ælfric *Homilies* the figures are different. The commonest orders are SvV 26 per cent, SVv 20 per cent, S(X)vVX 18 per cent, followed by SvOV 11 per cent, SvVO 9 per cent, and SOVv 8 per cent.

By showing statistically that SXV was already less than invariable in dependent clauses in *Orosius* and had declined still further by the time of Ælfric, well before the Norman Conquest, Smith can reason that 'while the influence of French powerfully aided the movement against transposition, it did not create the movement, but only fostered it' (1893: 230). He suggests a threefold explanation for the replacement of SXV by SVX in dependent clauses (1893: 238): the greater simplicity of SVX; analogy with main clauses; analogy with indirect affirmative clauses (which show higher proportions of SVX than other dependent clauses). The type he calls indirect affirmatives are *þæt*-clauses which follow a verb of saying, as in:

[7] *ÆCHom* I 3.46.2

We gehyrdon hine secgan þæt Crist towyrpð þas stowe
we heard   him say   that Christ destroys this place

'We heard him say that Christ will destroy this place.'

Perhaps they are not all truly dependent clauses; see Mitchell (1985:

§§1939–43) on the rather fluid boundary between true indirect speech and direct quotation.

4.4.2 Bacquet

The work of Paul Bacquet (1962) has been roundly criticised by Mitchell (1985: §3916 *et passim*), especially for its failure to acknowledge the subordinate-like behaviour of coordinate *ond/ac/ne*-clauses, and I shall not pursue the details of Bacquet's analysis here. Its importance lies in its thoroughness – it remains a major source of information on OE word order – and in the principle which Bacquet adopts, namely that for a given clause-type there is one order which is unmarked, and every other order must be in some way marked.

4.4.3 Mitchell

4.4.3.1

Bruce Mitchell's summary of the principles of OE word order runs as follows (1964: 119):[8]

> In the sentence or clause, Old English prose retained the three ancient Germanic word-orders – S.V. [. . .], S. . . . V., and V.S. But word-order in Old English is not as regular as that in Modern German, where S. . . . V. occurs only in subordinate clauses [. . .] and S.V. is the order of principal clauses except when some element other than the subject begins the sentence, when we have V.S. What are rules in Modern German are certainly tendencies in Old English prose. But (possibly under the influence of verse, where these rules do not apply, and as part of the process which led to the modern fixed word-order) S.V. and sometimes V.S. occur in subordinate clauses, while V.S. with initial verb can occur in principal clauses which are statements, not questions. [. . .]

Of course if Strang and others are right about early Old English, it is wrong (for that period at least) to use a classification which treats the position of the subject as fundamental.

Mitchell has been humorously but admiringly called the only living native speaker of Old English. Often his intuition about how to classify order types has anticipated later work, even if his classifications are not explicitly motivated. He points out, for example, that [8](c) is rare and that (therefore?) [8](d) is an equivalent of both [8](a) and (b) (1964: 124):

[8] (a) ic lufige God
          I love God
     (b) ic God lufige
     (c) ic lufige hine
          I love him
     (d) ic hine lufige

Van Kemenade's work on personal pronouns as ***clitics*** makes sense of the

behaviour of *hine* here: see §4.7.1.1 below. Another case in point is
Mitchell's classification of examples like [9] as S. . .V (1964: 120):

[9] *ÆCHom* I 3.44.29

þæt he tallice   word spræce   be   Moyse
that he blasphemous words might-speak concerning Moses

and be   Gode
and concerning God

'that he might speak blasphemous words concerning Moses and God'

He has chosen (but without real explanation) to ignore conjoined PPs that
come right at the end of what would otherwise be an SXV clause. Other
workers, notably Vennemann and Stockwell, have likewise regarded such
examples as variants of SXV in origin, but they have gone on to explain
both why they might have occurred and how their occurrence might have
contributed to the eventual demise of the SXV pattern.

One recurrent theme in Mitchell's work is the nature of OE clauses
beginning with *ond* 'and', *ac* 'but' or *ne* 'nor'. His suggestion is that they be
separately classified (1964: 118), since although coordinate in nature they
have a strong tendency to show the SXV order characteristic of
subordinates; see also Denison (1986: §2.2).

I shall not attempt to summarise the word order material in Mitchell's
great reference work (1985: Chapter IX). The approach is the same as in the
earlier article, but here Mitchell is at pains to show that so many order
possibilities can be attested in Old English that this reader at least is left
without a clear idea of what OE word order was like. For information on
the use of subjunctive verb forms in subordinate clauses – a possible test of
subordinate status which I shall not discuss here – see the many entries in
the contents pages of Mitchell's Volume 2 under 'Mood'. Subjunctives are
frequent, for example, in the subordinate members of correlative *ær* 'before'
. . . *ær* 'first' constructions (1985: §2540). Non-use is rarely decisive against
subordinate status, however.

4.4.3.2

Mitchell's important paper on the word order of the *Continuations* of the
Peterborough Chronicle (1964) is a highly traditional (if revisionist) study.
Where the *First Continuation*, dated 1122–31, might be regarded as very late
Old English, the *Second Continuation* of c1154–5 is often taken to be the
first Middle English text. Mitchell's purpose is to locate each *Continuation*
on a notional scale which runs from the norms of Old English to those of
Present-day English, and specifically to show that the *Second Continuation* is
less modern than had been claimed.

Various linguistic features are discussed in brief, but it is word order
patterns that dominate the article. A previous worker is condemned for 'not
appear[ing] to care whether the word-order in question is possible or not
today' (1964: 118). This criterion plays a major part in Mitchell's own
discussion, as can be seen from the conclusion that 'the word-order of the
two Continuations therefore contains much which is common to Old and

Modern English, much which cannot occur in Modern English, and nothing which cannot be paralleled in Old English' (1964: 138). Yet it is not necessarily helpful, since in principle at least the same pattern might be possible at different times for quite different reasons, as for example:

[10]   c1155 *Peterb.Chron.* 1137.42

    Wrecce men sturuen of hungær.
    poor   men died   of hunger

This word order could be produced either by V-2 syntax or by V-3, so that the modern-looking order of [10] might be coincidental and deceiving. Mitchell does observe that any *Peterborough Chronicle* word order which is found in Old English too is of no value as a test of modernity. He does not discuss the possibility that some word orders common to Old, Middle and Modern English might be due to fundamentally different word order principles in the different language systems. Only to some extent is this because of the limited purpose of his article: Mitchell's whole approach to word order makes discussion of underlying principles difficult.

4.5   Synchronic accounts within generative linguistics

Most transformational generative accounts of Old English syntax assume that the verb of every clause is generated in final position, despite the fact that V-F is not the most common of attested orders. In TG grammar, of course, a sentence may have a number of different syntactic structures, its underlying structure (initial structure, **deep structure**, **D-structure**) being transformed successively to its **surface structure** (**S-structure**) by means of explicit rules.[9] Details of tense marking and of notation apart, then, the underlying structure of *all* clauses in Old English is taken to be something like that of the subordinate clause illustrated in [11] (ignoring INFL):

[11]   (a)   *Gen 22.4*

    þa   hie   ða dune   gesawon
    when they(NOM) the hill(ACC) saw

    'when they saw the hill'

(b)

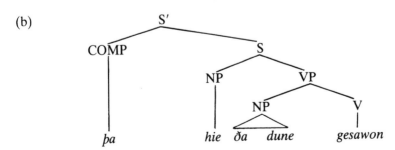

The subject of the clause – *hie* in [11] – is a *sister*[10] of the VP (verb phrase).
The VP may have a variety of internal structures – in [11] a simple object
NP, *ða dune*, as sister of V – but V is always its final constituent, at least if
sentence embedding is left out of account. Now the value of the V-F
analysis, first proposed for Modern Dutch and German, is that the typical
surface order of OE subordinate clauses is accounted for without further
cost, so that the surface structure of [11](a) is much like its underlying
structure.

Main clauses ('root clauses') require only a transformation from V-F to
V-2 order, and since COMP is typically empty of lexical material in main
clauses but occupied by a subordinator (conjunction) in subordinate clauses,
application of the movement rule can be made conditional on the COMP
node being empty. A common formulation is to treat the movement which
creates V-2 order as a two-stage process. First, V moves to COMP if COMP
is empty, making V the first constituent. Then one of the other constituents
is topicalised, that is, moved over V to a TOPIC position at the left
periphery of the whole structure, creating V-2 order. Support for,
refinements of, and problems with this analysis appear in numerous
publications, of which a selection of the ones concentrating on Old English
are discussed in the following pages. For a more general survey see Platzack
(1985).

4.5.1   Koopman

Willem Koopman has written a series of papers on Old English word order
(1985, 1990b, 1990c, 1990d, 1992), each working carefully through the
implications for a generative analysis of one small domain of syntax (and not
to be confused with influential cross-linguistic research on verbal syntax by
his sister, Hilda Koopman).

4.5.1.1

Koopman (1985) uses verb-particle combinations as a test case, where a
particle (henceforth 'prt') is a (usually) spatial adverb like *forð* 'forth,
forwards', *up* 'up', *ut* 'out'. Prior assumptions are that general base-
generated word order is SXV and that verb and particle are generated under
a single node (1985: §1), though the latter is perhaps a little dubious, since
most OE verb-particle combinations have nothing like the idiomatic unity of
many ModE phrasal verbs (Denison 1985b). In clauses where the verb-
particle combination is at the end and can therefore be presumed to
preserve its base-generated position, particle nearly always precedes verb, so
Koopman assumes that S-X-prt-V is the underlying order.[11] Particle and
verb, incidentally, are inserted as the following subtree:

[12]

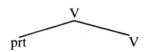

Given Koopman's working assumptions about underlying structure, the possible surface positions of prt are a useful pointer to the rules of OE syntax.

There are two main parts to his argument. In the first he looks at what happens to prt in clauses where V has moved to second position, as in:

[13] *ChronE* 135.10 (1003)

    ac he teah forð þa   his ealdan wrenceas
    but he drew forth then his old   tricks

    'but then he produced his old tricks'

He argues that the order of [13] is best accounted for by a Particle Movement rule to the left[12] rather than by Object Extraposition of *his ealdan wrenceas* to the right, thus:

[14] he [teah]$_{Vi}$ [forð$_j$]$_{prt}$ . . . his ealdan wrenceas [t$_j$]$_{prt}$ [t$_i$]$_V$

                     V-2

(In diagram [14] t stands for *trace*.) Koopman also claims that Particle Movement confines prt within the VP (1985: §§1.1–1.2).

4.5.1.2*

The variety of surface positions of prt within VP leads him to wonder if the internal order of VP could be left unspecified by the rules apart from the finality of V, but he decides against this and sticks with fixed underlying order and a rule of Particle Movement (1985: §2.1). (In a later paper on double object constructions, Koopman (1990d) goes the other way and argues for a VP with no internal structure.)

4.5.1.3

When prt appears to have escaped from VP altogether, as in:

[15] *Bede* 3 1.154.10

    þæt heo   onweg adyde þa gemynd   þara treowleasra
    that it[*sc.* the time?] away   did   the record(ACC) the faithless

    cyninga
    kings(GEN PL)

    'that it/they would strike out the record of those faithless kings'

Koopman's explanation is that the V-2 rule(s) have moved particle and verb as a unit, i.e. the higher V of [12] (1985: §1.2).

The second major strand of argument is rather more a problem of theory than of Old English, and it concerns the **landing site** for the movement of V (§2.2). The problem arises in subordinate clauses with SVX order (which suggest that V-2 applies only optionally in subordinates), some of which have an explicit subordinating conjunction: if COMP is already occupied by a subordinator, COMP cannot be the landing site for movement of V. An example Koopman cites in this context is [16]:

[16]   *ChronA* 46.5 (745)

        siþþan he onfeng bisc̄   dome
        after   he received bishop's authority

        'after he received the bishopric'

Koopman's eventual conclusion is that the landing site in both main and
subordinate clauses is INFL, the constituent which carries tense, with the
possibility of further movement of V + INFL to COMP and/or of
topicalisation of some other constituent.[13] The paper concludes with a brief
analysis of changes in Middle English (§§3–3.2).

    Koopman (1990c) deals with constructions involving a finite modal, an
infinitive of BEON, WESAN, WEORÐAN, or HABBAN, and a participle. Of
the six possible relative orders for the three verbal elements, two are rare
and one has not been found at all. Koopman's explanation of this, which
will be looked at in more detail in §15.3.1 below, relies heavily on the
technical notion of Verb raising, to be discussed in §4.7.1.2 below.

4.5.2   Pintzuk and Kroch

Having accepted that Old English had V-F underlying structure and a V-2
constraint, Susan Pintzuk and Anthony S. Kroch (1985, 1989) set out to
explain apparent departures from the orders predicted by it. Using a poetic
text, *Beowulf*, both because of its presumed archaism and because its metre
may provide clues to Old English intonation, they discuss why some main
verb complements can come *after* a verb which would otherwise be clause-
final, as in such examples as [17] (their [3]):

[17]   *Beo* 636

        Ic   gefremman sceal │ eorlic ellen
        I(NOM) perform   shall   heroic deed

        'I shall perform a heroic deed'

in effect giving a generative analysis of verb-late syntax. They consider in
turn four possible explanations:

(A)   variable word order in the base – but that cannot explain the complete
       absence of certain orders
(B)   'verb-attraction', a sort of topicalisation of the (non-finite) verb to the
       left periphery of the VP – but that too leaves certain examples
       unexplained
(C)   *Extraposition*
(D)   *Heavy-NP Shift*

The last two are different mechanisms for moving certain constituents to the
right periphery of VP. Since Extraposition in modern languages neither
moves NPs nor necessitates a strong intonation break between the moved
element and the preceding ones, they decide that Extraposition cannot
explain *Beowulf* examples which have an NP in the final position and/or a
metrical boundary between verb and complement. The rest of the paper is a
justification of the Heavy-NP Shift analysis. In Present-day English, only

when the NP to the immediate right of the verb is 'heavy' can it be shifted to the right, and then there is usually an intonation phrase boundary before the shifted NP.

Pintzuk and Kroch present evidence that half-line boundaries in *Beowulf* probably coincide with intonation phrase boundaries in speech, and they then make a statistical analysis of the presence or absence of half-line boundaries between clause-final NPs or PPs and their preceding clauses. Correlations between the metrical facts and various clause patterns lend support to three analyses: a Heavy-NP Shift analysis for final NPs in verb-late clauses; an Extraposition analysis for at least some final PPs; and, for clauses whose only verb is finite and not in final position, either a verb-seconding rule if there is a single constituent before the verb, or Heavy-NP Shift if there are more than one.[14]

4.6 Diachronic, non-generative explanations

4.6.1 Fourquet, Reszkiewicz and Strang[15]

Jean Fourquet's pioneering work (1938) on word order in early Germanic languages is of great importance, not least for his methodological assumptions. Fourquet looks for opposition(s) between an unmarked order and order(s) marked in some way. He allows for the convergence of unrelated developments, where speakers (unconsciously) identified new patterns accidentally formed and hence began to use new ordering principles, as well as for different ordering principles overlapping and being in conflict at a given time.

Texts from various Germanic languages are studied, including runic and Gothic material which represents the most primitive state of all. Within the historical period of English Fourquet studies the OE poem *Beowulf* and two sections of the *Anglo-Saxon Chronicle*, representing for him, respectively, an old, transitional and newer system of word order. In Fourquet's own summary (1938: 285–97) the primitive state is characterised by the importance of the VP ('*prédicat*'): OV order, the unmarked case, called attention to the whole VP, whereas VO order was used to draw attention to the individual constituents. Pronouns, however, behaved differently from other NPs and had their position determined by the other elements. Rather than discuss Fourquet's analysis of the succeeding three systems, let us move on to Barbara Strang, who relied on Fourquet's work in developing her analysis of word order developments in early Old English (1970: §192). Her dense but insightful argument resists further shortening. Here nevertheless is a brutal summary.

Prehistoric and early recorded Old English were V-F, with objects and complements – i.e. the rest of the VP – preceding the verb, and subject, if expressed, preceding *them*. Marking could be achieved by extraposing a focused element beyond the verb. A newer principle which grew up beside the older one was to put rhythmically light elements at the start of the clause; these included BEON and other auxiliary-like verbs. Contrastive marking for sentences ordered by weight was by means of V-1 order, a pattern appropriate for, and later specialised for, interrogatives. By the late ninth century a new pattern had developed for sentences which lacked light elements to put at the beginning. Where a heavy element opened the clause, the nominal elements of the VP closed it, leaving the verb contingently in medial position, i.e. V-2.[16] Increasingly V-2 became the norm for independent clauses, while verb-late began to be taken as characteristic of subordinate clauses.

For later Old English Strang leans on the work of Alfred Reszkiewicz (1966). His study of word order in the prose of Ælfric (c1000) concluded that the 'weight' of elements was a determining factor in their ordering. His ten-place template for unmarked declarative order – there is a succinct account of it in Strang (1970: §174) – is essentially a restricted version of SVX and is meant to apply to both main and subordinate clauses. The nucleus of the clause is the SV cluster, where V refers to the finite verb. A short function word, more or less what could be generated under COMP in a generative account, may precede the SV cluster. After the SV cluster are seven positional slots, available for items of increasing 'weight' as one moves further to the right. The first of them, for instance, is for items like personal pronouns, the last two for dependent and independent clauses. Like Fourquet and Bacquet, Reszkiewicz assumes that any deviation from the unmarked order he has intuited must have been marked in some way.

I see little prospect of confirming or disconfirming such a detailed specification, as the size of corpus which would be needed to produce reliable statistics and filter out all the distortions of marking, individual style, and interaction of factors would be enormous. If it could be done, it would certainly have to be computer-assisted, in order for statistical tests of correlation to be carried out on what would be a horribly multivariate distribution. Kohonen (1976/82, 1978) goes some way towards the goal, also confining himself (for Old English) to Ælfric.

A similar but less detailed view is very widely held. The two poles of Reszkiewicz's weight classification are represented by pronouns at the light end and clauses at the heavy. It is generally agreed that pronouns tend to come earlier in a clause than functionally equivalent full NPs during the OE period, whilst it is universally conceded that dependent (non-relative) clauses are final in the higher clause. Whether the manifest tendency of pronouns and clauses in Old English towards early and late placement, respectively, is a matter of weight or of givenness is harder to assess. Just as pronouns tend to be **anaphoric** and therefore given information, so clauses tend to be high in information content and therefore new information. Are their positional tendencies due to their weight or to the general linguistic fact that, other things being equal, theme (given) tends to precede rheme (new)? In probably the majority of cases, the positional predictions made by Reszkiewicz's weight classification will coincide with an ordering along a theme-rheme spectrum. However, they do not always coincide, and Kohonen has some interesting statistics on cases where a principle of end-weight seems to override considerations of givenness in the placement of adverbials (1976/82: 192).

I do not know whether weight *can* be separated from givenness: it may be that 'weight' can be factored into a component of 'rhematicity' and some measure of structural complexity. Whatever its theoretical status, the weight factor, or a reformulated principle or principles covering the same facts, ought to have its origin explained (which Strang at least does not do). Perhaps its appearance is due to a reinterpretation of common ordering sequences, originally determined by theme-rheme considerations, in terms of the *form* of the elements in question. But how, why, and indeed whether, remain unanswered questions.

4.6.2   Vennemann

4.6.2.1

Theo Vennemann (1974) suggests a development 'from SXV to SVX via TVX' as a general diachronic process but with obvious application to the history of English. His paper ranges rather wider than our immediate concerns, and we cannot summarise all of it. He develops a theory of basic word order which can make sense of the Greenberg universals, the so-called principle of natural serialisation. The principle concerns the relative order of operator and operand in binary constructions like P + NP, A + N, V + object, and so on. As defined in the article, **operator** is the partner which specifies or modifies, **operand** that which is specified or modified. This semantic definition is enhanced by a syntactic one: the operand is the partner which has the same (sort of) category membership as the combined construction. Thus in the NP *big feet*, the noun *feet*, being the same sort of category as the whole construction, is the operand; semantically too it is *feet* which is specified by *big*. With languages defined as XV if 'the normal position of the finite verb is the clause-final position in main declarative clauses' and VX otherwise (1974: 350), the principle states that operators will precede operands in a consistent XV language, and conversely for VX languages. (That many languages are 'inconsistent' is conceded and explained.)

Armed with this very powerful generalisation, Vennemann argues that English has been a clear VX language throughout its recorded history, even though its reconstructed distant ancestor, Early Proto-Indo-European, is thought to have been an XV language.[17] The word order changes we are interested in – relatively recent changes and all in the historical period – can then be seen as a move towards greater consistency as a VX language, as can other changes. Thus the growth of the *of*-possessive at the expense of preposed genitives (*the cover of the book* vs. *the book's cover*), as well as the growth of *to*-phrases at the expense of prepositionless indirect objects (*give a toy to the child* vs. *give the child a toy*), are both seen as predictable developments for a VX language, since both lead to operand-operator order.

The next stage of Vennemann's argument is to confine attention to the three most common types thrown up by Greenberg's survey, SXV, SVX and VSX, in all of which S precedes O in the unmarked situation. How can O be topicalised in such languages to give an emphatic or marked order? With SVX and VSX the marked order will be quite different from the unmarked. With SXV, however, there is a potential problem if the language cannot

reliably distinguish subject and object by morphological means (if it lacks
'S-O morphology'), for then both marked and unmarked order will be of the
form NP-NP-V. The relevant part of Vennemann's hypothesis is as follows
(1974: 359):

> A language with S-O morphology tends to be XV; as reductive phonological
> change weakens the S-O morphology, and does not develop some substitute S-O
> morphology, the language becomes a VX language. Since in VX languages order
> is a major grammatical marker, the order becomes increasingly rigid.

The way it becomes a VX language is for the verb to move to the position
after the topic in the marked sentences, i.e. TVX, after which V-2 order
may be generalised, and finally SVX order. Corroboration for the first stage
comes from the retention of XV order in subordinate clauses, where
topicalisation plays a smaller role. Bean (1983: 28) points to a problem with
Vennemann's theory, however, which is that a TVX stage with deficient
subject-object morphological differentiation is as bad as the NP-NP-V
ambiguity it was meant to solve, since now NP-V-NP will be ambiguous
between SVO and OVS.

The final section of Vennemann's paper concerns the TVX stage of
development. Vennemann looks at that characteristic feature of German
(and Dutch) grammar, the **sentence brace** (*Satzklammer*) formed by a finite
verb in (usually) second position and a non-finite verb or adverbial particle
at the end, enclosing between them most of the rest of the clause. I illustrate
the sentence brace construction from Old English:

[18]   *ÆCHom* I 1.20.1

On twam þingum hæfde God þæs mannes sawle gegodod
in two   things   had   God the man's   soul   endowed

'God had endowed man's soul with two things'

Vennemann suggests that the brace construction testifies to the fact that it is
the finite verb which has moved, since all other constituents remain in the
XV pattern. The brace construction has of course now disappeared from
English, but still-surviving remnants are the split verb-particle construction,
as in *look it up*,[18] and indirect-before-direct-object order (where the
principle of natural serialisation should predict the reverse). If the latter is a
remnant, however, it is worrying that its regularity should have *in*creased
between Old and Present-day English.

4.6.2.2

A later paper (Vennemann 1984) gives a plausible explanation of the rise of
the V-2/verb-late contrast and of what happened then: either its fall (English
and, to a lesser extent, Scandinavian) or its further strengthening (literary
German).[19] Everything is a long-term consequence of the early Germanic
formation of complex sentences by combining two sentences as a main and a
subordinate clause, with the latter introduced by a subjunction (subordinating
conjunction) which was etymologically a demonstrative. Most relevant for
the historical period of English are two ideas. Where subjunctions were
identical in form to demonstrative adverbs (I shall use the symbol

'ADV/COMP'[20] for such items), signalling of clause type by word order became a necessary disambiguating device, especially in writing, and the position of the finite verb became crucial. This is perhaps the origin of the V-2/verb-late contrast.[21] Main clause word order could safely be generalised to subordinate clauses provided that V-2 was maintained, for then main clauses would be V-2, and subordinates would be (literally) V-3 with the order ADV/COMP XV(X) (and ADV/COMP a subjunction). For V-2 to be lost in main clauses, however, with TV(X) becoming (X)SV(X), a new way of marking subordination was necessary, since the order ADV/COMP SV(X) would then have become ambiguous between main and subordinate clause. The new way found in English was a new set of subjunctions. Demonstratives and subjunctions became almost entirely distinct classes, so that the subjunction itself could be a sufficient marker of subordinate status.

4.6.3 Stockwell

4.6.3.1

Robert P. Stockwell's paper (1977) builds on Vennemann's work and tries to motivate both the TVX stage of development and the loss of the sentence brace construction. Although Stockwell talks informally of movement 'rules', his presentation does not invoke a specific, formal model of transformational grammar. Five conjectural stages intervene between a putative prehistoric SXV order for main clauses and the modern (X)SVX order for all clauses; they are summarised by Stockwell as follows (1977: 296):

[19] (a) SO(V)v → vSO(V) by Comment Focusing
     (b) vSO(V) → xvSO(V) by Linkage or Topicalization
     (c) TvX(V) → SvX(V) by Subject = Topic
     (d) SvX(V) → Sv(V)X[22] by Exbraciation
     (e) Subordinate Order → Main Order by Generalization (or, at least, elimination of whatever differences existed)

The meanings of the abbreviations are given as follows (1977: 292):

v   = modal, *have*, *be*/*become*, finite V (probably a restricted set of V, such as V of motion)
S   = subject
O   = object/verb complements
(V) = optional non-finite verb
[. . .]
x   = *then*, *there*, etc.

Let us take each stage in turn.

Process [19](a) 'would code some semantic content such as "vividness" of action: i.e. the action, not the participants, would be primary in the expression' (Stockwell 1977: 291). What remains unclear from the article is why only the restricted set of verbs subsumed under 'v' could be fronted to produce 'Comment Focusing'; note however the rather similar proposals of Strang on contrastive marking by V-1 order (see §4.6.1 above, also further data and analysis in Denison 1986: §2.4). For subsequent stages of the argument 'v' seems to mean any finite verb at all.

Process [19](b) produces V-2 order. Either an explicit linking word contextualises the heightened vividness of vSO(V), or topicalisation puts an object or adverb in the initial slot. The two separate processes [19](a–b) (or three, if linking ≠ topicalisation) are meant to give a more plausible explanation for the TVX stage posited by Vennemann (1974). A problem which Stockwell readily concedes is that there is little evidence for the stages immediately succeeding the initial SXV proto-stage and therefore for [19](a–b), and prose evidence for a V-1 stage even suggests an *in*crease in the late ninth century rather than the decrease predicted from the action of process [19](b).[23] Some tricky interpretation of the data is called for (1977: 296–8), which I tentatively interpret as follows. The apparently widespread V-2 of early Old English is illusory, since the proportion which are unambiguously the result of a TVX rule is actually negligible: either they have *þa* 'then', *þonne* 'then' or *þær* 'there' as first element and can be seen as examples of linkage and therefore 'really' V-1, or they have S in initial position and so can be seen as the output of [19](c). The effect of redistributing the apparent V-2 examples is to give more plausibility to the five-stage development of [19] by evening up the scores for the first three stages.

Process [19](c) results from the fact that two overlapping subtypes of V-2 happen also to be SVO and so permit the ***abduction*** of SVO as a new word-order rule (Stockwell 1977: 295):

[20] (i)   Those in which, as Vennemann notes above, topic is specialized to the primary topic case, namely the subject: i.e. TVX = SVO.
      (ii) Those in which the finite verb is simple so that there is no remnant of a complex verb in the final position: i.e. SvO(V) = SVO.

Stockwell distinguished the two subtypes in order to emphasise the contribution made to the rise of SVO ordering by two potentially independent developments: loss of V-2 and loss of the sentence brace (p.c. 1989).

It is the fourth and fifth stages, [19](d–e), which are of greatest interest. Process [19](d), exbraciation, means that 'rightward movement takes place to eliminate nominal and adverbial elements from within the brace [v. . .V], thus reunifying the auxiliaries and main verbs' (Stockwell 1977: 295). A number of contributory factors are later adduced (1977: 301–10). The first is that many V-2 sentences have only a simple verb [and the subject in first position] and therefore have all object and adverbial material *after* the verb, while true braced constructions are not very common. This is essentially the type described under [20](ii), of course, in the context of explaining [19](c). Therefore the Old English language learner 'had very good reason to abduce a rule of the following nature':

Nominal and adverbial complements follow their head verb. (1977: 305)

Then Stockwell brings in a number of 'rightward-movement rules which lifted constituents out of the sentence brace and destroyed the verb-final appearance of surface clauses' (1977: 305). These are the optional Extraposition to the very end of the superordinate clause of relative clauses, conjuncts (split constituents), appositives, adverbs and afterthoughts, and sentential subjects and objects. Here is one of his examples, with an *except*-phrase appearing as an afterthought:

[21]   *ChronA* 90.28 (897)

    on þæm   wæron eac þa men ofslægene
    on that-one [*sc.* ship that got away] were   also the men killed

    buton   fifum
    except-for five

    'On that one too all but five of the men were killed.'

As for process [19](e), note simply that the analogy proposed is for subordinate clauses to be influenced by main clause order. Stockwell is aware that the empirical support is weak, citing Bean (1976) for evidence that SVO was established *earlier* in subordinate clauses than in main clauses, and in later work (see §4.7.3 below) he and Minkova have actually suggested a converse direction for analogy.

4.6.3.2

Stockwell's later paper (1984) looks at constructions in Modern English which appear to obey a V-2 constraint. He finds some to be retained from Old English, others to be innovations. His scenario is that V-2 represented an optional norm in late Old English, 'probably a rhetorical norm for the introduction of a new or surprising subject' (1984: 583–4), and that there never was a genuine TVX stage in which NP-topics other than subject were commonly found in initial position. After late Old English there were two principal developments. V-2 instances that were SVX were reanalysed as marking subjecthood to the left of the finite verb, leading to the (X)SVX (i.e. V-3) syntax of Modern English. V-2 instances with initial negatives, affectives (?= semi-negatives like *rarely*) and interrogatives came to be regarded as being triggered by those particular initial elements, so that a grammaticised V-2 came to be limited to those domains. Two further modern types remain: V-2 after certain adverbs and after quotations has always been optional – there is no change here – and V-2 after **predicative** constituents (e.g. participles + modifiers, adjective phrases) is a ME or ModE innovation.

4.6.4 Canale

(William) Michael Canale (1976) builds on the work of Greenberg, Vennemann and others to test the validity of some hypotheses on implicational hierarchies. In particular, he suggests that there is an implicational hierarchy of word order patterns within the NP, another within the VP, and that both are reflected in observed chronological change. His English data come from early portions of the *Anglo-Saxon Chronicle* and produce the contradictory findings that within the NP domain the patterns

are consistent with an OV language type, while within the VP domain the
patterns mostly fit VO. There is some inconclusive discussion of how these
facts might be reconciled. Chapter 3 of Canale (1978) appears to be a
slightly updated version of the article.

It is Chapter 2 of Canale's dissertation (1978) which has been very
influential on generativists. (The thesis director was David Lightfoot.) Here
the corpus includes portions of the *Chronicle* extending through and maybe
beyond the OE period.[24] Canale uses the EST variant of Chomskyan
grammar and makes much of the notion of a **root S**, one not dominated by a
node other than S (i.e. Sentence, of course, not Subject). A main clause is
the obvious kind of root S, but other kinds of clause can be root Ss too.

On the grounds that the surface order of non-root Ss (i.e. most dependent
clauses) must reflect base order, Canale assumes that base order in Old
English was (S)XV (1978: 79–80). V-2 phenomena are dealt with by a rather
mechanical rule of 'Verb Seconding' (1978: 91–2), while clauses where the
non-finite verb has moved to a position next to the finite are derived by
means of 'Verb Attraction' (1978: 103–13). The essence of the argument,
however, is that transformations like these, which produce patterns
impossible as underlying orders, can only affect root clauses. (Canale quotes
with approval some studies that suggest that syntactic change affects main
clauses before subordinates.) He claims that in Old English up to the
eleventh century, VX patterns were more or less confined to root clauses.
Counter-examples have to be explained away somehow or other, for instance
as errors or the result of stylistic expressivity, or by extending the concept of
root S to include Causal clauses, Purpose clauses, *þæt*-complements to non-
factive verbs, as well as all SE relatives (1978: 69–74). In the twelfth-century
material, however, Canale finds that VX patterns had indisputably invaded
non-root Ss, and his preferred explanation is that base order had by
then changed to SVX (rendering Verb Seconding and Verb Attraction
redundant).

Certain details of the exposition are dubious. For example, relative
clauses with HATAN 'name, be called' have the name treated as object,
whether the verb is passive or active in form (1978: 59n.), thus presumably
both *Willelm of Curboil* and *Cicc* in the two instances in [22]:

[22]   *ChronE* 251.32 (1123)

    Ða cusen hi   an clerc Willelm of Curboil wæs gehaten. he was
    then chose they a cleric William of Corbeil   was called,   he was

    canonie of   an mynstre   Cicc hatte.   & brohten him toforen
    canon   from a monastery   Cicc was-called, and brought him before

    se kyng
    the king

    'Then they chose a cleric called William of Corbeil – he was a canon
    from a monastery called Cicc [= St Osyth's, Essex] – and brought him
    before the king.'

But inflected names are usually in the nominative case in these idioms
(Mitchell 1985: §§1473–5), so that 'predicative complement' would be a

better label than 'object'. Sentences whose only verb (or verbs) is (are)
BEON, HABBAN, WEORÐAN or a modal are said to develop (S)VX order
mysteriously earlier than others and are therefore ignored in most of the
tabulations (Canale 1978: 61–3). Some types of constituent do not show the
desired degree of freedom of movement and are ignored on that account:
pronoun objects because they favour pre-verb position too rigidly, PP and
AdvP constituents because their positioning is too free (1978: 66–7). There
is some nonsense (1978: 83) about treating *hie* in

[23] *ChronA* 91.17 (897)

& he   hie   ðær ahon   het
and he(NOM) them(ACC) there hang(INF) ordered

'and he ordered them to be hanged there'

as an indirect object (!) and *ðær ahon* as the direct object, with a false claim
of support from Callaway (1913); for the construction see Chapter 8 below.
Despite the acknowledged and unacknowledged weak points in Canale's
theory and his argument from data, his conclusion that base order changed
from SXV to SVX by the mid-twelfth century is taken over with little
comment by a number of generative grammarians of the 1980s.

Unlike many generative grammarians, Canale offers counts of different
patterns in his material. Among the interesting claims made is the
suggestion that the brace construction was actually rather rare. On Canale's
figures (1978: 58) the proportion of clauses with a sentence brace was
actually 11 per cent in his middle (tenth-/eleventh-century) period, but a
figure of just over 1 per cent in both the ninth- and twelfth-century periods
brings the overall proportion down to about 4 per cent.

4.6.5 Bean

Marian C. Bean's experiment (1983),[25] preceded by a useful review of
earlier work, is to test a number of conjectural theories of word order
change against the actual facts of Old English. Her method is appealing in
its simplicity. In brief she takes different portions of the *Anglo-Saxon
Chronicle* as representative of different stages of Old English, counts
instances of different orders in each portion, and tots up the number of
clauses consistent with various ordering principles, for instance T-V, V-1,
V-2, and V-3. When she finds that the history of main clauses in the
Chronicle does not present a neat development and is inconsistent with any
of the theories under investigation, she looks briefly and inconclusively at
some other studies and some other texts, before deciding that stylistic
factors have distorted her results and that the best explanation is that Old
English developed straight from being a V-F language to a V-3 one (as
English is now). But this takes us back to conjecture again – one that is
neither better nor worse than many other conjectures on offer – and utterly
undermines the careful data collection which is the basis of her work.

Bean's main research programme has considerable merit, but the results –
or rather the lack of a clear result – must be seen in the light of such
problems as the following:

(A)   a failure to distinguish clauses introduced by coordinating conjunctions from other main clauses (see e.g. §4.6.6 below)

(B)   a failure to distinguish pronouns from other NPs (see e.g. §§4.4.3, 4.6.1 above)

(C)   absence of generalisation about the polarity and the kind of finite verb often found in V-1 examples (see Denison 1986: §2.4)

(D)   counting two instances of X'SVXV$_n$ (where V = finite verb, V$_n$ = non-finite verb) as evidence of V-2 ordering (see Denison 1986: §2.1 n.7)

(E)   the assumption that *Anglo-Saxon Chronicle* annals for years prior to 892 are *linguistically* pre-892 as well

4.6.6 Kohonen

One of the fullest and most important non-generative accounts is by Vilho Kohonen (1978). As a dissertation it begins with valuable surveys of previous work and of word order theory. Careful methodology and reliable statistics permit the consideration of various possible explanatory factors for changes in word order between Old and Middle English. The Old English of Ælfric is contrasted with the early Middle English of *SWard* and *Vices & V.(1)*. Kohonen's model makes reference to Fillmore's Case Theory (see §3.1.3.1 above), to Functional Sentence Perspective (a theory centring on the theme-rheme continuum, see §4.1.4 above), and to work in transformational grammar which distinguished between main and subordinate clause phenomena (Kohonen 1978: 51–69).

The central chapters of the book offer statistical analyses of the word order patterns found, first on a syntactic basis, then according to thematic structure. The syntactic analysis deals with the positions of various clausal elements, tabulating the effects of syntactic function, length and meaning and of clause type, before considering the change from SXV to SVX syntax. Coordinate clauses (those introduced by *and* or *ac*) are always treated as a category in themselves; they shifted from showing statistical behaviour intermediate between main and subordinate clauses to being more like main clauses. The discussion of clauses with auxiliary verbs does not always make clear when it concerns main clauses, subordinate clauses, or all clauses. Kohonen tentatively suggests the following development: SXVv → SXvV → SvXV/vSXV → SvVX (1978: 104). The evidence for the first stage appears to come from subordinate clauses, and for the last stage from main clauses.

Kohonen argues that SXV first began to break down in main clauses but that the increase in SVX order was then faster in subordinate clauses, since main clauses retained XVS (V-2 order) for some time. He looks at various possible factors relevant to the breakdown of SXV order (1978: 123–32), namely syntactic function (subject complements move beyond the verb first); ambiguity avoidance (clauses with full nouns as S and O tend towards SVO order); afterthought phenomena; and length of clause (longer clauses tend towards SVO order). Most of these factors correlate strongly with a principle of end-weight, making it hard to untangle the causatory factors. While not denying their relevance, Kohonen downplays the importance of ambiguity avoidance and especially of afterthought phenomena (cf. §4.6.3.1).

The discourse analysis proceeds from a classification of constituents on a scale of givenness. The positional behaviour of various sentence constituents is then cross-tabulated against their givenness. One result is a criticism of Vennemann's suggested TVX stage of Old English (discussed in §4.6.2.1 above) on the grounds that some initial constituents and a fair proportion of pre-verbal elements were new (1978: 151). There was, however, 'a general tendency to arrange constituents in a given-new perspective' (1978: 191). Kohonen finds too 'that givenness was involved in the shift from SXV to SVX: new elements seemed to be the first to shift to the right of the verb, with the tendency being more pronounced in main clauses. But the shift can hardly be attributed to this factor alone' (1978: 191).

Kohonen's results form a useful database. A possible improvement might be the elimination of 'knock-out' factors before correlations among other factors are measured, as favoured in more recent work in variation analysis (e.g. Rydén and Brorström 1987). To give an example: if the relativiser *þe* in Old English (which Kohonen 1978: 107 treats as a pronoun) is always clause-initial and shows no positional variation, then clauses with *þe* could be removed from the count before the general, variable, positional behaviour of pronouns is examined.

4.6.7 Gerritsen

Marinel Gerritsen (1984) gathers some useful data on Germanic languages during their recorded histories and then tries to account for the varied fortunes of what she calls 'embraciation' (i.e. the brace construction in declarative main clauses vs. V-F in dependent clauses) and 'inversion' (i.e. V-2). For the modern languages she suggests that English alone has lost both; the Scandinavian languages have lost embraciation but retained obligatory inversion; while German, Frisian and Dutch have made both obligatory. Gerritsen's *forte* is the global view, not the precision of detail. She suggests that embraciation was lost in English because of an alleged late development of periphrastic verb forms, and especially a later and lesser use of the perfect than shown by contemporaneous forms of German and Dutch. If true it would reinforce Stockwell's [20](ii) (§4.6.3.1 above); however, I found reasons to doubt that periphrastic verb forms were at all infrequent in Old English (Denison 1986: §2.5). We shall look at the development of the perfect in Chapter 12. As for the loss of V-2, Gerritsen speculates that this was due either to creolisation in Middle English from the mixture of Old English, Scandinavian and French (cf. §2.4 above) or to direct French influence. What is interesting here is the treatment of the loss of V-2 as a later and separate development, an idea we shall see explored with more precision in van Kemenade's work (§4.7.1 below).

4.6.8 Danchev and Weerman

An influential study of second-language acquisition of German (Clahsen and Muysken 1986) suggested that adult Turkish learners tended to posit SVO order for German, despite the fact – or at least, the usual analysis – that both Turkish and German are OV languages. (Children behaved differently.) This led to the idea that SVO might somehow be the natural outcome of language contact when adult speakers of one language transfer to another. Andrei Danchev argues that SVO is 'simpler, less marked and more iconic than SOV (and other word orders)' (1991: 116), and he implies that Clahsen and Muysken's results support his more general claim that Middle English was a partly creolised language (see §2.4 above), where reduction of morphology and establishment of fixed SVO word order would be predictable outcomes. Apparently independently of Danchev, Fred Weerman gave a conference paper (1991) in which the Clahsen and Muysken results were extrapolated to the Danish settlements in England as an explanation for the SOV → SVO change in English.

Unfortunately, the relevant results of Clahsen and Muysken (1986) have been partially withdrawn. It appears from fuller collections of data that adult speakers of OV languages like Turkish and Korean do *not* tend to postulate VO when learning German. As Vainikka and Young-Scholten (1991: 20 n.16) report, 'since we found a good number of SOV structures in our data, Clahsen and Muysken's analysis is no longer descriptively adequate' – which rather pulls the rug out from under these promising speculations on the history of English word order.

4.7 Diachronic accounts within generative linguistics

4.7.1 Van Kemenade

4.7.1.1

Ans van Kemenade's dissertation (1987) is a major study within the framework of Government-Binding theory of, amongst other things, Old and Middle English word order. In her analysis two major changes distinguish Modern English from Old English. In the first place Old English had SOV (V-F) base order, whereas Modern English has SVO. In the second place there was a fully grammaticised rule of V-2 in main (root) clauses in Old English but not, of course, in Modern English. The two changes on the way to Modern English were not simultaneous.

The argument for SOV base order in Old English is largely as sketched above in §4.5. A base-generated complementiser prevents the application of the V-2 process, which is why most subordinate clauses have V-F order. Van Kemenade finds detailed corroboration of the V-F hypothesis in the behaviour of verb-particle constructions, where her material overlaps with similar work by Koopman, summarised in §4.5.1 above. She acknowledges that V-F could be weakened to surface verb-late if object NPs or PPs were moved beyond the verb (1987: §2.2; cf. §4.5.2 above).

The analysis of V-2 is a more technical matter (1987: §2.3.1). Many main clauses in Old English are clearly V-2 on the surface, but many are not. Van Kemenade suggests that the essence of 'V-2' is the movement of V to INFL – the component which includes tense – which in Old English is outside S, the clause proper:[26]

[24]

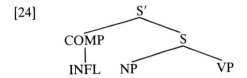

Subsequent topicalisation of some S-constituent (whether the subject NP or some constituent of VP) to first position in COMP will then give V-2 order, while failure to topicalise explains the fairly frequently attested V-1 order. Two major classes of exception remain. One involves NP constituents which are pronominal. Van Kemenade gives detailed argument for taking personal pronouns as clitics in Old English and therefore not independent words, which means that they should not be counted as constituents in assessing the position of the verb. Doing this removes a large number of cases where the verb is apparently in third or fourth position, though it also turns many examples which would otherwise have been V-2 into V-1 examples. Van Kemenade's work on OE and ME pronouns has been very influential and has revealed far greater regularity in word order patterning than had been achieved in previous analyses. That *some* OE personal pronouns nevertheless cannot be clitics is demonstrated by Koopman (1992).

4.7.1.2*

The second problem concerns embedded infinitive clauses. The analysis which van Kemenade follows takes verbs like CUNNAN 'can, know how' and MAGAN 'may, have power' – what in Present-day English would be called modal verbs – as ordinary lexical verbs in Old English. That means that an infinitive associated with a modal (or indeed with a perception verb like SEON 'see') is part of the complement of the modal. So the underlying structure of [25](a) is something like [25](b):

[25]   (a)   *Or* 48.18
             þæt he mehte his feorh generian
             that he might his life   save

             'so that he could save his life'

(b)

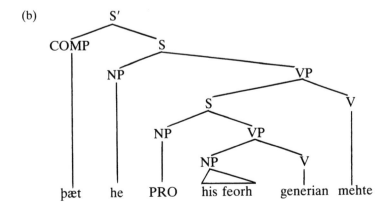

The element **PRO** which is subject of *generian* is a pronominal **anaphor** with no phonological form in surface structure, ***controlled*** by the NP *he* which is subject of *mehte*. Treating finite verb and infinitive as constituents of different clauses leaves certain properties of such sentences unexplained, especially the multiplicity of word orders attested. Van Kemenade therefore adopts a proposal made for Dutch and German, namely a transformation of **Verb raising**, which alters the structure to make finite verb and infinitive part of a single clause, thus perhaps as [25](c):

[25]   (c)

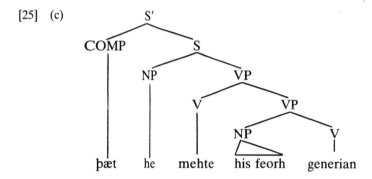

Verb raising seems to permit either V or VP to be raised into the higher VP, and as either left sister (German) or right sister (Dutch) of the finite verb. The details are not fully worked out for Old English; there is a little further discussion in van Kemenade (1985), and see now Koopman (1990c). I have actually borrowed structure [25](c) from van Kemenade's analysis of a West Flemish example (1987: 59).

4.7.1.3

The upshot is that the great majority of OE declaratives are consonant with underlying V-F order and a small number of transformational processes: V-2 (i.e. Verb-movement + Topicalisation), Extraposition (i.e. either Extraposition proper or Heavy-NP Shift), and Verb raising. It is perhaps worth pointing out that Koopman, whose approach is similar to van Kemenade's, finds very little evidence in any of the constructions he investigated of change *during* the OE period (1990a: 18).

As far as subsequent historical development is concerned, van Kemenade (1987: §6.1.1) accepts Canale's claim that a base order change from OV to VO was completed by 1200. Once base order had changed, surface SVO patterns had to be derived from underlying SVO by a two-stage V-2 process which left all constituents in the same relative order, though with the subject NP and finite verb now attached to different nodes of the tree (a 'string-vacuous' change). This derivation being somewhat opaque, the SVO/V-2 stage was unstable. Though it is well preserved in Chaucer's London dialect of the last quarter of the fourteenth century, in the contemporary Midlands dialect of Wyclifite writings there is evidence that pronouns were no longer being treated as clitics, and standard Modern English descends from Midlands varieties. By about 1400 V-2 had been lost. Van Kemenade associates the loss with a fundamental change in underlying sentence structure. Compare the pre-1400 structure of [24] with the proposed structure [26] for the modern period:

[26]

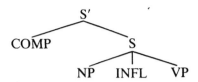

INFL is now in VP rather than being part of COMP.

4.7.2 Colman

Fran Colman's contribution (1988) to an understanding of word order change in Old English is couched in Case Grammar terms (see §§3.1.3.1–5 above). She sees Heavy-NP Shift as an important factor, renaming it 'Heavy Argument Shift' to include constituents other than NPs, and concentrating on the loss of V-F in subordinate and coordinate clauses.

The verb is analysed as head of its clause, and *all* other constituents are called arguments of the verb, since all are dependent on it, directly or indirectly, in this analysis. Colman makes use of a distinction between **participants** and **circumstantials**. Participants are those constituents which play a part in the classification of the verb, roughly what we have been calling *arguments* of the verb. Circumstantials are the remaining constituents, what we have been calling non-arguments. The discussion proceeds as follows.

Early Old English was essentially V-F, but this is a word order which can lead to particular perceptual problems. The clause nucleus of verb and non-subject participant arguments (cf. Strang 1970, discussed in §4.6.1 above) may be interrupted by circumstantials, illustrated graphically by the **tangling** of dependency lines. If one clause – e.g. a relative clause – is embedded inside another, verbs may pile up at the end of the construction if V-F is rigorously obeyed. Extraposition and especially Heavy Argument Shift were two strategies for alleviating these problems. Examples from an eleventh-century text of the *Anglo-Saxon Chronicle* are presented in two main groups, (S)XV order and (S)VX. Some of the dependency trees from the first group serve to illustrate the perceptual problems mentioned above, while the second group represents the solution. (Notice, though, that (S)VX order does not keep all Colman's examples free of 'tangling'.) Finally, Colman suggests, the movement was generalised from heavy arguments to light ones – i.e. pronouns – and SVX had been grammaticalised.

Colman's analysis is a helpful step towards making precise the 'leakage' by various rightward movements which is thought to have weakened and ultimately destroyed V-F word order. Since the distinction between participants and circumstantials seems to have some bearing on adverbial placement in Present-day English, it is promising to explore its utility for Old English. And it seems an improvement over many other formal accounts that the presence or absence of circumstantials is not treated as an irrelevance to the placement of participants.

Much more work remains to be done, however. 'Heaviness' in arguments is described as made up of two components, **lexical weight** and **constituent** weight (1988: 41–3). Essentially all NPs apart from bare pronouns have lexical weight, and all NPs apart from a bare pronoun or noun have constituent weight. Any non-pronominal NP is therefore eligible for Heavy Argument Shift, plus those pronominal NPs with quantifier or relative clause modification, so that practically any example of SVX order can be claimed as the outcome of the alleged process. (A *scale* of heaviness, together with statistical treatment of the incidence of Heavy Argument Shift, might make the explanation more falsifiable and therefore more convincing.) And the nature of the process is not made clear. Although Colman appears to set constituents in motion by the use of expressions like 'Extraposition', 'Heavy Argument Shift', and even 'move to the right of the V' (1988: 82), the movements implicitly represent a chronological change rather than a derivational process, since she is not working within a transformational theory. Heavy Argument Shift must presumably be interpreted as a constraint on possible word orders.

4.7.3 Stockwell and Minkova

Robert P. Stockwell and Donka Minkova have written several papers recently on word order development (1990, 1991, 1992). One of them focuses on the relationship between V-F order and subordinate clause status and offers the novel suggestion that V-3 word order, first grammaticised in subordinate clauses, influenced the development of V-3 in main clauses rather than vice versa (Stockwell and Minkova 1991). Their hypothesis can be summed up as follows, with arrows indicating the main directions of analogical influence:

[27]

order:	underlying	surface		
clause type:		main		subordinate
subject:		full NP	pronoun	NP/pronoun
OE	XSXV	XVS(X) or SVX	(X)SV(X)	XSXV
1200–1400	XSVX	SVX or XVS(X)	XSV(X)	XSVX
ModE	XSVX	(X)SVX	(X)SVX	XSVX

In Old English main clauses mostly obeyed a V-2 constraint, while subordinates mostly remained V-F. In the transition from Old English to early Middle English a new underlying order VX rather than XV was abduced for verb phrases. This happened because V-2 plus exbraciation of various kinds so frequently produced apparent SVX in main clauses (cf.

§4.6.3.1 above). When underlying structure changed, subordinate clauses ceased to be SXV and became SVX[27] – effectively a change in subordinate order on analogy with (frequent surface) main clause order. Main clause order was still actually V-2 at this stage, however, for with a non-subject topic the order was XVS(X), unless the subject was a personal pronoun and therefore a clitic (in which case XSV(X) conformed to the V-2 constraint).

In late fourteenth-century texts decliticisation of pronouns set in. In Chaucer's prose V-2 was maintained in main clauses but now without distinction between full NP and pronoun subjects, which both appeared in XVS(X) order when the topic was not S.[28] In Wyclifite texts, on the other hand, there was no XVS(X) order with non-subject topics, only XSV(X). That too at least suggests that subject pronouns were not clitics, since full NPs were now appearing in what had previously been a clitic position. Stockwell and Minkova suggest that what had happened was that subordinate order had been generalised to main clauses in this dialect. In subordinates it already made no difference whether the subject was a full NP or a clitic pronoun: either would precede the verb. The only place in the grammar of declaratives where subject had been able to *follow* the verb was XVS(X) for full NPs in main clauses – see the '1200–1400' line of diagram [27]. In the types of Middle English that underlie standard ModE syntax, this clause type came to conform to the (X)SV(X) found everywhere else. In other words, V-2 order in main clauses had disappeared and been replaced by V-3 (SVX).

4.8   Ramifications

Apart from its intrinsic importance, word order change is implicated in a number of syntactic changes. Changes in the relation between subject and finite verb are connected with the increasing association of pre-verbal position with subjecthood (see Part III of this book on changes in impersonal constructions and the development of indirect and prepositional passives). So too are changes in the relation between NP and infinitival verb, i.e. in the structure of embedded infinitive clauses, discussed in Part IV. The loss of final position for non-finites increases the frequency with which finite and non-finite verbs are contiguous and hence is relevant to the formation of auxiliary verbs such as modals and HAVE, on which see Part V. And increasing use of auxiliary verbs ties in with increasing fixity of S(. . .)VX word order (where V is now the *main* verb) for declaratives – positive and negative – and interrogatives, so that V is followed directly by its object(s) or complement(s). This brings us back round to the development of idiomatic expressions consisting syntactically of verb plus object or (part of) complement, for example phrasal and prepositional verbs.

4.9   Questions for discussion or further research

(a) Choose a stretch of OE prose and try counting the word orders that you find in it. What problems of classification do you have to solve (or ignore!)? To what extent do main clauses and subordinate clauses show

V-2 and V-F orders, respectively? Is there any evidence of SVO ordering?

(b) Make a careful analysis of the word order developments sketched by Strang (1970) and Stockwell (1977). Identify any logical flaws or gaps in their respective arguments, and correct or fill as appropriate.

(c) Suppose that Reszkiewicz's weight ordering principle is approximately empirically correct for Old English. Can you construct a plausible explanation of its development? Can you integrate the facts which it accounts for into a conventional generative model?

(d) If it is true that Old English obeys a looser version of the word order rules followed by Modern Dutch or German, should we assume that all three languages have shared similar developments? If so, is Old English at an earlier stage of development in this respect, at a later stage, or in some sense at both?

(e) Investigate the prevalence in other dialects of late-fourteenth-century English than Chaucer's and Wyclif's of (i) clitic pronouns and (ii) V-2 order.

(f) Consider the relationship between interrogative and declarative word order (and/or between imperative and declarative order) as declarative order changes over time. Have interrogatives and imperatives changed significantly during the historical period?

Notes

1. Bruce Mitchell (1985: §3887) prefers the term 'element order', since what is in question is the order of clause elements like 'subject' rather than of the individual words which make the elements up. This is a fair point (though we can note pedantically that some items discussed are not actually immediate constituents of the clause), but so far 'word order' remains the prevalent usage.

2. I retain the SVO labelling, as is normal in this field. Note, however, that synchronic descriptions of Present-day English in the British tradition of Halliday tend to reserve Verb for the *category* (on a par with Noun, etc.) and use the label Predicator for the *function* (on a par with Subject, Object, etc.). For a good discussion see Huddleston (1984: 5–9). However, Quirk et al. (1985) – the best-known exponents of (certain aspects of) the Hallidayan approach – actually use Verb for the function.

3. That is to say, for example, if a language is SOV in its basic clause order, then (usually? always? eventually?) its prepositional phrases will have the NP before rather than after the particle, its NPs will have adjective before noun, and so on.

4. For example, while Clahsen and Muysken (1986) carefully distinguish between 'underlying' and 'frequently used' or 'dominant' orders (1986), Vainikka and Young-Scholten say that they 'analyzed SVO as the canonical word order' (1991: 20 n.16).

5. I ignore the intervention of certain adverbs between subject and verb:

   (a) (Last year) Jimmy always spoilt his chances.

6. In contexts where O = object is inappropriate, some studies use X as a cover term for all elements other than subject and verb. Bean (1983) also uses X' for anything except S, V and O.

7. Topicalisation of adverbial particles as in [5] is blocked, for example, if the adverb is not literally directional in meaning or the verb is transitive:

(a) *Down piped the heckler after the speaker's riposte.
(b) *Down he ripped the flag.

8. I have made omissions at the three points indicated by [. . .].
9. At this stage I mention some more-or-less equivalent terms used by different sects without going into theological differences.
10. Root clauses (i.e. main clauses) allow topicalisation of certain constituents and thus require a Topic node. In some formulations Topic is a left sister of the topmost S', with both of them dominated by S'' ('S-double-prime'):

(c)

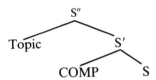

In other formulations Topic is a daughter of COMP. (For *COMP(lementiser)* see the Glossary.)
11. Koopman mentions four examples found by Hiltunen (1983: 116) with clause-final V–prt order. Two of them (*CP* 277.24 *toweorpeð ut* 'throws out' and *HomU* 18(*BlHom* 1) 9.33 *cwom forþ* 'came forth') can be explained by the attraction of the particle to an extraposed PP, as in *toweorpeð ut of hiere selfre*: PPs can of course be extraposed to the right of an otherwise-final verb quite easily in Old English. *ChronE* 248.21 (1119) involves the combination *coman togædere* 'came together'. I have argued (Denison 1981: 122-4) that forms like *togædere* are marginal to the particle system and show some behaviour indicative of their origins in prepositional phrases. That leaves just *ÆCHom* II 11.95.112 *teah ut*. (Cf. also van Kemenade 1987: 31–2.) Koopman's choice of prt-V as the base generated order is amply justified, therefore, given his other assumptions.
12. A rather sterile debate among transformational grammarians of the 1970s concerned the relationship in Present-day English between pairs like:

(a) Nixon pulled out the troops.
(b) Nixon pulled the troops out.

Is the underlying order as in (a), with (b) formed by Rightwards Particle Movement, or conversely is the (b) order basic and (a) formed by Leftwards Particle Movement?
13. However, Koopman has now abandoned this aspect of the analysis and adopted the Topic analysis sketched in §4.5 above, citing the following sentence as evidence:

(a)   *HomU* 20(*BlHom* 10) 113.2
       Hwæt he þonne sceal mid his saule anre Gode ælmihtigum riht   agyldan
       well he then   must with his soul alone God almighty   account render
       'Well then he must render to Almighty God an account with his soul alone.'

If INFL follows the subject directly, (a) shows that *sceal* cannot have moved to INFL. Rather *sceal* is in COMP, *he* and *þonne* in Topic (1990a: 6–8).
14. Pintzuk and Kroch assume that V-2 in early Old English meant that only one *stressed* constituent could precede the verb, and accordingly they analyse as V-2 those examples where additional elements preceding the verb are (unstressed) pronouns (1985: 105 n.12). Their assumption, which is stated in terms of rhythm, is restated in syntactic terms by van Kemenade. The revised paper introduces a

rule of Floating to move the unstressed elements (1989: 128).

15. Much of the material in this section is taken from Denison (1986), the passage on Reszkiewicz's weight ordering template almost *verbatim*.

16. Fourquet suggests that in sentences introduced by a heavy element in his 'transitional' stage – *Chronicle* to 891 – pronouns would come before the verb and form a group with it, effectively to be ignored in the counting of elements for V-2 (1938: 57, 91, 290): compare van Kemenade's clitic analysis, discussed in §4.7.1.1 below.

17. It is interesting to contrast Vennemann's theoretical view of (Old) English – as a VX language which reveals within itself historical traces of a chronologically much earlier XV stage – with the prevalent transformationalist view of Old English that we have examined in §4.5, a language whose generally VX main clauses derive *synchronically* from an underlyingly XV structure.

18. Once again we shall find transformational grammarians embodying similar diachronic claims in their synchronic derivations. That 'synchrony recapitulates diachrony' is a slogan once bandied about in this connection.

19. Also Dutch: see Weerman (1989). I am grateful to Willem Koopman (p.c., 30 October 1989) for the reference.

20. I take the term, an abbreviation for **adverb/complementiser**, from Stockwell and Minkova (1991).

21. Indeed correlative pairs formed with þa 'when' . . . þa 'then' and the like show almost 100 per cent consistent verb-late/V-2 contrast in Old English.

22. I have corrected an apparent slip here. This rule is actually printed as SvX(V) → SvVX in the summary; compare SvO(V) → Sv(V)O earlier in the text.

23. See Stockwell and Minkova (1992) for a discussion of V-1 in OE verse.

24. Canale gives the conventional label 'Early OE' to *Chronicle* annals 734–891 (1978: 56). He calls annals 892–1070 'Middle OE' (compare the conventional 'late Old English' for material of c1000), and the two *Continuations* of the *Peterborough Chronicle*, covering the annals 1122–1154, he labels 'Late OE' (where annals 1132–1154 in particular are often regarded as early Middle English).

25. Curiously, Bean mentions neither her own dissertation (1976), of which the book is a slightly revised version – it does not cite the important Kohonen (1978), for instance – nor the important published work of her dissertation supervisor, Stockwell, who for his part does acknowledge *her* ideas (1977: 312). I have commented in detail on Bean's book in Denison (1986). Certain portions of that somewhat inaccessible paper are reproduced here.

26. Structure [24] is quoted from van Kemenade's (1987: 49), where she summarises earlier work on modern Germanic languages. A later formulation at (1987: 173) puts COMP and INFL in a somewhat different structural relationship. Stockwell's discussion of the inconsistent presentation is helpful (1990: 96–7).

27. Stockwell and Minkova note that the verb brace 'persisted into late ME, more commonly in subordinate than in main clauses but not by any means confined to them' (1991: 397), and that it is a problem for syntactic theory to explain the occurrence of such 'old-fashioned' sentences.

28. Stockwell and Minkova's point here is that decliticisation is not a *sufficient* condition for the loss of V-2. Chaucer's word order is to be seen as a viable system, similar to that of Modern Swedish, which just happened to be a dead end in the history of standard English.

Part III

SUBJECT AND VERB PHRASE

Overview

The central topic in Part III is Chapter 6, Dative Movement and the Indirect Passive. The indirect passive is a construction peculiar to English (and mainland Scandinavian languages) which allows the indirect object of an active sentence to become subject of a passive:

[1]   She was never given a chance.

In studying its origins, late in the ME period, we must consider the loss of the morphological dative case, the relationship between case-marked noun phrases and prepositional phrases, the growing fixity of SVO word order, and the meanings of terms like 'transitive', 'object' and 'passive'. We are dealing with the syntactic relations holding between a verb and its nominal *arguments*, both subject and objects.

A very similar list of problems shows up in Chapter 5, Impersonals (though true impersonal verbs have no subject-verb relation, since all the arguments of the verb are within the verb phrase). Here as in Chapter 6 we find dative arguments in OE sentences whose ModE counterparts are in subject function. Not surprisingly, some scholars both in the philological tradition and in generative linguistics have tried to give essentially a single explanation for the rise of the indirect passive and the loss of impersonal verbs. The last part of Chapter 5 discusses the significance of dummy *hit* 'it' in OE impersonal clauses.

Another new and characteristically English passive appearing during the ME period is discussed in Chapter 7, the Prepositional Passive:

[2]   She was searched for everywhere.

Again there have been many attempts to find a single explanation for the origins of [1] and [2], and the last part of Chapter 7 concentrates on accounts which deal with both passives jointly. A key issue in the history of [2] is the more general phenomenon of 'preposition stranding', and that too is covered in detail in Chapter 7: much of the more technical discussion of this is not essential to an understanding of the general issues and may be skipped at a first reading.

Chapter 5

Impersonals

5.1 The problem

Deciding what the problem is turns out to be a problem itself: there has been little consensus on just what the impersonal verbs of Old English are – hence what changes have to be explained – and even on what 'impersonal' means as a linguistic term.

In the history of impersonal verbs at least two (related) matters are involved. One is that certain verbs in Old English have the potential for subjectless use,[1] whereas no verb in Modern English may be used without a subject in ordinary declarative main clauses. The other is a change in realisation whereby certain **arguments** formerly realised as non-subject come to be realised as subject of the verb.

Subjectlessness is the more straightforward notion: a subjectless clause is one whose verb takes 3 SG inflection no matter what NP arguments are present, and which lacks a nominative NP. The classic impersonal sentence is *rineð* 'rains', i.e. 'it is raining'. We must mention four potential difficulties with such a definition:

(A) A **dummy** subject (one without **anaphoric** reference)[2] is counted as a subject by some scholars but not others. Is *hit rineð* 'it is raining' subjectless or not?

(B) The status of certain clausal arguments is disputed:

[1] *ÆCHom* II 10.81.16

Ne gedafenað biscope   þæt he beo on dædum
not is-fitting   bishop(DAT) that he be in deeds

folces   mannum gelic
people(GEN) men(DAT) like

'it is inappropriate for a bishop to be like men of the people in deeds'

Is *gedafenað* subjectless in [1], or is the *þæt*-clause its subject?

(C) Certain subjectless usages might be considered characteristic either of the verb concerned or merely of the clause or discourse type (and therefore irrelevant). Should SECGAN 'say' be included in the ranks of potentially subjectless verbs on the strength of such examples as [2]?

[2] *BlHom* 65.27

Her sægþ, men þa leofestan, be   þisse halgan tide
here says   men the dearest   concerning this holy   time's

arwyrþnesse, hu . . .
honour   how . . .

'It says here about the honour of this holy time, dearest men, how . . .'

(D) Not all scholars regard nominative case and subject-verb concord as necessary conditions for subjecthood! I discuss such an account in §5.7.2 below, meanwhile retaining a morphologically more conventional use of the term **subject**.

Even subjectlessness, then, is a controversial term.

The term **impersonal** is even more so and is notoriously misused. The strictest syntactic definition of impersonalness would apply only to clauses (presumably subjectless ones) whose verbs have no personal argument at all. The term is often extended, however, to subjectless clauses whose verbs do have personal arguments. A further extension brings in clauses which do have a subject but whose subject is not a (characteristically) personal one for that verb.[3] And the widest usage employs 'impersonal' for any verb which *can* appear in any of the previously mentioned clause types, even when it is being used 'personally'.

The widest definition is not quite as all-inclusive as it might seem. It would not be normal to use the term 'impersonal' of an ordinary transitive verb both of whose argument NPs happened to be inanimate, nor of many verbs which can govern, say, the dative of a person. This is because semantic considerations play a part, explicitly or otherwise, in delimiting the field. Here is one semantic definition:

> The term 'impersonal' verbs refers to a class of verbs which have a common semantic core: they all express a physical or mental/cognitive experience which involves a 'goal', in this case an animate 'experiencer', and a 'source', i.e. something from which the experience emanates or by which the experience is effected (in this article we shall mostly refer to the 'source' as 'cause' . . .) (Fischer and van der Leek 1983: 346)

Scholars who have worked on impersonal verbs have had recourse to both syntactic and semantic considerations

It seems unnecessary to chart every variation of terminology that has been used. I shall adopt the wide syntactic definition of impersonal used by Fischer and van der Leek, as follows. Thus an **impersonal construction** is a subjectless construction in which the verb has 3 SG form and there is no nominative NP controlling verb concord; an **impersonal verb** is a verb which can, but need not always, occur in an impersonal construction (1983: 346-7). It will be clear from the preceding that some questions are being begged, but the definitions give a convenient starting point.

It will be useful to refer to arguments by semantic role. Fischer and van der Leek's analysis concentrates on two-*place* verbs and recognises an argument as an **Experiencer** if characteristically animate, otherwise as a **Cause**. We shall go further and tentatively distinguish Causes and **Themes** (see §5.6.2 below on the distinction). An Experiencer argument is always nominal; a Cause or Theme argument may be an NP or a clause. The same argument labels can usefully be employed in the description of the semantic structure of one-place impersonals.

The problems to be tackled can now be stated as follows. What types of impersonal verb were there in Old English? What constructions did impersonal verbs take part in, and what semantic differences are there among the competing constructions? Consider here these three examples of *OFHREOWAN 'rue' from Ælfric, handily gathered by John Anderson (1986: 170–1):

[3] *ÆCHom* I 8.192.16

him   ofhreow   þæs   mannes
to-him(DAT) there-was-pity because-of-the man(GEN)

[4] *ÆCHom* I 23.336.10

Þa   ofhreow   ðam munece   þæs hreoflian mægenleast
then brought-pity to-the monk(DAT) the leper's   feebleness(NOM)

[5] *ÆLS* II 26.262

se mæsse-preost þæs   mannes   of-hreow
the priest(NOM) because-of-the man(GEN) felt-pity

Example [3], a true impersonal construction, has no subject. The Cause is in the genitive, the Experiencer is in the dative. Example [4] has the Cause as nominative subject[4] and the Experiencer in the dative. Example [5] has the Experiencer as subject and the Cause in the genitive. Why did certain patterns disappear from the language, especially the impersonal construction? What are the origins of new patterns which became the norm in Middle English or Modern English? Where the patterns dominant in Modern English are not new ones, why is it they that survive at the expense of others? Examples of new or newly dominant patterns include:

[6] John liked the suggestions.
[7] John rued his mistake.

Both LIKE and RUE have become transitive verbs with the Experiencer in subject function. In Old English, by contrast, LICIAN would have had the *suggestions* NP as subject and *John* as dative object, while HREOWAN had three surface patterns in variation, as in [3]–[5].

5.2 The data

In this chapter, like the previous one, a neutral presentation of the data is an impossibility. My presentation is much influenced by Fischer and van der

Leek (1983), and I have found Ogura (1986) a useful source of examples. Fischer and van der Leek maintain that for some two-place verbs (they claim almost *all* of them) there are essentially three surface patterns, which they call types (i), (ii) and (iii). They are subjectless, Cause-subject and Experiencer-subject respectively and may be represented by examples [3]–[5]. We shall adapt this classification, but first we must consider an equivocal type.

5.2.1 Function of clausal arguments

5.2.1.1

If the Experiencer is oblique and the Cause (or Theme) is clausal there is no obvious way, pre-theoretically, of discriminating between types (i) and (ii), since the Cause may be regarded either as object or subject. In order not to prejudge what may be an important issue, therefore, we must treat examples like the following as indeterminate between types (i) and (ii):

[8]   *ÆLet* 7 24

> me   sceamað   þearle   þæt ic hit secge ðe
> me(DAT) shames(3 SG) grievously that I it tell   you

> 'it shames me grievously to tell you it'

I suggest the label 'type (i/ii)' for them (Denison 1990a); Anderson also notes that in examples like [8] 'the distinction [between types (i) and (ii): D.D.] is obliterated' (1986: 175). For many impersonal verbs type (i/ii) is the most frequent pattern of all.[5]

Precisely the same indeterminacy attaches to certain one-place impersonal patterns, as for instance:

[9]   *LS* 17.1(MartinMor) (*BlHom* 217.10) 702

> Þa   gelamp   æfter þon þæt þes eadiga wer Sanctus Martinus sum
> then happened after that that this blessed man Saint   Martin   a

> mynster   getimbrede
> monastery built

> 'Then it happened subsequently that this blessed man, St Martin, built a monastery'

5.2.1.2*

Fischer and van der Leek give three reasons for preferring the object analysis for such clauses, thus type (i) (1983: 348–9).[6] The only relevant reason applies to cases where a clausal Cause is anticipated by a provisional object in the genitive:

[10]   *Bo* 38.3

> . . . ðæt nanne mon   þæs   ne tweoð   þæt se sie
> . . . that no   man(ACC SG) that(GEN SG) not doubts(3 SG) that he is

strong on his mægene þe . . .
strong in his might   who . . .

'. . . that no man doubts (it) that he is great in strength who . . .'

Such clausal Causes are indeed objects and the examples are counted here as type
(i). (Coordinate constructions where an oblique NP Cause in one conjunct
parallels a clause in the other could also be taken as evidence of the object status
of the clause.) It is unsafe, however, to argue for the objecthood of *all* clausal
Causes from their consistent final position within the **higher** clause, since that
applies equally to clauses in apparent subject or complement function and
in apposition to nominative NPs (Traugott 1992). I give two examples of an
embedded clause whose object status is at least dubious:

[11]   *CP* 205.2

Đæm lytegan   ðonne is betere   ðæt hie . . .
the   cunning(DAT) then   is better(NOM/ACC SG NEUT) that they . . .

'It is better then for the cunning to . . .'

[12]   *HomS* 26 (*BlHom* 7) 83.7

. . . þæt seo wyrd   . . . geweorþan sceal, þæt se ilca Scyppend
. . . that the event(NOM) . . . happen   shall that the same Creator

gesittan wile on his domsetle.
sit   will on his judgement-seat

'. . . that the event shall happen . . . that the same Creator will sit upon his
seat of judgement'

We may also cite an embedded Theme clause which is split, with one part
appearing to the left of the higher clause and the rest in final position:

[13]   *Or* 14.29

Þa Finnas, him   þuhte, & þa Beormas spræcon neah an
the Lapps   him(DAT) seemed and the Biarmians spoke   nearly one

geþeode.
language

'The Lapps, it seemed to him, and the Biarmians spoke near enough one
language.'

Examples [10–13) involve finite embedded clauses. As for infinitival clauses,
Mitchell argues that they *can* be subject of an impersonal verb and *should* be so
analysed if they **commute** with a nominative NP (1985: §1542), though Fischer
argues that since impersonals can occur without a nominal subject, a plain
infinitive with an impersonal 'must presumably be looked upon as an object rather
than a subject' (forthcoming: §2).

Fischer and van der Leek's third reason for treating embedded clauses as
objects is that type (ii) is derived from type (i) by 'move NP' and is thus
unavailable for a sentential Cause; see §5.5.2 below. Whilst all discussions of

subjecthood and objecthood depend to some extent on the theory in use, this reason is entirely theory-internal and hence irrelevant here.

5.2.2 Taxonomy of construction types for impersonal verbs

To summarise the classification to be used here, I shall call a pattern subjectless if there is no nominative NP argument and either no clausal argument or a clausal argument heralded by an oblique pronoun: this is type (i). It is subject-full if there is a nominative NP in argument function, whether type (ii) (Cause- or Theme-subject) or type (iii) (Experiencer-subject). Otherwise it is indeterminate: type (i/ii). The pronoun *hit*, if in clear non-argument function, is ignored (but see §5.9 below). The taxonomy is appropriate for verbs with any number of arguments.

The number of arguments of an OE impersonal verb ranges from zero to two (but see §5.2.6.9 below). Typically, a weather verb like RIGNAN 'rain' occurs with no argument, a verb like HYNGRAN 'hunger' with a single NP argument, and a verb like TWEOGAN 'doubt' with two arguments, though each of these verbs can actually occur with a different number of overt arguments.

5.2.3 The impersonal verbs

Here I give a listing of OE impersonal verbs in rough semantic groupings, and in the following sections some OE and ME examples of impersonals.

The (typically) zero-place impersonals of Old English are the WEATHER verbs: ÆFENLÆCAN, ÆFNIAN 'grow towards evening', DAGIAN 'dawn', (GE)FREOSAN 'freeze', HAGALIAN 'hail', LEOHTIAN 'grow light', (GE)NIPAN 'grow dark', RINAN 'rain', SNIWAN 'snow', STYRMAN 'storm', SUMERLÆCAN/ WINTERLÆCAN 'draw on towards summer/winter', SWEGAN 'sound', (GE)SWEORCAN, ASWEORCAN, TOSWEORCAN 'become dark' [also mental], ÞUNRIAN 'thunder', A WEORÐAN 'become A'.

The remaining impersonal verbs can be one-place, two-place or either.

The HUNGER verbs

CALAN 'be(come) cold', HYNGRIAN 'hunger', ÞREOTAN, AÞREOTAN 'be weary', ÞYRSTAN 'thirst', GEYFLIAN 'become ill'.

The BEHOVE[7] verbs

(GE)BYRIAN, GEDAFENIAN, NEODIAN 'be necessary', *god/betere/betst* BEON 'be good/better/best' and further items listed by Elmer (1981: 42).

The RUE verbs

(GE)EGL(I)AN, ÆTEGLAN 'ail', EARMIAN, OFEARMIAN 'pity', (GE)HREOWAN, OFHREOWAN 'rue', LAÐIAN 'cause loathing', (GE)LUSTFULLIAN 'desire', LYSTAN 'desire', RECCAN 'care', (GE)SCEAMIAN, FORSCEAMIAN, OFSCEAMIAN 'shame', OFÞYNCAN 'be displeased', (GE)TWEOGAN/ (GE)TWEONIAN 'doubt', WLATIAN 'cause loathing', *ege* BEON 'fear'.

The HAPPEN verbs

GEBYRIAN, BECUMAN, AGAN, (GE)GAN(GAN), (GE)LIMPAN, (GE)SCEON, GESÆLAN, TOSÆLAN, (GE)SPOWAN 'turn out well', MISSPOWAN 'turn out ill', (GE)TIDAN, GETIMIAN, MISTIMIAN, (GE)WEORÐAN, MISWEORÐAN.

The SEEM verbs

ÞYNCAN 'seem', MISÞYNCAN, *cuþ* BEON 'be known'.

The DREAM verbs

BEIRNAN 'come (into mind)', MÆTAN 'dream', MISSAN 'escape notice', OÐIWAN 'appear', SWEFNIAN 'dream'.

The AVAIL verbs

DUGAN, FORSTANDAN 'avail', FREMIAN 'avail', ONHAGIAN 'have power, be convenient', LOSIAN 'be lost', *BENUGAN, *GENUGAN 'be sufficient', (GE)NYHTSUMIAN 'suffice', BEÞURFAN 'lack', *nyt* BEON 'be profitable'.

The PLEASE verbs

CWEMAN, MISCWEMAN 'please', LEOFIAN 'be dear', (GE)LICIAN, MISLICIAN, OFLICIAN, UNGELICIAN 'please', *deore* BEON 'be dear'.

If we include the subjectless use of SAY verbs, the relevant items are: CWEÐAN 'say', CYÐAN 'make known', MANIAN 'warn', MYNEGIAN 'mention', ONGINNAN 'begin', SECGAN 'say', (GE)TACNIAN 'betoken'. For examples see Visser (1963–73: §§10–11, 50).

5.2.4   Zero-place impersonals

5.2.4.1   Old English

[14]   *Or* 123.17

Þæt þridde wæs þæt hit hagolade seofon niht, dæges &   nihtes, ofer
the third   was that it   hailed   seven nights day and night over

ealle Romane.
all   Romans

[15]   *Sea* 31

norþan   sniwde
from-north snowed

'It snowed from the north'

5.2.4.2   Middle English

[16]   c1400(?a1300) *KAlex.*(Ld) 6440

Whan it snoweþ oiþer rineþ . . .
when it snows   or   rains . . .

[17]   c1450(?a1400) *Destr.Troy* 3691

Thunret   full   throly
thundered very severely

'It thundered very loud.'

5.2.5   One-place impersonals

5.2.5.1   OE type (i)

[18]   *Jn(WSCp)* 6.35

& ne þyrst þone   næfre ðe on me gelyfð.
and not thirsts the-one(ACC) never who in me believes

'and he who believes in me will never thirst'

[19] · *MSol* 271

Longað hine   hearde
yearns   him(ACC) grievously

'He feels great discontent'

[20]   *ÆCHom* I 4.72.30

Gyt me   tweonað
yet me(DAT/ACC) doubts(3 SG)

'I am still in doubt'

5.2.5.2   ME type (i)

[21]   (a1393) Gower, *CA* 1.459

Him   may fulofte   mysbefalle
him(OBL) may very-often suffer-misfortune

'He may very often suffer misfortune.'

[22]   (c1375,c1390) Chaucer, *CT.Mk.* VII.2039

. . . so thursted hym that he | Was wel ny lorn

'He was so thirsty that he was well-nigh lost'

[23]   ?c1425(?c1400) *Loll.Serm.* 3.78

Crist answerede, it semeþ, noȝt directli to þis questioun;
Christ answered   it appears not   directly to this question

5.2.5.3   OE type (i/ii)

[24]   *Bo* 101.22

Hit gelamp   gio   ðætte an hearpere wæs on ðære ðiode ðe
it   happened formerly that a harper   was in the   nation that

Ðracia hatte
Thracia is/was-called

'Once there was a harpist in the country called Thracia.'

[25] *GD(H)* 77.18

Gregorius cwæð: 'on sumum   timan gelamp,   þæt sum
Gregory   said   at a-certain time happened that a-certain

man forlet his eagena gesihðe'.
man lost   his eyes'   sight

'Gregory said: "Once it happened that a certain man lost his eyesight."'

5.2.5.4 OE type (ii)

[26] *BlHom* 91.34

& rineþ blodig regn   æt æfen.
and rains bloody rain(NOM) at evening

'and it shall rain bloody rain in the evening'

[27] *BlHom* 91.29

Þy ærestan dæge   on midne dæg gelimpeþ   mycel
the first   day(INST) at mid   day happens(3 SG) great

gnornung   ealra gesceafta
lamentation(NOM) all   creatures(GEN)

'On the first day at midday great lamentation of all creatures shall take place.'

5.2.5.5 OE type (iii)

[28] *JnGl(Li)* 19.28

cuoeð ic   ðyrsto.
said[?] I(NOM) thirst(1 SG)

Lat. dicit['says'] sitio

'He said, "I am thirsty." '

5.2.5.6 ModE type (iii)

[29] 1667 Milton, *Paradise Lost* 11.586

till in the amorous Net | Fast caught, they lik'd, and each his liking chose;

5.2.6 Two-place impersonals

5.2.6.1 OE type (i)

Example [3] above, and:

[30]   *Beo* 2032

Mæg þæs   þonne ofþyncan   ðeodne   Heaðobeardna
may that(GEN) then   displease(INF) lord(DAT) Heathobards(GEN)

. . . þonne . . .
. . . when . . .

'It may displease the lord of the Heathobards . . . when . . .'

5.2.6.2   ME type (i)

[31]   c1180 *Orm.* 10220

A33 lisste   himm   affterr mare
ever desires him(OBJ) for   more

'He always wants more.'

[32]   c1225(?c1200) *SWard* 152

ne of al þet eauer wa   is ne schal   ham   neauer
nor of all that ever woeful is not shall(3 SG) them(OBL) never

wontin
lack

'nor will they ever be in want of anything that is woeful'

A few verbs appear in type (i) apparently for the first time in Middle English:

[33]   c1230(?a1200) *Ancr.* 52a.15

&   swetest him   þuncheð   ham
and sweetest him(OBL) seem(s)/thinks(3 SG or PL) them(OBL)

'and sweetest they seem to him'

[34]   c1230(?a1200) *Ancr.* 90a.15

As ofte as ich am ischriuen: eauer me   þuncheð   me
as often as I   am confessed ever   me(OBL) seems(3 SG) me(OBL)

unschriuen
unconfessed

'However often I confess myself, still I seem to myself to be unconfessed'

[35]   (c1395) Chaucer, *CT.Cl.* IV.106

For certes,   lord, so wel us   liketh   yow | And al
for certainly lord so well us(OBJ) likes(3 SG) you(OBJ PL) and all

youre werk, and evere han   doon
your work and always have(PL) done

'For certainly, lord, we like you and all your works so much, and always have done.'

These and other blend-like examples are discussed in Denison (1990a: §5.2).

5.2.6.3   OE type (i/ii)

[36]   *GD(C)* 174.18

    me sylfum   þynceð, þæt ic na   ne ongyte . . .
    me self(DAT) seems   that I not-at-all not understand . . .

    'It seems to me that I do not at all understand . . .'

[37]   *ÆCHom* II 21.202.97

    ða oflicode   me ðearle   þæt ic eft to ðam lichaman sceolde
    then displeased me grievously that I back to the body   had-to

    fram ðære stowe wynsumnysse
    from that place joy(GEN)

    'then it was most displeasing to me that I had to return to the body
    from that place of joy'

5.2.6.4   ME type (i/ii)

[38]   ?c1425(?c1400) *Loll.Serm.* 1.247

    so it sufficeþ noȝt ynow   to prestis to preche trueli þe word of God
    so it suffices not enough for priests to preach truly the word of God

    'so it is not sufficient for priests to preach the word of God truly'

[39]   a1500(?c1450) *Merlin* 233.16

    sore hym   longed to wite how . . .
    sore him(OBJ) longed to know how . . .

    'he badly wanted to know how . . .'

A sporadic impersonal use of phrasal and modal verbs like HAVE *liefer*
'prefer', MUST, OUGHT, ÞURFE 'need' appears first in Middle English
(see Visser 1963–73: §§33, 40–41, 1715; Plank 1984: 322–3):

[40]   c1225(?c1200) *SWard* 242

    He easkeð ham ȝef ham   biluueð   to heren him ane
    he asks   them if them(OBL PL) pleases(3 SG) to hear him a

    hwile.
    while

    'He asks them if it pleases them to listen to him for a while.'

[41]   (c1395) Chaucer, *CT.CY.* VIII.946

    Us   moste   putte oure good in aventure
    us(OBL) must(SG) put   our goods in jeopardy

    'We have to put our goods at risk.'

[42]   a1450(?1348) Rolle, *FLiving* 99.83

    and if he have taken   grace, to use it noght als hym   aght
    and if he have received grace to use it not   as him(OBL) ought

    '. . . as he ought'

[43] (a1393) Gower, *CA* 3.1666

> Wher as him   oghte have be   riht fain
> whereas him(OBL) ought have been very glad

'Whereas he should have been very glad'

Type (i/ii) seems to have become available to a small group of verbs which had not normally been impersonals in Old English. (In fact the compound verb BILOVEN of [40] is not recorded in Old English at all.)

5.2.6.5 OE type (ii)

[44] *Or* 84.32

> hu him   se sige   gelicade
> how him(DAT) the victory(NOM) pleased

'how the victory had pleased him'

[45] *ChronE* 141.18 (1011)

> Ealle þas   ungesælða   us   gelumpon   þurh
> all   these misfortunes(PL) us(DAT) happened(PL) through
> unrædes . . .
> folly/evil-counsel(ACC PL) . . .

'All these misfortunes befell us through folly . . .'

5.2.6.6 ME type (ii)

[46] a1225(c1200) *Vices and V.(1)* 115.14

> Hi me reweð swa swiðe ðat ic reste ne mai habben.
> they me rue   so much that I rest not may have

'They [*sc.* souls] distress me so badly that I cannot have any rest.'

[47] (a1393) Gower, *CA* 1.1698

> godd wot   how that sche him pleseth | Of suche wordes as sche
> God knows how (that) she him pleases by such words as she
> spekth
> speaks

5.2.6.7 OE type (iii)

[48] *GD(C)* 244.27

> þonne seo sawl   þyrsteð   & lysteð Godes rices
> when the soul(NOM) thirsts-for and desires God's kingdom(GEN)

'when the soul thirsts for and desires the kingdom of God'

[49] *CP* 100.5

> ðæt ic   eac ðæs   ne scamige
> that I(NOM) also that(GEN) not shame

'that I also am not ashamed of that'

5.2.6.8 ME type (iii)

[50] (a1393) Gower, *CA* 3.1610

Mi goode fader, if ye   rewe | Upon mi tale, tell me now
my good father if you(SUBJ) feel-pity for my tale tell me now

[51] (c1387–95) Chaucer, *CT.Prol.* I.12

Thanne longen   folk to goon on pilgrimages
then   long(PL) folk to go   on pilgrimages

5.2.6.9 More than two arguments?

Is it possible for an impersonal verb to have more than the two arguments envisaged by Fischer and van der Leek (1983)? Consider these examples:

[52] *Bo* 119.6

Ac hu þincð   þe   ðonne be
but how seems/thinks(3 SG) you(DAT/ACC) then   concerning

ðæm   þe nanwuht goodes   næfð,   gif he hæfð sumne eacan
the-one who nothing good(GEN) not-has if he has an   increase

yfeles?
evil(GEN)

'But what, then, do you think about someone who has no goodness, if he has evil in addition?'

[53] c1230(?a1200) *Ancr.* 113a.18

Of   swuch witunge is muchel vuel ilumpen   ofte siðen.
from such   guarding is much   evil happened often

'From such looking-after [of possessions] much evil has often come about.'

Example [52] can be interpreted as having pronominal Experiencer, *þe*, and adverbial Theme,[8] *hu*, with an additional PP of (roughly) location and an *if*-clause both associated with the Theme, while in [53] we have a Theme-subject construction with an extra Source PP (and with no Experiencer expressed); see further Denison (1990a: §2.1), where these and similar cases are discussed.

5.3 Explanations

Among the numerous cross-currents in the scholarly treatment of impersonals, one stream dominates: Jespersen's and van der Gaaf's idea that non-subject NPs were reanalysed as subjects in the ME period. This explanation is accepted in whole or in part by Elmer, Krzyszpień, Lightfoot, von Seefranz-Montag, and Fischer and van der Leek (1987). Changes in word order are the ultimate cause of reanalysis. The earlier and probably better contribution by Fischer and van der Leek (1983) takes nominal morphology as the ultimate cause of the demise of the impersonals, which is seen purely as a loss and not as a reanalysis.

Elmer and von Seefranz-Montag consider certain OE non-nominative NPs to show subject properties, as does Allen, who rejects the Jespersen explanation and presents a very detailed account of the history of one verb, LIKE. In McCawley's account, also critical of Jespersen, it is the requirement for a surface subject which is crucial, together with changes in the coding of semantic roles. The relationship between morphological case and semantic role is the focus of the contributions of Anderson and Fischer and van der Leek (1987).

Finally there are some diverse contributions of which it can be said that they are largely descriptive. I include here those of Wahlén, Ogura, Denison, and van der Wurff.

5.4 Explanations involving reanalysis

5.4.1 Jespersen

Jespersen's statement of the problem has been very influential, especially in the version presented in his *Modern English Grammar* (1909–49: III 208–12, 352–5; VII 244–9). His discussion ranges very widely over a number of constructions which seem to show a shift whereby what was formerly an object becomes a subject. Impersonal verbs – though Jespersen regrets the use of the term – are the first but by no means the only verbs and constructions to be covered.

Jespersen's explanation involves three factors:

(A) 'the greater interest taken in persons than in things', which caused Experiencer to be placed before Theme or Cause

(B) the identity in form for many NPs of nominative (subjective) and oblique (objective) forms

(C) the neutralisation of remaining distinctions between subjective and objective forms when the NP in question is in an infinitive clause dependent on another verb and may owe its objective case to the *higher* verb

Factor C can be illustrated by [54]:

[54] c1430(c1380) Chaucer, *PF* 108

    . . . That made me to mete   that he stod   there
    . . . that made me to dream that he stood there

    '. . . that made me dream he was standing there'

In [54] *me* will necessarily be objective because of its relation to MAKEN, and we cannot tell from this example what case METEN 'dream' would normally require of its Experiencer.

Jespersen invents 'a typical sentence in its various stages', a sequence subsequently reproduced rather often (the gloss to [55](a) is mine):

[55] (a) þam cynge   licodon   peran
           the king(DAT) pleased(PL) pears(NOM PL)

(b) the king likeden peares
(c) the king liked pears
(d) he liked pears

In [55](a) *peran* is subject and *þam cynge* is clearly dative; in (b) *peares* is still subject, marked by verbal concord, though *king* has lost its explicit dative marking – Allen finds no evidence that this stage ever actually existed with LIKE (1986a: 396–7); in (c) either of the NPs could be subject as far as formal marking is concerned, but 'natural feeling' determined that it should be *the king*; (d) shows this development explicitly. Notice that a fourth factor has thus been brought in: increased scope for ambiguity of structure as verbs show less number differentiation.

The syntactic shift is accompanied by a semantic shift. Jespersen writes that 'in most cases the verb began by meaning "give an impression" and came to mean "receive an impression"'. It should be pointed out that there is not necessarily any change in the action or state that the verb describes: the alleged semantic shift only becomes apparent when the sentences are glossed word for word, and especially when the glossing language happens to have separate lexical items (here LIKE and PLEASE) which allow the original subject-verb relation to be maintained in the gloss. As Allen clarifies the matter (p.c., 13 December 1990), 'the major change has not been a change in the meaning (in the sense that the experiencer receives pleasure from the theme or cause) but rather a change in the assignment of semantic to grammatical roles'.

5.4.2 Van der Gaaf

The monograph by W. van der Gaaf (1904) actually predates the account of Jespersen described in §5.4.1 above; however, Jespersen had published the essentials of his explanation somewhat earlier, albeit with little data. Van der Gaaf's work is the first thorough descriptive account. It concentrates on what he too sees as a *change* in construction in the ME period, and therefore largely ignores OE verbs which died out by early Middle English, as well as zero-place WEATHER verbs which survived but underwent no change in case syntax. His explanation is the same as Jespersen's: reanalysis of clauses with topicalised objective NP, owing to the combined pressure of subject-oblique case *syncretism* and the increased fixity of subject-verb word order (1904: §3). He goes into far more detail, however, on the kinds of equivocal example permitting reanalysis and the morphological changes which encourage it (1904: §§32–7). He also provides collateral evidence in the form of instances of zero *anaphora* where a (formerly) impersonal verb is conjoined with an ordinary, personal verb (§§38–9):

[56] ?a1220 *HMaid* 21.28

Sone   se þu   telest   te   betere þen anoðer
as-soon as you(SUBJ) reckon(2 SG) yourself better than another

. . . ant hauest   of ei   ouerhohe, ant þuncheð
. . . and have(2 SG) for anyone disdain   and seems(3 SG)

> hofles   ant hoker   of   eawt   þet me seið þe
> unreasonable and contemptible concerning anything that one tells you
>
> oðer deð ȝetten,   þu   merrest   þin meiðhad . . .
> or   does moreover you(SUBJ) harm(2 SG) your virginity . . .

'As soon as you reckon yourself better than another . . . and feel contempt for anyone, and find unreasonable and contemptible anything that is said or moreover done to you, you defile your virginity . . .'

The very frequent ÞUNCHEN 'seem' is the earliest source of such examples (perhaps partly owing to confusion with ÞENCHEN 'think'), and from the end of the thirteenth century other impersonals behave likewise. (Actually Visser gives examples from Old English as well as Middle English (1963–73: §38).) Van der Gaaf will not go so far as to cite examples like [56] as proof of type (iii) use, merely claiming that the difference between his type A (subsuming our types (i, i/ii, and ii)) and ' "personal" use' (our type (iii)) was 'beginning to be lost sight of'. The next and longest chapter of his book gives a detailed history of many impersonal verbs and phrasal constructions from Middle English onwards, the data organised according as the Experiencer is (B) formally equivocal between subject or oblique, (C) prepositionally marked as oblique, or (D) subject (1904: §§42–170).

Two phenomena are acknowledged to confuse the Jespersen–Gaaf picture of change. One is a too-early use of type (iii): van der Gaaf mentions five verbs which show type (iii) use beside types (i–ii) already in Old English (1904: §§184–94). The other is the development of type (i–ii) patterns as late as the fourteenth and fifteenth centuries. In the case of some verbs van der Gaaf alleges blending, as for example with LIKEN in [35] (1904: §73). This is apparently type (i), standing outside what Jespersen and van der Gaaf regard as the main line of development from OE type (ii) to ModE type (iii). Other examples of 'anti-grammatical' constructions are given in §§171–3, especially of MOT 'must' and REMEMBREN 'remind, remember'. Impersonal use is said to develop for the first time in Middle English, and to become very common, for four verbs: OUEN 'ought', DEINEN 'deign', REPENTEN 'repent', and THURVEN 'need' (1904: §§174–83). (DEINEN and REPENTEN are borrowings from French not found in Old English.) The explanation offered is analogy with semantically similar verbs.

5.4.3 Elmer

5.4.3.1

Willy Elmer's monograph (1981) is based on a more explicit methodology than van der Gaaf's and Jespersen's. Having characterised van der Gaaf's reanalysis account as 'quite clearly correct' (1981: 4), Elmer seeks to give a more systematic description of subjectless sentences involving verbs like RUE and LIKE that typically have two arguments. Alive though he is to modern linguistic theory, he steers clear of formal, generative grammar. The logic of his book's structure may not be immediately apparent – tracking down individual points can be slow – but logical it is, as the following sketch should reveal.

He separates the synchronic description of Old English from the diachronic, especially the ME and eModE, development. Within each of the two parts of the monograph he first tackles those constructions with a clausal argument, then the ones where Cause or Theme is nominal. And within each chapter he divides the verbs under consideration into the five semantic sub-classes RUE, PLEASE/DESIRE, BEHOVE, HAPPEN and SEEM.[9] Semantics and syntax are throughout treated side by side. Given the nature of Elmer's approach it is hard to present specific findings. For example, the intricate account of post-OE developments covers both the overall behaviour of each class of verbs and individual idiosyncrasies in syntactic patterning, so that the RUE group alone requires over twenty pages (1981: 85–107).

As far as Old English is concerned Elmer claims that the positional behaviour of oblique-case experiencers is identical to that of subject NPs elsewhere in OE grammar (1981: 8), and he therefore calls the experiencer NP a 'pseudo-subject'. In support of Elmer's position we could cite the anticipation of a dative Experiencer in a 'Left Dislocation' structure by an NP, *ða ungelæredan preostas*, which is presumably nominative:

[57]   *ÆGenPref* 77.23

Ða ungelæredan preostas,   gif hi   hwæt   litles understandað
the ignorant   priests(NOM) if they somewhat little understand

of   þam Lydenbocum, þonne þingð   him   sona
from the Latin-books   then   seems(3 SG) them(DAT) immediately

þæt hi   magon   mære   lareowas beon
that they have-the-power famous teachers be(INF)

'The ignorant priests, if they understand a smattering of the Latin books, then it immediately seems to them that they can be famous teachers.'

Of course the NP is also anticipating a nominative, *hi*. Elmer takes the pattern when Cause or Theme is sentential (what I have called 'type (i/ii)' and Elmer 'type S') as the basis for the whole description, and a basic word order Experiencer-V-S (where S = **sentential** Cause or Theme) is identified. Deviations from this are ascribed to general factors in OE word order. See further §5.9.4 below on the (non-)use of *hit*.

5.4.3.2

In a later article (1983) Elmer deals with the behaviour of SEEM in Middle English. He argues that SEMEN 'seem' and THINKEN 'seem' were indistinguishable semantically but nevertheless occurred in a sort of complementary distribution. THINKEN was used when there was an Experiencer argument, whereas SEMEN was only used if there was not. This led to a difference in **thematic structure**, commonly in many languages a progression from 'theme'[10] (given) to 'rheme' (new information): the only lexical NP which could occur as theme with SEMEN was the Theme argument ('entity' for Elmer), whereas with THINKEN an Experiencer was often theme. These different preferences for particular thematic structures help to explain why THINKEN did not occur in *Raising* constructions,[11] whereas SEMEN did:

[58]   a1400(a1325) *Cursor* 5749

þe tre þat semed   to bren
the tree that appeared to burn

From the middle of the fourteenth century, as THINKEN 'seem' (OE ÞYNCAN) lost out to THINKEN 'think' (OE ÞENCAN), at least with nominative subjects, SEMEN gradually spread into all the syntactic patterns formerly used with THINKEN 'seem'.

5.4.4   Krzyszpień

Jerzy Krzyszpień (1984) works with Jespersen's assumptions about what happened to impersonals, including the famous invented sentences [55]. His contribution to an explanation depends on the thematic structure of a sentence. Taking an example like:

[59]   ?a1220 *HMaid* 4.1

þet te   schal laði   þi lif, ant bireowe þi   sið
that you(OBL) shall be-hateful-to your life and rue   your time

'that you shall loathe your life and rue your time'

he claims that 'the speaker announces that he is talking about his interlocutor and the theme is the Experiencer NP *te* (*þe*) appearing in initial position' (1984: 67). Experiencers are natural choices as the themes of utterances; themes naturally come in initial position. Therefore even after the establishment of SVO word order and the loss of morphological case in most NPs, Experiencers tend to remain in initial position, although they must now be syntactically reanalysed as subjects. Krzyszpień's observation is akin to Jespersen's 'greater interest felt for the person', if more amenable to proof.

   It is hard to see how circularity can be avoided, however. The analysis of example [59] and others like it suggests that an NP is in initial position because it is a theme, yet it is identifiable as theme (mainly? only?) because it is in initial position. To rebut such a charge one would need extracts longer than the clause snippets offered by Krzyszpień. Even then one would want to see some statistical support for the hypothesis that maintenance of thematicity is partially responsible for the reanalysis.

5.4.5   Lightfoot

David Lightfoot adopts Jespersen's account and repackages it in the Extended Standard Theory of TG (transformational generative) grammar (1979: §5.1). OE examples like [55](a) are said to have had an underlying structure something like:

[60]   *peran* [$_{VP}$ *þam cynge*(DAT) *licodon*]

A rule of NP Postposing moved the subject *peran* to the right. When SVO order had been adopted as underlying order in Middle English, the new initial structure was:

[61]   *peares* [$_{VP}$ *likeden the king*(DAT)]

Now the surface form could only be derived by NP Postposing of *peares* followed by NP Preposing of *the king*.[12] Such a derivation was too opaque – the two NP arguments had swapped places between initial (i.e. deep) and surface structure – and the 'Transparency Principle'[13] forced a reanalysis of structurally ambiguous sentences like [55](c). Indeed even morphologically unambiguous examples like [55](b) could behave, it is claimed, as if the topicalised oblique NP were in fact syntactic subject of the verb. Three pieces of evidence are offered, largely following Butler (1977):

(A)   sporadic instances of verb agreement triggered by an oblique pronoun
(B)   conjoining of personal and impersonal verbs, especially with null (i.e. zero) anaphora in one clause
(C)   sporadic instances like the first clause of [35], repeated here as [62]:

[62]   (c1395) Chaucer, *CT.Cl.* IV.106

For certes,   lord, so wel us   liketh   yow |
for certainly lord so well us(OBJ) likes(3 SG) you(OBJ PL)

And al youre werk
and all your work

one of whose NPs, given Lightfoot's assumption that they cannot be double-object patterns, must therefore be subject. (Fischer and van der Leek merely regard [62] as subjectless type (i), of course.)

For criticism of these kinds of evidence see especially Warner (1983), Allen (1986a: 389–94).

Various scholars pointed out theoretical objections to an analysis which moved an NP away from subject position, leaving behind a trace, and then replaced the trace by another NP moved out of the VP. In Lightfoot (1981) he disowns his earlier derivation of [55](c)[14] by two movement rules, since it violates the so-called Trace Erasure Principle by which the trace of a moved NP can only become the landing site of another movement rule if the new arrival is a 'designated' morpheme like expletive *it* or *there*, rather than a full lexical item (1981: 89–90). Under the revised formulation, reanalysis takes place unavoidably as soon as SVO word order enters base grammar in the shape of underlyingly verb-initial VPs.

Problems remain, however. In an excellent commentary appended to Lightfoot (1981), Susan Schmerling observes that the proposed derivation of [55](a) in Old English is no less problematic than the similar one for [55](c) in Middle English, whose difficulties Lightfoot acknowledges (1981: 121–2). Fischer and van der Leek highlight the false prediction of Lightfoot's account that one and the same author should never use both type (ii) and type (iii) for a given verb (1983: 342–3). They cite Chaucer (late fourteenth century); Pepys is still using both patterns with LIKE in the 1660s.

5.5 An explanation without reanalysis

5.5.1 Fischer and van der Leek (1983)

Olga Fischer and Frederike van der Leek's account is, like Lightfoot's, cast in the mould of GB theory (1983). Their lexical entry for an OE impersonal is my [63], their [20]:

[63]
$$\begin{bmatrix} \text{NP} & \text{NP} \underline{\hspace{1em}} (\text{S}') \\ & \text{NP: DATIVE: } \theta\text{-role: experiencer} \\ & \begin{cases} \text{NP: GENITIVE} \\ \text{S}' \end{cases} \theta\text{-role: cause} \end{bmatrix}$$

The entry encapsulates a number of claims. It suggests (as we have already noted) that OE impersonals are characteristically two-place verbs, with an Experiencer and a Cause argument. The Experiencer is a (typically animate) NP, the Cause is either an NP or a clause (for which Fischer and van der Leek tend to use $\bar{S}$) but not both (unless the NP is a provisional non-argument, that is, an NP with no referential function). Typical surface cases are dative for the Experiencer and genitive for a nominal Cause, though one can also find accusative for either argument and PP for Cause. This is Fischer and van der Leek's type (i) pattern. By means of syntactic processes in Government Binding theory to be discussed below, either argument of the verb may, if it is an NP, wind up as subject of the verb in the nominative, giving type (ii) or (iii). The range of examples [3]–[5] for *OFHREOWAN 'rue' is claimed to be typical of *all* OE impersonal verbs (four exceptions are noted at 1983: 344 n.7). No one had previously suggested that type (iii) was anything but a sporadic anomaly in Old English, or at most peculiar to a handful of impersonals. (Fischer and van der Leek were the first to tackle this problem using the Toronto *Microfiche Concordance* (Venezky and Healey 1980).)

Their account goes on to claim that type (i) died out in Middle English, and that eventually only one of types (ii) and (iii) survived for a given verb. This is to be contrasted with the traditional account, which assumes that type (i) or (ii) was basic in Old English and was reanalysed as type (iii) in the course of the ME period. In the accounts of Jespersen and his followers, LIKE rather than RUE is usually taken as the prototypical impersonal.

5.5.2 Syntax

Since their account has been justifiably influential, let us first try to summarise their explanation. They praise the methodology of Lightfoot (1981) but criticise both his data and his analysis (1983: 339–46). As far as

Old English is concerned it is *not* appropriate to use LICIAN sentences in OVS order as the basis of the account, since OVS patterns of Jespersen's invented [55](a) type are actually rather rare. Instead they assume essentially one underlying structure for all OE impersonal clauses:

[64]

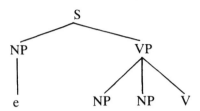

The verb must be subjectless, since there is no θ-role available for a subject NP. The verb is assumed to be clause-final (cf. §4.5 above), unless the Cause is a clause rather than an NP, in which case the Cause is base-generated *after* the verb. The two lexical NPs are unordered with respect to each other. Thus all impersonal clauses are regarded as underlyingly type (i). All order and case variants are to be explained transformationally.

What distinguishes an impersonal verb from other verbs in Fischer and van der Leek's view is that its assignment of lexical cases, as in [63], is not obligatory (1983: 357–8). If both NPs are in fact assigned lexical case – dative and genitive in the typical lexical entry [63] – then the surface form resulting is type (i), with word order OOV. If only one of the NPs is assigned lexical case, then the uncased NP moves by NP-Movement to the empty subject position, where it receives structural, nominative case through being **governed** by Tense (recall the discussion in §3.1.3.3 above).[15] Thus we can get either type (ii) or type (iii), according to whether the Cause or the Experiencer is moved to subject position. The word order then will be SOV. Fischer and van der Leek assume a rule of V-2 for main clauses, allowing them to account also for OVO in type (i) and SVO in types (ii) and (iii).

5.5.3* Chain-government

OSV cannot be generated in this way, however, and an elaborate mechanism of **Chain-government** is invoked to explain the occurrence of examples like:

[65]   *LS* 10.1(Guth) 12 148.45

and him	næfre syþþan . . .	seo	adle	ne eglode
and him(DAT)	never afterwards . . .	the	illness(NOM)	not troubled

'and the illness never troubled him afterwards'

Under this analysis the Experiencer *him* gets dative case from the verb. It may have been moved to subject position (this point is left vague, but the adverbs imply that it has – but cf. Allen 1986a: 386): if so it is assumed that structural nominative is *not* assigned to an argument already bearing lexical case (Fischer and van der Leek, 1983: 357). Meanwhile the Cause *seo adle* has remained in the VP as object but got nominative case because it is governed by V which in turn is governed by Tense. (There is no discussion of the verbal concord between this non-subject nominative and the verb.) Furthermore, the OVS order of Jespersen's invented [55](a), repeated here as [66]:

[66] þam cynge   licodon   peran
      the king(DAT) pleased(PL) pears(NOM PL)

is also explained by Chain-government, though it seems to me possible to derive [66] by movement of *peran* to subject position, then V-2 involving topicalisation of *þam cynge*. If a significant proportion of the allegedly rare OVS clauses are subordinates, however, then topicalisation would not provide a satisfactory explanation. Chain-government can be used to derive other types with oblique before nominative, for example putative variants of [65] like

[67] þære adle(GEN) he(NOM) eglode
[68] þære adle(GEN) eglode he(NOM)

These possibilities are not discussed.

5.5.4 Semantics

As to semantic differences among the three types, Fischer and van der Leek suggest that type (ii) expresses a greater degree of affectedness of the Experiencer than type (i) (though there is some confusion between surface dative and accusative in the discussion of this point), while type (iii) expresses a greater degree of volitionality on the part of the Experiencer than the other two (1983: 350). The three types differ in **transitivity** (in the sense of Hopper and Thompson 1980).

5.5.5 Diachrony

The demise of this system is explicitly decoupled from word order change, as the change from underlying SOV – or with impersonals, OOV – to SVO or OVO required no more than re-ordering of the lexical entry (1983: 361). What actually broke the system was the ME change in nominal morphology. As a result English lost the ability to assign lexical case (1983: 362), and since – by theoretical stipulation – a verb can assign only one case through government, i.e. structurally, a well-formed derivation now depended on the other NP being assigned nominative case by Tense. That is why type (i) died out. As for types (ii) and (iii), both remained grammatically possible, but the neutralisation of surface cases meant that they were no longer syntactically distinguishable. The consequence was that most impersonal verbs settled down with one type or the other but not both.[16] Four sample verbs are followed through to Modern English.[17]

Fischer and van der Leek made some notable improvements over previous accounts. They widened the data base, increased the generality and economy of the explanation, yet still managed to shift some of the burden of change from the syntactic to the lexical plane. (Loss of lexical case assignment remains presumably as a global phenomenon.)

5.6 Explanations involving semantics-based syntax

5.6.1 McCawley

Noriko McCawley concentrates on the semantics of impersonals (1976). She argues that the essential characteristic of (what we have been calling) Experiencer arguments is that the person referred to is 'unvolitionally/unself-controllably involved in the situation' (1976: 194). She casts doubt on Jespersen's reanalysis theory on the grounds that few instances in speech would have involved third person Experiencer NPs: most would have been first or perhaps second person, and these pronouns were not morphologically ambiguous (1976: 198–9). Her preferred explanation sees the Experiencer-subject construction as a *replacement* brought about by independently occurring changes in the language. These are:

(A) the loss of an OE syntactico-semantic principle that nominative case encodes Agent and dative case encodes Recipient,[18] and its replacement by a semantically obscure distinction between subjective and objective case (cf. Chapter 3 above)

(B) a new requirement that all sentences have a subject (1976: 200–201)

McCawley's criticism of the Jespersen–Gaaf account is useful, as are her cross-linguistic generalisations about the semantics of *impersonalia*, but the account of change from Old English to Modern English is more of a restatement than an explanation.

5.6.2 Anderson

Two papers of the prolific John Anderson will be considered here.

5.6.2.1

In Anderson (1986) he criticises certain aspects of Fischer and van der Leek (1983). He distinguishes between what he calls **true impersonals** (genuinely subjectless) and **quasi-personal impersonals** (with semantically empty *hit* subject) (Anderson 1986: 168–70).[19] (In the later paper he renames the latter **semi-impersonals** (1988: 8).) And he claims that the *subcategorisation frame* [63] is both redundant and misleading. He suggests that an alternation between nominal and clausal arguments is a general property of Causes, while the selection of dative and/or accusative case for the Experiencer shows sufficient generality for the relationship between surface case and θ-role not to be relegated to individual lexical entries (Anderson 1986: 172–3). That is, the subcategorisation frame for a verb simply needs to refer to the thematic roles of its arguments, not to their surface forms, which are predictable.

In order to achieve this economy in individual lexical entries, Anderson distinguishes between the RUE and most PLEASE/DESIRE verbs on the one hand and all other impersonals on the other. The former occur with Experiencer and Cause arguments, the latter with Experiencer and Theme. (With certain verbs the Experiencer or the Cause may be optional.) Unlike a Cause, a Theme is not marked by surface genitive or PP. The distinction is also supposed to have a semantic basis, in that a Theme is the semantically most neutral (deep) case:

[69]   *CP* 52.11

> Biscepe   gedafenað þæt he sie tælleas
> bishop(DAT) behoves   that he be blameless

'A bishop should be blameless.'

In [69] *þæt he sie tælleas* is a Theme in Anderson's analysis rather than the Cause of Fischer and van der Leek's, and it does seem counter-intuitive to treat blamelessness as the *cause* of the injunction on bishops. But the semantic distinction is not entirely straightforward. Anderson suggests that OE LICIAN 'please' occurs with a Theme argument rather than the Cause argument associated with LYSTAN 'desire' (1986: 175). The syntactic difference is clear – LICIAN does not occur with genitives – but it is not so obvious on semantic grounds that *ætes* in [71] should be a Cause but *þin modsefa* in [70] not:

[70]   *Beo* 1853

> Me   þin modsefa | licað leng swa wel
> me(DAT) your disposition(NOM) pleases longer so   well

'Your disposition has pleased me well for a long time/pleases me more and more.'

[71]   *Whale* 52

> ond þone aglæcan   ætes   lysteþ
> and the   monster(ACC) food(GEN) desires

'and the monster desires food'

(Fischer and van der Leek castigate Anderson's definition of Theme as circular (1987: 91–2).)

   In conclusion we should note that Anderson's main purpose in this paper is not to analyse OE impersonals for their own sake. Rather it is to use them as evidence that the syntactic notion of subjecthood is a derivative one, and that θ-roles – which he identifies with the deep cases of Case Grammar – determine syntactic structure.

5.6.2.2*

   The later paper (Anderson 1988) launches straight into Case Grammar, embedding within a discussion of subject formation in Modern English and elsewhere a classification of OE impersonal verbs on the basis of the different Case Relations (abs, erg, loc, abl – see §3.1.3.2 above) for which they are subcategorised. After a discussion of various subcategorisation frames Anderson concludes that they can be collapsed as follows (1988: 14):

[72]   → (abs → V)$_a$ (erg + loc)$_b$ (abl)$_c$

Term a is our Theme, realised either as an NP (abs) or a clause (V); term b is our

Experiencer; term c is our Cause. Each is (individually) optional, though there are co-occurrence constraints, for example that terms a and c are mutually exclusive.

Examples [3]–[5], here repeated as [73]–[75], are now explained as follows (1988: 15):

[73] *ÆCHom* I 8.192.16

> him   ofhreow   þæs   mannes
> to-him(DAT) there-was-pity because-of-the man(GEN)

[74] *ÆCHom* I 23.336.10

> Þa ofhreow   ðam munece   þæs hreoflian mægenleast
> then brought-pity to-the monk(DAT) the leper's   feebleness(NOM)

[75] *ÆLS* II 26.262

> se mæsse-preost þæs   mannes   of-hreow
> the priest(NOM) because-of-the man(GEN) felt-pity

In type (i) [73] the Experiencer is erg + loc and is expressed by default as dative, while the Cause is abl and therefore surface genitive. In type (iii) [75] the underlying case relations are the same, but the Experiencer argument has undergone optional subject formation and is thus surface nominative. In type (ii) [74], however, the Cause is not abl but erg, 'source of the action' instead of mere 'causative object'. (Erg-hood would have been associated with volitionality for animate referents, but with an inanimate like *mægenleast* the semantic distinction is less clear.) Since erg outranks erg + loc in the subject selection hierarchy (1988: 2–3), the Cause argument will become subject and therefore nominative.

Only a subset of OE impersonals allows all three surface forms. The option of an erg argument, leading to type (ii) surface form,

> is available only to verbs which otherwise take an obligatory abl, i.e. *scamian* verbs [and not to verbs like HINGRIAN with optional abl: D.D.]. Notice too that verbs like *gelimpan*, with optional erg + loc, and abs rather than abl, lack both [the [74] pattern and the [75]: D.D.] (1988: 16)

The comment on HAPPEN verbs is perhaps misleading, given the existence of two-place type (ii) examples like [45]: they have precisely the case syntax of [74] and in our typology come out the same. I take it that for Anderson they differ from [74] in having a nominative Theme (underlyingly abs) rather than nominative Cause (erg). Conversely LICIAN permits an erg (or erg + abl) argument and therefore type (ii) syntax, but lacking both abs and abl arguments it fails to conform to [72]. Consequently, type (i) is absent. Type (iii) only occurs in one-place use (i.e. if the erg argument is absent and so unavailable for subjecthood). And type (i/ii) occurs because sentential erg arguments do not subject-form and somehow block subjecthood for the Experiencer erg + loc argument too (1988: 16–17).

A diachronic point of some interest is Anderson's speculation on new accretions in Middle English to the class of impersonals, such as PURFE 'need', OUGHT 'have obligation' (see §5.2.6.4 above). His suggestion is that the option of impersonalness (impersonality?) was extended from verbs with erg + loc Experiencers to those with erg + abl Experiencers (1988: 10).

5.6.3　Fischer and van der Leek (1987)

Olga Fischer and Frederike van der Leek's second contribution to the debate (1987), or fourth if Fischer and van der Leek (1981, 1985) are taken into account, is far less specific in its formal analysis of impersonal verbs, perhaps because its main concerns are to advance a new theory of the semantic basis of case assignment. It begins with a critical survey of five earlier accounts, including their own. We shall skip this part (1987: 82–92).

The new analysis depends heavily on Plank (1981, 1983), already alluded to in §3.1.3.4 above, Kuryłowicz (1949, 1964), and Gruber (1976). Verbs are classified as motional or non-motional (in an abstract sense), with further subclassifications. Underlying case roles are now defined localistically as Theme, Source, Goal or Location, though the formal framework is still more or less GB Theory. Relevant NPs can have one of three different statuses. They may be subjective (*sister* to a tensed INFL and nominative in form), objective (adjacent sister to V and accusative in form), or adverbial (sister to V or P and genitive or dative in form). Adverbial NPs are not arguments of a verb, do not receive their θ-role from the verb, and are interpreted independently of it: they play outsider roles in the verbal process rather than participant roles.[20] The semantic differences among [73]–[75] are now explained as follows. In [73], type (i), there are no participants. Fischer and van der Leek provide the PDE gloss 'he was sorry for the man'. In [74], type (ii), the Source NP *mægenleast* (Cause in our terminology) is in the nominative and therefore has an interpretation as an active participant; the suggested gloss is 'then the leper's feebleness caused pity to the monk'. Finally, in [75], type (iii), the Goal NP *mæssepreost* (Experiencer in our terminology) is nominative, prompting the gloss 'the priest took pity on the man' (1987: 111).

The new theory is more flexible in that it requires the lexical entry of a verb only to specify the possible θ-roles associated with it, and whether these θ-roles are actually assigned by the verb. NP arguments receive their interpretation from their syntactic sister if they are nominative or accusative in form and therefore arguments of the verb, otherwise purely from the inherent meanings associated with the surface cases dative (Location or Goal) and genitive (Source). The theory suggests a slightly different syntactic-semantic basis for impersonalness:

> OE impersonal verbs form a class from a semantic point of view in that they do not require θ-role[-]bearing NPs which are directly involved in whatever the predicate expresses (McCawley 1976 speaks of unvolitional involvement); it is a class of verbs, in short, which can do without even one NP having argument status. (Fischer and van der Leek 1987: 112)

The analysis can now cope with impersonals associated with fewer than two arguments or with more (§§5.2.4–5, 5.2.6.9 above), so long as the semantic function of additional arguments is compatible with the meaning of the verb (1987: 100), while the possibility of alternation between NP and clausal arguments is handled by pragmatics and verbal semantics rather than by specific mention in the lexical entry. Accusative case for the Goal is now explicitly allowed for:

[76]   *GenA,B* 1276

>   Hreaw hine   swiðe | þæt . . .
>   rued   him(ACC) greatly that . . .

Fischer and van der Leek suggest that the Goal NP *hine* in [76] is to be interpreted as a participant, albeit a passive one: 'he was much grieved that . . .'. Why accusative never marks the Source remains unexplained, however (1987: 117 n.28).

As for the loss of the impersonal construction, Fischer and van der Leek actually revert to a reanalysis account! They cite the following factors: the change in word order from SOV to SVO (late twelfth century), leading to a change in the directionality of government from left to right, and the loss of oblique case inflections, leading to the loss of adverbial case on bare NPs (late Middle English). The two together meant that NP-V-NP strings without explicit oblique case-marking on the initial NP had to be interpreted as SVO, which led to a change in the lexical entry of the verbs from an impersonal type to a transitive personal type (1987: 113). The details are sketchy. Whether the explanation refers only to type (i) OVO patterns or to type (ii) OVS as well is left somewhat vague, as is the relationship between the reanalysed pattern(s) and those patterns which survived relatively unchanged.

5.7   Other syntactic approaches

5.7.1   Von Seefranz-Montag

Ariane von Seefranz-Montag's German dissertation is a cross-linguistic study of subjectless sentences (1983), partly summarised in English as von Seefranz-Montag (1984). Although not strictly generative or formal it is most conveniently placed here in our survey. There is some useful comparative and typological material, ranging over other Germanic languages and Indo-European and occasionally beyond. Most detail is reserved for English, German, Icelandic, and French, however.

As far as English is concerned von Seefranz-Montag accepts the conventional descriptive accounts but argues (like Elmer, Allen, and others) that Experiencers had already begun to develop subject properties even while still morphologically dative. The evidence for syntactic subjecthood includes that cited by Lightfoot (points A–C in §5.4.5) as well as apparent Raising examples involving non-nominatives:

[77]   *BlHom* 113.14

>   Þa   ongan hine   eft   langian   on his cyþþe
>   then began him(ACC) again long(INF) for his native-land

>   'Then he began again to long for his native land'

The implication is that [77] arises by Raising of *hine* out of subject position of the LANGIAN clause into subject position of the ONGINNAN clause. (There is a full survey of such examples in Old English in Denison 1990b.)

In explaining the history of impersonals von Seefranz-Montag argues that Old English had a TVX word order requirement which was moving towards an SVX requirement. Topicalisation of dative Experiencers was one response to this, introduction of dummy *(h)it* was another, reanalysis of topicalised obliques as nominatives a third. Reanalysis did not arise because of ambiguity, however, but was a belated acquisition of morphological subjecthood to match the already acquired syntactic subjecthood.

The bringing together of various diachronic 'strategies' for correcting an imbalance between different notions of subjecthood is a useful exercise. (Von Seefranz-Montag's list also includes the creation of reflexives and extensions to the passive.) In her view the other languages she considers are following English along a similar developmental path. The review by Fischer and van der Leek (1985) of the longer work makes detailed criticisms of some specific claims which I cannot actually find in von Seefranz-Montag's shorter, English piece, especially the allegation that she imposes a strict chronological order on what are in fact overlapping stages.

5.7.2 Allen

Cynthia Allen (1986a) concentrates on the history of LIKE in a paper which offers an alternative within Lexical-Functional grammar to Fischer and van der Leek's earlier Government-Binding approach.[21]

5.7.2.1 Problems with other accounts, OE analysis

Allen first presents damaging new evidence against the Jespersen–Lightfoot reanalysis theory. In LIKE-sentences with two nominal arguments, the proportion where both are of ambiguous case is relatively low: some 9 per cent in OE prose, 15 per cent in some early ME texts, and 3 per cent in Chaucer (1986a: 378–9), thus reinforcing McCawley's point, §5.6.1 above. Furthermore, in examples with at least one argument before the verb, the proportion where the Experiencer is in initial position is also fairly low and falling: 45 per cent in OE prose, 30 per cent in early Middle English, 20 per cent in Chaucer (these figures include both OSV and OVS) (1986a: 379–80).[22] The suggestion that ambiguity in OVS leads to reanalysis as SVO is not well supported by the figures, therefore.

There is more. The arrival of Experiencer-subject examples does not correlate with the postulated arrival of underlying SVO order in the late twelfth century: if morphological evidence of subjecthood is required, then clear nominative Experiencers appeared too late, as did dative Experiencers which appear to control verb concord (late fourteenth century); if syntactic evidence from zero anaphora is accepted, then (dative) subject Experiencers appeared too early (Old English). The only morphological development which followed closely on the word order change is 'the appearance of two pronouns in the dative case in one sentence' (1986a: 382), as in the thirteenth-century [33]–[34] with PINKEN, though examples like [35] with LIKE are not found before the fourteenth century (1986a: 381–2). Then again, Lightfoot has not explained the appearance of type (iii) sentences with clausal Cause, since an oblique Experiencer moved into an empty subject position would not violate the Trace Erasure Principle (1986a:

382–3). And finally, Lightfoot provides no explanation for the facts that BEHOFIAN 'need' underwent apparently the opposite change to that undergone by LICIAN, while LOSIAN 'lose' followed the same path as LICIAN but completed the change before LICIAN had started (1986a: 384).

Allen considers the possibility that reanalysis occurred first in type (i/ii) sentences with a dative Experiencer and a clausal Cause, but finds them to have no greater proportion of structurally ambiguous examples than those with two nominal arguments. In any event, nominative Experiencers occurred no earlier with a clausal Cause than with a nominal one (1986a: 382–3).

After a discussion of Fischer and van der Leek (1983), Allen moves on to her own LFG analysis. For Old English she assumes that with two nominal arguments, type (ii) was the only productive pattern with LICIAN, but that there were two possible assignments of semantic to grammatical relations, her [12] and [18] respectively:[23]

[78]   EXP   CAUSE
        Pred 'LICIAN <(OB)   (SB)>'
                        ↑ OB CASE=DAT
                        ↑ SB CASE=NOM

[79]   EXP   CAUSE
        Pred 'LICIAN <(SB)   (OB)>'
                                      ↑ SB CASE=DAT
                                      ↑ OB CASE=NOM

The more normal usage is represented by [78]: Cause is nominative subject, Experiencer is dative object, word order is SVO or SOV. But a less common usage, represented by the subcategorisation frame [79], had Cause as nominative object and Experiencer as dative subject, with Experiencer now preceding Cause. (Word order was nevertheless still SVO or SOV.) Frame [79] therefore introduces the unconventional idea of subject arguments marked by an oblique case in surface form (and conversely, objects with nominative marking). What is the justification for this?

5.7.2.2 Coordinate subject deletion

Perhaps the most valuable part of Allen's article is the careful argumentation (1986a: 391–4) which precedes the introduction of [79]. It hinges on the analysis of null anaphora, or coordinate subject deletion. Consider this example of Allen's:

[80] *ÆHom* II 20.644.71

      ac Gode   ne licode na   heora geleafleast,
      but God(DAT) not pleased not-at-all their faithlessness(NOM)

      . . . ac asende him to fyr of   heofonum
      . . . but sent   them to fire from heavens

      'but God did not at all like their faithlessness . . . and sent fire from heaven to them'

The unexpressed subject of *asende* 'sent' is anaphoric with (i.e. is deleted under identity with) the Experiencer argument of *licode* 'pleased', namely the dative noun *gode* 'God'. Lightfoot (1979, 1981) had argued that such examples (though in Middle English) proved that datives could in fact be subjects, on the assumption that the subject of the second conjunct could only have been deleted under identity with the *subject* of the first conjunct. Warner (1983) had contested this assumption as unsafe up to early Modern English.

What Allen does is to give statistical support to the assumption, at least for Old English. First she shows that subjects of second conjuncts are not in general freely omissible. Taking a sample corpus of OE prose and confining herself to sentences where the undisputed subject of a first conjunct is nominative and the subject of a second conjunct is either a pronoun or missing, she finds that omission of the second subject is highly correlated with coreference between the subjects: deletion occurs in 80 per cent of the examples with coreference but in only 1 per cent of those without (percentages based on large totals).[24] It follows that deletion under identity with undisputed *objects* is almost non-existent. Then she compares the incidence of deletion controlled by preposed dative Experiencers, and finds 73 per cent deletion in a small total. She concludes that preposed dative Experiencers in Old English behaved far more like subjects than like objects as far as control of coordinate subject deletion was concerned (compare Elmer's use of 'quasi-subject', §5.4.3.1 above) – hence her differentiation between preposed and postposed Experiencers, with the former treated as subjects despite their dative case-marking. There may be problems with split NP arguments as in:

[81]   *LawAfEl* 49.10 46

& hie ða   cwædon, þæt him   þæt licode   eallum
and they then said   that them(DAT) that pleased all(DAT)
to healdanne.
to keep

'And they then said that they were all content to observe that.'

Him is preposed Experiencer, but its adjective *eallum* is postposed. A transformational grammar would probably use a rule of **Quantifier Floating** to account for the position of *eallum*.

5.7.2.3   History of LIKE

There is some discussion of verb agreement in Old English and early Middle English, and of the 'double object' (type (i)) pattern in Middle English, with the conclusion that from the thirteenth to the fifteenth centuries, 'a preposed cause was marked nominative, and a postposed cause was marked dative' (1986a: 398). Allen argues that in Old English, nominative was the default case (cf. Anderson on subjecthood, §5.6.2 above), so that postposed Cause NPs, even though objects, got nominative case. In Middle English, on the other hand, case assignment to objects was structural, 'with the result that any declinable object got dative [i.e. objective: D.D.] case' (1986a: 398). The ME equivalents of verbal lexical entries like [78–79] no longer require equations defining the case of an object.

Following through into the fourteenth century, Allen finds the same patterns for LIKE as in early Middle English but with the addition of nominative Experiencer subjects. The latter became increasingly dominant in the fifteenth century, and 'after Shakespeare's time' the lexical entry only assigned the Experiencer to subject role (1986a: 401). In fact, as we have pointed out above, Pepys still allowed Experiencer objects in the 1660s, so the final demise of the type (ii) Experiencer-object pattern must have been a little later:[25]

[82]   1661 Pepys, *Diary* II 114.14 (4 Jun)

But the houses did not like us, and so that design at present is stopped.

For verbs like SEEM which retained relics of old dative-Experiencer patterns well into the ModE period, Allen suggests that it was the *form* rather than the case of the Experiencer that was specified in the relevant lexical entries (1986a: 402–3). She is referring here to *preposed* oblique NPs, so examples like [82] are not at issue.

Allen's criticism of Fischer and van der Leek (1983) is too dense to summarise properly (1986a: 401–2). In brief, she argues that the facts she has collected demand the recognition of preposed dative Experiencer subjects, and that acceptance of this would make Fischer and van der Leek's GB account a mere notational variant of her own.

A final point of note is Allen's explanation for the gradual preference for type (iii) over type (ii) with LIKEN. It hinges on a comparison with the near-synonymous CWEMEN, also usually glossed as 'please'. A survey of both verbs in Old English, early Middle English and Chaucer reveals that animacy of the Cause argument correlates with choice of verb: more usually CWEMEN (later PLESEN) for human Cause, LIKEN for non-human Cause. Given that a sample count of OE main clauses with dative objects revealed 83 per cent to have human subjects, LICIAN's preponderant assignment of subject to *non*-human role was unusual. Thus the shift towards Experiencer subjects with LIKEN helped to bring it in line with other verbs (1986a: 404–5).

5.8   Mainly descriptive accounts

5.8.1   Wahlén

The dissertation by Nils Wahlén (1925) is one of the standard works on the subject, or rather, the subject*less*, since he restricts himself to clauses lacking a nominal subject apart from dummy *hit*. Separate chapters consider synchronic (OE) description and diachronic (pre-OE) reconstruction. Within each chapter Wahlén distinguishes A 'simple sentences', our type (i), and B 'complex sentences', type (i/ii). Types (ii) and (iii) are excluded on principle, and there is nothing on post-OE developments. Wahlén systematically covers a very wide range of verbs in semantic subgroupings, offering good exemplification, a dated but insightful discussion of the semantics, and much comparative material and discussion of pre-OE origins.

5.8.2 Ogura

Michiko Ogura's recent monograph on impersonal verbs and expressions in Old English (1986) is traditional in outlook.[26] This work is valuable especially for its reliable citation of examples, its Appendix 3 on syntactic patterns found with each verb, its comparisons between Latin usage and OE translations, and its tables of statistics based on laborious combing of Venezky and Healey (1980). The verbs and phrases are divided into eight, semantically-based groups, and the main chapters of the book cover six principal syntactic types, classified in large part by the form of the impersonal (for example, finite verb vs. BE + adjective vs. BE + PA PTCP) but also partly by the accompanying arguments. As far as synchronic treatment of Old English is concerned, the work is essentially descriptive. Diachrony, confined to the Summaries of each chapter, is raised in connection with the loss of certain OE patterns. Ogura largely follows the syntactic treatment of van der Gaaf (1904), except where his coverage of OE
data is deficient. She adds some observations on lexical semantics, especially conflict of synonyms and overlap between classes (see e.g. 1986: 132–4).

5.8.3 Denison

In Denison (1990a) I questioned some of the generalisations made about impersonals and suggested the use of serial relationship (Quirk 1965) as an analytic and explanatory tool. An extensive summary follows.

5.8.3.1 Non-homogeneity of impersonals

There are problems in Fischer and van der Leek's claim that OE impersonals form a single and fully productive class (Denison 1990a: §2). For example, LICIAN is very rare in type (i) and occurs in type (iii) only in the Latinate syntax of glosses, as in [83]:

[83]   *MkGl(Ru)* 1.11

þu eart sunu min leof   on ðe ic   wel licade
you are son my beloved in you I(NOM) well liked(1/3 SG)

Lat. . . . in te complacui

'You are my beloved son, in whom I am well pleased.'

Otherwise LICIAN is overwhelmingly type (ii). Then again Fischer and van der Leek claim that [84] shows ÞYNCAN occurring in passive type (iii), whereas I regard [84] and also [85] as non-passive type (ii), which fits in much better with the usual case syntax of those verbs:

[84]   *ChronE* 233.28 (1097)

& se leoma   þe him   ofstod.   wæs swiðe lang
and the light(NOM) that it(DAT) from-shone was very long(NOM)

geþuht   suðeast   scinende
seemed/thought(PA PTCP) south-east shining(NOM)

'And the light which shone from it (had) seemed very long, shining towards the south east.'

[85] *Or* 65.25

Ic nat   . . . for hwi eow Romanum   sindon þa   ærran
I not-know . . . for why you Romans(DAT) are(PL) those earlier

gewin   swa wel gelicad   &   swa lustsumlice
conflicts(NOM PL) so   well pleased(PA PTCP) and so enjoyable

. . . to gehieranne
. . . to hear

'I don't know why those earlier conflicts are so pleasing and so enjoyable for you Romans . . . to hear'

Thus in [84–85] I suggest that the past participles are *in*transitive and the verb BEON is more like a perfect than a passive auxiliary; see further §12.4.3 below. I showed too that impersonals are not always two-place verbs with Experiencer and Cause, as claimed by Fischer and van der Leek. There are clear cases of one-place use, as in §5.2.5.1, as well as examples with extra arguments, as in §5.2.6.9.

Having denied the homogeneity of impersonal verbs, I then showed that subclassifying them, as attempted by Elmer (1981), Ogura (1986), Anderson (1986), etc., whether on a syntactic or semantic basis, is equally unsatisfactory, since it inevitably separates patterns which belong together (Denison 1990a: §3).

5.8.3.2 Impersonal ~ non-impersonal demarcation

Furthermore there is no clear demarcation between impersonals and other verbs (Denison 1990a: §4). For example, Fischer and van der Leek had excluded zero-place WEATHER verbs as being obviously different from the kinds of impersonal they wanted to explain (1983: 346–7 n.8). But RIGNAN 'rain', say, at least shares with *OFHREOWAN 'rue' the noteworthy property of often occurring in a subjectless construction or with a *hit* subject. It can certainly have a cognate object (or maybe subject), and in glosses the verb may be used with a lexical subject and even a dative Recipient:

[86] *PsGII* 77.24

&   he rinde heom   þane heofonlican mete to etanne
and he rained them(DAT) the   heavenly   food to eat

Lat. et pluit illis manna ad manducandum

The verb SWEORCAN 'grow dark' is semantically like a WEATHER verb except that it frequently has a lexical subject and even a dative:

[87] *And* 372

Wedercandel swearc
weather-candle darkened

'the sun grew dark'

[88] *Beo* 1736

> ne him   inwitsorh | on sefan sweorceð
> nor him(DAT) malice-sorrow in heart darkens

'nor does (a problem caused by) malice darken his heart'

Him in [88] is a dative of possession or interest (disadvantage), but it is not unlike the dative Experiencers subcategorised for by certain impersonal verbs (cf. *Wand* 41 *Þinceð him on mode þæt* . . .). The subjectless use of SAY verbs, as in [2] and [89], is very similar to an impersonal type (i/ii) or (ii):

[89] *BlHom* 19.27

> Þæt us   tacnaþ þæt he . . .
> that us(DAT/ACC) signifies that he . . .

'That signifies to us that He . . .'

I also drew attention to the sometimes very similar syntax of impersonal and non-impersonal verbs, allowing them to share arguments by *verb conjunction*. Thus the verb EGL(I)AN 'ail' is an impersonal, the verb DERIAN 'harm, injure' is not:

[90] *CP* 199.12

> & ðeah sua sua hit him   no   ne derige, ne ne egle
> and yet   such that it them(DAT) not-at-all not injure nor not ail

'and yet so that it does not injure or annoy them at all'

Similarly, SCEAMIAN 'shame' is an impersonal while FÆGNIAN 'rejoice in' and WEOPAN 'bewail' are not:

[91] *Bo* 68.15

> oððe forhwy hi   ne mægen hiora   ma   scamian   þonne
> or   why   they not may   them(GEN) more feel-shame than
> fægnian
> rejoice

'or why they may not be more ashamed of those things/themselves than glad'

[92] *GD(C)* 130.4

> . . . ongan his scylde   weopan   &
> . . . began his offence(ACC/GEN) bewail(INF) and
> scamian
> be-ashamed-of(INF)

'. . . began to bewail and be ashamed of his offence'

The verb LYSTAN 'desire' is impersonal, GITSIAN 'covet' and FRICLAN 'desire' are not, yet all take a genitive of the object desired. In LYSTAN's rare type (iii) occurrences its subcategorisation is just like the other two. LICIAN 'please' is usually classed as an impersonal, CWEMAN 'please' is not. In fact their normal subcategorisations are identical:

[93]   *Ps* 34.14

And ic   . . . him   tilode to licianne, &   to cwemanne
and I(NOM) . . . them(DAT) strove to please   and to please

'And I . . . strove to please them.'

5.8.3.3   Serial relationship

The impossibility of classifying impersonals satisfactorily either in one or in
several classes, despite the evident family resemblance, led me to suggest
plotting them individually in a matrix which could represent *degrees* of
similarity. Thus one could describe and to some extent explain the
behaviour of the various impersonals. I reproduce two examples of such
matrices:

[94]   *pattern*:   1   2   3

verb

	1	2	3
SLEAN 'strike'	+	–	–
GEYFLIAN 'injure, suffer'	+	+	–
CALAN 'grow cold'	–	+	–
*ÞREOTAN 'grow weary'	–	+	–
HYNGRIAN 'hunger'	–	+	?
AÞREOTAN 'grow weary'	–	+	+
ÞYRSTAN 'thirst'	–	+	+
TWEOGAN 'doubt'	–	+	+
ONHAGIAN 'be convenient'	–	+	+

1 = NOM Cause, ACC Experiencer/Patient[27] (type (ii))
2 = Ø Cause, ACC Experiencer/Patient
3 = GEN/S' Cause, ACC Experiencer/Patient (type (i))

Matrix [94] ranges from the personal verb SLEAN 'strike' to the impersonals
*ÞREOTAN 'grow weary' and ONHAGIAN 'be convenient'. Consider now
the intermediate verb GEYFLIAN 'suffer', which can be an impersonal verb
with just an Experiencer argument, like *ÞREOTAN. The Cause
argument of GEYFLIAN, however, appears in the nominative if expressed,
giving the type (ii) pattern, and the verb can then equally be viewed as an
ordinary, personal, transitive verb – 'injure' – like SLEAN. [94] gives a simple
illustration of serial relationship from personal to impersonal verbs. A
second example is [95]:

[95]   *pattern*:   1   2   3   4   5

verb

	1	2	3	4	5
BEFEOLAN 'apply (o/s) to'	–	–	–	–	+
CWEMAN 'please'	–	–	–	–	+
HELPAN 'help'	–	–	–	+	+
LAÞIAN 'loathe'	–	–	–	+	+
MÆTAN 'dream'	–	–	?	+	+
(GE)LICIAN 'like, please'	?	?	?	+	+
HREOWAN 'rue'	+	+	+	+	+

1 = NOM Experiencer, PP/GEN Cause – type (iii)
2 = DAT Experiencer, PP/GEN Cause – type (i)
3 = DAT Experiencer, ACC Cause – ?type (i)
4 = DAT Experiencer, S' Cause – type (i/ii)
5 = DAT Experiencer/Patient,[27] NOM Cause/Agent – type (ii)

Some allegedly Latinate uses of (GE)LICIAN discussed above (example [83]) make more sense if fitted into a context such as that of [95]. The matrix makes clear that (GE)LICIAN is much like HELPAN in syntax but overlaps sufficiently with HREOWAN to allow the sporadic analogical use of impersonal-like syntax. (Allen has made a similar suggestion (1986a: 387–8). She also makes interesting observations on a statistical difference between LICIAN and CWEMAN as far as potential volitionality on the part of the Cause argument is concerned (1986a: 404); this is consistent with the different placings of the verbs in [95].)

Variation is the prerequisite for change. Whereas most synchronic generative syntax idealises variation away, mappings of serial relationship like [94]–[95] actually focus on it. A further example will be given in §9.4.3 below. My hope was that future work along these lines would fill in some of the gaps left by generative linguistics. These ideas might now perhaps be reframed in terms of Prototype Theory or Grammatical Construction Theory (Rosch 1978, Lakoff 1987: 58–67).

5.8.4   Van der Wurff

Elmer (1981), Ogura (1986) and Denison (1990a) discuss the use of phrasal impersonals alongside the simple impersonal verbs. Wim van der Wurff (1992a) specifically concentrates on phrasal impersonals with adjective + infinitive, using a full collection from Venezky and Healey (1980). The article offers careful, detailed analyses for various patterns and individual examples, many of them never previously given a systematic modern treatment. While not going deeply into syntactic theory, van der Wurff's article has pointers towards conclusions of theoretical importance for GB theory.

Van der Wurff's main classification distinguishes dummy *hit*-subject (type A), complete absence of subject (type B), and full lexical subject (type C). Type C is subclassified according to the syntax of the subject of the matrix verb, that is, whether it is to be interpreted as (i.e. whether it *controls*) the subject of the infinitive, the object of the infinitive, the object of a preposition, or part of an unrealised PP. There is also some discussion of the matrix verb, usually BEON but occasionally PYNCAN or one of a scattering of other verbs, or even absent altogether. Frequencies are gathered with a view to establishing any restrictions on use of particular patterns, including what is 'original OE' as opposed to the Old Englishes of translation and glossing. Van der Wurff examines such factors as text-type, order of constituents, presence or absence of dative NP, and nature of infinitive.

5.9 Dummy *it*

In this section we shall go back over the history of impersonals, looking at the status of dummy *it* (OE *hit*). Previously we have made the simplifying assumption that dummy *it* is distinguishable from anaphoric *it*, has non-argument status, and can be ignored. Now we reconsider the difference between clauses with and without *it*. Most scholars who regard at least some instances of *it* as syntactic dummies have suggested that its use in Old English is correlated with one or more of these syntactic developments:

(A) the rise of V-2 word order in main clauses
(B) the rise of SVO word order
(C) a growing requirement for a surface subject in every finite clause

Impersonals are of course one of the most important sources of subjectless sentences.

5.9.1 The data

Kohonen has a collection of OE and eME examples of type (i) impersonals and impersonal passives without and with dummy *hit* (1978: 178–9). Further examples can be found in Visser (1963–73: §§3, 10, 29–64). There is also the occasional use of *hit* as an existential dummy:

[96] a1225(c1200) *Vices and V.(1)* 65.14

    Ac hit bieð sume ðe   bieð swiðe wise ihealden . . .
    but it   are some that are   very   wise held . . .

    'But there are some who are considered very wise . . .'

5.9.2 Meaning of *hit*

Wahlén treated *hit* as a semantically empty element (1925: 8–11), as does Mitchell (1985: §1031). Several scholars have questioned whether *hit/it* can ever be a true dummy element. Bolinger has proposed that *all* occurrences of *it* in Present-day English, including 'weather *it*', are meaningful and therefore have reference (1977b: 66–90). Even if some uses of *it* in Present-day English are genuinely non-argument NPs, there seems to be a gradience from dummy to fully anaphoric use. Similar considerations apply to OE *hit*, as argued by Bennis (1986: 284) – reference from Wim van der Wurff (p.c.).

5.9.3 Use and non-use of *hit*

Wahlén reckoned that 'the state of things in this respect [namely, use or non-use of *hit* in Old English: D.D.] is next to chaotic', apart from the virtual absence of *hit* with impersonals of physical or mental affections, but other scholars have detected some tendencies. It is generally agreed that non-use is rare with WEATHER verbs, while the use of dummy *hit* is rare with two-place impersonals of the HUNGER, RUE, DREAM and

PLEASE classes, and the SAY verbs. Visser's material (1963–73: §58a) contains no examples from Old English of *hit* co-occurring with an Experiencer argument, but cf. Elmer (1981: 34) BEON *sorhlic* and examples of the BEHOVE class:

[97]   *ÆLS* I 17.260

     hit ne gerist nanum ricum   cynincge   þæt . . .
     it not befits no   powerful king(DAT) that . . .

     'It befits no powerful king to . . .'

Anderson's generalisation is that:

> 'formal *hit*' alternatives are typical of those constructions where otherwise no non-impersonal variant would be available: the predicate is argumentless or takes a sentential one. (1988: 9)

In a plea for the study of discourse units longer than the clause, Lagerquist suggests tentatively that the use of *hit* with HAPPEN verbs in Old English 'may indicate that the action described proceeds logically or causally from what has gone before' (1985: 130).

5.9.4 Elmer

Elmer always considers the significance of *(h)it*, treating it as a dummy in type (i/ii) but apparently as a pronominal NP in types (i), (ii) and (iii). He regards the use of *it* in type (i/ii) as very rare with the RUE verbs in Old English but possible from Middle English or early Modern English (1981: 34, 86–7). Use of *it* was non-existent with PLEASE/DESIRE verbs until perhaps the thirteenth century (1981: 39), available with BEHOVE from late Old English onwards (1981: 42–3, 122–5; 1983: 161), absent with HAPPEN – unless with *þæt* for *hit* – until the twelfth century (1981: 44, 129–31), and very rare indeed with SEEM until the thirteenth or fourteenth century (1981: 44–45, 133–35). For tables of occurrence with individual verbs see Elmer (1981: 46, 86, 94, 109, 116, 122, 130, 134). An interesting observation is that RUE verbs which only entered widespread use in Middle English were more likely to prefer *it* in type (i/ii), perhaps because of the then stronger influence of SVO syntax, whereas the long-established members of the class preferred non-use.

Why was *hit* used? In type (i/ii) without Experiencer argument, Elmer claims that *hit* was optional in Old English and was more frequently *not* chosen (1981: 52–7), especially in the pattern of [101]:[28]

[98]   *GD(H)* 11.3

     Hit gelamp   geo   . . . þæt . . .
     it happened formerly. . . that . . .

[99]   *ChronE* 148.15 (1016)

     Ða gelamp   hit þet . . .
     then happened it that . . .

[100] *KtPs* 16

    Gelamp   þæt . . .
    happened that . . .

[101] *gedafenaþ hit þæt . . .
    is-fitting   it   that . . .

Non-occurrence of [101] – and indeed the vanishing rarity of [100] – argues in favour of the 'force of the verb-second target' (1981: 55), though that cannot be the explanation for the use of *hit* in [99]. But in any case Elmer has other reasons for arguing that 'in OE *it* is still not used purely to produce verb-second order' (1981: 71, and cf. also 62).

5.9.5 Allen

Cynthia Allen (1986b) examines main clauses in OE prose containing GELIMPAN 'happen' for their use or non-use of dummy *hit*. She finds that out of a total of 227 instances, dummy *hit* assures V-2 order by its presence in only 58 examples, actually prevents V-2 order in 65, is irrelevant to V-2 in 75 – and does not appear at all in 29. *Hit* thus makes no contribution to V-2 in 71 per cent of its occurrences. The conclusion is that dummy *hit* cannot in fact be explained on the basis of a V-2 target (which is offered as a received view), especially since it is no less frequent in subordinate clauses, where no V-2 constraint is expected.

Instead Allen puts forward two other hypotheses to explain the presence or absence of dummy *hit*. She concludes 'that dummy *hit* was obligatory, or very nearly so, when nothing else protected the verb from being sentence-initial in a declarative sentence, and highly favored, but not completely obligatory, in other situations, regardless of the position of the verb' (1986b: 468). Conversely, dummy *hit* was virtually absent from clauses containing a preposed dative Experiencer – 0/17 occurrences in main clauses, 1/11 in subordinates – despite being frequent with other sorts of preposed constituents (140/169 in main clauses, as I interpret her figures). This, she says, may be because preposed Experiencers were in fact subjects, despite their dative case. In §5.7.2 above we saw her reach the same conclusion by another route.

5.10 Questions for discussion or further research

(a) With a view to testing the hypotheses of Krzyszpień (details in §5.4.4) and Lagerquist (§5.9.3), investigate the correlations between discourse givenness and (i) initial position for Experiencers of impersonals, (ii) use of *hit*, in any one Old English text. (You could use the listing of impersonals in Ogura 1986. For (i) a Middle English text would be equally suitable, especially one with a full glossary.)

(b) If Allen's (1986a) analysis of LIKE were to be accepted in essentials, what would be the consequences for verbs like RUE?

(c) Try to repeat Allen's investigation of dummy *hit* in main clauses (discussed in §5.9.5 above, details in Allen 1986b), but with the following changes:

    (i)   allow for possible clitic status of *hit* in some instances, on the lines suggested by van Kemenade (brief discussion §4.7.1.1 above, details in van Kemenade 1987, Koopman 1992). Can the positional distribution of *hit* be accounted for? Is there still a negative correlation between the use of *hit* and V-2?

    (ii) replace the verb GELIMPAN by one or more phrasal impersonals involving BEON/WESAN (where clause-initial position for the verb might seem more likely). What are the results now?

(d) What patterns for the (non-)use of *hit* can you glean from the material in Ogura (1986)?

Notes

1. That is, a potential by virtue of the choice of verb. We are not here considering certain kinds of OE subjectless sentence which are possible, independently of choice of verb, by virtue of discourse factors or type of clause, for example imperatives, certain infinitival clauses, verb phrase conjunction (as in PDE *He saw the mess and lost his temper*).

2. The status of *hit* 'it' as dummy subject may even be controversial: see §5.9.1 below.

3. The hedge '(characteristically) personal' is meant to allow for an OE clause of the type:

    (a) *GD(C)* 85.35

        . . . þæt he   licode   þam ælmihtigan Gode
        . . . that he(NOM) pleased the almighty   God(DAT)

        '. . . that he might be pleasing to Almighty God'

Although the subject NP *he* is animate, it fills an argument position, Theme, which need not be animate and in fact usually is not (Allen 1986a: 404). Cynthia Allen, worried by animacy as a defining characteristic of Experiencerhood, points out that the *non*-Experiencer argument of CWEMAN 'please' is generally personal too (p.c., 13 December 1990). To this I would answer, firstly that CWEMAN is not really an impersonal verb (see further §5.8.3.2), and secondly that there are a few examples like (b) with an inanimate in that argument position:

    (b) *MSol* 165

        . . . ðeah ðe him   se wlite   cweme
        . . . although him(DAT) the brightness(NOM) please(SUBJ SG)

        '. . . even if the brightness pleases him'

    (c) *GD(C)* 129.14

        mid þy þa   word   gecwemdon his earum
        with that those words(NOM) pleased   his ears(DAT)

Indeed even the Experiencer in (c), *earum* 'ears', is not literally personal!

4. N.B. another MS. has *non*-nominative *mægenleaste*, so [4] may not be an ideal example of this type, but they exist. Cynthia Allen suggests the following (p.c., 13 December 1990):

(a) *ÆCHom* I 13.192.17

Ac him ne ofhreow na　　　ðæs deofles hryre
but him not rued　　not-at-all the devil's fall/death

'But he did not regret the devil's fall at all.'

5. Indeterminacy between types (i) and (ii) may also result from non-distinctiveness of nominal inflections, principally nominative and accusative. Non-systematic indeterminacy between other types is also found occasionally, for example between types (i) and (iii):

(a) *LS* 20(AssumptMor) 88

Þa　þæt folc　　　　　　　　ongan tweogan　on heora heortan
then the people(NOM or ACC SG) began feel-doubt in their　heart

'Then the people began to feel doubt in their hearts'

6. If their tentative claim that S's are objects in OE is accepted, we should note its consequences for the analysis of examples where a sentential Cause occurs in initial position in ME: either the ME patterns must be analysed quite differently from the OE, or Intraposition must be invoked. And in Old English where a provisional subject argument is used, it cannot then be regarded as in apposition with the S' (unless provisional *hit*, *þæt*, etc. are treated as accusative rather than nominative).

7. Cynthia Allen (p.c., 13 December 1990) says that BEHOFIAN itself was not impersonal before the twelfth century.

8. See Anderson (1986: 174) for an analysis of SEEM verbs as occurring with Experiencer and Theme, not Cause, arguments.

9. Unfortunately Elmer's and Fischer and van der Leek's systems of syntactic labelling are confusingly similar. The main correspondences are as follows:

Fischer and van der Leek	*Elmer*
type (i), neutral	$\begin{cases} \text{type N (Cause is NP)} \\ \text{type S (Cause is clause)} \end{cases}$
type (ii), cause-subject	variant type I (Cause is NP)
type (iii), experiencer-subject	$\begin{cases} \text{variant type II (Cause is NP)} \\ \text{variant with nominative subject} \end{cases}$ (Cause is clause)

Note too that Elmer tends to use **NPa** – i.e. '(typically, necessarily) animate NP' – for what we have been calling 'Experiencer'.

10. In §§5.4.3.2 and 5.4.4 I use **theme** in a sense which has to do with discourse structure and is similar to the notion of topic (cf. also §4.1.4). Here and elsewhere in the chapter I shall reserve **Theme** (with capital T) for a quite different usage, a label for the semantically most neutral argument of a verb.

11. *Tre* in [58] is an argument not of *semed* but of *bren* and appears therefore to have been 'raised' out of the lower clause. (Elmer does not use the term 'Raising'.) See Chapter 9.

12. The same rule of NP Preposing is invoked to explain the arrival of new transformational passives; see §7.6.2 below.

13. See Plank (1984) for a withering review of parts of Lightfoot (1979), especially the much-vaunted, often-promised, but never actually produced Transparency Principle.

14. The famous Jespersen *king-pears* sentences [55](a–d) are slightly altered in Lightfoot (1981), though stages (a)–(d) are the same in essentials.

15. The derivation is ill-formed if *neither* NP gets lexical case in deep structure, since only one can then get structural nominative, and by the *Case Filter* all NPs must have exactly one case.

16. Faarlund (1990: 53–4) points out that Modern Norwegian NP-V-NP sentences involving LIKE 'like' can remain ambiguous in principle between SVO and topicalised OVS readings. Both readings are type (iii) in our terms, so the ambiguity is different from the one discussed by Fischer and van der Leek. Nevertheless its effects are very similar on the surface, so it is interesting to note that in practice, according to Faarlund, the potential Norwegian ambiguity is never a problem, since it is resolved by context or by the use of an auxiliary verb (which allows word order to discriminate the readings) or by the choice of a case-marked NP.

17. They assume without discussion that ModE SEEM fills precisely the same lexical slot in the system as OE ÞYNCAN (Fischer and van der Leek 1983: 366). It should be observed that SEEM when first borrowed from Old Norse was a member of the BEHOVE class, and that in the first 150 years or so of its use it had a different distribution from THINKEN in that it could not occur with an Experiencer argument (Elmer 1983: 164–5, discussed in §5.4.3.2 above). No explanation is given for the fact that SEEM – unlike SHAME, BECOME or the ME borrowings PLEASE and GRIEVE – requires an Experiencer object to be marked by *to*:

    (a) It seems/*pleases to me that . . .
    (b) It *seems/pleases   me that . . .

18. McCawley subsumes the semantic category represented by our label Experiencer under the category Recipient. Certainly the two are closely related both in their semantics and in their case syntax in Old English.

19. Beware a minor notational trap. In the first part of his 1986 article Anderson's classification into 'types (*a*), (*b*) and (*c*)' hinges on whether the verb has, respectively, 0, 1 or 2 arguments associated with it. Later he uses 'types *a*, *b* and *c*' in the sense of our types (i), (iii) and (ii), respectively.

20. One can also have adverbial NPs which are pure circumstantials (sister of VP, not of V).

21. Neither Allen (1986a) nor Fischer and van der Leek (1987) makes reference to the other.

22. Allen excludes from the figures two Chaucer examples with preposed Experiencers that are in clear subjective case (1986a: 380 n.7).

23. I quote Allen's explanation of the arrows: 'The upward pointing arrows refer to the node immediately dominating the node to which the equation is assigned; thus the first equation in [entry [78]] is interpreted "the case of the object of the verb is dative" ' (1986a: 388).

24. Even the 1 per cent (= 4 out of 313 examples) can often be explained as mistakes.

25. *OED* s.v. *like* v.[1] gives examples up to the nineteenth century.

26. The rather tortuous terminological distinctions of the title are explained at (1986a: 16).

27. I use 'Experiencer/Patient' as a crude device to represent an obligatorily animate, non-agentive argument.

28. Some of Elmer's citations of patterns [98]–[101], for example his [112] (= *Bo* 45.4), [123], are useless for discussions of word order because an initial element has been omitted. Venezky and Healey (1980) has just one example with clause-initial *gedafenað* (but no *hit*):

    (a) *HomM* 11(PetersonVercHom 14) 192 (*DOE*)

        Gedafenað us eac . . ., þæt we . . .
        is-fitting   us also . . . that we . . .

        'It is fitting for us also . . . to . . .'

Chapter 6

Dative Movement and the indirect passive

6.1 The problem

For three-*place* verbs like GIVE, Modern English tends to allow two different kinds of active complementation:

[1] (a) Tom gave presents to Mary.
     (b) Tom gave Mary presents.

Traditionally the NP *Mary* has the syntactic status of indirect object in [1](b) at least.[1] Its semantic role may be labelled as Recipient, or more generally, **Benefactive**. The direct object *presents* has a semantic role which can be called **Theme**. Reference to NPs by semantic roles will simplify comparison of active and passives. Early transformational grammars of English related [1](a) and (b) by a transformation known by some such name as Dative Movement, with [1](a) usually taken as closer to the underlying form, and [1](b) derived transformationally by permutation of the two object arguments and deletion of the preposition.

There are corresponding passives for both patterns in [1]:

[2] (a) Presents were given to Mary (by Tom).
     (b) Mary was given presents (by Tom).

We may call [2](a) a **direct passive**: it is the conventional sort of passive whose subject (the Theme) corresponds to direct object in the active. Type [2](b) is often known as an **indirect passive**, since it takes as its subject an NP (the Benefactive) corresponding to the indirect object in the active.

What was the position in Old English? The answer probably varies with different subgroups of three-place verbs. Types [1](a) and [2](a) appear to be lacking for the verb GIEFAN 'give' and its close synonyms. Old English used dative case marking rather than prepositional marking for its Benefactive NP, but a Benefactive occasionally appears in a *to*-phrase with verbs like FORLÆTAN 'surrender' and CWEÐAN 'speak'. The equivalent of [1](b) was normal. As for the indirect passive, [2](b), this is not found in Old English, nor in most western European languages. However, Old English did have a passive where the Benefactive remained in the dative case. Two main possibilities are conceivable, each represented below by pseudo-ModE examples where either Theme or Benefactive is in topic position:

[3]   (a)   Presents(OBJ) was given her(OBJ).
      (b)   Her(OBJ) was given presents(OBJ).
[4]   (a)   Presents(SUBJ) were given her(OBJ).
      (b)   Her(OBJ) were given presents(SUBJ).

Patterns [3](a,b) are sometimes called **impersonal passives**, since the finite verb is 3 SG and lacks a nominative subject. Patterns [4](a,b) are direct passives: the finite verb is not subjectless, since a nominative NP in the role of Theme is subject of the passive. My made-up examples deliberately involve a Theme NP which is not 3 SG, allowing [4] to be distinguished from [3] by presence or absence of verbal concord.[2] In many actual OE examples the Theme is either a clause or a singular NP of uncertain case, and the verb is 3 SG, thus neutralising the distinction between types [3] and [4]. (I have found no clear impersonal type [3] passives with GIEFAN 'give' and doubt whether they occur with similar verbs either.) Of course in Modern English [4](a) is lexically and dialectally restricted, while [3](a,b) and [4](b) are impossible.

The problem, then, is to account for the appearance in Middle English of new forms with *to*, [1](a) and [2](a), and a new indirect passive form [2](b), and also to explain the loss – if it is a loss – of the passives [3](a,b) and [4](b). Since the question crucially involves the relation between a (three-place) verb and a dative NP in Old English, it seems wise to consider first the simpler problem of datives governed by two-place verbs.

6.2   The data

6.2.1   Two-place verbs

A number of verbs in Old English took a single object in the dative case, either invariably or in variation with other cases, for example SWICAN 'betray', WIÐHABBAN 'withstand, resist'. There are lists of such verbs in Visser (1963–73: §§316, 323) and Mitchell (1985: §1092). If these verbs occurred in the passive, an NP which would have been marked dative in the active retained its dative case in the passive,[3] and the verb was 3 SG:

[5]   *CP* 225.22

Ac ðæm   mæg beon suiðe hraðe   geholpen from his lareowe
but that-one(DAT) may be   very quickly helped   by   his teacher

'But that one may be helped/it may be remedied very quickly by his teacher'

[6]   *ÆCHom* I 3.52.31

. . . on urum agenum dihte hu   us   bið   æt Gode
. . . in our   own   power how us(DAT PL) will-be(3 SG) by God

gedemed
judged

'. . . in our own power as to how we shall be judged by God'

Dative marking was sporadically replaced from early Middle English onwards by the use of the preposition *to*, especially in the active:

[7]   (1340) *Ayenb.* 26.28

    . . . uor to kueme kueadliche to þe wordle.
    . . . for to please sinfully   to the world

'. . . to please the world sinfully'

On the other hand, from Middle English onwards these verbs also began to show properties of transitive verbs, for example sharing an object with a true transitive verb (though the value of such evidence is disputable):

[8]   c1225(?c1200) *St Juliana* (Bod) 13.131

    ne nulle   ich neauer mare him lihen   ne leauen
    nor not-will I   never more him prove-false-to nor leave

'nor will I ever more prove false to him or leave him'

LEVEN 'leave' has always been transitive, but LIEN 'lie, tell untruth' was often in Old English (and is again now) intransitive. More conclusively, formerly dative-governing verbs also appeared in direct passives:

[9]   c1225(?c1200) *St Kath.(1)* 196

    Þe king wes swiðe icwemet, ant wolde witen . . .
    the king was very pleased and wished know . . .

[10]   (c1395) Chaucer, *CT.Sq.* V.666

    Ne hadde he ben holpen by the steede of bras
    not had   he been helped by the steed   of brass

'had he not been helped by the steed of brass'

In example [9], admittedly, it is not certain – despite the following clause – that the NP *þe king* is in subjective case, but the pronominal *he* of [10] is conclusive. Examples like [10] started to appear from the thirteenth century, possibly with dialectal and/or lexical variation.

6.2.2 Three-place verbs in the active

There are numerous OE examples of Benefactives marked with dative:

[11]   *ÆCHom* I 7.116.13

    hi   offrodon Criste   gastlice recels,   and noldon
    they offered   Christ(DAT) spiritually frankincense and not-wished

    him   gold   offrian
    him(DAT) gold(ACC) offer

'they offered Christ frankincense spiritually and did not wish to offer Him gold'

[12] *ÆCHom* I 7.118.4

Ðam acennedan Cyninge   we bringað gold.
the born   king(DAT) we bring   gold(ACC)

. . . Stor   we him   bringaþ, gif . . .
. . . incense(ACC) we him(DAT) bring   if . . .

'To the born King we bring gold. . . . Incense we bring to him, if . . .'

[13] *WPol* 2.1.1 49, §17

þonne cyðe   hit   man   þam cyninge
then   tell(3 SG SUBJ) it(ACC) one(NOM) the king(DAT)

'then let one tell it to the king'

[14] *GD(C)* 69.25

. . . þæt heo hæfde henna . . . ac þa   hire
. . . that she had   hens . . . but them(ACC PL) her(DAT)

afyrrde   &   bereafode an fox
took-away and robbed   a fox(NOM)

'. . . that she kept hens . . . but a fox robbed her of them and took
them away'

It is not clear whether GIVE verbs should be discriminated from DEPRIVE
verbs (as Visser does, 1963–73: §§682–3).

With the loss of explicit dative inflections the construction continues to
the present day with the Benefactive in common (or if a case-marked
pronoun, objective) case:

[15] c1180 *Orm.* 3352

To kiþenn ȝuw þatt all follc   iss Nu cumenn mikell blisse
to inform you that all people is now come   great bliss

'to inform you that to all people great bliss has now come'

[16] c1400(?c1390) *Gawain* 920

God hatz geuen vus his grace godly   for soþe
God has given us his grace graciously indeed

[17] The warders denied the prisoners all privileges.

(Example [15], like some of the OE examples, shows topicalised word
order.)[4] Most verbs of depriving now belong to different subcategories of
verbs, requiring one of the objects to be prepositionally marked:

[18] The fox stole some hens from the woman.

[19] The fox robbed the woman of some hens.

As for Benefactives in *to*-phrases, it is not always easy to discriminate
between a true Benefactive (for which the *to*-phrase was rare) and an
adverbial Goal adjunct (for which the *to*-phrase was normal). Two
neighbouring early examples which look like Benefactives are:

[20]   *Or* 147.27

&   [Dioclitianus &   Maximianus] leton þa onwealdas
and Dioclitianus and Maximianus left   the jurisdiction/dominions

to Galeriuse &   to Constantiuse
to Galerius and to Constantius

[21]   *Or* 148.3

&   for þæm he forlet   his agnum willan Italiam &   Affricam
and for that he relinquished his own   volition Italy   and Africa

to Galeriuse.
to Galerius

'and for that reason he relinquished Italy and Africa to Galerius of his
own volition'

The following, more recent example just might contain separate expression
of Benefactive (*me*) and Goal (*to me*), though simple error is more likely:

[22]   1660 Pepys, *Diary* I 231.3 (24 Aug)

I find at home that Captain Bun hath sent me four dozen bottles of
wine to me today.

Use of *to*-phrases is discussed by Visser (1963–73: §687) and Mitchell (1985:
§1210).[5]

Now from the fourteenth century *to*-phrases with clear Benefactives
became more common:

[23]   a1425(a1382) *WBible(1)* Gen 29.19

Betir is that Y ȝyue hir to thee than to another man
better is that I give her to you than to another man

Several of the earliest examples with GIVEN involve the giving in marriage of
a woman to a man – precisely a context where Theme and Benefactive are
both animate nouns and where explicit marking of function is useful.

6.2.3   Three-place verbs in the passive (Benefactive ≠ subject)

For Old English we must distinguish in principle between the direct passive
(Theme as subject) and the impersonal passive (Theme as retained object).
There are numerous direct passives, i.e. type [4]:

[24]   *Beo* 1677

Ða wæs gylden hilt   gamelum rince | . . . on
then was golden hilt(NOM) old   warrior(DAT) . . . in

hand gyfen
hand given

'Then the golden hilt was handed to the old warrior'

[25]   *Lk(WSCp)* 1.45

þa ðing   þe ðe   fram drihtne gesæde synd;
the things(PL) that you(DAT) from God   said   are(PL)

'the things which are told you from God'

[26] *GD(H)* 82.27

&   þam þeo   wæs agifen seo ærre   hælo
and that thigh(DAT) was granted the earlier health(NOM)

'and health was granted the sooner to that thigh'

[27] *ÆCHom* II 6.57.154

. . . þæt ðam godum   þe hit gehealdan willað, ne sy oftogen
. . . that the good(DAT) that it hold   will   not is withheld

seo gastlice depnyss
the spiritual profundity

'. . . that spiritual profundity is not withheld from good men who wish
to observe it'

[28] *ÆCHom* II 36.306.1

ðe   bið   seo bodung   oftogen.
you(DAT) will-be the preaching withheld

'Preaching shall be withdrawn from you.'

Examples [24]–[28] include both GIVE and DEPRIVE verbs (which may be
thought of as antonyms of GIVE). Both groups also appear, fairly
infrequently, in impersonal passives of type [3], although, it would seem,
only when the Theme is genitive[6] or with the group-verb LÆTAN *blod*:

[29] *ÆCHom* I 23.330.29

ac him   næs   getiðod ðære lytlan lisse
but him(DAT) not-was granted that small favour(GEN)

'But he was not granted that small favour'

[30] *ÆHex* 484

and him   wæs swa forwyrned ðæs inganges   syððan
and him(DAT) was thus prevented the entry(GEN) subsequently

'and thus he was denied entry from then on'

[31] *Bede* 5 3.392.2

Sægde þæt hiere   niowan blod   læten wære in earme
said   that her(DAT) newly   blood(ACC) let   was in arm

'She said that she had lately been bled blood from the arm'

See also Visser (1963–73: §§1959 (1), 1963 (1)), from which [30]–[31] come.
    There are occasional, apparent impersonal passives in Middle English and
perhaps even later:

[32] 1395 *EEWills* 5.14

out-tak the forsayd   matyns bookis that is bequethe
except the aforesaid [*sc.* pair of] matins books that is bequeathed

to Thomas my sone
to Thomas my son

[33]   a1450(c1410) Lovel. *Grail* 46.356

Celidoine to this maide was wedded . . . and ʒoven   hem
Celidoyne to this maiden was married . . . and given[?] them(OBL)
pocesciowns   Manye &   fel
possessions(PL) many   and numerous

'Celidoyne was married to this maiden . . . and many and numerous
possessions were . . . given to them'

[34]   1523–5 Berners, *Froiss.* I.xi.11.25

Than there was brought to the quene her owne chyldren

Examples [32]–[34] resemble my hypothetical [3], though only the dubious
[33] has the Benefactive without *to*. Of course we may be dealing here with
failures of subject-verb concord (the reason for their citation by Visser), but
then with full NP arguments that is the only possible symptom of an
impersonal passive.

   From Middle English onwards the impersonal passive disappeared,[7] apart
from examples with dummy *there* or *it* anticipating an extraposed *that*-
clause:

[35]   1375 Barbour, *Bruce* 13.671

For thar wes fra   thine   send him worde |That the riche   Erll
for there was from thence sent him word   that the powerful Earl

of herfurde, |And othir mychty als, wes thar.
of Hereford   and other mighty also was there

'For there he was sent word that the powerful Earl of Hereford was
there, and other mighty ones too.'

[36]   1660 Pepys, *Diary* I 146.10 (18 May)

Observing that in every house of entertainment there hangs in every
room a poor-man's box and desirous to know the reason thereof, it
was told me that it is their custom to . . .

(Of course [35] could be taken as a direct passive with subject *worde*,
though not if final *-e* on *worde* is significant.) Notice the failure to use an
indirect passive *I was told* in [36] – which [54] shows to have been available
to the writer – despite the preceding participial clause and adjectival phrase.

   The direct passive remained a possibility:

[37]   c1230(?a1200) *Ancr.* 106a.6

Þis scheld is iʒeuen us aʒein   alle temptatiuns
this shield is given   us against all temptations

[38]   (c1390) Chaucer, *CT.Pard.* VI.920

I have relikes and pardoun in my male, . . . Whiche were me yeven
I have relics and a-pardon in my bag . . . which were me given

by the popes hond.
by the pope's hand

It may be that the direct passive is sometimes a deliberate and slightly artificial avoidance strategy for the somewhat stigmatised indirect passive:

[39]   1883(1875–6) Trollope, *Autobiography* v.84.3

and the fact that opportunities had been given me of seeing the poor-houses in Ireland

[40]   A doll was given the girl.

The passive type illustrated in [39]–[40] has as its subject an NP which in the corresponding active would be direct object but not immediately post-verbal. In PDE direct passives it is more common to use a *to*-phrase for the Benefactive than an oblique NP (examples from Quirk et al. 1985: §16.55):

[41]   A doll was given to the girl.

However, there may be a dialectal difference within Britain at least in direct passives, with (roughly speaking) [41] preferred in the south of England but [40] quite acceptable in the north (where, incidentally, direct object *is* sometimes immediately post-verbal in the active).[8]

6.2.4   Three-place verbs in the passive (Benefactive = subject)

There are no examples of the indirect passive in Old English (Mitchell 1985: §839). Apparent examples date from early Middle English, all involving group-verbs like DO (*somebody*) *good*, LET (*somebody*) *blood*:

[42]   c1230(?a1200) *Ancr.* 48b.2

ȝef me is iluuet mare þen an oþer . . . mare idon god   oðer menske.
if   one is loved more than an other . . . more done good or   honour

'if one is loved more than another, done more good or honour'

[43]   c1230(?a1200) *Ancr.* 31a.8

þa   he wes þus ilete blod
when he was thus let   blood

Such V + N group-verbs behaved differently from other verb + object *syntagms*.[9] The first reasonably clear[10] examples with verbs like GIVE and TELL are late fourteenth century, and they remained rare until late in the fifteenth century:

[44]   (1375) *Award Blount* in *ORS* 7 205.30

Item as for the Parke she is a lowyd Every yere a dere and xx Coupull of Conyes and all fewell Wode to her necessarye To be Takyn in a Wode callidde Grenedene Wode.

'Item: as for the park, she is allowed a deer each year and twenty pair

of rabbits and all fuel wood [= firewood] necessary[11] for her, to be
taken in a wood called Greendene Wood'

[45]   ?c1450(?a1400) *Wycl. Clergy HP* 383.34

playnly þu art forbodyn boþe
plainly you are forbidden both

[46]   (1418) *Let. War France* in *Bk. Lond. E.* III.xvi 77.8

and þey shall be assigned redy shippyng and passage
and they shall be allotted ready shipping and passage

[47]   a1450 *Aelred Inst. (2)* (Bod) 846

Now is he nayled to the cros and youen eysel   medled with galle
now is he nailed to the cross and given vinegar mixed with gall

to drynke
to drink

[48]   a1500(?a1450) *GRom.* (Hrl) 88.18

tyll tyme þat I be paied fully my salary.
till time that I be paid   fully my reward

'till the time that I am paid my reward in full'

[49]   (c1453[not before]) *Paston* 47.9

if Ser Thomas thynk that he shuld be a-lowyd mo, he shall be
if Sir Thomas think that he should be allowed more he shall be

'if Sir Thomas thinks that he should be allowed more, he shall be'

[50]   (a1470) Malory, *Wks.* 699.19

and whan he   was gyvyn the gre   be my lorde kynge
and when he(SUBJ) was given the prize-for-victory by my lord King

Arthure[12]
Arthur

'and when he was given the prize by my lord, King Arthur'

The spread of indirect passives to more and more verbs is documented by
Visser (1963–73: §§1967–75), though see note 19 for a caution on the
validity of his earliest citations. And even our fifteenth-century citations
need care.

The French loan PAY was at first a two-place verb meaning 'satisfy,
please'. *MED* does not record an indirect passive s.v. *paien* v., while Visser
(1963–73: §1972) has no example before 1835. In [48] we may therefore
suspect some influence from the attested ME usages *be paid* 'be satisfied'
(very common) and *be paid of* (*a sum of money*) (cf. ALLOW). In a similar
way, the French loan INFORM was originally more like LÆREN 'teach' than
TELL, in that the person informed was a Patient (Theme) rather than
Recipient, and thus again a direct object in the active. It is unclear,
therefore, whether examples like the following are true indirect passives:

[51]   c1450(?a1400) *Destr.Troy* 3011

He was enformyt before   of þat fre   lady, | þat ho . . .
he was informed beforehand of that noble lady   that she . . .

[52]   (c1451[not after]) *Paston* 476.1

And for asmuche as we be enformed that . . .
and inasmuch   as we are informed that . . .

'and inasmuch as we are informed that . . .'

Furthermore, Allen (in prep.) argues that indirect passives where the
Theme is clausal – as in [52] – should be treated separately from those where
the Theme is nominal.
   Some later examples of indirect passives:

[53]   1660 Pepys, *Diary* I 140.2 (15 May)

where we were showed the place where the States-generall sit in
council.

[54]   1660 Pepys, *Diary* I 146.20 (18 May)

. . . the thing that hangs up like a bushell in the Stathouse, which I
was told is a sort of punishment for some sort of offenders . . .

Compare [54] with [36] above, part of the same diary entry. Visser quotes a
number of condemnations of the construction by twentieth-century grammarians but notes that few earlier grammarians even discussed it (1963–73:
§1974 and n.1) – for details see now Sundby et al. (1991: 240). My
impression is that careful writers from the eighteenth century onwards were
wary of using the indirect passive in print, and it might be worth trying to
document the history of stigmatisation (Question (g) in §6.4 below).
Example [55] is stylistically interesting, as it continues with a *was being
changed* construction which was certainly stigmatised in print at the time
(§14.2.4.4):

[55]   1817 Mary Shelley, *Six Weeks' Tour* 110.11
We were allowed two hours for dinner

6.3 Explanations in non-generative linguistics

Jespersen, van der Gaaf and Visser base their accounts on the loss of
accusative ~ dative contrast and the increasing fixity of SVX word order.
Visser and Mitchell each discuss possible OE precursors of the indirect
passive, though they choose different sorts of example. Marchand concentrates on the verb + direct object grouping. Marchand and Visser suggest a
far earlier date for the advent of indirect passives than most scholars accept.
   A forthcoming account by Allen (in prep.) in the Lexical-Functional
Grammar framework is briefly mentioned at the end of this chapter. Since all
published generative work on the indirect passive tackles the prepositional

passive at the same time, we shall postpone consideration of generative analyses to §7.6, after we have introduced the problem of the prepositional passive.

6.3.1 Jespersen

Otto Jespersen's account of the origins of the indirect passive runs as follows (1909–49: III 299–311).

6.3.1.1

As soon as the distinction between accusative and dative had been lost in early Middle English, two-place verbs which had had a dative object in Old English developed passives where that argument was subject. Then three-place verbs with an indirect object in the active began to develop indirect passives (said to be 'extremely rare before the MnE period', but cf. §6.2.4 above). Various reasons are offered for this. One is the effacement of any formal distinction between dative and accusative, which is presumably meant to imply a reanalysis of *active* examples by which all objects, indirect or direct, became equally eligible for subjecthood in a corresponding passive. Another is an alleged parallel between the indirect passive of a verb like SHOW and a rather different passive of 'the same' verb, as in [56] and [57], respectively:

[56]   We were shown the evidence.
[57]   We were shown upstairs.

This seems at best unimportant. A third factor, and the one given most attention, is 'the greater interest felt for the person' (cf. §5.4.1 above). This is offered as the explanation for the typical ordering at all periods[13] of Benefactive before Theme in the active:

[58]   He offered the girl a gold watch.

It is also held to explain front position of the dative in passives like [59](a,b) in Old English:

[59]   (a)   Her was offered a watch.
       (b)   The girl(DAT) was offered a watch.
       (c)   The girl(NOM) was offered a watch.
       (d)   She was offered a watch.

(Notice that Jespersen's [59](a,b) are equivocal between my [3](b) and [4](b) types, i.e. as to whether *a watch* is retained object or subject.) A passive like [59](c), Jespersen argues, resulted from pressure to interpret the NP in pre-verbal position as subject, an interpretation made possible or easy by the loss of subject ~ non-subject distinctions in full NPs. Pattern [59](d) is explicit evidence of the arrival of the indirect passive. The factor under consideration therefore promoted reanalysis of *passive* sentences. Notice that [59](b) could only be reinterpreted as [59](c) if there was no person/number conflict between Benefactive NP and verbal inflection, otherwise the verb form would have had to be altered. The verb BE has always maintained a wide range of person-number distinctions.

6.3.1.2*

Jespersen also cites Deutschbein's suggestion of an analogy between [60] and [61]:

[60]   If I were permitted a glance at the book.
[61]   He was permitted to go.

Now PERMIT is a three-place verb with a similar meaning in both sentences, but the superficial similarity is outweighed by some diverse evidence of difference between NP and clausal arguments. In Present-day English a verb like GIVE in the active, which corresponds to the [60] use of PERMIT, may have the Benefactive in a *to*-phrase, whereas PERSUADE, corresponding to [61], may not:

[62]   I gave a copy to her.
[63]   *I persuaded to her that she was wrong/*I persuaded that she was wrong to her.

In Old English whereas GIVE-type verbs consistently took dative of the person, PERSUADE-type verbs varied. In Dutch, which, like Old English, has no indirect passive, a PERSUADE-type verb can have a personal passive when the Theme is a clause, as in [64](a), but not when it is an NP, as in (b):

[64]   (a)   De mensen werden   verzocht hun jassen daarop te hangen.
             the people were(PL) requested their jackets on-it   to hang

             'The people were requested to hang their jackets on it.'

       (b)   ?*De mensen   werden iets   verzocht.
             the people(SUBJ) were(PL) something requested

       (c)   De mensen   werd   iets   verzocht.
             the people(OBJ) was(SG) something requested

             'Something was requested of the people'

Instead an impersonal passive, [64](c), is necessary. I am grateful to Olga Fischer (p.c.) for the Dutch examples.

For reasons like these it seems prudent to give a separate treatment – as part of the history of 'Control' verbs in Chapter 8 below – of PERSUADE-type verbs with clausal complements. Nevertheless a possible relevance must be kept in mind. Verbs like PERMIT and TELL with two NP objects are clearly three-place verbs. When one of the object arguments is a clause there is some evidence of two-place, causative-like behaviour as early as Old and Middle English; see §8.8.4.2 below. A two-place structure (no indirect object in the **higher** clause) might facilitate a 'second passive' (passive of the higher verb), which in turn might promote the indirect passive of the same verb with nominal arguments.

6.3.1.3

Jespersen quotes a number of actual examples of the indirect passive, nearly all from the ModE period, verb by verb. In noting that the construction has been gaining in favour throughout Modern English without yet having spread to every eligible verb, he cites as unlikely such passives as *He was sent a note* or *He was written a letter*. Perhaps they were unlikely in 1927, but they are both quite acceptable now – which proves his point.

6.3.2 Van der Gaaf

6.3.2.1

W. van der Gaaf's two-part analysis of the problem (1929) remains a major contribution to the early history. Old English and Middle English are covered in detail, and examples from Modern English range only as far as the beginning of the seventeenth century.

Van der Gaaf's analysis is not greatly different from Jespersen's. The first, and longer, instalment of his article deals with the history of verbs governing a dative, mainly in two-place use. Four verbs are singled out: QUEMEN 'please', HELPEN 'help', THANKEN 'thank', BEDEN 'offer, command'; idiosyncrasies in their histories are covered in detail.

6.3.2.2*

All occurred occasionally in Middle English with a *to*-phrase in the active (what van der Gaaf calls a 'dative substitute'), but more often with a personal object in common case without preposition. All developed personal passives in early Middle English. For QUEMEN and HELPEN, he says, the passive resulted from their transitivation: the personal object of the active had been reinterpreted as a direct object. For THANKEN the passive was rather the result of reanalysis of an impersonal passive. The passive of BEDEN was due in part to its longstanding confusion with transitive BIDDEN 'ask, pray'.

6.3.2.3

Further verbs of this type like COMMAND, PRAY, etc., were borrowed into Middle English from Old French. They too showed sporadic use of *to*-phrase for the 'recipient' in the active, reflecting the NP's indirect object status in Old French (cf. here Visser 1963–73: §§325–6), but on the other hand they tended to allow a personal passive, suggesting that they had become ordinary transitive verbs. The conclusion we are invited to draw from these facts is that the formerly dative NP was fluctuating between indirect objecthood (explicit marking with *to*) and direct objecthood (could be made subject of passive). Developments in the syntax of these two-place verbs are the background to van der Gaaf's account of three-place verbs.

In the case of three-place verbs great importance is attached to word order. Van der Gaaf adduces passives whose Benefactive NP is a topicalised dative, as in Jespersen's made-up examples [59](a,b) above. He argues that 'there can have been no other motive' for topicalisation than 'the desire to draw special attention to the personal object' (1929: 60), a claim which deserves critical scrutiny; cf. Chapter 4 and also §6.3.3 below. Whether or not van der Gaaf's explanation of the motivation for such examples is right, their existence is clear enough – what about frequency, however? – and many from about 1300 on show the structural ambiguity of [59](b,c). Eventually, van der Gaaf argues, NPs in that fronted position came to be interpreted as subject of the verb, and he gives corroboration from two sources. One is the notoriously difficult area of zero ***anaphora***.[14] Van der Gaaf is properly cautious about the analysis of cases like [65]:

[65]   a1450 *Rich.*(Cai) 1315

þe Duke Myloun was geuen hys lyff, | And ffley3 out off lande wiþ
the Duke Myloun was given his life   and fled   out of land with

hys wyff
his wife

'Duke Myloun was given his life and fled the country with his wife'

He calls *þe Duke Myloun* a retained object, not a subject, but suggests that
it could hardly still have 'been distinctly felt to have a datival function' by
someone capable of writing [65] (van der Gaaf 1929: 61). Further
corroboration comes from some manuscript variants in *Cursor Mundi* (1929:
62). For example:

[66]   (a)   a1400(a1325) *Cursor* 19019

Yow   sal   for-giuen be yur sake
you(OBJ) shall forgiven be your sin

(b)   a1400 *Cursor*(Frf) 19019

ye   shulle for-yevyn by your sake
you(SUBJ) shall   forgiven be your sin

Two MSS of the (early) fourteenth century have the (a) reading (spelling
variants aside), while three MSS of the fourteenth or early fifteenth
centuries have the (b) reading. (It is possible to run on to the following
clause and read FORYEVEN as a control verb here.)

  Van der Gaaf observes that the great majority of his passive examples
from two-place verbs (and, he might have added, from three-place verbs as
well) lack an agent-phrase, making them equivalent to active sentences with
an indefinite subject. Now the principal expression of an indefinite subject in
Middle English was the pronoun MAN (*man, mon, me*), but MAN lost
ground during the period and had all but disappeared by the end of the
fifteenth century (Mustanoja 1960: 219–22). Van der Gaaf sees an obvious
connection between the obsolescence of MAN and the preference for passive
constructions with an indefinite logical subject (1929: 59), though he makes
no attempt to sort out cause and effect: did the loss of MAN foster the
growth of these and other passives, or did the new passives render MAN
redundant and lead to its obsolescence?[15] Or indeed both – one of those
snowball developments which go to completion? I too have nothing to
contribute on this question. He also notes that the indirect passive was
established in informal writings in the fifteenth century but was infrequent
then in formal prose or conventional poetry, as 'is generally the case with
innovations' (1929: 63).

6.3.3 Marchand

Hans Marchand (1951) builds on van der Gaaf's analysis but parts company
from him and Jespersen in discussion of examples with topicalised
Benefactive. Recall Jespersen's examples [59], repeated here as [67]:

[67]   (a)   Her was offered a watch.
       (b)   The girl(DAT) was offered a watch.

    (c)   The girl(NOM) was offered a watch.
    (d)   She was offered a watch.

Marchand casts doubt on the alleged emphatic nature of many of the topicalised examples (1951: 77–8), noting – correctly, I think – that pronominal examples like [67](a) greatly outnumber instances like [67](b) with full dative NPs in topic position; this is what we should expect from our discussion of word order (Chapter 4 above).[16] He thus finds a weakness in Jespersen's argument, namely that it is examples like [67](b) whose syntactic ambiguity must motivate reanalysis as (c), whereas in fact unambiguous examples like (a) are in the majority. (Compare McCawley's objection to Jespersen's rather similar history of impersonals (§5.6.1 above).) Marchand prefers to offer an alternative account of the origin of the indirect passive.

    According to Marchand the significant fact about early indirect passives is that verb and direct object ('retained object' = 'RO', later 'verb auxiliary') formed a syntactic ('functional') unit, a sort of group-verb, and in the case of passives of LETEN *blod* 'let blood', even a semantic group. Indeed he extends the claim to indirect passives of all periods. Thus in

[68]   He was offered a seat.

the pronoun *he* is crucially subject not of *was offered* but of *was offered a seat* (1951: 80–1). (Marchand later implies that OFFER *a seat* forms a semantic as well as syntactic group.) The argument seems to be that once accusative ~ dative distinctions disappeared, any object could in principle become subject of the passive, and it was more natural that it should be the *in*direct object that did so, in order that the verb + direct object unit should remain undisturbed.[17] It is certainly noteworthy that the eME examples of §6.2.4 above involve lexicalised group-verbs where verb and direct object have fused. The suggestion of *semantic* unity of verb and direct object becomes less persuasive as we move towards Present-day English, where the indirect passive may be used freely with verbs and direct objects that do not regularly or predictably *collocate* together and so are less plausibly thought of as a semantic unit:

[69]   Max was promised an ice-cream.

    Marchand also makes the remarkable claim that the type exemplified by [67](d) 'was in use long before 1300' (1951: 79) and was historically prior to [67](a), the latter being a mere hypercorrection in writing of a tabooed [67](d). This I find quite implausible: there was utter consistency of dative marking of topicalised Benefactives in Old English and early Middle English, then a period when equivocal instances became common, and only later still the first clear instances of Benefactive as subject of the passive. One early example which Marchand (1951: 71) borrows from van der Gaaf (1929: 62) is misinterpreted by both of them (and indeed by Visser 1963–73: §1968 and by Lieber 1979: 686):

[70] *ÆLS* I 9.136

   . . . swa ic   eom forgifen fram þam ælmihtigan gode nu þyssere
   . . . so I(NOM) am given   by   the almighty   god now this

byrig   siracusan   eow   to geþingienne
town(DAT) Syracuse(DAT) you(DAT) to intercede

'. . . so now I am given by Almighty God to this town of Syracuse to intercede for you'

Crucially van der Gaaf omitted the NP *þyssere byrig siracusan* when he quoted the passage, perhaps therefore leading him to translate 'so *am I allowed* by Almighty God . . . to intercede for you'. Van der Gaaf did not regard [70] as an indirect passive, but he did see it as a blend. Marchand seems to imply that it probably was indeed an indirect passive, and Visser and Lieber are in no doubt at all. However, restoration of the dative[18] NP *þyssere byrig siracusan* makes clear that FORGIEFAN means here 'give' rather than 'allow', that the infinitive clause is an adjunct of purpose rather than an argument of the verb, and that the NP *ic* is Theme rather than Benefactive. Example [70] is a direct passive.

6.3.4 Visser

Frederik Theodoor Visser as usual gives a very full collection of data (1963–73: §§316–23, 325–6, 1933–5 on two-place verbs; §§682–97, 1963–85 on three-place verbs), though certain crucial citations are misleading. In particular, most of his early examples of the indirect passive are either downright mistaken, or ambiguous instances of the [67](b,c) type, or else have an infinitival or finite clause as Theme.[19] Visser's explanation of the origins of the indirect passive (1963–73: §1967, cf. §1966) largely follows Jespersen's.

6.3.5 Mitchell

Bruce Mitchell has some observations on those OE three-place verbs which sometimes but not invariably take an accusative object, especially those with 'a variety of meanings and constructions' (1985: §§856–8). He calls [71] a 'transitional example' (from impersonal to personal):

[71] *Exhort* 26

gif heo   inne wyrð | feondum   befangen,
if it(FEM) [*sc.* your soul] within gets   enemies(DAT) surrounded

frofre   bedæled, | welena   forwyrned.
comfort(?GEN) deprived   happiness(GEN PL) denied

'if it gets surrounded within by enemies, deprived of comfort, denied happiness'

Despite the fact that FORWYRNAN in the sense 'deny, deprive of' usually marks the Benefactive by dative and the Theme by genitive, example [71] gives the verb a personal passive with Benefactive as subject. Mitchell seems to suggest that [71] is an understandable error caused by the long separation of *forwyrned* from the auxiliary *wyrð*; by confusion with the personal passive appropriate to the preceding verb, BEDÆLAN 'deprive of' (which can mark the Benefactive by accusative case); and by confusion with two-place, accusative-governing uses of FORWYRNAN 'withhold, prevent'.

Another verb which he describes as similar is actually crucially different. According to him, OFTEON can mean 'take/deny something(ACC) from/to someone(DAT)' or 'deprive someone(DAT) of something(GEN)', so that the Benefactive argument is always marked dative, while the Theme may be accusative or genitive. Having illustrated the different passives appropriate to the two uses, he continues:

> As the case sysem progressively collapsed, such verbs would obviously serve as a bridge between verbs which took the accusative and so had the personal passive and those which took a genitive or dative and so had the doomed impersonal passive. (Mitchell 1985: §858)

Note, however, that both OE passives of OFTEON are like our [3]–[4]. None would have had the Benefactive argument as subject, and so their contribution to the history of the indirect passive is at best tangential.

6.3.6 Allen

A book by Cynthia Allen (in prep.) is a major study of the indirect passive, impersonal verbs, and related topics. She kindly sent me an early draft of some portions. As a result I have reconsidered the early examples of the indirect passive and added to my §6.2.4, but since this chapter was already virtually complete and her work was still in progress, I have not thought it appropriate to take full account of her analysis. One interesting point is that, rather than distinguishing my types [3] and [4] according to whether there is subject-verb agreement, Allen distinguishes my [3]–[4](a) from (b), according to whether the dative NP is fronted or not (cf. her earlier published work on preposed Experiencers with LIKE, §5.7.2.2 above). (Her choice of labels for the patterns is also, unfortunately, rather different from mine.) On this basis she observes that the **dative-fronted passive** became infrequent in the thirteenth century and did not coexist in most registers with the indirect passive. This argues against a reanalysis explanation for the indirect passive.

6.4 Questions for discussion or further research

(a) Two-place verbs which in Old English had governed a dative object show some evidence of intransitive use in Middle English (*to*-phrase object) and some evidence of transitivation (verb phrase conjunction, direct passive). Is the same verb ever used in both ways by the same author? Look for instances. Is the result what you expect?

(b) Are the impersonal passive (examples [3] above) and the direct passive (examples [4]) ever alternatives for the same three-place verb in Old English, or does each verb permit only one or the other? Check suitable past participles in Venezky and Healey (1980).

(c) Gather statistical information on direct passives in Old English and/or Middle English. How frequent are topicalised Benefactives? What proportion of topicalised Benefactives are pronouns? What proportion are apparently fronted for reasons of thematic emphasis? Assess Jespersen's and van der Gaaf's claims in the light of your data.

(d) The two main approaches to the origins of the indirect passive involve reanalysis of actives and reanalysis of (existing) passives. Is it possible that both should be correct?

(e) Look at early instances of the indirect passive to see whether they lend any support to Marchand's assertion that verb and Theme (direct object) in such examples form a close unit.

(f) Historically speaking, dative marking of indirect objects is ancient, and Benefactive *to*-phrases are a later innovation. In some TG descriptions of Present-day English, the *to*-phrase is basic and the *non*-prepositional structure is derived. Does the chronological priority of the non-prepositional construction have any legitimate bearing on the transformational analysis of Present-day English?[20] (Or, to phrase the question as a slogan, does synchrony recapitulate diachrony?)

(g) Try to detect and measure evidence of conscious avoidance of the indirect passive in the various centuries of its existence. You could make use of texts subclassified by genre and date in the Helsinki Corpus, or perhaps compare private letters and diaries with published works by the same author.

Notes

1. As Cynthia Allen pointed out to me (p.c., 13 December 1990), what is traditionally called 'indirect object' in [1](b) is merely a (direct) object in some current approaches, for example Lexical-Functional Grammar.

2. In a GB approach it may be necessary to distinguish the order of [4](a) from [4](b). Koopman (1990b: 208), citing Szalai-Smits (1988), notes that the former order is common, as in (a) below, whereas the latter – (b) and (c) – is not:

   (a) *GD* 289.23

   for hwylcre scylde se   cniht   wæs geseald swylcum ehterum
   for which   crime the boy(NOM) was given   such   persecutors(DAT)

   'for what crime the boy was given to such persecutors'

   (b) *ÆEtat* 192 (*DOE*)

   Eallum þam sawlum   is seo yld   forgifen . . .
   all   the souls(DAT PL) is that age(NOM SG) granted . . .

   'That same age is granted/restored to all the souls . . .'

   (c) *GD(C)* 15.35

   þa   þam Godes mæn   his agen hors   gegifen wæs
   when the God's man(DAT) his own horse(?NOM) given   was

   'when the servant of God was given back his own horse'

   Szalai-Smits's study of some 60 three-place verbs found only about 30 independent examples like (b) or (c). Of these, some are explicable by topicalisation of the dative NP, e.g. (b), leaving a mere 13 like (c) which cannot be so explained and which are problematic for a GB analysis.

3. According to Mitchell (1985: §851), the verb FULTUMIAN 'help' is one verb which

took a dative object in the active in Old English – there are also ambiguous accusative ~ dative NPs but no unambiguously accusative ones – but which had clear personal passives with nominative subject.

4. Example [15] is morphologically ambiguous, and it is not perhaps immediately obvious that *all follc* is a topicalised Benefactive or Goal rather than the subject. Although it would make sense to speak either of joy coming to the people or of people coming to (a state of) joy, context suggests the former, as does comparison with:

(a)   c1180 *Orm.* 719

   . . . &   all þatt blisse þatt uss   comm   Þurrh þatt he comm onn
   . . . and all that bliss that us(OBL) came(SG) through that he came on
   eorþe
   earth

'. . . and all that bliss that came to us because he came to earth'

The verb morphology of [15] is inconclusive, since the noun *follc* is often singular in *Orm.* (e.g. 445) and only sometimes plural (e.g. 263). The decisive test is that apart from animates and words like *ham* 'home', a Goal argument with CUMENN is always prepositionally marked (e.g. by *till*), so *blisse* must be subject.

5. Mitchell points out that *to*-phrases occur with verbs of speaking and with BRINGAN, SENDAN, etc.; here we can reasonably assume Goal status. Mitchell also notes the use of *to*-phrases with AGIFAN 'give', but only when the NP refers to a monastery or other place, not to a person, which argues against Benefactive role. And *to*-phrases occur with LÆTAN 'let, leave', with personal NPs. I speculate that *to*-phrases were possible with LÆTAN and FORLÆTAN (as in [20]–[21]), despite the apparent Benefactive nature of the role, because of the potential misinterpretation of a personal argument without prepositional marking as Patient of a causative construction (LÆTAN + NP + infinitival clause).

6. According to Anderson, genitive marking precludes analysis as a Theme: see §5.6.2.1 above. I retain it as a convenient label for the 'thing' given or denied.

7. As briefly noted in §6.3.6, Cynthia Allen (in prep.) has a more precise account of the loss of the impersonal passive.

8. Visser states: 'When both the objects [in the active] are pronouns it seems always to have been the rule to put the direct object before the indirect object' (1963–73: §686). In my own (London) speech the reverse order is much more common even with two pronouns.

9. Note, for example, the group-verb FIND *fault* illustrated in (a), which is a two-place verb, or better a one-place verb, with *fault* not counted as an argument. In (b) it has an apparently impersonal passive:

(a)   1490 Caxton, Prol.*Eneydos* 110.1

   . . . to correcte adde or mynysshe where as he or they shall fynde faulte
   . . . to correct   add or subtract wherever he or they shall find   fault

'. . . to correct, add or subtract wherever he or they shall find fault'

(b)   1490 Caxton, Prol.*Eneydos* 109.28

   where as shalle be founde faulte
   wherever shall   be found   fault

Jespersen points out (1909–49: III 312) that LET *blood* never occurs with *blood* as passive subject; Allen (in prep.) mentions the likelihood of object incorporation with this syntagm.

10. I am indebted to Cynthia Allen for reminding me of Visser's examples [44]–[46].
    In relation to [44] and [49], note that the only examples of passive ALLOW in
    MED with Benefactive as subject have the Theme in a PP with *of* or *for* rather
    than as direct object (s.v. *allouen* v. 4).
    Note too that [47] is only an indirect passive if the ellipted NP is a subject,
    while Lightfoot points out (1979: 260–1 n.1) that [50] was printed by Caxton (in
    1485) with *him* for *he*, turning it into a direct passive with topicalised
    Benefactive.
11. Example [44] predates slightly *MED*'s earliest citations s.v. *necessari(e*, whether
    as the noun 'required amount' or as the adjective. My gloss assumes the latter.
12. It may be significant for Marchand's hypothesis that the noun *gre* '(prize for)
    victory' occurs 17 times in Malory, all but once with the verbs WIN (×7), GIVE
    (×6), or HAVE (×3). Furthermore GIVE frequently occurs with synonyms like
    prize. GIVE *the gre* may therefore be regarded as a fairly close-knit combination.
13. Whether Benefactive typically precedes Theme in Old English is doubtful. Smith
    (1893: 218) assumed that Benefactive before Theme was the norm in his two
    texts when both are full NPs, though he quotes one counter-example:

    (a)   *Or* 65.18

          he sealde his dohtor   Alexandre þæm cyninge his agnum
          he gave   his daughter(ACC) Alexander the   king   his own
          mæge
          kinsman(DAT)

          'he gave his daughter to King Alexander, his own kinsman'

    The figures in Koopman (1990d) suggest that the two orders were roughly evenly
    balanced: 54 per cent DAT before ACC, 46 per cent ACC before DAT.
14. For further discussion see §5.7.2.2 above and Warner (1983: 205–6), Allen
    (1986a: 389–94).
15. If the obsolescence of MAN helped to promote a greater use of passive
    constructions, we must then explain – perhaps in terms of discourse structure and
    information flow – why the indirect passive came to be preferred over the pre-
    existing direct passive. The indirect passive was arguably a better replacement
    for the MAN active, because in both of them Benefactive typically preceded
    Theme, whereas in the direct passive the relative order was reversed.
16. Koopman's totals (1990b) for the ratio of pronominal to nominal datives with
    three-place verbs taking an accusative and a dative object are worth citing here:
    2576 : 1808, or only about 59 per cent pronominal. The figures do not bear
    directly on Marchand's point, since they specifically exclude both passives and
    actives with any object topicalised (and also those where the accusative object is
    clausal or the dative is a relative clause with included antecedent). Nevertheless
    the proportion of nominal datives is not small.
17. Marchand's claim can be formulated as a reanalysis much akin to that discussed
    in Chapter 7 below, and indeed Marchand explicitly puts his explanation of the
    indirect passive on the same footing as the explanation of the prepositional
    passive. For him the direct object in the indirect passive and the preposition in
    the prepositional passive are both 'verb auxiliaries'. I have discussed this point in
    Denison (1985a: §4.1).
18. Russom labels *siracusan* genitive (1982: 678), which is possible, but apposition
    with case-agreement seems more likely (Mitchell 1985: §§1290, 1437). The point
    at issue is unaffected.
19. Some of Visser's early examples in (1963–73: §1968) are examined and rejected
    by Mitchell (1979), Denison (1981: 225), or Russom (1982). All the OE
    examples and the first paragraph of ME examples are suspect for one reason or

another, so that hardly any safe examples in this section are pre-1400. Visser misquotes an apparent fourteenth-century example of *as I am told* in an unexpected place (1963–73: §1935), but the actual form is not an indirect passive because it contains the verb LEREN, not TELLEN:

(a)   a1500(?a1400) *SLChrist* 10429

> he Apered | helder in fourme   of fir . . . |þen in other   element, As
> he appeared rather in the-form of fire . . . than in another element as
> I am lered, | As clerkes   techen sothe to say.
> I am taught as learned-men teach truth to tell
>
> 'he appeared rather in the form of fire than in another element, as I have been taught, as learned men teach, truth to tell'

The OE verb LÆRAN 'teach' had taken two accusative objects, so Experiencer-subject passives in Old and Middle English were ordinary direct passives (Denison forthcoming: §2.4). Allen (in prep.) says that there were no Experiencer-subject passives of LÆRAN in Old English when the Theme was an NP rather than clausal.

20. Faarlund (1990: 22–3) argues that in a context where competing forms exist, there is no necessary correlation between **oldest/original** and **underlying/basic** after the first generation which permitted variation.

Chapter 7

The prepositional passive

7.1 The problem

Modern English has numerous examples of verb-preposition *collocations* which appear to act as units as far as their complementation is concerned. The most striking manifestation is the **prepositional passive**, where the subject of the passive corresponds to the object of a preposition in the active:

[1]   Jim was laughed at.

Further evidence is provided by what we might call *verb conjunction*:

[2]   They voted against and defeated all the proposals.

In [1] and [2] the collocations LAUGH *at* and VOTE *against* appear to behave syntactically very much like an ordinary transitive verb such as DEFEAT, though verb conjunction is not as secure a test as passivisation. The standard explanation for the active equivalent of [1] is that reanalysis has occurred, with P entering into *constituency* with V, as in structure [3](b), rather than with NP object, as in [3](a):

[3]   (a)   [VP [V *laugh*] [PP *at* [NP *Jim*]]]
        (b)   [VP [V *laugh at*] [NP *Jim*]]

Thus V and P together make up a **prepositional verb**. The theoretical nature of such a reanalysis is a matter of dispute, which we shall look at in §7.4.2. A full collection of syntactic and semantic tests for the relative cohesion of the V-P and P-NP *syntagms* in Present-day English is to be found in Vestergaard (1977).

In [1] the preposition *at* is **stranded** at the end of its clause: the term **preposition stranding** is frequently used for cases where a preposition is not followed by an NP object. Modern English provides numerous other syntactic opportunities for preposition stranding, as for example in relative clauses:

[4]   (a)   the house which I live in
        (b)   the house that I live in
        (c)   the house I live in

clauses of comparison:

[5] (a) This is the same sort of house as I live in.
     (b) He owns more houses than I've ever lived in.

wh-questions, exclamatives, and free relatives (i.e. nominal relative clauses):

[6] (a) Which (house) does he live in?
     (b) What a house I live in!
     (c) What he lives in is *his* business.

infinitive clauses:

[7] (a) I need a house to live in.
     (b) a pleasant house to live in
     (c) a house pleasant to live in

topicalisation:

[8] That house I could never live in.

The history of the prepositional passive is closely bound up with the history of preposition stranding, and both will be discussed below. Where a preposition appears in a fronted position together with its complement, as in

[9] the house in which I live

the phenomenon is whimsically called **pied piping**, in reference to the transformationalists' view that the *wh-* word has moved and taken the particle with it.

The prepositional passive is not found in 'Standard Average European' (though there is something similar in mainland Scandinavian languages), nor is it found in English prior to the ME period. Preposition stranding is also freer in modern English than in most other European languages. What then is the explanation for these peculiarities of English?

7.2 The data

7.2.1 The prepositional passive

Here is a selection of the earliest examples of the prepositional passive. I know of 39 examples of 24 different collocations dated c1400 or earlier:[1]

[10] c1225 *St.Juliana* (Roy) 22.195

þer wes sorhe te seon hire leoflich lich faren so reowliche wið
there was sorrow to see her dear body dealt so cruelly with

[11] c1330(?a1300) *Arth. & M.*(Auch) 849

Þis maiden . . . feled also bi her þi | Þat sche was   yleyen bi
this maiden . . . felt also by her thigh that she had-been lain   by

'this maiden felt by her thigh that she had been lain with'

[12] a1400(c1303) Mannyng, *HS* 1033

And þe comaundment ys brokun, | And þe halyday, byfore
and the commandment is broken   and the holy day previously

of spokun.
of spoken

'The commandment is broken, and the holy day previously spoken of.'

[13] a1400(a1325) *Cursor* 14216

Bot nu þan   am i after send
But now when[?] am I after sent

'But now when I am sent for'

[14] c1450(1352–c1370) *Winner and W.* 27

He schall be lenede   and louede and lett   of a while | Wele
he shall be listened-to and loved and thought of a while   rather

more   þan þe man that made   it hymseluen
more [= more highly] than the man who composed it himself

[15] c1400(a1376) *PPl.A(1)* 11.29

Litel is he louid or lete   by þat suche a lessoun techiþ
little is he loved or thought of who such a lesson   teaches

'He is little loved or valued who teaches such a lesson.'

[16] a1500(?c1378) *Wycl.OPastor.* 440.14

for nobley in vertues shulde be coueytid &   worldly nobley litil
for nobility in virtues should be coveted and worldly nobility little

teld by
told by [=valued]

[17] ?a1425(c1380) Chaucer, *Bo.* 4.pr1.22 (and sim. ibid. 4.pr1.25)

how worthy it es to ben wondrid   uppon
how worthy it is to be   wondered at

[18] (a1387) Trev.*Higd.* VII 7.ix.385.14

he was piled   and i-robbed, and fare wiþ as it   were a
he was plundered and robbed   and dealt with as-if (he) were a

þeef
thief/as-if it were a thief (they were dealing with)

[19] (1389) *Lond.Gild.Ret.* in *Bk.Lond.E.* 52.52

ʒif þe wardeyns of þat ʒeer ben sent after
if the Wardens for that year are sent for

[20] c1390 Hilton, *ML*(Vrn) 272.37

              vnarayed, vnkept,   & not tended   to as hem ouʒte
[*sc.* feet] unclothed unwatched and not attended to as them ought

for   to be;
(for) to be

'[feet . . .] unclothed, unlooked-after, and not tended as they should be'

[21] a1425(?a1400) *Cloud* 3.20

&   how it may not be comen to
and how it may not be attained

[22] c1400 *Pep.Gosp.* 44.9

no prophete is so mychel   leten   of in his owene cuntre
no prophet is so much [= well] thought of in his own   country
as . . .
as . . .

[23] ?a1425(c1400) *Mandev.(1)* 190.27 (and sim. ibid. 90.23)

But after the firste nyght þat þei ben leyn by . . .
but after the first   night that they are slept with . . .

[24] a1500 *Tundale* (Adv) 2300

How þei schuld be wyt don as Goddes wyll wolde.
how they should be with done as God's   will wished

'how they should be treated as God's will intended'

[25] c1475(?c1400) *Wycl.Apol.* 31.9

Steuyn, and silk oþer þat is redd of in apostlis dedis
Stephen and such other that is read of in apostles' deeds

'Stephen, and other such who are read of in Acts of the Apostles'

[26] a1425 *Wycl.Serm.* I 39.26

and aftyr   he was turmentyd, and aftyr   he was spyt vpon
and afterwards he was tormented   and afterwards he was spat upon

For the complex prepositional passive – *She was made fun of, She is being made up to*, etc. – see §7.5 below.

7.2.2 Verb conjunction and ellipsis

As was said earlier, verb conjunction may be another sign of the formation of a prepositional verb; Mitchell's discussion (1985: §§1572–9) is too brief for our purpose here. Unfortunately not all examples involving an object NP shared between a transitive verb and a verb-preposition collocation should be analysed as verb conjunction; some are simply the result of ellipsis in the clause lacking an object, as in PDE:

[27] Jim approached the fence and scrambled under.

In OE and ME examples where an object is apparently shared between a transitive verb and verb-preposition collocation it can be difficult to

discriminate between verb conjunction (suggestive of V-P unification) and
ellipsis (irrelevant). In the following selection [30] and [38] may illustrate
verb conjunction, the remainder probably lean towards mere ellipsis:

[28] *Bo* 56.3

þætte ælces monnes ingeþanc wenð þætte good sie, &   æfter higað,
that each man's   mind   thinks that good is   and after thinks
&   wilnað to begitanne
and wishes to acquire

'that each man's mind thinks that it is good and hankers after it and
wishes to acquire it'

[29] *Bo* 36.30

þæt he wolde   ælcne cuman swiðe arlice   underfoon & swiðe
that he wanted each arrival very honourably receive   and very
swæslice wið   gebæran
lovingly towards behave

'that he wanted to receive very honourably, and to behave very
lovingly towards, each arrival'

[30] *GD* 232.1

&   eac symble wiðstodan &   ongen fuhton heora agnum
and also always withstood and against fought their own
synlustum
sinful-desires

'and also always withstood and fought against their own sinful desires'

[31] *WHom* 3.34

And forðy   us eac swencað &   ongean winnað manege gesceafta
and therefore us also trouble and against struggle many   beings

'And therefore many beings also trouble and struggle against us.'

[32] *ChronA* 40.14 (694)

Wihtred feng   to Cantwara rice,   & heold .xxxiii. wintra
Wihtred succeeded to Kentish kingdom and held 33   years

'Wihtred succeeded to the Kentish throne and held it for 33 years'

[33] *ChronA* 86.21 (894)

Þa foron hie to & gefliemdon þone here
then went they to and put-to-flight the army

'then they went there and put the army to flight'

[34] *WHom* 15.15

ðær   he geseah Godes englas & wið spæc
where/there he saw   God's angels and with spoke

'where he saw God's angels and spoke with them'

[35]   c1230(?a1200) *Ancr.* 115b.23

    ne lokin feaste o na mon; ne toggin .wið ne pleien.
    not look hard at any man not tussle[?] with nor play

    'not look directly at any man, not tussle or play with one'

[36]   c1225(?c1200) *St.Juliana* (Bod) 13.144

    Ah ich him luuie &   wulle don. & leue   on as o lauerd
    but I   him love and will do and believe in as in lord

    'But I love him and will do, and I believe in him as in the Lord'

[37]   c1225 *St.Juliana* (Roy) 12.96

    an þet ichulle treowliche to halden ant wið uten les   luuien
    and that I-will truly   to hold and without falsehood love

    'and that I will truly hold to and truly love'

[38]   a1250 *Ancr.*(Nero) 57.4

    saul ðet is ðe ueond hateð &   hunteð efter   hire
    Saul that is the devil hates and hunts for[=pursues] her

[39]   c1250 *Owl and N.* 959

    Þar   lauerd liggeþ &   lauedi | Ich schal heom singe &   sitte bi.
    where lord   lies   and lady   I   shall them sing and sit by

    'Where lord and lady lie, I shall sing to them and sit near by.'

7.2.3   No nominal object

The following active clauses given by van der Gaaf (1930a: 15) and Visser
(1963–73: §394) suggest that verb and preposition are acting as a unit,
since the preposition is not followed directly by a nominal object:

[40]   *Or* 153.12

    het   þeh   sendon   æfter, þær he
    ordered(3 SG) though send(INF) after where he

    ænigne   libbendne wiste
    anyone(ACC SG) living   knew

    'he ordered, though, to send where he knew anyone to be living'

[41]   c1475(a1400) *Wycl.Pseudo-F.* 300.3

    &   herfore wake ȝee, &   þenke onne hou bi þre ȝeer nyȝt &
    and herefor wake you and think on   how for three years night and

    day y ceessede not bi teris monestynge ilche of ȝou
    day I ceased   not by tears admonishing each of you

[42]   (1482) *Let.Cely* 177.12

    wherffor we loke afftyr here that ther schall com a ffellyschypp
    wherefore we look for   here that there shall come a fellowship

    owte off Ynglond schorttly
    out of England shortly

'for which reason we here expect a company to come from England shortly'

[43]   (1482) *Let.Cely* 195.9

and how sone thay wyll cawll apon for the xx s.   of the
and how soon they will call   upon for the 20 shillings of the

sarpller   I connot say
bale-of-wool I cannot say

'and how soon they will demand the 20 s. for the bale I cannot say'

7.2.4   Preposition stranding in Old and Middle English

First we must explain the useful shorthand expression '**relativising** a clause **on** a particular NP'. Consider the main clause [44](a) and some relative clauses derived from it:

[44]   (a)   The man put the car in the garage.
       (b)   (the man) who put the car in the garage
       (c)   (the car) which the man put in the garage
       (d)   (the garage) which the man put the car in

[44](b) is relativised on the subject NP, (c) on the direct object, and (d) on the prepositional object.

   Now, stranding patterns found in both Old and Middle English include clauses relativised on the object of a preposition:

[45]   *ChronA* 84.1 (893)

se   micla here. þe   we gefyrn ymbe spræcon
the great army that we before about spoke

'the great army that we spoke about before'

[46]   *LawAf 1* 6 52

&   slea   mon þa hond of ðe   he hit mid gedyde.
and strike(SUBJ) one   the hand off that he it   with did

'and let one strike off the hand that he did it with.'

[47]   *Bede* 3 16.228.5

Þyslic wæs seo syn, þe   se   cyning fore ofslegen wæs
such was the sin   that the king   for slain   was

'Such was the sin for which the king was slain'

[48]   c1180 *Orm.* 461

þiss gode prest, Þatt we nu   mælenn offe
this good priest that we now speak   of

[49] c1180 *Orm.* 11818

summ hefiȝ sinne | Þatt he me maȝȝ wel eggenn to
some mortal sin   that he me may well egg   towards

'some mortal sin that he may well egg me on to do'

[50] c1180 *Orm.* 3550

þatt soþfasstnessess ham Þatt mann wass shapenn inne
that faithfulness's   home that man was created in

'that home of truth in which man was created'

Examples [45]–[47] are OE examples, [48]–[50] ME examples, of an active
clause containing an intransitive verb, an active clause containing a
transitive verb with direct object, and a passive clause whose subject
corresponds to the direct object of the active. As my examples suggest, P-V
order is characteristic of Old English, V-P of Middle English.

A similar range of stranding constructions is found in *as-* (or *than-*) and
infinitive clauses:

[51] *Jn(WSCp)* 5.4

. . . fram swa hwylcere untrumnysse swa he on wæs
. . . of   whatever   infirmity   as he in was

'. . . of whatever infirmity he had'

[52] *Bo* 24.15

Þeah he nu nanwuht elles næbbe   ymbe to sorgienne
though he now nothing else not-have about to sorrow

'though he may now have nothing else to grieve about'

[53] a1450(?c1348) Rolle, *FLiving* 104.43

For I hope þat God will do swilk thoghtes in þi   hert als he es
for I think that God will put such thoughts in your heart as he is

payde of
pleased with

[54] c1155 *Peterb.Chron.* 1140.4

ðat me lihtede candles to æten bi
that one lit   candles to eat by

Again I have given OE and ME examples of each, in P-V and V-P order,
respectively, though P-V order occurs sporadically through the ME period.
Another possibility is illustrated by [55] below:

[55] *Or* 88.27

him   com   on Godes wracu
them(DAT PL) came(3 SG) on God's vengeance(NOM SG)

'God's vengeance descended on them'

Here we seem to have a light NP fronted to maintain V-2 order (see
Chapter 4). Technically this may be topicalisation, but the NP *him* does not
seem to be highlighted in any way – if anything it is *Godes wracu* which has
the focus.

7.2.5   New preposition stranding patterns in Middle English

Various stranding constructions apart from the prepositional passive make
their first appearance in Middle English. The non-subject contact clause (a
clause relativised on an object position and lacking a relativiser) is very rare
in Old English but more common in Middle English (Dekeyser 1986), and
for that reason alone it may be that stranding patterns in contact clauses first
appear in Middle English:

[56]   a1225(?a1200) Lay.*Brut* 15517

  nis   nan feirure wifmon: þa whit sunne scineð on
  not-is no fairer woman the white sun   shines on

  'there is no fairer woman the bright sun shines on'

Stranding in *wh*-relatives is first found in Middle English too:

[57]   a1325(c1250) *Gen. and Ex.* 3715

  And getenisse men ben in ebron | Quilc men mai get wundren on.
  and gigantic men are in Hebron which men may yet wonder on

  'and there are gigantic men in Hebron that men may still wonder at'

[58]   a1400(a1325) *Cursor* 145

  how god bigan þe law hym gyfe | þe quilk the Iuus in sul   life
  how God began the law him give which   the Jews in were-to live

  'how God gave him the law by which the Jews were to live'

An example of a free relative (i.e. one without an antecedent) is:

[59]   c1225(?c1200) *SWard* 311

  Hwamse heo biseched fore is sikerliche iborhen
  whoever she intercedes for is certainly saved

Topicalisation with focus on the topicalised NP rarely co-occurs with
stranding in Old English (one example is given below as [60]) but becomes
more common in early Middle English:

[60]   *MCharm* 11.37

  Freond ic gemete wið
  friend I meet   with

  'May I meet with a friend!'

[61] c1230(?a1200) *Ancr.* 103a.22

þulliche   dunes þe gode pawel spek of;
those-very hills   the good Paul   spoke of

[62] a1400(a1325) *Cursor* 654

Bot yhon tre   cum   þou nawight to, | Þat standes in midward
but that tree come thou not   to   that stands in the-middle-of

paradis
Paradise

'but do not approach that tree which stands in the middle of Paradise'

[63] a1400(a1325) *Cursor* 1826

Þe saulus he wald   haf   of merci
the souls he would have of mercy

'The souls he would have mercy on'

See Allen (1980b: 286–91 and n.30).
   We might also include here the topicalisation of an infinitival clause
serving as prepositional object:

[64] c1225(?c1200) *SWard* 30

Forte breoke þis hus   efter þis tresor   . . . is moni þeof abuten
for-to break   this house after this treasure . . . is many thief about

'Many a thief is engaged in breaking into this house for this treasure'

7.2.6 Repeated preposition

The repetition of a preposition in both 'pied piped' and stranded positions is
an interesting and not uncommon phenomenon:

[65] c1225(?c1200) *St.Marg.(1)* 38.1

& sei me hwer þu wunest meast; of hwet cun þu art ikumen
and tell me where you live   mostly from what kin you have come

of
from

[66] a1400(a1325) *Cursor* 467

For in þat curt, þat es sa clene, | May na filth in dwell
for in that court that is so clean   may no filth in dwell

'for in that court [*sc.* heaven] which is so pure, no dirt may remain'

[67] (a1470) Malory, *Wks.* 1005.16

Also they founde there namys of ech lady, and of   what bloode
also they found there names of each lady and from what blood

they were com   off.
they had   come from

[68]   (a1470) Malory, *Wks.* 1234.1

all thes   be ladyes for whom I have foughten for
all these are ladies for whom I have fought   for

'all these are ladies on whose behalf I have fought'

Sporadic repetitions of this kind occur in Modern English too, especially in speech or careless writing:

[69]   1790 Woodforde, *Diary* III 228.5 (20 Nov)

. . . Mr. Hardy's the Mason's Lad, to whom I gave a Shilling to last Saturday

They are regarded as errors.

7.3   Explanations in non-generative linguistics

The concerns of generative grammarians being rather different, it will be convenient to discuss non-generative treatments first, separately. Most scholars suggest some process of reanalysis which links V and P as a unit, and most make some connection with the phenomenon of preposition stranding. They differ as to whether they regard word order change as crucial or not. Van der Gaaf, Mustanoja (1960: 113, 441; not discussed here) and Thornburg seem to take the replacement of P-V by V-P order in stranding constructions as a virtual prerequisite for the development of the prepositional passive, while de la Cruz and Denison explicitly deny this; Visser, though muddled, is with the latter. Denison does relate the *spread* of the construction to the fixing of SVX order, however.

Loss of the accusative ~ dative distinction is mentioned by virtually everyone, as also the loss of indefinite MAN 'one'. De la Cruz brings in the idea – attacked by Denison – that the prepositional passive arose by reanalysis of an impersonal passive. Several scholars attempt to relate the development of the prepositional passive, *She was sent for*, to a pre-existing passive, *A messenger was sent for her*, corresponding to the active syntagm V + NP + PP (van der Gaaf, de la Cruz, Thornburg – again with Denison dissenting). Denison and Thornburg discuss the semantic roles (deep cases) which license passives, the former also discussing an individual prepositional verb and associated lexical set which might have formed a bridgehead for the development of the prepositional passive.

7.3.1   Van der Gaaf

An early and still important account is that of W. van der Gaaf (1930a). Here we have much of the relevant data, well analysed as far as most individual examples are concerned but with discontinuities in the argument and too many impressionistic statements.

Van der Gaaf regards the object of a prepositional verb in the active as an ordinary direct object, and he likens English prepositional verbs to the separable compound verbs of Dutch and German. He rightly gives a lot of attention to preposition stranding (though not under that name), in particular in relative clauses relativised on the prepositional object, in comparative clauses introduced by *swa*, and in infinitive clauses of various types; see §7.2.4 above. These are patterns where 'the preposition is detached from the element of the sentence to which it belongs, and is joined to the verb' (1930a: 2), a positional effect which seems obviously relevant to the reanalysis of [3].

His examples show that the lexical verb is typically clause-final in these patterns in Old English, and that the preposition immediately precedes it and therefore comes *after* any object:

[70]   (O) (. . .) P V

He emphasises the fact that occasionally in late Old English, and increasingly in Middle English, the place of the stranded preposition tends to be post-verbal rather than pre-verbal:

[71]   (O) (. . .) V P

He claims that preposition stranding with the particle in V-P order is 'a potent factor in the origin and development' of the prepositional passive (1930a: 8), though it is not made clear exactly what the change in particle position has to do with the prepositional passive. In fact in his frame of reference the positional effect of preposition stranding should be as potent in P-V order as in V-P order, since P is still next to V and usually separated from any O.[2] After all, the separable compounds of Dutch and German show semantic and syntactic unification, and their stranding possibilities have P-V order. More telling still, at least six prepositional passives in Middle English actually have P-V order themselves (among them examples [12]–[13] and [24] above), all in texts where P-V is found in other stranding constructions. It is the stranding which is significant, not the relative order of P and V.

The central argument of van der Gaaf's article seems to run as follows, though some of the logical steps elude me. OE 'separable compounds' of preposition and verb were to some extent synthetic forms. The change of P-V to V-P position was part of the general ME tendency to substitute analytic (multi-word) for synthetic (single-word) forms, since V-P order at least puts a clear word boundary between V and P. Analytic replacements with V-P order sometimes went on to become unified, and when they did, syntactic connection and semantic change often went hand in hand, as in STANDAN + *bi* 'support, assist'. Even in Old English there had been examples suggesting that a prepositional object was already equivalent to a direct object, though the small total is due to the comparative rarity of accusative-governing prepositions. *Ymb* is one such, and in [72] SECAN *ymb* 'seek after' looks like a prepositional verb:

[72]   *CP* 350.8

swæ hiene swiður		lyst	ðisses andweardan lifes,	swæ he læs
as him	more-strongly	desires	this present life	so he less

secþ ymb þæt ece.
seeks after the eternal

'the more he desires this present life, the less he seeks after the eternal'

In Middle English there are rather more such examples, partly because of the loss of nominal inflectional endings. Further evidence of syntactic reanalysis comes from certain examples where the object of a preposition is ellipted or is a clause, constructions which 'would have been impossible if the verb and preposition had not syntactically become a unit' (1930a: 15): see [40]–[43] above.

There are several dubious claims here. The development of analytical constructions does not 'explain' the replacement of e.g. ONLOCIAN by LOKEN *on*, it merely subsumes it. Anyway it is misleading to suggest that many ME verb-preposition collocations were replacements of OE compounds (1930a: 12–13): few ME collocations are developed from OE *inseparable* compounds, and ME descendants of OE '*separable* compounds', which had simply been verb-adverb or verb-preposition collocations,[3] merely reflect general changes in verb-particle word order.

Van der Gaaf closes his paper with detailed histories of the combinations STANDEN *ayein* 'oppose' and LIGGEN *bi* 'have sexual intercourse with', and then a wide selection of passive collocations from the fourteenth to the sixteenth centuries.

Two last points from van der Gaaf's paper are worth noting. He observes that most instances of the prepositional passive have as agent 'an individual that cannot or need not be specified' (1930a: 19) – this applies to all but 2 of my 39 early examples – and so the function of such passives is similar to actives with the indefinite pronoun subject MAN (*man, mon, me*) 'someone, one, people', as in:

[73]   c1230(?a1200) *Ancr.* 111a.23

Me let   leasse of þe þing þet me haueð ofte.
one thinks less   of the thing that one has   often

'One thinks less highly of the thing that one often has.'

Therefore the rise of the prepositional passive is connected with the fall, so to speak, of MAN, something already discussed in the previous chapter (§6.3.2).

The second point I wish to comment on is as follows. Van der Gaaf sets a ModE active declarative beside its passive relative transform:

[74]   (a)   They packed the goods in bales.
         (b)   the bales (that) the goods were packed in

He asserts that the passive of a *transitive* verb + preposition can produce a connection between verb and preposition more intimate than in the active. The existence of such passives as [74](b) in Middle English is a probable factor, he suggests, in the origin of the prepositional passive, which is the passive of an *intransitive* verb + preposition (1930a: 9–10). We shall return to this in §7.3.4 in de la Cruz's more precise formulation, pausing only to disprove one of van der Gaaf's assertions. He attributes 'the evident preference that Middle English evinced for such constructions' over pied-piped alternatives to a feeling 'that the preposition belonged to the verb rather than to the relative' (1930a: 11).[4] But the constructions occur from early Old English onwards, even – as his own examples show – with combinations of V and P that betray no other sign of unification:

[75=47]   *Bede* 3 16.228.5

>   Þyslic wæs seo syn, þe se cyning fore ofslegen wæs
>   such was the sin that the king   for slain   was

'Such was the sin for which the king was slain'

The juxtaposition of V and P merely follows from the choice of uninflected relative (OE *þe*, ME *þat*) as clause connective, which debars pied piping. However, the frequency of examples with repeated preposition (§7.2.6 above) may perhaps testify to a feeling that the preposition belonged with the verb *as well as* with the relative.

7.3.2 Jespersen

Otto Jespersen's observations on preposition stranding and the prepositional verb are scattered over several volumes of his *Modern English Grammar* (1909–49).[5] He notes some semantic differences between verbs used transitively and the same verbs used with a preposition (III 252–72). He notices the significance of verb conjunction, though he states wrongly that it is rare in Middle English (III 272) – for OE and ME examples see §7.2.2 above. He suggests that examples of interruption of the P-NP sequence demonstrate close V-P connection (III 274–6). Otherwise there is nothing which van der Gaaf's more systematic treatment does not have.

7.3.3 Visser

F. Th. Visser deals with the prepositional passive at length (1963–73: §§1947–57), providing more in the way of data than explanation. Active patterns relevant to the prepositional verb, especially stranding construc-tions, are exemplified in a different volume (§§393–416, 632–3). He amplifies the list of constructions where, as he puts it, 'the preposition would find itself hanging in the air, if it were not part and parcel of the verb' (1963–73: §394) – examples were given in §7.2.3 above. One minor observation is that not all verbs which form part of prepositional verbs are *in*transitive when used alone: some are normally or often transitive (§1949).

Visser's pre-1400 material must be treated with great caution. His discussion of passives with P-V order in Old and Middle English is hopelessly muddled (§1947): of ten examples, one is of a phrasal verb, four are of inseparable compound verbs, and one (*GD* 51.14) is a freak of translation, leaving just four valid examples (which he regards as a possible prototype of the passive with V-P order). As for his examples of early prepositional passives in V-P order, several must be rejected. (For details see Note 1 and Denison 1981: 220–2; 1985a.)

7.3.4 De la Cruz

Juan M. de la Cruz has dealt with the history of the prepositional passive in a structuralist framework.[6] His work makes hard reading but contains much of value. De la Cruz (1973) provides a detailed analysis of the English prepositional passive and will be our main concern, while de la Cruz (1972) draws parallels between English and other languages and expands on one important but erroneous component of the other account.

De la Cruz is at pains to show where the prepositional passive fits in to the *system* of ME syntax. The typological change from synthesis to analysis covers the replacements not just of compound verbs by prepositional verbs but also of compound verbs by phrasal verbs and of case inflection by prepositional marking (1973: 161–4). The development of phrasal verbs and the development of prepositional verbs are related, in that both are verb-particle structures[7] largely equivalent to compound verbs in Old English. On one score in particular prepositional verbs can be regarded as functional replacements of OE compound verbs: both can serve as 'transitivating' devices, converting what is usually an intransitive simplex verb into a transitive verbal unit (1973: 164–5). Incidentally, an interesting blending of old and new is shown by:

[76]   (1389) *Lond. Gild. Ret.* in *Bk. Lond. E.* 49.47

þat ȝif þe wardeyns of þat ȝeer be of sent after
that if the Wardens for that year are sent   for

This uniquely seems to combine the transitive verb OFSENDEN 'send for' with its synonymous replacement SEND *after* (used by itself in [19]).

De la Cruz mentions the great expansion of prepositional use during the ME period, both in numbers of prepositional particles and frequency and range of use, noting that it affects both the nominal and verbal realms (1973: 168–9). Increased use of PPs links the development of the prepositional verb to the demise of nominal inflections; see §3.2.2 above.

His next point is that prepositions can become partly adverbialised through stranding, quite apart from adverbialisation by ellipsis of the object NP, and that the prepositional passive is a 'rather adverbialized structure' too. Building on van der Gaaf's suggestion, he suggests that the prepositional passive arose for reasons of structural symmetry (1973: 170–2). He considers three different kinds of main clause verb phrase: transitive V + direct object + P + prepositional object (e.g. *send somebody for* NP), intransitive V + P + prepositional object (e.g. *send for* NP – our prepositional verb), and transitive verb + prt + direct object (e.g. *pick up* NP – the transitive phrasal verb). The distribution of these kinds of VP is then tabulated in three constructions, which can be taken to stand for all the stranding constructions, and in which de la Cruz believes the particle is partly or wholly adverbialised – hence his treatment of P and prt as a single category. To illustrate the constructions with the first kind of VP:

[77] (a) (the man) that I sent somebody for
      (b) (the man) that somebody was sent for
      (c) (a suitable man) to send somebody for

(Some OE and ME examples of stranding in the first two types were provided in §7.2.4 above.) De la Cruz notes that the word order change from P-V to V-P affects all three VP types, correctly points out that it need play no part in his argument, but unfortunately allows it to confuse an already complicated diagram on p. 172, which I simplify to the following schema for Old English/early Middle English:

[78]	*send* NP$_j$ *for* NP$_i$	*send for* NP$_i$	*pick up* NP$_i$
active REL clause relativised on NP$_i$	+	+	+
passive REL clause relativised on NP$_i$	+	−	+
active INF clause relativised on NP$_i$	+	+	+

The argument runs as follows. The clause types listed at the left of the diagram remove NP$_i$ from its basic position next to the particle in a main clause. Only one combination of VP type and clause type fails to occur, namely the passive relative clause equivalent to PDE

[79] (the man) that was sent for

Hence there is systemic pressure for the gap to be filled on analogical grounds, and prepositional passives will be the result.

Parts of the argument are weak, however, as the proposed 'system' lacks homogeneity and coherence. In particular, it is misleading to identify the adverbial particle of a phrasal verb (*up* in *The book which she picked up* – 'prt' in my account) with the prepositional particle of a prepositional verb (*for* in *The book which she sent for* – 'P' in my account), since there is only limited overlap between the two classes of particle in Middle English, and the syntactic relation between particle and NP is quite different for the two classes. On de la Cruz's logic the earliest prepositional passives should occur in relative clauses with the relative as subject, yet only five of the 39 early examples are relatives or reduced relatives of this type.

Other useful points which are worth noting are the observation that both compound verbs and prepositional verbs can permit a difference of object with respect to the simplex[8] (1973: 164); the citation of examples showing parallel function of the old and new structures (1973: 174); the discussion, and ultimately rejection, of the possibility of Celtic influence on English (1972: 172, 175–9).

One major element requires critical comment, however, and brings us back to the relationship with case syncretism (on which see §3.2.1 above). De la Cruz argues that the loss of case marking in nouns plays a crucial role in the history of the prepositional passive by effacing the distinction between nominative and oblique, especially dative, case. This permitted both the prepositional (and indeed the indirect) passive to enter the language by conversion of an impersonal to a personal passive (1973: 166–8). The point is clearest in his comparison of Icelandic, which shows what he alleges to be the transitional stage (1972: 177):

[80]   hana   var talað   við
         her(ACC) was spoken with

Here we have an impersonal passive in which the NP has retained the oblique case it would have had in the active. If that had been the route which English followed, however, one would expect to find some evidence that prepositional passives developed as follows (adapting the Jespersen sentences of §6.3.1.1):

[81]   (a)   *her was spoken with
         (b)   *the girl(DAT/ACC) was spoken with
         (c)   the girl(NOM) was spoken with
         (d)   she was spoken with

Yet the first two kinds simply do not occur.[9] De la Cruz has over-egged the pudding by proposing a new source for the prepositional passive, namely reanalysis of an impersonal passive, when the obvious source, reanalysis of existing active patterns, is far better attested and provides an adequate explanation. The double source is more relevant to the history of the indirect passive, already discussed in the previous chapter.

7.3.5 Denison

Denison (1985a) is a densely written reaction to the preceding items and others, not intended to stand by itself as a history of the prepositional passive. I think three points from that paper might be brought into the present discussion, two of them drawing on my 'corpus' (see Note 1) of 39 pre-1400 prepositional passives.

7.3.5.1   (A) Semantic roles

The first concerns the semantic classifications of NP functions which are set up by Vestergaard (1977) and Couper-Kuhlen (1979) in a Case Grammar framework. For a range of PDE prepositional passives they analyse the roles of what we might call the active subject (the NP which would have been the subject in the active) and the passive subject (the subject of the passive = the NP which would have been prepositional object in the active) to see which combinations of deep cases permit a prepositional passive. Couper-Kuhlen claims that semantic configuration is the most important factor determining whether a prepositional passive is acceptable, though lexical choice and contextualisation play their part too. I suggested extending the approach to Middle English. In my corpus there seemed to be a very limited number of deep case combinations, and only two main types. In one, exemplified by [15] above, the passive subject would be Stimulus[10] in Couper-Kuhlen's system and the active subject would be Experiencer. The other type is the semantic relationship usually thought of as typical of the passive, with the passive subject as Patient or Goal (or, once, Benefactive) and the active subject as Agent, as in [10]. The only departure from these two types was a biblical (Latin-influenced?) example with Path as passive subject:

[82]   a1425(c1395) *WBible(2)* Ezek. 47.5

> depe watris . . . that mai not be waad ouer.
> deep waters. . . that may not be waded over

In addition two examples of *smitten through* had an active subject (*spear*, *lance*) which could be classed as Instrument, but I suggested that both are anyway dubious as prepositional passives because of the confused categorial status of the particle *through*, which can be prefixal or adverbial as well as prepositional in collocations which mean 'transfix'. I drew the tentative conclusion that the narrow range of deep case pairings in my sample argued in favour of lexical diffusion of the prepositional passive as against across-the-board adoption of a purely syntactic rule.

7.3.5.2   (B) LETEN *of* and related verbs

A more specific argument is provided by a cluster of closely-related prepositional verbs: LETEN *of/by*, SETTEN *of/by*, TELLEN *of/by* 'regard, esteem, think of'. They supply 12 of the 39 early passives, and a further 14 that I know of in the fifteenth century, and their semantic and even phonological similarity to one another supports the idea of lexical diffusion of the construction.

The most common collocation of all is one of their number, LETEN *of*, which I claimed had special properties: the verb LETEN had long been in transitive use with particles, e.g. LETEN *doun* 'let down', and in early Middle English even transitively by itself in the sense 'regard'; it already occurred in the passive in the anomalous construction LETEN *blod* 'let blood'; and non-spatial *of* was being used elliptically and 'quasi-elliptically' (a term explained in §7.3.5.3 below), including in collocation with LETEN. So LETEN *of* in early Middle English was an unusual prepositional verb, in that its verbal element was already familiar in the passive, and its particle already had a non-prepositional use similar to that needed for the prepositional passive. In the light of these facts I suggested that LETEN *of* had special suitability as a 'bridgehead', a collocation likely to be involved in the *actuation* of the prepositional passive (even if it does not, as often claimed, provide the earliest recorded instance).

7.3.5.3*   Quasi-ellipsis

I digress to explain the term **quasi-ellipsis** mentioned in connection with B above, abridging Denison (1985a: §5.2).

There are clear cases of prepositions and adverbs introducing a clause:

[83]   c1230(?a1200) *Ancr.* 14a.28

> tis uuel of dynacom nawt of þet ha seh sichen emores sune
> this evil of Dina came not from that she saw Sichem Hamer's son

> 'This evil of Dina's did not come from her seeing Sichem, Hamer's son.'

[84]   c1230(?a1200) *Ancr.* 95a.17

Þe deade   nis   noht   of;   þah   he ligge unburiet. &   rotie
the dead(OBL) not-is nothing from though he lie   unburied and rot
buuen eorðe
above ground

'It does not matter at all to a dead man if he lies unburied and rots above
ground.'

In [83] *of* is prepositional, with a *that*-clause as object, whereas in [84] it is
adverbial or elliptical, since the *though*-clause cannot logically be its prepositional
object. However, there are intermediate cases, whose syntax I gave the pre-
theoretical name 'quasi-ellipsis':

[85]   c1180 *Orm.* 10047

ȝiffþatt teȝȝ nohht ne blinnenn off   To follȝhenn Godess wille
if   that they not   not cease   from to follow   God's   will

'if they do not stop following God's will'

[86]   c1230 *Ancr.*(Corp-C) 29a.7

& heo schal beo greattre ibollen. leafdiluker   leoten of   þen
and she shall be greater swollen more-ladylike behave(INF) than
a leafdi of hames[11]
a lady   of homes

'and she shall be more self-important, shall behave in a more ladylike way,
than a lady of property'

[87]   c1230(?a1200) *Ancr.* 60a.19

ȝet is meast dred of hwen þe sweoke of helle eggeð to a þing
yet is most fear of when the deceiver of hell incites to a thing

'Yet there is most fear when the Deceiver of Hell incites one to
something'

[88]   ibid. 60b.10

bringeð hire on to gederin.   &   ȝeouen al earst to poure
draws   her on to collect(INF) and give   all at-first to poor

'draws her on to collecting and giving it all at first to the poor'

[89]   ibid. 82b.17

ah ful wel he let   of hwen ei   seið þet . . .
but full well he thinks of when anyone says that . . .

'but he is very pleased when anyone says that . . .'

In [85]–[89] the clause is partly like a prepositional object, partly an adjunct or
complement of the verb; thus, for example, BLINNEN *off* in [85] may be analysed
either like PDE CEASE *from* or like LEAVE *off*. Although quasi-elliptical particles
before clauses are not confined to early Middle English (see §7.2.3 above), non-
spatial *of* seems to be used in that way for only a short time. For instance, every

one of my examples from the Corpus Christi MS. of *Ancr.* is modified or omitted in at least one other MS. of the text, though most are vouched for in the Cleopatra MS., corrected by the author. Furthermore, at about the same time non-spatial *of* was being used with clear ellipsis of its object NP:

[90]   *ChronD* 93.29 (1076)

    Ac se kyngc let   lihtlice of oð þæt he com to Englalande
    but the king   thought lightly of until that he came to England

    'but the king made light of it [*sc.* his offence] until he came to England'

[91]   c1230(?a1200) *Ancr.* 47b.1

    ha walde awilgin   elles oðer to wel leoten of
    she would grow-over-confident else   or   too well think of

    'she would grow overconfident or else think too well of herself'

[92]   ?a1220 *HMaid* 18.12

    Ne þunche   þe   nan uuel of
    not seem(3 SG PRES SUBJ) you(OBL) no harm of

    'Do not think badly of it'

As far as I can tell, elliptical and quasi-elliptical use of non-spatial *of* is confined to late Old English and early Middle English. It may simply have been one unsuccessful experiment among the particularly widespread changes undergone by *of* in the course of the ME period – witness the many new functions taken on and the incipient differentiation of strong and weak forms (*off* and *of*, respectively), later recast into a distinction between (broadly speaking) spatial and non-spatial meanings.

7.3.5.4   (C) Word order

A final point from Denison (1985a) is the suggestion that two late ME/early ModE processes would have been mutually supportive. One is the spread of idiomatic prepositional verbs (as well as such other verb-complement idioms as phrasal verbs and the HAVE *a look* type). The other is the fixing of SVX order followed by the rise of auxiliary verbs and the regulation of DO. The further each process advanced, the more often a complete lexical item could appear in all sentence patterns in a fixed sequence without interruption. The real period of growth of the prepositional verb, for instance, was between 1300 and 1700, which coincides with the rise and regulation of DO. Arguing that the rigidification of word order fostered the *spread* of the prepositional verb is compatible with denying its relevance to the *formation* (actuation) of the prepositional passive.

7.3.6 Thornburg

Linda Thornburg (1985) reaches a useful conclusion by a dubious route, taking data and analysis largely from van der Gaaf and Visser, errors included.[12] She claims that the order NP-P with prepositions is more common that P-NP when the NP is a pronoun, and that a dative pronoun conditions the order NP-V-P. Reference to Mitchell (1978: 251–4) would have shown that these are exaggerations. She also claims that dative pronouns are always **anaphoric** to animate NPs, which is largely true in relevant examples only because *þær* rather than a third-person pronoun is the normal form for an inanimate prepositional object. She concludes 'that the environment that conditioned post-verbal Pr[eposition] placement generalized in late Old English from "animate pre-verbal (Pro) object" to "animate pre-verbal NP" to "pre-verbal NP" ' (1985: 331). This led to productive preposition stranding in relative clauses, under a definition of preposition stranding which implicitly excludes P-V order; cf. §7.3.1 above. Thornburg then follows van der Gaaf in looking at clauses passivised on a direct object and relativised on an agent NP – cf. example [74](b) – and argues that 'by analogy' with them 'it was a short step to prepositional passives' (1985: 331). This logic has been criticised in §7.3.4 above.

More helpful is her conclusion that the prepositional passive must be understood in relation to transitivity, which has a prototypical semantic structure. In prepositional passives, she says, the referent of the passive subject (= active object) is usually Affected, and the active subject is usually Agentive. I would add to this the Stimulus-Experiencer type. I miss too any reference, at least in Thornburg (1985), to the pioneering work of Bolinger (1977a), Vestergaard (1977) and Couper-Kuhlen (1979).

7.4   Explanations in generative linguistics

Relevant generative work on prepositional constructions has centred on two main areas, stranding and reanalysis, and we shall organise the discussion on that basis.

7.4.1   Preposition stranding

7.4.1.1

Consider these ModE relative clauses:

[93] (a) (the book) that I spoke of
      (b) (the book) I spoke of
      (c) (the book) which I spoke of
      (d) (the book) of which I spoke

Patterns [93](a–c) involve preposition stranding, (d) pied piping. A transformational derivation of types [93](c,d) would involve **movement** of the *wh*-phrase from an underlying structure something like:

[94] I spoke of which

The movement rule has gone under various names as the theory has evolved: '*Wh* Fronting', '*Wh* Movement', 'Move α'. Its **landing site** is usually assumed to be the complementiser position COMP.[13] If just the NP is moved we get [93](c); if the whole PP, (d).

Even if the surface relativiser is not a *wh*-word, a movement analysis is still possible: [93](a,b) could be derived by movement of *wh* followed by its deletion, in which case all four types would have a similar origin. The form *that* in [93](a) would be a complementiser, optionally absent in the zero relative [93](b) in just the same way that complementiser *that* is optional elsewhere.[14] Alternatively, [93](a,b) could be derived without any movement by **deletion** in the VP, taking the underlying form of the clause to be something like:

[95] I spoke of it

In that case the *wh*-relatives and non-*wh*-relatives would have rather different derivations. What is at stake, then, is whether the best analysis of [93](a,b) involves movement (and deletion in COMP) or just deletion (in VP).

It is worth mentioning that this general introduction to the analysis of relative clauses would serve equally well for simple transitive verbs like REVIEW by the substitution of *reviewed* for *spoke of* in [93](a–c) (of course there would be nothing corresponding to the (d) pattern). It would also cover verbs like PUT which can take both direct and prepositional object (substitute, say, *put the bookmark in* for *spoke of*).

The basic choice identified above could be extended backwards in time at least to late Middle English. Before that time the discussion would have to take account of differences in distribution. Pattern [93](b), stranding with zero relative, is with one exception not found before early Middle English,[15] while pattern (c), stranding with a *wh* (inflected) relative, does not enter the language until a little later. Furthermore it is not obvious that patterns [93](a,d) are found in Old English either. Claims that they are rest on two assertions of equivalence between OE and ME/ModE relative clauses. The first, relatively uncontroversial, is that the OE *þe*-relative is equivalent to the later *that*-relative of [93](a). The second is that the OE SE-relative is equivalent to the later *wh*-relative [93](d), though their properties differ in important ways.[16] Contention about the correct analysis of stranding constructions has produced a stream of articles, many in *Linguistic Inquiry*, often with syntactic theory rather than the details of English as their major concern. Van Kemenade (1987: ch. 5) has a good summary.

7.4.1.2* Vat & co.

Let us go no further back than Chomsky and Lasnik (1977), who argue for a movement analysis of *that*-relatives in ModE and extend it to *þe*- and *that*-relatives in OE and ME. Their position is criticised by Joan Maling (1978) on the basis of modern Scandinavian relative and interrogative clauses which behave differently with respect to certain constraints. She argues from this that some relative clauses at least must be derived by deletion, including ModE *that*-relatives and OE *þe*-relatives. Jan Vat (1978), a pseudonym for an eight-member seminar, concentrates 'his' fire on one paragraph of a footnote in Maling's paper. The problem concerns the status of *þær* 'there, where' in OE, which could be a relativiser in a clause type that has no counterpart in PDE:

[96] *Dan* 717

    þæt tacen . . . þær   he to starude
    the sign . . . where he to gazed

'the sign . . . at which he gazed'

This kind of relative, accorded only marginal mention in the earlier accounts, becomes the linchpin of Vat's analysis.

Chomsky and Lasnik had asserted that OE *þær* 'is clearly a relative pronoun' (1977: 496 n.122). Maling claimed that on the contrary this was 'far from obvious' (1978: 79 n.2), though her reasoning is confusing. Vat retorts, this time with Modern Dutch in support, that OE *þær* is indeed a pronoun in relative clauses like [96], and mounts an ingenious case for deriving even *þe*-relatives in OE from *þær*-relatives. Vat's argument runs as follows.

First, the morphosyntactic feature [±P] functions in the same way as [±WH] in ModE (1978: 695 n.2), and [+P] can surface as the SE pronoun or as *þær*. Second, *þær* is a proform which can amongst other things replace an NP within a PP, as in [97]:

[97]   *CP* 337.12

ne he   self nanne wæsðm ðær   ofer ne bireð
nor it [*sc.* figtree] self no   fruit   there over not bears

'And it bears no fruit above it itself.'

Third, most PPs in OE have the order P-NP, and extraction from PP (i.e. movement of an NP out of a PP) is normally disallowed. The order NP-P occurs only with *r*-pronouns (*þær*, *her*, *hwær*) and personal pronouns,[17] and it is precisely those two classes of prepositional object which allow preposition stranding, i.e. instances where P and NP are not adjacent at all, as in:

[98]   *Bede* 3 4.164.31

þær   stod micel seolfren disc on
there stood large silver   dish on

'A large silver dish stood on it'

The correct analysis, Vat argues, should build on the distributional similarity between inverted PPs and preposition stranding. In Vat's analysis preposition stranding is a two-stage process which involves the inversion of a PP. First a pronoun (if one of the two eligible types) moves to the left of its preposition, putting it in the only 'escape-hatch' which permits an NP to leave PP altogether. Then, given that a non-locative *r*-pronoun is considered to be a special case of the *þ*-pronouns (1978: 708), it can undergo *Wh* Fronting. To get a surface *þær*-relative like [96], the complementiser *þe* is deleted. The last flourish of Vat's argument is to derive ordinary *þe*-relatives with stranding in essentially the same way: for Vat they are *þær*-relatives which have undergone *Wh* Fronting and then had *þær* rather than *þe* deleted from COMP. Example [100] is a skeletal derivation *à la* Vat of the *þe*-relative in [99]:

[99]   *Or* 22.4

(meolc) þe hy   mæst bi libbað
(milk) that they mostly by live

'(milk) that they mostly live on'

[100]   (a)   [$_{COMP}$ +P þe] hy mæst bi þær libbað ⇒ (PP Inversion [not Vat's term])

(b)   [$_{COMP}$ +P þe] hy mæst þær bi libbað ⇒ (P-Movement)

(c)   [$_{COMP}$ þær$_i$ þe] hy mæst e$_i$ bi libbað ⇒ (P-Deletion)

(d)   [$_{COMP}$ e þe] hy mæst e bi libbað

(The 'e' symbols in this derivation represent *empty nodes*, in this instance *traces*.) Recall the very similar movement analysis for ModE *that*-relatives sketched out above.

The advantages of Vat's analysis are that it gives a unified account of all OE clauses relativised on a prepositional object, and relates preposition stranding in relative clauses to other instances of PPs in NP-(. . .)-P order where the NP is a pronoun. The disadvantages are that absence of complementiser þe in þær-relatives becomes an unexplained fact which must be handled by an arbitrary surface filter (1978: 710), while in þe-relatives an underlying þær must be posited without overt evidence for its presence. As pointed out by Bresnan and Grimshaw (1978: 375 n.14) and Allen (1980b: 315) among others, this deleted þær must be able to refer to human or non-human antecedents, whereas þær as surface pronoun is only ever anaphoric to inanimate NPs; furthermore, there is no explanation of the absence of þær-relatives with human antecedents. These are serious problems.

7.4.1.3*   Allen

An alternative analysis is provided by Cynthia Allen (1980b). She claims for OE that

in all constructions in which there was an item on the surface which had clearly been moved, pied piping of prepositions was obligatory, while preposition stranding is found in those in which the affected item was deleted (1980b: 265)

assuming in a footnote to the above quotation that

an item has clearly been moved if it appears "out of place" in the sentence and furthermore exhibits the case marking we would expect from its logical underlying position

Her description of relative clauses in OE is a model of precision and clarity.

In order to sustain her basic claim, she must argue that relative clauses with stranding have a complementiser and not a relative pronoun, since case-marked pronouns are assumed to have been moved. One problem to be disposed of is instances of stranding after þæt, a relativiser which one might assume to be pronominal. Allen cites some examples where relative þæt *cannot* be a pronoun and generalises from them to the claim that 'ðæt is an undeclinable relative complementizer, a less common alternative to ðe' (1980b: 274–5). On that basis she can argue that stranding in relatives is wholly correlated with the use of a complementiser. She then deals systematically with a succession of constructions – infinitival clauses, free relatives, questions, topicalisation, and þær-relatives – covering examples with and without prepositions. Like Vat she suggests that prepositions can permute with personal pronouns and locatives (Vat's r-pronouns), but she differs in her treatment of the latter. Recall that for Vat non-locative þær, her, hwær are all special cases of þ-pronouns and therefore of wh-pronouns, and all can permute with prepositions. For Allen þær and her are

[−wh], not [+wh]. Second, *hwær* cannot permute with prepositions in OE, only in ME; see Allen (1980b: 293 n.42, 310–12) for discussion of *hwær*. Allen also proposes a readjustment rule of PP Split to turn a permuted PP, i.e. one in NP-P order, into a non-***constituent***, thus enabling subsequent movement of the NP.

In the light of her analysis of these five constructions, with topicalisation as the crucial case, Allen proposes to derive SE-relatives in OE by *Wh* Movement; *þær*-relatives by Locative Inversion, PP Split and Topicalisation; and *þe*-relatives and infinitival clauses by deletion in VP (***controlled unbounded*** deletion, deletion under identity). Her derivation of [99], therefore, will run as follows:

[101=99]   *Or* 22.4

(meolc) þe hy mæst bi libbað
(milk)   that they mostly by live

[102]   (a) [COMP þe] hy mæst bi NP libbað ⇒
            (b) [COMP þe] hy mæst bi e libbað

The changes in ME are handled only briefly in Allen (1980b), and we must turn to the related Allen (1980a). In this revision of her doctoral dissertation, Allen argues that the extension of preposition stranding in ME to new constructions (§7.2.5 above) can be explained as follows. OE had a constraint on movement of NP out of PP (apart from the special circumstances of PP Split), so that certain stranding constructions were then unavailable. Apparent counter-examples where a case-marked pronoun co-occurs with stranding can be explained satisfactorily as having the pronoun as antecedent – therefore not moved – and a relative complementiser. The types in question are exemplified as follows:

[103]   *ÆCHom* II 19.175.55

for ðan ðe we nabbað ða   ðe   he on ðrowade
because   we not-have that(FEM ACC SG) which he on suffered

'because we do not have what he suffered on'

[104=51]   *Jn(WSCp)* 5.4

se . . . wearþ gehæled fram swa hwylcere untrumnysse swa he on
he . . . became healed of   whatever   infirmity(DAT) as he in
wæs
was

'he . . . was healed of whatever infirmity he had'

In example [103], Allen argues, we do not have a SE *þe* relative, rather a *þe* relative whose antecedent happens to be the pronoun *ða* (FEM ACC SG of SE); in [104] the indefinite NP *swa hwylcere untrumnysse* is the antecedent of a relative clause whose complementiser is the second *swa*. Both have preposition stranding, but the constraint is not violated because there has been deletion of a prepositional object NP within the relative clause rather than movement of a pronoun. In ME the *wh* pronouns came to be used in all kinds of relative clause, and the first *swa* in indefinite relatives was lost. All relative clauses now used the same pronouns and looked superficially similar, which prompted speakers to extend stranding from clauses like [103]–[104] to relatives which did involve movement (1980a: 235–6). This meant that the constraint on movement out of PP was dropped (1980a: 359), so that stranding could spread to yet other constructions, amongst them the previously impossible prepositional passive. Allen's explanation, then, is based on language learners drawing an analogy between similar-sounding surface structures and taking this as evidence that the language lacked a constraint on movement out of PP.

7.4.1.4* Van Kemenade

Ans van Kemenade (1987: 164–71) provides yet another GB analysis of the phenomenon. Having argued that personal pronouns and *þær* in Old English were clitics in certain well-defined clitic positions (in COMP, at the left periphery of VP, left-adjacent to P), she now suggests an empty clitic pronoun, i.e. one that is phonologically null, as object of the preposition. This is the empty category *pro*. Pro could move to the clitic position to the left of P and in suitable circumstances from there to COMP. Van Kemenade offers example [105](a) with the underlying structure [105](b):[18]

[105] (a)   *Or* 150.4

> (þære) scole þe he on leornode
> (the)   school that he in learnt

'(the) school that he learnt in'

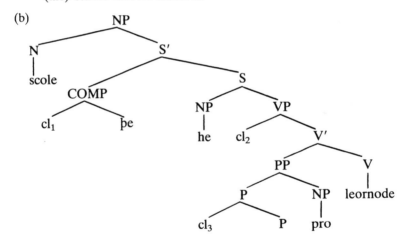

What happened in the derivation of [105](a) is that pro cliticised on to P, leaving behind a trace, and subsequently moved to COMP, where its person/case/gender/ number features could be identified by *þære scole*. Van Kemenade argues that such derivations were possible in relative clauses, infinitival relatives, and (with subject rather than antecedent as identifying argument) *Tough-Movement* constructions; lack of a suitable identifying element is what blocked this kind of derivation, and hence preposition stranding, in *wh*-relatives and topicalisation. The prepositional passive was blocked both by the lack of an identifying element and by Case Theory, as discussed in §7.6.5 below.

The change of VP word order in Middle English meant that V assigned θ-role to the right (its object was to its right), just like P. Where P was itself a thematic dependent of V and was governed by it, then it too could in some vaguely defined way become a 'proper governor' (1987: 216–17), and that in turn allowed preposition stranding by movement to COMP, for example in *wh-c*onstructions.

7.4.1.5* Van Riemsdijk

A different kind of explanation for differences between OE and ME preposition stranding is offered by Henk van Riemsdijk (1978), a leading light of the Jan Vat group, though his real concern is with Modern English and Dutch (his section on diachronic English changes overlaps largely with the more readily accessible Vat 1978). Van Riemsdijk's account distinguishes stranding as a result of NP Movement and of *Wh* Movement.

Stranding by *Wh* Movement involves an 'escape hatch' (from an otherwise escape-proof PP). We have discussed the escape-hatch analysis of Old English in §7.4.1.2 above. In his diachronic sketch, prepositional objects which precede their governing preposition are taken to be the norm in Proto-Indo-European. In Old English they were merely a remnant of the older NP-P order and were now characterised by the morpho-syntactic feature [+R] (i.e. the *r*-pronouns). Later '[i]n the history of English the remnant position was reinterpreted in terms of the feature [+WH], that is as COMP, presumably as a consequence of the rise of the *wh*-pronouns in the ME period. Of the *r*-pronoun escape hatch only a few fossilized relicts remain such as *hereby, thereupon, whereabouts,* etc.' (Vat 1978: 296). Stranding by *Wh* Movement in Present-day English (and presumably from Middle English onwards) is explained by positing a COMP node within PP (P''', or P-triple-bar) which can act as the escape hatch for the moved *Wh* item (1978: 226–31). Presumably, though he does not develop the point, the new patterns involving preposition stranding after *wh*-words would be accounted for along these lines (for data see §7.2.5 above).

For van Riemsdijk, stranding by NP Movement is explained by means of reanalysis, which is dependent on adjacency. Van Riemsdijk's work has been independently followed up in two articles which also place the burden of explanation on word order changes.

7.4.1.6 Fischer and van der Leek

Fischer and van der Leek (1981: 327–9) correlate the advent of the prepositional passive with the change from VPs which are underlyingly verb-final to VPs which are verb-initial, on which see Chapter 4 above. The point is a simple one. Recall the generative analysis of word order in §4.5. In the older (OE) underlying order an intransitive verb with PP complement will appear in the configuration:

[106] [$_{VP}$ [$_{PP}$ P NP] V]

In the later (ME) order the equivalent VP configuration is:

[107] [$_{VP}$ V [$_{PP}$ P NP]]

Crucially P is adjacent to V in [107] but not adjacent in the older [106]: adjacency is a prerequisite for reanalysis, and reanalysis, it is argued, is a prerequisite for preposition stranding by NP Movement. A similar point is made by van Kemenade (1987: 212–13). This leads us in to the next section, on reanalysis.

7.4.1.7* Koma

Before that we must mention the work of Osamu Koma (1981), who observes that the asymmetry between movement and deletion processes is considerably weakened in Middle English by the appearance of stranding in *wh*-relatives (genuine *wh*-words now rather than the SE forms of Old English). Cynthia Allen had, of course, observed that too. Koma independently uses the word order argument of van Riemsdijk to account not just for the prepositional passive but also for new stranding constructions like *wh*-relatives. In other words he takes reanalysis to be a crucial stage in *all* stranding patterns, whether the movement rule is NP Movement or *Wh* Movement. However, the intuitive justification for reanalysis seems to be far greater in prepositional passives than in the less constrained processes of stranding in relative and interrogative clauses and *Tough*-Movement. Compare [108](a) with (b–d):

[108] (a) *Slums can't easily be lived near.
       (b) (The slums) that you live near (are decaying).
       (c) Who do you live near?
       (d) Slums are difficult to live near.

Type (d), not known by Koma to exist in Middle English (1981: 135 n.5), can in fact be found then:

[109] c1230(?a1200) *Ancr.* 13a.9

þe blake cla ð . . . is þiccre aȝein þe wind & wurse to seon þurh.
the black cloth . . . is thicker against the wind and harder to see   through

7.4.2 Reanalysis

7.4.2.1

The mechanism of reanalysis is adopted from Chomsky by van Riemsdijk (1978: 218–26). It is the optional introduction at the level of lexical insertion of 'an extra pair of V-brackets around contiguous strings of words that are listed in the lexicon as semantic units' (1978: 222). Examples of **semantic words** (or **units**) or **natural** (or **possible**) **predicates** which are said to be amenable to reanalysis include ModE LOOK *into* 'investigate', TAKE *advantage of*, and the like, and indeed the LAUGH *at* of [3](b), repeated here for convenience as [110]:

[110] [$_{VP}$ [$_V$ *laugh at*] [$_{NP}$ *Jim*]]

The closing V-bracket interrupts the PP *at Jim*, invalidating the constraint which normally blocks extraction from PP and opening the way for *NP movement* of *Jim* to give a prepositional passive. Hornstein and Weinberg present the concept of reanalysis in much the same way, confining themselves to Modern English (and Dutch), apart from one footnote (1981: 67–8 n.16) which extends the analysis to Old English.[19]

As we have already seen, the concept of reanalysis is harnessed to an analysis of word order change by Fischer and van der Leek (1981) and van Kemenade (1987) to provide an explanation for the sudden appearance of the prepositional passive in the thirteenth century, and indeed Koma (1981) also uses it to account for new stranding patterns in *wh*-constructions.

7.4.2.2*   Inada

Toshiaki Inada (1981), however, poses some cogent problems for the reanalysis approach, though his objections have most force against analyses like Koma's which bring reanalysis into *Wh* Movement constructions. First Inada claims that reanalysis cannot apply in the base, since it must follow NP Movement in the derivation of:

[111]   The bale that the goods were packed in went bad.

Furthermore it must both precede and follow *Wh* Movement in:

[112]   (a)   Which cellar were the books hard to keep in?

derived as follows:

  (b)   the books$_i$ were hard to keep *wh*$_i$ in which cellar ⇒ (*Tough*-Movement = *Wh* Movement on a then-common assumption)
  (c)   the books$_i$ were hard *wh*$_i$ to keep t$_i$ in which cellar ⇒ (reanalysis)
  (d)   the books$_i$ were hard to [$_V$ keep t$_i$ in] which cellar ⇒ (*Wh* Movement)
  (e)   which cellar$_j$ were the books$_i$ hard to keep t$_i$ in t$_j$

Then follows a more general objection. Reanalysis is an option which makes a preposition a constituent of a prepositional verb rather than of a PP. If the option of reanalysis is taken up for, say, INSIST *on*, then problems are posed by the unacceptable sentences below:

[113]   (a)   *John insisted on that you be here on time.
        (b)   John insisted that you be here on time.
[114]   (a)   John insisted on the fact that he was neutral throughout the discussion.
        (b)   *John insisted on throughout the discussion the fact that he was neutral.

The standard way of deriving [113](b) is by obligatory deletion of *on* from the structure underlying [113](a), but *on* should not be deletable if it has become a constituent of a prepositional verb: why then is [113](a) impossible? As for [114], a restriction against applying **Heavy-NP Shift** to an NP within a PP would normally block derivation of [114](b) from the structure underlying [114](a), but after reanalysis the NP *the fact that he was neutral* is no longer inside a PP. Nevertheless [114](b) is impossible. Inada's conclusion is that reanalysis in active structures is unworkable. In a subsequent publication which I have not seen, he expounds his view that prepositional passives and related facts can be accounted for by morphological redundancy rules applying to participle-preposition strings. A problem which he does not address is the role of the trace t$_i$ in [112](c), where reanalysis apparently has to proceed despite the non-contiguity of *keep* and *in*.

7.4.2.3*   Van der Wurff

In the course of an analysis of *Tough*-Movement constructions (as in [117] below), Wim van der Wurff (1992b) brings in the concept of borrowing across social networks. Such borrowing is not exactly 'external', since no foreign source is assumed, but crucially it involves borrowing from speakers with a different grammar rather than relying solely on reanalysis within a single dialect, as did his earlier studies. In the terms of Samuels (1972a) it is 'extrasystemic' rather than 'intrasystemic'.

Van der Wurff's scenario runs as follows. He imagines two networks of speakers, A and B, both of which used the prepositional passive, [115], but only one of which, a, had preposition stranding in infinitive clauses, [116]–[117]:

[115]   This was dealt with.
[116]   This is still to deal with.
        'This still has to be dealt with.'
[117]   This is easy to deal with.

Network A speakers analysed [115]–[117] as passives.[20] Network B speakers had a narrower range of passive constructions which did not extend to [116]–[117]. Van der Wurff then conjectures that construction [117] but *not* [116] might have been adopted by network B as a result of numerous weak-tie contacts with A-speakers. Lacking [116], the B-speakers could not interpret [117] as a passive and had therefore to analyse it as having undergone *Wh*-Movement. Once *Wh*-Movement was admitted into this area of their grammar, however, they (but not the A-speakers) could generate new sentences of the type

[118]   This is easy to get results with.

With the new analysis established in B, subsequent borrowing of the [116] type from A would have reinforced it.

There are two interesting features of this scenario. One is the curious leapfrog development, in which network A initially has the wider range of preposition stranding constructions and yet does not develop the last one, [118], because its underlying analysis of [115]–[117] would not permit it. The other is the proposal that surface patterns are likely to spread from one group of speakers to another in a particular order, specifically [115], then [117], and only later [116] (and perhaps in subsequent spread to a network C, [118]). The relative salience and frequency demanded do not seem implausible to my PDE intuitions, and the model of borrowing via weak ties holds out great promise.

7.5   The complex prepositional passive

A good account of the origins of the prepositional passive should carry over to the complex prepositional passive, a construction exemplified by:

[119]   The school was set fire to.
[120]   Jim was taken advantage of.

All the scholars mentioned in §7.4 claim to deal with both at once. Reanalysis now involves not a V-P unit but a V-X-P unit, of course, with X most often but not invariably nominal. Thus for [119]:

[121]   (a) $[_{VP} [_V set] [_{NP} fire] [_{PP} to [_{NP} the school]]]$
        (b) $[_{VP} [_V set fire to] [_{NP} the school]]$

If X is an adverbial particle we have a so-called **phrasal-prepositional verb**, FALL *in with*, PUT *up with*, etc. As I pointed out in Denison (1985a: §6), however, there is a problem with dates. Complex prepositional passives arrived much later than ordinary prepositional passives. For nominal X the first, mostly problematic passives are fourteenth century, and no other safe examples are found before the fifteenth century – a time lag of some 150 years from the appearance of the prepositional passive:

[122]   a1450(?1348) Rolle, *FLiving* 86.43

when any . . . haves envy to   þam þat es spokyn mare gode
when any . . . feel   envy towards them that are spoken more good

of þan of þam;
of than of them

'when any . . . are envious of those who are praised more than them'

[123]   a1425(a1382) *WBible(1)* I Sam.[=I Kings] 3.14

. . . that the wickidnes   of hys hows shal not be doon a seeth
. . . that the wickedness of his house shall not be made amends

before with slayn sacrifices . . .
for   with slain sacrifices . . .[21]

'that the wickedness of his house shall not be purged with sacrifices.'

[124]   ?c1450(?a1400) *Wycl. Clergy HP* 369.1

and þes   oþer wordis of þis bischop ouȝte to be taken hede to.
and these other words of this bishop ought to be taken heed to

[125]   c1440 *PLAlex.* 15.4

so thi   name &   thi   dedes schall be made mynde of to the
so your name and your deeds shall be made mind   of to the

worldes end.
world's end

'in the same way your name and your deeds shall be remembered to the end of the world'

Notice that [122] would be a perfect example were it not for the following *than*-clause, whose form is appropriate not to a preceding prepositional passive but to a clause with a normal PP (thus either a direct passive or an active). Precisely the same reluctance to embrace the prepositional passive fully is seen in this example of the simple prepositional passive:

[126]   c1450(c1400) *Vices and V. (2)* 131.33

for he was fouliche fare wiþ, as wiþ a þef.
for he was foully   dealt with as with a thief

Returning to the complex prepositional passive, for X = adverbial particle,[22] phrasal-prepositional verbs, passives do not appear until much later still:

[127]   c1613 (1502) *Plumpton Let.* 130 164.11

I understand there there [*sic*] was a servant of yours, and a kynsman of myne, was myschevously made away with

[128]   1662 Patrick, *Latitude-Men* 12.13

and then if their Neighbors will not follow their example, . . . they shall be cryed out on for disaffected;

[129]   1668 Pepys, *Diary* IX 45.11 (31 Jan)

and after it was read, the Deane made the service be gone through with

The absence of such passives when ordinary prepositional passives were proliferating is not due to lack of suitable idiomatic units in the active, so one must fall back for explanation on the lower overall frequencies of occurrence and on vagaries of survival of text. If simultaneity of appearance is such powerful corroboration of elegant generative analyses, this might be felt to be a disappointment.

7.6   Indirect and prepositional passives

For reasons already alluded to in Chapter 6, the temptation has been strong – and for most generative grammarians, irresistible – to provide a single explanation for the advent of indirect and prepositional (and indeed other) passives. The details vary quite considerably. We will start by recalling two discussions from outside the generative tradition, then move on to formal approaches, apart from one contribution in the Relational Grammar framework – that of Bennett – which is couched in fairly informal terms.

7.6.1   Marchand and de la Cruz

We saw in §6.3.3 how Marchand attempted to treat the indirect and prepositional passives alike by regarding both as the passive of a group-verb formed in the active from a verb and what he called a 'verb-auxiliary': verb + direct object and verb + preposition, respectively. His account of the indirect passive was decidedly strained. In §7.3.4 we discussed de la Cruz's attempt to bring the two constructions together by regarding both as instances of reanalysis in the passive. This time it was the prepositional passive for which the explanation was implausible. Non-generative work on these passives has not succeeded in providing a unified explanation of their histories.

7.6.2   Lightfoot (1979)

David Lightfoot gave a section of his influential book over to English passives (1979: §5.2.3), and all subsequent contributions make reference to it. His analysis makes great play of a distinction between **lexical** and **transformational** passives (1979: §5.2.2), drawing largely on Wasow (1977) (see Lieber 1979: 668 for an excellent summary). Simplifying greatly, we can state the distinction as follows. A lexical passive is derived by a local rule, that is, a rule which affects constituents (verb and NPs) that are grammatically related, so that the NP moved into subject position must be an *argument* of the passive verb. Lexical passives may be idiosyncratic, since the behaviour of each verb is stated in the lexicon. A transformational passive on the other hand is derived by a much more general syntactic process that moves an NP from the VP into subject position. The lexical ~ transformational distinction (which is theory-internal, of course) is said to correlate approximately with two other distinctions of more general application: those between stative and dynamic passives and between adjectival and verbal passives. These latter terms should be transparent. By and large, lexical, stative and adjectival go together, and likewise transformational, dynamic and verbal, but these are no more than associations – a transformational passive may be stative rather than dynamic in meaning, for instance. (See further Chapter 14 below.)

Lightfoot's original thesis, published in several forms but most conveniently available in Lightfoot (1979), is that Old and Middle English had only a lexical passive rule, so that nothing but direct objects of an active verb could be related to subjects of a passive. In the early ModE period – 'fifteenth to sixteenth centuries' – a transformational passive entered the grammar of English, accounting at a stroke for a number of simultaneous developments, amongst others the indirect and prepositional passives. Such an account fits in with a view of syntactic change influenced by Catastrophe Theory, a branch of mathematical topology. Independent, small-scale, random changes accumulate in a language over time, to the point where language learners constructing their own internal grammars make some radical alteration by comparison with previous generations, in order to render the grammar more 'transparent'. Such a change brings in its train a large number of simultaneous changes in the output of the grammar, that is, in attested utterances. Many scholars have doubted the alleged simultaneity of the developments that Lightfoot tries to bring together. As far as the indirect and prepositional passives are concerned, the dates revealed above in §§6.2.4, 7.2.1, 7.5 do not overlap very closely. We shall not pursue this version of Lightfoot's account any further, since he later made substantial theoretical changes.

7.6.3 Bennett

Paul Bennett works with the historical data of Lightfoot (and Visser) and largely accepts the ModE analysis proposed by Wasow. For two-place verbs Bennett explicitly claims that 'there is a remarkable coincidence in the dates at which unmarked (direct) objects appear with these verbs and the first occurrences of subjectful passives' (1980: 104). In other words, loss of dative inflections converts an indirect object into a direct object. A similar argument is advanced, more tentatively, for three-place verbs. Loss of explicit dative inflection, dated to 1150–1200, leads to the emergence of V-NP_i-NP_j structures where the NP_i is recipient (Benefactive). Bennett assumes that these are derived by Dative Shift (= Dative Movement) from the new V-NP_j-[$_{PP}$ *to*-NP_i] structures which emerged around the same time, and that the Benefactive NP_i in V-NP_i-NP_j is a (derived) *direct* object. His brief, conventional account of the prepositional passive likewise assumes that NPs can be direct objects of verb-preposition units. He accepts a distinction between lexical and transformational passives but finds no reason to doubt that both have been part of English grammar since OE times. His explanation for the emergence of new passive constructions is that the passive rules have always converted the direct object of an active verb into subject of the passive: all that is new is the increased scope of the relation 'direct object'. He shows that Lightfoot's use of the term 'direct object' is inconsistent and problematic, since direct object is not a *primitive* in TG. The analysis is rather reminiscent of Marchand's (cf. §6.3.3 above).

There are errors of fact in Bennett's analysis, however. His apparent examples of the indirect passive in Lay.*Brut*, taken direct from Visser, are all mistaken; the *Rich.* example, taken from van der Gaaf, is not morphologically unambiguous; and at least two of his prepositional passive examples are erroneous (1980: 105–6; cf. §6.3.2, Note 19 of Chapter 6, Note 1 of this chapter). The dates need adjustment too. Bennett says that '[t]he earliest examples of indirect object passives date from the same period as the establishment of the Dative alternation' (1980: 105). For GIVE verbs it seems that the Dative alternation, as he terms it, was uncommon before the fourteenth century (§6.2.2 above), while the indirect passive was not found until the late fourteenth and was uncommon till the fifteenth. It may still be possible to show that the two phenomena grew up together over the same period, but that period will be somewhat later than the loss of dative inflections and the emergence of direct passives for two-place verbs like HELPEN. Another problem, not necessarily damaging to the main line of reasoning, is that it seems somewhat contorted to have V-NP$_i$-NP$_j$ structures, abundant since OE times, suddenly becoming derived forms in Middle English – derived, moreover, from a nascent V-NP$_j$-*to*-NP$_i$ pattern which was at best infrequent as a surface string at the time.[23]

7.6.4 Lieber

Rochelle Lieber (1979) stays within the TG framework in her critique of Lightfoot (1979). Like Bennett she assumes that a transformational passive rule has been operative since Old English. Six kinds of passive, she says, should only be possible by virtue of a transformational passive rule: indirect passives, predicative passives (*John was considered a fool*), dynamic passives, raising passives (*John was expected to win*), complex prepositional passives, and prepositional passives. Her strategy is to show that they did not appear at the time – fifteenth to sixteenth centuries – required by Lightfoot's approach, often because they were already in existence in Old English. Her reasoning is clearly presented, but some crucial evidence is suspect.

Lieber demonstrates that predicative and dynamic passives were possible in Old English. She explains the uncertainties surrounding the analysis of putative raising passives in Old English and leaves open the question of whether they are an eModE innovation. (We also defer these matters to Chapters 8 and 9 below.) She points out that prepositional passives from the thirteenth and fourteenth centuries cannot be ignored. So far so good.

On complex prepositional passives she attacks Lightfoot from two sides.

First she suggests that they appeared too early: there are as many as fifteen examples in Visser from the fourteenth century. This is a legitimate criticism, since Lightfoot had argued that both kinds of passive in [130] should be derived transformationally (1979: 267–70):

[130] (a) John was found fault with.
       (b) Fault was found with John.

However, she does not observe that almost all of the early passives are of the (b) type, not the (a) (Denison 1985a: 202 n.9). Whether or not Lightfoot's analysis of [130](b) in Modern English is correct, *early* examples of the pattern are most simply taken as ordinary direct passives which have no bearing on the formation of a group-verb or the existence of a transformational passive rule. Then Lieber suggests that complex prepositional passives appeared too late, since 'the real period of growth seems to begin in the eighteenth and nineteenth centuries' (1979: 671). This is a genuine problem.

On indirect passives, however, her presentation is less happy, largely because her data is taken uncritically from Visser.[24] Lieber's transformational passive rule is merely Move NP (1979: 678), subject to such conditions as the *Case Filter*. (For brief discussion of Case Theory see §3.1.3.3 above.) Two-place verbs in Old English like HELPAN 'help' and three-place verbs like OFTEON 'withhold, take away' appear to fit the predictions of the theory. They assign dative case lexically in underlying structure, so the only passives of such verbs should be impersonal ones (1979: 681–5). (Apparent exceptions, namely personal (direct) passives, involve verbs which permit the alternative of accusative marking in the active for the argument which is passive subject: accusative, like nominative, is not lexically assigned but structural.) On the other hand the Benefactive NP argument of a three-place verb like GIEFAN 'give' is said to get its dative case at surface structure and not by lexical assignment (1979: 681). Therefore the indirect passive should have been possible in Old English, since a Benefactive moved to subject position will be assigned nominative case. Lieber claims that indirect passives were rare but attested in Old English (1979: 685–6). Her examples, all from Visser, have been thoroughly examined by Russom (1982) (overlapping partly with Mitchell 1979): none survives scrutiny.

7.6.5 Lightfoot (1981)

Lightfoot (1981) is a reformulation of his earlier proposals in the light of Lieber (1979) and other critiques. The date of introduction of a transformational passive rule, Move NP, is subtly shifted from 'fifteenth to sixteenth centuries' (1979: 278) via 'end of Middle English' (1981: 95) to 'late Middle English' (1981: 96), mitigating the force of some of the chronological objections. Then the date is abandoned altogether with the new claim that *all* passives are, and always have been, derived by Move NP (1981: 97–8). The explanation for the appearance of new surface types in Middle English must lie elsewhere, therefore.

The new explanation makes use of Abstract Case (recall §3.1.3 above).

Nominative case is assigned at surface structure under government by tense (**government** is a technical term which I shall not go into here): essentially, nominative case is assigned to the subject of a finite verb. Objective case is assigned structurally to an NP governed by V, effectively to the object of a verb, and in some languages (but not Old English) it may be assigned to the object of a preposition. Unlike nominative and objective, oblique case is assigned lexically in the base: this will account for datives and genitives in Old English assigned by verbs or prepositions, and notice that the Benefactive NP in a GIVE sentence is assumed to get its dative case by *lexical* assignment, *contra* Lieber. There can be no prepositional or indirect passive in Old English because a putative derivation of one would produce a case conflict on the moved NP: base-assigned oblique case but structural nominative case. The relevant historical changes in English are accounted for by assuming the loss of base-assigned oblique case (1981: 106), probably as a consequence of surface morphological changes in Middle English (1981: 107). The derivation of (complex) prepositional passives involves reanalysis *à la* Hornstein and Weinberg (1981), a process logically independent of, and perhaps prior to, loss of oblique case.[25] Schmerling (1981) points to some difficulties in the Lightfoot-Vat account of preposition stranding, and suggests that prepositional and indirect passives have rather different histories (1981: 124–5). Recently Lightfoot's explanation in terms of abstract case has been developed by Roberts (1985a) in an obscurely published paper. A similar theory, though with greater semantic sophistication, is put forward by Fischer and van der Leek (1987), involving the loss of 'adverbial Case' on bare NPs.

Even though Lightfoot's later theory makes use of the loss of abstract Oblique case rather than the introduction of Move NP, it is still a 'catastrophic' explanation which predicts near-simultaneity of change in various parts of the grammar – unless, that is, the ability to govern Oblique case can be lost verb by verb rather than 'across the board'.

7.7 Questions for discussion or further research

(a) Does the history of the prepositional passive suggest across-the-board introduction or lexical diffusion? What are the consequences for synchronic linguistic theory?

(b) What is the significance of negative data, for example the lack of prepositional passives in Old English, or the near-absence of complex prepositional passives from fourteenth- and fifteenth-century material? (Consider here Lieber 1979: 671–2, Lightfoot 1981: 115–16 n.7, Warner 1982: 2–6, and §7.5 above.)

(c) Can the origins of the prepositional and indirect passives in English be given a unified explanation?

(d) Can the origins of the prepositional passives in English and in Scandinavian be given a unified explanation? Should they?

(e) What part should semantic factors play in an account of the prepositional passive?

(f) Visser suggests that in the sixteenth century the prepositional passive 'appears to have been a special favourite in familiar letters and other texts written in a colloquial style' (1963–73: §1953). Comment on the correctness, and – if it is correct – the significance, of this observation.

Notes

1. The often-cited example of LETEN *of* from *Ancr.* is not passive at all: see discussion of [86] and Note 11. My list is based on Visser's citations with composition dates up to c1400 (1963–73: §§1950–51), discounting the erroneous *leten of (Ancr.)*, *ronnen aboute (Cursor)*, *seruede with-alle* (Mannyng *HS*), *ymedlid wiþ* (Trev.*Barth.*), the unsafe *smyten þorgh* (Mannyng *Chron.Pt.2*), *forgiven till (Cursor)*, and the wrongly attributed *lukede to* (c1440 Hilton *ML*(Thrn), given as 1340 Rich. Rolle). I include four citations in P-V order from his §1947, namely a1400(a1325) *Cursor* 8324 (SPEKEN *of*), ibid. 14216 (SENDEN *after*), ?a1400(a1338) Mannyng *Chron.Pt.2* 195.13 (LETEN *of*), c1450(c1380) Chaucer *HF* textual note to 911–12 (SPEKEN *of*), and add the following: c1225 *St Juliana*(Roy) 22.195 (FAREN *wið*), ?c1430(c1383) *Wycl.Leaven Pharisees* 7.29 (DISPENSEN *wiþ*), c1400 *Pep.Gosp.* 44.9, c1450(1352–c1370) *Winner and W.* 27 (LETEN *of*), ?a1425(c1380) Chaucer *Bo* 4.pr1.22 (WONDER *uppon*), c1390 Hilton *ML* 272.37 (TENDEN *to*), c1450(c1400) *Vices and V.(2)* 131.33 (FAREN *wiþ*), c1400(?a1387) *PPl.C* 3.204 (LETEN *by*).
2. The only items which normally intervene between P and V are the *to* of an infinitive or the *ne* of a negative, both **proclitic**, that is, unstressed and phonologically part of V.
3. An argument that the category 'separable compound verb' is redundant and indeed unworkable in the description of OE syntax is given in Denison (1981: 53–60).
4. Van der Gaaf probably did not mean the claim to apply to *all* relative clauses with preposition stranding, as I assumed in earlier work (Denison 1981; 1985a: 192). In Denison (1981: 237–43) I gave some statistical backing to my claim that stranding in relatives is a consequence of choice of relativiser and not (at least before the prepositional verb became established) of mutual V-P attraction.
5. The main ones are III 139, 161, 184–95, 252–77, 312–17; V 483–7; VII 72–6.
6. His many articles on verb-particle constructions are based – without explicit acknowledgement – on an unpublished thesis (de la Cruz Fernández, 1969), which is full of valuable insights but tiresome to use. Terminological idiosyncrasies in de la Cruz's work include 'preverbial structures' for compound verbs, 'prepositional object' for both particle and NP rather than just NP, 'phrasal verb' for all verb-particle constructions, 'phrasal verb proper' for phrasal verb.
7. To make the distinction clear, compare:

   (a) He called his friend up.
   (b) He called on his friend.

   CALL *up* is a phrasal verb, CALL *on* is a prepositional verb.
8. A **simplex** verb has neither a prefixal nor a prepositional particle.
9. If topicalisation occurs it is the whole PP which is fronted:

   (a) (c1390) Chaucer, *CT.Mcp.* IX.226

   To Alisaundre was toold this sentence, that . . .
   to Alexander was told this maxim   that. . .

10. The case role Stimulus seems quite similar to the Cause role discussed for impersonal verbs in the previous chapter. Couper-Kuhlen finds that PDE

prepositional passives are possible when the active subject is Experiencer and the passive subject Stimulus, and when the active subject is Agentive and the passive subject Benefactive, Comitative, Goal, Instrument, Objective/Patient, or Replacive (1979: 90–7).

11. LETEN *of* probably means 'behave' here, as in the near-contemporary French translation of this passage and as at *Ancr.* 36a.18, although it could also means 'think of (herself)', cf. example [91] below. Either way *leoten* is an infinitive, not a past participle, and *of* is elliptical.

12. Thornburg's examples (4, 5, 8, 16, 36, 38, 39) are misclassified or inappropriately glossed.

13. Allen considers the possibility of a landing site at the front of S', before COMP (1980b: 272).

14. Absence of *that* in [93](c,d) in Modern English is handled by a prohibition on doubly filled COMP in surface form: one at most of *that* and a *wh* pronoun can remain.

15. Visser (1963–73: §412a) implies that the construction is hardly known before Shakespeare, but more ME examples appear in his §632, apparently independently compiled. Further early examples include:

(a=56)   a1225(?a1200) Lay.*Brut* 15517

nis   nan feirure wifmon: þa whit sunne scineð on
not-is no fairer woman the white sun   shines on

'there is no fairer woman the bright sun shines on'

(b)   (c1300) *Havelok* 253

þe knictes he micte tristen to
the knights he might trust   in

(c)   c1400(?c1380) *Cleanness* 62

Alle excused hem   by þe skyly he scape by moʒt.
all   excused themselves by the skill he escape by might

'Each excused himself with the pretext by which he might escape.'

16. The particle *þe* in Old English is a relativiser showing no case/gender/number variation; it also appears as a constituent of many subordinating conjunctions. Thus it seems quite appropriate to take *þe* as the equivalent of ModE *that* and to analyse them similarly. However, relative clauses in Old English could also be formed using the demonstrative SE, with or without *þe*. SE inflected for case, gender and number, and its case marking as sole relativiser was determined by its rôle in the relative clause (Mitchell 1985: §2123). Hence SE is a rough equivalent of later *wh-* relatives with their *who/whom* (case) and *who/which* ('gender') alternations. When SE + *þe* was used to form relative clauses, the case of SE was that appropriate either to both clauses or to the **higher** clause alone (Mitchell 1985: §2154). Allen gives a reason for treating *þe* in combination with SE as a complementiser and suggests that the SE relative was essential a SE *þe* relative with *þe* deleted (1980b: 272).

17. Actually there are some instances of *nouns* preceding their governing prepositions: see Mitchell (1978: 250–2).

18. I have made trivial corrections to van Kemenade's diagram [105](b).

19. Hornstein and Weinberg (1981) refer to Weinberg and Hornstein (forthcoming) 'Reanalysis as a parameter of grammar'. I have been unable to trace this paper.

20. The infinitive is passive in the technical, GB sense of not case-marking its direct object NP (which must therefore move to a case-marked position), and the infinitive is head of an S and not contained in an S'.

21. Example [123] is problematic. To interpret it as a complex prepositional passive we must assume that *before* is being used in the place of *for*: the normal phrase is DON *asseth for* 'make amends for' (*MED* s.v. *asseth* n.2). But I can find no record of such a substitution.

22. A number of combinations like SET *light/little/much/more by/of* are found in prepositional passives from the later fourteenth century (Visser 1963–73: §1986). Different examples could be classified as ordinary V-P passives with optional adverbial, as complex V-X-P passives with X = adverbial, or as V-X-P passives with X = NP.

23. Note, however, that Fischer and van der Leek also distinguish between the V-NP$_i$-NP$_j$ structures of Old English and those of later English (1987: 116 n.25), though on different grounds.

24. Visser cannot be blamed for her apparent attribution to Old English of several crucial examples from *Orm.*, a text that is firmly early Middle English.

25. Van Kemenade follows Lightfoot in finding significance in the alleged fact that both new kinds of preposition stranding (in *wh*-constructions and in the prepositional passive) appeared 'simultaneously' (1987: 213). However, as far as reanalysis is concerned she writes (1987: 212):

> The fact that V and P are adjacent, and assign θ-role in the same direction, and that this case is exclusively structural, paves the way for a rule of V-P reanalysis along the lines of Hornstein and Weinberg [(1981)]

In other words, for her the loss of abstract case was one of the prerequisites for reanalysis.

Part IV

COMPLEX COMPLEMENTATION

Overview

Where Part III concentrated on the relationship between a verb and its (mostly) nominal **arguments**, Part IV deals with verbs (**catenatives**) which have one argument that is sentential. We concentrate on embedded clauses headed by an infinitive, leaving aside other kinds of complex complementation – by *-ing* forms, past participle forms, finite clauses. Infinitive clauses are of major interest in their own right, and they provide the background for the rise of some of the auxiliary verbs studied in Part V.

Chapter 8, VOSI and V+I, discusses various types of construction of the pattern V̲erb + O̲bject/S̲ubject + I̲nfinitive, as in

[1]   Alex told Jezebel to concentrate on her homework.

where the NP *Jezebel* appears to be both object of the verb *told* and subject of the infinitive *concentrate*. It also looks at what I call the V+I (catenative verb + infinitive) pattern, where there is no object/subject NP intervening between verb and infinitive, and takes a special interest in examples like [3] where the subject of the *higher* verb and understood subject of the infinitive are not the same:

[2]   Miriam wanted to follow her brother.
[3]   Amy said to be careful.

Sentence patterns like [1]–[3] are sometimes referred to as *Control* structures, since the empty pronoun subject of the infinitive assumed by *GB theory* may be 'controlled by' an NP in the higher clause (*Jezebel* in [1], *Miriam* in [2], but arbitrary in [3]). The V+I pattern will turn out to be of importance in the origins of DO (Chapter 10).

Chapter 9, Subject Raising, also concerns sentences with a verb followed by an infinitive and hence superficially like [2] and [3], but here with the understood subject of the infinitive clearly the same as the surface subject of the higher verb:

[4]   Weeds seem to thrive in my garden.

The difference between [2] and [4] has to do with the semantic role of the higher subject NP: in [2] it is an argument of the higher verb, in [4] not. The name Subject Raising refers to a grammatical process said to raise an NP out of underlying subject position in the embedded clause into subject position in the higher clause. The history of Subject Raising interacts particularly with that of impersonals (Chapter 5), control verbs (Chapter 8), and modals (Chapter 11).

Chapter 8

VOSI and V+I (control verbs)

8.1 The problem

The patterns which we shall study in this chapter can be exemplified in Present-day English (PDE) by [1]:

[1] (a)   Bob expected Liz to bring the car.
     (b)   Bob said to bring the car.

What [1](a,b) have in common is an infinitival clause embedded in the VP of a *higher* clause, the underlying subject of the infinitive differing from that of the higher verb. Where they differ is in whether the subject of the infinitive is explicit (present in surface structure) or implicit ('understood', absent in surface structure). The surface patterns can be formulated as in [2]:

[2] (a)   . . . V NP (*to*) V_{INF} . . .
     (b)   . . . V (*to*) V_{INF} . . .

There are many labels in use, none wholly satisfactory; pattern [2](a) in particular has long been known as the **accusative cum** (or **and**) **infinitive** or **aci**. Visser talks of 'indirect consecution' of higher verb and infinitive and calls pattern [2](a) **VOSI** (= Verb + Object/Subject + Infinitive), his name for the NP intended to suggest that it is simultaneously object of the higher verb and subject of the infinitive (1963–73: §2055). Despite Mitchell's legitimate objection to the term (1985: §3722, etc.), I shall adopt it *faute de mieux* and use the analogous term V+I (not in general use) for the direct consecution of pattern [2](b), confining attention to instances where V (higher verb) and I (*lower* verb) do not share the same underlying subject. My working assumption is that the V+I type is parasitic on the VOSI type.

The VOSI pattern was less freely and less often used in Old and Middle English than it is in PDE, whereas V+I was *more* widespread then than now. The problems addressed in this chapter, then, are the rise of the VOSI pattern in at least some of its variant types, and the decline of the V+I pattern. (In relation to the particular verb DO the converse questions come up in Chapter 10.)

Note that I shall include under VOSI those patterns where the object-subject NP is not actually located in between the two verbs, as in

[3]   a1425 *Wycl.Serm.* I 12.56

for men deef in Godis lore   he made to here what God spaak in
for men deaf to God's teaching he made to hear what God spoke in

hem, . . .
them . . .

'For he made men who were deaf to God's teaching hear what God
spoke in them . . .'

[4]   c1640 Jonson, *Discoveries* VIII 621.1889

Words . . . are to be chose according to the persons wee make speake

[5]   (the actor) who we expected to appear
[6]   We never expected to appear such an incredibly inept bunch of amateurs.

Rearrangement of the strict order higher V – OBJ-SUBJ NP – INF occurs
most readily in Old English, though as [5]–[6] illustrate, *Wh*-Movement and
Heavy-NP Shift can affect VOSI order even in PDE. Conversely, there are
OE and ME examples where an NP, though appearing between the two
verbs, does not function as subject of the lower verb (most often it is *object*
of the lower verb). In such cases the NP does not count towards a VOSI
analysis and we have a V+I pattern. See further §8.3.2 below.

We exclude examples containing an infinitive of purpose (or 'final
infinitive'), though the borderline is not always clearcut:

[7]   Sally invited her brother to save money.
[8]   Peter took his children to see the circus.

Example [7] is ambiguous between a VOSI and an infinitive of purpose,
depending on whether the brother or Sally is to save money. One test in
PDE for an infinitive of purpose is that *in order to* makes an acceptable
substitute for *to*. Example [8] is near the borderline.

8.2   VOSI

8.2.1   Object control and Object raising

The VOSI pattern is very widespread, and many grammarians recognise two
or three major variants in PDE, exemplified by [9]–[11] below:

[9]   Bob expected Liz to tickle Jim.
[10]   Bob persuaded Liz to tickle Jim.
[11]   Bob saw Liz drive away.

Let us begin with the difference in PDE between [9] and [10].

It has been widely assumed that there is a difference in complementation
between EXPECT and PERSUADE. In the VOSI construction EXPECT is a two-
place[1] verb: its two **arguments** are an Experiencer (*Bob*) and a clausal
Source (*Liz to tickle Jim*). The NP sandwiched between higher and lower
verb (*Liz*) is an argument only of the lower verb. PERSUADE, on the other
hand, is a three-place verb: its three arguments are an Agent (*Bob*), a
Recipient or Theme (*Liz*), and a clausal Theme or Goal (*Liz to tickle Jim*).[2]

The NP sandwiched between the verbs has two semantic roles and is separately an argument of each verb. The two structural patterns can be represented in various ways. In transformational theory, for example, the structure of [9] is roughly:[3]

[12] Bob$_i$ [$_{VP}$ expected [$_{S'}$ [$_S$ Liz$_j$ to tickle Jim$_k$]]]

There is, however, some syntactic evidence that the NP *Liz* can behave like an object of the higher verb. This is handled in some grammars by assuming a syntactic rule that raises the NP out of the lower clause and into the higher clause, a rule often known as **Raising to object** (see §8.2.4 below). Example [9] is therefore an 'Object raising' sentence.

The structure of [10], on the other hand, is:

[13] Bob$_i$ [$_{VP}$ persuaded Liz$_j$ [$_{S'}$ [$_S$ PRO$_j$ to tickle Jim$_k$]]]

The element PRO is a pronominal *anaphor* with no phonological form in surface structure, **controlled** by – that is to say, co-indexed with and taking its reference from – the NP *Liz* which is object of PERSUADE. Control theory is a module of the GB framework which provides a semantic explanation of our knowledge that the object of PERSUADE and the subject of TICKLE have the same referent. Older versions of transformational grammar, before the invention of PRO, required a second occurrence of *Liz* in deep structure in the embedded clause, deleted by a rule known as 'Equivalent NP deletion' or 'Equi'. Whether the relationship between the two argument positions is handled by rules of interpretation ('object control') or by rules of syntax ('Equi') need not trouble us here. The jargon 'Equi-construction' is still in wide use for sentences like [10].[4]

In Present-day English there are a number of differences between [9] and [10] which have been used as diagnostics for structure. I give a selection in [14]:

[14] (a) *commutation* of the embedded infinitival clause with an NP
      (b) paraphrase relation with a finite clause
      (c) paraphrase relation if the embedded clause is passivised
      (d) selectional restrictions imposed by higher verb on following NP
      (e) possibility of dummy NP *there* or *it* in that position
      (f) use of reflexive pronouns to test for clause membership
      (g) behaviour in 'pseudo-cleft' construction
      (h) passivisation in higher clause (sometimes called 'second passive')
      (i) intuition about number of semantic roles associated with higher verb

Examples to illustrate these tests are given in [15], using '*' for non-acceptability, '?' for dubious acceptability, and '!' for inappropriateness as paraphrase:

[15] (a)   Bob expected/*persuaded a scandal.
      (a′) Bob *expected/persuaded Liz of his rightness/to his point of view.
      (b)   Bob ?expected/*persuaded that Liz should tickle Jim.
      (b′) Bob *expected/persuaded Liz that she should tickle Jim.
      (c)   Bob expected/!persuaded Jim to be tickled by Liz.
      (d)   Bob expected/*persuaded a scandal to ensue.

(e)   Bob expected/*persuaded it to rain.
(e')   Bob expected/*persuaded there to be a scandal.
(f)   Bob expected/persuaded himself to tickle Jim.
(f')   Bob expected/persuaded Liz to tickle herself/*himself.
(g)   What Bob expected/*persuaded was (for) Liz to tickle Jim.
(g')   What Bob *expected/?persuaded Liz was for her to tickle Jim.
(h)   Liz was expected/persuaded to tickle Jim.
(i)   EXPECT: expecter, expectation
(i')   PERSUADE: persuader, persuadee, suggestion

Tests [14](c–e), for example, suggest strongly that the NPs between the two verbs – *Liz/Jim, a scandal, it,* respectively, in [15](c–e) – are arguments of PERSUADE but not of EXPECT.

There has been wide agreement on the basic difference between two- and three-place verbs with infinitival complementation, though there are problems with verbs of the ALLOW, ORDER type, which show conflicting evidence of both two- and three-place use. For further, relatively theory-neutral discussion see the chapter on 'The Catenatives' in Palmer (1988).

8.2.2 Perception verbs

In the tests of [14] above, perception verbs like SEE tend to pattern more like EXPECT than PERSUADE, but they also show conflicting evidence of three-place use. An example like [11] would normally imply that Bob saw Liz. We may contrast this with

[16]   Bob believed Liz to be a liar.

which of course does not entail that Bob believed Liz. BELIEVE is clearly a two-place verb. Does it follow, then, that SEE is a three-place verb, with the sandwiched NP, *Liz,* a separate object of the perception verb as well as subject of the embedded clause? Probably not, since the seeing of Liz is not really separable from seeing her drive away. Contrast

[17]   Bob persuaded Liz to run away.

where the persuasion and the running away are conceptually separable, for example by happening at different times. This is not true of SEE + NP + infinitive. Semantically, then, perception verbs are probably two-place, and finite clause complements generally support a two-place analysis.

Note, however, that Mitchell (1985: §§3734–8) gets entangled in this question for Old English, and Kopytko (1985) actually asserts that perception verbs have been three-place throughout the history of English on the basis of such ME evidence as:

[18]   a1425(a1382) *WBible(1)* Gen. 12.14

Egipciens sawen the woman that she was ful   fayre;
Egyptians saw   the woman that she was very beautiful

'The Egyptians beheld the woman that she was very fair.'

Here we have both an NP object and a (finite) clausal complement of SEE, which might suggest – as with test [14](b) above – that SEE is like

PERSUADE. However, these patterns look much more like Warner's CLAN-sentences, in which NP and clause are not really independent arguments (§8.8.2.3 below). Fischer's rejoinder (1987) to Kopytko makes a convincing case for SEE being two-place even in examples like [18].

Another difference between EXPECT and perception verbs like SEE is that the latter take a plain rather than *to*-infinitive, except when in the passive. This property applies also to the causatives LET and MAKE, which seem to fall somewhere between the EXPECT and PERSUADE patterns. All in all the oldest causatives have a lot in common with perception verbs. On the possible significance of *to*-infinitive vs. plain infinitive see §8.9 below.

VOSI with perception verbs goes back at least to Germanic (Mustanoja 1960: 526–7).

8.2.3 Subject Control

With a few three-place verbs the sandwiched NP in the VOSI construction is co-referential not with the object (Recipient) of the higher verb but with its subject (Agent):

[19] Max promised Jim to return the car.

to be analysed as

[20] Max$_i$ promised Jim$_j$ [PRO$_i$ to return the car$_k$]

PROMISE can also be used without expressed Recipient:

[21] Max promised to return the car.

Subject Control verbs will not be studied in detail.

8.2.4 Raising to object

Raising to object is a somewhat theory-bound analysis which concerns two-place verbs in patterns like [15](e,f,h). The sandwiched NP, *Ted* in [22] below, is claimed to have no direct underlying relation to the higher verb. Yet sometimes that NP appears to behave like a genuine direct object of the higher verb, as with reflexivisation in the parallel [23], which on certain assumptions implies that *Bob* and *himself* must be clausemates:

[22] Bob expected Ted to get elected.
[23] Bob expected himself to get elected.

That in turn implies that the NP had been raised out of the embedded clause into object position in the higher clause.

Important evidence comes from dummy subjects like *it* and *there*. In simple clauses these are always in subject position, so the natural assumption in examples like:

[24] I expected it to rain.
[25] I expected there to be trouble.

is that there too they originate in subject position in the lower clause. If such dummy NPs behave elsewhere like direct objects of the higher verb, as in passives like:

[26]   It was expected to rain.

this is taken as good evidence of Raising to object. Allen (1984) gathers some historical data on examples like [24]–[26].

The standard account of Object raising is Postal (1974), heavily criticised by Lightfoot (1976). Fischer points out that GB theory disallows Object raising, since it would involve movement to a θ-*position* (1989: 185 n.39). For discussion of further problems with Subject-to-object raising see Radford (1988: 549–51). One is that the theory disallows movement across an S′ boundary, to which the answer is either to delete the S′ node transformationally – see §8.7.3.1 below – or to do without it altogether by saying that two-place verbs are complemented by an *exceptional clause* (Radford 1988: 317–24). These expedients enable the subject of the lower verb to take part in passivisation or reflexivisation in the higher clause, because there is no S′ boundary to cross. In demonstrating a distinction between two-place verbs and control verbs, Radford confines himself to the most convincing two-place examples, namely verbs of saying and thinking like KNOW. Use of VOSI with these verbs is rather uncommon outside formal usage. However, the example verb we have been using, EXPECT, is probably intended to be analysed in the same way. Verbs like WANT go like EXPECT in the earlier transformational accounts, but they are classed separately in some more recent versions (e.g. Chomsky 1981), which assume an underlying *for* in the COMP of the embedded clause, an analysis no doubt suggested by the Americanism

[27]   Jim wanted for me to leave.

In this analysis there is virtually a prepositional verb WANT *for*, like HOPE *for*, with *for* deletable under certain circumstances.

8.3   V+I

8.3.1   Present-day English

In most PDE instances of a verb followed directly by an infinitive, the underlying subject of the infinitive is the same as that of the higher verb:

[28]   Bob can drive the car.
[29]   Bob expects to drive the car.

The V+I type with underlying subject of the infinitive *different* from the subject of the higher verb is more or less confined in PDE to constructions involving HELP, SAY, and fossilised constructions like HEAR *tell*, LET *go*, MAKE *believe*, MAKE *do*:

[30=1(b)]   Bob said to bring the car.
[31]   Bob helped (to) load the car.
[32]   Bob let go immediately.
[33]   Bob made believe that all was well.

In this chapter we shall be concerned only with V+I structures like [30]–[33], not the far more common [28]–[29].

The structural analysis of [30] is unclear. We could make these assumptions:

(A) that there is an underlying Recipient argument, as overtly expressed in the corresponding TELL sentence:

[34] Bob told Paul to bring the car.

(B) that such a Recipient would be co-referential with the subject of the lower verb.

Then we could posit the following structure:

[35] Bob$_i$ [$_{VP}$ said pro$_j$ [$_{S'}$ [$_S$ PRO$_j$ to bring the car]]]

However, the pronominal *pro* ('little pro') cannot – as it should – commute with a full NP:

[36] *Bob said Paul to bring the car.

and [36] becomes only marginally acceptable with the NP *Paul* replaced by a PP *to Paul*. This casts doubt on assumption A. An analysis along the lines of [35] looks more promising for [31] – at least the version with *to*:

[37] Bob$_i$ [$_{VP}$ helped pro$_j$ [$_{S'}$ [$_S$ PRO$_j$ to load the car$_k$]]]

Arguably PRO has a split antecedent here – PRO$_{i+j}$ – in that Bob too does some loading, blending Subject and Object Control, which would jeopardise assumption B.

Alternatively we could attempt a two-place analysis with the arbitrary element as subject of the lower verb:

[38] Bob$_i$ [$_{VP}$ said [$_{S'}$ [$_S$ PRO$_{arb}$ to bring the car]]]

However, PRO$_{arb}$ is not appropriate in GB theory for reference which is not truly arbitrary, and little pro must be used (cf. §10.3.5.2). However, the lower subject position in [38] is an ungoverned position and pro cannot appear there. Perhaps SAY governs an exceptional clause:

[39] Bob$_i$ [$_{VP}$ said [$_S$ pro to bring the car]]

How then would we guarantee a non-lexical subject for the lower clause? I leave further consideration of these analyses.

8.3.2 Old English

There has been much argument over whether the dependent infinitive in a V+I construction should ever be regarded as passive in function even when active in form. The question arises in relation to examples like the following, where the object of the lower verb is placed before it:

[40] *GD* 341.36

| gif | hi | letað | hi | selfe | bebyrgan | on | haligre | stowe |
| if | they | cause | them | selves(ACC) | bury(INF) | in | holy | place |

'if they have themselves buried in holy ground'

mainly because the readiest translation into modern English (though not German or French) involves a passive in the embedded clause, which seems a poor reason for calling something 'passive'. I have never had difficulty in regarding an infinitive like *bebyrgan* in [40] as active in sense as well as in form. For complementary defences of this viewpoint and references to other voices from both camps see Fischer (1991: §§0, 2.3.3.2) and Mitchell (1985: §§3762–5, 937–43). A possible late example with this word order is:

[41]   1667 Pepys, *Diary* VIII 24.31 (22 Jan)

> I heard them [*sc.* a set of lessons] play[ed] to the Duke of York this Christmas at his lodgings

where the past participle ending on *play* is apparently editorial and may be unnecessary.

8.4   The data

Useful sources of examples include Callaway's monograph (1913), which surveys virtually the whole OE corpus and moreover gives a complete listing of citations; and Visser (1963–73), who covers all historical periods. Both authors organise their material by means of a semantic classification of the higher verb plus some formal distinctions. Zeitlin (1908) is another convenient source of citations. Only some of the PDE diagnostics listed and illustrated in [14]–[15] can be applied to historical material in order to determine argument structure.

8.4.1   VOSI

See Callaway (1913: 107–31), Visser (1963–73: §§2055–81).

8.4.1.1   VOSI with causatives

The VOSI construction is found in Old English with the causative LÆTAN and a few other verbs:

[42]   *ChronE* 116.10 (963)

> & leot   him locon þa gewrite þe ær   wæron gefunden
> and caused him look-at the writings that earlier were   found

> 'and had him look at the writs which had been found'

[43]   *ÆCHom* I 31.468.20

> Swa swa ðu dydest minne broðor his god forlætan . . .
> as   as you made   my   brother his god forsake . . .

> 'Just as you made my brother forsake his god . . .'

Scholars differ on which other verbs to include in the class, for example BEBEODAN, which occurs with inanimate sandwiched NPs in [54]–[56]. It is conjoined with HATAN in:

[44]   *Bede(B)* 1 7.36.30

het   ða & bebead raðe   menn swingan   & tintregian ðone
ordered then and ordered quickly men beat(INF) and torture   the

Godes andettere
god's confessor/praiser

Lat. cædi sanctum Dei confessorem a tortoribus præcepit

'he quickly ordered and commanded men to beat and torture the praiser of God'

(In the base MS. *menn* is omitted from [44], making this a V+I construction.)

New items entered the list of causative verbs during the ME period, including CAUSE (but see §8.8.1.2), GER, GET, HAVE, MAKE, SUFFRE, while DO continued to be used as a causative until the sixteenth century:

[45]   (a1399) *Form Cury* 2.59.5

& after   do   it boyle in god   breth of buf oþer of pork.
and afterwards make it boil in good broth of beef or   of pork

[46]   a1425 *Wycl.Serm.* I 12.55

for he made   deef men to here
for he caused deaf men to hear

[47]   (a1449) Lydg. *Epistle Sibille* 18

femyninytee | Cawseþe slowþe frome housholdes for to flee
femininity   causes   sloth   from households   to flee

[48]   (c1300) *Havelok* 189

Þer-on   he garte þe erl suere | Þat
on-it [*sc.* the massbook, etc] he made the earl swear that

he sholde . . .
he would . . .

[49]   (c1300) *Havelok* 542

Jesu Crist, þat makede to go | Þe halte and þe doumbe
Jesus Christ who made   to walk the halt and the dumb

speken, . . .
speak . . .

'Jesus Christ, who made the lame walk and the dumb speak, . . .'

[50]   ?a1425(c1380) Chaucer, *Bo.* 1.m7.18

lat non of thise foure passiouns overcomen the or blenden the
let none of these four passions overcome you or blind   you

[51]   ?c1425(?c1400) *Loll.Serm.* 1.237

but þorou   true prechynge of Goddes word þei   maden many
but through true preaching of God's   word they made many

þousendes come to feiþ, and leue   here erroures, and be
thousands come to faith and leave-behind their errors   and be

baptised;
baptised

One test for causative rather than three-place status is an embedded clause which does not express an action that can be executed or controlled in some way by its subject (Fischer 1992b: 52), as in (theology apart):

[52]   a1500(a1460) *Towneley Pl.* 298.166

Bot to the Iues I gaf   counsayll | That thay shuld cause hym dy;
But to the Jews I gave counsel   that they should cause him die

'But I advised the Jews to have him put to death'

[53]   a1500(?c1400) *Florence* 92

Many a crowne Y schall gar   crake
many a crown I shall cause crack

'I shall cause many a crown to crack'

Most passive infinitives would pass that test. Conversely, it might be argued that [48] shows a three-place verb rather than a causative.

The following OE examples appear to show an inanimate sandwiched NP, which is taken as an indication of a two-place higher verb:

[54]   *And* 729

Nu ic bebeode beacen   ætywan, | wundor   geweorðan on
now I command beacon(s) show(INF) wonder(s) happen   in

wera   gemange
men(GEN PL) midst

'Now I command tokens to appear, marvels to take place among men'

[55]   *Ps* 41.9

On dæg bebead God his mildheortnesse cuman   to me
in day ordered God his mercy   come(INF) to me

'In the daytime God commanded his mercy to come to me.'

[56]   *Ps* 43.6

þu þe bebude   hælo   cuman   to Iacobes cynne
you who commanded well-being come(INF) to Jacob's kin

[57]   *HomU* 34 (Nap 42) 196.1

and treowa   he deð   færlice   blowan
and trees(ACC) he causes suddenly bloom(INF)

'and he makes trees burst into bloom'

[58]   *MSol* 100

. . . læteð flint brecan | scines sconcan
. . . causes rock break(INF) devil's legs

'. . . makes a rock break the devil's legs'

And for some scholars occurrence with a plain rather than *to*-infinitive can be an indication of causative status.

8.4.1.2 VOSI with perception verbs

The VOSI construction is normal from the earliest records with a plain infinitive, though a *to*-infinitive is now used where the perception verb is in the passive:

[59] *Bede* 2 23.144.4

> þære gen to dæge mæg mon geseon þa weallas stondan
> there still today can one see the walls stand(INF)

[60] *Bede* 4 21.322.2

> þa semninga gehyrdon we þa abbudissan inne hludre stefne
> then suddenly heard we the abbess inside loud voice
>
> cleopian . . .
> call(INF)
>
> 'then suddenly we heard the abbess calling inside in a loud voice . . .'

[61] *ÆCHom* I 2.42.26

> Þa geseah heo þæt cild licgan on binne, ðær . . .
> then saw she the child lie in manger where . . .

[62] *BlHom* 15.14

> gehyrde myccle menigo him beforan feran
> heard great multitude him before go
>
> 'He heard a great multitude go in front of him'

[63] ?c1425(?c1400) *Loll.Serm.* 2.674

> whanne ʒe seon þese dredful tokenes biginne to come
> when you see these dreadful tokens begin to appear

For further examples see Visser (1963–73: §2067).

8.4.1.3 VOSI with two-place verbs (≠ causatives or perception verbs)

VOSI is rare in Old English with two-place verbs other than perception verbs and causatives and is virtually confined to Latin-influenced texts:

[64] *ÆColl* 203

> . . . ic hæbbe afandod þe habban gode geferan . . .
> . . . I have proved you have(INF) good companions . . .
>
> Lat. . . . probaui te habere bonos socios . . .
>
> '. . . I have proved you to have good companions . . .'

[65] *PsCaA* 1 (Kuhn) 13.5

> ... ðorh   ðone   usic arisan   holde mode   we
> ... through him/whom us arise(INF) devout mind(INST) we
> gelefað
> believe

Lat . . . per quem nos resurgere deuota mente credimus

'. . . we devoutly believe that through him we will rise again'

For poetic examples after WITAN 'know' see Fischer (1989: 201–2):

[66] *Jul* 91

> ... þær he glædmode   geonge   wiste | wic
> ... where he gentle-minded young(ACC) knew   dwelling-place
> weardian.
> inhabit(INF)

'. . . where he knew that the gentle-minded young woman lived'

VOSI with verbs of saying and thinking is hardly found in the early ME period, in poetry mainly in one poem closely based on its Latin model (Bock 1931: 231):

[67] a1325(c1250) *Gen. and Ex.* 2632

> Ghe wiste of   water it boren ben.
> she knew from water it born   be

'She knew it [*sc.* the child Moses] to have been born from water.'

[68] a1450(a1338) Mannyng, *Chron.Pt.1* 3861

> Elydour feyned hym   sik to lye | & seide he hopede forto deye.
> Elidour feigned himself sick to lie and said he expected to   die

'Elidour pretended to be lying sick and said that he expected to die.'

[69] a1400(a1325) *Cursor* 17981

> Helle, make þe   redy | To receyue iesu hastily, |Þat boost
> Hell   make yourself ready to receive Jesus shortly   who boasts
> him   goddes sone to be.
> himself God's son to be

'Hell, make yourself ready to receive Jesus shortly, who boasts that he is the Son of God.'

Bock argues from this distribution that this construction had died out in spoken language since the OE period (1931: 231). In later Middle English examples are a little easier to find. The following examples are cited by Bock (1931: 239, 242), Warner (1982: 147/247 n.5) or Fischer (1992b):

[70] ?a1425(c1380) Chaucer, *Bo.* 5.pr3.99

> yif that any wyght   wene a thing to ben oothir weyes than it is
> if that any creature think a thing to be   otherwise   than it is

Lat. si quid aliquis aliorsum atque sese habet existimet

'if any creature thinks something to be otherwise than it is'

[71] ibid. 3.pr12.108

> . . . hym that we han graunted to ben almyghty
> . . . him that we have conceded to be almighty

Lat. quem potentissimum esse concessimus

[72] ibid. 5.pr6.159

> whan that God knoweth any thing to betide
> when that God knows   anything to happen

[73] ibid. 5.pr6.44

> thilke   same is iwitnessed and iproevid by right to ben eterne
> the-very same is witnessed and proved   by right to be   eternal

[74] (1464) *Paston* 118.2

> . . . 3eluerton knowlacheyd it to be Sire John Fastolfe is dede opynly
> in þe Eschekere

> '. . . Yelverton acknowledged it openly in the Exchequer to be Sir
> John Fastolf's deed'

In Modern English the construction is common in more formal styles:

[75] 1667 Pepys, *Diary* VIII 518.17 (4 Nov)

> and he owning Sir W. Coventry in his opinion to be one of the
> worthiest men in the nation

[76] 1667 Pepys, *Diary* VIII 546.5 (24 Nov)

> . . . and that what I said would not hold water in denying this Board
> to have ever ordered the discharging out of the service whole ships
> by ticket

8.4.1.4 VOSI with three-place verbs

Old English examples of VOSI which are probably to be analysed as three-place:

[77] *Bede* 5 20.472.6

> ðara þinga, ðe he oðre   lærde to donne
> those things that he others(ACC) taught to do

> 'those things that he taught others to do'

[78] *Bo* 149.21

> &   tæc me þinne willan to wyrcenne
> and teach me your will   to perform

> 'And teach me to perform thy will.'

[79] *ÆLS* II 32.104

> þe   forbead petre mid wæpnum to winnenne . . .
> who forbade Peter with weapons to fight . . .

'who forbade Peter to fight with weapons . . .'

[80] *Mt(WSCp)* 19.8

moyses for   eower heortan   heardnesse. lyfde
Moses because-of your(PL) heart's(GEN SG) hardness   allowed

eow eower wif   to forlætenne;
you your   wives to abandon

[81] *Mk(WSCp)* 6.45

Ða sona   he nydde his leorningcnihtas on   scyp
then straight away he forced his disciples   aboard ship

stigan
climb(INF)

'Then straight away he forced his disciples to board the ship'

[82] *ChronE* 173.14 (1048)

se cyng . . . bead heom cuman   to Gleaweceastre
the king . . . bade them come(INF) to Gloucester

'the king . . . told them to come to Gloucester'

Some Middle English examples:

[83] c1180 *Orm.* 6624

Herode king Badd ta   þreo kingess sekenn   Þatt ȝunge king . . .
Herod king bade those three kings   seek(INF) that young king . . .

&   buȝhenn himm o cnewwe
and bow   him   on knee

'King Herod told those three kings to look for that young king . . .
and to bow down to him on their knees.'

[84] ?c1425(?c1400) *Loll.Serm.* 1.150

Þis castel þat he bad   hem goo intoo . . .
this castle that he bade them go   into . . .

8.4.1.5 VOSI with verbs indeterminate between two and three place

[85] c1225(?c1200) *SWard* 8

ne nalde   he nawt þolien þe þeof forte breoken   hire.
nor not-would he not permit the thief to   break-into it [*sc.* his house]

'nor would he allow the thief to break into it.'

[86] ?a1425(c1380) Chaucer, *Bo.* 1.pr1.47

Who . . . hath suffred   aprochen to this sike man thise comune
who . . . has permitted approach to this sick man these common

strompettis . . . ?
strumpets . . .

'Who . . . has permitted these common strumpets . . . to come near this sick man?'

8.4.1.6 Dative, etc., case marking

For most classes of matrix verb the unmarked form of the sandwiched NP is accusative in Old English, common case subsequently. There is no particular reason to attribute the NP's case to the higher verb. Examples with a different case marking, such as dative, or with the sandwiched NP in a prepositional phrase, serve in some analyses as proof that the NP is *subcategorised for* by the higher verb:

[87] *ÆCHom* I 29.416.4

Ða færlice het he his gesihum,
then suddenly ordered he his companions(DAT PL: read *gesiðum*?)

ðone biscop mid his preostum samod geandwerdian
the bishop with his priests together oppose(INF)

'then he suddenly ordered his companions to oppose the bishop together with his priests'

[88] *ÆCHom* II 25.232.74

for ðan ðe us is beboden . . . ofsittan and
because us(DAT[/ACC]) is commanded . . . repress(INF) and

fortredan ða gewilnigendlican lustas
tread-down(INF) those desirable/concupiscent pleasures

'because we are required . . . to repress and tread down the pleasures of desire'

[89] a1400(a1325) *Cursor* 11559

He commandid til his knyghtes kene | To sla þe childer al be-dene
he commanded to his knights brave to slay the children all together

'He commanded his brave knights to kill all the children together'

[90] ?c1430(c1400) *Wycl.Spec.Antichr.* 112.18

but he comaundiþ to prestis for to preche þe gospel . . .
but he commands to priests for to preach the Gospel . . .

See Visser (1963–73: §2063), Fischer (1989: 188). On an increase in prepositional marking in Middle English see Fischer (1989: 171). On the converse *loss* of a preposition or reanalysis of a preposition so that it is no longer (entirely) head of a PP see Marchand (1951) and also Chapter 7 above.

8.4.2 Finite complementation

Clues to the analysis of infinitive complementation can be gleaned from alternatives with a finite clause. As noted in discussion of [14]–[15] above, the sandwiched NP of a VOSI construction will correspond to the subject of a finite embedded clause and possibly also to a co-referential object NP in the higher clause. If the NP does appear separately as object in the higher clause – possibly with its case determined by the higher verb – that would suggest that it is an argument of the higher verb, which is accordingly a three-place verb. Conversely, lack of separate expression in the higher clause may be taken as evidence – perhaps weaker than the positive case – for the higher verb having a two-place argument structure. However, causative verbs hardly occur at all in Old English with finite complementation, apart from DON; later there were *that*-clauses also after MAKE, CAUSE, SUFFER (Fischer 1992b: §2.2.1.2.1; 1989). (We should note that for many verbs the converse is true, namely that in Old English finite complementation was far more common than infinitival.) For a large collection of finite clause complements in Old English see Wülfing (1894–1901: II 88–101), and for a systematic comparison of *that*-clause and infinitival complementation in Middle English see Manabe (1989), useful for data and numbers but otherwise unsatisfactory.

8.4.2.1   V + NP + finite clause

These are examples with both an NP object in the higher clause and a separate – though usually co-referential – subject in the lower clause. Visser collects some examples in (1963–73: §2059).

[91]   *Bede* 5 2.388.10

ða heht   he his geferan,   ðæt hio sohton sumne earmne
then ordered he his companions(ACC) that they sought some   poor

ðearfan
wretch

'then he ordered his companions to look for some poor wretch'

[92]   *ÆCHom* I 38.594.30

and bebead   ðam cwellerum   þæt hi   hine mid wiððum
and commanded the executioners(DAT) that they him with cords

handum and fotum   on þære rode gebundon
hands   and feet(DAT) on the   cross bound

'and commanded the executioners to bind him hand and foot to the cross with cords'

[93]   *ÆCHom* I 1.16.3

. . . and het   ða eorðan   þæt heo sceolde forðlædan cuce
. . . and ordered the earth(ACC) that she should bring-forth live

nytenu
animals

'. . . and ordered the earth to bring forth live animals'

Two similar examples from late Old English, cited by Fischer (1989: 188 n.44) as if *fyrst* were an adverb, 'first', are not in fact germane:

[94]   *ÆCHom* I 19.268.32

```
. . . and læt      him            fyrst        þæt he his mandæda geswice
. . . and allow him(DAT) time(ACC) that he his crimes      abandon
```

'. . . and allow him time to abandon his crimes'

The *þæt*-clause is actually dependent on the noun *fyrst*, not on LÆTAN.
  Examples like the following suggest that ModE MAKE can be three place:

[95] 1667 Pepys, *Diary* VIII 105.18 (9 Mar)

  . . . which made me I durst not put them on.

[96] 1667 Pepys, *Diary* VIII 221.18 (17 May)

  but only want of practice makes her she cannot go through a whole
  tune readily.

8.4.2.2 V + finite clause

These are examples without a separate object NP in the higher clause.
Visser collects some examples in (1963–73: §2058). Both of the following
examples would on semantic grounds count as three-place verbs despite the
absence of an explicit Recipient argument in the higher clause:

[97] *Or* 140.11

```
he forbead ofer  ealne his onwald    þæt mon nanum cristenum men
he forbade over  all    his dominion that one  no    Christian man

ne  abulge
not offend
```

  'he forbade throughout his whole dominion that anyone should offend
  a Christian man'

[98] *ÆCHom* I 2.38.27

```
Englas geþafodon ær       Drihtnes to-cyme þæt mennisce men him
angels granted   before Lord's   arrival  that mortal   men them

to feollon
to fell
```

  'Before the Lord's advent angels allowed mortal men to fall down
  before them'

8.4.2.3 Finite clause or VOSI?

From Middle English the subjunctive and the infinitive were frequently
identical in form. One kind of finite complementation – with subjunctive
verb in a contact clause (that is, without complementiser *that*) – could
therefore in some circumstances be mistaken for one kind of VOSI
construction, namely with plain infinitive. Syntactic ambiguity of this kind
might have played a part in the spread of the VOSI construction:

[99] (c1390) Chaucer, *CT.Mil.* I.3226

```
And demed hymself been lik  a cokewold
and  judged himself be    like a cuckold
```

[100]   a1450(1391) Chaucer, *Astr.* Prol. 56

> And preie God save the king

[101]   a1425(?a1400) *RRose* 11

> And whoso   saith or weneth it be | A jape, or elles nycete
> and whoever says or thinks it be a joke or else foolishness

[102]   (a1393) Gower, *CA* 1.501

> . . . in here avys | Thei wene it be a Paradys

> '. . . in their opinion they think it to be/think that it is a Paradise'

[103]   ?c1430(c1400) *Wycl.Prelates* 66.22

> þat men supposen alle þes   passen þre   fiftenþes
> that men suppose all   these exceed three fifteenths

Both Bock (1931: 234) and Fischer (1992b: §2.4) suggest that the
subjunctive interpretation is preferable in most of these instances apart from
those like [99]. Other doubtful cases in Chaucer's *Boethius* are cited by
Bock (1931: 239–40), all translations of Latin infinitives, but all of them
interpretable as English VOSIs only with a plain infinitive rather than the
expected *to*-infinitive.

8.4.2.4 Finite clause coordinated with VOSI

Visser collects some examples in (1963–73: §2061), and see also Mitchell
(1985: §3732):

[104]   *Or* 59.14

> . . . siþþan gelicade eallum folcum   þæt hie
> . . . then   pleased   all   peoples(DAT PL) that they

> Romanum   underþieded wære, & hiora æ   to behealdanne
> Romans(DAT) subjected   were and their law to observe

> '. . . then all the peoples were content to be subjected to the Romans
> and to observe their law'

[105]   *ÆLS* II 32.52

> Nu het   he þe dælan   þine digelan goldhordas . . . and
> now commanded he you share(INF) your secret   goldhoards . . . and

> þu beo   his underkyning
> you be(PRES SUBJ) his underking

> 'Then he commanded you to share your secret hoard of gold . . . and
> that you be his underking.'

[106]   c1450(c1380) Chaucer, *HF* 1815

> And prayed her to han good fame, | And that she nolde
> and prayed her to have good reputation and that she not-would

doon hem no shame
cause them no shame

'and asked her to keep her good reputation and that she would not
bring shame on them'

The finite clause of Mitchell's example [105] may actually, as he observes,
be direct speech and not dependent on *het*. There are also many examples
where VOSI and V + finite clause are used in parallel:

[107]   ?a1425(c1380) Chaucer, *Bo*. 3.m12.3

The poete . . . hadde makid the ryveris to stonden stille, and hadde
the poet . . . had   made the rivers to stand   still   and had

maked the hertes and the hyndes to joynen dreedles here sydes to
made the harts and the hinds   to join   fearless their sides to

cruel lyouns. . . and hadde maked that the hare was nat agast
cruel lions . . . and had   made that the hare was not terrified

of the hound,
of the hound

8.4.2.5   V + *that* + OSI

My shorthand heading refers to some curious examples, attested from c1200
to the sixteenth century, with the complementiser *that* followed subsequently not by a finite clause but by NP and infinitive:

[108]   a1450(c1410) Lovel.*Merlin* 6344

this goodman. . . preyde his wyf ful   tendirlye | that a Norse to
this man   . . . begged his wife very tenderly   that a nurse to

geten hire   in hye
get   her   in haste

This construction is taken by Visser to be 'clearly a hybrid of a VOSI and a
that-clause' (1963–73: §2060); cf. also Mitchell (1985: §3731) and references
and discussion in Fischer (1989: 173–4).

8.4.3   V + NP + Pred

An important kind of complementation for many potential VOSI verbs
involves a direct object NP and a *predicative* adjunct (usually an NP or AP),
what I shall call the 'V + NP + Pred' construction. It is arguable whether
these structures are two-place (with NP and Pred forming a single
constituent, as in the fashionable '*small clause*' analysis, Radford 1988:
324–8), or three-place: perhaps there are two different types. Visser has a
sensible discussion of the syntax and gives a fair range of examples classified
by (semantic) type of verb (1963–73: §§646–59). I give a few examples
below:

[109]   *Beo* 617

bæd hine   bliðne   æt þære beorþege
bade him(ACC) happy(ACC) at the   beer-taking

'told him to be happy at the beer-drinking'

[110]   *ÆCHom* I 1.18.29

ac God hine   let frigne
but God him(ACC) left free(ACC)

[111]   *HomU* 34(Nap 42) 197.19

. . . Apollinis, þe hi   mærne god   leton;
. . . Apollo   that they great god(ACC) considered

'. . . Apollo, whom they considered a great god'

[112]   c1400 *PPl.B* 12.193

. . . &   knewliched hym   gilty.
. . . and acknowledged himself guilty

[113]   a1425(c1385) Chaucer, *TC* 2.371

. . . Wol deme it love of frendshipe in his mind

'. . . will judge it affection between friends in his mind'

Some verbs, for example LÆTAN 'think, reckon', are common in the construction from Old English onwards. The majority of verbs in Visser's collection have no OE attestation. The significance of V + NP + Pred in this chapter is as a possible forerunner of VOSI and as a clue to argument structure. An apparently similar construction is found with impersonal ÞYNCAN 'seem' (see Chapter 5 above and §9.3.1.1).

8.4.4 Passives

Passive morphology in the lower clause (sometimes called the 'first passive') may be of significance for the analysis of the higher verb (see test [14](c) above), as well as bearing on possible ambiguity in ordinary active VOSI examples. Passive morphology in the higher clause ('second passive') indicates in some analyses that the passive subject corresponds to a direct object in the active equivalent, which is sometimes taken as an indication of Raising to object (see [14](h) above). The terms 'first' and 'second passive' presumably refer to the transformationalists' view that transformations like passivisation take place 'from the bottom up', i.e. in embedded clauses before superordinate ones; they were apparently introduced by Lees in 1960 (Warner 1982: 244 n.4).

8.4.4.1 Passive in lower clause

Mitchell (1985: §3742) cites Callaway's figure of fifty-two examples with passive in the lower clause only (1913: 120), all but two outside poetry:

[114]   *BlHom* 33.9

. . . se eca   Drihten . . . se   hine sylfne   forlet
. . . the eternal Lord   . . . who him self(ACC) caused/permitted

from deofles leomum, &   from yflum mannum beon   on rode
by   devil's limbs   and by   evil   men   be(INF) on cross

ahangenne
hanged(PTCP, MASC ACC SG)

'. . . the eternal Lord . . . who permitted himself to be hanged on the
cross by the limbs of the devil and by evil men'

[115]   *GenA,B* 2196

Ne læt þu þin ferhð wesan | sorgum   asæled
not let you your spirit be(INF) sorrows(DAT) bound

'Do not let your spirit be bound with sorrows'

It is commonly stated that this construction was Latin-inspired and was not
native to Old English (Callaway 1913: 213–14, Bock 1931: 225). For further
OE examples see Callaway (1913: 120–4), Mitchell (1985: §3753 and
references §3754).

In Middle English examples remained infrequent at first but became more
common later in the period:

[116]   a1250 *Wooing Lord* 269.7

feirnesse and lufsum   neb . . . makes moni mon beo luued te
fairness and attractive face . . . makes many man be loved the

raðer.   and te mare
more-readily and the more

'Beauty and facial attractiveness . . . causes many a man to be
more beloved, and more readily'

[117]   ?a1425(c1380) Chaucer, *Bo.* 5.pr4.92

. . . any necessite. . . that constreynith or compelleth any of
. . . any necessity. . . that constrains   or compels   any of

thilke   thingis to ben don so
those-very things to be done thus

[118]   a1425 *Arth.& M.*(LinI) 1159

Y schal hire don   anon   beo knowe
I shall her cause at-once be known

'I shall make her confess at once.' (*MED*: 'reveal her identity' s.v.
knouen v. 14b.(a), but 14c 'confess' fits context better)

[119]   ?c1425(?c1400) *Loll.Serm.* 1.326

euery man . . . wole cese and suffre þe asse beo loosed   and be
every man . . . will cease and permit the ass be unloosed and be

brouȝt to Goddis werk.
brought to God's work

'every man . . . will stop and allow the ass [*sc.* sinful flesh] to be
unloosed and brought to God's work'

For further Middle English examples see Fischer (1991: §2.2).

8.4.4.2 Passive in higher clause

An impersonal passive has already been cited as [88]. Personal passives include:

[120] *Bede* 5 13.424.2

> . . . forðon þe ic soðlice from deaðe aaras &   eam eft   forlæten
> . . . because I truly   from death arose and am   again permitted
>
> mid monnum liifgan
> with men   live(INF)

> '. . . because I truly arose from death and am again permitted to live among men'

[121] *GD(H)* 104.21

> hi   . . . wæron geneadode niwe þing   to smeagenne
> they . . . were   compelled new things to consider

> 'they . . . were compelled to consider new things'

[122] *ChronE* 235.13 (1100)

> &   to þam Pentecosten wæs gesewen innan Barrucscire æt anan
> and at the Pentecost   was seen   within Berkshire   at a
>
> tune blod weallan of   eorþan
> village blood well(INF) from earth

> 'and at Pentecost blood was seen welling from the earth at a village in Berkshire'

[123] 1667 Pepys, *Diary* VIII 501.9 (25 Oct)

> but were bid to withdraw

> 'but we were asked to withdraw'

Further examples are given by Callaway (1913: 59–60).

Some rather different examples have as subject of the higher verb what is underlyingly the *object* of the lower verb:

[124] *Bede* 3 14.206.16

> . . . of   eallum þon, þe   on halgum bocum beboden   is to
> . . . concerning all   that that in holy   books commanded is to
>
> healdanne
> hold

> '. . . concerning everything that is ordained in the scriptures to be kept'

[125] *Lev* 11.6

> Hara   & swyn synd forbodene   to
> hare(SG) and swine are forbidden(PA PTCP, NOM PL) to

æthrinene.
touch

'It is forbidden to touch hare and pig.'

This looks rather like **Tough-Movement**. (Example [124] might be an impersonal passive.)

Some ME examples of the second passive are:

[126]   a1425(a1382) *WBible(1)* Baruch 6.39

Hou therfore is it to be gessid,   or to be saide, hem for to be
how therefore is it to be guessed or to be said   them for to be
goddis; . . .
gods

Lat. Quomodo ergo aestimandum est, aut dicendum, illos esse deos?

'How therefore is to be guessed or said that they are gods?'

[127]   a1425 *Wycl.Serm.* II 59.28

A man is seyd to loue hys lyf, þat loueþ it more þan oþur þing;
a man is said to love his life that loves it more than other thing

'A man is said to love his life if he loves it above any other thing'

For further ME examples see Warner (1982: 136). In GB analyses they can be seen as essentially Subject raising sentences – cf. §9.2 below – though [126] is an odd example.

8.4.4.3   Passive in both clauses

For examples see Visser (1963–73: §2183).

[128]   *Bede* 1 16.78.3

. . . heo wæron bewered heora weorum   gemengde beon
. . . they were   prohibited their men(DAT) mixed   be(INF)

'They were prohibited from having intercourse with their menfolk'

[129]   *GD* 203.22

þæt he nane þinga næs   gelyfed beon   gefylled . . .
that he none things not-was believed be(INF) filled . . .

'that he was not believed to be provided at all . . .'

[130]   1530(c1450) *Mirror Our Lady* 141.19

Endelesly before all tymes. I was forknowen and ordeyned of god to be made.

'Endlessly, before all times, I was foreknown and ordained to be made by God.'

[131]   1667 Pepys, *Diary* VIII 445.2 (23 Sep)

which is a book that Mrs. Pierce tells me hath been commanded to be burnt.

[132]   1667 Pepys, *Diary* VIII 461.25 (4 Oct)

. . . the ill state of my Lord Sandwich, that he can neither be got to be called home nor . . .

A rather different type is shown by:

[133]   (c1449) Pecock, *Repr.* 524.14

But so it is,that sectis . . . to be mad   with inne the comoun
But so it is that sects . . . to be made   within   the common

Cristen   religioun . . . is not . . . weerned and forboden bi Holi
Christian religion   . . . is not . . . refused   and forbidden by Holy

Scripture
Scripture

'But so it is, that for sects to be formed within the common Christian religion . . . is not . . . refused and forbidden by Holy Scripture'

Here the whole (passive) lower clause is acting as subject of the passive higher clause.

8.4.5   Nominal complementation

Another reasonable test for the valency of an infinitive-governing verb is to examine its behaviour when used with similar meaning with straightforward NP and PP complementation. By the usual *commutation* test we prefer to assume that the number of arguments with nominal complementation is the same as with clausal complementation.

8.4.5.1

Thus [134]–[135] give conflicting evidence as to whether LETTE 'prevent, hinder' has two or three argument places:

[134]   a1425 *Wycl.Serm.* II 58.60

Nyle   ȝe   . . . do   þing þat schilde lette   þis wirk.
not-wish you . . . do(INF) thing that should hinder this work

'Do not . . . do anything to hinder this work'

[135]   a1425 *Wycl.Serm.* II 122.100

so þis fourþe hungryng   lettuþ   men fro   coueytyse;
so this fourth being-hungry hinders men from covetousness

'so this fourth, being hungry, prevents covetousness in men.'

On the other hand [136] confirms that PERSUADE is a three-place verb:

[136]   1667 Pepys, *Diary* VIII 506.20 (28 Oct)

whereupon the King did command him to . . . persuade him to it

8.4.5.2 NP/PP coordinated with infinitival clause

A particularly convenient source of data is where an embedded clause and NP/PP complement(s) are actually coordinated under the same higher verb, as in:

[137]   a1425 *Wycl.Serm.* III 128.32

Ion mouyde men to mekenesse and to þenke on þe day of dom, . . .

'John moved men to meekness and to think about the Day of Judgement . . .'

8.4.6 V+I

See the examples in Visser (1963–73: §§1195–1249).

8.4.6.1 Old English

See Callaway (1913: 28–72). In Old English the unexpressed subject of the infinitive is usually vague or recoverable from context:

[138]   *Or* 34.13

het   hiene   þa niman   & ðæron bescufan
ordered him(ACC) then take(INF) and therein cast(INF)

'ordered him then to be taken and cast inside'

[139]   *ÆCHom* I 20.284.10

Þonne ðu gehyrst nemnan   þone Fæder . . .
when you hear   name(INF) the   father(ACC) . . .

'When you hear the Father named . . .'

[140]   *Bede* Pref. 1.2.1

Ic Beda Cristes þeow   and mæssepreost sende gretan   ðone
I Bede Christ's servant and masspriest   send greet(INF) the

leofastan   cyning Ceoluulf
most-beloved king   Ceolwulf

'I, Bede, Christ's servant and masspriest, send greetings to the most beloved King Ceolwulf'

Mitchell gives three instances where 'the subject accusative has to be understood from a preceding clause' (1985: §3747), that is, where V+I is apparently formed by ellipsis from VOSI, for example:

[141]   *ÆCHom* I 1.12.3

and se Ælmihtiga Scyppend hi   ealle   adræfde of
and the Almighty Creator   them all(ACC PL) expelled from

heofenan rices   myrhðe, and let befeallan on þæt ece
heaven's kingdom's delight and let fall(INF) into the eternal

fyr . . .
fire . . .

'and the Almighty Creator expelled them all from the delight of the
kingdom of heaven and let them all fall into eternal fire . . .'

But clear ellipsis of a specific NP is not the normal source of V+I.
  There is at least one example of V+I with a subjectless verb:

[142]   *Mt(WSCp)* 5.45

& he læt   rinan   ofer þa rihtwisan. & ofer þa
and he causes rain(INF) over the righteous and over the

unrihtwisan;
unrighteous

'and he makes it rain on the just and the unjust'

Another half-dozen examples are syntactically ambiguous between VOSI
and V+I, depending whether an accusative NP is taken as subject or object
of the lower verb:

[143]   *Exod* 9.24

& Drihten let   rinan   hagol wið fyr gemenged
and Lord   caused rain(INF) hail with fire mixed

'and the Lord made it rain hail mixed with fire'

[144]   *Or* 87.10

þæt mon geseah weallan   blod of   eorþan & rinan meolc of
that one saw   well(INF) blood from earth and rain milk from

heofonum
heavens

'that blood was seen to well from the ground and milk to rain from
the heavens'

In [144] it is more likely that *blod* is subject than object of WEALLAN, which
is normally intransitive, suggesting that RINAN is perhaps intransitive in all
of [142]–[144]. On the other hand RINAN is clearly used with the nouns *ryne*
'flow, flux' and *re(ge)n* 'rain' as (cognate) *object* in such examples as:

[145]   *HomS* 44 69 (*DOE*)

and hit þonne onginneð rinan blodegan rine.
and it then   begins rain bloody flux(ACC/DAT?)

'and it will then begin to rain a shower of blood'

[146]   *HomU* 35.2(Nap 44) 216.32

and hit agan þa   rinan xl. daga and xl. nihta tosomne þæm mæstan
and it began then rain 40 days and 40 nights together the greatest

rene
rain(DAT)

'And it then began to rain very heavily for forty days and forty nights
together'

so that the status of *hagol* in [143] and *meolc* in [144] remains open to question.

8.4.6.2   Middle English

The V+I construction continued into Middle English:

[147]   c1225(?c1200) *St.Juliana*(Bod) 69.753

    þer lette sophie.from þe sea a mile.setten   a chirche
    there caused Sophia from the sea a mile erect(INF) a church

    'There a mile from the sea Sophia had a church built'

[148]   c1225(?c1200) *St.Juliana*(Bod) 59.648

    & bed   binden   hire swa þe fet & te honden
    and ordered bind(INF) her thus the feet and the hands

[149]   c1225(?c1200) *St.Marg.(1)* 8.18

    & het   biliue bringin   hire biforen him.
    and ordered at-once bring(INF) her before him

    'and ordered her to be brought before him at once'

[150]   a1425 *Wycl.Serm.* III 162.27

    order axiþ   to bygynne at þe manhed   of Crist . . .
    order requires to begin   at the manhood of Christ

    'Order demands beginning at the manhood of Christ'

[151]   a1425 *Wycl.Serm.* II 121.55

    Crist preyuþ not to take hem   ȝeet out of þe world, but to
    Christ prays   not to take them yet out of the world but to

    kepe   hem here . . .
    preserve them here . . .

8.4.6.3   Modern English

Towards the end of the ME period different-subject V+I became more and more uncommon, eventually surviving only after one or two verbs (SAY, HELP) or in set phrases like LET *fly*. However, Visser has ModE (though not PDE) instances of V+I, some of them unique attestations, after BID, CAUSE, COMMAND, FORBID, GAR, ORDAIN, PERMIT, SEND, TEACH, URGE (1963–73: §§1195–1249). Here is an example with BID:

[152]   1667 Pepys, *Diary* VIII 249.25 (3 Jun)

    nor do they spend many words themselfs, but in great state do hear what they see necessary, and say little themselfs but bid withdraw

Two set phrases are of recent introduction rather than survivals: LEAVE *go*, a nineteenth-century variant of LET *go*, and twentieth-century MAKE *do*.

8.4.6.4   Passive of V+I

Can V+I occur in the passive? A first passive would only be possible if the passive subject were ellipted, since the first passive of V+I with transitive lower verb is a VOSI construction. The second passive ought to be impossible without the first passive as well, otherwise there would be no higher subject. If [153] has omission or ellipsis of *wesan* 'be'(INF) – but see Mitchell (1985: §3776) – then it would be a double passive of V+I, and [154]–[158] look like second passives, though the lower verb remains formally active:

[153]   *Beo* 991

Ða wæs haten   hreþe Heort innanweard | folmum
then was ordered quickly Heorot inwardly   hands(DAT)

gefrætwod
decorated

'Immediately Heorot was ordered to be decorated inside by men's hands.'

[154=124] *Bede* 3 14.206.16

. . . of   eallum þon, þe on halgum bocum beboden
. . . concerning all   that that in holy   books commanded

is to healdanne
is to hold

'. . . concerning everything that is ordained in the scriptures to be kept'

[155]   c1330(?c1300) *Amis* 1216

A strong fer þer   was don   make
a great fire there was done(PA PTCP) make(INF)

'a great fire was caused to be made there'

[156]   a1450(a1338) Mannyng, *Chron. Pt.1* 15957

Hertly   were þey halden   waken
vigorously were they held(PA PTCP) watch(INF)

'They were carefully kept watch on'

[157]   c1400(a1376) *PPl.A (1)* 2.179

He was . . . |Oueral   yhuntid & yhote   trusse
he was . . . everywhere hunted and ordered tie-up

[158]   1603 Knolles, *Hist. Turks* (1638) 322 (*OED* s.v. *hear* v. 3c)

He was . . . neuer afterwards seene or heard tell of.

8.5 Explanations

It is agreed that VOSI was native to Old English after verbs of perception and at least some verbs of causation. Some scholars have argued for a two-place argument structure in Old English with subsequent extension to three-place patterns (Ard, Terasawa), while the converse picture also has its champions (Kageyama, Lightfoot, Schmerling). Extension to other three-place verbs has been ascribed to syntactic reanalysis (Bock) or Latin influence (Visser). Fischer sees basic word order change as the ultimate reason for VOSI to be used with three-place verbs in Middle English, and she and many others have seen analogical behaviour in verbs which straddle the two-place ~ three-place distinction.

The use of VOSI in Old English with two-place verbs of saying and thinking is generally regarded as a Latinism, though Bock sees certain usages as survivals of a native pattern. For (re)appearance in late Middle English all sorts of explanation have been put forward: Latin influence again (all scholars), extension of the V + NP + Pred construction (many scholars), confusion between subjunctive and infinitive (Bock, Warner, Fischer), analogy with perception verbs (Zeitlin, Ard, Fischer), and even analogy with verbs like ORDER (Kageyama) and loss of case marking in NPs (Ard). Use in least salient contexts, e.g. where the sandwiched NP is fronted, is the mechanism of introduction advocated by Warner.

It will be convenient to look first at traditional philological accounts, mostly with an impressionistic semantic basis. Despite his formulaic structural analyses for Modern English, Jespersen belongs here because his diachronic material is based on Zeitlin's. Then we consider a group of scholars who concentrate on syntax and offer formal analyses of other peoples' data. Lastly comes a group who pay close attention to texts without neglecting questions of syntactic structure.

8.6 Philological and semantics-based accounts

8.6.1 Wülfing and Zeitlin

J. Ernst Wülfing's massive study of Alfredian (early) Old English prose (1894–1901) has a great deal of useful data on VOSI and V+I as on so much else, but the work is wholly taxonomic and synchronic.

Nor do I regard Jacob Zeitlin's dissertation (1908), consisting largely of classified lists of examples, as of much explanatory value. After the collections of material a short summary (1908: 108–13) gives some elementary syntactic analysis based essentially on semantics, without offering any account of syntactic *change*. The only explanations advanced for change involve the use of VOSI with verbs of mental perception by analogy with verbs of sense perception, by analogy with the V + NP + Pred construction, and under Latin influence, all of which are more precisely taken up by other scholars.

8.6.2 Callaway

The monograph of Morgan Callaway jr. on the infinitive in Old English (1913) is a thorough piece of scholarship, careful enough to be of lasting value. His major syntactic distinctions are traditional and easily translated into modern equivalents, but the subdistinctions are not the ones which I have concentrated on in this chapter, since Callaway classifies by the *semantic* class of the higher verb and does not use its valency. This means, for instance, that verbs of causing (two-place?) and verbs of permitting (three-place?) are often treated together. Bock (1931: 157–8) is critical of a different aspect of the classification, Callaway's often inconsistent attempts to distinguish between 'objective' (VOSI) and 'final' (purpose) infinitives; see further §8.8.1 below. On the other hand word order, the presence or absence of *to*, and any Latin original are carefully documented.

Callaway considers VOSI ('the predicative infinitive with accusative or dative subject') in his Chapters 8 and 9. He finds about 1527 examples with accusative object-subject NP, of which 1512 have an uninflected infinitive (1913: 107 and Appendix D). He does not give a total for examples with a dative NP.

Callaway tackles V+I in his Chapter 2 ('the objective infinitive'). His total of about 3238 examples, of which 2709 have an uninflected infinitive (1913: 28), is not very useful, since it throws together both same-subject and different-subject V+I patterns, as well as second passives of VOSI constructions and VOSI constructions with a dative sandwiched NP. I have not tried to work out how many of the examples are different-subject V+I.

The origins of the various infinitival constructions are the subject of Callaway's Chapter 14. On grounds of distribution (kind and date of text, correspondence or not to Latin, cognate Germanic languages), he argues for native origin of VOSI with HATAN and other verbs of commanding, (FOR)LÆTAN, HIERAN and SEON, and certain verbs of mental perception. Latin influence is suggested for most of the rest (1913: 203–13). Scheler, treating VOSI within a general discussion of syntactic Latinisms in Old English, reaches similar conclusions after a much shorter discussion, though his list of verbs whose use of VOSI must be due to Latin is longer (1961: 99–100).

As for V+I, Callaway argues for a native origin after HATAN, LÆTAN, verbs of sense perception, and verbs of mental perception other than GETEON 'determine' which take a plain infinitive, although numbers of the last group are very low. Among verbs that can or must take a *to*-infinitive there are long lists of probably native and of probably Latin-influenced types (1913: 183–92).

8.6.3 Royster

James Finch Royster wrote two articles on causative verbs in Old English. The first (1918) deals mainly with HATAN, not usually regarded as a causative. He cites such V+I examples as

[159]   *Beo* 198

>   Het   him   yðlidan | godne gegyrwan
>   caused him(DAT) ship   good prepare(INF)

>   'he had a good ship made ready for him'

as evidence that HATAN could be causative in meaning. The crucial point for him is not that *gegyrwan* has no expressed subject but that HATAN is **perfective**, in the sense that the proposition expressed in the lower clause was fulfilled, and indeed that its fulfilment – rather than the giving of an order – was what the poet meant to express. He contrasts [159] with a more conventional example of HATAN in the sense 'order, command' (also, as it happens, a V+I example):

[160]   *Bede* 5 17.456.4

> . . . Balthild seo cwen . . . het   þone bysceop ofslean
> . . . Balthild the queen . . . ordered the   bishop kill(INF)

'. . . Queen Balthild . . . ordered the bishop to be killed'

The continuation of the text makes clear that HATAN is imperfective in [160], since the order to kill the bishop was not carried out. The remainder of the article considers the close semantic and etymological relationships among verbs of causing, forcing and ordering.

Royster (1922) extends the topic to non-embedding causatives like WIERMAN 'make warm' (which can be regarded as semantically equivalent to 'cause' + WARMIAN 'get warm') and – more to our purpose here – to DON, LÆTAN, MACIAN and other causative verbs taking embedded clauses.

Royster believes that DON + NP + predicate adjective – an instance of V + NP + Pred – is frequent enough in Old English to be called well established and is more likely to be a precursor of DON + NP + BEON + adjective than a reduced form of it (1922: 336–7 and n.41). He confirms that where DON takes embedded clauses it is predominantly *þæt*-clauses, but he conjectures from the evidence of Middle English that causative DON + infinitive was probably already present in colloquial Old English.

Causative use of LÆTAN seems to be outweighed greatly in Old English by the fuller 'allow' sense, though what probable examples there are tend to be found in the more nearly colloquial *Chronicle* and especially from after 1040. In Middle English causative use is easy to find (1922: 351–3). The verb MACIAN 'make' was rare altogether in Old English, rarer still as a causative, and is never found with an infinitive (1922: 353–4). Its fixation as the general causative towards the end of the ME period coincided with the specialisation of DO and LET in auxiliary uses. Other causatives and verbs of related meaning in Old English which are briefly discussed are hardly ever used with an infinitive (1922: 354–6).

Royster asserts that HATAN and probably LÆTAN could be mere tense-auxiliaries, that is, causatives bleached of all meaning. He cites the use of HATAN + verb in parallel with a simple verb in [161] and in translation of a simple verb in [162]:

[161]   *ChronE* 146.2 (1015)

> se cyng þa genam eall heora æhta.   & het   nimon
> the king then seized all   their possessions and caused seize(INF)
>
> Sigeferðes lafe
> Sigeferth's widow

[162]   *Gen* 12.18

> Farao   þa het   clypian Abram
> Pharaoh then ordered summon Abraham
>
> Lat. vocavitque Pharao Abram

'though its development in this direction was later arrested' (1922: 351). Similarly, LÆTAN in the V+I construction 'is scarcely more than a periphrasis for the passive voice' (1922: 353). I have not been able to trace a promised (1922: 356) follow-up article on ME causatives.

8.6.4 Jespersen

Otto Jespersen's contribution to the study of the VOSI construction falls into three parts: an overview of the history based on Zeitlin (1908), a selection of ModE data, and some insightful syntactic analysis (1909–49: V 277–94, issued in 1940).

For Modern English Jespersen recognises three major syntactic types of VOSI:

(A) two-place, as with perception verbs and causatives
(B) three-place with sandwiched NP as indirect object, as with ALLOW
(C) three-place with sandwiched NP as direct object, as with FORCE

The classification is not without problems – see Fischer (1989: 151–5) – though it should be noted that Jespersen denies the existence of clear boundaries between the classes, allowing for the appearance of the same verb in different types. He also has some descriptive material on V+I (1909–49: V 294–7).

8.6.5 Visser

F. Th. Visser (1963–73) has in general little to say on the two-place ~ three-place distinction and merely classifies by surface form. There is some material on parallels with finite complementation (1963–73: §§2058–61) but no systematic collection of *that*-clauses. A number of *that*-clauses are to be found, incidentally, in his discussion of the subjunctive (1963–73: §§869–70).

Visser suggests that only a dozen or so verbs occurred in the VOSI in early Old English, principally verbs of physical and mental perception and of commanding (1963–73: §2056). In late Old English there was a great increase of use – but cf. Mitchell (1985: §3742) – possibly due to the insertion of an explicit NP in the V+I construction. Visser thus suggests that V+I is at least as old as VOSI. (Addition of an NP to V+I to give VOSI is scornfully dismissed by Fischer 1989: 162–3.)

According to Visser there was a further expansion of VOSI during Middle English, probably under French and then Latin influence. With verbs of causing and ordering there were changes in the inventory of verbs appearing in the construction, largely through the dying out of certain OE members and the accretion of French and Scandinavian ones. According to my interpretation of Visser's material, when a new verb joined the group, either both VOSI and V+I were used, or perhaps VOSI preceded V+I, but the evidence is not full enough to detect clear patterns.

8.6.6 Mitchell

Mitchell's discussion of the OE data is intricate and in the end indecisive (1985: §§3722–86), both as regards structure and origin.

On V+I Mitchell has nothing to say on priority *vis-à-vis* VOSI (1985:

§§3755–65), merely that it was a construction of ancient (PIE) lineage (1985: §3765). He argues forcefully that V+I is a form of VOSI with NP unexpressed. Verbs of commanding form the largest group (§3757).

8.7 Accounts in generative syntax

8.7.1 Kageyama

Taro Kageyama's account (1975) is linguistically tidy, though its citation of OE and ME material is secondhand and the translations unreliable. He divides matrix verbs into four groups – causatives, physical perception verbs, mental perception verbs, verbs of declaring – and attempts to decide whether particular VOSI constructions were due to Equi or Raising. He argues that OE verbs of causing had a three-place structure with Equi (what would now be Control verbs of the PERSUADE type), basing his claim on the absence of dummy NPs as 'causees' and on examples with the causee expressed both in the higher clause and as subject of an embedded finite clause, as in §8.4.2.1. (Examples like those in §8.4.2.2 are explained by a deletion rule, 1975: 179 n.1.) Physical perception verbs are analysed on rather unconvincing grounds as three-place. It is suggested that verbs of mental perception and of declaring, however, especially in late Old English, may have been two-place with Object raising.

  In Middle English, verbs of 'letting' (causation?) now show evidence of two-place structure in addition to three-place + Equi. The new two-place analysis is justified by the appearance of inanimate NPs in the sandwich position of the VOSI construction. But such objects can be found already in Old English: see §8.4.1.1 above. Verbs of mental perception also give better evidence of two-place structure with the increasing frequency of non-finite complementation.

  The closest Kageyama comes to an explanation is his suggestion (1975: 176) that verbs like BELIEVE formed a VOSI pattern by analogy with verbs like ORDER. Otherwise his paper offers more on Subject raising; see §9.4.6 below.

8.7.2 Ard

The dissertation of Josh Ard (1977: 9–28, 46–8) has a slightly better grip on the philology – likewise without original data – but a weaker logic to its argument.[5]

  Following Postal (1974), Ard divides the matrix verbs of the Old English VOSI construction somewhat arbitrarily into semantic classes (1977: 16–17):

'B verbs': supposed to be verbs of saying and thinking (1977: 10), but represented solely by mental perception verbs like ONGIETAN 'perceive', WITAN 'know'

'N verbs': verbs of negative causation like FORWYRNAN 'prevent'

'W verbs': two-place WANT-type verbs

'C verbs': (what I would call three-place) PERSUADE-type verbs like
BEBEODAN 'command'. Physical perception verbs like GEHIERAN 'hear',
GESEON 'see' are included without explanation among the C verbs.

The verb GEFRIGNAN (cited as *gefrægnan*) 'learn by enquiry' is felt by Ard
to be problematic for his classification, purely because it has no obvious
PDE equivalent; see §8.8.2.5 below. N and W verbs lack representatives in
eOE VOSI patterns.

A puzzling paragraph suggests that the spread of VOSI to N verbs and W
verbs in late Old English is 'more a growth through the lexicon than through
semantic and/or syntactic classes, since all classes are represented in Old
English' (1977: 17). A few pages later we get a curious syntactic proposal.
Ard suggests that C verbs (and W verbs, though evidence is lacking) were
two-place verbs underlyingly. He is unwilling to derive OE and ME VOSI
by Object raising, however, because of the existence of finite complementation after C verbs with optional separate expression in the higher clause of
the animate argument (cf. §8.4.2 above). So he proposes that the optional
NP be introduced into the higher clause as a heralding element by a copying
transformation – this is out of tune with current ideas on the inability of
transformations to alter structure – and that the original NP (subject of the
lower clause) may then be deleted in non-finite examples by the Equi
transformation (1977: 23–7). A later chapter suggests, however, that this
optional heralding NP was 'an integral part of the higher sentence' (1977:
70).

The transition to Modern English is dealt with extremely vaguely but
seems to involve VOSI patterns becoming associated with the semantically
similar finite complement types, while the sandwiched NP in VOSI became
semantically associated more and more with the lower clause and less and
less with the higher one, until somehow a new derivation by Object raising
came into being for the C verbs (1977: 27, 70–2). Another muddled
paragraph seems to suggest both that V+I in Old English may have
influenced the spread of VOSI, and that V+I may have *been* influenced
(semantically?) by VOSI (1977: 27). The spread of VOSI to N verbs was
'[p]resumably . . . affected by factors similar to the ones which affected C
verbs and W verbs' (1977: 29).

As for B verbs, they permit *To-be*-Deletion in Modern English (1977:
31–2):

[163]   John believed Fred to be a fool.
[164]   John believed Fred a fool.

(I have substituted *fool* as predicative in [163]–[164], since Ard's *plumber*
sounds awkward in my dialect in the [164] type.) Ard suggests that the V +
NP + Pred [164] type, analysed in Present-day English as a reduced form of
[163], was actually historically prior to the [163] type. On this question see
Mitchell (1985: §§3772–6). Ard cites two of Visser's OE examples of
predicative adjuncts (1963–73: §648) (garbling one), and suggests that they
were common in Old English. Agreement in case of adjunct and object
serves to prove for Ard that no raising had taken place and that object and
adjunct originated in the same clause:

[165]   *WHom* 20.2 264.113

þe læt   hine silfne   rancne & ricne   & genoh
who thinks him self(ACC SG) noble   and powerful and very

godne . . .
good . . .

'who has thought himself noble and powerful and very good . . .'

Verbs of saying and thinking probably 'developed the predicative adjunct
complement type by analogy to the complement types found after verbs like
make and *name*' (1977: 37), where the two NPs in a sentence like

[166] Jim made his son his heir.

are regarded as an embedded copulative sentence lacking an explicit copula.

On the other hand the VOSI pattern he believes to have been at best
peripheral to the grammar of Old English, a Latinate borrowing (1977: 34).
It increased in frequency after the loss of case distinctions, because
previously the necessity for the complement of BE to be in the accusative
had hindered its acceptability. (Why?) Full acceptance was not due to Latin
influence but rather to a 'three-pronged analogy' (1977: 44). The first
ingredient was verbs of saying and thinking with finite sentential complements, presumably providing a sentence pattern ripe for reduction. The
second ingredient was perception verbs in the VOSI, which not only
provided the structural analogy but also a semantic analogy because of
examples like

[167] I found her to be gone.

In [167], since *her* is clearly not an argument, FIND is a two-place verb and
has a meaning close to a verb of thinking. The third and final ingredient was
verbs of saying and thinking with NP + Pred complementation, which
explains why the lower verb was virtually restricted to BE and certainly to
statives. Although this last factor has been invoked by earlier linguists too,
its relevance has been criticised because the V + NP + Pred construction
was infrequent before the second half of the ME period. For references see
Fischer (1989: 174), and for a contrary view Bock (1931: 243), who cites a
remarkable parallel use of VOSI and V + NP + Pred (and of V + NP +
that-clause too?!):

[168] ?c1430(c1400) *Wycl.Prelates* 61.4

but ȝif þei clepen . . . þe deuelis chirche to be holy chirche, as þei
but if they call   . . . the devil's church to be holy church as they

clepen hem self   men of religion and þat þei forsaken þe world
call   themselves men of religion and that they forsake   the world

What about an example like this?

[169] c1225(?c1200) *SWard* 209

and þet Ich demi riht ant wisdom to donne.

'and that I consider to be right and wise to do'

8.7.3 Lightfoot

8.7.3.1

David Lightfoot (1981: 107–13) argues that there were no two-place +
Raising types in Old English and early Middle English at all, and that many
of the verbs associated now with such an analysis did not appear in the
appropriate constructions until the ModE period (but cf. §8.4.1.1–3). As
two-place verbs they could not appear in surface VOSI constructions, since
the sandwiched NP would not have been assigned any case (it cannot be
governed by the higher verb across an S′ barrier and there is no INFL in its
own clause to govern it), thus falling foul of the *Case Filter*. If such
sentences nevertheless entered the language, for example in translating the
Latin aci, then a rule of 'S̄ Deletion' would enter the grammar in order to
accommodate them. Such a rule prunes an embedded S′ node dominating
an empty COMP, thus an S′ (circled in [170]) whose only non-empty
constituent is S:

[170]

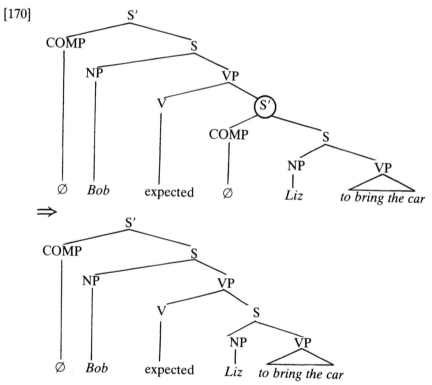

With the S′ barrier removed the NP *Liz* could receive structural accusative
case from the higher verb.

8.7.3.2 Objections to Lightfoot

Schmerling (1981: 123) assumes that a three-place + Equi analysis –
something already available in the language – would have sufficed at first for
EXPECT-type verbs, and that there is no evidence for the two-place +

Raising analysis before the nineteenth century, but Allen (1984) demolishes that dating.

Fischer (1988, 1989: 161) is critical of Lightfoot's reliance on Latin influence as an explanation for such a radical syntactic change.

8.8 Text-based, structural accounts

8.8.1 Bock

While Callaway's monograph remains the main data source for Old English, Hellmut Bock's investigation (1931; in German, with Table of Contents at p.249), which makes use of Callaway's material, has had most influence on recent work. For Middle English Bock cites a selection of his own collection of material.

The bulk of Bock's article is concerned with the origin, functions and spread of the particle *to* as accompaniment to an infinitive (1931: 114–217) and will not be relevant till later (§8.9), though a discussion of VOSI constructions with dative intervening NP belongs here. In the second and shorter part Bock gets on to the (strictly) accusative and infinitive construction (1931: 217–47), though again mainly in relation to the *to*-infinitive. His discussion divides the history into four periods: Germanic, Old English, twelfth/thirteenth century, and fourteenth century.

8.8.1.1   Old English

Bock identifies three types of VOSI construction on unspecified but apparently semantic criteria (1931: 220):

Type 1: NP more closely linked to higher verb than to infinitive
Type 2: NP and infinitive form equivalent complements[6] of higher verb
Type 3: NP + infinitive together form single complement of higher verb

Bock intends the typology to be valid for all periods. We shall take them in turn.

Type 1 may be exemplified by:

[171]   *Bede* 1 13.54.30

he sende A. . . . bodian   Godes word
he sent A. . . . preach(INF) God's word(ACC)

Ongolþeode
English-people(DAT)

Lat. misit A. . . . praedicare uerbum dei [. . .]

The particle *to* spread rapidly in Old English and retained its original final meaning (indeed Bock deliberately ignores as unhelpful the distinction between VOSI and purpose infinitives, 1931: 158). Not many verbs were used in this construction, and most modern members of the class appeared in Middle English, of romance origin. There is a large overlap between Bock's type 1 and our three-place category.

Type 2 involves causatives and perception verbs. Bock's characterisation of the structure captures the observation that the action referred to by the infinitive and the sandwiched NP are in a sense each, separately, objects of causation or perception. Our discussion in §8.2.2 above showed that it is not necessary to assume three-place structure for such verbs. Bock discusses the different ways that BIDDAN and BEBEODAN were drawn into this class, and he argues (against the traditional separation of verbs of sense perception from those of mental perception) that certain verbs of mental perception are indistinguishable in their behaviour from SEON 'see':

[172] *Beo* 118

Fand   þa þær inne æðelinga   gedriht |
found(3 SG PA) then there in   princes(GEN PL) troop

swefan   æfter symble
sleep(INF) after feast

'Then he found in it a troop of princes sleeping after the feast.'

[173] *And* 1061

oððæt he gemette   be mearcpaðe | standan   stræte neah stapul
until   he came-across by road   stand(INF) street near pillar

ærenne.
brazen

'until by the roadside he came across a pillar made of brass, standing near the paved road'

[174] *Rid* 68.1

Ic þa   wiht geseah on weg feran
I that being saw   away   go

'I saw that being/creature go away'

However, since these examples all involve concrete perception, they argue for a reclassification of individual instances rather than (necessarily) for abandonment of the distinction.

Type 3 is the accusative and infinitive in the strict sense after verbs of saying and thinking. Bock's analysis of its distribution across texts leads him to the conclusion that the remains of a native construction survived in OE poetry but were replaced in prose by *þæt*-clauses. The few examples in original prose are either the last remnants of the native construction or are to be ascribed to indirect Latin influence; all other instances are imitations of corresponding Latin constructions. Bock also includes here some isolated examples of VOSI after verbs of wishing and emotion and all occurrences of causative (GE)DON, apart from the DO *to wit* construction (§10.2.2.3 below).

8.8.1.2 Early Middle English

After a penetrating discussion of the collapse of the OE literary language and of literary/linguistic conditions in early Middle English, Bock introduces what is apparently a fourth type. He comments on the astonishingly low survival rate beyond the start of the thirteenth century of verbs of forcing and persuading which could appear in VOSI. He suggests for verbs in these (and other) semantic areas that a new VOSI pattern emerged from verbs which had governed a dative NP in connection with an infinitive. The infinitive was reanalysed as dependent on the higher verb rather than on the NP (which Boch confusingly calls *Akkusativobjekt*, anticipating his next point). For various reasons, among them phonetic, accusative case replaced dative, and the infinitive-marker *to* became common. We are to infer that this fourth type became assimilated to type 1.

The plain infinitive was increasingly confined to a small class of verbs, those which had formed type 2 in Old English, though with the noteworthy addition of MAKEN, which he says is first found in VOSI in [175]:

[175] 1175 *Lamb.Hom.* 159.17

swa makeð þe halie gast þe Mon bi-halden up to houene
so makes the holy ghost the man look   up to heaven

'so the Holy Ghost makes the man look up to heaven'

(Visser's earliest citations are from the same text, 1963–73: §2068.) Notice that Bock classifies CAUSE under type 1 rather than with the causatives in type 2, perhaps because (at least in late Modern English) it has regularly been used with a *to*-infinitive, and that is an important criterion for him.

8.8.1.3 The fourteenth century

Bock discusses the rise of English as a prestige language, and of a new literary dialect. The pressure to use VOSI was greater in translation than in original works, and after verbs of saying and thinking much greater in philosophy than in sermons. Some syntactic borrowings in the new prose literature were ephemeral, however. In type 1 examples where the sandwiched NP had a 'dative character', this could be marked externally by *to*, as in [90], and an influx of French verbs increased numbers greatly. Bock mentions the V+I pattern and its replacement by VOSI with a passive infinitive (1931: 236–7). Use of finite complementation was also common – c150 *that*-clauses as against c16 VOSIs after verbs of saying and thinking in Chaucer's *Boethius* (1931: 241) – and Bock notes the potential ambiguities caused by formal coalescence of infinitive and subjunctive (cf. §8.4.2.3 above).

As for verbs of saying and thinking, it is possible that imperceptible transitions between verbs of thinking and of perception had allowed a weak tradition of VOSI after verbs of thinking to survive through from Old English (1931: 244), but it is clear that the re-establishment of the pattern on a small scale in the fourteenth century cannot be explained without Latin influence. Bock also emphasises that the revival of VOSI must have resulted from connection with V + NP + Pred, basing his argument on these observations (1931: 242–3):

(A) overwhelming frequency of BEN 'be' + predicative nominal as lower clause – in *Boethius* only KNOWEN occurs with an infinitive other than BEN, as in [72]
(B) use of V + NP + Pred since Old English
(C) greater frequency of V + NP + Pred in all texts

The more a fourteenth-century work was intended for a wider, unlearned audience, the less it used VOSI (1931: 245 n.2). Bock suggests that this would prove a revealing stylistic test for later writings too.

8.8.2 Warner

Anthony Warner (1982) provides a careful, semi-formal analysis of verbal complementation in Wyclifite Sermon English c1400, together with a lucid discussion of the necessary procedures for making linguistic judgements on texts from a dead language. For example, Warner's discussion of root sentences, and whether subordinate clauses can qualify as such, is of general interest (1982: §4.2.1). That brings in indirect discourse, and the question of how *direct* speech is embedded under a higher verb of reporting is discussed later (1982: §7.1). Another discussion which may be of more general use is that of the relation between the Early and Late versions of the *Wyclifite Bible* and their evidence for relative acceptability, especially of Latinate constructions, in late-fourteenth-century English (1982: 138–40). The study is corpus-based, and an appendix classifies every occurrence in the 60,000-word corpus of a clause embedded in object position.

8.8.2.1 Argument structure

Warner makes much of the two-place ~ three-place distinction (n.b. see Note 1), using distributional information from within his corpus as much as possible. For example, the verb SEE in the VOSI is analysed as two-place because it occurs with roughly the same meaning either with a simple NP as object or with a *that*-clause as object, thus always monotransitively (1982: 36). Matrix verbs are assigned to a number of classes on the basis of tests such as that. A few examples from the full list (1982: 100–14):

(A) VOSI, two-place: HEERE 'hear', MAKE, SEE
(B) V+I, two-place: AXE 'ask', BIDDE 'bid', STIRE 'urge', TECHE 'teach'
(C) VOSI, three-place: BIDDE, BINDE 'compel', COMANDE, NEDE 'compel', SEIE 'order'. Some of this last group have the sandwiched NP governed by a preposition, as in

> [176]   a1425 *Wycl.Serm.* III 158.107
>
> God seyþ þanne to his seruauntis to brynge forþ . . .
> God says then to his servants   to bring forth . . .

(D) VOSI, neutral or unassignable to two- or three-place: ENFORCE, LETE 'permit, suffer', ORDEYNE

Notice that some verbs, e.g. BIDDE, can be both two-place and three-place in different examples.

8.8.2.2 Structural analyses and derivation

Warner's analysis of infinitival clauses treats them as S's which are sole constituents of an NP. The structure he assigns to [177] is in essentials [178] (1982: 25):

[177]   a1425 *Wycl. Serm.* II.64.105

and as þe wolf . . . makeþ schep to flocke   for dreede, . . .
and as thewolf . . . makes sheep to flock-together out-of fear

[178]

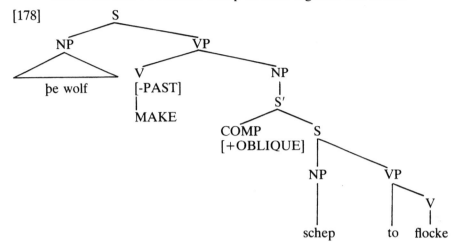

The [NP S′] in structure [178] reflects both the sentential internal structure of the embedded clause and its essentially NP-like distribution (1982: 31, 58–68). The same subtree can occur in underlying subject position, possibly with Subject raising verbs (see §9.4.9 below), or – with PRO as lower subject – as second complement of a three-place verb.

Warner finds much evidence that the string NP (*to*) VP can behave as a surface constituent (1982: §3.2.2), which is an argument against the old Raising-to-object analysis:

[179=133]   (c1449) Pecock, *Repr.* 524.14

But so it is, that sectis . . . to be mad   with inne the comoun
But so it is that sects . . . to be made within   the common

Cristen religioun . . . is not . . . weerned and forboden bi
Christian religion . . . is not . . . refused   and forbidden by

Holi Scripture
Holy Scripture

'But so it is, that for sects to be formed within the common Christian religion . . . is not . . . refused and forbidden by Holy Scripture'

The appearance in [179] of the whole infinitive clause, including subject, as subject of the passive higher verbs *weerned* and *forboden* suggests that it is a constituent. He finds very little evidence for Raising to object (1982: 31), what there is occurring outside his corpus in cases like:

[180]   (c1387–95) Chaucer, *CT.Prol.* I.513

So that the wolf ne   made it nat myscarie; . . .
so that the wolf not made it not miscarry

'so that the wolf did not make it come to harm'

The sandwiched NP *it* in [180] appears within the *made . . . nat* of the higher clause. Warner suggests that Raising may apply only to pronominal NPs, though he prefers a model which can dispense with Raising altogether (1982: 47).

On the analysis of the V + NP + Pred construction, as in

[181]   a1425 *Wycl.Serm.* I E33.50

And þus þe feend þinkiþ hym   sure of synful men . . .
and thus the devil thinks himself sure of sinful men . . .

Warner decides against a rule of *To-Be*-deletion on the grounds that some verbs have the V + NP + Pred construction but show no evidence of occurring with BE + predicate embedded clauses (1982: 89–90).

8.8.2.3* CLAN-sentences

There is some discussion of what Warner calls 'CLAN-sentences' (1982: 91–9):

[182]   a1425 *Wycl.Serm.* II 73.95

þei schulden schame   of   þese dedis, how þei   ben
they would   feel-shame about these deeds how they[= the deeds] are
aʒenus God.
against God

'CLAN' stands for 'clause and nominal', and the idea is that a finite clause (in [182] a *how*-clause) and a nominal (in [182] the PP *of þes dedis*) stand in apposition to each other and together occupy a single position in the argument structure of the higher verb; the clause contains a pronoun coreferential with (part of) the nominal. This idiosyncratic construction (which has restricted parallels in PDE) tends to occur with verbs of knowing and seeing. See also Denison (1990a: 115–16) and §9.3.8.2 below.

8.8.2.4 VOSI after verbs of knowing, thinking and declaring

The spread of VOSI with these two-place verbs is the subject of Warner's Chapter Six (1982: 134–57). He looks at Wyclifite Sermon English, at Chaucer's English (examples of his like [72]–[73] are claimed to be the earliest for the higher verbs in question), and above all at differences between the two versions of the *Wyclifite Bible*, the earlier one a highly literal translation from the Latin *Vulgate*, the later one (which explicitly aimed at clarity) frequently rejecting a VOSI construction used in the earlier version.

Warner argues that VOSI with verbs of knowing, thinking and declaring was only just beginning to become grammatical again in the late fourteenth century. Various factors are discussed which appear to conduce towards use of VOSI with these verbs at the time. The most important are the following:

(A) Latin model
(B) lower verb is BE
(C) sandwiched NP is fronted.

Factor A has been widely cited by other scholars, and Warner demonstrates that VOSI was particularly appropriate to translation from Latin (1982: 140–2). Factor B is not new either. Factor C means that the subject of the lower verb has been removed by Topicalisation, Relativisation, or Passivisation (second passive) from a presumed underlying position immediately before its verb. The second passive is for some verbs more frequent than the active and indeed less confined to Latin translation (1982: 136). An example showing both B and C is:

[183]   a1425 *Wycl.VOct.* 316

but þis pope or þese prelatis we schulde not byleue to be of Cristus
but this pope or these prelates we should not believe to be of Christ's

chirche;
church

Warner suggests that his data show an early stage of syntactic change, with an ***implicationally ordered*** variability (1982: 147–8). Speakers of English familiar with Latin sought to accommodate their language towards the Latin accusative and infinitive without yet being able to use VOSI in normal English. The introduction of VOSI with these verbs was most acceptable if brought about by minimal alteration of existing forms, as for example by insertion of *to be* in a V + NP + Pred construction. Another possible minimal alteration was the reinterpretation of a finite lower verb as infinitive (and insertion of *to*), claimed to be more probable in examples with a fronted NP because the surface identity of the lower clause would be less noticeable. Much the same constraints have operated ever since,[7] though their longevity raises problems (1982: 149–57).

8.8.2.5   Objection to Warner

Ruta Nagucka (1985) tests Warner's methodology for tracing Latin influence in Middle English, by trying a similar exercise on samples of the OE Ælfric and *Beowulf*. She finds that *Beowulf* does not show significantly less use of VOSI after verbs of saying and mental perception than the apparently more Latinate Ælfrician texts and draws the conclusion that Latin influence did not play a part. However, Fischer points out (1989: 194 n.50) that the only VOSI verb of saying and mental perception in *Beowulf* is GEFRIGNAN 'learn by enquiry'. Fischer makes a case (1989: 194–9) for classifying GEFRIGNAN with the (physical) perception verbs (which had had the VOSI construction from proto-Germanic times) rather than with verbs of knowing (which probably accepted VOSI in part under Latin influence), thereby removing the force of Nagucka's objection.

8.8.3   Terasawa

Jun Terasawa (1985) compares the causative use of MAKE with infinitival and various other sorts of complementation in eight biblical translations from the *West Saxon Gospels* to the *New English Bible*. By showing that the relative proportions of causers and causees that are agentive both increase over time, he suggests that in addition to its original pure causative, two-place structure, MAKE has developed an agentive causative, three-place structure. In this context the early ModE examples [95]–[96] become rather interesting. Terasawa notes that the history of HAVE shows some parallels to MAKE.

8.8.4 Fischer

Olga Fischer has dealt with infinitive constructions in a series of substantial and overlapping articles, of which Fischer (1987, 1991, 1992b, forthcoming, and especially 1989) are most relevant here and make up the best modern treatment of the topic. With such a large body of material, though – and even within some of the longer individual pieces – it is difficult to see the wood for the trees. The synopsis that follows was written before the appearance (late 1990) of a PhD dissertation which reprints several of these papers and includes Fischer's own overview. Fischer's theoretical standpoint is if anything Chomskyan, but her discussion is eclectic and much of it non-formal. The thorough examination of philological accounts of the VOSI construction in Fischer (1989: §2) usefully complements my §8.6 above.

8.8.4.1 Old English

Fischer assumes a fourfold categorisation of matrix verbs in Old English (1989: 174–5):

(A) perception verbs
(B) causative verbs
(C) three-place verbs like PDE PERSUADE
(D) two-place verbs like PDE EXPECT

I summarise her discussion of them.[8]

The perception verbs had long been used in the VOSI construction, always with an accusative sandwiched NP (which could be inanimate) and always with a plain infinitive. VOSI could not be used if the time reference of the infinitive differed from that of the higher verb, i.e. if the perception was not direct: in those circumstances finite complementation was *de rigeur*. The finite variants prove that they were two-place verbs (1989: 185–7; 1987; forthcoming).

Causative verbs embrace only LÆTAN, FORLÆTAN, and DON. They resembled perception verbs greatly in all the above respects, except that LÆTAN failed to show finite complementation,[9] and that DON was occasionally followed by a *to*-infinitive (perhaps when used under Latin influence). Finite complementation after DON, and inanimate sandwiched NPs after DON and LÆTAN (as in [57]–[58]), show clearly that in the sense 'cause' they, and by inference FORLÆTAN, were two-place verbs. Fischer suggests (1989: 203–4) that an attractive analysis for OE perception and causative verbs might be to derive their complementation structures via Verb raising (see §4.7.1.2 above). A later paper finds word-order support for the analysis in specific examples (1991: 170):[10]

[184]   *HomU* 15(Robinson) 10

> and him mon þonne lete hangian   þæt heafod andune niþer
> and him one then let hang(INF) the head   down   below

> 'and one was then to make his head hang downwards/him hang head downwards'

PERSUADE-type verbs were three-place, normally occurring with an animate sandwiched NP (often dative) and a *to*-infinitive. This category includes the use of LÆTAN in the sense 'allow, permit'. The contrast between causatives and the PERSUADE type is drawn out in Fischer (1989: 187–90).

Finally, when EXPECT-type verbs occurred in the VOSI pattern it was 'almost exclusively in glosses and literal translations from Latin' (1989: 190). Occurrences of the 'few verbs . . . which seem to form an exception to this statement', namely FINDAN (GEMETAN) 'find', WITAN 'know', GEFRIGNAN (GEASCIAN) 'learn by asking', ONGIETAN 'perceive', are individually explained away – in part following Bock (1931: 222–5)[11] – as belonging with the perception verbs and/or as poetic or Latin-influenced (1989: 191–202). This is an ingenious and largely convincing way of removing some distracting irregularities from the OE system.

8.8.4.2 Middle English

In trying to account for new VOSI possibilities which appeared in the ME period, Fischer rejects Latin influence as more than a facilitating factor, since Latin influence was just as strong in Old English and in the history of Dutch and German. She presents a clutch of changes in Middle English which might have resulted in ambiguous surface structures and hence allowed a reanalysis in which the sandwiched NP might become an argument solely of the lower verb (1989: 168–74). And she discusses the spread of the construction from perception verbs to mental perception verbs to verbs of desire and wishing (1989: 168). None of these is a sufficient condition for the development of the 'genuine aci' (VOSI pattern with EXPECT-type verbs). Lexical diffusion (analogy) *within* a group of verbs could not be the explanation either, since the VOSI construction hardly existed at all in certain groups.

For Fischer the crucial change – the only one unique to English as opposed to Dutch and German – is the word order change SOV → SVO (on which see Chapter 4 above). It is this which she says led eventually, through a rather intricate chain of causation, to the adoption of the VOSI pattern with EXPECT-type verbs (1989: 205–12). The bones of the argument are as follows.

Fischer invites us to compare OE examples like [185] and [186]:[12]

[185]   *Bede* 1 14.58.8

    þa   het   he hi   bidan   on þæm ealonde
    then ordered he them(ACC) wait(INF) on the   island

    'Then he commanded them to wait on the island'

[186]   *ÆLS* II 25.40

    Moyses forbead . . . þa nytenu   to etanne
    Moses forbade . . . the animals(ACC) to eat

    'Moses forbade . . . anyone to eat the animals'

In both sentences there is an accusative NP before the infinitive. Since BIDAN 'wait' is intransitive, [185] must be a VOSI construction and *hi* the subject of *bidan*. While [186] as it stands could in theory be a VOSI construction with *þa nytenu* as sandwiched NP and subject of *to etanne*, it is – Fischer says – a V+I construction with no expressed subject for *to etanne*, and *þa nytenu* is *object* of the lower verb.[13] Fischer claims that other things (context, cultural awareness, transitivity of lower verb) being equal, an NP in front of an infinitive in Old English would by default be interpreted as its object, because of the underlying SOV order. An implicit claim is that this default interpretation was unfavourable to the spread of the VOSI construction in Old English.

After the change to SVO, sentences like [186] would tend to be misinterpreted as if *þa nytenu* were subject of the lower verb, i.e. '!Moses forbade the animals to eat anything'. Accordingly some change was necessary. If an infinitive structure was to be retained, a different word order – and more in accord with SVO – would have resolved the ambiguity. Such a pattern was the one seen in

[187]   Moses forbade to eat the animals.

but it was never widely used (see §8.8.4.3 below.) Alternatively, an explicit, if non-specific, subject for the lower verb could be inserted to turn the V+I into a VOSI pattern (1992b: 55):

[188]   Moses forbade anyone/everyone/people to eat the animals.

[189]   (a1470) Malory, *Wks.* 215.6

He alyght   off   his horse and toke hym in hys armys and there
he alighted from his horse and took him in his arms and there

commaunded knyghtes to kepe   well the corse.
commanded   knights   to watch-over well the body

(Fischer points out that the *knyghtes* of [189] play no further part in the story.) Or then again, the infinitive could be made passive, as in

[190]   Moses forbade the animals to be eaten.

This last option was increasingly resorted to in Middle English for all four kinds of higher verb. (For fuller details see Fischer 1992b: §§2.2–2.3.) But a consequence was that the higher verb then had to be subcategorised as a two-place verb. After all, in [190] *the animals* is not an argument of FORBID.

Here the four groups of verbs seem to dissolve and the picture in Fischer (1989) becomes a little blurred, though Fischer (1992b: §2.3) helps to bring it back into focus, in particular by a discussion of causative-like properties in certain ME PERSUADE-type verbs. (For a similar tendency in Old English see Fischer 1989: 186 n.41.) What seems to be suggested is that VOSI with EXPECT-type verbs became possible because of the following facts and analogies between groups of verbs:

(A)   PERSUADE-type verbs were already used in a VOSI construction
(B)   causative verbs were already used with passive embedded clauses = 'first passive' (Fischer 1992b), especially in replacement of the [186] pattern
(C)   (some) PERSUADE-type verbs resembled causative verbs in several ways
(D)   [from B + C] some PERSUADE-type verbs now sporadically occurred with embedded passive infinitives
(E)   [from D] these PERSUADE-type verbs developed the possibility of a two-place, causative-like argument structure

(F) EXPECT-type verbs already had a two-place argument structure
(G) [from A + E + F] EXPECT-type verbs developed a VOSI construction

In the more fine-grained analysis of Fischer (1992b: §2.4) we find other reasons being offered for the extension of the VOSI construction to verbs of mental perception and declaring. Perhaps we should interpret A–G as providing the systemic framework which *allowed* the VOSI construction to be extended, with various additional incentives for the actual exercise of the option. These include Latin influence in the case of formal, legal documents:

[191] (1471) *Paston* 260.13

> know ye me the seid John Paston, knyght, feithfully to promytte
> know you me the said John Paston knight   faithfully to promise
>
> and graunt by thiez presentes . . .
> and grant   by these present . . .
>
> 'Know that I, the said John Paston, knight, will faithfully promise and grant as witnessed by these people present . . .'

and a host of individual explanations for particular cases, such as the ease with which the long-accepted V + NP + Pred construction could be elaborated; several examples of ambiguity between an infinitive and a contact-clause subjunctive, as in §8.4.2.3; the influence of the neighbouring perception verb SEE on the complementation of UNDERSTAND in

[192] (a1470) Malory, *Wks.* 380.9

> . . . but they wepte to se and undirstonde so yonge a knyght to
> . . . but they wept   to see and understand so young a knight to
>
> jouparté hymself for theire ryght.
> risk   himself for their just-cause

and even occasional causative-like behaviour among these verbs (though is A(D)VENTURE a verb of mental perception at all?):

[193] (1460) *Paston* 156.8

> for she dare not aventure here money to be brought vp to London for feere of robbyng . . .

(On the two-place-ishness of three-place verbs see also §6.3.1.2 above.)

In accepting Warner's hypothesis of accommodation to a model by minimal alteration (§8.8.2.4 above), Fischer adds to his external, Latin model a second, internal model, namely causative verbs (1992b: §3.1). But when she tries to rationalise his account of the minimal alterations themselves, she is less successful (1989: 210–12). Several factors he identifies as increasing the acceptability of new VOSI constructions could all boil down to avoidance of ambiguity in the function of sandwiched NP, which in Old English could have been object rather than subject of the lower verb. That, she says, is why the new VOSIs favoured intransitive lower verbs, including BE and passives. I cannot see why, logically, transitive verbs should have been disfavoured, since a separate explicit object for the verb would serve very well to confirm the subject role of the sandwiched NP. Nor does this seem consistent with the next claim, that VOSI examples with moved NP were more acceptable than otherwise, because such surface patterns had always been possible with an NP moved from object position. If ambiguity was now being avoided in non-moved examples, why should it be tolerated with moved NPs? And anyway the ambiguity being avoided should have ceased with a word-order change allegedly completed two hundred years previously.

8.8.4.3   V+I

As we have seen, V+I constructions play a significant part in Fischer's account of the history of VOSI. In Old English, complements of the lower verb in a V+I construction could precede the higher verb if they were pronominal or topicalised or *Wh*-moved, or could follow the lower verb if heavy or clausal, but their unmarked position was in between higher and lower verbs (1992b: §2.2.1.2). From Middle English the unmarked position for complements was increasingly *after* the lower verb, leaving both verbs adjacent (1992b: §2.2.1.2.1).

Fischer speculates on the reason that such patterns did not prosper (1989: 207–10; 1992b: 44). The V+I construction, she says, involves arbitrary PRO [perhaps better, 'little pro']; see §8.3.1 above. She suggests that adjacency of two verbs was increasingly being confined to like-subject constructions where the non-finite verb, if an infinitive, had as its subject *controlled* PRO. This could occur with 'true auxiliaries such as modals, etc.'[14] and – especially later in Middle English – with Equi verbs:

[194]   c1230(?a1200) *Ancr.* 2b.1

> ha hit mei do þah
> she it   may do though
>
> 'she may do it, however'

[195]   ?a1425(c1380) Chaucer, *Bo.* 3.pr11.192

> But . . . thilke thing that desireth to be and to duelle   perdurably,
> but . . . that   thing that desires to be and to survive permanently
>
> he desireth to ben oon.
> he desires   to be   one

Thus the V+I pattern in its new word order became anomalous and hence obsolescent. Nevertheless ME LETEN shows a slight preference for adjacency to its embedded infinitive. In earlier examples this is ascribed to a partial auxiliation of LETEN, and in later Middle English to the formation of fixed idioms like LET *go*.

8.8.5*   Pintzuk and Kroch

Susan Pintzuk and Anthony S. Kroch (1985, 1989) are not principally concerned with infinitival complementation, but one point in their article is pertinent here. They suggest that the object-subject NP in examples like [196] has been moved rightwards by Heavy-NP Shift:

[196]   *Beo* 864

> Hwilum heaþorofe   hleapan   leton | on geflit faran
> at-times battle-brave(NOM PL) gallop(INF) caused in rivalry go(INF)

fealwe mearas
bay   horses(ACC)

'At times the warriors let the bay horses gallop, run races'

(In this typical OE example of poetic variation there are two appositive infinitives, *hleapan* and *faran*; the NP *fealwe mearas* follows both.) Their justification is a difference between Old English and Modern German. The object-subject NP apparently cannot be postposed beyond the lower verb in German, which would follow neatly if Heavy-NP Shift were absent from its grammar (1985: 97–8; 1989: 124–5 and nn.14–15).

8.9   Infinitive ± *to*

What is the significance of the choice between a plain infinitive and a *to*-infinitive? – for a small collection of data see Visser (1963–73: §897).

8.9.1   Old English

In Callaway's view one factor stands out as predisposing to the use of a *to*-infinitive, namely when the higher verb (or, if a compound, its simplex) governs a case other than the accusative when it has a nominal argument (1913: 60–71). Bruce Mitchell reviews the OE evidence for the *to*-infinitive in VOSI, excluding cases where the sandwiched NP is or may be dative and where the infinitive is or may be final (i.e. purposive). With these stipulations the surviving examples are very meagre indeed (1985: §§3748–51). As we have observed, Hellmut Bock (1931) includes VOSI and final infinitives together, so he has more examples to play with, for all of which he suggests that a *to*-infinitive retains its original meaning. He discusses the spread of *to* with two-place control verbs (same-subject V+I), suggesting that in Old English a verb like LEORNIAN 'learn' took a plain infinitive as complement but a *to*-infinitive when it had an NP object on which the infinitive was in turn dependent (1931: 166). On the question of choice between plain and *to*-infinitive in Old English, Bruce Mitchell has a useful table of references (1985: §971) to other sections of his grammar which deal with the various uses of the infinitive.

8.9.2   Middle English

Moving on to Middle English and to VOSI, Bock observes that the plain infinitive was increasingly confined to a small group of verbs, to which MAKEN acceded. He ascribes alternation between plain and *to*-infinitive with MAKEN to its membership of two different groupings, his types 1 and 2 (our three-place and causative, respectively) (1931: 228–30). By late Middle English we find SUFFREN sometimes being used with a plain infinitive, either through analogy with the causatives or through the influence of a French model (1931: 234–5). Svartvik and Quirk give a table showing the possible infinitive markings associated with different matrix verbs in the VOSI construction (1970: 401).

That there is some apparent randomness in Middle English can be seen from pairs like [197]–[198]:

[197]   (a1399) *Form Cury* 2.76.4

&   make hem to boyle togedere
and make them to boil   together

'and boil them together'

[198]   (a1399) *Form Cury* 2.78.4

&   mak it boyle
and make it boil

For extensive data on Chaucer's English see Kenyon (1909).

Greater-than-usual distance between higher and lower verb is often put forward as an explanation for the use of a *to*-infinitive. In support of such claims is the existence of same-subject V+I examples like

[199]   a1400(c1303) Mannyng, *HS* 10414

And preyd she my3t hys messe here, | And for here housbunde
and prayed she might his mass hear   and for her   husband's

soule to synge
soul   to sing

where a second coordinated infinitive is marked by (*for*) *to* even though the first conjunct is not (if indeed the last clause of [199] really does have the same subject rather than the ellipted subject *him* [*sc*. the friar]). There are occasional examples of coordinated infinitives in VOSI which show the same effect:

[200]   ?c1425(?c1400) *Loll.Serm.* 3.99

Goob and seieb to John bat I make blinde men see, and crokede
go   and say   to John that I make blind   men see and crooked

men to goo
men to go

See Ohlander (1941/42) and Visser's discussion of BID/BEODAN (1963–73: §2078). However, Svartvik and Quirk (1970: 402–3) and Warner (1975: 213, 1982: 128–9) analyse coordinated pairs of infinitives in Chaucer and Wyclifite sermons, respectively, and both find two tendencies, each of which rather contradicts the distance hypothesis:

(A) that the second infinitive should have the same (lack of) marking as the first
(B) that the second infinitive should have *fewer* particles than the first (Ø instead of *to*, Ø or *to* instead of *for to*)

(These results concern infinitives in all sorts of grammatical functions, not just the ones that have formed the subject-matter of this chapter.) Looking at conjoined infinitives, Warner finds separation of the second infinitive *from its conjunction* to be a significant factor, greater separation correlating with greater use of particle (*to, for to*) marking (1982: 129–32).

Jespersen cites the distance between *subject* and lower verb as one factor explaining the prevalence of *to*-infinitive marking in second passives even where the corresponding active would have had the plain infinitive (1909–49: V 315). A second factor he adduces is the less colloquial nature of the passives. An interesting example with plain infinitive is:

[201] 1667 Pepys, *Diary* VIII 562.9 (3 Dec)

He says also, that this day [it] hath been made appear to them that . . .

(Incidentally, was the editor right to insert *it* in [201]?) Jespersen also has some second passives with plain infinitive, mostly – apart from BE *let pass* – obsolete in PDE.

Olga Fischer (forthcoming) argues from a full study of Chaucer and *Paston* that in most cases of variation between plain infinitive and (*for*) *to*-infinitive, use of the plain infinitive correlates very well with direct perception or causation, and a (*for*) *to*-infinitive with indirect causation, perception or whatever. 'Direct' implies simultaneity of the activities expressed in the lower clause and the higher clause, and/or that the activity expressed in the lower clause is directly perceivable or is directly caused by the subject of the higher verb, and/or actuality of the lower clause activity. The two clauses constitute a single event. (Other factors of lesser generality which she discusses include the use of *to*-infinitive to distinguish causative DO from periphrastic DO in texts which use both, the auxiliation of LET, and passive in the higher clause.) She refers to Callaway's observation, noted in §8.9.1 above, that in Old English the bare infinitive commutes with accusative NP objects while the *to*-infinitive commutes with genitive or dative NPs, and links it with van der Leek's claim that, of the non-subjective cases in Old English, only accusative marks a direct participant in the process expressed by a verb (see §§3.1.3.6, 5.6.3 above). Taken together she suggests that the claims fit in nicely with her analysis of the fourteenth/fifteenth-century position.

8.10 Questions for discussion or further research

(a) Do some sample counts in texts of the twelfth, thirteenth and fourteenth centuries to test the relative frequencies of the V + NP + Pred construction (§8.4.3 above) and VOSI after verbs of saying and thinking.

(b) Look for evidence on the appropriate classification of the verb CAUSE in Middle and Modern English, including the examples in *OED*, *MED* and Visser (1963–73: §2068). In what ways does it pattern like FORCE and in what ways like a two-place causative?

(c) Is there a GB analysis of different-subject V+I in PDE which is theoretically kosher (see §8.3.1 above)? If so, does it offer any insight into the widespread use of the construction in earlier English and its subsequent decline (§8.4.6)?

(d) Give a formal analysis of the apparent second passives of V+I in [154]–[158].

(e) Does the history of VOSI in the Scandinavian languages shed any light on Fischer's hypothesis (§8.8.4.2 above) on the effect of word order change on the spread of VOSI in English?

Notes

1. Beware an alternative use of 'n-place' to describe the complementation rather than the valency of the verb, i.e. counting only the items in the VP and *not* the subject. In some of the works cited here, for example Warner (1982), this alternative convention is followed and thus EXPECT is described as a one-place verb, PERSUADE as a two-place verb. I prefer to count *all* the NP arguments, in order to be consistent with previous chapters.

2. For once the labelling of arguments by semantic role makes unhelpful distinctions. The only relevant fact for us is that all PERSUADE-type verbs take two object arguments, one of them an animate NP, the other at least sometimes a clause. With FORCE one could argue that the roles are Theme and Goal, respectively; with PERMIT they might be Source and Theme – thus Fischer (1987: 62 n.5), following Gruber (1976) – or in my view Recipient and Theme; while PERSUADE seems to fall somewhere between FORCE and PERMIT.

   Jespersen's grammatical labelling produces similar conflicts: thus after ALLOW the NP is indirect object and the clause direct object, while after FORCE the NP is direct object and the clause an adverbial (1909–49: V 279).

3. The validity of the S′ bracket round the subordinate clause in [12] is controversial: see §8.2.4 and §8.7.3.1 for two different approaches to the question. In more recent GB work S′ has become CP (i.e. complementiser phrase) and S has become IP (i.e. INFL phrase). I have not adopted this notation.

4. Ard (1977: 14–15) offers yet another viewpoint, suggesting that the Equi analysis is essentially the same as the *apo koinou* (ἀπὸ κοινοῦ 'in common') of Greek and Latin grammar, in that the intervening NP functions as an argument of both higher and lower verbs. However, other criterial features of *apo koinou* are absent, such as the requirement that the *koinon* (here the intervening NP) should make both constructions semantically complete and should be in the same case for each of them (Meritt 1938: 16–17 [170–71]). It is noticeable that Mitchell (1985: §§3789–3803) never mentions VOSI constructions in the context of *apo koinou*.

5. The overall thesis under test is whether synchronic derivations recapitulate diachronic developments; the last third of the dissertation deals with Slavic languages.

6. I have translated Bock's '*Ergänzung*' as 'complement', though perhaps 'completion' would be safer; he certainly wishes to distinguish it from 'object' (1931: 155 n.2).

7. Part of the demonstration is Table 6.8 (Warner 1982: 154), whose figures seem to imply that factors B ('NP TO *be*') and C ('NP fronted') are mutually exclusive, but of course they often co-occur, as in the very first item counted (under ACCOUNT, example dated 1531, in Visser 1963–73: §2079).

8. The terminology includes a bewildering variety of near- and non-synonyms. Fischer distinguishes 'EXPECT type verbs' [large caps] (= types A, B and D = 'aci in the broad sense', i.e. all two-place verbs) from '(pure) *expect* type verbs' (= D only = 'aci in the narrow sense' = ' "learned" aci' (1992b), i.e. two-place verbs which are neither causative nor perception verbs). I will use 'EXPECT-type verbs'[small caps] only for the latter. The following are also used: ' "ordinary" aci' (1992b) = perception verbs + causatives. Note also *verba sentiendi et declarandi* (1992b) = verbs of mental perception and saying, which seems to embrace three narrower categories: *verba declarandi et cogitandi* (1989: 158ff.) = 'verbs of saying and thinking', verbs of mental perception, and verbs of wishing (1989: 205).

9. Fischer suggests without giving evidence that LÆTAN was only able to have a complement in the same tense domain, something which would have made the finite/non-finite distinction redundant. Williams has concocted a possible counterexample (1984: 141, cited by Arimoto 1989: 121 n.9):

  (a) If I could rewrite Russian history, I would let the revolution have already taken place by the time Lenin was born.

It would be worth checking whether LÆTAN was ever actually used for the perfectly conceivable kind of indirect causation where what is caused is not simultaneous with the act of causing.

  Manabe (1989: 115, 157) claims two ME occurrences of LETEN with finite complementation, one of which he quotes:

  (b) a1225(c1200) *Vices and V.(1)* 53.20

  . . . ic ne mai swa laten ðat tu of hire   ȝiet more ne
  . . . I not may so   permit that you of it [*sc.* virtue of humility] still more not
  gehiere;
  hear

  '. . . I cannot permit that you do not hear more about it'

10. The dissertation reprint silently alters the selection of examples (Fischer 1990: 193–4).
11. Fischer has independently reached essentially the same insight as Gorrell (1895: 395, 475–6), who lists WITAN, GEACSIAN, etc. under 'Verbs of Direct Perception' and who asserts of VOSI with perception verbs:

  . . . by the use of this construction the writer portrays the events narrated in the strongest manner, as actually taking place before our eyes; it is mainly the picturesque style of poetry. (1895: 476)

  (Reference due to Lightfoot (1991: 81).)
12. In Fischer (1991: §0) the example of V+I used to set the scene for this same argument is truncated. In full it runs:

  (a) *Rid* 13.1
  Ic seah turf tredan,   X wæron ealra, | VI gebroþor ond hyra
  I saw turf tread(INF) 10 were   in-all(GEN PL) 6   brothers and their
  sweostor mid; | hæfdon   feorg cwico.
  sisters   with   had(PA PL) lives alive

  and is arguably therefore a VOSI rather than V+I, with *VI gebroþor ond hyra sweostor mid* the 'intervening NP', though of course extraposed, and *X wæron ealra* a parenthetic clause. The example – in truncated form and with the reference '*Rid* 14.1' – comes originally from Callaway (1913: 35), where it is classified under 'The Objective Infinitive', i.e. V+I.
13. Actually Fischer misrepresents [186], since the text continues with a dative NP, *þam ealdan folce* 'the old people', which is subject of *to etanne*. There is no ambiguity in this particular example and it should be analysed as VOSI. So as not to obscure her logic I have followed her in truncating the citation.

  There is an argument that the infinitive in [186] should be analysed as 'passive' in GB terms despite its lack of passive morphology, that is, capable of occurring with an agent-phrase and not capable of assigning case. For a rebuttal see Fischer (1991: §2.3.3.2).
14. Not all of Fischer's 'true auxiliaries' would normally be classified as such in GB theory, nor would all be analysed as having a controlled PRO subject in the embedded clause. See further Chapters 9 and 11 below.

Chapter 9

Subject Raising

9.1 The problem

9.1.1

It is a truth universally acknowledged (well, almost) that the surface subjects of the following sentences are not 'really' subject of the **higher** verb:

[1]   Tim appeared to shun publicity.

[2] (a) Max seems to own a number of houses.
     (b) A number of houses seem to be owned by Max.

[3]   There happened to be understudies available.

In [1] it is not 'Tim' who 'appeared'. What 'appeared', surely, is that 'Tim shunned publicity'. *Tim* is an **argument** only of SHUN, not of APPEAR. Similarly, the equivalence in truth-value of sentences [2](a,b) is explained if we assume that SEEM is here a one-**place** verb whose sole argument is roughly the clause *Max owns a number of houses*. The difference between the sentences depends on whether or not that embedded clause has been passivised, but SEEM itself is indifferent as to which NP winds up as its subject. Assuming a similar argument structure for HAPPEN and an embedded clause *there were understudies available* explains the possibility of a dummy surface subject *there* in [3]. Dummy *there* cannot be an argument. Its presence is licensed – or not, as in [4] – by the **lower** clause rather than by HAPPEN:

[4] *There happened to find understudies available.
[5] The director happened to find understudies available.

(Example [5] shows that [4] is not ruled out simply because of some incompatibility between HAPPEN and FIND.)

These and other semantic and syntactic arguments are deployed to justify the claim that the subjects of the higher clauses [1]–[3] have been 'raised' there from underlying subject position in an embedded clause. Such an analysis has been proposed for a number of verbs in many languages, and – with appropriate technical devices – in a variety of theoretical frameworks.

Subject raising is overall more persuasive than the Object raising discussed in §8.2.4.

In Present-day English the verbs which are generally given a Raising analysis are SEEM, CHANCE and their synonyms, *aspectual* verbs like START, CEASE when used with non-agentive subjects (Brinton 1988: ch. 2 has a good discussion of the issues), plus a number of predicates like BE *certain*, BE *likely*, etc. ('LIKELY predicates'). One task in this chapter will be to trace the history of such constructions as

[6] Bob seems to hate fireworks.
[7] Bob is unlikely to lose the race.

Another problem is the history of such constructions as

[8] Bob happened to win the race.

since the equivalent in Old English might well have had *Bob* as dative Experiencer of an impersonal verb rather than nominative; see §9.3.4.1 below. Somewhat similar is

[9] She failed to notice it.

which Jespersen (1937: §16.2) analyses as parallel to PDE HAPPEN, though to my mind the surface subject has a better case to be taken as an argument of the higher verb with FAIL than with HAPPEN, cf. *her failure*. (FAIL was a ME borrowing from French with an impersonal use, much like OE LOSIAN, though with neither FAIL or LOSIAN have I found a type (i/ii) impersonal use with infinitive.)

Once we consider transitions from dative to another case we bump into the history of sentences like

[10] It's good for people to eat polyunsaturates.

and the eventual development of 'inorganic *for*', as in:

[11] It's good for this idea to be tried out.

To help keep the book within bounds I have reluctantly had to neglect this important and much-studied topic. Fischer (1988) offers a full historical analysis and reference to previous work. I have also had to excise most of my material on *Tough-Movement*, the transformation held to underlie pairs like:

[12] (a) Exceptions are difficult/easy/tough to ignore.
      (b) It is difficult/easy/tough to ignore exceptions.

apart from §7.4.2.3. For some discussion see Quirk et al. (1985: 1226–30), and for historical comments Mitchell (1985: §§930–31, 937–43, 1539), van der Wurff (1987, 1990, 1992b), Fischer (1991).

9.1.2 Modals

Finally we must keep in mind the similarities between Raising verbs like SEEM and certain auxiliary verbs. It is quite common to make the comparison between SEEM and a modal verb like MAY, both of which can apparently leave their surface subject to be selected by, and be an argument of, the following verb. Compare [2](a,b) with:

[13] (a) Max may own a number of houses.
     (b) A number of houses may be owned by Max.

This similarity has led some to claim that the so-called auxiliary verbs are just Raising verbs, like them having an embedded clause as argument.

9.1.3* Passive BE

It is even possible to regard passive BE as a Raising verb. Radford (1988: 444–6) outlines an analysis in which the sentence [14] has the simplified derivation [15]:

[14]   Nobody will be arrested.
[15] (a) [$_{NP}$ e] will be [$_{SC}$ [$_{NP}$ e] arrested nobody]
     (b) [$_{NP}$ e] will be [$_{SC}$ [$_{NP}$ nobody] arrested t]
     (c) [$_{NP}$ nobody] will be [$_{SC}$ [$_{NP}$ t] arrested t]

(Here 'SC' stands for *small clause*.) NP-Movement applies twice successively to *nobody*, the first time within the lower clause (= Passivisation) transforming [15](a) to (b), the second time (= Raising) transforming (b) to (c). This analysis is applied by van der Wurff (1990) to Old English.

9.2 Raising

With Raising verbs there have been various proposals as to underlying structure. In some analyses the embedded clause is the subject of the higher verb, leading to the characterisation of examples like [1]–[3] as 'split-subject' sentences, since the embedded clause appears in two separate fragments. In other analyses the lower clause is part of the complement, not the subject, of the higher verb.

In current transformational theory Raising does not exist as a separate transformation. What used to be called Raising sentences are given the following derivations by Andrew Radford (1988: 426, 435ff), with parallel analyses for [16] and [17]:

[16] John is considered to be incompetent.
[17] John seems to me to be unhappy.

Both are derived by NP Movement from underlying structures with empty higher subjects, in other words, by Subject raising, though the underlying position of the subordinate clause is post-verbal:

[18] [$_{NP}$ e] is considered [$_S$ John to be incompetent]
[19] [$_{NP}$ e] seems to me [$_S$ John to be unhappy]

Notice that the subordinate clause is an *Exceptional Clause*, that is, an S rather than an S′.

9.3 The data

9.3.1 SEEM verbs

9.3.1.1 Old English

It has been assumed (e.g. by Fischer and van der Leek 1983: 366 n.18, Allen 1984: 464, Anderson 1988: 14) that Subject raising is already found in Old English with ÞYNCAN 'seem' in such examples as:

[20] *Beo* 866

ðær   him   foldwegas   fægere
where them(DAT) earthways(NOM PL) beautiful(NOM PL)

þuhton
seemed(PL)

'where the paths seemed beautiful [*sc.* suitable for galloping] to them'

[21] *CP* 24.9

&   ðynceð   him   swiðe leoht   sio
and seems(3 SG) them(DAT) very light(NOM) the

byrðen   þæs lareowdomes
burden(NOM SG) the being-a-teacher(GEN)

'and the burden of teaching seems very light to them'

The details are not spelled out, but the implication is that the nominative
NPs *foldwegas* in [20] and *seo byrðen* in [21] are not arguments of
PYNCAN but originate in a lower clause as arguments of the predicate
adjectives *fæger* and *leoht*, respectively. (Whether a verb BE is underlyingly
present and later deleted is wisely not gone into.) For further examples see
Visser (1963–73: §235).

If [20]–[21] are analysed instead as type (ii) impersonals with a ***predicative
complement*** (cf. §§5.2, 8.4.3 above), they need not contain an embedded
minor clause and are not Raising sentences. This alternative analysis – which
Fischer and van der Leek had earlier preferred (1981: 337, 347 n. 64) – is
not available for examples with an unmistakable embedded clause, such as
PDE

[22] Your cough seems to be better.

but such examples are hard to find in Old or early Middle English. Anthony
R. Warner (1992: 196) points to one:

[23] *GD* 179.8

. . . swa þæt me   þynceþ of   gemynde beon
. . . so   that me(DAT) seems out-of memory be(INF)

Paulines   wundor   Nolane burge biscopes . . .
Paulinus's(GEN) miracle(NOM) Nola   city   bishop(GEN) . . .

Lat. ita ut Paulini miraculum, Nolanæ urbis episcopi, . . . memoriæ
defuisse videatur

'. . . so that the miracle of Paulinus, bishop of the city of Nola, seems
to me to have been forgotten'

The text is one with a fairly close adherence to its Latin original. Warner's
other examples of Raising are discussed in §9.3.2 below. As he concedes
himself, Subject raising was rare before the second half of the Middle
English period.

9.3.1.2 Middle and Modern English

In late Middle English and Modern English examples start to reappear, now no longer always in close dependence on a Latin original:

[24]   ?a1425(c1380) Chaucer, *Bo.* 4.pr6.166

that alle thingis semen to ben confus   and trouble to us men
that all   things seem to be confused and trouble to us men

'that all things seem to us men to be confused and disturbed'

[25]   ?a1425(c1380) Chaucer, *Bo.* 5.pr5.32

But the ymaginacioun cometh to remuable   bestis, that
but the imagination   comes to capable-of-movement beasts that

semen to han talent   to fleen or to desiren any thing.
seem   to have inclination to flee   or to desire   any thing

'But imagination comes to beasts that can move, when they seem to have an inclination to flee or to desire any thing.'

[26]   (c1395) Chaucer, *CT.Mch.* IV.1632

And shapen that he faille nat to spede
and contrive that he fail   not to prosper

[27]   (a1398) Trev.*Barth.* 140a/b (*MED* s.v. *faillen*, but ?*fall*)

The tretys   . . . falliþ   to speke somwhat of þinges þat . . .
the treatise . . . fails/falls to speak somewhat of things that . . .

[28]   a1500(a1415) Mirk, *Fest.* 230.17

for þeras   hit was semyng forto be ynpossybull þat . . .
for whereas it was seeming to   be impossible   that . . .

[29]   (c1443) Pecock, *Rule* 46.21

and wheþer þese skilis   proceden and proven what þei þus semen
and whether these reasons proceed   and prove what they thus seem

to prove, y leeve to þe   discussioun of oþere men
to prove I leave to the discussion   of other men

[30]   (1447) *Shillingford* 33 101.26

which offence preveth to be done by the consent of some of the saide Comminalte . . .

[31]   1502–3 *Receyt Kateryne* 1.12

Thympacient wiendes of that coostis shold seme to have ben   greatly
the-impatient winds   of that region would seem to have been greatly

aggreved and not peasably to suffer the bifore-desired   passage
aggrieved and not peaceably to permit the previously-desired journey

of the said Princesse to the coostes of Englond
of the said princess   to the coasts   of England

[32]   1533 More, *Wks.* IX 84.4 [885 C1]

some waye y^t appered at ye firste to mow stande the realme in great
stede

'some way that appeared at first to be able to stand the realm in good
stead'

[33]   1724 Defoe, *Roxana* 214.35

I warrant you it shall not look to be upon your Account;

Arguably [28] should be treated as an example of raising with BE +
adjective, as in §9.3.3. And some examples may in fact not involve a one-
place higher verb at all:

[34]   a1425(c1385) Chaucer, *TC* 1.747

Ek som   tyme it is a craft to seme fle | Fro   thyng whych in effect
also some time it is a trick to seem flee from thing which in fact

men hunte faste.
one hunts eagerly

'Furthermore sometimes it is a trick to appear to flee from something
which one in fact is eagerly hunting.'

[35]   1667 Pepys, *Diary* VIII 571.12 (8 Dec)

That the Duke of Albemarle seems to be able to answer them [*sc.*
papers contradicting his story]

where SEEM probably means 'present oneself as'. Such examples are same-
subject V+I constructions; cf. a similar problem with HAPPEN verbs noted
in §9.3.4.3 below.
   Many but by no means all of the examples have BE as the lower verb. As
with the VOSI constructions there are many examples of the same set of
higher verbs (APPEAR, LOOK, PROVE, SEEM, etc.) with a predicative
complement, as in

[36]   a1425(c1395) *WBible(2)* Isa. 59.15

And the lord si3, and it apperide yuel in hise i3en
and the Lord saw and it appeared bad in his eyes

For further examples see Visser (1963–73: §235, chronological chart §236).
It is noticeable that for a given higher verb, V + Pred always came into use
earlier than V + infinitive.

9.3.1.3   New impersonal uses in Middle English

The verb SEEM was sometimes used in what looks like a Raising structure of
the kind discussed in §9.3.1.2, but with an oblique case instead of subjective
NP:

[37] (c1300) *Havelok* 2917

Hire   semes   curteys   forto be, | For she is fayr so flour
her(OBL) seems/befits courteous to   be   for she is fair as flower

on tre:
on tree

[38] a1400(c1303) Mannyng, *HS* 10641

By hys semblant   and feyre beryng | Hym   semed weyl to be a
by his appearance and fine bearing him(OBL) seemed well to be a

lordyng
lord

[39] a1425(?1400) *RRose* 305

Hir   semede to have the jaunyce.
her(OBL) seemed to have the jaundice

[40] c1440 *Degrev.* 422

Knyghte aunterus, | The   semys   to be envyous
knight   valiant   you(OBL) seems(3 SG) to be envious

[41] ?c1450 *St.Cuth.* 7364

Him   semed to be a kynges ayre
him(OBL) seemed to be a king's heir

It is possible that the first two examples at least involve the verb SEMEN in
its sense 'beseem, befit', which would, unlike the classic Raising verbs under
discussion in this section, be a two-place verb. Where the meaning really
does suggest the one-place verb SEMEN 'seem, appear', however, the
oblique case must be ascribed to blending or contamination (*OED* s.v. *seem*
v.[2] 8b annotates the usage '?by confusion'.) Something very similar
happened with modal verbs at around the same time (see §5.2.6.4), and
both usages may be compared to a similar pattern occurring with HAPPEN
verbs (§9.3.4.1 below).

9.3.2 Second passive of two-place verbs

9.3.2.1 Passive of VOSI

Warner claims (1992: 196) to find in Callaway (1913)

> a handful of undoubted examples of 'subject-raising' type catenative constructions
> with infinitives (including 'second passives' in glosses and close translation (*Bede*
> and Wærferð's *Gregory*) (esp. 1913: 59–60, 72, 82)

(For *catenative* see Glossary.) Of at least ten good examples all but one –
our [23] – involve a higher verb of mental or physical perception in the
passive: SEON 'see', ÆTEAWAN 'show', (GE)LIEFAN 'believe', ONGIETAN

'understand'.[1] And as with [23], most – though not [45] – occur in texts which are close translations of a Latin original. I give a selection below:

[42]   *Bede* 1 12.142.4

þæt he wæs gesewen Criste   þeowian   & eac deofelgeldum
that he was seen   Christ(DAT) serve(INF) and also devil-images

Lat. 116.7 Christo seruire uideretur et diis

'that he seemed to serve both Christ and images of the devil'

[43]   *GD* 203.21

an þing wæs, þæt gesewen wæs on him tælwyrðe   beon,   þæt
one thing was that seen   was in him reprehensible be(INF) that

full oft   swa mycclu blis in him wæs gesægenu beon,   þæt he . . .
very often such great   bliss in him was seen   be(INF) that he . . .

Lat. unum erat quod in eo reprehensibile esse videatur, quod nonunquam tanta ei lætitia inerat, ut illis tot virtutibus nisi sciretur esse plenus, nullo modo crederetur

'there was one thing which seemed to be reprehensible in him – that very often he seemed to be in such a state of bliss that he . . .'

[44]   *Bede* 1 16.88.5

þonne bið   ongyten   ðær syn gefremed beon
then   will-be understood there sin performed be(INF)

Lat. 61.15 tunc peccatum cognoscitur perfici

'then sin will be understood to be being perpetrated there'

[45]   *ChronE* 235.13 (1100)

&   to þam Pentecosten wæs gesewen innan Barrucscire æt anan tune
and at the Pentecost   was seen   within Berkshire   at one village

blod weallan   of   eorþan
blood well(INF) from earth

'and at Pentecost blood was seen welling from the earth at one village in Berkshire'

(Example [45] appears also in §8.4.4.2.)
    Now in current TG these are underlyingly passive (and one-place), and a Subject raising analysis is appropriate, but in earlier TG work their passiveness would have been a derived property, and underlyingly they would have been two-place verbs – as discussed in Chapter 8 – whose surface subject arrived there for example via Object raising and Passivisation.

9.3.2.2   Passive of V + NP + Pred

The construction V + NP + Pred, discussed in Chapter 8 as a precursor of the Object raising VOSI, can undergo a passivisation comparable to the second passive of a VOSI. There are examples in Visser (1963–73: §§1937,

1942, 1946). The resultant pattern can be regarded as an instance of Subject
raising, and Cynthia Allen cites what she calls an 'early' example with
dummy subject (1984: 463), our [56]. But there are several examples in Old
and Middle English. In the following collection [49]–[52] have clearly
anaphoric subjects, but the rest have some claim at least to have dummy
subjects:

[46] *Jud* 285

Her ys geswutelod ure sylfra   forwyrd, | toweard getacnod
here is revealed   our selves(GEN) destruction imminent betokened

þæt . . .
that . . .

'Here our own destruction is revealed, shown to be imminent that
. . .'

[47] *ÆLS* I 25.479

Hit is halig geðoht and halwende to gebiddenne for ðam
it   is holy thought and salutary to pray   for the

forðfarendum
departed

'It is thought holy and salutary to pray for the departed.'

[48] a1400(c1303) Mannyng, *HS* 8614

For sacrylege, alle ys hyt tolde
as sacrilege all is it   reckoned

'it is entirely reckoned as sacrilege'

[49] a1400(c1303) Mannyng, *HS* 11160

hyt   ys holde yn þe more prys
it [*sc.* matrimony] is held   in the greater value

[50] ?a1425(c1380) Chaucer, *Bo*. 3.pr.2.101

And power, aughte nat that ek to be rekned   among goodes?
and power ought not that also to be reckoned among benefits

[51] (a1387) Trev.*Higd*. I 1.xi.83.16

and in þat contray þat   is acounted þe fairest
and in that country that [*sc.* being buried alive]is reckoned the best

hap   and [. . .] worschippe þat eny wyf myȝte haue.
good-fortune and . . . honour   that any wife might have

[52] (a1398) *Trev.Barth*. 310b/b (*MED*)

Atramentum . . . is acounted amonges feynede colours.

[53] (a1398) *Trev.Barth*. 104b/b (*MED*)

Þe ouer parties of þe world is j countid more noble &   worthi
the higher parts   of the world is accounted more noble and worthy

[54] a1450 *St.Kath.(3)* 5

Hit was seen nedeful   to require þe sayde kynge Constaunce to . . .
it   was seen necessary to ask   the said   King C.   to . . .

cease þat rebellion.
crush that rebellion

[55]   1480 Caxton, *Descr. Ireland* (1520) 6/1 (*OED*)

[It] is acounted for a myracle that lechery reygnethe not there as wyne reygneth.

[56]   1545–68 Ascham, *Works* 235.2

that there it is counted good pollicie, when there be foure or fiue brethren of one familie, one, onlie to marie:

9.3.3   NP BE LIKELY + infinitive

There are scrappy collections in Visser (1963–73: §§341–2, 939); cf. also Wülfing (1894–1901: II 197–200). In Present-day English we can argue from

[57]   (a)   The weather is likely to improve.
         (b)   It is likely that the weather will improve.
         (c)   That the weather will improve is likely.
         (d)   *The weather is likely.

that the surface subject of BE *likely* in [57](a) is underlyingly subject of the lower clause but not of the higher one. BE *likely* is a one-place predicate with (here) a clause as sole argument.

9.3.3.1   Old English

When did this construction arise? Consider a curious OE use of *toweard* 'future' noted by Callaway: 'Occasionally *beon* (*wesan*) plus *toweard* represents the future indicative' (1913: 105). (In a brief aside Visser (1963–73: §1379) apparently takes it as a substitute for BEON + *to*-infinitive.) Examples are cited below as [58]–[60] and appear to resemble Raising usages inasmuch as their surface subject can be considered a non-argument of the adjective:

[58]   *Bede* 4 3.268.34 (and sim. *Bede* 3 16.224.19, *Chad* 188)

hwonne he . . . toweard sy in . . . wolcnum . . . to demanne cwice
when   he . . . about   is in . . . heavens . . . to judge   quick

and deade
and dead

Lat. uenturus est . . . ad iudicandos uiuos et mortuos

'when he . . . will in the heavens . . . judge the quick and the dead'

[59]   *BlHom* 81.35

we eac witon þæt he is toweard to demenne, &   þas world to
we also know that he is about   to judge   and this world to

geendenne
end

[60] *ÆCHom* I 12.190.29

Godes sunu, seðe wæs toweard to alysenne ealne middangeard fram
God's son   who was about   to redeem all   earth   from

deofles anwealde
devil's power

Note that examples [61]–[64] (from Toller 1898), especially [64], support such
an analysis of *toweard* – more strongly, at least, than the distributions of
æmettig 'free, at leisure', *fus* 'eager', *gearo* 'ready', etc.:

[61] *Mt(WSCp)* 3.7

. . . fram ðan toweardan yrre
. . . from the future   anger

Lat. a futura ira

'. . . from the vengeance to come'

[62] *Mt(WSCp)* 3.11

Se ðe   æfter me towerd ys
he who after me to-come is

Lat. quis post me venturus est

[63] *Bo* 24.16

þæt he nat   hwæt him   toweard bið
that he not-knows what him(DAT) imminent is

'that he does not know what will happen to him'

[64] *Mt(WSCp)* 2.13

Toweard ys. þæt Herodes secð þæt cild to forspillenne;
imminent is that Herod   seeks the child to destroy

However, an alternative analysis would treat the infinitival clause in
[58]–[60] as a purpose adjunct, so that the surface subject of BEON *toweard*
would actually be an argument of *toweard*, as in [62]. In any case it is
apparently an idiom of translation and of limited currency. Goossens asserts
that no LIKELY adjectives were in use in Old English (1982: 76).

9.3.3.2 Middle and Modern English

With the possible exception of OE examples with *toweard* there are, on the
evidence I have collected so far, no examples like [7] until Middle English,
when the new 'probable' senses of *likely* (borrowed from Old Norse) and
like (influenced by Old Norse) both had a Raising usage; see here Fischer
(1991: §2.4.2). In semantics the participial adjective *wont* resembles the
LIKELY group, especially when predicated of inanimates (*OED* s.v. *wont*
pa.pple. 2(b)), but it does not seem to occur in the *it*-construction; cf. also
§9.3.5.2. In early Modern English or even later some other adjectives,
mostly French or Latin borrowings, developed similar usage, often

shortlived. Only *certain, fated, (un)likely, sure* seem to have maintained it
(Huddleston 1984: 307, Quirk et al. 1985: §1679).

[65] a1400(a1325) *Cursor* 3452

   Hir lijf was lickest   to be ded.
   her life was likeliest to die

[66] a1400(a1325) *Cursor* 4877

   I sai it noght for-qui   þat yee | Ne ern lickli lel   men to be
   I say it not   for-the-reason that you not are likely loyal men to be

[67] (c1385) Chaucer, *CT.Kn.* I.1692

   thider was the hert wont   have his flight
   thither was the hart in-the-habit have his flight

   'the hart tended to run away in that direction'

[68] a1425(c1385) Chaucer, *TC* 3.1268

   . . . thow me . . . Hast holpen, there I likly   was to sterve
   . . . you me . . . have helped where I likely was to die

[69] 1395 Purvey, *Remonstr.*(1851) 84 (*OED*)

   The noueltees of this Innocent ben vnlicli to be sothe.

[70] c1425(c1400) *Ld.Troy* 15612

   Thei myȝt ther-fore be sur &   bold | To scle the kyng &   brenne
   they might therefore be sure and bold to slay the king and burn

   Ilyoun.
   Ilioun

[71] (1478) *Paston* 312.10

   . . . þat ther is like   to be troble in the maner off Oxenhed
   . . . that there is likely to be trouble in the manor of Oxnead

[72] a1500 *Imit.Chr.* 94.21

   And he þat . . . demeth himself more unworþi . . ., he is more apte
   and he that . . . judges himself more unworthy. . . he is more likely

   to receiue gretter ȝiftes.
   to receive greater gifts

[73] 1512 *Helyas* in Thoms *Prose Rom.*(1828) III.131 (*OED*)

   Yf ye be able and possible to reedifie the churches of God.

[74] 1524 Wolsey in *State Papers* (1836) IV.197 (*OED*)

   The high benefites . . . apparant to ensue unto theym.

[75] 1528 More, *Wks.* VI 348.4 [248 F3]

   yet be such workys . . . apte to corrupt and infecte the reder.

[76] 1538 Henry VIII in *Wyatt's Wks.*(1816) II.498 (*OED*)

Unjust . . . demands, and unlike to proceed out of a willing heart to conclude.

[77]   1623(1595–6) Shakespeare, *Rom* I.v.135

My graue is like to be my wedding- [*Folio:* wedded] bed.

[78]   1653 Walton, *Angler* ii.49 (*OED*)

I'l be as certain to make him a good dish of meat, as I was to catch him.

[79]   1653 Gauden, *Hierasp.* 114 (*OED*)

These rustick and rash undertakers . . . are only probable to shipwrack themselves.

[80]   1667 Milton, *Paradise Lost* 9.359

Firm we subsist, yet possible to swerve

A large group of examples has passive infinitives in the lower clause. There is a good collection in van der Gaaf (1928: 133–7):

[81]   a1500(a1415) Mirk, *Fest.* 73.34

þe pepull ys combyrt   wyth þe same synne, and ys full like   to
the people are encumbered with the same sin   and are very likely to

be smytten wyth þe same vengeans . . .
be struck   by   the same vengeance . . .

[82]   (?a1439) Lydg. *FP* 6.2843

Calipurnia . . . | Hadde a drem . . . | How that hir lord was likli to be lorn | Be conspiracy . . .

'Calipurnia . . . dreamt . . . how her lord was likely to die as a result of a conspiracy . . .'

[83]   a1500(?a1450) *GRom.* 88.31

. . . he come by   a   depe water, Þat was impossible to be passid
. . . he came upon some deep water that was impossible to cross

[84]   (?1450) *Paston* 456A.10

what were   most necesary to be desierid   of   the Kyng . . .
what would-be most necessary to be requested from the King . . .

'what would be most necessary to request from the King . . .'

[85]   (1465) *Paston* 324.18

. . . that ther wer   leek to be do   gret harme on bothe ouyr
. . . that there would-be likely to be done great harm on both our

pertyes
sides

'. . . it would be likely for great harm to be done on both of our opposing sides'

[86]   a1500 *Imit.Chr.* 94.30

Thou knowist what is expedient to be ȝouen to euery body
you know   what is expedient to be given   to everybody

[87]   1616 Sheldon, *Mirr. Antichr.* Pref. ¶¶jb (*OED*)

Such Conuerts . . . are sure to bee beset with diuerse sorts of Aduersaries.

[88]   1852 Smedley, *L. Arundel* xxvii.204 (*OED* s.v. *safe* a. 12b 'certain')

Society had better shut up shop at once, for it's safe to be 'uprooted from its very foundations'.

9.3.4   HAPPEN verbs

9.3.4.1   Non-subject Experiencer

From Old English to early Modern English the HAPPEN verbs had a type (i/ii) construction (in the classification of §5.2.2 above) with a clausal Theme, and a dative (or oblique) Experiencer argument in the higher clause. The Theme argument could be non-finite and therefore subjectless only if the unexpressed subject was coreferential with ('controlled by') the Experiencer NP. Examples with non-finite Theme are very rare in Old English, to judge from Ogura's material (1986):

[89]   *Bede* 4 33.382.11

ða   gelamp   him   semninga mid gife þære godcundan
then happened him(DAT) suddenly with gift the   divine

arfæstnesse þurh   reliquias ðæs halgan fæder Cuðbryhtes
faith(GEN) through relics   the holy   father Cuthbert(GEN)

gehæledne beon
healed   be(INF)

Lat. contigit eum subito divinæ pietatis gratia per sanctissimi Patris Cudbercti reliquias sanari

'then suddenly with the gift of divine faith he happened to be healed by means of relics of the holy father Cuthbert'

[90]   *HomU* 51 154.10

ac þam cilde   ne becymð næfre into heofonan rice
but the child(DAT) not happens never into heaven's   kingdom

becuman.
come(INF)

'but the child will never manage to get into the kingdom of heaven'

[91]   (c1395) Chaucer, *CT.CY.* VIII.649

Ful oft   hym   happeth to mysusen it
very often him(OBL) happens to misuse   it

[92]   (c1390) Chaucer, *CT.Pard.* VI.885

it happed hym, par cas, | To take the botel ther   the poyson was
it befell   him by chance to take the bottle where the poison was

[93]   (a1470) Malory, *Wks.* 272.35

And at the laste by fortune hym   happynd . . . to com to a
and at the last   by chance him(OBL) happened . . . to come to a

fayre courtelage
fair   courtyard

'And eventually by chance he happened . . . to come to a fair
courtyard'

[94]   1590–96 Spenser, *FQ* 1.ii.12.5

At last him chaunst to meete vpon the way | A faithlesse Sarazin . . .

This construction with infinitival Theme is found occasionally with other
classes of impersonal verb in Old English and has survived with some of
them to the present day, now with obligatory dummy subject:

[95]   *CP* 99.19

hu flæsclicum monnum   gedafonode on hira burcotum &
how carnal   men(DAT PL) behoved(SG) in their chambers and

on hiera beddum to donne
in their beds   to do

'what was proper for carnal men to do in their chambers and beds'

[96]   *ÆCHom* I 27.394.15

ac hit ne fremede him   swa gedon
but it   not profited him(DAT) so   do(INF?)

'but it did not benefit him to do so'

[97]   *ÆCHom* II 16.161.20

ne gedafonode criste   swa ðrowian.   and swa faran
not befitted   Christ(DAT) thus suffer(INF) and thus go(INF)

into his wuldre
into his glory

[98]   *ÆCHom* II 33.284.168

& us   ne gebyrað   to ameldigenne ða
and us(1 DAT/ACC PL) not behoves(3 SG) to make-known the

scyldigan
guilty

[99]   c1180 *Orm.* 5554

& hu þe   birrþ   uppo þin fend All
and how you(2 SG OBL) behoves(3 SG) in   your enemy all

hatenn woh & sinne
hate   crime and sin

'and how it behoves you wholly to hate crime and sin in your enemy'

[100] It behoves me to mention this.

The higher verb is a two-place verb.

9.3.4.2 Raised subject ≠ Experiencer

From late Middle English onwards one finds examples with a subject NP in
the higher clause which cannot be an argument of the higher verb. The
clearest cases have dummy subject NPs, which cannot be an argument of
any verb:

[101] c1450(?a1400) *Destr. Troy* 742

And oft   in astronamy hit auntres to falle, | Þat domes men
and often in astronomy it   happens to befall that fate   men

dessauis   and in doute bringes.
deceives   and in fear   brings

[102] 1553 Eden *Treat. New Ind.* (Arb.) 5 (*OED*)

There chaunsed . . . to come to my handes, a shiete of printed paper.

(Examples [71] and [85] with LIKELY predicates involve dummy subjects
too.)

   Inanimate NPs can hardly be Experiencer arguments and may therefore
be assumed not to be arguments of the higher verb:

[103] a1400(c1303) Mannyng, *HS* 75

Þe ȝeres of grace fyl þan to be | A þousynd & þre   hundred &
the years of grace fell then to be   one thousand and three hundred and

þre.
three

'It happened then to be 1303 A.D.'

[104] a1400 Lanfranc 100.10

ofte tymes alle þese causis happen to come togiders
often   all   these causes happen to come together

The higher verb must be a one-place verb.

   Notice the following example apparently *without* Raising of *the seyd
patentes*, the inanimate subject of the lower verb:

[105] (?1455) *Paston* 51.8

And for asmeche as it fortowned be grase the seyd patentes to be
and for as much as it chanced   by grace the said patents to be

mystake so þat they were not laufull ne suffycyent . . .
faulty   so that they were not lawful nor sufficient . . .

'and given that it chanced by grace of God that the said documents
were faulty, so that they were not lawful or sufficient . . .'

9.3.4.3   Raised subject ?= Experiencer

Animate NPs are more difficult. If they are in subjective case, they clearly differ from the non-subject Experiencers discussed in §9.3.4.1, but in principle they at least *could* still be Experiencers:

[106]   (a1470) Malory, *Wks.* 1046.19

> for I may happyn to ascape

> 'for I may happen to escape'

[107]   c1450(?a1400) *Destr. Troy* 5369

> Teutra . . . | Þat Achilles, with a chop, chaunsit to sle
> Teutra . . .   that Achilles with a blow   chanced to kill

[108]   1667 Pepys, *Diary* VIII 572.25 (8 Dec)

> . . . for he doth happen to be held a considerable person of a young man, both for sobriety and ability.

Under such an analysis there would be a two-place structure for the higher verb, with – in TG terms – PRO in the lower clause under subject control. Alternatively such examples may be – and for PDE usually are – grouped with the one-place examples of §9.3.4.2.

9.3.5   Aspectual verbs

9.3.5.1   BEGIN verbs (ingressive)

Aspectual verbs occur in Old and Middle English in patterns which could involve Subject raising. Examples are the more convincing the less agentive the subject of the higher verb and hence the less likely that the NP is an argument of the higher verb:

[109]   *HomS* 25.96 (*DOE*)

> þonne hit on morgene ærest dagian   onginneð
> when it in morning first   dawn(INF) begins

> 'when dawn first begins to break in the morning'

[110]   c1180 *Orm.* 4782

> & war & wirrsenn toc anan   ut off hiss lic   to flowenn
> and pus and corruption took at-once out of his body to flow

> 'and pus and corruption at once began to pour out of his body'

[111]   c1225(?c1200) *St Marg. (1)* 22.4

> Hire bleo   bigon to blakien
> her countenance began to grow-pale

[112]   c1330 *Orfeo* 247

> þei   it comenci   to snewe and frese
> though it commence to snow and freeze

[113]   a1400(a1325) *Cursor* 24414

þe   aier gun   durken and to blak
the   air   began darken and to turn-black[?]

[114]   ?c1425(?c1400) *Loll.Serm.* 2.670

Wanne þese þyngis bigynnen for   to be doon
when   these things begin   (for) to be done

Perhaps we should include a wholly subjectless example here:

[115]   c1175(?OE) *HRood* 2.1

HER ONGINNÆÐ to sæcgæn be þæm treowe þe   ðeo rode wæs
here begins   to tell   of the   tree   that the cross was

of   iwroht. . . . hu . . .
from made   . . . how . . .

'Here it begins to tell about the tree that the cross was made of, . . .
how . . .'

The aspectual verb ONGINNAN/AGINNAN 'begin' occurs in Old English
with the infinitive of an impersonal verb in such sentences as:

[116]   *ChristA, B, C* 1414

Ða   mec   ongon hreowan þæt . . .
then me(ACC) began rue   that . . .

'Then I began to feel regret that . . .'

[117]   *LS* 35(VitPatr) 330

Þa   ongan   me   langian for   minre hæftnyde
then began(3? SG) me(ACC) grieve because-of my   imprisonment
and ic   ongan   gyrnan, þæt . . .
and I(NOM) began(1 SG) yearn   that . . .

'Then I began to find my imprisonment tedious and I began to yearn
that . . .'

Of some fifteen instances of ONGINNAN/AGINNAN + type (i) or (i/ii)
impersonal (Denison 1990b: §2.2.2), eight have an Experiencer argument.
As discussed in that paper, the behaviour of ONGINNAN with impersonals
suggests that case assignment within these sentences is being determined
entirely by the argument structure of the impersonal verb.

Similar sentences are found in Middle English, even apparently once with
BIGINNEN:

[118]   c1225(?c1200) *St Marg.(1)* 42.10

Him   bigon to gremien,   & o grome gredde
him(OBL) began to grow-angry and in rage   cried-out

'He began to grow angry and cried out in rage.'

[119]   c1380 *Firumb.(1)* 49

On herte him   gan   to nuye

in heart him(OBL) began to be-vexed

'He became vexed in heart'

[120]   c1380 *Firumb. (1)* 978

Ac wan   Charlis hit wiste &   seȝ; for hymen hym   gan   to
but when Charles it   knew and saw for them   him(OBL) began to

maye
dismay

'But when Charles saw it and took it in, he was dismayed for them.'

As Ogura (1991) points out, some examples lend themselves to analysis
either as impersonal or reflexive.

The 'transparency' of ONGINNAN, a one-place verb with clausal argument,
is very reminiscent of the behaviour of Raising verbs in Modern English.
Can we therefore analyse [116]–[120] as Raising sentences? If we do, we
must recognise one of the following:

(A) 'Subject raising' of non-subject NPs
(B) Subject raising of NPs with non-nominative morphology
(C) Verb raising (as discussed in §4.7.1.2 above)

Option A, though it would widen the definition of Subject raising
alarmingly, is probably tenable in more modern versions of TG which do
not distinguish Subject raising from other sorts of NP Movement; it would
be best simply to use the label NP Movement.

Option B is the one favoured by von Seefranz-Montag, who takes the
existence of sentences like [116]–[117] as confirmation of the subjecthood of
certain non-nominative Experiencer arguments (see §5.7.1 above). Note
that Allen's analysis of the impersonal LICIAN (§5.7.2 above) treats a non-
nominative Experiencer as subject only if in preverbal position. In these
eight examples we have *two* verbs in the clause, of course, a possibility not
discussed in Allen (1986a). Four times out of eight OE examples the
Experiencer follows ONGINNAN (as with [117]), but it always precedes the
lexical verb.

Option C is presumably favoured by van Kemenade, since she posits Verb
raising for modal verbs in Old English, and in this respect ONGINNAN
behaves exactly like the modals. See further §11.3.9.6 below.

Brinton (1988) concentrates on the semantics and does not provide
detailed syntactic analysis of historical examples.

Visser gives examples of verbs of hesitating, etc. (1963–73: §1252), which
Ard chooses to treat as Raising verbs. All naturally have human subjects.

9.3.5.2 Continuative/iterative and egressive verbs

Various examples:

[121]   c1180 *Orm.* 14564

Fowwerrtiȝ daȝhess all onnann   Ne blann itt nohht to reȝȝnenn
forty   days   all continuously not ceased it not   to rain

'For forty days together it did not stop raining'

[122]   (a1393) Gower, *CA* 4.507

love is welwillende |To hem that ben continuende | With besy herte
love is benevolent   to those who are continuing   with busy heart

to poursuie . . .
to pursue . . .

[123]   1604 Bacon, *Apol.* Wks. 1879 I.436 (*OED*)

A sonnet directly tending and alluding to draw on her Majesty's
reconcilement to my lord.

[124]   1662 Stillingfl. *Orig. Sacr.* III.iv.§10 (*OED*)

It may further tend to clear the truth of the Scriptures.

[125]   1689 *Sc. Acts* (1875) XII. 61/2 (*OED*)

Letters . . . ordering the Judges to stoppe and desist sine die to
determine causes depending before them.

One verb worth focusing on is OE GEWUNIAN (once, WUNIAN) 'be
accustomed', which without the prefix survived into the ModE period as
WONT (latterly virtually replaced by BE *wont*). Visser gives examples of
GEWUNIAN + infinitive (1963–73: §§1331–2), claiming: 'The subject of the
sentence exclusively refers to living beings.'

[126]   *Or* 23.27

Ða sæde he Pompeius þæt . . . he gewunode   monigc wundor
then said he Pompeius that . . . he was-in-the-habit many   marvel(s)
to wyrcenne
to perform

'Then Pompeius said that . . . he [Joseph] was in the habit of
performing many marvels.'

[127]   *Bede* 1 15.62.4

in þære   cirican seo cwen gewunade   hire   gebiddan
in the/that church the queen was-in-the-habit herself pray(INF)

'the queen was in the habit of praying in that church'

But Callaway notes four examples of GEWUNIAN where the lower infinitive
is passive *beon* (1913: 87), and in at least three of them the subject is
inanimate:

[128]   *Bede* 3 6.172.26

monig weorc . . . &   monig tacen . . . wundra   . . .
many deeds . . . and many signs . . . miracles(GEN). . .
gewuniað   . . . sægd   beon
are-accustomed . . . said(PA PTCP) be(INF)

Lat. 143.3 solent opera . . . et signa . . . narrari

'many deeds . . . and many signs . . . of miracles tend to be told of'

[129]   *Bede* 4 3.270.32

gewuniað   . . . wundor hælo   geworden   beon
are-accustomed . . . miracles health become(PA PTCP) be(INF)

Lat. 212.9 solent . . . miracula operari

'miracles of healing are in the habit of being done'

[130] *Bede* 5 20.474.13

þe hie næfre ær   gewunedon   in þæm stowum
that they never before were-accustomed in those places

weorþade   beon
honoured(PA PTCP) be(INF)

Lat. 348.4 nunquam . . . celebrari solebat

'who had never been customarily honoured in those places before'

[131] *GD* 183.17

be   þam ylcan Iohanne þis wundor gewunode
concerning this same John   this miracle was-accustomed

beon   sæd fram urum witum
be(INF) told by   our   wise-men

Lat. 224A De quo etiam illud mirabile . . . narrari solet

Semantically it is tempting to regard the higher subject as an argument only
of the lower verb, though this cannot be proved. If accepted, that would
make GEWUNIAN a Raising verb. Semantically it could be seen as an
aspectual with iterative meaning. There is no evidence of an *it*-construction
(Extraposition) with GEWUNIAN, though that follows from the fact that
GEWUNIAN is not an impersonal (and would not in any case be demanded of
an aspectual).

9.3.6 Modal verbs

Modal verbs get Chapter 11 to themselves, so it will suffice here to say that
several of the OE modals occur in patterns amenable to analysis as Subject
raising, both with nominative subjects and with oblique (?)'subjects' like
those in [116]–[117]. Good examples with nominative subjects include those
where the modal has epistemic meaning, for then the semantics imply that
the only argument of the modal is the embedded clause, not an NP, or with
inanimate subjects:

[132] *Bo* 116.3

Sio hi   sædon sceolde   bion swiðe drycræftigu
she they said   was-supposed-to be   very skilled-in-magic

[133] *ÆCHom* II 40.339.131

Gif we deoplicor   ymbe ðis sprecað. þonne wene we þæt hit wile
if   we more-deeply about this speak   then think we that it   will

ðincan ðam ungelæredum   to menigfeald
seem   the unlearned(DAT) too complicated

'If we speak about this more deeply, we think that it will seem too
complicated to/for uneducated people'

There are nearly 150 examples with non-nominative Experiencers in Old
English (Denison 1990b):

[134]   *LS* 34(SevenSleepers) I 23.93

    . . . þe   wolde þincean færunga swilce . . .
    . . . you(DAT)[2] would seem   suddenly as-if . . .

    '. . . it would suddenly seem to you as if . . .'

[135]   *Or* 115.30

    his   me   sceal aþreotan for Romana gewinnum
    it(GEN) me(DAT/ACC) shall weary   for Romans' conflicts

    'I must weary of it because of the conflicts of the Romans'

The options for analysis seem to be the same as those outlined in §9.3.5.1
above, except that it is possible to find the word order where Experiencer
follows both verbs:

[136]   *OrW* 21

    ne sceal þæs   aþreotan þegn modigne, | þæt
    not shall that(GEN) irk(INF) thane proud(ACC SG MASC) that

    he . . .
    he . . .

    'It shall not be irksome to a brave nobleman that he . . .'

[137]   *ÆIntSig* 61 400

    Ic axige hwæðer hit mihte gedafenian abrahame þam halgan were.
    I ask whether it might befit   Abraham the holy   man(DAT)

    þæt he . . .
    that he . . .

    'I ask whether it might have been fitting for Abraham, the holy man,
    to . . .'

Examples with non-subjective Experiencers continue to be found well into
the ME period:

[138]   (c1395) Chaucer, *CT.Cl.* IV.908

    Hym   wolde thynke   it were a disparage | To his estaat
    him(OBL) would seem/think it was   a disgrace   to his estate

    'It would seem to him a disgrace to his estate.'

9.3.7   Was there Raising in Old English?

Apart from [23], then, the existence of Raising with Old English
ÞYNCAN remains open to question, depending as it does on the precise
relationship between examples like [20]–[21] and those like [24]–[33]. This is

sometimes handled in terms of a transformation of *To-be*-Deletion; see for example Borkin (1973) and also §8.8.2.2 above.

Van Kemenade flatly describes the following as instances of Subject raising in Old English (forthcoming: 296–7):

[139]   *CP* 177.19

. . . ða   ðe   him   ðyncð   micel
. . . those who themselves(DAT) seems(3 SG) great

earfoðu   & micel gesuinc to habbanne
hardship(NOM/ACC NEUT PL) and great labour to have

'. . . those who think it[*sc.* transitory authority] a great hardship and trouble to hold'

[140]   *Or* 132.10

ne ferþan þætte ænigum folce   his ægenu æ gelicade
not even that any   people(DAT SG) its own   law pleased

to healdenne
to hold

'that it did not even please any nation to keep its own law'

But [139]–[140] are poor candidates for Raising, given that the dative NP in the higher clause seems to be an argument of the higher verb; better to regard them as involving control by the Experiencer argument, as discussed in §9.3.4.1 above.

There is limited evidence of Raising in second passives (§9.3.2), and arguable instances with BEON *toweard* (§9.3.3.1), aspectuals (§9.3.5), GEWUNIAN (§9.3.5.2), and modals (§9.3.6).

9.3.8   Finite complementation

9.3.8.1

Vilho Kohonen (1978: 196 n.7) gives the following examples of *that*-clauses where later usage would prefer infinitival complementation:

[141]   *ÆCHom* I 3.56.1

Micel gedeorf bið me   þæt ic minne feond lufige
great hardship is me(DAT) that I my   enemy love

'It is a great hardship for me to love my enemy'

[142]   *ÆCHom* I 4.74.15

tima is þæt þu mid ðinum gebroðrum wistfullige on minum
time is that you with your   brothers   feast   at my

gebeorscipe
banquet

'It is time for you to feast at my banquet with your brothers'

[143] *ÆCHom* I 5.86.22

> Wearð þa eac his læcum   geðuht   þæt hi on
> became then also his leeches(DAT) seemed/thought that they in
> wlacum   ele hine gebeðedon
> lukewarm oil him bathed

'It then seemed good to his leeches to bathe him in lukewarm oil'

9.3.8.2*   Topicalisation or raising?

In Denison (1990a) I offered the following example as a possible blend construction:

[144] c1225(?c1200) *SWard* 66

> ant euch her þuncheð þet stont in his heaued up.
> and each hair seems   that stands in his head   up

'and it seems that (= as if) each hair on his head stands on end', 'and each hair on his head seems to stand on end'

It looks as if *euch her* in [144] is functioning as subject of the higher verb, which would mean that – exceptionally – it had been 'raised' out of a *finite* clause (= second translation). However, Aimo Seppänen and Gunnar Bergh have pointed out to me (p.c., 4 March 1990, 12 May 1990) that an alternative analysis is possible here and has wider applicability, namely that *euch her* has been topicalised rather than raised (= first translation). Example [144] would then be a straightforward instance of PUNCHEN in subjectless use with a *that*-clause complement, apart from the unusual position of the subject of the *that*-clause.

In support of the topicalisation analysis Seppänen offers some comparable instances, of which [146] is closest:

[145] a1225(?a1200) *Trin.Hom.* 65.25

> þis us bihoueð þat we eche dai don.
> this us behoves that we each day do

[146] a1425(?a1400) *Cloud* 59.10

> Alle men   him   þink ben   his freendes, &   none his foen
> all   men(PL) him(OBL) seem be(INF) his friends   and none his foes

Further examples provided by Seppänen have an empty subject position in *that*-clauses because of *Wh*-Fronting rather than Topicalisation:

[147] a1425(?a1400) *Cloud* 36.4

> ȝif it be a þing þat þee   þink greueþ   þee or haþ greued
> if it be a thing that you(OBL SG) seem grieves(3 SG) you or has grieved
> þee before.
> you previously

[148] ?a1425(c1380) Chaucer, *Bo.* 1.pr4.126

> Now what thyng semyth myghte ben likned to this cruelte?

'Now what thing does it seem might be likened to this cruelty?'

[149] ?a1425(c1380) Chaucer, *Bo.* 3.pr1.14

And tho   remedies whiche that thou seydest herbyforn that weren ryght
and those remedies which   you said   previously that were very

scharpe, . . .
sharp . . .

'And those remedies which you said previously were very sharp . . .'

But Seppänen points out that the Raising analysis also has support:

[150] ?1528 Tyndale, *Obedience* 241.24

if I do the works which are prophesied that Christ should do when he
cometh

though [150] would have to be Raising out of *object* position in a finite clause, or
just a parasitic gap.

A somewhat similar construction is common in Old English in apparent
avoidance of (passive) VOSI after SECGAN 'say':

[151] *GD(C)* 307.12

witodlice se   Tiburtius   wæs sægd, þæt he underlæge a   &
indeed   that Tiburtius(NOM) was said   that he submitted-to always and

hyrde   symble þam lichamlicum lustum.
followed always the bodily   desires

'Indeed this Tiburtius was said always to submit to and follow carnal
desires.'

Here, though, a pronoun copy is left in the lower clause, so that [151] is almost a
second passive of a CLAN-construction (see §8.8.2.3), except that the higher
subject could not have been a direct object in the active.

9.4 Explanations

There is relatively little written on the history of Subject raising, and not
much disagreement. These sources are offered:

(A) passive of VOSI with verbs of perception and saying and thinking, with
    a possible precursor in the passive of V + NP + Pred
(B) SEEM verbs + Pred
(C) loss of argument status for the oblique Experiencer with HAPPEN
    verbs, associated with cessation of impersonal behaviour
(D) loss of argument status for the subjective Experiencer with LIKELY
    predicates, especially BE *sure/certain*
(E) loss of argument status for the subjective Theme with SEEM verbs
(F) Scandinavian influence on the semantics and syntax of *like(ly)* and of
    HAPPEN, and borrowings from romance of other LIKELY adjectives

They overlap to some extent, so that for instance A, C, D and E all
arguably bear on the use of *wont* 'in the habit of' + infinitive, a word often
indeterminate between adjective and verbal past participle. The main areas
of contention are whether PYNCAN + Pred in Old English should be

analysed as a Raising structure, and how far the history of SEEM verbs ties
in with HAPPEN verbs.

9.4.1 Zeitlin and Callaway

Jacob Zeitlin's dissertation (1908) has a little material relevant to Subject
raising, namely some second passive examples in the chapter on the
accusative with infinitive, and some ME examples of infinitival complementation with impersonal or formerly impersonal verbs. The latter appear in
the chapter on 'inorganic *for*', where Zeitlin does have something to say.
Otherwise there is little of explanatory value. A selection of Zeitlin's
examples appears in §9.3.

Morgan Callaway jr.'s dissertation (1913) has a great deal of OE material
efficiently organised, but little in the way of historical explanation. What
there is is confined to discussion of choice between plain and *to*-infinitive,
and of native origin vs. Latin influence.

9.4.2 *OED*, Jespersen

9.4.2.1 Reanalysis of impersonals

Otto Jespersen deals with certain aspects of Subject raising under the
heading of 'Nexus. Subject' (1909–49: III 208–20, published in 1927). This is
where he advances his reanalysis hypothesis for impersonal verbs with
nominal arguments, already discussed in §5.4.1 above. The same explanation is clearly intended to stand for verbs like HAPPEN with an infinitival
complement, namely that a preposed oblique Experiencer (as in §9.3.4.1)
was reanalysed as subject (as in §9.3.4.2). *OED* has this explanation too,
s.vv. *chance* v. 1c (published 1888–93), *hap* v.¹ 2, *happen* v. 3. Jespersen has
further synchronic material on the analysis of PDE 'split subject with
infinitive' in (1909–49: V 268, 315–19) and in (1937: 55–7).

9.4.2.2 Semantic change

Jespersen does not intend this explanation to apply to predicates like BE
sure, BE *certain*, since they do not seem to have been used with oblique
Experiencers. Instead, following *OED* s.v. *sure* a. 12, they are discussed
only in terms of semantic change (1909–49: III 212–13). Thus Jespersen
assumes that an earlier type [152]:

[152]   He is sure to return.

    'He is sure of returning.'

changed in some unexplained way to the present construction [153]:

[153]   He is sure to return.

    'It is certain that he will return.'

In other words, *he* is an argument – Experiencer – of BE *sure* in [152] but not
in [153]. Once the type [153] had come into existence, however, it had the
same structural analysis as modern instances of Subject raising with

HAPPEN verbs (1909–49: III 227–9). (Jespersen cites similar usage with *safe*, *like(ly)* and even nonce instances with *improbable*, *inevitable*, though without making clear what their origins might be.)

In fact, though, Jespersen's accounts of HAPPEN verbs and BE *sure* predicates have a lot in common. Both are seen as originally two-place predicates with an Experiencer argument, and both come to be one-place predicates with only a clausal Theme as argument.

9.4.2.3 Objections to Jespersen

Kageyama (1975: 173–4) has three criticisms of Jespersen's account of the history of HAPPEN verbs, two of which are not cogent. One concerns examples with inanimate and dummy subjects, as in [24]–[25], [27]–[33]. Kageyama points out that these subjects cannot be Experiencers, which is self-evidently true. However, since such examples do not predate the alleged reanalysis they do not invalidate it: Jespersen was offering a diachronic explanation, not a synchronic derivation.

Another of Kageyama's objections depends on finite complementation examples where the Experiencer in the higher clause is not coreferential with the subject of the lower clause:

[154]   *BlHom* 113.7

Þa   gelamp   him   þæt his lif wearð   geendod
then happened him(DAT) that his life became ended

'Then it befell him that his life was brought to an end.'

[155]   a1225(?a1200) Lay.*Brut* 1643

me   þuncheð þat mi fæder. nis   nowhit
me(OBL) seems   that my father not-is not-a-bit
felle
excellent/worthy

'I think that my father is utterly unworthy.'

[156]   1568 Grafton, *Chron.* II. 122 (*OED*)

It chaunced him that as he passed through Oxfoorde, the schollers picked a quarrell unto his servauntes.

In such examples there is no possibility of 'personalization', i.e. reanalysis of the Experiencer as subject of the higher verb. Kageyama takes this to prove that the subject of the lower verb is not the Experiencer in *any* example. But in other examples it clearly is co-referential with the Experiencer, and when the embedded clause is non-finite – the only kind covered by Jespersen – the unexpressed subject of the lower verb is *always* coreferential with the Experiencer of the higher verb (thus also Fischer and van der Leek 1981: 338).

Where Kageyama is on stronger ground is in highlighting Jespersen's inadequate treatment of SEEM, for Jespersen appears to neglect what is nowadays seen as a central type of Subject raising:

[157]   He seemed to be crazy.

As Kageyama points out, *he* is not an Experiencer in [157], and indeed an Experiencer can be added:

[158]   He seems to be crazy to me.

Since these patterns are not very old, at least not *with* an embedded infinitive but *without* a predicative adjective (§9.3.1), Kageyama's observation may show no more than that Subject raising has been extended to new verbs.

9.4.3   Denison

In Denison (1990a: §7.4) I pointed out that the different constructions illustrated in §§9.3.4.1 and 9.3.4.2 coexisted for some time. An account which enforces a rigid distinction between them cannot do justice to the surface structure relationships of [159]:

[159]   1530(c1450) *Mirror Our Lady* 8.9

Therfore yf eny suche parsone happen to se this boke . . .

'Therefore if any such person happens to see this book . . .'

Examples like [159] with an animate but non-case-marked NP represent a striking surface overlap between two different constructions. I suggested that the surface overlap exemplified in [159] must have played an important (though unspecified!) part in the history of Subject raising. In this connection note these examples of coordinate subject deletion cited by Visser (1963–73: §899):

[160]   c1400(?c1390) *Gawain* 1239

Me   behouez   of   fyne force | Your seruaunt be,
me(OBL) behoves(3 SG) from pure necessity your   servant   be(INF)

and schale.
and shall

'It behoves me from pure necessity to be your servant, and I shall be.'

[161]   c1450 *Alph.Tales* 57.18

hym   happend   to be hurte with ane arow, &   was bown
him(OBL) happened to be hurt by   an arrow and was about

to dye.
to die

Another example is [119] above. On the interpretation of such evidence see §§5.4.2, 5.7.2.2 above.

9.4.4   Fischer and van der Leek

Olga Fischer and Frederike van der Leek have some useful observations of the history of Raising with HAPPEN verbs in their review article (1981) on Lightfoot (1979). They assume that a dative Experiencer NP was reanalysed as subject of HAPPEN and that the two-place control verb HAPPEN was then reanalysed as a one-place Raising verb (1981: 338–9). In support they cite:

[162]   c1450(?a1400) *Destr.Troy* 10288

Miche harme . . . happit   to falle | On aither part with pyne
much harm . . . happened to fall   on each side with pain

'It happened that great and grievous injury befell each side'

[163]   c1450(?a1400) *Destr.Troy* 13421

There   hym   happyt   to here of his harme first
there/where him(OBL) happened to hear of his injury   first

Example [162] must be a Raising sentence, since *miche harme* is inanimate. They argue that it is reasonable to analyse [163], from the same text but with 'a dative NP in subject position', as a Raising sentence too. It is not clear to me exactly what analysis they have in mind.

They write that they have not found any ME examples of HAPPEN like [154]–[156], namely with oblique Experiencer and subject of the embedded clause (finite or non-finite) *not* co-referential (1981: 338). (Any such examples would, of course, damage the claim that the Raising pattern originated with reanalysis of an oblique Experiencer as subject.) And they cite an interesting nonce occurrence from another text:

[164]   ?c1450 *Knt.Tour-L.* 29.1

And after she happed she deied

'and afterwards it happened (to her) that she died'

They base the following claim on [164]: 'The subject of *happed* cannot be the result of [Subject raising], therefore it must have developed from the original dative' (1981: 338). Of course, [164] might simply be an error due to change of construction (anacoluthon).

Fischer and van der Leek observe that the reanalysis of HAPPEN sentences 'went hand in hand with a slight shift in meaning from "befall" (semantically a two-place predicate) to "chance" (semantically a one-place predicate)' (1981: 339). A footnote acknowledges that the 'befall' meaning still survives in PDE sentences like

[165]   What has happened to you?

This mild polysemy of HAPPEN, associated with differences in argument structure, may apply equally to FAIL and so help us to classify sentences like [9].

9.4.5 Traugott

Elizabeth Traugott (1972: 102) writes of Old English:

Unquestionable instances of subject-raising with verbs like *þync-* 'seem' are hard to find. Their rarity appears to be more than chance textual skewing as translators clearly had difficulty with finding the correct OE form to correspond with Latin subject-raised structures. Of the few sentences likely to involve subject-raising, most can be interpreted as having surface complements rather than subjects . . .

(cf. discussion and examples in §9.3.1 above). One of her arguments against Raising is the existence of examples like:

[166]   *Or* 66.1

Þonne þuhte   eow   þas tida
then   seemed(SG) you(DAT PL) these times(NOM/ACC PL)

beteran þonne þa
better than   those

where, she says, *þas tida* is not subject of ÞYNCAN, because of lack of concord (though note that the glossary of Bately's edition marks this instance of *þuhte* as SUBJ PL).

Of the ME/eModE period, Traugott writes (1972: 152):

Subject-raising from the complement to the main clause, as in *It seems that he is a phoney* → *He seems to be a phoney*, came to be used extensively whereas in OE it is scarcely evidenced at all.

9.4.6 Kageyama

Taro Kageyama (1975: 171) follows Traugott in denying the existence of Subject raising in Old English. He dismisses most examples involving aspectual verbs with this representative example:

[167]   *Gen* 9.20

Noe ða   yrðlingc began to wyrcenne ðæt land
Noah then farmer   began to work   the land

This he sees as an Equi sentence, or in more recent terms, subject control, because it has an agentive subject – Agent with respect to both verbs. (He also adduces an example with a finite clause in place of the embedded infinitival, but that evidence is for verbs like HRAÐIAN 'hasten' and not BEGINNAN/ONGINNAN 'begin'.) As for examples with inanimate subjects like

[168]   *Bede* 3 1.154.34

& sona   on morne, swa hit dagian   ongan
and immediately in morning as it dawn(INF) began

'And in the morning, as soon as it began to dawn'

Kageyama suggests that they are more likely to show a non-aspectual, quasi-auxiliary ONGINNAN, bleached of most meaning, and that therefore they do not constitute evidence for Subject raising. By the eME period, however, examples like [168] are so common, and with verbs that clearly remain aspectuals, that Kageyama regards the existence of Subject raising as certain (1975: 172).

His explanation for this apparent innovation depends on the assumption that the clause out of which an NP is raised must itself be subject of the higher verb. Thus a structure like:

[169] [John to live in the same street] chanced

must, he argues, underlie

[170] John chanced to live in the same street.

Since clauses as subject were vanishingly rare in Old English, whether finite or non-finite (Kageyama implicitly takes initial position as criterial for subjecthood), Raising to subject could not take place. A somewhat confusing passage suggests that the NP V NP V_{INF} patterns already produced by Equi and Raising to object were structurally identical to potential NP V V_{INF} patterns which would arise from Raising to subject: both are reducible to NP X V_{INF}, which is 'presumably the simplest structure to express complex ideas which are underlyingly described by multiple sentence embedding' (1975: 175). Once the source structures for Raising to subject (namely, clauses as subject) became available in Middle English, the transformation would be made use of because of a *conspiracy* to generate parallel surface structures.

9.4.7 Ard

Josh Ard's dissertation has a chapter on Raising to subject (1977: 49–66). He sees two main historical sources for Raising verbs.

One is verbs which occurred in the correct surface syntactic frame

[171] NP V V_{INF} X

but with semantics incompatible with Raising. This turns out to apply to predicates like BE *certain* and BE *sure*, since Ard follows Jespersen and *OED* in seeing what is essentially a semantic change as having forced a change from an Equi to a Raising analysis (1977: 57–9). The verb HESITATE belongs here as well. This is said to be a probable Raising verb in the second reading offered for

[172] He hesitated to throw the ball.
       (i) 'He hesitated in order to throw the ball.'
       (ii) 'He was hesitant [*Ard*: "reticent"!] in throwing the ball.'

(My intuition is that *he* is semantically an argument of HESITATE even under the (ii) reading.) The rather loose justification given is analogy with aspectuals like CEASE, STOP (1977: 56, 61).

The second source of Raising verbs is two-place impersonal verbs whose oblique NP argument became 'subjectified' – essentially the Jespersen scenario of §9.4.2.1 for HAP and HAPPEN.

What about SEEM? In the sense 'befit' which *OED* lists as the earliest one in English, Ard proposes that SEEM underwent a development of subjectification akin to that with HAPPEN. We are then meant to apply his very sloppily stated 'principle of polysemy' (1977: 53), which (I think) suggests that SEEM 'appear' should have come to share the same privileges of occurrence as it had in its other meaning. We are also to assume that French SEMBLER, possibly one influence on the semantics of the verb, had 'a major influence' on the syntax too (1977: 62–3). As for APPEAR (1977: 63–4), this verb is said to have developed into a Raising verb for three reasons: on the analogy of SEEM (the 'principle of synonymy', 1977: 53), because of French influence, and – mystifyingly – by Equi-NP deletion from the (finite!) sentence type

[173]   1623(1609–10) Shakespeare, *Cym* IV.ii.47

   This youth . . . appeares he hath had Good Ancestors.

To take discussion of Raising on this level seriously is hard.

9.4.8   Lightfoot

9.4.8.1

In his earlier analysis David Lightfoot deals with SEEM constructions by a transformation of 'NP Preposing' (1979: §6.1). NP Preposing had already been introduced in Lightfoot's discussion of impersonal verbs and passives (see §§5.4.5 and 7.6.2 above). Its introduction into the grammar of English can be seen as the explanation for the appearance in late Middle English or early Modern English of Subject raising with SEEM. Lightfoot appears to quote with approval Jespersen's and Traugott's views on the history of SEEM verbs, of HAPPEN verbs, and of EASY adjectives. The development of the Raising construction with HAPPEN verbs – and, though this is not quite clear, SEEM verbs – 'was part of the demise of the impersonal verbs', while Raising with LIKELY adjectives may have been influenced by the prior existence of Raising with HAPPEN-sentences (1979: 300). He argues that if

[174]   John happened to leave.

is formed by NP Preposing, then Kageyama's examples [154]–[156] prove that *John* must have been in subject position, not 'dative position', beforehand (Lightfoot 1979: 300–1), though I think he makes the same error here as Kageyama – on which see §9.4.2.3 above.

9.4.8.2

In a later analysis he assigns to [175] the underlying structure [176], transformed by S' deletion (which entered the grammar in late Middle English) and NP Movement (which is now said to have been available throughout English history) to the surface structure [177] (1981: 110):

[175]   John seems to be happy.
[176] $[_{N''}$ e] Pres $[_{V'} [_V$ seem] $[_{S'}$ e$[_S [_{N''}$ John] to be happy]]]
[177]   John Pres $[_{V'} [_V$ seem] $[_S [_{N''}$ t]   to be happy]]

(For S' deletion see §8.7.3.1 above.) Notice that [176] is like Radford's [19] apart from the S' node (and Lightfoot's more cheerful view of John!).

9.4.9 Warner

Anthony Warner (1982: 71–4) looks at the analysis of SEME sentences in
Wyclifite Sermon English, offering two possible underlying structures for the
post-COMP part of [178]:

[178] a1425 *Wycl.Serm.* II 55.81

for ʒif suche men semon to doon yuele, . . .
for if such men appear to do   evil

namely [179] and [180]:

[179] [$_{NP}$ [$_{S}$ suche men to doon yuele]] [$_{VP}$ SEME]
[180] [$_{NP}$ e] [$_{VP}$ SEME [$_{S}$ suche men to doon yuele]]

In [179] SEME is intransitive and has a sentential subject. This embedded S is
extraposed to the right periphery of the higher S, and then by a second
transformation its subject, the NP *suche men*, is Raised into the empty
subject position of the higher clause. Under analysis [180], however, all that
is required is to move the NP *suche men* to the higher subject position by a
rule of NP preposing.[3]

Warner finds arguments running both ways. The Raising analysis is
supported by the general equivalence in distribution of NP and S (recall the
decision, noted in §8.8.2.2, to analyse all embedded clauses as an S' inside
an NP), though as it happens no examples in his corpus with SEME,
CHANCE, HAP or HAPPEN surface with a clause embedded in subject
position; the best he can offer is abstract lexical noun subjects for these
verbs. As for Lightfoot's now-rejected NP preposing analysis, see §9.4.8.1
above.

9.5 Questions for discussion or further research

(a) Examine in detail the three transformational analyses of sentences
    [116]–[117] discussed in §9.3.5.1 above.
(b) Compare the relationship between Pred constructions and infinitival
    clauses as manifested in Raising (this chapter) and in VOSI (Chapter 8).
(c) Is the material discussed in §9.4.3 above (merely) evidence in favour of
    reanalysis of HAPPEN sentences, as proposed by *OED* and Jespersen
    (§9.4.2.1)?

Notes

1. I am not sure whether examples like the following (Callaway 1913: 82) are
   exceptions to this generalisation:

   (a) *GD* 181.13

   grene wyrta he is gewunod   me   to bringanne
   green herbs he is accustomed me(DAT) to bring

   Lat. herbas mihi ad prandium deferre consuevit

   'He is in the habit of bringing me green herbs.'

Is GEWUNIAN 'accustom' a two-place verb, and is it passive in (a)? It is hardly a verb of mental perception.

2. It is possible that *þe* in [134] is not a 2 SG pronoun but a conjunction, but the interpretation of *wolde* is unaffected; cf. Mitchell's discussion of this example (in another context) (1985: §1960 n.8).

3. Structure [180] is much like Radford's [19], though Warner leaves it a little unclear whether an S' level is omitted on principle or as irrelevant. There is an inconclusive discussion in the previous chapter (1982: 48–69).

Part V

AUXILIARIES

Overview

Part V discusses the main auxiliary verbs of Present-day English. All derive historically from full verbs with complex complementation.

Chapter 10, Origins of Periphrastic DO, examines a variety of proposals, including a possible syntactic origin in the V+I construction discussed in Chapter 8. Chapter 11, Modals, compares modal verbs syntactically both to control verbs and raising verbs (Chapters 8–9). Chapter 12, Perfect, discusses perfect HAVE and BE (and WEORÐAN) + past participle. The origins of the perfect are traced to predicative constructions, and the rivalry between HAVE and BE and eventual triumph of HAVE are important elements in the history. Chapter 13, Progressive, looks at BE (and WEORÐAN, etc.) + -ing, considering possible origins in predicative constructions, including prepositional structures (BE on hunting, etc.). Also involved are the relationships among what are traditionally called present participles, gerunds and verbal nouns. Chapter 14, Passive, deals with passive BE (and WEORÐAN and GET) + PA PTCP.

Chapters 10–14 therefore examine the development of auxiliary status for each verb or set of verbs, taking first the most general or default auxiliary of Present-day English and then – in their relative order in verbal groups – the remaining auxiliaries. (The order by date of grammaticisation is different: probably modals/perfect HAVE, then DO, passive BE(?), progressive BE, passive GET.) Each historical development can be seen as essentially independent, just as descriptions of Present-day English often imply that speakers have five independent binary choices (present ~ past tense, ±modal, ±perfect, ±progressive, ±passive), with use of DO conditioned by failure to select any other auxiliary in certain constructions. In reality both assumptions are oversimplistic. The tense/mood/aspect/voice selections in Present-day and earlier English are not wholly independent of each other, nor are the historical origins of the various auxiliaries. Chapter 15, Multiple Auxiliaries, Regulation of DO, makes an attempt to integrate the various developments, examining their interaction and combination and showing how a category **auxiliary verb** established itself in the language.

Chapter 10

Origins of periphrastic DO

10.1 The problem[1]

DO plays a central role in Present-day English verbal structure. Its use as a periphrastic auxiliary is one of the most striking features of PDE syntax as compared with Standard Average European or with older stages of English itself. In PDE it is the auxiliary *par excellence*, or rather the **operator** (Quirk et al. 1985: §§2.48–9, 3.21–8). An operator is required in any finite clause showing negation, inversion, post-verbal ellipsis (see further §10.2.7 below) or emphatic polarity – illustrated in [1]–[4], respectively. This function can be carried out by most uses of BE and the modals and by certain uses of HAVE. In the absence of any other potential operator the empty operator DO is required (the insertion of which in some transformational grammars is known as DO-Support):

[1]   Max didn't see the car.
[2]   (a)   Did Max see the car?
       (b)   Scarcely did Max see the car (when . . .)
[3]   (a)   (Tim saw the car) and Max did too.
       (b)   (Tim hardly saw the car.) Nor did Max.
[4]   (A. I don't believe Max saw the car.) B. Max *díd* see the car.

Operator-like behaviour in these four tests is sometimes known collectively as the 'NICE' properties (Huddleston 1976: 333), an acronym formed from Negation, Inversion, Code (= post-verbal ellipsis), Emphasis.[2]

   At the Old English stage there would be little justification for calling DON an auxiliary verb (though cf. Warner 1992), since its only operator-like quality then was occurrence in post-verbal ellipsis, a context which does *not* involve cooccurrence with a main verb in a clause. By the end of the ME period, if not before, DO had become an auxiliary in some of its uses. The problem to be tackled in this chapter, then, is the *origin* of DO as an auxiliary verb, and specifically one of such neutral meaning that it could become the default auxiliary. There is an interesting diversity of opinion on the origins of so-called **periphrastic DO**, with a tendency for scholars to pursue lines of inquiry suggested by their own previous research on other topics. We shall look at the circumstances of its appearance – date, dialect, register, the questions of foreign influence and creolisation, and so on – as well as the purely syntactic source(s) of the construction. Since several such sources have been proposed, our selection of data must cover a wide range of patterns. (The establishment in the eModE period of the operator ~ non-operator distinction, or equivalently, of the NICE properties, is tied in intimately with the **regulation** of DO. That will be one subject of Chapter 15.)

10.2   The data

10.2.1   Full verb DO

Two uses of DO found throughout the recorded history of English must always be kept in view. **Full verb** DO in early intransitive use meant something like 'act' (*OED* s.v. B.15), and was usually *cataphoric* or *anaphoric* for another verb. A typical transitive meaning is something like 'perform, accomplish' (*OED* B.6) or else, in early texts, 'put, place' (*OED* B.1):

[5]   c1123 *Peterb.Chron.* 1123.73

þis he dyde eall for þes biscopes luuen.
this he did   all for the bishop's love

'This he did all for love of the bishop.'

[6]   c1155 *Peterb.Chron.* 1137.23

Me dide cnotted strenges abuton here hæued
one put knotted strings   about   their head

'Knotted strings were tied around their heads'

[7]   (1478) *Let.Cely* 22.34

Y most <u>do</u> as hothyr men dothe, ar ellys Y most kepe stylle.
I   must do as other   men do   or else I must be   inactive

'I must do as other men do or else I must be inactive.'

The 'act, accomplish' senses simply mean that DO can be a very general verb of action, in fact the most general verb of all – what Visser (1963–73: §1412) calls **factitive** DO. Note that PDE full verb DO does not have the NICE properties and requires operator DO in the appropriate contexts:

[8]   Max didn't do his homework.

10.2.2   Causative DO

Until the ModE period DO could be used as a causative, usually in the form DO (+ NP) + *that*-clause 'cause (NP) that NP should. . .'. There was a rarer VOSI variant DO + NP + infinitive. (For a good discussion of both see

Royster 1922: 332–53.) Even rarer still, there was a V+I variant of the infinitive construction where the NP (which would have referred to whoever was made to perform the action) was not expressed. Ellegård (1953: 54) and others have argued that the OE use of causative DO with an infinitival clause – as opposed to the more common DO + *that*-clause – was probably due to Latin influence, though Visser (1963–73: §1212) is less sure.[3]

10.2.2.1   Causative DO in VOSI

[9]   c1155 *Peterb.Chron.* 1140.22

þe biscop of Wincestre . . . dide   heom cumen   þider.
the bishop of Winchester. . . caused them come(INF) thither

'the bishop of Winchester . . . had them come there'

[10] c1400(?a1300) *KAlex.*(Ld) 7681

Þis ymage is made after þee. | J dude   it an ymageoure | Casten
this image is made after you   I caused it a   sculptor   cast(INF)

after þi   vigoure
after your face

'This sculpture is made in your likeness. I had a sculptor cast it in likeness of your face.'

[11] (1460) *Paston* 55.4

preyng you þat ye wole do   them spede them   in þat matier.
praying you that you will cause them speed themselves in that matter

'asking you to cause them to hasten/succeed in that matter'

DO in VOSI is found rarely in Old English, commonly in some varieties of Middle English, especially eastern ones, but became obsolete by the sixteenth century (Visser 1963–73: §2068).

10.2.2.2   Causative DO in V+I

Causative DO, unlike ModE CAUSE and MAKE, resembled such causatives as OE/ME LÆTAN/LETEN, cognates of LET in Dutch and German, and Fr FAIRE, in the possibility of leaving the subject of the infinitive unexpressed. Possible examples include:[4]

[12] a1225(c1200) *Vices and V.(1)* 25.10

Ðis hali mihte ðe   dieð   ilieuen ðat . . .
this holy virtue that causes believe that . . .

'This holy virtue which causes one to believe that . . .'

[13] a1400 *Ancr.Recl.*(Pep) 184.22

and for alle þat it heren. oiþer reden. oiþer writen oiþer done
and for all   that it hear   or   read   or   write or   cause

writen.
write(INF)

'and for all that hear or read or write it or have it written'

[14] (1418) *Grocer Lond.* in *Bk.Lond.E.* 198.121

Al so it is be comun   assent of the Fraternite that no man   of
also it is by common assent of the Fraternity that no member of

the Fraternite take, ne be Frawde do   take, hys neighbourʒ hows . . .
the Fraternity take or by fraud   cause take his neighbour's house . . .

[15] (1480) *Paston* 229.39

and wulleth that if the seid Thomas paie or do   paie to the seid
and wills   that if the said Thomas pay or cause pay to the said

Margaret yerly   xviij li. as is aboveseid, . . .
Margaret yearly £18   as is abovesaid . . .

'and wills that if the said Thomas pays or has paid £18 yearly to the
said Margaret as is said above . . .'

The chronological distribution of V+I is similar to that of VOSI, except that
it was very rare indeed in Old English (Ellegård 1953: 17, 48; Visser
1963–73: §1212), while unambiguous examples were not common in Middle
English either. A similar pattern with other verbs of causation was
widespread in Old English and Middle English, however (Visser 1963–73:
§1195, and see Chapter 8).

10.2.2.3* DO *to wit*

The idiom DO *(sb.) to wit/understand/etc.* 'bring to somebody's knowledge' is
causative: literally 'cause sb. to understand', cf. ModE *let (sb.) know*. Ellegård
makes a convincing case for treating it differently from other causative DO
examples, however, mainly on the strength of its quite different geographical and
chronological distribution (1953: 39–40). He mentions the possibility that the
subject of the infinitive in this construction in Old English was a dative rather
than the accusative usually associated with the NP sandwiched in a causative
construction; thus also Bock (1931: 226). (On datives see Mitchell 1985: §§3782–6
and §8.4.1.6 above.) In support of this I can cite impersonal passives from early
Middle English:

[16] c1180 *Orm.* 3892 (sim. 3896, 3902, 16042, 16048)

Þurrh   þatt wass uss   don þær full wel To sen &
through that was us(OBL) done there full well to see and

tunnderrstanndenn . . .
to-understand . . .

'By this means we were made there to see and to understand very clearly
. . .'

I shall not consider the DO *to wit* pattern further.

10.2.2.4* *Did do* V

Late in the ME period, and especially in the works of Caxton, frequent use is made of a double DO construction:

[17]   1490 Caxton, Prol.*Eneydos* 108.14

And also my lorde abbot of westmynster ded do shewe to me late
and also my lord   Abbot of Westminster 'did do' show to me recently

certayn euydences   wryton in olde englysshe
certain pieces-of-evidence written in old   English

'and also my lord, the Abbot Westminster, had me shown recently certain pieces of evidence written in ancient English'

(In some examples either the first or the second verb is not DO but LET or MAKE.) I follow Ellegård (1953: 110–15) in reading *did do* examples as an attempt to mark causative meaning at a time when the periphrasis was on the increase and simple causative use of DO open to misunderstanding.

10.2.2.5* DO + past participle

A curious construction in (mostly) late Middle English has a past participle rather than an infinitive after DO:

[18]   c1275 *Ken.Serm.* 129

yet ha deþ mani   time maked   of   watere wyn gostliche
yet he does many-a time made(PA PTCP) from water wine spiritually

. . . so ha maket of   þo watere, wyn.
. . . so he makes from the water   wine

[19]   c1330 *KTars* (Auch) 997

&   þer fore haþ don   sent me bi sond
and therefore has done [= caused] sent me by messenger

'and therefore has had sent to me by messenger'

[20]   c1400 *Brut*-1333(Rwl B.171) 64.31

. . . wiþ michel honoure, þat he hade done   made in remembrance of þe
. . . with great honour   that he had caused made in remembrance of the

Britons . . .
Britons . . .

[21]   (1426) *Paston* 4.4

I haue . . . doon   dwely examyned þe jnstrument by þe wysest I coude
I have . . . caused duly examined the instrument by the wisest I could

fynde here
find   here

'I have had the document duly examined by the wisest men I could find here'

It is particularly common with DO in the perfect or past perfect, and also occurs after other causative verbs; see Ellegård (1953: 141–3). (Rynell 1964 shows that alleged instances of DO + past tense can nearly all be explained as misreadings, irrelevant, or instances of DO + past participle.)

10.2.3 Equivocal DO

Some examples of DO with an infinitive are indeterminate between a causative (different-subject V+I) and a periphrastic (same-subject) reading. They are what Engblom calls **ambiguous** DO (1938: 71) and Ellegård (usually) **equivocal** DO (= Visser's 'edi' type), though at times Ellegård distinguishes between 'equivocal' and 'ambiguous' uses. I think the distinction matters. The meaning of the DO + verb syntagm is usually **vague** rather than ambiguous:[5]

[22] ?a1300 *Fox and W.* 51

> I do þe lete blod ounder þe brest
> I 'do' you let blood under the breast [*you* = object of *lete blod*]

> 'I have you bled beneath the breast/I bleed you beneath the breast'

[23] (c1300) *Havelok* 761

> Gode paniers dede he make, |On til him,   and oþer þrinne | Til
> good baskets 'did' he make   one for himself and others three   for
> hise sones
> his   sons

[24] (1386) *RParl.FM* in *Bk.Lond.E.* 34.25

> And in the nyght next after folwynge he did carye grete quantitee of Armure to the Guyldehalle

[25] a1400 *Usages Win.* 9 50.24

> Also, non of þe Citee ne shal don werche qwyltes ne   chalouns
> also none of the city not shall 'do' make quilts nor blankets
> by-þoute þe walles of þe Citee
> outside   the walls of the city

[26] (1470) *Paston* 343.19

> look that ye   spare for no cost to do serche   for itt
> look that you spare for no cost to 'do' search(INF) for it

> 'Make sure you spare no expense to have it searched for/search for it.'

Equivocal DO is found from the thirteenth century onwards, at first in verse (Ellegård 1953: 55; Visser 1963–73: §1213). For corrections to Visser's list of citations see Denison (1985c: 58 n.3).

10.2.4 Anticipative DO + appositive V

This is a use of main verb DO:

[27] *CP* 397.19

Ægðer he dyde, ge   he egesode ða   ðe on unryht
both   he did   both he terrified those who in wickedness

hæmdon, ge he liefde   ðæm   ðe hit forberan ne meahton
fornicated and he permitted those(DAT) who it forgo   not could

'He did both; he both inspired with fear those who committed
fornication, and gave permission to those who could not forgo it'

[28] *BenR* xlvi 71.15

gif he aðor   dyde, oððe ofergimde, oððe forgeat, oððe
if he any-of-the-following did   either neglected or   forgot or

tobræc ænig þing
violated any thing

[29] *WHom* 7.1

Leofan men, doð swa eow   micel þearf   is, understandað þæt
dear   men do as you(DAT) great necessity is understand that

ælc cristen   man . . .
each Christian man . . .

'Beloved men, do as is very necessary for you, understand that each
Christian man . . .'

[30] a1225(?a1200) *Trin.Hom.* 179.34

Hire   ne dide noðer. ne   oc.   ne smeart. þo   þe hie
her(OBL) not did neither neither ached nor smarted when   she

bar ure louerd ihesu crist. . . . Ac elch oðer wimman doð. akeð.
bore our lord   Jesus Christ. . . . But each other woman   does aches

and smerteð sore. þan hie beð mid childe   bistonden.
and smarts sorely when she is with child(birth) afflicted

Such examples occur from early Old English onwards. In Old English and
Middle English the explanatory verb is in the same tense or non-finite part
as DO. Notice that the first DO at least in [30] takes on the impersonal syntax
of the two lexical verbs which it anticipates.

10.2.5 Anticipative DO + infinitival V

It is doubtful whether there are any examples of this construction in Old
English or Middle English. Visser offers such as the following (1963–73:
§1413):

[31] *Bo* 14.17

. . . wiðstent. Swa doð nu ða þeostro þinre gedrefed nesse
. . . withstands as 'do' now the darkness your disturbance(GEN)

wiðstandan   minum leohtum   larum.
withstand(INF?) my   light [= enlightening] teachings

[32] *WHom* 8c.125

ac utan don swa us   þearf   is, gelæstan hit georne.
but let-us do as us(DAT) necessity is perform it eagerly

'but let us do as we must, carry it out eagerly'

[33]   *WPol* 2.1.1 123, §§173–4

Riht is þæt munecas . . . don, swa heom   ðearf   is:
right is that monks   . . . do   as   them(DAT) necessity is

carian   æfre, hu hi   swyðost magan Gode gecweman
take-care(INF) always how they most   may   God please

[34]   *WPol* 2.1.2 200, §55

And we læraÞ, þæt preostas swa dælan   folces   ælmessan, þæt
and we instruct that priests so share-out people's alms   that

hig ægÞer don, ge   God gegladian ge folc   to ælmessan gewænian
they both do both God gladden   and people to alms   treat

In eight lOE examples like [32] the infinitive is most plausibly to be
regarded as dependent on *uton*: cf. [29], where *uton* is absent. Bruce
Mitchell has criticised Visser's analysis in detail (1985: §666), arguing that
[33] and [34] probably contain present subjunctives and are therefore
anticipative DO + appositive verb, while [31] is causative DO with idiomatic
omission of *þe* (= subject of the infinitive). If it were not so isolated one
might find [31] a plausible example of anticipative DO + infinitive.[6]

For Middle English Visser offers:

[35]   a1225(?a1200) *Trin.Hom.* 179.2

Swo don in þis woreld þe riche þe   ben louerdinges struien þe
so   do in this world the rich who are petty-lords destroy the

wrecche men þe   ben underlinges. and naðeles   bi hem libben.
wretched men who are underlings and moreover off them live

and habbeð of   here swinche hundes . . .
and have   from their toil   hounds . . .

[36]   a1225(?a1200) Lay.*Brut* 4990

heom heo . . . brohten to þen kinge. | þat þe king heom sculden:
them they . . . brought to the king   that the king them should

don: oÞer slan oÞer hon
do   either slay or   hang

'They brought them to the king, so that the king should have them
either slain or hanged.'

[37]   ibid. 6613

for heo ne dursten for   Gode: don þer þa   misbode. | nime þane
for they not dared before God   do there that offence   take the

munec child: &   makien Brut-londes king.
monk child and make Britain's   king

'for they dared not commit that offence before God, take the monk-
child and make him King of Britain'

[38] ibid. 7442

buten þat heo sculde wel don: luuien þene Cristindom
except thatshe should well do love   the Christendom

'except that she should do well, love Christianity'

[39] ibid. 8389

ȝif þu þet nulle: do þine iwille. | whaðer-swa þu wult don: þa
if   you that not-wish do your will   whichever you wish do either

us slan þa us an-hon.
us slay or us hang

'If you don't want that, do your will, whichever you wish to do, either
slay us or hang us.'

[40] ibid. 9353

þenne heo sculde don: swa ne deð na wif-man. | mid æie vnimete:
then she should do as not does no woman   with fear immense

halden luue swete.
hold   love sweet

'Then she would have to do what no woman does: harbour thoughts of
sweet love together with immense fear.'

[41] c1230(?a1200) *Ancr.* 60a.22

Swa he deð as ofte as he ne mei wið open uuel cuðen
thus he does as often as he not can with open evil make-known

his strengðe.
his strength

'Thus he does as often as he can, with open evil make known his
strength.'

[42] c1400 *PPl.B* 17.209

And as wex and weke and warm fir togideres | Fostren forþ
and as wax and wick and warm fire together foster   forth

a flawmbe and a fair leye |. . . | So dooþ þe Sire and þe sone
a flame   and a fair blaze. . . so do the Lord and the son

and also *spiritus sanctus* | Fostren forþ amonges folk   loue and bileue
and also holy spirit   foster forth among   people love and belief

. . .
. . .

[43] c1400(?c1384) *Wycl.50 HFriars* 384.10

And þus deede beggers, freris, lippen   up to kynges power, and
and thus did   beggars friars leap/leapt up to king's power and

mony tymes more þen þo kyng dar do, and maken þo kyng þo
many times more than the king dare do and make   the king the

fendis tormentour to prisoune trewe men, for   þei seyn þe sothe.
devil's tormentor to imprison true   men because they say the truth

There is doubt about whether [35]–[36], [42]–[43] actually contain infinitives at all,[7] while all the other examples contain a 'modal' or other verb which may be responsible for the infinitive, until we reach the mid-fifteenth-century examples:

[44]   ?c1450 *Knt.Tour-L.* 2.24

And so thei dede bothe deseiue ladies and gentilwomen, and
and   so they did   both deceive ladies and gentlewomen and

bere forthe diuerse langages   on   hem
make   diverse allegations about them

[45]   1463–77(a1450) *Yk.Pl.* 9.111

Woman, why dois þou þus? | To make vs more myscheue?
woman why do you thus   to make us more mischief

And Ellegård (1953: 133) regards example [44] as unambiguously periphrastic, while [45] has a *to*-infinitive. Now it is entirely possible that some of Visser's earlier examples do in fact contain anticipative DO + infinitive, but it is noteworthy that no examples before the fifteenth century are certain and that many have *to*-infinitive rather than plain infinitive.[8] Another possible example is discussed as [101] below. What may be a related construction, DO + *but* + infinitive (Visser 1963–73: §1414a), also fails to provide a secure example before the fifteenth century.

10.2.6 Periphrastic DO

This is the construction whose origin we wish to explain (Visser's 'pdi' type). It is first found in thirteenth-century rhyming verse from the southwest of England.

10.2.6.1 Positive declaratives

[46]   c1300(?c1225) *Horn* 1057

His sclauyn   he dude dun   legge
his pilgrim's-cloak he did   down lay

'He laid down his pilgrim's cloak'

[47]   c1300 *SLeg.Jas.* (Ld) 45.380

His menbres, þat he carf of : euer-eft   he dude misse, | Bote
his members that he cut off ever afterwards he did   miss   apart-

       a luytel wise   ȝware-þoruȝ he miȝhte : ȝwane he wolde, pisse.
from a little amount through-which he might   when he wished piss

[48]   c1300 *SLeg.Patr.Purg* (Ld) 205.191

toward þe stude þat þe sonne : In winter does a-rise.
towards the place that the sun   in winter does arise

10.2.6.2   Negatives

In negative declaratives periphrastic DO is found from the end of the fourteenth century, a little later than in positive declaratives. Visser (1963–73: §1438) cites one example from the late thirteenth century which is rejected as a scribal error by Davis (1961), plus two from the late fourteenth that could well be DO + noun. Here are some safe examples:

[49]   c1460(?c1400) *Beryn* 557

    that were   grete vnry3te, | To aventur oppon a man þat with hym
    that would-be great wrong   to venture against a man that with one

    did nat fi3te.
    did not fight

[50]   (1423) *Doc.Brewer* in *Bk.Lond.E.* 181.1286

    . . . þoo persones . . . þe wheche were nought present atte   seide
    . . . those persons . . . who   were not   present at-the said

    dyner ne neyther deden nought heren þe same acountes
    dinner nor neither did   not   hear the same accounts

In connection with the low absolute frequency of negative examples, it may be that Tottie's (1983) evidence for PDE, that negation is considerably less common in written than in spoken form, holds for earlier periods too.

10.2.6.3   Interrogatives and inversion

As a verb of inversion, periphrastic DO is found certainly from the fourteenth century (Visser 1963–73: §1434). In direct questions with subject-verb inversion it is first found 'about the end of the fourteenth century' (Visser 1963–73: §1451; examples §§1457, 1458, 1464):

[51]   c1380 *Firumb.(1)* (Ashm) 3889

    How dost þow, harlot, þyn erand   bede?
    how do you rascal your message deliver

    'What kind of message are you delivering, rascal?'

[52]   1635 Wimbledon *Serm.* A8r.23

    Why . . . doe men put their sons to the Civill Law . . . ?

[52'] c1450 Wimbledon *Serm.* (Hat) 7.1

    why . . . puttyn men her sonys raþir to laue ciuile . . .?

[53]   c1460(?c1400) *Beryn* 2148

    Beryn . . . doist þow sclepe, or wake?

    'Beryn . . . are you sleeping, or awake?'

Ellegård (1953: 168n.) and Visser (1963–73: §1450) agree that no separate explanation is needed for the *origin* of DO in questions, which they see as simply the natural interrogative form of the periphrasis. However, Ellegård does show that periphrastic DO was relatively more common in interrogatives (and negatives) than in positive declaratives from the earliest period when all three types are recorded (1953: 161–2), and work by Kroch et al. (1982) has supported Ellegård's belief that the interrogative was crucial to the *spread* of the DO periphrasis; see further Chapter 15.

10.2.6.4 Emphasis

The introduction of emphatic periphrastic DO is very hard to date, as it is almost impossible to distinguish it objectively from non-emphatic cases. In PDE at least three uses can be distinguished, though often only the first is mentioned:

(A) to assert the truth of a proposition, or to mark a polarity contrast
(B) to give contrastive emphasis to the tense or lack of modality of a verb
(C) to give emotive or exclamatory emphasis

(Quirk et al. 1985: §§18.16, 18.56). I do not mean to imply that the distinctions are rigid ones. Examples of the three uses:

[54] .. but I *díd* lock the door.   (A)
[55] I did and do take great care of it.   (B)
[56] You do make a fuss about things.   (C)

To prove that we have an A type, affirming = polarity contrast, we need to find positive periphrastic DO contradicting a preceding negative, or vice versa. I have no early examples of this. Alternatively, we can look for the inverted pattern illustrated by

[57] c1475 *Gregory's Chron.* 222.20

    but rewarde hym he dyd . . .

which is taken by Mustanoja to be a certain case of emphatic DO (1960: 606), but there are no examples before the late fifteenth century – thus also Visser (1963–73: §1423) – and so they do not help our discussion of the origins.

    For the B type, tense/modality contrast, periphrastic DO must be used in parallel with another auxiliary verb or tense. Alleged examples are unsafe if they contain what may be substitute or anticipative DO, e.g.:

[58] (1417) *Let.War France* in *Bk.Lond.E.* III.ix 69.29

    it hath stonde, yit doth, and euer   shal . . . in as gret   pees and
    it has   stood   yet does and always shall . . . in as great peace and

    tranquillite as euer ded   Cite . . .
    tranquility as ever did (a) city . . .

They are better if a periphrastic analysis is the likeliest:

[59] (1460) *Paston* 705.80

    But in fayth I knowe wele the iuge, W. Wayte hise mawment, hise
    but in faith I know well the judge W. Wayte his puppet   his

    boy Yimmys,   with here hevedy and fumows langage haue and dayly
    boy Yimmys[?] with their heady and volatile language have and daily

do vttyr lewd and schrewd dalyauns, &c.
do utter lewd and schrewd dalliance etc,

'But indeed I know well that the judge, William Wayte, his puppet, and his boy Yimmys, with their hasty and volatile language have and daily do utter ignorant and malicious gossip, etc.'

[60]   (1478) *Let.Cely* 26.18

At thys day I haue schepyt x   sarplerys woll and dayly do schepe
at this day I have shipped 10 bales   wool and daily do ship

'Today[?] I have shipped ten bales of wool and do so daily'

Visser says that coordination of DO with another auxiliary 'has been common since the beginning of the fifteenth century' and gives both good and bad examples mixed indiscriminately (1963–73: §1424; further examples in §§1738, 1746, 1751, 1756, 1764). Once again we have no firm evidence for the thirteenth or fourteenth centuries.

The C type, emotive/exclamatory effect, which Ellegård believes to have developed later than the others (1953: 172n.), is very similar to positive imperative DO. Objective proof of its early use is lacking, other than in imperatives.

I have found it convenient to identify these three types of emphatic DO. Usually they are not distinguished. Thus Engblom finds his first example of emphatic DO, a B type, in 1460 (1938: 50). Ellegård doubts that there are any certain examples before c1400 (1953: 24, 147–8), while Visser starts his citations of the B type c1400, and of the A type with some rather dubious examples of the late fifteenth century (1963–73: §§1424–5, but cf. §1423). *MED* has a number of possible examples s.v. *don* v. 11a.(a), likewise Mustanoja (1960: 601–2). The first wholly convincing example of the A type which I have seen is the second *do* in:

[61]   a1500(?c1450) *Merlin* 101.25

Loke ye,   do not lye; and thow   do lye, I shall it knowe wele
look you(PL) do not lie   if   you(SG) do lie   I shall it know   well

The importance of dating the beginnings of emphatic DO is that it has often been regarded as the forerunner of unstressed periphrastic DO.

10.2.6.5   Imperatives

Imperatives are awkward for any analysis, synchronic or diachronic. In Present-day English, for instance, it is doubtful whether imperative *do* + V and *don't/do not* + V belong with periphrastic DO, even for cases where there is no juncture between DO and V. The doubt arises because although imperative DO is very similar to periphrastic DO, imperative DO can co-occur with BE and with perfective HAVE, while periphrastic DO cannot (except in the *Why don't you* and *If you don't* constructions):

[62]   Do/don't be careful.
[63]   Don't have prepared yourself beforehand.
[64]   ?Do have prepared yourself beforehand.

[65] *He *díd*/didn't be careful.
[66] *He *díd*/didn't have prepared himself beforehand.

It is also arguable that there is a semantic difference between positive imperative DO and most examples of emphatic periphrastic DO (Ellegård 1953: 148; Huddleston 1980: 69). The difficulty is well illustrated by Quirk et al., who tentatively list imperative forms under the heading of DO-Support (periphrastic DO) but later deny that imperative DO is an operator (1985: §§3.37, 11.30 note [a]). See further Warner (1985: §6.21) for arguments that the V following imperative *do* or *don't* is an infinitive but that imperative DO is distinct from other uses of DO.

In Old English and Middle English it is not always clear whether imperative DO followed by another verb belongs under full verb or anticipative or even periphrastic DO (cf. Ellegård 1953: 132–3). Indeed, Ellegård argues that positive and negative imperative DO have different histories (1953: 177–8).

Visser decides not to discriminate morphologically among different possible forms of V (imperative? infinitive? subjunctive?), and instead divides the examples according to whether DO_{IMP} + V forms a 'syntactical entity' (1963–73: §1426). On that basis there is only a single OE example, and that in the translation English of the Bible:

[67] *Jn(WSCp)* 8.11

& se hælend cwæð . . . do   ga   & ne synga   þu
and the saviour said . . . do(IMP) go(IMP) and not sin(IMP) you

næfre ma;
never more

'and the Saviour said . . . go on, go, and do not sin ever again'

In early Middle English there are several examples in the *Katherine Group*, e.g.

[68] c1225(?c1200) *St.Juliana*(Bod) 35.381

Do sei me qð þe meiðen hwa sende þe to me
do tell me said the maiden who sent you to me

and a continuous history from then on, e.g.

[69] c1325 *A wayle whyt* (Hrl 9) 38

Whose wole of loue be trewe, do lystne   me.
whoever wishes of love be true   do listen-to me

However, Visser cites in his discussion a number of 'mere juxtapositions' of DO and V, e.g.:

[70=29] *WHom* 7.1

Leofan men, doð swa eow   micel þearf   is, understandað
dear   men do as you(DAT) great necessity is understand

þæt ælc cristen   man . . .
that each Christian man . . .

'Beloved men, do as is very necessary for you, understand that each Christian man . . .'

Here presumably the interpolated clause is taken to be evidence of a prosodic and syntactic boundary between DO and the following verb, and it is not unreasonable to class these under anticipative DO.

Negative imperative DO + V is found (apart from an isolated fourteenth-century example) from the fifteenth century (Visser 1963–73: §1447a). With BE, negative imperative DO occurs from the end of the sixteenth century (Trnka 1930: 50, Visser 1963–73: §1447b), and positive imperative DO is found from the mid-eighteenth century (Visser 1963–73: §§1426–7). With HAVE, imperative DO is found from the sixteenth century (Visser 1963–73: §1427). Imperative DO + HAVE considerably predates periphrastic DO + HAVE.

What is the historical relationship between imperative and periphrastic DO? The best argument for involving imperative DO in the origin of the periphrasis is that from early times imperative DO could be used before and adjacent to another verb, something which has not been demonstrated for other kinds of anticipative DO prior to the thirteenth century. It is also a fair guess that imperative DO was relatively more common in speech than surviving written records suggest. But the form of the lexical verb was not an infinitive; parallel constructions with GO, etc., suggest an absolute, non-auxiliary function (Ellegård 1953: 132-3); and the form of DO was itself presumably stressed and its function affective. I am inclined to follow Ellegård in the belief that periphrastic DO had more influence on imperative DO than the other way round (Ellegård 1953: 132, 148).

10.2.6.6   The paradigm of DO

Periphrastic DO in Present-day English has no non-finite parts. Any non-finite occurrences at some earlier stage might be important in determining its origins. Here are some reasonably likely examples of infinitive and past participle periphrastic DO prior to 1500:

[71]   (c1300) *Havelok* 1747

He . . . bad him . . . Hauelok wel yemen   and his wif, | And
he . . . bade him . . . Havelok well look-after and his wife and

wel do wayten   al the nith
well 'do' watch-over all the night

'He . . . asked him . . . to look after Havelok and his wife well and to guard them well all night.'

[72]   a1400(a1325) *Cursor* 2818

Þe angls badd loth do him flee.
the angels bade Lot 'do' him flee

[73]   (c1395) Chaucer, *CT.Sq.* V.45

He leet the feeste of his nativitee |Doon cryen thurghout Sarray his
he had the feast of his nativity 'do' cry   throughout Tzarev his

citee.
city

[74]   ?c1425(?c1400) *Loll.Serm.* 2.592

... þat resenable men ... schul þanne do make hem   redy
... that rational   men ... shall then   'do' make themselves ready

aȝen þe comynge of þe Lord.
for   the coming of the Lord

[75]   (?1456) *Paston* 558.12

The parson wyth yow shall do   well sort my maister
the person with you shall do(INF) well sort my master's

evidenses
pieces-of-evidence

'The person with you will certainly sort my master's evidence for him'

[76]   ?a1475 *Ludus C.* 283.339

and þis ȝe knowe now All and haue don   here | þat it stant in þe
and this you know now all and have 'done' hear   that it stands in the

lond of galelye.
land of Galilee

[77]   a1500 *Partenay* 2367

behold | ho   shall doo gouerne And rule this contre
behold who shall 'do' govern and rule this country

See further Visser (1963–73: §§1414a, 2022, 2133). The past participle
construction gained some vogue in sixteenth-century Scottish poetry, and we
find examples like:

[78]   1568(1500–20) Dunbar *Poems* 55.13

Thow that hes lang done Venus   lawis teiche ...
you   that have long 'done' Venus's laws teach ...

as well as examples of the present participle, gerund and infinitive of
periphrastic DO. Some Scots dialects even now allow non-finite forms of
modal verbs like CAN, and it seems likely that the non-finite use of DO must
be tied in with this. If some Scots dialects have been able to use periphrastic
DO with fewer restrictions than other varieties of English, it seems almost
paradoxical that 'the Scotch language used periphrastic *do* much more
sparingly than the dialects South of the Humber even in the 16th and 17th
centuries' (Ellegård 1953: 46, and cf. 164, 200n., 207n.).

10.2.6.7 Impersonals

From early on periphrastic DO could occur with an impersonal verb or with
a dummy *it* subject, a strong indication of auxiliary status. There are several
examples in the early material (Ellegård 1953: 57ff.):

[79]   c1300 *SLeg.Nich.*(Ld) 245.177

sone it dude bi-falle | Þat þare cam to heom a schip
soon it did   happen that there came to them a ship

[80]   c1300 *SLeg.*(Ld) 377.29

for þar-of   me   deth agrise;
for of-that [*sc.* going to India] me(OBL) does feel-terror

'for I am terrified of that'

[81]   a1325(c1280) *SLeg.Pass.*(Pep) 1713

and ȝif hit so doþ byffalle | Þat his disciples his body stele
and if   it so does befall   that his disciples his body steal

[82]   a1400(?a1350) *Siege Troy(1)*(Suth) 219

Þrouȝ eritage   him   dide falle | To be king of Troyens all.
through inheritance him(OBL) did befall to be king of Trojans all

The behaviour illustrated in [79]–[82] is quite compatible with either of the two principal suggestions for the ancestor of periphrastic DO. Anticipative DO stands for an impersonal verb in [30], and I have several examples of causative verbs (once DO itself) taking impersonal complements:

[83]   *Mt(WSCp)* 5.45

& he læt   rinan   ofer þa rihtwisan. &   ofer þa unrihtwisan;
and he causes rain(INF) over the righteous and over the unrighteous

[84]   a1225(c1200) *Vices & V.(1)* 3.14 (cf. ibid. 3.11, 71.9 for impersonal use of OFÞENCHEN)

hie   makeð ðane religiuse man . . . sari . . . and ofte doð
they make the   religious man . . . sorry. . . and often make

ofþenchen þat he æure swo haueð idon
regret   that he ever so has   done

[85]   (a1420) Lydg. *TB* 1.1646

And sodeinly sche coude make it reyne
and instantly she could make it rain

Another related example is [90] below.

10.2.7 Substitute DO

When DO is used anaphorically for another verb in conjunction reduction and other constructions, the term **substitute** DO (= vicarious DO = proverb(al) DO = propword DO) is often employed; see *OED* B.24d for examples that 'serve to connect' main verb DO and substitute DO. Ellegård confines it to cases 'when *do* can be exchanged for a verb appearing in the foregoing context, without any other change in the construction of the sentence being necessary' (1953: 124). In Ellegård's terms substitute DO is a verb-substitute. Elsewhere it looks more like a VP-substitute, and after intransitive verbs the distinction may be neutralised. Similar possibilities hold for other auxiliaries, and a more general consideration of terminology is in order. Compare the following examples (from Warner 1992: §2.1):

[86] — Is Paul bringing Mary?
      — If he isn't, I'll tell him he should.
[87] — I just hope it will make you happy.
      — Hasn't it you?

Example [86] contains two examples of **post-verbal** (or **post-auxiliary**) **ellipsis**; for these terms and a rejection of the common **Verb Phrase Deletion** see Huddleston (1984: 138), Warner (1985: 55). In example [87] there is 'a partial ellipsis. Here some of the complementation of the missing head is retained' (Warner 1992: §2.1). Warner adopts the term **pseudogapping** for the latter. DO can occur in either construction (*If he doesn't . . ., Didn't it you?*), and I include both patterns under the heading of substitute DO.

Substitute DO has a complete paradigm and can copy the construction of the verb which it stands for:

[88] *ÆHom* II 27.779.116

      him   sceal   on Domes-dæg sceamian . . . swa þam
      him(DAT) shall(3 SG) on doomsday   shame   . . . as   that
      menn   dyde þe . . .
      man(DAT) did   who . . .

[89] c1127 *Peterb.Chron.* 1127.55

      &   Þær he wunede eallriht swa drane doð on hiue
      and there he dwelt   alright as   drone does in hive

      'and there he lived exactly as a drone does in a hive'

[90] c1155 *Peterb.Chron.* 1135.5

      &   sæden   ðat micel þing sculde cumen herefter: sua dide,
      and said(PL) that great thing should come   hereafter as did

      for þat ilc   gær warth   þe king ded
      for that very year became the king dead

      'and said that a major event should follow, which it did, for that very year the king died'

[91] c1225(?c1200) *SWard* 208

      ah þah ha ne trust nawt on hire ahne wepnen, ah deð o Godes
      and yet she not trusts not in her own weapons but does in God's
      grace
      grace

[92] c1250 *Owl & N.* 1779

      'Ah ute   we þah   to him fare, | . . . . ' | 'Do we,' þe Niȝtegale
      but let-us we though to him go   . . .   do we   the Nightingale
      seide;
      said

      ' "But let us go to him, though," . . . . "Let's," the Nightingale said.'

[93] ?a1300 *Fox & W.* 67

Þe þurst him dede   more wo | Þen heuede raþer his hounger <u>do</u>.
the thirst him caused more woe than had   earlier his hunger done

[94] c1440(a1349) Rolle, *Bee* 55.19

Arestotill sais þat þe bees are feghtande agaynes hym þat will
Aristotle says that the bees are fighting   against him that wishes

drawe þaire hony fra   thaym. Swa sulde we do agaynes devells þat
take   their honey from them   so   should we do against devils that

. . .
. . .

[95] (1468) *Paston* 238.25

And asfore any wryghtyng fro   the Kyng, he hathe promysyd þat
and as for any writing   from the King he has   promised that

þer   schall come non; and iff ther do hys vnwarys,
there shall come none and if there do which-he-is-unaware-of

yowr answere may be thys, . . .
your answer   may be this . . .

'And as for any message from the King, he has promised that none will
come; and if any should which he is unaware of, your answer may be
as follows . . .'

[96] (1479) *Let.Cely* 74.11

Thys I wryte to you of   my payne and grefe as ȝe haue doyn vnto
this I write to you about my pain   and grief as you have done to

me of   yowrs.
me about yours

'I write this to you about my pain and grief, as you have done to me
about yours.'

Substitute DO is found at all periods of the language.

DO cannot normally be a substitute for the modals or for BE, nor until
recently for HAVE. A rare example of substitution for BE, missed by Visser
(1963–73: §188), is [97]:

[97] (c1469) *Stonor* 98 I 103.15

. . . thynkyng þat ye shulde be þe better willed   for my sake,
. . . thinking that you should be the better disposed for my sake

the which I wyll veryly   trust ye will doo.
which   I will certainly trust you will do

'. . . thinking that you would/should be the better disposed for my
sake, which I certainly trust you will be'

See also §13.2.4 below. In connection with tests for such semantic features
on verbs as ±ACT(IVITY) (where +ACT refers to a controllable state of
affairs and roughly equals 'agentive'), Schendl (1988: 130–1) notes that

substitute DO could occur in Old English with −ACT verbs as well with +ACT ones.

10.2.8

The origin of periphrastic DO has been sought in the anticipative use, the causative, the full verb use, and the substitute use – hence the need for such a wide range of data. It should be pointed out that the boundaries between these uses are not always clearcut. For example, Huddleston (1980: 72) notes a problematic distinction between periphrastic and substitute DO in:

[98]   They said he would win and win he did.

10.3   Explanations in non-generative linguistics

10.3.1   Koziol, Marchand, Rissanen

H. Koziol (1936) thought that periphrastic DO would be stressed in early use. Hans Marchand (1938–9, 1939:123) suggested that although early (literary) examples of periphrastic DO were colourless, the unattested colloquial usage was emphatic.[9] Traugott (1972: 140), who unlike them accepts that periphrastic DO was probably of causative origin, argues that it was from the first a marker of emphatic asseveration ('affirming *do*'). Matti Rissanen has shown that use of the periphrasis in seventeenth-century American texts is largely motivated by emotion, emphasis and euphony (1985). He extrapolates back from this to suggest that the origins of periphrastic DO cannot be separated from emphatic use, and to argue against literary origin. However, register and function can change enormously in three hundred years, and I am not convinced that the later evidence is germane to discussion of the origins.

A priori, however, an emphatic, colloquial origin is conceivable for periphrastic DO. As we have seen (§10.2.6.4), though, there is no hard evidence for it at all. Ellegård observes that most early examples of periphrastic DO occur in verse in unstressed position (1953: 121). Of course lack of metrical stress does not rule out being a marker of asseveration, but it does make it unlikely (cf. Ellegård 1953: 24). Ellegård believes that emphatic DO developed naturally as an optional stressed form of the pre-existing, unstressed periphrastic auxiliary (1953: 148), while Samuels believes that its origins are 'not directly connected with the original unstressed periphrasis' (1972a: 176n.2).

In a later article Matti Rissanen (1991) reformulates his case for the spoken origin of periphrastic DO, quoting favourably from the work of Tieken (1988), on which see §10.3.7 below. He suggests three structural patterns which might have contributed to development of the periphrasis:

(A) causative use, 'even though it seems an unlikely candidate for the sole or primary source of the periphrasis' (1991: 335)
(B) (imperative) DO + imperative
(C) DO + action noun.

Now C had been dismissed as of little importance by Ellegård (1953: 144), but Rissanen reasserts its significance on two grounds: the frequency of finite DO + action noun or adjective in Old and Middle English, and the ease of reinterpretation 'as *do* + infinitive structures in Early Middle English, after the collapse of the verbal ending system' (1991: 337).

Although Rissanen is correct to point out that most of his examples of DO + noun/adjective are close to being semantic variants of a simple verb, few of the nouns and adjectives [how many?] could have been interpreted as verb forms even in a period when formal distinctions in verbal endings were in a state of flux. There are some, of course:

[99]   a1400(c1303) Mannyng, *HS* 5215

Þat þefe alle manere wys   dyd synne
that thief all   manner ways did sin

'that thief sinned in all manner of ways'

In fact the majority of Langenfelt's best examples involve the word *synne* 'sin' (1933: 117–18). I see no grounds for associating such patterns with the *origins* of the periphrasis; see Ellegård (1953: 143–5). In my opinion such patterns could at best have strengthened a DO + infinitive pattern which had already come into existence.

10.3.2 Preusler

Various features of English are ascribed to Celtic influence by Walther Preusler in a series of articles in German (1938–9, 1942, 1944), collected and revised as Preusler (1956). One of these features is periphrastic DO. Preusler argues (1956: 334–6) that it was *calqued* on the common Old Welsh GWNEUTHUR 'do' + verbal noun construction, a periphrasis with three meanings in Modern Welsh: future/volitional, emphatic, and more-or-less empty. Survival of the DO periphrasis in unstressed affirmatives in modern south-western English dialects confirms for him that Celtic (Welsh and Cornish) influence was responsible for the entry of the construction into English. (The frequency of a TUN periphrasis in southern German dialects must therefore also be due to Celtic influence, he says.)

Preusler speculates that the distribution of English periphrastic DO (he does not separate origins and regulation) might have been an indirect consequence of Celtic morphology. The verbal periphrases of Welsh (involving the verb BOT 'be') contain a *d*-element when negative and/or interrogative in the perfect and when negative ± interrogative in the imperfect. This *d*-element could very easily have been felt to be a characteristic of the form and translated into the DO periphrasis by English-speaking Britons. Indirect confirmation of this 'bold supposition' comes from the striking absence of DO periphrases in Scots English despite a frequent meaningless periphrasis with the equivalent of DO in the substrate Celtic: absence of any *d*-element in Scots Gaelic removes the motivation for calquing. Ellegård dismisses the *d*-element argument as based on mere phonetic resemblance (1953: 120 n.2).

Preusler's general theory has been considered by both Ellegård (1953:

119–20) and Visser (1963–73: §1415). Ellegård does not reject the Celtic factor out of hand but relegates it to at best a minor role, on the grounds that the English DO periphrasis appeared several hundred years after the period of more probable English-Celtic contact; Visser concurs. The hypothesis of Celtic influence has been revived in modified form by Poussa: see §10.3.6 below.

10.3.3 Visser

Visser derives periphrastic DO from a cataphoric use of factitive DO (1963–73: §1412–14a). Such a development from loose parataxis towards tight syntax would have many parallels.

10.3.3.1

Visser claims that OE factitive DO could take as its object a nominal, an imperative, or a finite verb form. He claims that 'it is only natural to assume' that factitive DO in Old English could take an infinitive as object too, except that the pattern 'had nothing to recommend itself because it expressed nothing more, or better, than' the simple verb. In Visser's OE material it is noticeable that when DO precedes non-contiguous imperatives or finite verbs, it always has a complement within its own clause, such as *swa*, a *swa*-clause, *oþer þæra*, or whatever. The placing of *ægðer/aðor* in [27, 28] is at least suggestive that it was perceived as the object of DO (thus Ellegård 1953: 133 and cf. Mitchell 1985: §1545). And anticipative DO is very rarely adjacent to the explanatory verb. The premise that OE factitive DO could take a verbal 'object' other than a verbal noun is highly dubious, therefore. Fischer and van der Leek have commented on the paucity of evidence for the alleged nominal character of the OE and early ME infinitive (1981: 318–21).

The next stage of Visser's argument seems to be that this alleged potential for factitive DO + infinitive, latent at least from OE times, was finally exploited in Middle English when a useful purpose was found for it, namely rhyming verse. Visser claims support from the fact that reduction of stress on non-adjacent anticipative DO and deletion of material intervening between DO and infinitive would give periphrastic DO (§§1412–14a). Thus, for example, [100](a) would yield [100](b):

[100] (a) a1450 *Wor.Serm.* 23.54

         þat we do rythe als þe childyr of Israel dede, gedder vs
         that we do right as the children of Israel did   gather us

         to-gedre
         together

         'We do just what the children of Israel did, gather ourselves
         together'

       (b) we do gedder vs to-gedre

It is not clear whether he regards this process as an actually occurring event or as merely theoretical support for his hypothesis. Why should it happen?

10.3.3.2   Objections to Visser

The main problem with Visser's hypothesis is that it depends on the presence of anticipative DO + infinitive in Old English and early Middle English, and yet all of his apparently copious collection of examples can, and many should, be discounted (see §10.2.5 above). The first secure examples are fifteenth-century. The distinction between the two appositive constructions is neutralised if DO is itself in the infinitive: that accounts for some of Visser's examples. But if that particular subgroup had been the ancestor of periphrastic DO, one would expect early periphrases to show frequent infinitival DO. Also, if examples like [100](a) were really implicated in the development of periphrastic DO, it is odd that practically every early example outside Malory should have nothing (or just the subject) intervening between DO and the lexical verb (Ellegård 1953: 146).

Not only is anticipative DO + appositive verb much more common than anticipative DO + infinitive verb until at least the fifteenth century, but according to Ellegård (1953: 145–6) the loss of distinctiveness of verbal inflection which might have helped to efface the distinction advanced fastest in northern dialects, which are precisely the ones slowest to adopt periphrastic DO. I am not sure that this is very persuasive, as different permutations of person, number and tense fell together with the infinitive for different verbs in different dialects. If Ellegård is right, though, it would be evidence against Sweet (1898: §2172), who assumed without evidence that the appositive construction was actually reanalysed as the infinitive one. Also against Sweet is the early prevalence of *to*-infinitives in anticipative DO + infinitive examples.

Is it fair to comment on the match between Visser's explanation and his previous scholarly interests (a comment that would seem to apply equally to the work of Poussa, Tieken and myself)? Consider this rather unusual occurrence of DO with BE, *dyd not . . . be reformed*:

[101]   1532–3 More, *Wks.* VIII 469.32 [563 C8]

> For ellys yf Tyndale sayd trew, that euery elect person wolde be reformed at the fyrste / it muste folow that who so euer dyd not when he were better taught, retourne and be reformed at the fyrste, were a fynall reprobate . . .

Here we may have partial neutralisation of anticipative and periphrastic DO. I suspect that Visser's immersion in the language of More, which shows very free use of anticipative DO at a time when periphrastic DO was already flourishing, may have predisposed him to look for the origins of the latter construction in the former. Visser's general line of argument and many of his examples are taken wholesale from his study of More (1946–56: II 503–6), actually written before the war.

10.3.4   Engblom and Ellegård

Victor Engblom's study (1938) is a useful source of data and of discussion, but as his explanation is developed and refined by Alvar Ellegård (1953) it need not be discussed further here, except to note Engblom's belief that emphatic DO (but not periphrastic DO in general) developed out of substitute DO (1938: 44–61). The most generally accepted account is that of Ellegård, based on a very thorough survey of the written evidence. Visser and Ellegård essentially developed their accounts independently of each other.

10.3.4.1 Semantic change

Ellegård's argument runs as follows. Most of the possible causative (V+I) DOs in Middle English must strictly be classified as equivocal DO. Thus there are many opportunities for **permutation**[10] of a DO + verb string, whereby without overall change of meaning the lexical verb could itself be interpreted causatively and the DO taken as an empty auxiliary. One of the classic examples is:

[102]   ?a1400(a1338) Mannyng, *Chron.Pt.2* 97.22

Henry . . . | þe walles did   doun felle, þe tours   bette he doun.
Henry . . . the walls 'did' down fell   the towers beat he down

'Henry . . . felled the walls, he beat down the towers.'

Did felle in [102] could be interpreted either as *did* 'caused' + *felle* 'to fell/be felled' or as *did* 'past tense' + *felle* 'cause to fell/be felled'. The motivation for the semantic change (Ellegård does not consider the syntax) was not strictly linguistic at all: periphrastic DO was a convenience in rhyming verse, as it allowed the lexical verb to appear as an infinitive in rhyming position and also offered a bit of metrical padding. Once the construction had come into use in south-western poetic texts, it spread gradually to other areas and to prose. At this stage it was unemphatic and entirely synonymous with the simple verb.

10.3.4.2 Objections to Ellegård

Ellegård's theory requires a sufficient frequency of equivocal DO for the semantic change to be possible, but without too high a frequency of causative DO for it to be inhibited. This is somewhat problematic, though Ellegård argues that the southwestern dialect area meets these criteria. There are other problems. First, as Ellegård admits (1953: 37, 55), clear cases of causative (V+I) DO are rare. Second, equivocal and periphrastic DO appeared more or less simultaneously. Therefore in the putative development causative → equivocal → periphrastic, we have little evidence for the first stage, while the chronological support for the second stage is weaker than one would like. The problem is acknowledged but not, I think, solved.

I am not convinced by Visser's objections to causative origin, however (1963–73: §1417). First he claims that there are few examples of equivocal DO before 1400, and in particular, few suitable and plausible ones. For a detailed rejoinder to Visser see Denison (1985c: §1.5.2). Visser also writes: 'The weak point in this theory is the assumption of the possibility for *fell* to mean "cause others to fell".' Now I see no problem there, particularly in the light of the parallel *bette doun* in [102] and modern examples like:

[103]   Nixon bombed Cambodia.

Marchand actually found the semantic change causative → periphrastic a 'mental impossibility': ' "Causing a thing to be done" is fundamentally different from "doing a thing" ' (1939: 123). Yet GET or HAVE + PA PTCP can show the same equivocation in Present-day English between doing something oneself and having it done by another:

[104]   I will get/have the work finished on time.

What the modern comparison shows is that language *can* tolerate a vagueness of this kind; for a similar view see Royster (1922: 346).[11]

The whole change is envisaged as taking place in poetic language. Ellegård argues that periphrastic DO was 'a peculiarity of the poetic diction, belonging to the paraphernalia of the verse-maker's craft' (1953: 146, though cf. 208). The implication is that but for the advent of rhyming verse there would have been no motivation for the semantic change which produced periphrastic DO. An arbitrary fact of cultural history seems a poor explanation for the appearance of what was to become a central feature of the English verbal system. That does not mean that Ellegård was necessarily wrong. After all, a GAN periphrasis also developed in Middle English rhyming verse, as widespread as periphrastic DO and serving a very similar metrical purpose, yet without leading to any permanent effect on anything except the language of ballads. (Similarly, though less common, COMSE.) But we would be happier to find specifically linguistic, structural factors. Finally, the development of DO is essentially an accidental and isolated phenomenon, and no real explanation is given by Ellegård for the spread of the DO periphrasis to prose and ordinary speech.

10.3.5 Denison

I tried to dispose of some problems in Ellegård's account by concentrating on the syntax (Denison 1985c). My conjectural reconstruction ran as follows.

10.3.5.1 Syntactic origin

Causative DO + NP + infinitive (VOSI) entered late Old English probably as a Latinism, and since it clashed neither with OE syntax nor with the semantics of DO, it gradually entered more general use. By the thirteenth century it had spawned a variant construction with subject of the infinitive unexpressed, what we have called a V+I construction. Development of V+I would have been a natural development from VOSI given the examples particularly of HATAN and LÆTAN and perhaps also French FAIRE. That is, there was a systemic gap to be filled. I regard causative DO (V+I), equivocal DO and early examples of periphrastic DO as all the same construction: DO + infinitive. After all, all three appeared virtually simultaneously. That fact is inconvenient for both Visser and Ellegård, Visser because he assigns separate origins to the periphrasis, and Ellegård because he needs a time lag for the proposed semantic change.

Then, picking up a hint of Visser's, I suggested that its meaning was factitive, with purely contextual clues as to whether or not an intermediary actually performed the action. Note therefore that a thirteenth-century DO

+ infinitive is *not* assumed to be structurally the same as a fifteenth-century periphrasis: it might have been a *catenative* rather than the real auxiliary verb it certainly later became.

10.3.5.2 Argument structure

It would have had a two-clause structure. In 1985 I suggested that in GB terms the subject of the infinitive would be **PRO**, carrying the index *arb*. This was not an ideal choice, since PRO_{arb} was intended by theoreticians as an empty category of truly arbitrary reference, e.g. as the unstated subject of *have* in *It's nice to have friends*, but the alternative, **pro**, presents technical difficulties too. DO would probably have been a two-place verb:

[105]   NP [DO $[_{S'}$ $[_S$ PRO_{arb} VP]]]

(I am ignoring I/INFL and other niceties.)

10.3.5.3 Semantics and morphology

The contemporary (Middle English) interpretation of the pattern depended on the verb and the context. The majority were equivocal between direct agency and action through an intermediary, a distinction which the construction itself left unspecified. In some examples a causative reading (i.e. action through an intermediary) is ruled out lexically or pragmatically, and we now tend to assume with hindsight that these must be empty DO periphrases. In other cases (much fewer, and often in translated and legal texts), context rules out direct agency and we have been able to classify the examples as causative DO. Returning to my modern GET/HAVE + PA PTCP analogy, we could compare contextual interpretations of:

[106]   I got my car professionally resprayed. [+ intermediary]
[107]   I got the wheelnuts unscrewed.   [± intermediary]
[108]   I got my hand stuck in the gearbox.   [− intermediary]

In the formation of DO + infinitive from VOSI no semantic change was required. The VOSI pattern has the surface form:

[109] NP_1 DO NP_2 VP
        'NP_1 cause NP_2 to VP'

Usually but not necessarily $NP_2 \neq NP_1$. If NP_2 is omitted, then we have DO + infinitive:

[110] NP_1 DO VP
        'NP_1 cause unspecified-NP to VP'

The semantics of [110] follow predictably from those of [109].[12]

I surmised that DO + infinitive was used to focus not on who performed an action but on what happened, and that its meaning might at first have been perfective, something like 'achieve (the action of the infinitival VP)' but without agentive associations. In support I pointed out that a development from a word meaning 'do' or 'done' to a perfective marker would be widely paralleled cross-linguistically, and could perhaps even be paralleled within Middle English for certain lexical uses of *done*.[13] Second, the eleventh to the thirteenth centuries witnessed the development of various new **aspect-** and **Aktionsart**-marking devices in parallel with the obsolescence of the OE prefixal system; see Samuels (1972a: 160–5) for a long list. The new DO + infinitive construction could be seen as an experimental form of Aktionsart marking, later altered in structure and function.[14] And thirdly, Fischer (1992a: 274), citing Royster (1918), has pointed out that examples of DO + verb where DO is in the perfect (§10.2.2.5 above) may support the idea of a relationship between causation and perfectivity. Royster compares OE HATAN with ME DON in their sporadic occurrence with a following past participle, implying that such occurrences are blends provoked by the writer's attention shifting from the giving of the order to the accomplishment of the action (1918: 89–90 n.28). He writes: 'The causative verb affirms accomplished action; it is a perfective verb' (1918: 84).

Perfective meaning, I argued, could then be used to explain co-occurrence restrictions, as it ought to be incompatible with 'activity' and state verbs.[15] The thirteenth- and fourteenth-century occurrences of DO + infinitive broadly support the hypothesis (Denison 1985c: §4.4.2), and this might explain the origin of the constraint against DO + HAVE, BE or modals.[16]

DO itself had a full paradigm, however, occurring in infinitive, past participle and imperative as well as finite forms up to the sixteenth century (see §10.2.6.5–6 above), and this too is what we would expect.

10.3.5.4 Reanalysis

With the subsequent loss of the V+I construction with most verbs other than DO, if not the verbs themselves, plus the loss of VOSI with DO, the supporting framework fell apart, leaving DO + infinitive isolated. Then DO + infinitive was reanalysed as a true auxiliary, on the analogy of the modals.[17] From then on it was the subsystem of the modal auxiliaries which 'held it in place', and loss of non-finite parts was to be expected.

10.3.5.5 Objections to Denison

Denison (1985c) did not account for the geographical location of the early examples, though I wondered whether DO + infinitive had in fact started in the east as a two-clause (catenative) structure, given the far higher frequency of VOSI with DO there, and been reinterpreted more readily as a probably one-clause (auxiliary) structure when it spread to the west. It also left undiscussed the near-complete loss of the V+I construction with verbs other than DO, now discussed in Chapter 8. For present purposes, though, this is just a fact which can be used to help explain changes in DO.

10.3.6 Poussa

10.3.6.1 Language contact

Patricia Poussa (1990) has an entirely different conjecture. She believes that the DO periphrasis started in the west, and moreover was in colloquial use in Old English as an originally simplificatory device in Saxon-Celtic contact. On the extent of Celtic survival she refers (1990: 418) to Gelling (1978) and others. She gives some evidence that speakers in a language-contact situation where lexical verbs from a second language are being incorporated

into the speech chain have often found it convenient to use an auxiliary verb
for tense marking. The use of DON as an auxiliary might have derived from
substratal influence of the Celtic tense/aspect system, which had three
different durative verbal forms.[18] The DO periphrasis might then have been
originally habitual in meaning – a usage still found in modern southwestern
dialects. It is also found in Pembroke in southwest Wales (Parry 1979:
148).[19]

The absence of periphrastic DO from Old English is treated as non-
significant, since OE texts were largely literary and standardised and so
would tend not to use a low-status construction. On the other hand the first
appearance in the west is explained, as is the later and greater extension of
the DO periphrasis to contexts from which it has been lost in standard
English (DO + BE, habitual DO, DO in unemphatic declaratives, etc.). The
success of the DO periphrasis in standard – that is, London – English, as
compared with the marginalisation of cognate periphrases in Dutch and
German, can then be ascribed in part to dialect mixture in London and the
renewed utility of a verbal periphrasis at a period of great uncertainty as to
verb conjugation.

10.3.6.2 Objections to Poussa

Poussa does not give a syntactic origin for periphrastic DO: that is, she does
not explicitly point to an existing pattern in the language which might have
been adapted to the needs of a creole. The parallel she draws with ME GAR
and GAN is unsafe, since both GAR and GAN were already in use with a
following infinitive. Furthermore, it is doubtful whether GAR was ever a
pure dummy: rather it was a causative allowing VOSI and V+I
complementation and thus at best equivocal. If the analogy of German is to
be taken seriously, it would presumably be the full verb and/or substitute
uses of DO which provided the material for a periphrasis, but without
offering an existent DO + infinitive pattern. We are left with DO + infinitive
as a syntactic calque on Welsh GWNEUTHUR 'do' + verbal noun.

That DO might have been a perfective marker in the early attested
material (Denison 1985c: §4.4) is not an insuperable objection either, since
functions do change, though it would not help her case. On the other hand,
there are quite a few early examples which would support a habitual
reading.

It could be argued that Poussa's account does not explain why the
periphrasis first appeared in verse. (Stein 1990: 19 suggests that French
influence – FAIRE – may be significant here.) On the other hand, in some
ways the early rhyming verse was less formal than much of the prose, and
we cannot neglect the pressure of metrical demands for the use of such a
convenient device, if it existed.

Poussa suggests that the fertile periods for creolisation were early Old
English and early Middle English and specifically not late Middle English.
The dearth of other traces of contact with Celtic – lexical or otherwise – is
unfortunate and must presumably be ascribed to a difference between
written Old English and the more creolised lower lects in the continuum.
There is another inconvenient lack of positive evidence in early Middle
English. If I understand her correctly, this period includes the thirteenth

century when the periphrasis first appeared: one of her arguments is that
other dialects made use of alternative dummy auxiliaries, suggesting that
dummy aux formation is a universal tendency. But then we have no
explanation for the apparent fact that early use of the DO periphrasis shows
no particular preference for foreign loan words.[20] There is also an argument
to the effect that weakening, contraction and loss happen first in
phonologically non-prominent forms like the weak affirmative; that loss in
the weak affirmative argues for the written data representing a much older
spoken form; and that therefore a first appearance in written Middle English
suggests a spoken origin that predates the ME period. But the eME data do
not show loss in the weak affirmative: in fact that is the only form recorded.
Loss of the weak affirmative is a ModE phenomenon, and although it is
reasonable to project backwards from that loss if one assumes an
implicational hierarchy of environments for DO, it is not made clear why a
decline starting in the middle of the sixteenth century should provide
evidence about spoken usage prior to the thirteenth century.

Poussa suggests at one point (1990: §3.4) that habitual DO + verb in
Somerset may have derived through decreolisation by deletion of BE from
DO + BE + V, and that the resulting DO + V spread eastwards. It is implied
that the V in DO + BE + V would have been in present participle form. Now
progressive BE + PRES PTCP *is* found in Old English, but at far lower
frequencies in non-translated texts than in early Modern English and later
(see §13.3.1.1 below). This more specific hypothesis puts an even greater
burden on largely absent data.

Finally, use of DO as a tense marker is not confined to language contact
situations. In my paper I referred to observations by myself and others that
DO in early Modern English often seems to be used to avoid repetition of
the tense marking on coordinated verbs, and Samuels has suggested that the
efflorescence of use in the sixteenth century coincided with a period of great
uncertainty as to tense marking on irregular and Latinate verbs (1972a:
174). (Of course the absorption of Latinate vocabulary is a kind of language
contact.)

10.3.7 Tieken

Ingrid Tieken-Boon van Ostade (1988) makes a number of similar points to
Poussa. She wants to argue, however, that the DO periphrasis was common
Germanic in origin (a position already taken by Hausmann 1974: see
§10.4.1 below) and is continually reformed by children in the language
acquisition phase. She even goes so far as to suggest that causative DO
developed out of the periphrasis, which seems to me to go against the
evidence.

An important plank in her argument is the use of substitute DO in
common Germanic, which is certainly a fact. Now I think that this is
misleading. It is true that substitute DO is one of the NICE properties
('code') which distinguish present-day operators, a set largely co-extensive
with syntactic auxiliaries. But it occurred in Old English long before there
was any trace of auxiliary use of DO in written English, and it was used
freely with stative verbs, and even perhaps occasionally with HAVE:

[111]   (1340) *Ayenb*. 196.31

Þe holi man . . . ne   hedde none ssame of þe poure / ase <u>doþ</u> zome
the holy man . . . not had   no   shame of the poor   as do some

greate lhordes of þis wordle. þet wel   doþ elmesse to poure /
great lords of this world that certainly give alms   to the-poor

ac alneway his   habeþ ine onworþnesse uor hare pourehede.
but always   them hold   in contempt   for their poverty

In [111] DO may also be anticipative, of course. It was not really an auxiliary verb at all and should not be brought into the history of the periphrasis.

Tieken gives evidence of a DO periphrasis in Dutch dialects and in the pre-two-year speech of her son, suggesting that he lost it partly through pressure of stigmatisation. She appears to be unaware that weak affirmative DO is also common with English children of about three (Poussa 1990 cites Fletcher 1979; I would cite my elder daughter). I want to suggest, however, that the child data is not really pertinent. For a modern English child to overgeneralise DO is a natural inference given the importance of DO in adult language (cf. Ihalainen 1982, discussed in §10.3.8 below). It is the unemphatic declarative which is the real difference from adult language, plus the absence of certain co-occurrence restrictions. (My daughter at around five was still quite often saying *Did you be quiet?, I didn't be naughty*.) Auxiliary DOEN in use by a Dutch child is rather different, since it seems to be emphatic and may be confined to imperatives, though simplification of tense marking may play some part. In standard Dutch the use of DOEN usually coincides with topicalisation of the lexical verb or with an afterthought construction, and furthermore the infinitive in Dutch has a much more nominal character than the English infinitive, taking a definite article to form an NP, for example.

Tieken rests much of her case on Chaucer's famous examples of the DO periphrasis in the language of a three-year-old child:

[112]   (c1375,c1390) Chaucer, *CT.Mk*. VII.2431

His yonge sone, that thre yeer was of age, | Unto hym seyde,
his young son   that three years was of age to   him said

'Fader, why do ye   wepe? | Whanne wol the gayler bryngen our
father why do you   weep   when   will the gaoler bring   our

potage? | Is ther no morsel breed that ye   do kepe?'
soup   is there no morsel bread that you do keep

'His young son, three years of age, said to him, "Father, why are you weeping? When will the gaoler bring our soup? Isn't there a little bit of bread left that you are keeping?" '

This, she suggests, indicates that to Chaucer the usage was one appropriate to children, since he does not use the empty periphrasis elsewhere (Tieken 1988: 14–15). (Poussa cautiously takes a similar line.) The evidence is, as she admits, scant, but it *is* interesting. Whether it proves an origin in language simplification or merely a change coming up from below, I cannot judge. Ellegård's discussion of this passage (1953: 21–2) concludes that the exceptional demands of the rhyme scheme at this point caused Chaucer to lapse into what he otherwise evidently regarded as a cheap metrical device.

10.3.8 Ihalainen

Ossi Ihalainen (1982) discusses a development in which periphrastic DO might be extended to simple affirmatives, neatening the pattern in that *all* main clauses would then contain an operator, and making the derivation of interrogatives more transparent. (Such a development is hypothetical for standard Modern English but is actually attested in child language, second language acquisition, and – partially – Middle and early Modern English.) He mentions five factors which favour periphrastic formations of the type *went → did go*:

(A) availability of a syntactic pattern
(B) a need to integrate a lot of foreign lexical material
(C) a need for communicative simplification (pidginisation)
(D) existence of a learning problem
(E) a cross-linguistic tendency for VO languages to have prefixes rather than suffixes, hence perhaps favouring pre-position of tense marking

I think A is important. Once a construction exists then uses can be found for it which may alter immeasurably its meaning, its distribution, and ultimately its form, but few, if any, syntactic innovations come out of nothing. B, as we have seen, is cited by Poussa. It was true for the period in question, but there is no apparent association with the use of DO. Ihalainen is unsure whether C is true of ME Anglo-French contact. (Poussa thinks not.)

Factor D is central to Tieken's argument. Whether it applied to Middle English depends on whether there was an auxiliary category. Ihalainen is not sure whether there was, citing Lightfoot's material on modals. I think that there was an auxiliary category. The evidence of OE non-finite impersonals suggests strongly that ONGINNAN and the modals were already a separate semantic and syntactic subclass in Old English (cf. §§9.3.5–6 above). However, it does not appear that DON was then a member, and there were no NICE properties to distinguish one subset of verbs from another, so there probably was not any learning problem. See further Chapter 11.

I have no comment on E, but I repeat a point I have made in a quite different context – the history of the prepositional verb – that the rise of DO and its utility as a device to keep lexical verb and complementation uninterrupted coincides with either the formation or the rise of verb-complement idioms like the phrasal verb, prepositional verb, verb + noun (+ preposition), etc.

10.4 Explanations in generative linguistics

10.4.1 Hausmann

One of the first generative accounts is that of Robert B. Hausmann (1974). The interest here is the early gathering together of evidence to suggest that periphrastic DO is a common Germanic phenomenon, with standard Modern German somewhat comparable to Old English, and German dialects more like Modern English. Since in his framework PDE periphrastic and substitute DO both involve the DO-Support rule (here called *do*-insertion), Hausmann is led to the assumption that periphrastic DO somehow developed out of substitute DO.

He then goes on to couch a description of some of the facts in a now-outdated generative framework, ascribing everything to purely syntactic changes involving rule reorderings. (Fischer and van der Leek attack the lack of explanatory value, 1981: 305.) That is, Hausmann assumes that the relative order of such transformations as Tense Attachment and Question Formation has altered between Old and Modern English, while the transformation of DO-Support has existed from the earliest times. On this assumption it is not necessary or indeed possible to explain the origin of substitute DO within English (1974: 174). Hausmann considers the possibility that periphrastic DO actually existed in Proto-Germanic but was too heavily stigmatised in the earliest periods of the daughter languages to appear in writing (1974: 175–6), but he plumps instead for independent, if largely parallel, development within English, German and Dutch.

10.4.2 Lightfoot

In his frequent discussions of the modals David Lightfoot has been unwilling to commit himself to an account of DO:

> . . . one might argue that English had a phrase structure rule Aux → T [i.e. Tense: D.D.] from the earliest times and that *do* was attached first only to a T where there was no verb in the clause, then to any T (except before *be* or *have*), and finally only to a T not immediately preceding its verb. (1979: 119n.)

Presumably the DO-Support rule has to be obligatory in Old English, optional in Middle English and obligatory in Modern English again. And although the arguments for placing PDE progressive BE and perfect HAVE in the VP-*constituent* rather than in Aux are familiar, no justification is given for the special behaviour of DO *vis-à-vis* BE and HAVE in Middle English as opposed to Modern English (cf. 1979: 113).

10.4.3 Lenerz

Jürgen Lenerz works backwards from Present-day English to Old English, claiming that DO 'acts like a modal verb in OE, ME and NE alike' (1982: 215). This is already highly dubious. Even if we grant the existence of modals in Old English, they consistently took a plain infinitive, whereas causative DO – which was not at all common and may have been at first a Latinism – could occur with *to*-infinitives, and in any case had a different argument structure. The auxiliary DO proposed by Lenerz has to be given causative interpretation by the semantics and is different from substitute ('dummy') DO, which is taken to be a main verb use. But since the existence of substitute DO was the only real justification for positing a potential for auxiliary DO in Old English in the first place, the basis of the argument has fallen away, and we have an extremely counter-intuitive proposal.

10.4.4   Warner

Anthony Warner (1990, 1992) makes a careful and precise examination of evidence for a category 'auxiliary' in early stages of English, coming to the overall conclusion that there is sufficient justification for treating auxiliary verbs as a subsidiary-level category (in the cognitive terms of Rosch and associates) in Old English. In Warner (1992) three formal properties are analysed: post-verbal ellipsis, pseudogapping, and transparency to impersonal constructions. Pseudogapping corresponds to DO as verb-substitute (as e.g. example [88]), while post-verbal ellipsis involves the ellipsis of the whole of the VP rather than just V, though the two may be neutralised (as in my [92] above). The third property concerns constructions like:

[113]   *Bo* 26.12

    þætte nænne mon   þæs   tweogan   ne þearf
    that   no   man(ACC) that(GEN) doubt(INF) not needs(3 SG)

    þætte . . .
    that . . .

    'that no man need doubt that . . .'

where the case syntax of the impersonal TWEOGAN 'doubt' is apparently unaffected by the presence of the finite ÞEARF 'need'. OE DON is *not* found in the position of *þearf* in sentences like [113]. Accordingly (and also on morphological grounds) DON is regarded as a non-central member of the auxiliary category.

In these papers Warner does not explicitly address the question of the origin of periphrastic DO. With an acknowledgement of Hausmann's insistence on the relevance of substitute DO, however, he does suggest that one source of the failure of periphrastic DO to co-occur with auxiliaries may have been that even in Old English DON would not act as substitute for a modal (1992: 204).[21]

10.5   Questions for discussion or further research

(a) Is it legitimate to ignore interrogatives, negatives, imperatives and emphatic sentences (as for instance does Denison 1985c: §3) in discussing the syntactic origins of periphrastic DO?

(b) What would constitute good evidence for choosing between the conjectures of Denison (1985c) and Poussa (1990)? Does such evidence exist? Are the conjectures compatible? (Dieter Stein 1990 suggests a polygenetic origin, with the periphrasis being introduced both from above (Latin-influenced, two-clause structure) and below (creole-continuum, simplification device).)

(c) Studies on the origins of periphrastic DO seem to concentrate either on the intra-systemic (largely syntactic) mechanisms which could have produced the form, or on the sociolinguistic circumstances which could have made use of the function. Comment on the methodology.

(d) Go through valid pre-1400 examples of periphrastic DO in Visser (take note of Denison 1985c: 58 n.3), testing for possible Aktionsart values. Note down what proportion must be and what might be (i) perfective, (ii) habitual.

(e) Examine a portion of one of the Robert Mannyng texts to correlate use or non-use of DO with (i) a borrowed lexical verb, (ii) perfective Aktionsart, (iii) habitual Aktionsart. (Count only clauses with a finite lexical verb or with DO + infinitive.)

Notes

1. Some parts of this chapter follow Denison (1985c) closely.
2. The four NICE properties go together most of the time but not always. Thus, for example, NEED rarely behaves as an operator in the affirmative assertive contexts of [2](b), [3](a) or [4], though it can satisfy the remaining NICE tests.

   The class of operators in Present-day English largely overlaps with, but is not quite identical to, the class of auxiliaries. Operators are defined purely in terms of the NICE properties. An example of an operator which is not an auxiliary is main verb BE as sole verb. A possible auxiliary which is never an operator is passive GET. See later chapters in Part V.
3. Visser's labels are **cdsi** and **cdi**, standing for causative DO (±subject-of-the-infinitive) + infinitive.

   Royster claims that causative FACERE was 'practically never used' + infinitive in formal classical Latin but rather + finite clause or + predicate NP and adjective, though the infinitival construction was used colloquially and became the favoured construction in medieval Latin (1922: 333–4). He advances the conjecture that causative DON + infinitive was probably used in colloquial Old English – as evidenced by its widespread use in Middle English texts – but was considered stylistically unsuitable for formal writing in Old English (1922: 337–45).
4. For [12] cf.

   (a) a1225(c1200) *Vices & V.(1)* 25.8

      hie   iliefð   ðat hie næure niseih
      it/she [*sc.* Faith] believes what it   never not-saw

   suggesting that the personified virtue can be subject of ILEVE and thus weakening the evidence for causative use. [15] is in the possibly archaic legal language of an indenture of lease (cf. Ellegård 1953: 71).
5. A sentence is **ambiguous** if the hearer/reader cannot tell which of two (or more) meanings was intended but can assume that the speaker/writer intended only one of them. It is **vague** if the speaker/writer did not choose between the meanings and left the semantics underdetermined. A standard test is to conjoin a DO *so too* clause and see whether the original clause and the conjoined clause can carry different meanings. Thus (following Kempson 1977: §8.2 or Lakoff 1970) the sentence

   (a) Johnny saw her duck.

   has two readings ('Johnny saw the duck she owned'/'Johnny saw her lower her head') and is ambiguous between them, since

(b)   Johnny saw her duck and Will did so too.

cannot have the reading 'Johnny saw the duck she owned and Will saw her lower her head' (or vice versa). Compare (a) with

(c)   Johnny killed a bird today.

which also has two readings at least ('John intentionally/accidentally killed a bird today') but is vague as to which, since

(d)   Johnny killed a bird today, and so did Susie.

would be appropriate even if Johnny had done it on purpose and Susie not.

6. Mitchell's suggestion that [31] is a sort of causative V+I is not much better supported than Visser's, given that the pattern is very rare in Old English. And as Mitchell himself points out, the parallel metrical OE version offers *willað* . . . *wiðstandan*: WILL *must* have the same subject as WIÐSTANDAN. But this is hardly conclusive. The relevant Latin prose passage is even more distant:

(a)   *Bo* (Lat.) I 6, 21

ex   quibus [falsis opinionibus] orta perturbationum caligo   verum
out-of which   risen of-perturbations darkness true

illum confundit intuitum
that   confuses intuition

'out of which [false beliefs] the darkness arising from perturbations confuses that true insight'

No help there. On *any* of the possible readings – anticipative, causative, even periphrastic (also sometimes proposed) – [31] stands in virtual isolation for its period.

7. In [35], *struien* and *libben* may be PRES (likewise *fostren* in [42], *lippen* in [43]): cf. *habbeð* in the next clause, not printed by Visser. Both *-en* and *-eð* are used for PRES PL in this manuscript, though conceivably *libben* INF (as 183.9) contrasts with *liuen* PRES PL (as 179.2). In [36], *sculden* may be responsible for the infinitive, or the structure may be VOSI. MS. Otho has no metrical punctuation before *don*. Example [43] is a strange one. PA PL is usually *-en*, so why *deede*? PRES PL regularly ends in *-en* in this text, INF is usually -Ø or *-e*.

8. Compare:

(a)   c1180 *Orm.* 13087

&   didenn   alls he seȝȝde, | To lokenn whære he wass   att inn
and did(PA PL) as he said   to look   where he was   at inn

'and did as he said, to look where he was staying'

again with *to*-infinitive. But this may not even be anticipative DO + infinitive at all but instead derived elliptically from SAY 'order' + NP + infinitive, which was extant at this time (Visser 1963–73: §2078 and cf. §1241).

9. Compare Marchand's claim that the indirect passive too was in colloquial use long before its first surviving attestation (§6.3.3 above).

10. The idiosyncratic term is due to Stern, who defines it as follows (1931: 261):

> Permutations are unintentional sense-changes in which the subjective apprehension of a detail – denoted by a separate word – in a larger total changes, and the changed apprehension (the changed notion) is substituted for the previous meaning of the word.

11. Note too that Royster accepts the primacy of causative origin but suggests that

the period of causative use and potential reinterpretation as tense auxiliary began earlier, in (largely unattested) colloquial Old English.

12. Here's another analogy for the vagueness of DO + infinitive in Middle English:

   (a) He painted the wall.   (affected object)
   (b) He painted a portrait.   (effected object)
   (c) He painted his family.   (some other kind of object)

   The wall in (a), *a portrait* in (b), and *his family* in (c) are all direct objects of PAINT, yet the *semantic* relation to PAINT varies greatly from one example to the next. Syntactically, however, (a–c) show exactly the same construction.

13. Jones (1972: 157) cites:

   (a) ?a1300 *Fox & W.* 106

        Ac nou of   me idon   hit hiis!
        but now concerning me done [*sc.* finished] it   is

        'But now it is all over with me!'

14. Professor Samuels points out that the southern origin of DO + infinitive does not lend support to the hypothesis of Aktionsart value (personal communication).

15. For the fourfold distinction of **accomplishments** (telic), **achievements** (punctual), **activities**, and **states**, see Vendler (1967) as elaborated in Dowty (1979).

16. Of over 400 examples, around 20 look more like 'activity' verbs, and under 10 look like 'state' verbs. These latter include the verbs MEAN, MISS (as in [47]) (cf. Goossens 1984: 155–6).

17. Kroch et al.'s formulation fits in well with my [42]: 'Eventually, PRO comes to be obligatorily controlled by the matrix subject . . .' (1982: 284). However, it implies an alternative analysis of modern sentences with modal verbs as two-clause structures with subject control; see further Chapter 11.

   Stein elaborates my perfective hypothesis by suggesting that reanalysis to a one-clause structure would have been particularly likely in second-person usage in a 'setting of authority', where someone is required to see that a job gets done (1990: 23–6).

18. Old Welsh had three compound verb forms made up of forms of BOT 'be' + verbal noun which could have durative meanings; also a synthetic verb form with durative or futural meaning; also a non-durative compound form made up of GWNEUTHUR 'do' + verbal noun; see Wagner (1959). I am very grateful to my colleague Pat Williams for clarification of the Celtic facts.

19. I owe this reference to Pat Poussa (p.c., 8 February 1990), who attributes the information to Clive Upton. Poussa observes that Pembroke is an area settled by the English during the eME period, and suggests that in this respect it is a relic area comparable with Somerset.

20. Poussa's rejoinder to this (p.c., 4 February 1990) is that 'substratum effects will be felt for a very long time, centuries after language death', and that modern Irish English DO + BE forms, which are generally agreed to reflect substratal Celtic influence, do not *collocate* with Irish loanwords. She also refers to comments by Lesley Milroy (1987: 144–5) on the rarity in spontaneous Irish English speech of the DO + BE construction. But the fact remains that DO provides no evidence for a *Middle* English phase of creolisation.

21. Warner implicitly rejects Visser's lone example of DON as substitute for MOT (1963–73: §187):

   (a) *Sat* 622

        Menað   þæt heo moten to þære mæran byrig | up to englum swa
        think(3 PL) that they may   to the glorious town up to angels as

oðre   dydon
others did

'They will think that they may be permitted to go up to the glorious city to the angels, as the others had done'

presumably on the grounds that *dydon* may be a substitute for an ellipted verb of motion.

Chapter 11

Modals and related auxiliaries

11.1 The problem

Modal verbs in Present-day English belong to a class that shows major differences from other verbs in syntax, morphology and semantics. The central set consists of CAN, MAY, WILL, SHALL, MUST. Other verbs with – for differing reasons – more peripheral membership include OUGHT, USED, IS, HAVE, NEED, DARE, DO, LET.

Amongst the interrelated problems to be addressed in this chapter are:

(A) changes in individual verbs on the way to their present properties, both syntactic and semantic
(B) global changes that led to a class identity of modals
(C) the dating of B
(D) whether modals are main verbs or auxiliaries in Old English and later
(E) changes in the membership of the class, both losses and gains

Terminology is a bugbear, as ever, with labels for the OE precursors of PDE modals a particular difficulty. Amongst those offered have been 'pre-modals' (Lightfoot), ' "modal" auxiliaries' (Mitchell), 'preterite-present verbs' (various). For simplicity I shall stick to **modal**, without inverted commas. The list of verbs included and the properties they have will be the subject of §§11.2–3.

11.2 Modals in Present-day English

The features which distinguish modals from other verbs in Present-day standard English can be summarised as follows. For fuller accounts see Huddleston (1980, 1984), Palmer (1988).

11.2.1 Morphology

Modals have no non-finite forms at all. Most have two tensed forms, present and past, though without person-number marking in 3 SG PRES and with great irregularity in the formation of the past: *can/could, may/might,*

shall/should, will/would.[1] MUST has only the form *must.* Negated forms
(*can't, shouldn't, won't,* etc.) are traditionally analysed as modal + **enclitic**
not, though a persuasive recent analysis treats them as special inflectional
forms (see Zwicky and Pullum 1983, Huddleston 1984: 87–8). WILL (and
SHALL?) can be cliticised to *'d* [d, əd] and *'ll* [l, əl], and most modals have
forms with reduced vowel: [kən], [kəd], [məst], [ʃəl], [ʃəd], [wəl], [wəd].

11.2.2 Syntax

A modal is complemented by a plain infinitive. Given the absence of non-
finite forms, one modal clearly cannot follow another in the same verbal
group. Another consequence is that there can be no perfect or progressive
of a modal, and no passive. Or, to put it another way, a modal must always
be the first verb of a finite verbal group. There are no imperatives.

Modals are **operators,** they have the 'NICE' properties. They can be
negated by a following *n't/not,* take part in subject-verb inversion, survive
post-verbal ellipsis, and be stressed for emphatic polarity:

[1] N: Mel can't sing a note.
[2] I: Can Mel dance at all?
[3] C: (Mel will arrive late) and so will Bob.
[4] E: Mel *cán* be trusted.

They share these properties with BE (almost all uses), HAVE (perfect
auxiliary and some main-verb uses), and DO (periphrastic auxiliary only).

In unreal conditional constructions such as

[5] If Mel wasn't/hadn't been such a no-hoper, the show would be/would
     have been a smash hit.

it is a requirement that the first verb of the main clause (*apodosis*) should be
a modal in the past tense.

11.2.3 Semantics

A distinction is often drawn between **epistemic** meanings, which concern the
truth, probability, possibility, etc. of the whole proposition, and other uses,
the latter either called **root** meanings in the TG literature or subdivided as
deontic, dynamic, etc. Deontic modality involves permission given or
obligation imposed performatively by the speaker/writer (or in a question,
the hearer/reader). Dynamic modality lacks this performative element.
Examples [6]–[8] illustrate epistemic, deontic and dynamic CAN, respectively:

[6] That can't be the time!
[7] Can I have some sweets?
[8] John can speak good French.

Modals also appear in many contexts where some other European languages
would use a subjunctive mood (e.g. . . . *requirement that . . . should be*
. . .). For discussion see Palmer (1979, 1988).

The relationship between present and past tense in modals is different from that in other verbs, being further removed from notions of time. A past-tense modal in a main clause, unlike other verbs, need have no reference to past time. Indeed there are relatively few modals which even *can* show a present ~ past distinction semantically comparable to ordinary verbs. Here are some examples where modals do show an 'ordinary' use of tense:

[9]   (a)   (Now) I can cycle up the Isle of Skye Road with some difficulty.
      (b)   (When I was younger) I could cycle up the Isle of Skye Road quite easily.

[10] (a)   Students *wíll* ask the most awkward questions.
      (b)   (In those days) students *wóuld* ask the most awkward questions.

But in Present-day English a sentence like [12] is no longer the natural past-time variant of the [11] type:

[11]   Foreign nationals may not enter without a visa.
[12]   !Napoleon might not leave Elba.

Indeed *may* and *might* are frequently almost interchangeable:[2]

[13]   Ronald may not have known where the place was.
[14]   Ronald might not have known where the place was.

One of the few non-historical arguments for treating, say, *may* and *might* as different tense-forms of a single lexeme MAY is the so-called 'sequence-of-tenses' or 'backshifting' rule after a past-tense verb of reporting, etc. In this respect MAY in [15] behaves just like the ordinary lexical verb HATE in [16]:[3]

[15] (a)   'I may write another two chapters this morning.'
      (b)   He said that he might write another two chapters that morning.
[16] (a)   'I hate scribbles in library books.'
      (b)   He said that he hated scribbles in library books.

11.2.4 Non-standard English

There are dialects of Present-day English which permit 'double modals' of various limited kinds:

[17]   You might would say that.
[18]   I don't feel as if I should ought to leave.
[19]   Ye'll   can   cum   neist weik?
       you-will be-able-to come next week
[20]   If wey had cuid   cum.
       if we   had been-able-to come

Typical forms are *might* + infinitive and *might* + past tense/past participle modal in the southern United States, as in [17] (see Butters 1973), and CAN with complete non-finite morphology in Scotland and certain English dialects, as in [19]–[20] (see Ščur 1968, Brown and Millar 1980).

11.3 The data

11.3.1 Inventory of modals

The membership of the class modal varies slightly over the centuries. By labelling verbs as 'modal', 'marginal' or (implicitly) 'non-modal', I run inevitable risks of arbitrary classification.

11.3.1.1 Old English

Amongst the verbs which Mitchell includes under his heading 'The "Modal" Auxiliaries' are CANN 'can, know' (> PDE CAN), DEARR 'dare' (> PDE DARE), MÆG 'have power' (> PDE MAY), MOT 'can, must' (past *moste* > PDE MUST), SCEAL 'must' (> PDE SHALL), ÞEARF 'need' (now obsolete), WILE 'wish' (> PDE WILL) (1985: §§990–2).[4] The glosses I have given are fairly rough and ready. Unlike Mitchell I shall treat AGAN 'have, own' as a marginal modal, because its syntactic properties were significantly different from the rest. See further §11.3.9.1 below. Mitchell has much useful information on the OE modals (1985: §§990–1024).

ÞEARF is confined largely to negative and interrogative contexts, much like PDE modal NEED. As for DEARR 'dare', because it has a root (dynamic) meaning rather remote from common epistemic modal meanings, the type (ii) usage in [21] – where the subject is inanimate Theme rather than animate Experiencer – is unexpected:[5]

[21] *GD* 232.7

be þam ne dorste us   nan wen   beon
by which not dared(SG) us(DAT) no expectation(NOM) be

geðuht,   þæt hi   mihton beon dælnimende þæs heofonlican
seemed/thought that they might be   partaking   the heavenly

wuldres
glory(GEN)

'in consideration of which we should not dare think it likely that they might partake in the glory of heaven'

However, something very similar occurs with ModE DARE, which sometimes shows the voice-neutrality associated with epistemic modals and raising verbs:

[22] 1668 Pepys, *Diary* IX 154.5 (6 Apr)

And I wonder how it [*sc.* a libel] durst be printed and spread abroad

[23] c1977 att. by A. Radford

Inflation is a problem which dare not be neglected.

As Palmer observes of [23], ' . . . the semantics make this most unlikely. This is yet another indication of the auxiliary nature of the modals' (1979: 184). Example [21] shows that it is an indication valid for Old English too, even though BEON *geðuht* is probably perfect rather than passive (see §12.4.3 below). The evidence of [21]–[23], the fact that DEARR/DARE can occur with a following plain infinitive in a like-subject construction, and its semantic similarity to other dynamic modals (capability, intentionality, possibility, etc.) seem sufficient justification for including this verb with the modals in all periods.

As far as historical morphology is concerned, all the OE modals except WILE were preterite-present verbs, a set of verbs with a present tense just like the past (preterite) tense of a **strong** verb (apart from the *-st* of the 2 SG), and a past tense formed on an irregular stem with the endings of the **weak** past. WILE was of different origin but similarly irregular. Some sample indicative forms are given below:

[24]

	pret.-pres.	WILE	strong	weak
[PDE citation form	*can*	*will*	*swim*	*hear]*
1 SG PRES	ic cann	wille	swimme	hiere
2 SG PRES	þu canst	wilt	swimst	hierst
3 SG PRES	he cann	wil(l)e	swimð	hierð
1/2/3 PL PRES	we cunnon	willað	swimmað	hierað
2 SG PA	þu cuþest	woldest	swumme	hierdest
3 SG PA	he cuðe	wolde	swam	hierde

Admittedly the PL PRES of WILE had the normal inflection of strong and many weak verbs, while its 3 SG PRES indicative was not endingless, but like the preterite-presents and unlike almost all other verbs, its 3 SG PRES indicative inflection did not end in -ð. So the precursors of two distinctive PDE traits – 3 SG PRES -Ø rather than -*s*, and irregular past tense formation – already tended to place WILE with the preterite-presents in Old English.

However, the set of preterite-presents in Old English included several non-modal verbs: BENEAH/GENEAH 'suffice', DEAH 'avail, be of use', GEMUNAN 'remember', (GE)UNNAN 'love, grant', WITAN 'know'. BENEAH/ GENEAH and GEMUNAN did not survive the Conquest.

11.3.1.2 Middle English

The list of modals in Middle English should include the preterite-present MUN (*MED monen* v.(2)) 'must' (now obsolete in the standard language) and some instances of NEED. The OE verb ÞEARF 'need' survived, often in forms without the final *-f* and sometimes – through confusion with DARE – with initial *d-* rather than *þ-/th-*. See *OED* s.v. *tharf, thar* v., Visser (1963–73: §1343). The verb became obsolete (except in Scotland) by the end of the fifteenth century.

Most non-modal preterite-presents died out in the course of the ME period. UNNEN 'grant, wish', despite having meanings close to certain modals, had never been complemented by an infinitive; it had disappeared by the early fourteenth century. DOUEN (*OED dow*) 'avail, be of profit', which had been chiefly impersonal, became obsolete by maybe the end of the ME period except in northern and Scottish English. Interestingly, however, it developed a modal use 'have the strength or ability, be able':

[25] a1400(a1325) *Cursor* 23771

Fight he aght   ai   quils he dught, | And fle   quen he langer
fight he ought always while he was-able and flee when he no-longer

ne moght.
not could

[26] 1637 Rutherford, *Lett.*(1862) I.203 (*OED* s.v. *dow* v.[1] 5)

Ye may not, ye cannot, ye dow not want Christ.

WIT 'know' died out by the nineteenth century except in the phrase *to wit*
'namely'. One minor use in the sense 'know how to' required a following *to*-
infinitive, but WIT was never modal-like in its syntax. In morphology,
however, it probably retained its *s*-less 3 SG PRES to the last: see *OED* s.v.
wit v.[1] A.2.[6]

11.3.1.3 Modern English

The principal change in the late ModE period is the loss of 2 SG inflection,
though use of the 2 SG *thou* forms had been on the decline for some time.
With these forms all person-number marking was lost.

  In Present-day English it is common to assume that there are two
homonymous and synonymous verbs DARE and NEED, the modal seen
in [27] and the non-modal seen in [28]:

[27] Dare/need we wait any longer?
[28] Do we dare/need to wait any longer?

The modal form tends to occur in non-assertive contexts (negatives and
questions); see Huddleston (1980), Palmer (1988). The picture is a little
messy, since there are sentences which have both DO (typical of non-modal
DARE) and a following plain infinitive (typical of modal DARE):

[29] 1932 Greene, *Diary* xxix.431.25

Frere-Reeves hopeful of the Book Society, but I do not dare hope, or
rather I hope but do not believe in the actuality of the hope.

Another 'mixed' example, in a southern AmE dialect, is:

[30] 1989 Gurganus, *Confederate Widow* III.i.2 339

Some of our children . . . stood in the doorway, not daring interrupt
for once . . . .

  Visser cites the following example of DARE in the apodosis of an unreal
conditional, suggesting that ' "[h]e dare not" instead of "he dared not" or
"would not dare" . . . deserves notice' (1963–73: §861):

[31] 1905 Shaw, *Man of Destiny* 155b.4

He dare not keep you waiting if he were at liberty.

The obvious explanation for [31] is that the conditional construction
required a past tense modal, but that *durst* was ruled out by its obsolescence
and *dared* because it looked like a non-modal past; see Visser (1963–73:
§796). Similarly, [32] requires an operator because of the inversion:

[32]   1959 Norton, *Borrowers Afloat* xx.504.11

She could not, at that moment, find words to thank him, nor dare she take his hand.

Compare [33], where *dared*, though the sentence is hypothetical, is not in a position which demands a modal:

[33]   1905 Shaw, *Man of Destiny* 163a.9

suppose I . . . were to . . . cover up my weakness by playing the magnanimous hero, and sparing you the violence I dared not use!

For PDE *need*, *dare* as past tense forms see Jespersen (1909–49: IV 12–13), Palmer (1988: 135, 155).

11.3.2   Modal + infinitive

11.3.2.1   Epistemic meanings, with subject

Goossens claimed that 'the OE modals *magan*, *sculan* and *willan* show the first traces of epistemic use, but that none of them can be regarded as an established carrier of epistemic meaning' (1982: 79). His candidates for possible epistemic interpretation, not all of them in construction with an infinitive, are [36]–[41], to which we can add a couple of others:

[34]   *ÆCHom* I 12.182.15

And hi   ða   ealle sæton, swa swa mihte beon fif ðusend wera.
and they then all   sat   as as might be five thousand men

'And then they all sat, maybe five thousand men.'

[35]   *ÆCHom* I 23.330.9

Sume beladunge   mihte se rica   habban his uncyste,
some excuse(ACC) might the rich-man have   his stinginess(DAT)

gif se reoflia wædla ne læge   ætforan his gesihðe:
if the leprous beggar not lay(PA SUBJ) before his sight

'The rich man might have had some excuse for his stinginess if the leprous beggar had not been lying before his eyes:'

[36]   *Bede* 2 1.96.23

Wel þæt swa mæg
well that so   may

'That may well be so'

[37]   *Sat* 22

Ðuhte him   on mode þæt hit mihte swa, | þæt hie weron
seemed them(DAT) on mind that it   might so   that they were

seolfe   swegles brytan, | wuldres waldend.
themselves heaven's governors glory's rulers

'It seemed to them that it might be the case that they were themselves governors of heaven, rulers of glory.'

[38] *BlHom* 21.17

Swiþe eaþe   þæt mæg beon þæt sume men þencan . . .
very eas(il)y that may be   that some men think . . .

'It may very well be that some men think . . .'

[39] *Gen* 2.17

ðu scealt deaðe sweltan.

'thou shalt surely die'

[40] *Jul* 425

Wende ic þæt þu þy wærra   weorþan sceolde . . .
thought I that you the more-ware become should . . .

[41] *PPs* 123.2

wen   is, þæt hi   us lifigende lungre wyllen | sniome
expectation is that they us living   quickly intend at-once

forsweolgan
swallow-up

'It is likely that they will swallow us up at once'

[42] *Or* 15.26

eastewerd hit mæg bion syxtig mila brade oþþe hwene brædre
eastward it may be   sixty miles broad or   a-little broader

Arguably [34]–[38] should be treated as subjectless and moved to the next
section, though they differ somewhat from the examples treated there.
Traugott is cautious about the early development of epistemic meaning:

> All the same, there are very few instances of OE *magan, willan* or **sculan* where
> the meaning without question expresses the speaker's assessment of probability
> and nothing else. . . . We may note that in PDE, it is only with inanimate subjects
> that prediction is the primary meaning of *will* (cf. *It will rain tonight*). There do
> not appear to be any such sentences with inanimate subjects in OE. (1992: 196–7)

Goossens adds 'that also in Middle English clear epistemic examples are
difficult to find' (1982: 78), citing only [43]–[46] below:[7]

[43] a1225(?a1200) Lay.*Brut* 2250

Sone hit mæi ilimpen
soon it may happen

[44] a1400(a1325) *Cursor* 289

And if þou wynus it mai not be | Behald þe sune, and þou mai se
and if you think it may not be behold the sun   and you may see

[45] a1400(a1325) *Cursor* 11963

Vr neghburs mai þam   on vs wreke
our neighbours may themselves on us avenge

[46]   a1425(?a1350) *7 Sages(2)* 2843

Sen þou ert both ȝong and fayre, | Þou mai haue childer to be þine
since you are both young and fair   you may have children to be your

aire.
heir(s)

[47]   (1472) *Stonor* 123 I 126.36

þough þe fflame of the ffyre of love may not breke out so þat it may
be seyn, . . .

[48]   ?c1425(?c1400) *Loll.Serm.* 1.168

Þe enbatelynge aboute . . . mai wel be her   feyned holynesse
the battlements around . . . may well be their feigned holiness

wherbi   þei colouren al her   euele.
by-means-of-which they disguise all their evil

For Modern English, examples are readily to be found in the handbooks.

11.3.2.2   Epistemic meanings, without subject

Subjectless instances are found quite widely in Old English and in Middle
English, dying out with the increasingly fixed requirement that all English
main clauses should have a surface subject (imperatives and elliptical
utterances apart). For the OE material see Denison (1990b).

[49]   *Beo* 2032

Mæg þæs   þonne ofþyncan ðeodne   Heaðobeardna |
may that(GEN) then   regret   lord(DAT) Heathobards(GEN PL)

ond þegna   gehwam   þara leoda, | þonne he . . .
and thanes(GEN PL) each(DAT) the   people(GEN PL) when he . . .

'The lord of the Heathobards and each nobleman of the people may
regret it when he . . .'

[50]   *ÆLet* 2(Wulfstan 1) 147 122.11

Nu mæg eaþe getimian, þæt eower   sum   ahsige, hwi . . .
now may easily happen   that you(GEN PL) someone ask   why . . .

'It may well be that one of you will now ask, why . . .'

[51]   *LawGer* 12 454

[Me mæig] . . . &   raðe   æfter ðam, gif hit mot gewiderian,
[one may] . . . and quickly after that if it   may be-fine-weather

mederan settan . . .
madder sow

'. . . and promptly afterwards, if the weather may be fine, plant
madder . . .'

[52]   *ÆIntSig* 61 400

Ic axige hwæðer hit mihte gedafenian abrahame þam halgan were.
I ask   whether it might befit   Abraham the holy   man(DAT)

þæt he . . .
that he . . .

'I ask whether it might have been fitting for Abraham, the holy man,
to . . .'

[53]   *Bo* 46.5

Þōn mæg hine   scamigan   þære brædinge
then may him(ACC) shame(INF) the   spreading(GEN/DAT)

his hlisan
his fame(GEN)

'then he may be ashamed of the extent of his fame'

[54]   *Bo* 142.2

Hu wolde   þe   nu lician   gif . . .
how would(3 SG PA) you(2 SG DAT) now please(INF) if . . .

'How would it please you now if . . .?'

[55]   *HomS* 25 412 (*DOE*)

. . . þæt we þa   þing   don þe us   to ecere hælu
. . . that we those things(PL) do   that us(DAT PL) to eternal salvation

gelimpan mote
happen   may(SUBJ SG?)

'. . . that we do those things which may lead to eternal salvation for
us'

[56]   *HomM* 5(Willard) 57.6

. . . ðæt us   ne ðurfe sceamian
. . . that us(DAT/ACC) not need shame

'. . . that we need not feel shame'

[57]   *HomU* 37(Nap 46) 238.12

. . . hine   sceal on domes dæg gesceamjan beforan gode . . . swa
. . . him(ACC) shall on doom's day shame   before God . . . as

þam men   dyde, þe . . .
that man(DAT) did   who . . .

'. . . he shall feel shame before God on the Day of Judgment . . . as
did the man who . . .'

[58]   *ÆHom* I 2.235.112

. . . ne him   hingrian   ne mæg
. . . nor him(DAT) hunger(INF) not may

'. . . nor may he be hungry'

[59]   *HomU* 14(Holt) 4

. . . þonne sceal þe   spowan   & þe
. . . then   shall you(ACC/DAT SG) succeed/prosper and you/the

bet   limpan
better happen

'. . . then you shall prosper and it will go (the) better for you'

[60]   1175 *Lamb.Hom.* 243.18

Ac se þe   geð into fihte wið-ute heretoche. him   mai sone
but he who goes into fight without leader   him(OBL) may soon
mislimpe.
go-amiss

'But he who goes into battle leaderless may soon come a cropper.'

[61]   c1225(?c1200) *St.Juliana*(Bod) 51.551

grisen   him   mahte þet sehe hu . . .
feel-horror him(OBL) might that saw how . . .

'He who saw how . . . might feel horror.'

[62]   a1300 *Þo ihu crist* 85.24

ne schal him   þurste neuere.
not shall him(OBL) thirst never

[63]   a1300 *Sayings St.Bede*(Jes-O) 83.336

Vs   schal   euer   smerte
us(OBL) shall(SG) always feel-pain

[64]   a1500(?c1300) *Bevis* (Cmb) p.83, textual note to 1583–1596

hym shall not gayne

'It will do him no good.'

[65]   a1300 *A Mayde Cristes* (Jes-O) 96

Ne þurhte þe   neuer rewe, | myhtestu do þe   in his
not needed you(OBL) never rue   might-you put yourself in his
ylde.
protection

'You would never need regret putting yourself in his protection.'

[66]   a1400(a1325) *Cursor* 17553

Mai fall   sum gast awai him ledd, | And es vnto þe felles fledd.
may happen some spirit away him led   and is into the hills fled

'Maybe some spirit led him away and he(?) has fled into the hills.'

[67]   c1450(1369) Chaucer, *BD* 256

Hym   thar not nede   to turnen ofte.
him(OBL) need not necessarily to turn   often

'He needn't necessarily turn often.'

[68]   (a1393) Gower, *CA* 1.457

Him   may fulofte   mysbefalle
him(OBL)   may very-often suffer-misfortune

'he may very often suffer misfortune.'

[69] (c1395) Chaucer, *CT.Cl.* IV.908

Hym   wolde thynke   it were a disparage | To his estate
him(OBL) would seem/think it was   a disgrace   to his estate

'It would seem to him a disgrace to his estate.'

[70] a1425 *Daily Work* 144.1

ware þe drink nere   sa gode, him   wold wlat   þer-with
were the drink never so good him(OBL) would disgust with-it

'however good the drink, he would find it disgusting'

ME examples like [65] and [67] may reflect impersonal use of THURVEN rather than, or as well as, impersonal use of the *lower* verb (see §11.3.8 below). It is not always easy to distinguish epistemic usage, and examples [63]–[64] could equally be glossed by a PDE root modal.

11.3.2.3   Root meanings

Root meanings of modals in Old English are very common. Here are a few examples:

[71] *Mart* 3 178.41

& he næfre hine ofersuiðan meahte
and he never him overcome   could

'and he was never able to overcome him'

[72] *CP* 225.22

Ac ðæm   mæg beon suiðe hraðe   geholpen from his lareowe[8]
but that-one(DAT) may be   very quickly helped   by   his teacher

[73] *BlHom* 67.33

þu scealt on æghwylce tid   Godes willan wercan
you must   at each   time God's will   perform

[74] *And* 1215

Ne magon   hie ond ne moton . . . | ðinne lichoman, . . . |
not have-power they and not are-permitted your   body

deaðe   gedælan
death(DAT) deal(INF)

'They cannot and may not kill you bodily.'

Root meanings continued, of course, throughout Middle English, though there were gradual changes of meaning for several of the modals. For example, MOT lost the sense of permission which MAY had developed (later also CAN), CAN lost the sense of knowledge, and so on. Traugott has a useful discussion of meanings, summarised in a handy chart (1972: 68–72, 114–18, 168–72, 198–9). Here are some ME examples:

[75]   a1400(a1325) *Cursor* 5987

> Gas þan, sin   yee wil   þider   ga.
> go   then since you wish thither go

> 'Go then, since you wish to go there.'

[76]   ?c1425(?c1400) *Loll.Serm.* 3.323

> . . . and wiþ her   feyned disputacions and false exposicions scleen
> . . . and with their feigned disputations and false expositions destroy

> it in hemself   and in oþere as miche as þei may
> it in themselves and in others as much as they may

The Modern English examples below show that change has continued in recent centuries:

[77]   1816 Austen, *Emma* I.xviii.145.16

> . . . but I dare say he might come if he would.

> '. . . but I dare say he would be able to come if he wanted to.'

[78]   1816 Austen, *Emma* I.xviii.146.28

> but if he wished to do it, it might be done.

> 'but if he wished to do it, it could be done'

11.3.2.4   Futural meanings

I put these under a separate heading because they seem to have affinities both with root and with epistemic meanings. Principally WILL and SHALL belong here. By late Old English, if not earlier, each had developed a use which was almost a compound future tense:

[79]   *Bede* 4 29.366.4

> Gif me   seo godcunde geofu in ðære stowe forgifen beon wile
> if   me(DAT) the divine   gift   in that place granted be   will

> . . ., ic ðær   lustlice wunige.
> . . .   I there happily dwell

> 'If the divine gift is granted to me in that place . . ., I will happily remain there.'

[80]   ?c1425(?c1400) *Loll.Serm.* 2.699

> Alle þoo þat haue be,   and beþ, and schul be into þe Day of
> all   those that have been and are   and shall be until the Day of

> Doom,   pursueris of true cristen   peple, ben of þe
> Judgment persecutors of true Christian people are of the

> generacioun of Caym;
> generation of Cain

Although the history of WILL and SHALL as prime exponents of futurity – and their changing fortunes over the centuries – is of great importance in the history of English, detailed discussion of the *syntactic* development is not necessary here.

11.3.3 Modal without object or infinitive

11.3.3.1 With directional adverbial

Modal + directional adverbial is often used in Germanic languages as if a
verb of motion is to be understood. The usage is virtually dead in Present-
day English (consider proverbial *Murder will out*, or with non-modal WANT
the AmE *Bugsy wants out*) but was common in earlier periods. See Visser
(1963–73: §§178–9) and the dictionaries.

[81] *ÆLS* I 5.328

and he begeat ða   leafe þæt he of   þam lande   moste.
and he got   then leave that he from the   country could

'And then he got permission to leave the country.'

[82] (c1390) Chaucer, *CT.ML.* II.281

Allas, unto the Barbre nacioun | I moste   anoon
alas   to   the pagan world   I had-to [*sc.* go] at-once

[83] (a1470) Malory, *Wks.* 62.14

but the swerde wolde nat oute.

'but the sword would not come out'

[84] 1623(1607–8) Shakespeare, *Cor* I.iii.71

I will not out of doores . . . Ile not ouer the threshold . . . I will not
foorth.

11.3.3.2 Without directional adverbial

See Visser (1963–73: §§176–7). The verbs SHALL and MAY are occasionally
intransitive:

[85] *Med3* 37 114.20

þeos seolf mæg   wið   ælces cynnes   untrumnysse ðe
this salve is-efficacious against each kind(GEN) illness(es)   which

eagan eigliað.
eyes   afflict(PL)

'This salve is good for all manner of infirmities that affect the eyes.'

[86] c1180 *Orm.* 8043

Þatt ifell gast maȝȝ   oferr[9] þa   Þatt follȝhenn barrness
that evil spirit has-power over   those that follow   children's

þæwess . . .
customs . . .

[87] 1667 Pepys, *Diary* VIII 549.27 (26 Nov)

This I confess is strange to me touching those two men, but yet it may
well enough, as the world goes;

See also examples [36]–[37] above.
   There are also examples which appear to show ellipsis of the infinitive BE:

[88] *Mald* 312

> Hige   sceal þe heardra, . . . | mod sceal þe mare,   þe   ure
> thought must the harder   . . .   spirit must the greater the-more our
>
> mægen lytlað.
> might dwindles

> 'Resolution must be the fiercer, . . . spirit the greater, the less our
> might grows.'

This too is a Common Germanic pattern. On all these types see also
Mitchell (1985: §§1006–7).

11.3.4 Modal + direct object

11.3.4.1 Nominal object

There are examples and discussion in Visser (1963–73: §§548–73). Examples
[92]–[99] below seem to be among the latest for those verbs.

[89] *MCharm* 9.14

> Binnan þrym nihtum cunne   ic his mihta
> within three nights know(PRES SUBJ) I his powers

> 'Within three nights may I know his powers'

[90] *Lk(WSCp)* 5.39

> And ne drincð nan man eald win &   wylle sona   þæt niwe.
> and not drinks no man old   wine and wants immediately the new

[91] c1230(?a1200) *Ancr.* 107b.25

> wult tu   castles. kinedomes. wult tu   wealden al þe world?
> want you castles kingdoms   want you rule   all the world

> 'Do you want castles, kingdoms? Do you want to rule the whole
> world?'

[92] (?c1422) Hoccl. *ASM* xxiii.695

> the leeste   ferthyng   þat y men shal
> the smallest farthing [quarter-penny] that I men owe

[93] c1470 Henry, *Wallace* III.396 (*OED* s.v. *may* v.[1] B.1b)

> For all the power thai mocht.
> for all the power they had-power

> 'for all the power they had'

[94] c1530 *Crt. of Love* 131 (*OED* s.v. *shall* B.1b, given in square brackets)

> By the feith I shall to god.
> by the faith I owe   to God

[95] 1577 Grange, *Golden Aphrod.* I iij b (*OED* s.v. *will* v.[1] B.1)

> Who   wil   the curnell of the nut must breake the shell.
> he-who wants the kernel of the nut must break   the shell

[96] 1600 Fairfax, *Tasso* X.iv.180 (*OED* s.v. *can* v.[1] B.1b)

The way right well he could.
the way very well he knew

[97] 1643 [Angier] *Lanc. Vall. Achor* 18 (*OED* s.v. *will* v.[1] B.22)

When we would no Pardon they laboured to punish us.

[98] 1649 Lovelace, *Poems* (1659) 120 (*OED* s.v. *can* v.[1] B.1b)

Yet can I Musick too; but such | As is beyond all Voice or Touch.

[99] 1654 Whitlock, *Zootomia* 44 (*OED* s.v. *will* v.[1] B.1)

Will what befalleth, and befall what will.

In the phrase CAN *skill of/in* 'be skilled in', CAN + direct object is recorded up to 1710(1709). Late occurrences of WILL in [100]–[101] may show post-verbal ellipsis rather than a direct object (and perhaps non-modal WILL in the *willing* of [101]):

[100] 1692 Washington tr. *Milton's Def. People* xii.238 (*OED* s.v. *will* v.[1] B.22)

To perform, not what he himself would, but what the People . . . requir'd of him.

[101] 1734 tr. *Rollin's Anc. Hist.* V.31 (*OED* s.v. *will* v.[1] B.1)

He that can do what ever he will is in great danger of willing what he ought not.

11.3.4.2 Modal + *it/that*

One particular kind of object is *it/that* standing for VP material, as in:

[102] (a1470) Malory, *Wks.* 696.27

'That shall I nat,' seyde sir Dynadan

' "That I won't", said Sir Dynadan.'

[103] 1534 More, *Wks.* XII 13.31 [1143 H6]

I pray you good vncle, procede you farther in the processe of your matter . . . . That shall I cosin with good wille.

[104] 1567 T. Stapleton, *Counterblast* 116v (Visser 1963–73: §573)

the Bisshops could not remoue him. – Yes, M. Horn, that they might.

[105] 1818 Scott *Br. Lamm.* xxi (*OED* s.v. *shall* v. B.28b)

'His Mastership will do well to look to himself'. 'That he should', re-echoed Craigengelt.

[106] 1872 Carroll, *Looking-Glass* viii.219.24

"You ought to have a wooden horse on wheels, that you ought!"

[107]   1955 Norton, *Borrowers Afield* xviii.323.4

"We should have pulled down the screen," whispered Arrietty. "We should that," agreed Pod.

Plank describes them as possible 'about until the end of the 18th century or even longer' (1984: 336) and suggests that the modal is never epistemic. Visser advances a case for treating these constructions as a sort of Gapping, with the modal a substitute for the main verb of a preceding clause (1963–73: §573). In fact the construction is perfectly possible when the main verb in question is intransitive, as in Visser's own examples [103] or [105], so that Plank's interpretation of the pronouns as 'pro-forms of constituents in the scope of a modal' is preferable.

11.3.5   Modal + *that*-clause

MAY and especially WILL have been able to govern a *that*-clause instead of an infinitive:

[108]   *Or* 74.25

Ac þæt hie magon   þæt hie þas   tida leahtrien
but that they have-power that they those times blame(SUBJ)

'but all they can do is blame the times'

[109]   *Bo* 92.7

Hwa mæg   þæt he ne wundrie swelcra gesceafta   ures
who has-power that he not wonder such   creations(GEN) our
scyppendes
creator(GEN)

'Who can help wondering at such creations of our Creator?'

[110]   *Or* 38.10

. . . ic wolde þæt þa   ongeaten   þe . . . hwelc mildsung
. . . I would that those might-understand who . . . what mercy
siþþan   wæs, siþþan se   cristendom wæs
afterwards was after   the Christianity was

'I would like those who . . . to understand what kind of mercy there was after the coming of Christianity.'

[111]   c1230(?a1200) *Ancr.* 18a.13

Ich chulle þet ȝe speoken seldene ant þenne lutel.
I   I-will that you speak   seldom and then   little

'I desire that you speak seldom, and then little.'

[112]   ?c1425(?c1400) *Loll.Serm.* 3.84

. . . þerforre Crist wolde þei were sped   of   here
. . . therefore Christ would they were successful concerning their
axynge most spedili   to here profite;
asking most quickly/successfully to their profit

[113]   1682 Bunyan, *Holy War* (1905) 263 (*OED* s.v. *will* v.[1] 23)
He would that Captain Credence should join himself with them.

See also example [37] above.

11.3.6   The paradigms

Modals have always had positive finite forms, though as we have seen, some (MUST, the marginal OUGHT, perhaps DARE) have lost the possibility of tense contrast.

11.3.6.1   Negative + modal

The primary pattern of negation has changed from OE *ne* + finite verb to ModE operator + *not*; for some discussion see §15.2.2 below. Both negators have formed single-word contractions with modals.

Contraction of negative *ne* and modal WILL occurred from Old English to early Modern English, surviving vestigially in PDE *willy-nilly*. *Ne* could also contract with AGAN. There are examples in the dictionaries and in Visser (1963–73: §§1577, 1600). Similar contraction occurred with the non-modals BE (forms beginning with vowel or *w-*), HAVE, WITAN 'know', and with various non-verbs like *æfre* 'ever'.

Contraction of a modal with a following *not* is first recorded from the fifteenth century with assimilation or elision of part of the modal. Forms showing loss of vowel in *not* are first recorded at the very end of the sixteenth century. The dates of earliest occurrence in the following lists are in some cases considerably earlier than those usually cited, e.g. 'about 1660' (Jespersen 1909–49: V 430), and no doubt there are even earlier examples to be found:[10] c1420 *shulnot* (= *should+not*) / 1628 *shouldn't*, c1420 *wynnot* (= *will+not*) / 1647 *won't*, 1597 *can't*, c1631 *mayn't*, 1664 *sha'nt* [sic] / 1668 *shan'not*, 1694 *cou'dn't* / 1800 *couldn't*, 1704 *wou'dn't* / 1828 *wad-n't* / 1836 *wouldn't*, 1741 *mustn't*, 1778 *needn't*, 1837 *oughtn't*, 1840 *daren't*, 1848 *durstn't*, 1865 *mightn't*, 1886 *usen't*. See also Jespersen (1917: 117) for metrical evidence of contraction in Shakespeare. Similar contraction occurs with other operators like BE, HAVE, DO. In Scots there is an alternative contraction with *na*: 1588 *canna*, 1725 *needna*, 1591 *wald ne*/1785 *wadna*, a1796 *shouldna*, 1807 *darena*, 1864 *durstna*.

11.3.6.2   Non-finite modal

Non-finite forms of modals are dealt with by Visser in his (1963–73: §§1649–51, 1684–7, 1722–3, 1839, 2042, 2134). Some examples:

[114]   *ÆColl* 8

Leofre ys us   beon   beswungen for lare   þænne hit ne
dearer is us(DAT) be(INF) flogged   for learning than   it not

cunnan.
know(INF)

'We would sooner be flogged for learning than not know it.'

[115]   c1180 *Orm.* 2958

. . . Þatt I shall cunnenn   cwemenn   Godd
. . . that I shall have-ability(INF) please(INF) God

'. . . that I shall have the ability to please God'

[116]   c1330 *Floris*(Auch) 259

He moste   conne   wel mochel of art │ Þat þou woldest ȝif
he must(PA) be-skilled very greatly in artifice that you would   give

þerof ani part!
of-it any part

'Someone would have to be very astute to get you to give up any part
of it!'

[117]   ?c1425(?c1400) *Loll.Serm.* 2.325

but it sufficeþ too hem to kunne her *Pater Noster*, and to bileeue
but it suffices   to them to know   their Paternoster   and to believe

wel.
well

[118]   (1445) *Paston* 14.3

. . . that ho so euer   schuld dwelle at Paston schulde have nede to
. . . that whosoever should dwell at Paston should   have need to

conne   defende hymselfe.
know-how-to defend   himself

'. . . that whoever lived at Paston would need to know how to defend
himself'

[119]   c1450 *Pilgr.LM*(Cmb) 1.467

And whan ye wole go withoute me   ye   shul wel
and when you will go without   me [*sc.* Reason] you shall well

mown   avaunte yow
be-able-to be-boastful

[120]   (c1463) *Paston* 66.16

. . . and wythowte I knowe þe serteynté I chal not conne
. . . and unless   I know   the truth   I shall not be-able-to

answere hym.
answer   him

'. . . and without knowing the truth I shall not be able to answer
him.'

[121]   c1483(?a1480) Caxton, *Dialogues* 3.37

Who   this booke shall wylle lerne . . .
he-who this book   shall wish   learn . . .

'He who wishes to master this book . . .'

[122]   1528 More, *Wks.* VI 26.20 [107 H7]

yf we had **mought** conuenyently come togyther / ye wolde rather haue chosyn to haue hard my mynde of myne owne mouthe

[123]   1532 Cranmer *Let.* in *Misc.Writ.* (Parker Soc.) II.233 (*OED* s.v. *may* v.[1] A.1β)

I fear that the emperor will depart thence, before my letters shall may come unto your grace's hands.

[124]   1533 More, *Wks.* IX 84.4 [885 C1]

some waye y^t appered at ye firste to mow stande the realme in great stede

[125]   1556 *Aurelio & Isab.* (1608) M ix (*OED*)

Maeyinge suffer no more the loue & deathe of Aurelio.

Note that [114] and [116]–[117] show modal + NP (as in §11.3.4.1) rather than modal + infinitive. The modal in the infinitive is non-epistemic (only examples [119] and [123]–[124] above show any possibility of an epistemic interpretation); cf. Plank (1984: 314). Modal + infinitive is apparently not found with the modal item in the progressive, i.e. *BE + modal + V, though Visser has a few examples of the appositive present participle of MAY, of which [125] is the latest. Visser observes that with three-verb clusters of modal + modal + V, the first modal is almost always SHALL (1963–73: §2134). The only exceptions Visser gives for the ME and eModE periods are the following:

[126]   a1400 *Lanfranc* 17.2

Also he muste kunne   evacuener him þat is ful of yuel
also he must   know-how-to free   him that is full of evil

humouris.
humours

[127]   (c1443) Pecock, *Rule* 375.2

infantis mowe receive . . . þi   sacrament of baptym eer   þei
infants may   receive . . . your sacrament of baptism before they

mowe kunne   worschipe þee.
may   know-how-to worship   you

[128]   c1454 Pecock, *Fol.* 129.5

if y se my neiȝbour   goyng . . . forto drenche him silf, y oughte
if I see my neighbour going . . . to   drown   him self I ought

. . . forto wille defende him fro   drenching. . .
. . . to   wish prevent him from drowning . . .

References are given to *may can* V, etc., in current American English dialects. Elsewhere, however (1963–73: §1357), he notes infinitival modal DARE, as seen for instance in:

[129]   1871 Macduff, *Mem. Patmos* xi. 153 (*OED*)

We cannot dare read the times and seasons of prophecy.

11.3.7 Apodosis of conditional

It was pointed out in §11.2.2 above that PDE unreal conditionals require a past-tense modal in the apodosis. Certain modals have been found in that position from early times:

[130]   *Met* 20.107

Ne meahte on ðære eorðan awuht   libban, |. . . gif þu . . . |wið
not could   on the   earth   anything live   . . . if   you. . .   with

fyre hwæthwugu foldan and lagustream |ne mengdest togædre
fire somewhat earth and water   not mixed   together

'Nothing could live on earth . . . if you had not mixed earth and water together with fire.'

[131]   *WHom* 13.44

Ealle, we scoldan   forweorðan ecan   deaðe,   nære
all   we would-have-to perish   eternal death(DAT) not-were

þæt Crist for us deað þrowode.
that Christ for us death suffered

'We would all have had to die eternal death, had not Christ suffered death for us.'

Visser records *should*, *might* from Old English, *would* from the thirteenth century, *could* only from the sixteenth century, and does not appear to give the relevant information for *must*, *ought* (1963–73: §§1532, 1607, 1638, 1672). Here are some examples with *must* and a rare one with *ought*:

[132]   c1386 Chaucer, *CT.Sq.* V.38

It moste   been a rethor   excellent, |That koude his
it would-have-to be   a rhetorician excellent   that knew his

colours longynge   for that art, | If he sholde hire discryven every
colours appropriate to that art   if he was-to her describe   every

part.
part

'It would have to be an excellent rhetorician that knew his "colours" appropriate to that art, if he was to describe her fully and properly.'

[133]   1694(1671) Tillotson II 428.12

And if we would preserve our selves from the infection of this vice we must take heed how we scoff at Religion

[134]   1528 More, *Wks.* VI 251.22 [205 B15]

But he wolde haue asked how ye know y^t. – Than must I quod he haue sayd the same that I dyd, that . . .

[135]   1532–3 More, *Wks.* II 78.7 [65 E9]

. . . verely trustyng . . . none of them ani thing would intende vnto hym warde, where with he ought to be greued.

For *durst/dared* see Visser (1946–56: §542; 1963–73: §1361) and also the discussion of [31] above.

What has changed is that formerly the structure did not serve as a test of modal status, since the past – probably past subjunctive – of other verbs could occur there too. Visser gives examples of 'hypothetical statements' in two places (1963–73: §§815, 861), according to whether the form of the verb is (possibly) indicative or subjunctive, the latter type specifically described as unreal conditionals. This pattern was 'frequently' or 'extensively' used in Old and Middle English, widely used in early Modern English, then 'tend[ed] to become first archaic and then obsolete'.

[136] *ÆCHom* I 8.130.5

gif ðu her andwerd wære, nære   ure broðer forðfaren
if you here present   were not-was(SUBJ) our brother departed

'If you had been present here our brother would not have died'

[137] *BlHom* 33.35

gif þæt deofol hine ne gesawe   on ure gecynde, ne costode
if that devil   him not saw(PA SUBJ) in our form   not tempted

he hine
he him

'if the devil had not seen him in our form, he would not have tempted him'

[138] c1230(?a1200) *Ancr.* 55a.8

for ȝef ich schulde writen alle; hwenne come ich to ende
for if   I   should   write all   when   came I   to end

'for if I were to write them all [*sc.* words], when would I come to the end?'

[139] a1450(?1348) Rolle, *FLiving* 107.4

My hert, when sal   it brest for lufe? Þan languyst   I na mare.
my heart when shall it break for love   then languished I no more

'My heart, when shall it break for love? Then I would languish no more.'

[140] 1532–3 More, *Wks.* II 90.5 [70 A15]

and in what peril yᵉ duke stode if he fell once in suspicion of yᵉ tiraunt.

[141] 1901 Lang, *Tennyson* v.74.23

It were superfluous labour to point at special beauties, . . .

It is noticeable that every single ME and ModE example cited in §861 has the verb *were* – and most of the OE ones too. To some extent this reflects Visser's self-imposed requirement to find unambiguously past subjunctive forms, and in his §815 collection there are other verbs used, including clear subjunctives in [137]–[138]. The later examples, however, may indicate that *were* was the last item able to *commute* with past tense modals in the apodosis of an unreal conditional.

11.3.8 Impersonal use

In Middle English a number of verbs which had not been impersonal (or had not existed) in Old English developed impersonal uses, and many of them were modals or quasi-modal; see §§5.2.6.4 (where further references are given) and 5.6.2.2 above. Examples include:

[142]   a1450 *Rich.*(Cai) 3524

nouȝt on . . . þat hym   hadde leuere haue ben at home, . . .
not   one . . . that him(OBL) had   rather have been at home . . .
þenne . . .
than . . .

'not one . . . who would not rather have been at home . . . than . . .'

[143]   a1400(c1303) Mannyng, *HS* 2837

So had hym better . . . | For to haue broke þat yche vowe

'So it would have been better for him . . . to have broken that very vow'

[144]   a1450(?1348) Rolle, *FLiving* 99.83

and if he have taken   grace, to use it noght als hym   aght
and if he has   received grace to use it not   as him(OBL) ought

[145]   a1450(?1348) Rolle, *FLiving* 108.17

Þe   thare   noght covayte gretely many bokes;
you(OBL) behoves not   covet   greatly many books

[146]   (c1390) Chaucer, *CT.Mel.* VII.998

us   oghte   . . . have pacience.
us(OBL) ought(SG) . . . have patience

[147]   a1425(?a1400) *RRose* 5392

Hym   hadde lever asondre shake, | . . . | Than leve   his
him(OBL) had   rather apart   fall   . . .   than let-go his
richesse in his lyve.
riches   in his life

[148]   c1450(?a1400) *Parl.3 Ages* 653

And haues gud daye, for now I go; to graue moste me wende;

'and good day to you, for now I go; to the grave I must go'

[149]   c1450 *Jacob's W.* 46.23

me   muste speke wyth þe.
me(OBL) must speak with you

[150] a1500 *Mirror Salv.* 948

Me   nedes fro   hire presence withdrawe me   prively.
me(OBL) needs from her presence withdraw   myself unobtrusively

11.3.9 Marginal modals

11.3.9.1 AGAN/OUGHT

I regard this verb as a marginal modal throughout the history of English
because it has always been morphologically and syntactically different from
the central modals. Semantically, though, in the sense of obligation it
resembles the modals MUST and SHOULD quite closely; see the data in Visser
(1963–73: §§1711–21). Mitchell discusses the evidence for an obligation
meaning in Old English (1969; 1985: §§932–3), dismissing examples before
the late tenth century which had been cited by Callaway and Visser but
tentatively accepting some lOE ones:

[151] *HomU* 46 291.27

þæt we æfre   sculon mynegjan and tyhtan eow . . . hu ge
that we always must   remind   and exhort you . . . how you

agan   her on life rihtlice to libbanne;
ought(PRES) here in life rightly   to live

[152] *ChronA* 204.9 (1070)

Ða ða Landfranc crafede fæstnunge his gehersumnesse mid
when Landfranc craved pledge   his submission   with

aðswerunge. þa   forsoc he. & sæde þæt he hit nahte   to donne.
oath-swearing then refused he and said that he it   not-had to do

'When Landfranc demanded a pledge of his obedience on oath, he
refused and said that he did not have to do it.'

There is solid evidence for the modal meaning in Middle English:

[153] ?c1425(?c1400) *Loll.Serm.* 3.67

I owe   to be baptiside of þe, and þou comest to me to be
I have-obligation to be baptised by you and you come   to me to be

baptisid?
baptised

Once established in the fixed form *ought* – lexical verbs OWE, OWN having
become entirely distinct items by the eModE period – it came even more to
resemble MUST in its use of a historically past tense as (perhaps) a modal
present (though see here Jørgensen 1984). It nearly always occurs with a *to*-
infinitive.[11] In Modern English it only intermittently shows the NICE
properties, so that, for example, for different speakers both *oughtn't* and
didn't ought are possible.
  A possible view of the development of OUGHT is of divergent trends in
both morphology (A versus B) and semantics (C versus D):

(A) preterite-present morphology in Old English and modal morphology in
    Modern English
(B) development of regular verb morphology
(C) retention of typically non-modal meanings 'possess', 'owe', with
    nominal complementation
(D) development of a typically modal meaning, with verbal complementa-
    tion

Overall we could say that trends A and D have gone together, likewise B
and C, culminating in the lexical separateness of OUGHT (A+D, 'old'
morphology, new semantics) and OWE and OWN (B+C, old semantics, new
morphology). In the ME period, however, it is by no means obvious that
there was such a tidy bifurcation. To judge from the examples in *MED* s.v.
ouen v., regular morphology *was* relatively less common in modal than non-
modal uses of the verb in early Middle English, but by the fifteenth century
the combination of modal semantics and regular (non-preterite-present)
morphology was not uncommon:

[154]   (a1438) *MKempe* 42.36

> whan God visyteth a creatur wyth terys of contrisyon . . . he may
> when God visits   a creature with tears of contrition . . . he may
>
> &   owyth to leuyn   þat þe Holy Gost is in hys sowle.
> and should   believe that the Holy Ghost is in his soul

The combination only died out with the complete loss of present-tense OWE
in modal meaning. Whether this serves as evidence of the growing strength
of a category 'modal' – not strong enough in the early fifteenth century to
resist the spread of regular verb morphology, but strong enough in the
sixteenth to extinguish a combination which could combine non-modal
morphology with modal semantics – is a question I leave open.

11.3.9.2   HAVE 'be obliged'

The obligation sense of HAVE comes very close to the modals semantically,
and since HAVE can be an operator, there is often some syntactic
resemblance too.

  Whether OE HABBAN + *to*-infinitive could have the sense 'be obliged to
V' has been much discussed, notably by van der Gaaf (1931). The classic
example is:

[155]   *BlHom* 91.13

> Uton we forþon   geþencean hwylc handlean   we him   forþ
> let-us we therefore consider   what recompense we him(DAT) forth
>
> to berenne habban
> to carry   have(PRES PL SUBJ)
>
> 'Let us therefore consider what recompense we may have to bring
> him'

Many writers analyse this with *to berenne* as complement of *habban* 'are
obliged', and *hwylc handlean* as object of *berenne*. Others read it as *habban*
'possess' + direct object *hwylc handlean*, and the infinitive dependent on

that NP. Mitchell gives full references to the discussion, all the relevant examples, and comes down for the latter analysis (1985: §§950–3). For proof that the infinitive is a complement of HAVE we need an intransitive infinitive and/or a context which rules out the possession sense. These are not found until Middle English:

[156] (a1393) Gower, *CA* 7.1530

> Gramaire ferste hath forto teche | To speke upon congruite
> grammar first has to teach to speak about congruity

> 'Grammar has first to teach how to speak about congruity'

(TECHE in example [156] is not an ideal example of an intransitive, since it is introducing a V+I construction.)

In Present-day standard English the HAVE of obligation rarely has the NICE properties, though in northern BrE dialects and quite recent southern standard it can:

[157] You haven't to say anything.

(For discussion see Visser 1963–73: §1467, though he gives no NICE examples like [157] prior to 1875. In fact almost *all* earlier examples of HAVE had the NICE properties.) Furthermore it has a full paradigm, finite and non-finite, and patterns with a *to*-infinitive. A paper by Laurel Brinton (1991) is devoted to modal HAVE.

11.3.9.3 BE of necessity, obligation, or future

This verb too is a marginal modal, patterning with a *to*-infinitive to express meanings otherwise often expressed by modals. For Old English see Mitchell (1985: §§934–49), and more generally Visser (1963–73: §§1372–83). One complication is that the **syntagm** BEON + *to*-infinitive is used both personally [158] and impersonally [159]:

[158] *Mt(WSCp)* 11.3

> . . . &   cwæð eart   þu   þe   to cumenne eart
> . . . and said   are(2 SG) you(2 SG) that(REL) to come   are(2 SG)

> Lat. . . . ait illi tu es qui uenturus es

> '. . . and said: "Are you he that is to come?" '

[159] *ÆLS* I 10.133

> us   nys to cweðenne þæt ge unclæne syndon
> us(DAT) not-is to say   that you unclean are

> 'It is not for us to say that you are unclean.'

In Middle and Modern English this BE had a full paradigm:

[160] 1660 Pepys, *Diary* I 193.7 (5 Jul)

> . . . the King and Parliament being to be intertained by the City today with great pomp.

[161] 1667 Pepys, *Diary* VIII 452.6 (27 Sep)

Nay, several grandees, having been to marry a daughter, . . . have wrote letters . . .

[162] 1816 Austen, *Mansfield Park* I.xiv.135.30

You will be to visit me in prison with a basket of provisions;

Visser states that syntagms with infinitive *be* are 'still current' (1963–73: §2135), but although there are a few relevant examples later than Jane Austen (1963–73: §§1378, 2135, 2142), most are of the fixed idiom BE *to come*, as in:

[163] But they may yet be to come.

See also §14.3.7.2 below.

11.3.9.4 UTON

The OE verb UTON (*utan, uton, wuton, witon*, etc.) is only used as a 1 PL form with plain infinitive, with or without expressed subject *we*, and is usually translated as 'let us . . .'. According to Holthausen (1934) and other dictionaries, UTON is historically a form of the rare strong verb WITAN 'depart, die' (*wītan*) rather than a form of the preterite-present (but non-modal) WITAN 'know' (*witan*), though the morphology certainly looks preterite-present. For discussion of the OE syntax and examples see Mitchell (1985: §§916, 916a):

[164] *PPs* 94.1

wutun cweman gode
let-us please   God(DAT)

'Let us be pleasing to God'

[165] *ÆCHom* I 1.16.12

Uton gewyrcan   mannan to ure anlicnysse
let-us create(INF) man   in our likeness

[166] *ÆCHom* I 28.414.29

Ac uton we beon   carfulle
but let-us we be(INF) careful

'But let us be careful'

The usage is rather like a first-person imperative, and UTON is also modal-like in both syntax and meaning and indeed commutes with other modals:

[167] *ÆHom* I 8.357.12

Nu sceole we gehyran þæt   halige godspell
now shall   we hear   the/that holy   gospel

'Now we are to hear the holy gospel'

[168] *ÆHom* I 5.296.174

Nu ne þurfe we astigan to sticolum   muntum
now not need we ascend to steep/lofty mountains

[169]   a1225(?a1200) *Trin.Hom.* 45.31

Wille we mid þese þre lokes cuðlechen us wið alre kingene king.

'Let us with these three gifts make ourselves friends with the king of all kings.'

The verb survived into early Middle English:

[170]   a1225(?a1200) Lay.*Brut* 10296

Uten we heom to liðe
let-us we them to travel

'Let us go to them'

[171]   a1300 *I-hereþ ny one* (Jes-O) 173

Ariseþ vp . . . and vte   we heonne go.
rise   up . . . and let-us we hence   go

'Get up . . . and let us go from here.'

It was replaced principally by forms with LET.

11.3.9.5 LET

Olga Fischer observes that ME LETEN 'allow, cause' scarcely occurred 'by itself': it was used in VOSI constructions, or with a particle, or in idiomatic combinations with a noun, like LETEN *blod*, or in quite different senses like 'leave', 'lend'. As she puts it, LETEN was 'gradually reduced to more or less auxiliary status' (Fischer 1992b: 29). The usages which invite consideration as a marginal modal are developments in the ME period of the second-person imperative:

[172]   c1250 *Owl & N.* 258

Lat þine tunge   habbe spale![12]
let your tongue have   rest/splinter[?]

'Give your tongue a rest!'/'May your tongue get a splinter in it!'

[173]   c1450(c1380) Chaucer, *HF* 1761

Leet men gliwe on us the name – |Sufficeth that we han the fame.
let   men glue on us the name   it-suffices that we have the fame

'Let people attach that name to us! It is enough that we have the reputation.'

[174]   (c1390) Chaucer, *CT.ML* II.953

lat us stynte   of Custance but a throwe, | And speke we of
let us stop-talking of Custance for a short-while and speak we of

the Romayn Emperour.
the Roman   Emperor

[175]   (a1393) Gower, *CA* 3.292

If that my litel Sone deie, | Let him be beried in my grave | Beside me, . . .

[176]   (c1449) *Paston* 37.35

<u>Let</u> hym let his master know þat . . .

[177]   a1475(?a1430) Lydg. *Pilgr.* 12105

At ffenestrallys & at cornerys, | Lat be hangen out banerys | Off the croos

'Let Banners of the Cross be hung out at windows and at corners.'

Examples [172]–[177] are strictly speaking VOSI structures because of the intervening objective NP, but LET + NP + infinitive seems to serve as the equivalent of a subjunctive or imperative, most commonly third person or first person. In 'optative/third-person imperative' use LET commutes with MAY. In 'hortative/first person imperative' use it commutes with SHALL and typically is replaced by SHALL in a tag question (Palmer 1988: 171):

[178]   Let's go, shall we?

As a subjunctive- or modal equivalent, then, and one which occurs with plain infinitive, LET seems rather like a modal. There are some scattered examples in Visser's (1963–73: §§846, 853), but for useful collections one must turn to *OED* s.v. *let* v.[1] 14, *MED* s.v. *leten* v. 10a, 10b. From these sources it appears that the usage appeared sporadically in early Middle English and became established by the late fourteenth century.

To say that LETEN commutes with certain modals is not to claim that the meanings are identical. The real difference, however, is that true modals like SHALL and MAY require a subjective NP.[13] Occasionally LET occurred with a subjective rather than an objective NP (a development which has become standard with the cognate Dutch verb LATEN):

[179]   a1225(?a1200) Lay.*Brut* 9176

&   leten we vs   ræden; of   ure misdeden.
and let   we us(REFL) advise about our misdeeds

'and let us confer about our misdeeds'

[180]   c1250 *Þene latemeste dai* 98

Messes lete we singen
masses let   we sing

'Let us sing masses.'

[181]   1634 *Malory's Arthur* IV.iii (*OED*)

Let we [1485 lete vs] hold us together till it be day.

[182]   1678 Bunyan, *Pilgrim's Progress* I 136.12

Let thee and I go on . . .

Examples are given in *MED* s.v. *leten* v. 10a.(d) and *OED* s.v. *let* v.[1] 14b (the latter with the comment 'incorrectly used'), and by Visser, intermixed with other LET patterns (1963–73: §2062). Presumably such examples reflect a feeling that LET *was* virtually an auxiliary. However, other factors are involved too, including avoidance of repetition when there is a reflexive *us* in the complement of the infinitive, and the fairly common hypercorrect use in non-subject position of *you and I* and similar coordinations, as in my example [182].

Visser notes the following type, a second-person equivalent, as an Irishism (1963–73: §1427):

[183]   1905 Synge, *Well* II 103.9

Let you come out here and cut them yourself . . .

11.3.9.6   OE ONGINNAN, ME GINNEN

As far as Old English is concerned, I have mentioned already (§9.3.5.1 above) the evidence provided by the use of ONGINNAN 'begin' with subjectless impersonals, as in:

[184]   *LS* 35(VitPatr) 330

Þa   ongan   me   langian   for   minre
then began(3? SG) me(ACC) grieve(INF) because-of my

hæftnyde
imprisonment

'Then I began to find my imprisonment tedious'

The obvious semantic analysis of the [184] type takes ONGINNAN as a one-place verb with clausal argument, since none of the NPs in such sentences seem to be arguments of ONGINNAN or even to take their case from any function in the *higher* clause. (Mossé 1938a: §238 claims in passing that in earlier Old English ONGINNAN was used only with lexical verbs of durative meaning.) Syntactically it is possible to treat ONGINNAN as an auxiliary and so adopt the V-raising analysis of van Kemenade. There are no examples which cannot be made to fit, though some require special discussion. Thus [184] would presumably involve Verb-projection raising of the whole LANGIAN clause, followed by Extraposition of the PP *for minre hæftnyde*. Similarly, if *þæt folc* is accusative in

[185]   *LS* 20(AssumptMor) 88

Þa   þæt   folc   ongan tweogan on heora heortan
then that/the people(ACC/NOM) began doubt   in their heart

'Then the people began to doubt in their hearts.'

the sentence could be derived by V-Raising of TWEOGAN to the right of *ongan*, followed by Extraposition of the PP. Alternatively we might take *þæt folc* as nominative, making [185] a type (iii) occurrence of TWEOGAN and a possible two-place example of ONGINNAN.[14] In the case of

[186]   *GD* 181.2

   ... &   hine   ongan wel his worda   lystan
   ... and him(ACC) began well his words(GEN PL) cause-pleasure

   '. . . and his words began to please him well'

there must (in van Kemenade's terms) have been Verb-projection raising to
the right of *ongan*, which should have taken *hine* along with it, but *hine* may
have moved to a clitic position.

All of the above examples have ONGINNAN + plain rather than *to*-
infinitive, as do most OE uses of ONGINNAN/(A)GINNAN: in Callaway's
statistics (1913: Appendix A), 1006 out of a total of 1048 examples. Note,
however, that with the rarer BEGINNAN the plain infinitive was already in
the minority in Old English: only 28 out of 85.

In Middle English the simplex (or shortening) GINNEN came to be used as
a mere auxiliary, a dummy of little or no meaning, alongside the inchoative
meaning 'begin'. (Bleaching of meaning can be argued for in some instances
of OE ONGINNAN, though Mitchell is doubtful that complete bleaching can
be demonstrated for Old English, 1985: §§675–8.) With the virtually fixed
form *gan*, sometimes *can* (a possible blending of forms from GINNEN and
modal CAN), and occasionally plural *gunne(n)/gonne(n)*, it was used
especially as a metrical filler in rhyming verse:

[187]   c1300(?c1225) *Horn* 938

   he ferde | To wude for to schete; | A knaue he gan imete.

   'he went to the woods to go shooting [*sc.* with bow and arrow], and
   he met a knave'

The ME use of GINNEN is discussed by Mustanoja (1960: 610–15), Visser
(1963–73: §§1477–82), and others, with disagreement as to whether non-
inchoative examples are empty of meaning, are lexically meaningful, or have
significance as a discourse marker. Fischer, citing some of the recent work,
gives reasons for doubting that they are anything but a metrical filler (1992a:
265–7).

The vast majority of examples have (I)GINNEN (and perhaps occasionally
BIGINNEN) with a plain infinitive, though Visser suggests that the empty slot-
filler could sometimes occur in Middle English with a *to*-infinitive. By
contrast the fully meaningful inchoative use was increasingly – though again,
not exclusively – coming to require a *to*-infinitive and indeed the BIGINNEN
form (1963–73: §§1257, 1260, 1269, 1482). The empty use of GINNEN lost
ground in late Middle English and died out in the early ModE period, being
effectively replaced by DO.

11.3.9.7   DO

I have devoted the whole of Chapter 10 to DO and will not repeat
observations on the resemblances and differences between DO and modals.
Suffice to say that there is at least one historical semantic account,
Penhallurick (1985), which treats periphrastic DO as a modal with the
meaning 'occurrence questioned', while in the 1970s particularly it was
fashionable to analyse Present-day English as having an obligatory modal
element (with DO one of the 'modals' which could be chosen), and rules of

DO-Deletion and of DO-Replacement (by HAVE or BE) for deriving those surface patterns which lacked an explicit 'modal'.

11.3.9.8   USED

The verb USE 'be in the habit of' had both a present and past tense until at least the eighteenth century:

[188]   1668 Pepys, *Diary* IX 215.1 (27 May)

> . . . a fat man, whom by face I know as one that uses to sit in our church

The present tense is obsolete in this sense. (Transitive USE [juːz] is perceived as a separate lexeme.) The past tense form has survived as an almost invariable *used*, normally pronounced with enclitic *to* as [juːstə], and virtually equivalent to a past habitual with the additional sense that the situation no longer prevails. One meaning of the full modal WILL is similar, though *would* frequently cannot be substituted for *used to*. In informal or non-standard usage the verb co-occurs with DO or modals – *didn't use(d) to, couldn't use(d) to*, etc. – whereas in rather old-fashioned usage it can have the NICE properties – *usedn't, Used she to . . . ?* It hovers on the margins of the auxiliary verb system of Present-day English, frequently negated by *never* rather than *not/n't* in order to avoid uncomfortable decisions about its syntax. Structurally it bears closest resemblance to OUGHT. For details see Visser (1963–73: §§796, 1333–41).

11.3.9.9   Other verbs

Callaway mentions (1913: 87) seven examples with plain passive infinitive used 'in a way quite similar to that with the genuine auxiliaries' after the non-auxiliaries GEDAFENIAN 'be fitting', (GE)WUNIAN 'be wont', and WEORÐAN 'become'. Now GEDAFENIAN is an impersonal verb close to deontic modality in its semantics, (GE)WUNIAN is a possible aspectual and Raising verb (§9.3.5.2 above), while the WEORÐAN example is plain odd[15] and probably an error, suggesting strongly that *beon* and *weorþan* are tautological variants:

[189]   *HomU* 35.2(Nap 44) 217.9

> þæt þeos weoruld mihte eft   beon   geedstaþoled
> that this   world   might again be(INF) restored(PA PTCP)
>
> weorþan   and eft   of   awecnigan
> become(INF) and again from [*sc.* Noah and his progeny] revive(INF)

I don't think further discussion is necessary.

11.3.10   Modal substitutes

Many verbs and verbal groups have been more or less close synonyms of modals in the history of English without sharing their morphosyntactic properties. New modal equivalents appeared during the ME period. Visser lists some equivalents of CAN/MAY, MUST and OUGHT (1963–73: §§1646, 1710b, 1725). Mustanoja (1960: 453) quotes a list of 'subjunctive equivalents' by Wilde (1939–40). I give a few examples below:

[190]   *Mt(WSCp)* 20.22

mage gyt   drincan þone calic   ðe   ic to drincenne hæbbe
may   you-two drink   the   chalice that I to drink   have

'Are you able to drink from the cup which I must/shall drink from?'

[191]   ?c1425(?c1400) *Loll.Serm.* 2.168

. . . for þei hauen no desir after gostli helþe, but han myche leuere to heere oþer to speke vanites, þat litel profiten, or nou3t, þan prechyng of þe word of God.

'. . . for they have no desire for spiritual health but much prefer to hear or to speak vain things which do little or no good, rather than the preaching of God's word.'

[192]   a1425(a1382) *WBible(1)* Matt. 20.22

Mowen 3e drynke the cuppe that I am to drynke?

[193]   a1425(c1395) *WBible(2)* II.Tim. 2.2

. . . feithful men, whiche schulen be also able to teche othere men.

[194]   1667 Pepys, *Diary* VIII 572.4 (8 Dec)

for if they do look to the bottom and see the King's case, they think they are then bound to give the King money;

[195]   1667 Pepys, *Diary* VIII 591.24 (27 Dec)

and now the King would have the Parliament give him money, when they are in an ill humour and will not be willing to give any, nor are very able;

The syntagm *will not be willing* in [195] shows an interesting co-occurrence of modal WILL (here in a future sense) and the lexical verb WILL, or rather the verb + adjective combination BE *willing*. Notice too how *would* in the first clause is modal WILL in the root, volitional sense, here combined with a conditional sense.

Where the modal substitute has BE or HAVE as its verbal element, as many do, it may even share with the true modals the property of being an operator in ModE. As the NICE properties have become institutionalised, several modal substitutes have entered into what is almost a ***suppletive*** relationship with particular modals, replacing the modal where an infinitive or participle is required, e.g. MUST ~ HAVE *to*, CAN ~ BE *able*:

[196]   1667 Pepys, *Diary* VIII 575.14 (11 Dec)

. . . *Cattelin*, which is to [be] suddenly acted at the King's House; and all agree that it cannot be well done at that House, there not being good actors enow, and Burt acts Cicero, which they all conclude he will not be able to do well.

'. . . *Catiline*, which is to be acted in a short while at the King's House; and all agree that it cannot be done well at that theatre, there not being enough good actors, and Burt will act Cicero, which they all conclude he will not be able to do well.'

11.4   Explanations

The syntactic history of the modals inevitably (in my opinion) involves semantics too, though I shall neglect studies which concentrate on the semantics alone (for example Jespersen 1909–49 IV, Wilde 1939–40, Tellier 1962, Aijmer 1985, Kytö 1987, and of course the dictionaries). One scholar who has attempted to concentrate on the syntax has been David Lightfoot, and his account of English modals – one of the earliest systematic attempts, later modified somewhat – has been extremely influential. For many linguists inside and outside the transformational generative camp, Lightfoot's picture of a drastic syntactic reanalysis has been treated as definitive, or at least as an essential jumping-off point, while for others, especially those sceptical about the autonomy of syntax, it has been a notorious butt. Accordingly, it takes a privileged place in what follows.

11.4.1   Allen

Cynthia Allen (1975) offers a generative analysis of modal sentences in a corpus of Ælfric's writings. Her working hypothesis is that basic clause order was SOV, and her mechanism for deriving SVO order in main clauses and optionally in subordinates is merely to move the verb from clause-final to post-subject position by a rule called 'SVO'. (Principles and parameters were not yet *de rigeur*.) The significant decision is to treat modal verbs in the same way as any other verbs. Allen's reasons for this are various:

(A) OE modals did not have the NICE properties
(B) OE modals could occur independently of other verbs
(C) ordering facts

Point A – Allen expresses it differently – is one we can neglect. It is not so much that modal verbs have subsequently developed the NICE properties as that non-operators have lost them, and even now the operators and the auxiliaries are not quite co-extensive. Point B is a fair one, though all the examples Allen cites show dynamic meaning. It is C we shall explore here.

Allen assumes that OE modals were two-place verbs – so also Wagner (1969: 64) – and most of her examples involve modals plus another verb that takes a single object. Note that the four **constituents** S, M, V and O could in principle occur in twenty-four different orders,[16] and Allen's contribution is to explain why only some are found. She offers the underlying structure [198] for [197] (and any other sentence with those four constituents):

[197] *ÆHom* I 6.327.334

His leorningcnihtas woldon gelettan þone Hælend
his disciples   wished hinder the Saviour

[198]

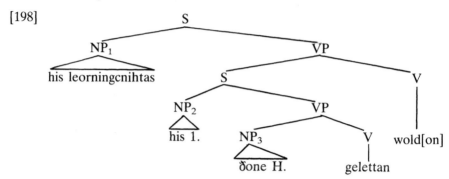

The derivation proceeds by applying the SVO transformation to the lower sentence, then deleting the second occurrence of *his leorningcnihtas* by the rule of Equi NP deletion (see §8.2.1 above: this is equivalent to having NP_2 as PRO controlled by NP_1), and finally applying SVO to the higher clause. That is how SMVO order is achieved. Since the SVO rule is optional for subordinate clauses, the analysis correctly predicts that some examples will surface without reordering of the embedded clause, giving SMOV order on the surface. These are the only possible main clause orders for modals.

If a structure like [198] is itself in subordinate position (which for Allen also includes second-conjunct position), then the optionality of the SVO rule on both cycles will permit four different surface orders: SOVM (application on neither cycle), SVOM (lower only), SMOV (upper only), and SMVO (both). The problem is that SVOM does not actually occur in her corpus, whereas SVMO – which shouldn't – does occur in 'subordinates':

[199] *ÆHom* I 3.251.62

. . . for þæm ðe hi   wyrcan sceoldon gode wæstmas Gode
. . . because   they make   should   good fruits   God(DAT)

'. . . because they should make a good harvest for God'

So does SOMV, usually with further clause material following V:

[200] *ÆHom* I 9.381.61

þeah ðe he mihte eall mancynn ahreddan butan   his agenum deaðe
though he might all mankind save   without his own   death

'though he had the power to save all mankind without his own death'

Two extra rules are needed to turn SVOM into SVMO and to permit SOMV(X). Both are somewhat *ad hoc*, though Allen does find some use for the latter in sentences without modals. The framework is one that later workers in the same tradition would regard as too unrestrictive. Nevertheless this early attempt to systematise some complex ordering facts gave added momentum to the modals-as-main-verbs hypothesis.

11.4.2 Lightfoot

11.4.2.1

David Lightfoot's analysis of the history of English modals has gone through a number of rewritings since its first appearance in 1974, virtually simultaneous with Allen's account of the OE phase. I shall discuss the version in Lightfoot (1979).

He too argues that the modals were full verbs in Old English. They had, he says, full person-number agreement, infinitives, and normal complementation including nominal direct objects. In Present-day English, on the other hand, they are merely auxiliary verbs. The transition from OE full verb to PDE auxiliary is seen as a purely syntactic phenomenon (1979: 100) which had three phases (here my presentation resembles that of Plank 1984: 347–8):

(A) (mainly Middle English) a gradual increase in exceptionality as a result of independently occurring surface changes spaced out over time
(B) (sixteenth century) a radical restructuring of syntactic categories and sentence structure, resulting in a clutch of simultaneous surface changes
(C) (approximately sixteenth century) further transformational and lexical innovations consequent on the restructuring of B

What is the evidence for each phase?

I number the five changes of A as follows, summing them up in Lightfoot's own words (1979: 109):

(A1) loss of all the direct object constructions with pre-modals
(A2) loss of all the preterite-presents except the pre-modals, thereby isolating the latter as a unique inflectional class
(A3) increased opacity of the past tense pre-modals *might, could, should, would* and *must*
(A4) special marking of epistemic pre-modals to avoid otherwise expected SVOM or *it* M [NP . . .]s structures
(A5) the development of *to* infinitives with almost all verbs except the pre-modals

What is being claimed here is straightforward enough, apart perhaps from A4, though the dates and significance of some alleged changes will need scrutiny in the light of the data presented in §11.3. The 'change' A4 is theory-specific and unconvincing, depending on the assumption that epistemic modals are one-place Raising verbs with an embedded clause in subject position. Lightfoot predicts that in Old English the underlying structure [clause SOV] M would surface as SOVM in subordinates, with various additional possibilities if a V-2 process applied. In Middle English underlying [clause SVO] M should give SVOM, but this word order is rare.

An alternative scenario with Extraposition and Raising would explain the more frequently attested word order SMVO but would then leave unexplained' the absence of Extraposed but unRaised *it* M [$_{clause}$ SVO]. Or epistemic modals might have become two-place predicates **subcategorised** for an empty subject. In any event 'some special mechanism would be needed to distinguish the epistemic pre-modals from other one-place predicates' (1979: 108).

Lightfoot adds one more property shared by modals but also some other verbs (e.g. TRY):

(A6) the subject NP of the S they dominated was never phonologically realised in surface structure, i.e. was obligatorily PRO

He gives the following PDE examples:

[201] (a) Bill could _____ do that
       (b) it may _____ be that Bill left
       (c) Bill tried _____ to do that

(Sentences with PDE DARE, NEED and WILL which contradict A6 involve non-modal homonyms.) As quoted above, A6 is inconsistent with Lightfoot's own analysis of OE epistemic modals! This is easily solved by restating it as follows:

(A6') finite modal and non-finite verb could not have non-co-referential surface subjects

The build-up of exceptionality in A conflicted with a nebulous 'Transparency Principle', leading to phase B, a restructuring of the grammar. The restructuring consisted of the following grammatical changes (1979: 113):

(B1) a new lexical category M(odal)
(B2) a new phrasal category Aux(iliary), a **sister** of the main verb, containing the constituents T(ense) and optional M
(B3) reformulations of the rules of Negative placement and Inversion to refer to auxiliaries rather than (finite) verbs

The evidence consists of four changes 'taking place simultaneously in the sixteenth century' (1979: 110):

(B4) loss of infinitives of modals
(B5) loss of *-ing* forms of modals
(B6) loss of multiple modals – but this clearly follows from B4
(B7) loss of perfect HAVE + past participle forms of modals

Three further changes, C, are apparently to be taken as *consequences* of B, though the dating of C1 and C2 is not so confidently stipulated:

(C1) loss of negatives of the form *John took not the bread*, temporary development of negatives of the form *he not spoke*
(C2) loss of inversion with non-modals
(C3) appearance of 'quasi-modals' like BE *going to*, HAVE *to*, BE *able to*

with the semantics of modals but 'all the usual properties of other verbs' (an unfortunate claim for group-verbs whose verbal item is BE or HAVE)

(Later, though, B4–B7 and C1–C3 become 'seven simultaneous changes' (1979: 129 n.1).)

Finally there are some desultory remarks on the rise of periphrastic DO and the likelihood that DO-Support 'was introduced at the same time as the modal category' (1979: 116).

11.4.2.2   Objections to Lightfoot

Paul Bennett's comments (1979) on Lightfoot's analysis are primarily theoretical. He argues against Lightfoot's notion that a Transparency Principle intervened to remedy a situation where deep and surface structure had got too far apart, by showing that none of Lightfoot's (A1–A5) actually increased deep-surface distance. Rather he suggests that what happened was that modals and DO became more and more exceptional as verbs and were assigned to a new category; see also Warner's analysis, §11.4.5.2 below.

Now let us take three review articles with detailed objections to offer. Anthony Warner picks his way critically around several sections of Lightfoot's book, including a survey (1983: 194–200) of Lightfoot's 'modals story', while Frans Plank (1984) concentrates an uncharacteristic degree of sarcasm on that one target. In a shorter contribution, Louis Goossens (1984), like Plank, spotlights the semantic issues so conspicuously ignored by Lightfoot.

Warner points out that A1, the loss of subcategorisation for direct objects, was completed rather later than Lightfoot claims, so that it would fit better in phase B than A. Plank, on the other hand, while noting the misleadingness of Lightfoot's dating, observes that epistemic and perhaps deontic modals have *never* taken NP objects in English;[17] that epistemic modals have *never* had non-finite forms; and that modal + object NP was confined to restricted uses of certain modals with notional meanings (1984: 310–11, 314). Much the same point is made independently by Goossens (1984: 150). Furthermore, Plank observes, modals have never occurred in the passive – a mystery if they were ordinary transitive verbs. Warner shows that A4 is weakened by its poor syntactic defence of a root ~ epistemic distinction.

Warner corrects Lightfoot on the dating of loss of non-finite forms, B4–B7 (see §11.3.6.2 above). Plank notes the spread of dates too but then suggests that whatever simultaneity there is is natural, since effectively all of B4–B7 amount to one change: the loss of non-finite forms. Warner observes that eModE modals still showed subject-verb agreement in 2 SG forms, while ordinary verbs continued to show the older patterns of negation and inversion, so that modals were more like ordinary verbs than they later became and the justification for B is less persuasive than it might be. And both Warner and Plank seize on Lightfoot's idealisation of the date of C3.

Plank goes on to list a number of other changes not covered by Lightfoot, all of them interesting and the last two, on his reckoning and mine, the most important:

(D) the loss by the modal verbs of all non-modal notional meanings
(E) the loss of the inflectional subjunctive from the English verbal system
and increasing use of modal verbs where previously a subjunctive
inflection would have been expected

He claims that even during the OE period there was an increasing tendency
to use a (subjunctive) modal + infinitive instead of subjunctive main verb,[18]
and that ever since then the subjunctive has been recessive, being
supplanted by the indicative, by modals, and by other alternatives. The
following example of SCEAL as a subjunctive equivalent is given by Traugott
(1992: 195):

[202] *ChronE* 235.13 (1100)

& to þam Pentecosten wæs gesewen . . . blod weallan of   eorþan.
and at that Pentecost   was seen   . . . blood well-up from earth

swa swa mænige sæden þe   hit geseon sceoldan
as as many   said that(REL) it see   should

'and at Pentecost . . . blood was seen welling up from the ground, as
many said who supposedly saw it'

Incidentally, present and past tense of SCEAL may have differed even in Old
English: Goossens argues that 'the degree of grammaticalization is markedly
higher for *sceold-* than for *sceal/scealt/sculon*' (1987: 136).
More recently, W. Scott Allan's paper (1987, in English) gives a long
resumé of Lightfoot's analysis (§1), a detailed critique of his dating (§2),
arguments against excluding semantics (§3), and comments on Lightfoot's
analysis of Old English (§4). Most of the points had already been made
elsewhere and do not require further comment here.
Allan argues that modals *with modal meaning* have undergone little
change since Old English: what has changed is the loss of semantic and
therefore syntactic properties associated with *non*-modal uses. Modals in
epistemic and probably deontic meanings – those translatable by PDE
modals – have never taken objects or occurred in non-finite forms. What
changes there have been are best captured by a lexical diffusion model, with
different properties being lost by different verbs at different times. Taken as
a whole, Lightfoot's changes A1 and B4–B7 show an S-curve pattern of
change.
Allan gives the following explanation for the failure of modals to occur
more than sporadically with *to*-infinitives even after *to* had lost its
prepositional sense (1987: 133–5). *To* is a marker of complement clauses and
so appropriate for a two-clause, two-proposition structure like

[203] I want to go to Christchurch.

But modal verbs are not independent predicates, so that MAY in

[204] I may go to Christchurch.

merely indicates the speaker's attitude to the single proposition expressed.
Hence a *to*-infinitive would be inappropriate. The evidence Allan gives in

support of a difference between WANT and MAY is pseudo-cleft sentences like

[205]   What I want is to go to Christchurch.
[206]   *What I may is to go to Christchurch.

and VOSI constructions like

[207]   I want John to go to Christchurch.
[208]   *I may John to go to Christchurch.

Arguably, though, both [206] and [208] fail because MAY can no longer take a direct object, and in any case the explanation does not account for

(A) the presence of *to*-infinitives with verbs like BEGIN
(B) the failure of verbs like AIM, PRETEND, TRY to occur in pseudo-cleft or VOSI patterns
(C) the absence of *to*-infinitives in VOSI constructions with verbs like MAKE and SEE

Finally in this long catalogue of objections to Lightfoot's modal story, a reminder that in Denison (1990b) I argued that the behaviour of modals (and ONGINNAN) with impersonals in Old English was a powerful argument for treating them semantically and syntactically as being more like auxiliaries than main verbs. For data and discussion see §§9.3.5–6, 11.3.2.2, 11.3.9.6 above.

11.4.3 Roberts

Ian G. Roberts develops Lightfoot's scenario with the aid of more up-to-date theoretical apparatus (1985b). Roberts argues that modals are ordinary verbs and always have been. The category change assumed by Lightfoot appears in Roberts as a change in the 'thematic grid' (i.e. argument structure) of modals between Middle and Present-day English, with consequent structural changes somewhat similar to those proposed by Lightfoot. A significant advance over Lightfoot is the integration of the loss of subjunctives into the scheme.

11.4.3.1* Theoretical assumptions

The theoretical core of Roberts's analysis is his 'V-Visibility Condition' (1985b: 29):

[209]   V assigns θ-roles iff ['if and only if': D.D.] V is governed.

Condition [209] holds at *S-Structure*. What it means is that a verb must assign thematic roles if it appears in certain structural configurations, otherwise it cannot and is 'invisible' (we have used 'transparent' in a similar context elsewhere) as far as thematic roles are concerned. He gives as clear an account as can be expected of some other essential theoretical prerequisites – Government, C-Command, the θ-Criterion, the Projection Principle, 'minimal maximal projections'.

The essence of Roberts's claim is that finite verbs in Middle English (and earlier too, presumably) were morphologically governed by the person/number/tense/mood affixes they could attach to by movement from VP to INFL. Modals were like other verbs and appeared in structures like [211] below. The modal or other V moved into INFL in the course of derivation, where it was morphologically governed by Af [= <u>Af</u>fix]. Being governed at S-Structure means, by [209], that it could in turn assign a θ-role to its complement, whether a direct object NP or VP/clause.

In ModE ordinary verbs became syntactically governed by AGR(eement) or Aux(iliary) – new abstract features residing within INFL – without having to move to INFL. Modals, on the other hand, were reanalysed as auxiliaries which did not assign θ-roles. Condition [209] forced them to occur in an ungoverned position, so now they were base-generated in INFL.

Root modals are somewhat problematic for this analysis. Noting that 'root readings, assigning a θ-role and appearing in nonfinite forms are correlated' (1985b: 50), Roberts suggests that they do not themselves assign (normal) θ-roles but can optionally assign 'adjunct θ-roles' to arguments already given a θ-role by the main verb. Adjunct θ-roles are not considered to be violations of [209].

11.4.3.2 Historical analysis

Roberts starts in Middle English with some hesitation as to which structure to assign to modals, [210] or [211]:

[210]

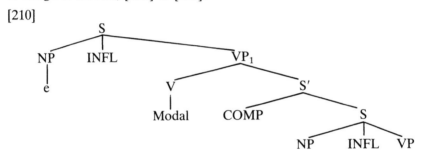

In [210] modals are Raising verbs subcategorised for an S'.[19] The analysis of [211] is the one followed up, with the modal subcategorised for a VP complement:

[211]

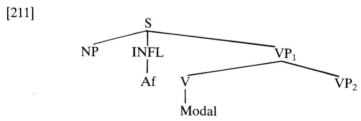

Here 'Af' stands for 'Affix', signifying the full agreement morphology of ME modals. (A third analysis involving restructuring is sketched but not developed, 1985b: 38–9.)

In the transition to Modern English, various changes *conspired* to affect the analysis of modals:

(A) longstanding morphological irregularity of modals

(B) loss of agreement in modals
(C) loss of the subjunctive from ordinary verbal morphology and its
     functional replacement by modal + infinitive
(D) increased frequency of other verbal periphrases (DO, perfect, pro-
     gressive, passive)

'The change was from a morphological agreement system to a syntactic
system' (1985b: 46).
   Reanalysis as auxiliaries led to a new structural configuration for
epistemic modals:

[212]

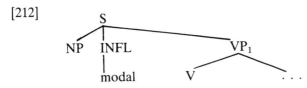

Notice, therefore, that although Roberts announces early on that his
analysis will treat modals as verbs throughout history, [212] inserts PDE
modals in a monoclausal structure as auxiliaries, not main verbs.[20]

11.4.4 Van Kemenade

Ans van Kemenade has developed her Verb-raising analysis of OE modals in
several works (1985, 1987, forthcoming); see also §4.7.1.2. In her (forthcoming: 298) the underlying structure assumed for OE sentences is [213]:[21]

[213]

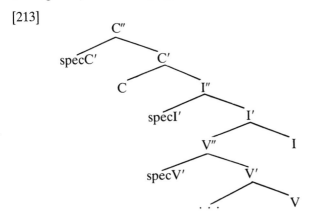

Deontic modals are regarded as control verbs and are inserted under V in
[213], with the constituent shown as '. . .' then a clause with PRO subject.
The process of V-raising may destroy the separateness of the embedded
clause and lead to word orders where material from the originally embedded
clause is discontinuous. Epistemic modals – a minority of examples – are
regarded as auxiliaries and are inserted under I.
   In Middle English three developments occurred:

(A) increasing range and frequency of epistemic uses to make up for the obsolescent subjunctive
(B) virtual loss of surface word order distinctions between deontic and epistemic uses
(C) loss of verb-second

The relevance of development C is a little vague: 'INFL in some sense becomes . . . more prominent' than COMP, facilitating the change of modals to auxiliaries, i.e. INFL elements. However, A and B at least, together with the loss of crucial main verb properties at the end of the ME period (here essentially the Lightfoot account is assumed), mean that 'the auxiliary pattern is readily available to be adopted by all the modals' (forthcoming: 304).

11.4.5   Warner

11.4.5.1

Anthony Warner (1982: 115–23) gives a careful assessment of the status of modals in Wyclifite Sermon English. He suggests that MOT and SHAL 'might be seen as the central modals' (1982: 118), citing such evidence as the probable complete absence of non-finite forms in Old and Middle English, the uniformity of occurrence with a plain infinitive (except when separated from the infinitive), the absence of NP objects (granted that SHAL 'owe' is a separate lexical item), and failure of the infinitive complement to commute with NP or PP. Other modals deviated to a greater or lesser extent. His conclusion is that modals in that dialect were verbs (as shown by concord, negation and inversion) but which could only be finite. He suggests that the eModE loss of WITEN 'know' effectively completed the correlation of endingless 3 SG PRES morphology with modalhood, leading to the complete loss of non-finite forms of verbs which could be modals.

CAN, WILL and MUN, he suggests (offering the comparison of PDE DARE and NEED) were modal/non-modal doublets in Wyclifite Sermon English, the non-modals responsible for non-finite forms and occurrence with objects. Support for this comes from the fact that all four instances of CAN or WILL with an adjacent[22] to-infinitive are non-finite:

[214]   a1425 *Wycl.Serm.* I 51.7

Al þe hardnesse of þis matere is to konnen   parfiȝtly to axson in
all the difficulty of this matter is to know-how perfectly to ask   in

Cristus naame
Christ's name

'The whole difficulty of this matter is to know fully how to ask in Christ's name.'

[215]   a1425 *Wycl.Serm.* III 144.4

whanneeuere men fasten þei shulden not wille to be sorowful
whenever   men fast   they should not wish to be sorowful

as   ipocritis
as/like hypocrites

'whenever men fast, they should not wish hypocritically to be sorrowful'

11.4.5.2

In a more recent article (1990) Warner explores the idea that it is useful to view the history of modals in the light of the theory of human categorisation developed by Eleanor Rosch and associates. For example, in the hierarchy which runs, say, furniture – chair – kitchen chair, the category 'chair' is **basic** because it has most distinctive properties and is most internally coherent, its membership is most clearly defined, it is more quickly retrieved in psychological experiments, and so on. **Subordinate** and **superordinate** categories are less central to human categorisation.

Warner's discussion fluctuates between consideration of the modals and consideration of all auxiliaries, of which modals are taken to be the prototypical members. Warner regards BE in all its uses and possessive HAVE as members of the auxiliary category. His major claims are that:

(A) auxiliary verbs in Old English formed merely a subordinate-level category to the basic category **verb**
(B) as a result of a *conspiracy* (not Warner's term) of successive changes, English-speakers came to perceive auxiliaries as a basic-level category in their own right by the sixteenth century
(C) subsequent changes have served to widen the gap between auxiliaries and non-auxiliaries

Much (not all) of Warner's evidence is more or less familiar: it is then the cognitive framework which is new. The main OE evidence for A which he cites is:

(A1) transparency to case with impersonals and passives
(A2) use of modals as sentence modifiers
(A3) use of modals as subjective epistemics

The eModE evidence for B includes:

(B1) loss of non-finite forms of modals
(B2) loss of non-modal senses and constructions
(B3) adoption of DO periphrasis
(B4) appearance of cliticised modals (*we'll*, *thou'rt*, etc.)
(B5) appearance of contracted negatives (*won't*, *shan't*, etc.)
(B6) loss of passive of HAVE
(B7) replacement of *ben*(3 PL PRES) by *are*[23]
(B8) development of tag questions

The later ModE evidence of C is:

(C1) loss of the last non-auxiliary preterite-present, WITE 'know'

(C2) generalisation of DO
(C3) loss of modal + directional adverbial
(C4) erosion of tense distinctions in modals
(C5) loss of agreement in modals with disappearance of *thou* forms

Other evidence concerns properties of BE.

It is worth comparing this approach, involving what I have called stages A to C, with Jean Aitchison's reformulation (1980: 141–2) of Lightfoot's material:

> STAGE 1. A slow moving away of the premodals from other verbs between OE and the end of the 15th century.
>
> STAGE 2. A much faster withdrawal of (pre)modals from other verbs in the 16th century.
>
> STAGE 3. A continued, slowed-down moving away of (pre)modals from other verbs in the late 16th and 17th centuries. This looks much more like an S-curve of the type we are now familiar with in phonology than [David Lightfoot]'s catastrophe scenario.

(The same point is made by Allan 1987: 139–41.) See also Warner (1992), discussed in §15.3.3 below.

11.4.6 Individual histories of modals

It is worth drawing together observations from a number of scholars (among others Warner, Plank, Allan, L. Roberts) which tend to show that the modals have not followed a uniform chronology in their historical development. Thus at the earliest historical period, Plank (1984: 310) quotes Standop (1957: 66) as finding only six out of 22 instances of CANN in *Beowulf* occurring with an infinitive complement, as against 79 out of 83 with MÆG. In the ModE period Warner notes that WILL and CAN are the last to lose the ability to take an object, an ability he correlates with the existence of non-finite forms. Linda Roberts (a student in my University) has observed a different correlation (1990: 47):[24] 'It is interesting to note that WILL and CAN are the last of the English "modals" to lose non-finite forms, and that precisely the same modals . . . show tense distinctions in PDE.' MUST and SHALL, on the other hand, seem to have attained unequivocal modalhood much sooner. MAY falls somewhere between the two pairs. And other items have shown varying degrees of modalhood in the different periods of English history.

As Frans Plank observes, many of the changes in English modals have been spread out over a very long period, and some are still going on at present. In Denison (1992) I discuss one current change in detail, the use of *may have* in counterfactual conditionals where previously *might have* would have been necessary:

[216]   1985 Blake, *ES* 66: 171

> Equally, if the order and allocation of tales were changing, it is quite likely that both may have been subsequently changed by Chaucer in some further revision if he had lived to make one.

I suggest there that the following four long-term changes form part of the context for this one:

(A) possible loss of *may* in favour of *might*, within which counterfactual *may have* is a reverse, 'death-throe' phenomenon
(B) disruption associated with the probable gradual obsolescence of the whole MAY paradigm
(C) splitting of modal tense-pairs into separate, perhaps tenseless, auxiliaries
(D) weakening of sequence-of-tense rules (if true, and if separable from C)

The differential behaviour of different modals tends to support lexicalist, semantic and cognitive approaches against the purely syntactic 'catastrophe' approach.

11.5 Questions for discussion or further research

(a) Allan (1987: 131–2) complains that Lightfoot (1979: 101–2) concentrates on the 3 SG PRES inflection, or lack of it, whereas the OE modals differed from both strong and weak verbs throughout their paradigms (see §11.3.1.1 above and any handbook of Old English). Furthermore, Allan denies that the morphology of modals can have contributed to increased opacity, both because it was an inherited difference and because it did not provoke them to adopt strong verb morphology. Examine the force of these objections.

(b) In Modern English we can say that absence of double modals and of perfect, progressive and passive modals follows from the defectiveness of the morphological paradigm. Alternatively, we can give a syntactic statement of these gaps and relate the morphology to the syntax. Does the history of modals favour one or the other viewpoint?

(c) Develop the speculation advanced in §11.3.9.1 on the changing relations between syntax, semantics and morphology in ME OWE/OUGHT.

(d) See whether the OE sentences [184]–[186] in §11.3.9.6 can be derived by (a combination of) the following analyses: Verb raising, Clitic climbing, Extraposition, and a suitable analysis of verb-second. See van Kemenade (1987), Koopman (1990c) for details of the individual analyses.

Notes

1. I neglect analyses of Present-day English which treat, say, *can* and *could* as two independent verbs or even not as tensed verbs at all. Although there are merits in such approaches, there is sufficient evidence for treating them as different tenses of a single lexeme CAN, and historically that is the only defensible position to take.
2. Recent evidence of confusion between *may* and *might* is discussed in Denison (1992).
3. In Standard English, at any rate. Increasingly, however, *may* is not backshifted at all: see Denison (1992).

4. Mitchell's citation form for these verbs is the infinitive, asterisked if unattested. I prefer to cite them under their 3 SG PRES form.
5. This paragraph is borrowed, with additions, from Denison (1990b: §4.3).
6. Lightfoot suggests that it lost its preterite-present morphology in Middle English, since he found no endingless 3 SG PRES forms after that time (1979: 102). But *OED* at least records no levelled -*s* forms either, and the 1 SG form remained typically *wot*, with vowel change from the infinitive.
7. For [44] Goossens gives only the second line (from *MED*), when the first line is actually a better candidate.
8. Example [72] apparently combines deontic meaning with subjectless syntax, which is surprising from a GB standpoint; see Denison (1990b).
9. For discussion of the idiom MAY *over* 'have power over' see Dickins (1926: 342), Clark (1970: 107–8), Bennett and Smithers (1968: xxxiii), Toller (1921) s.v. *ofer-mæg*, *OED* s.v. *may* v[1] B.1.
10. I have checked Visser (1963–73) and the *OED* entries for the modals. Most of the antedatings come by using the quotations in *OED* (the CD-ROM version) as a corpus to be searched. The citations may be found in *OED* as follows: CAN s.vv. *adjective* a. B.1, *pilgarlic*, *swap*, *swop* v. 8β; DARE s.vv. *call* v. 17d, *death-bell*, *upwith* adv. A; MAY s.vv. *carry* v. 1c, *yerk*, *yark* v. 6b, *read* v. 13b; MUST s.v. *must* v.[1] 7; NEED s.vv. *na* adv.[3], *ninny*[1]; SHALL s.vv. *shall* A.6b and A.9b, *rot* v. 4b; WILL s.v. *will* v.[1] A.6b and A.10b, *fob* v.[1] 1, *gemini* 4. For USED see Visser (1963–73: §796). The reference for *oughtn't* is 1837 Dickens, *Pickwick* vi.81.27; the one for *durstn't*, due to Jespersen (1917: 124), is 1848 Dickens, *Dombey* ix.119.16. For *canna*, *wald ne* the citations are in *DOST* s.vv. *na* adv.[4] and *ne* adv.[3].
11. Mitchell (1990: 3) cites four examples of AGAN + plain infinitive found by Ono (1989: 71–5).
12. Example [172] is Visser's earliest citation (1963–73: §846). It does not actually belong here if *spale* means something like 'rest, time off', and even if *spale* means 'splinter' it is still possible that *let* is a straightforward 2 SG imperative.
13. Compare here

    (a) They let her out.
    (b) Murder will out!

    LET is here rather similar to the modal in that both allow ellipsis of an intransitive verb of motion.
14. Because of the syntactic ambiguity I did not count [185] in my tally of subjectless ONGINNAN sentences in Denison (1990b).
15. Koopman (1990c: 271 n.1) independently comments on the strangeness of [189], the only four-verb cluster he found in Old English.
16. Allen uses M for 'modal' (an abbreviation which Lightfoot retains despite his preference for the label 'pre-modal'). S, V and O are used with familiar values.
17. Van Kemenade (forthcoming: 293) does not find deontic modality to be wholly inconsistent with taking an object in Old English.
18. To what extent modal + infinitive was interchangeable with subjunctive in Old English is a vexed question to which Mitchell returns again and again, quoting sympathetically earlier studies which deny full equivalence (1985: §§1014, 1995–9, 2081, 2764, 2824, 2974–5a, 2980). In these sections and others listed in his Index he gives generous references to the monograph literature on OE subjunctives and OE modals.
    As for change during the period, only two indications are cited by Mitchell. He quotes statistics by Gorrell (1895: 457–8) which give a ratio of 3:1 for subjunctive : modal+infinitive in Alfredian prose (early Old English) as against 2:1 in Ælfrician (later) Old English, suggesting a considerable increase in

frequency of modal usage; an opposite tendency to use *fewer* modals in the revision of the translation of Gregory's *Dialogues* can be ascribed to a closer adherence in the revision to the Latin (Mitchell 1985: §1998 n.24). He also cites (1985: §3950) Horgan's data on replacement of the subjunctive by modals in later manuscripts of *Cura Pastoralis*. She only gives three examples (1981: 219): 97.22 *sie* 'is'(SG PRES SUBJ) replaced by *sceal beon*; 235.9 *ofsloge* 'would kill'(SG PA SUBJ) replaced by *wolde ofslean*; 293.6 *weoxsen* 'grew'(PL PA SUBJ) replaced by *woldon wexan* in an eleventh-century manuscript and also (for the first two) in a possibly tenth-century one.

However, a recent monograph by Ogawa (1989) argues strongly against the idea that modals were – increasingly or otherwise – used as a substitute for the subjunctive during the OE period. As far as he is concerned, they only became substitutes *after* the period.

19. Had he made the complement a plain S – cf. the analysis given in §9.2 – his problem with lack of tense in the embedded clause would have disappeared. On the other hand, the disparity between what he calls 'the general "epistemic" meanings of the modals' (Roberts 1985b: 37) and the actual examples he gives, mostly deontic, is apparently missed.

20. The halfway status of aspectuals between main verbs and auxiliaries is noted but left unresolved (1985b: 30–1).

21. Cynics may feel that [213] betrays the effects of lingering too long at the X-bar. In line with much current GB work, it is somewhat overladen with nodes which are phonetically null.

22. Warner, following Svartvik and Quirk (1970: 403–4), ignores a single short word or inverted subject in judging whether higher and lower verb are adjacent (1982: 127).

23. The logic here is that the correspondence *thou art* ~ *they are* turns into a preterite-present sort of patterning, since PRES 2 SG and 1/2/3 PL are now set off against 1/3 SG (Warner 1990: 540).

24. Roberts's superb undergraduate dissertation on the theory of finiteness and its application to the history of English will, I trust, appear in published form.

Chapter 12

Perfect

12.1 The problem

Though there is little disagreement on the history of the HAVE/BE + past participle constructions, the material is perfectly capable of filling a modest chapter. What we have to cover includes the following:

(A) the relationship between HAVE as a full verb and HAVE as auxiliary of the perfect
(B) the date of grammaticisation of the HAVE perfect
(C) the relationship between the HAVE perfect and certain other HAVE + past participle constructions
(D) the choice between HAVE and BE as auxiliaries
(E) the date of grammaticisation of the BE perfect

For brevity in what follows I shall often refer to *collocations* of HAVE/BE + past participle as 'perfects' even where (as in Old English) it is uncertain or even unlikely that there is full grammaticisation of HAVE/BE and thus a true perfect.

12.2 The HAVE perfect

The HAVE perfect is a *syntagm* made up of HAVE and a lexical past participle.[1] It has the same argument structure as the lexical verb used alone and differs from a simple present or past in time reference and/or 'aspect' or 'phase':[2]

[1] America has found a role.

The received view on the origins of the HAVE perfect in sentences like [1] is of a reanalysis from [2](a) to [2](b) (ignoring certain details of analysis):[3]

[2] (a) America $[_{VP}$ $[_V$ has $]$ $[$ $[_{NP}$ a role $]$ $[_A$ found $]]]$
     (b) America $[_{VP}$ $[$has $[_V$ found $]]$ $[_{NP}$ a role $]]$

In [2](a) HAVE is a normal verb of full lexical meaning, roughly 'possess'. It is head of its VP, and transitive. Its object is the NP *a role*, modified by the adjectival passive participle *found* 'in a state of found-ness'. In [2](b) the head of the VP is the transitive verb FIND, and *a role* is object of the verbal syntagm *has found*. So HAVE has become a mere auxiliary in a syntagm which is essentially a complex form of the active transitive verb FIND, while V has become head of its phrase. From occurrence in sentences like [1] the perfect could then spread to other VP types.[4]

In sentences for which analysis [2](a) holds we might expect to find the following, writing 'V' for the participle even in adjectival use:

(A) a sentence brace in main clauses, with non-adjacency of finite HAVE and non-finite V
(B) accusative adjectival inflection on V
(C) a stative context where HAVE can mean 'possess' and both HAVE and V can refer to states

Analysis [2](b) would be supported by the occurrence of some of the following:

(D) adjacency of HAVE and V
(E) no adjectival inflection on V
(F) similar patterns in a non-stative context
(G) similar patterns with subjects that cannot be possessors
(H) similar patterns with objects that cannot be possessed
(I) similar patterns with Vs that do not take an accusative direct object

Properties F-I are consistent with the idea that HAVE is transparent to verbal restrictions: meaning and complement structure come from V.

12.3   Other HAVE + past participle constructions

Other HAVE + past participle constructions are of possible relevance to the history of the HAVE perfect as precursors, competitors, or subsequent developments. All but the first are distinguished from the perfect in Present-day English by word order amongst other factors – HAVE-NP-V as opposed to HAVE-V-NP – except where the NP is fronted. What follows is just one way among several of classifying them. For a fuller exposition with references to the handbooks see Brinton (forthcoming: §§4.1–2).

12.3.1   HAVE *got*

Historically HAVE *got* is the perfect of GET, but in the ModE period and especially in recent years it has come to be virtually synonymous with HAVE in a number of uses. Example [3] illustrates an early stage in the process, showing the potential for the later equivalence with HAVE:

[3]   1667 Pepys, *Diary* VIII 524.5 (10 Nov)

       . . . do hear that the Duke of York hath got and is full of the small-pox.

For our purposes I think it adequate to do little more than mention HAVE *got*, since the perfect is one use of HAVE which faces no competition from it in the standard language. Visser records the following as exceptional instances (1963–73: §2011):

[4]   1768 Sterne, *Sentimental Journey* I.3.11

by three I had got sat down to my dinner upon a fricassee'd chicken

[5]   1960 Lee, *Mockingbird* xxii.226.21

"I'da got her told," growled Dill, . . ., "but she didn't look much like tellin' this morning. . . . ."

A possible analysis of [4] is as (what is now northern dialectal) BE *sat down* 'be sitting down, be seated', but with BE replaced by GET. Compare the discussion of ambiguous GET + PA PTCP in §14.2.2.3 below. Example [5], which is clearly non-standard, looks like a variant of the conclusive perfect from the point of view of word order, though perhaps not of meaning.

12.3.2   Causative HAVE

As a causative verb HAVE may be used either with an infinitive in the VOSI pattern or with a past participle. It is the latter construction which concerns us here:

[6]   She'll have you arrested.

HAVE is agentive, the participle is passive. The construction is absent with participles of intransitives like DISAPPEAR, FALL, though Visser has a dozen examples from the sixteenth to the early eighteenth centuries (1963–73: §2121):

[7]   1711 Swift, *Jnl. to Stella* 230.27 (3 Apr)

He . . . would have had me dined [*edn*: dine] with him

Blending seems the obvious explanation here (or – in this example but not others – transitive DINE), though the editor assumes merely a printer's error.

12.3.3   The HAVE passive

For writers such as Brinton (who calls it 'the indirect passive with *have*'), this construction is reserved for three-place verbs with meanings like 'give':

[8]   I had a present given me.

Brinton distinguishes 'the passive of experience' as a later offshoot:

[9]   He had his head cut off.

but for my purposes it seems more convenient to include both [8] and [9] under the same heading, as they have much in common. Furthermore, an example like

[10]   1667 Pepys, *Diary* VIII 501.9 (25 Oct)

and there I had no more matters asked me

seems to straddle Brinton's distinction.

With the HAVE passive the subject of HAVE is Experiencer or Patient, and usually there is a co-referential pronoun or possessive adjective in the complement of the participle. The participle is passive; an agent-phrase is optional.

The difference between causative HAVE and the HAVE passive, generally quite clearcut, is purely one of agentiveness. Formally they are very similar, except that passive HAVE sometimes shows the NICE properties. For his classification Visser relies on the apparent meaning of HAVE, and because both 'cause' and 'experience' fit his contrived example *I am glad that I have had my shoes soled, heeled and shined*, he puts causative HAVE and the HAVE passive together (1963–73: §2118); for further examples of the HAVE passive see also his (1963–73: §§1964 (3), 1979).

12.3.4 The conclusive HAVE perfect

This is the construction seen in

[11] 1965 Capote, *In Cold Blood* iii.213.18

> The way he kept on, he had me almost convinced Hickock and Smith were innocent

There is little sense of causation – the subject of HAVE need not be agentive – though there may be some sense of possession. Since the subject of HAVE is coreferential with the logical subject of the participle, there is no opportunity for an agent-phrase. If we compare it with the ordinary perfect in Present-day English, some differences are clear:

[12] Poirot has the police convinced of your innocence.

[13] Poirot has convinced the police of your innocence.

The conclusive perfect, [12], is incompatible with reduced forms of HAVE and with the adverb *recently*, in contrast with the ordinary perfect, [13]. The conclusive perfect has a purely stative reading. (Brinton forthcoming: §1 cites McCoard 1978: 218–22, 250 and others on such differences.) Nevertheless there are some PDE examples where the semantic differences are small.

In earlier periods, when the criterion of word order is less reliable, the distinction between the ordinary and conclusive HAVE perfects can be very difficult:

[14] *ChronA* 48.4 (755)

> & hie ealle on þone Cyning wærun feohtende oþ þæt hie hine
> and they all on the king were fighting until they him
>
> ofslægenne hæfdon.
> slain   had
>
> 'and they all fought against the king until they had killed him'

The unreanalysed [2](a), putative source of the ordinary perfect, is sometimes identified with the conclusive perfect. The question then arises as to whether modern examples like [11]–[12] can be traced in continuous descent from Old English to the present day, although we note at once that the modern usage does not always involve literal or even figurative possession.

12.4   The BE perfect

12.4.1   BE

In Germanic languages generally, including Old English, the perfect of certain verbs was formed not with HAVE but with BE. These verbs were intransitive verbs, typically with meanings in the area of movement and change of state.[5] Visser lists many intransitive verbs which have been conjugated with BE to form a perfect or, as he terms it, Resultative Form (1963–73: §§1898–1904); he also cites early uses, if any, of those verbs with HAVE. The lists are long but not exhaustive: Mitchell points out Visser's omission of OE STANDAN 'stand' from §1899 (1985: §722 n.169); our [19] antedates Visser's ME citation of GELIMPAN 'befall' in §1901.

The history of the BE perfect in English has been one of continuous retreat in the face of the advancing HAVE perfect. Nowadays, in contrast to Standard Average European, the PDE BE perfect is pretty much archaic: Quirk et al. (1985: 170 n.[a]) actually call the surviving remnants 'pseudo-passives'![6]

12.4.2   WEORÐAN

An apparent variant of the BE perfect is a similar construction with WEORÐAN 'become'. Visser records it from Old English to the early fourteenth century (1963–73: §1897):

[15]   *Or* 117.11

On þæm swicdome wearþ Numantia   duguð gefeallen.
in that treachery became Numantines' nobility fallen

'By that treachery the flower of the Numantines died.'

[16]   c1250 *Owl & N.* 399

An was oferd þat hire answare | Ne wrþe   noȝt ariȝt
and was afraid that her answer   not become(PRES SUBJ) not right

ifare.
gone

'and was afraid that her answer was not going to go right'

It is fairly uncommon in Old English and rare in Middle English (Mustanoja

1960 does not mention it). Mitchell speculates on the possibility that
WEORÐAN 'never became a true auxiliary in this function' (1985: §739).
It is interesting that *ne* never seems to have cliticised to WEORÐAN
despite the initial *w-* (and cf. Chapter 14).[7]

12.4.3* Perfect ~ passive

There are a number of collocations of OE BEON/WESAN/WEORÐAN + past
participle which are on the face of it ambiguous between perfect and passive
readings:

[17] *ÆCHom* II 11.95.107

> and him   wæs geðuht þæt seo cæppe   hine atuge of   ðam streame
> and him(DAT) had seemed that the cap/hood him pulled from the stream

> 'and it seemed to him that the cap pulled him out of the stream'

Mitchell cites [17] under the heading of 'impersonal passive' (1985: §1965; for
explicit discussion see §§1049–51, 734–5, 739, 777–81). As noted in §5.8.3.1
above, I prefer an active reading for the participle, though certainty is not
possible. I grant that [17] looks very similar to a clear impersonal passive like

[18] *ÆCHom* I 23.330.29

> ac him   næs   getiðod ðære lytlan lisse
> but him(DAT) not-was granted that little   favour(GEN)

> 'but he was not granted that small favour'

but whereas [18] involves non-expression of what would have been subject
argument in the active – a typical function of passives – [17] does not. For me the
resemblance of [17] to the BE perfect of [19] is more persuasive:

[19] *ÆCHom* I 22.316.30

> and nyste   hu hire were   gelumpen wæs
> and not-knew how her husband(DAT) happened was

> 'and did not know what had happened to her husband'

See also Visser (1963–73: §1900 *weorðan/worth*), Denison (1990a: §2.2; 1990b:
§2.2.3), and for a complete descriptive survey of the *wæs geðuht* pattern in Old
English texts, Ide (1984, 1985).
Different classes of ambiguity are represented by:

[20] *ChronE* 221.28 (1086)

> . . . þa Dænescan . . . wurdon awende to þære meste   untriwðe
> . . . the Danes   . . . were   turned to the greatest treachery

[21] 1611 *Bible* Deut. 31.18

> . . . they are turned vnto other gods.

[22] *ChronE* 197.13 (1066)

> &   man cydde   Harolde cyng hu hit wæs þær   gedon &
> and one informed Harold king how it was there done and

geworden
?happened/?made

'and King Harold was informed how things had gone there'

In [20], as Mitchell points out (1985: §735), *awende* could represent either the passive of a transitive verb or the perfect of an intransitive: AWENDAN is recorded in both uses. Here the passive ~ perfect distinction is neutralised. The same goes for [21]; more examples can be found in Jespersen (1909–49: IV 41), Rydén and Brorström (1987: 24). In [22] and some similar examples which are cited by Mitchell, the individual probabilities seem to be that *gedon* is a passive participle 'done' and *geworden* an intransitive perfect participle 'happened' – yet they are coordinated complements of a single occurrence of BE. Such examples actually call the distinction into question.

12.5   Data on the HAVE perfect

12.5.1   Inflection

In Old English the participle in a HAVE perfect may agree with an accusative direct object. Mitchell reports a consensus of early workers that 'inflected forms are in a clear minority' and states furthermore that '[e]xamples with an inflected participle become less common with the passing of time' (1985: §710). Here are some examples with inflection:

[23]   *CP* 441.30

Ic hæbbe ðe   nu   todæg gesetne   ofer rice . . .
I have   you(ACC SG) now today set(ACC SG) over kingdoms

'Today I have set you over kingdoms . . .'

[24]   *Bede* 1 12.54.7

&   heo hæfdon utamærede   þa bigengan   þisses
and they had   expelled(ACC PL) the inhabitants(ACC PL) this
ealondes
island(GEN SG)

'and they had expelled the inhabitants of this island'

Mitchell suspects scribal error in his sole, doubtful case of agreement with a *non*-accusative NP:

[25]   *Exod(L)* 32.29

Todæg ge habbað Gode   gecwemede   &   eowere handa
today   you have   God(DAT) pleased(DAT?) and your   hands
gehalgode.
hallowed

'Today you have pleased God and sanctified your hands.'

He points out that *gecwemedum* rather than instrumental *gecwemede* would be the expected form if dative, and that another MS – our [46] – has uninflected *gecwemed* (1985: §709 n.161).

Some examples without inflection:

[26] *Beo* 1294

Hraðe heo æþelinga   anne   hæfde | fæste befangen
quickly she nobles(GEN PL) one(ACC SG) had   fast   seized

'Quickly she grasped firmly one of the nobles'

[27] *ChronA* 84.31 (894)

hæfde se cyning his fierd on tu tonumen
had   the king   his army in two divided

'The king had divided his army into two.'

[28] *ÆCHom* I 20.276.33

Nu habbað ge gehyred þa Halgan Þrynnysse
now have   you heard   the Holy   Trinity(ACC SG)

'Now you have heard about the Holy Trinity'

An example where the inflection, if present, would certainly have been zero (Ø) anyway:

[29] *ÆCHom* II 11.106.507

Hwæt hæfst þu gedon?

'What have you done?'

This happens with all neuter singulars, but the number of relevant examples may actually be greater, since adjectival inflections in general had an increased tendency to appear as zero on polysyllables, at least by Middle English (see Mossé 1952: §74). Past participles almost invariably have two syllables at the least: a minimum of one for the stem and a high likelihood of one more for the *-ed/-en* morpheme and/or another for *ge-* or some other prefix. Brunner states that participles are mostly endingless when predicative (1965: §306 Anm.1).

Finally I give an example showing the coordination of an uninflected and an inflected participle:[8]

[30] *ÆCHom* I 38.578.24

Fela Godes wundra   we habbað gehyred and eac gesewene
a-lot God's wonders(GEN PL) we have   heard   and also seen

'Many of God's miracles we have heard and also seen.'

Further examples of conjoined or parallel participles which are not parallel in inflection are given by Mitchell (1985: §711).

By early Middle English *all* adjectival inflection had disappeared apart from certain monosyllables (cf. §3.2.1), and entirely from predicative adjectives (Brunner 1963: §43). However, the *ge-* (now *i-*) prefix had also been dropped in the northern part of the country, which might have increased the possibility of participial inflection there. But hardly any is found.

12.5.2 Word order

Mitchell classifies the possible order patterns for Old English perfects in his (1985: §§706–21). In the light of the putative origin discussed in §12.2 above, the crucial patterns – involving transitive verbs – are Mitchell's [1], *hæfþ*-PTCP-NP (§712), and [4], *hæfþ*-NP-PTCP (§716). Other possible arrangements are less significant for our purposes and are anyway less common. Brinton (forthcoming: §3) claims that word order and presence or absence of inflection do not correlate. To the extent that each of the main orders can be found with both inflected and uninflected participles, this is true: see Tables 1–3 in Mitchell (1985: §706). But Mitchell himself suggests a certain statistical correlation (1985: §710):

> Caro (1896, pp. 404–6, and table V – which is not to be trusted completely) gives figures which confirm the reasonable expectation that the order object-participle produces a higher percentage of inflected forms (twenty-seven per cent) than the order participle-object (fifteen per cent).

Presumably it is 'reasonable' to expect some correlation between the factors A and B mentioned in §12.2 above.

In Middle English the picture remains blurred. In general the language lost the 'sentence brace' which had formerly tended to place *all* non-finite verbs in clause-final position; see Chapter 4. I would assume that in prose at least the order HAVE-PTCP-NP became dominant. However, older word orders survived, especially in poetry, throughout the ME period and probably beyond:

[31] (c1387–95) Chaucer, *CT.Prol.* I.52

Ful ofte tyme he hadde the bord   bigonne | Aboven alle nacions in
very often times he had   the board begun   above   all nations in
Pruce;
Prussia

'Very often he had sat in the place of honour in Prussia above all the nationalities.'

[32] 1609(1592–9) Shakespeare, *Son* 100.10

If time haue any wrincle grauen there

In some cases the HAVE-NP-PTCP order survived as a dialect form: Anglo-Irish is often cited in this context (Visser 1963–73: §2001, Harris 1984). In most dialects, including the standard language, that word order was increasingly associated with the conclusive perfect. Visser suggests that the decline of the HAVE-NP-PTCP order for true perfects may have set in through the likelihood of confusion with causative HAVE (1963–73: §2001).

12.5.3 VP types

We may classify types of VP which occur in the perfect in Old English according to the semantics of HABBAN and the valency of the main verb.

Examples where HABBAN may mean 'possess' are said to be only seven in number (Hoffmann 1934: 27–8, as reported with some scepticism by Mitchell 1985: §725). Two of the seven are:

[33] *CP* 45.12

    ðonne hæbbe we begen fet gescode suiðe untællice
    then   have   we both   feet shod   very blamelessly

[34] *Bede* 4 23.328.6

    . . . hwæðer he . . . þa stafas mid him awritene   hæfde
    . . . whether he . . . the letters with him written-out had

Mitchell adds some indeterminate examples like:

[35] *ChronA* 48.4 (755) (= second clause of [14])

    . . . oþ þæt hie hine   ofslægenne   hæfdon
    . . . until   they him(ACC SG) killed(ACC SG MASC) had

But in most cases HABBAN need not, and in some cases cannot, mean 'possess':

[36] *ChronA* 85.23 (894)

    Ac hie hæfdon þa . . . hiora mete genotudne
    but they had   then . . . their food used-up/eaten

    'But they had then . . . used up their food.'

[37] *ÆCHom* I 10.152.23

    þin geleafa hæfð ðe gehæled
    your faith   has you healed

    'Your faith has cured you.'

[38] *ÆCHom* II 34.289.31

    . . . and hæfde ær   his ðing þearfum   gedælede
    . . . and had   earlier his things the-poor(DAT PL) distributed

    '. . . and had earlier given his things away to the poor'

The second parameter to consider here is the complementation of the participle: whether it goes with an accusative direct object, an NP of some other case, or no NP at all. Examples with complementation other than accusative NP:

[39] *CP* 183.9

    Forðæm oft se welega   & se wædla habbað sua gehweorfed
    because often the wealthy(SG) and the poor   have   so changed

    hira ðeawum . . .
    their natures . . .

[40]   *Or* 9.18

Scortlice ic hæbbe nu   gesæd ymb þa þrie dælas ealles þises
briefly   I have   now spoken about the three parts all   this
middangeardes
middle-earth(GEN)

'I have now briefly described the three parts of the earth'

[41]   *Or* 132.17

Nu ic hæbbe gesæd . . . hu . . .
now I have   said   . . . how . . .

[42]   *Or* 104.29

Þa   Scipia hæfde gefaren   to ðære niwan byrig Cartaina
then Scipio had   travelled to the new   city Carthage

[43]   *CP* 407.19

Ongean ðæt sint to manigenne ða   ðe   ðonne giet ungefandod
against that are to admonish those who then yet untried
habbað flæsclicra scylda[9]
have   carnal   sins(GEN)

'Those, on the contrary, who have not yet tried carnal sins, are to be
admonished'

[44]   *Gen* 31.54

Þa   hi   eten hæfdon, hi   wunedon ðær
when they eaten had   they remained there

[45]   *Exod* 32.7

þin folc   hæfð gesyngod
your people has sinned

[46]   *Exod* 32.29

To dæg ge   habbað Gode   gecwemed, & eowre handa
today you(PL) have   God(DAT) pleased   and your hands
gehalgode
sanctified(ACC PL)

'Today you have pleased God and sanctified your hands.'

(Note that [46] shows phrasal coordination of a dative-governing verb and
an accusative-governing one, both lexical verbs sharing a single auxiliary
HABBAN.) These examples have mostly been taken from early OE texts.
Mitchell is impatient with aspectual or semantic classifications of verbs that
can occur with HABBAN, such as ± perfective, ± mutative: 'The important
point is that intransitive verbs are used with *habban* throughout the OE
period . . .' (1985: §722). Compare Visser's claim that the HAVE perfect
spread from A to B to C as follows (1963–73: §§2001–3):

(A) transitive verb (found from earliest Old English)
(B) transitive verb used without object expressed (from c1000)

(C) intransitive verb (from c1100)

Visser states that C is first recorded with the perfect of BE:

[47]   *ChronE* 232.18 (1096)

Þær beteah Gosfrei Bainard Willelm of Ou þes cynges mæg
there accused Geoffrey Baynard William of Ou the king's kinsman

þæt he heafde gebeon on þes cynges swicdome
that he had   been   in the king's treachery

'There Geoffrey of Baynard accused William of Ou, the king's kinsman, of having been a traitor to the king.'

But he himself seems to offer instances of the C type from poetry – some of it surely early Old English – under BRECAN 'break' and the verbs of motion FARAN, GAN, LIÐAN, WADAN (1963–73: §1902).

I have looked at the HAVE perfect in Sweet's *Oldest English Texts* (1885), apart from the *Vespasian Psalter*. I found only five examples (quoted here from the editions used by *DOE*):

[48]   *Rec* 6.5 12

ða hwile ðe God gesegen hæbbe   ðæt fulwiht æt
while   God seen   may-have(PRES SUBJ) that baptism at

ðeosse stowe beon mote
this   place be   may

'while God may have seen fit that baptism may continue at this place'

[49]   *Ch* 1200(HarmD 7) 10.20

Ðonne hebfað Eadwald & Cyne   ðas wisan   ðus
then   have   Eadwald and Cynethryth these arrangements thus

fundene mid hira friandum.
found   with their friends/relatives

'Now Eadwald and Cynethryth have devised the following arrangements with the help of their friends.'

[50]   *Ch* 1197(HarmD 4) 8.3

Se man se   ðis healdan wille & lestan   ðet ic beboden hebbe an
the man who this hold   will and perform that I decreed have in

ðisem gewrite . . .
this   document . . .

'He who is willing to observe and perform what I have commanded in this document . . .'

[51]   *Ch* 1482(HarmD 2) 5.2

Heregyð hafað ðas   wisan   binemned ofer   hire deg &
Heregyth has   these dispositions stipulated beyond her day and

ofer   Abban ðæm higum   et Cristes cirican
beyond Abba's the monks(DAT) at Christ's church

'Heregyth has specified the following terms for the community at Christ Church after her death and Abba's'

[52]   *Ch* 1508(HarmD 10) 14.32

Gif ðe̜t ðonne God ællme̜htig geteod habbe   ... þe̜t ...
if   that then   God Almighty decreed have(PRES SUBJ) ... that ...

'If, however, God Almighty has ordained . . . that . . .'

In none of them does HABBAN mean 'possess'. All of the lexical verbs are ones that take an accusative object, though SEON in [48] appears to be complemented by a *þæt*-clause.

Many intransitive verbs were conjugated always or sometimes with BE rather than HAVE, but exclusive reliance on BE became increasingly rare as the HAVE perfect was generalised. Nowadays *all* verbs can be employed in the HAVE perfect, apart from some auxiliaries and the occasional lexical verb which lacks a past participle (BEWARE, STRIDE).

12.5.4   Other evidence of grammaticisation

What other evidence can we find for the grammaticisation of the HAVE perfect? Of course, **grammaticisation** is a problematic notion. It could reasonably be applied to various stages of development of the perfect:

(A) when the HAVE perfect became available for any lexical verb which did not conjugate with BE (late Old English?)
(B) when it had come to be a pure tense equivalent (late Old English?)
(C) when it had developed approximately its present-day meaning (seventeenth century?) – which involved the *loss* of B
(D) when it became available for every non-auxiliary verb (late Modern English)

I am content to regard A as indicating the stage when perfect HAVE had become an auxiliary verb, since it suggests that HAVE was being used transparently, i.e. without an argument structure or selectional restrictions of its own.

The relation of the perfect to the simple past may be significant. In such examples as [53]–[57] the present perfect appears to be *commuting* with a simple past. The evidence is provided by parallelism with a simple past or by occurrence with an adverbial of definite past time:

[53]   *ÆCHom* I 22.316.26

Annania, deofol bepæhte ðine heortan, and ðu   hæfst alogen þam
Ananias devil seduced your heart   and you have lied-to the

Halgan Gaste.
Holy   Ghost

[54]   (a)   *ÆCHom* I 10.152.23 (= [37])

þin geleafa hæfð ðe gehæled
your faith   has you healed(PA PTCP)

(b) *ÆCHom* I 10.158.32

þin   geleafa ðe gehælde
your faith   you healed(PA SG)

[55] a1400(a1325) *Cursor* 16952

. . . als i haf   tald yow ar
. . . as I have told you earlier

[56] (c1390) Chaucer, *CT.ML.* II.1107

I am youre doghter Custance . . . |That whilom ye han sent unto
I am your   daughter Custance . . . that once   you have sent to

Surrye.
Syria

[57] a1450(c1400–25) Legat *Serm.PD* 19.37

&   schewe to him fullich . . . al þat euer þat   þu
and show   to him fully   . . . all that ever that [= whatever]you

hast doon þat ʒer
have done that year

Further examples can be found in Mitchell (1985: §723), Visser (1963–73: §§805–11). Visser writes that, with occasional deviations,

> [i]t is only after the time of Shakespeare that the preterite and the *have* + past participle construction are used as they are used nowadays: the first when the past event is circumstantially related, the second when a particular happening of the past has a bearing on the present . . . . (1963–73: §805)

Frequency of use may also be appealed to, though for English the results are inconclusive. In colloquial Modern German and French the present perfect has virtually replaced the simple past and can be used with an adverb of definite past time:

[58] Ich habe es voriges Jahr gesehen.
I   have it last   year seen

'I saw it last year.'

[59] Je l'ai   vu   l'année dernière.
I it-have seen the-year last

This constitutes an argument for treating the perfect as part of the tense system of those languages. The present perfect in English cannot now be used in this way:

[60] *I have seen it last year.

Nor has it ever displaced the past tense to such an extent. Gerritsen actually claims that English developed a [fully grammaticised] perfect more slowly than either German or Dutch, and used it less often and in fewer functions (1984: 122–4). The ratio of simple past to present perfect in two late ME literary texts was reckoned at about 10:1 by students of Mustanoja's (1960: 480, 505). (Past perfects and especially passive perfects were relatively less frequent still.) But as he points out, 'the frequency of the perfect is somewhat higher in everyday speech'.

12.5.5 The paradigm of perfect HAVE

The paradigm of perfect HAVE has always included finite forms, of course, and from OE times an infinitive was possible, always in collocation with a modal (Mitchell 1985: §922):

[61] *LS* 34(SevenSleepers) I 23.254

for his micclan wundrum. þe eft   he gedon habban   wolde
for his great   wonders that afterwards he done   have(INF) would

'for the great wonders which afterward He willed to do'

[62] a1400(a1325) *Cursor* 22353

Quen þat þis ilk   dughti dring | Sal haf an hundret winter king |
when that this same brave man   shall have a hundred winters king

Ben and tuelve, þan sal   he fare | To iursalem
been and twelve then shall he travel to Jerusalem

[63] 1759–67 Sterne, *Tristram Shandy* IV.i.218.12

knowing right well, that when I shall have told it, and my reader shall have read it thro' – 'twould be even high time for both of us to shut up the book;

Visser observes (1963–73: §2010) that the type seen in [62]–[63] is generally disfavoured, with WILL/SHALL usually absent after certain conjunctions:

[64] 1712 Addison, *Spect.* 279 II 585.17

it is my Design as soon as I have finished my general Reflections . . . to give particular Instances . . .

Other uses of the infinitive – absolute, as adjunct to a noun or adjective, in collocation with a *catenative* verb – came later (Visser 1963–73: §§2043–50). The paradigm widened in the early sixteenth century to include a non-finite *-ing* form (Strang 1970: 207, Visser 1963–73: §§2051–3). Some early examples of these patterns:

[65] c1230(?a1200) *Ancr.* 86b.9

ich . . . schulde bi rihte beo mare scheomeful to habben ispeken ase
I . . . should by rights be more shameful   to have   spoken as
ich spec.
I   spoke

[66] c1325(c1300) *Glo.Chron.A* (Clg) 674

. . . þat betere him adde ibe | Abbe   bileued   þer doune þan
. . . that better him had   been have(INF) remained there down than

ilerned vor to fle
learned for to fly

'. . . that it would have been better for him to have remained down
there than to have learned to fly'

[67]   a1400(a1325) *Cursor* 1105

Þai thoght þat kynd him mond for-bede | To haf don suilk a nogli
dede;

'They thought that nature would have prevented him from doing such
an ugly deed'

[68]   c1528 More, *Wks.* VI 200.24 [183 C1]

Nowe . . . yf some infydels . . . hauyng herde of Crystes name / dyd
longe to knowe his scrypture . . .

Perfect HAVE does not itself occur in the progressive, the perfect,[10] or the
passive, and an imperative is at best marginal.

12.5.6 Unreality

A very interesting correlation has developed between unrealised action and
the use of the HAVE perfect in certain contexts. Some examples are unreal
conditionals, where HAVE may appear in the *protasis*, the *apodosis*, or both,
but the usage is not confined to conditionals:

[69]   c1230(?a1200) *Ancr.* 13b.24

hwa   se   hefde iseid to eue . . . 'A eue went te   awei . . .',
anyone who had   said to Eve . . . O Eve turn yourself away . . .

hwet hefde ha iondsweret?
what had   she answered

'If anyone had said to Eve . . . "O Eve, turn away" . . . What would
she have answered?'

[70]   (1448) *Paston* 128.21

. . . and told here þat ʒe had sergyd   to a   fownd wrytyng
. . . and told her   that you had searched to have found writing

þer-of and ʒe kwd   non fynd in non wyse.
thereof and you could none find in no way

'. . . and told her you had gone searching to find written evidence of
it, and you could not find any anywhere'

[71]   (1454) *Paston* 84.17

Neuer the lesse he bode   lenger than he sayd hymself he schull
never the less he remained longer than he said himself he should

a   do.
have done

'Nevertheless he remained longer than he himself said he was going
to.'

[72]   (1478) *Let.Cely* 34.5

and thay spake to me, and desyryd to haue had iij sarpelers . . .[11]
and they spoke to me and desired to have had 3 bales (of wool) . . .

'and they spoke to me and asked to have three bales . . .'

[73]   1660 Pepys, *Diary* I 102.18 (3 Apr)

This day came the Lieutenant of the *Swiftsure* (who was sent by my
Lord to Hastings, one of the Cinque ports, to have got Mr. Edw.
Mountagu to have been one of their burgesses); but could not, for
they were all promised before.

[74]   1660 Pepys, *Diary* I 216.27 (7 Aug)

Here I endeavoured to have looked out Jane that formerly lived at Dr
Williams at Cambrige, whom I had long thought to live at present
here; but I found myself in an errour, meeting one in the place where
I expected to have found her, but she proves not she, though very like
her.

[75]   1667 Pepys, *Diary* VIII 344.21 (19 Jul)

and I had great mind to have gone back to have seen, but yet would
correct my nature and would not.

[76]   1667 Pepys, *Diary* VIII 446.5 (23 Sep)

the glass was so clear that she thought it had been open, and so run
[PA: D.D.] her head through the glass and cut all her forehead.

Many of Visser's examples of HAVE + past participle fall into the category
of unrealised action;[12] see especially his (1963–73: §§2030–50, 2154–6, 2188).
A few of his types begin with isolated late OE instances, but most of them
did not appear until Middle English.

The prescriptive tradition frowns upon some of the patterns with double
use of HAVE (e.g. *would have liked to have gone*), even though each pair of
adjacent verbs conforms to the standard morphosyntax of English verbal
groups. However, the tendency to use HAVE may even be strong enough to
produce two adjacent instances (ignoring non-verbs) of perfect HAVE, a
pairing which certainly contravenes what is now a clear rule in the standard
language:

[77]   a1425 *Dial. Reason & A.* 9.2

Hadde neuere infirmite haue asailed Job &   Tobye: here holinesse
had   never infirmity have assailed Job and Tobias their holiness

hadde not ȝit be   fully opened.
had   not yet been fully revealed

'If infirmity had never assailed Job and Tobias, their holiness would
not yet have been fully revealed.'

[78]   (1446) *Paston* 16.21

. . . the valew of the heye, yf
. . . the value of the hay   if

it   had well a   be
it [*sc.* a meadow not cultivated in good time] had well have been
dite.
cultivated

'. . . the value of the hay, if the meadow had been properly cultivated'

[79]   1837 Dickens, *Pickwick* xxvi.393.27

"Well, I raly would *not* ha' believed it, unless I had ha' happened to ha' been here!" said Mrs. Sanders.

[80]   1848 Dickens, *Dombey* xxxii.445.12

Little Dombey was my friend at old Blimber's, and would have been now, if he'd have lived.

[81]   1987 Wolfe, *Bonfire* xix.456.31

I wish we hadn'ta moved so fast with the sonofabitch.

The syntagm seen in the last clause of [80] is variously expanded as *had have* V*ed* and *would have* V*ed*, both by syntacticians and in attested instances, though it is commonest with contracted '*d* for the first verb. See Visser (1963–73: §2157), Wekker (1987), and also some comments in Denison (1992).

  Suppose we treat the construction as involving double HAVE (certainly correct for [81]). One analysis would treat the first HAVE as modal, since it appears to be followed by an infinitive. It is then anomalous in lacking an obligation sense and in not requiring *to*, as in the pattern

[82]   They have to have a swim every day.

An alternative analysis of [80]–[81], which I prefer, takes both HAVEs as perfect, the first marking anteriority (central use of the perfect) and the second unreality (secondary use): each function is separately realised. The morphological oddity then consists in the fact that the second auxiliary is an infinitive rather than a past participle despite being in the HAVE perfect, rather as Dutch auxiliaries followed by an infinitive behave when they themselves have a perfect auxiliary (Geerts et al. 1984: 523–5):

[83]   Ik had het moeten   zien.
       I   had it   must(INF for PA PTCP) see(INF)

       'I ought to have seen it.'

[84]   Ik ben wezen   kijken.
       I   am be(INF[13] for PA PTCP) look(INF)

       'I have been to have a look.'

In the English double HAVE pattern we might expect to find forms where the second auxiliary is a past participle:

[80']   *If he'd had lived . . . / *If he'd'd lived . . .
[81']   *I wish we hadn't had moved so fast . . .

The usual handbooks do not mention any, but Visser (1946–56: §710b) has two somewhat similar examples:

[85]   1442 *Let.Bekynton* II. 213 (*OED* s.v. *have* v. B.26)

He might never have had escaped. [modern spelling suspicious]

[86]   1535 Joye, *Apol. Tindale*(Arb.) 30 (*OED* s.v. *swerve* v. 3b)

He wold . . . neuer haue had so farre swaruen from his principal,
he would . . . never have had so far   swerved from his principle
as . . .
as . . .

'He would never have strayed so far from his principle, as . . .'

But they are clearly most unusual. Why? Among the reasons may be:

(A) phonetic awkwardness and/or avoidance of repetition
(B) residue of historical confusion in *'d* of *had* and *would*, the latter of which would have collocated with an infinitive, not a past participle
(C) possible association of infinitival rather than other forms of HAVE with unreality

Factor B could only be relevant for examples from around 1600 onwards, when contracted auxiliaries are first recorded. Factor C might be a consequence of the frequent use of a modal in unreal clauses.

12.5.7 The conclusive perfect

It is very difficult to find examples prior to Modern English which *must* be treated as statives and thus not ordinary perfects. Brinton regards the conclusive perfect as rare in early texts and essentially a seventeenth-century development (forthcoming: §4.1.3). The seven OE examples represented by [33]–[34] would qualify if HABBAN does indeed mean 'possess'. Certain adverbial or contextual clues would presumably indicate stative meaning:

[87]   While the attackers had them bottled up, they could do nothing.

I have not searched for such examples. A PDE test cited by McCoard (1978: 221, 250 n.7):

[88]   John has the toast all burnt.
[89]   *John has all burnt the toast.

could not be applied to earlier periods without a careful study of the prevailing patterns of so-called *Quantifier Floating*.

12.6   Data on the BE perfect

12.6.1 Examples

Instances of the BE perfect are common throughout Old, Middle and early Modern English:

[90] *Phoen* 363

oþþæt wintra   bið | þusend   urnen
until   winters(GEN) is   thousand run

'until a thousand years have passed'

[91] (c1375,c1390,etc.) Chaucer, *CT.Mk.* VII.2735
Whanne he escaped was

[92] c1440(?a1400) *Perceval* 977 (*OED* s.v. *uprisen*)
Up-resyne es a sowdane, | Alle hir landes hase he tane.
uprisen   is a sultan   all   her lands has he seized

[93] 1623(1598–9) Shakespeare, *Ado* III.iv.86
yet *Benedicke* was such another; and now is he become a man

[94] 1849 Ch. Brontë, *Shirley* i.22.12
As it cleared away he looked again for the soldiers, but they were
vanished;

For further examples see Mitchell (1985: §§734–42), Visser (1963–73:
§§1898–1904), Fridén (1948), Rydén and Brorström (1987). Despite
Mitchell's objection to the term (1985: §§722, 740), it is helpful to make the
generalisation that the majority of lexical verbs appearing in the BE perfect,
especially after the OE period, are **mutative** verbs (i.e. signifying a change
of state) and/or verbs of motion. See Question (b) below in §12.8.

Some intransitives of motion could already be used with HABBAN in Old
English, as in [42] above. All types of verb in the BE perfect have been
gradually moving over to the HAVE perfect, a process effectively completed
in the nineteenth century. For a careful statement of overall frequencies and
tendencies in the period up to the sixteenth century see Rydén and
Brorström (1987: 16–18).

12.6.2 Inflection

By contrast with the HAVE perfect, if the participle in a BE perfect shows
agreement it will be with a *nominative* NP. 'In general it is uninflected in the
singular and has *-e* in the plural . . .', writes Mitchell (1985: §737). This is
not unexpected, since the strong masculine and neuter nominative singular
inflection of adjectives was -Ø anyway, while the *-e* of masculine plurals was
often generalised to feminine and neuter plural adjectives too. Examples
that fit:

[95] *CP* 7.15

. . . hu   sio lar   Lædengeðiodes
. . . how the teaching(NOM SG FEM) Latin-language(GEN SG)

ær   ðissum afeallen wæs
before this   fallen-off was

'. . . how the teaching of the Latin language had formerly declined'

[96] *ÆCHom* I 5.88.27

Þa   sind forðfarene, þe . . .
they are passed-away who . . .

[97] *PPs* 106.24

beoð heora yþa   up astigene
are   their waves(NOM PL FEM) up climbed

'Their waters will have mounted up.'

Exceptions:

[98] *CP* 3.13 (cf. [95])

Swæ clæne   hio   wæs oðfeallenu . . .
so   completely it(NOM SG FEM) had declined . . .

[99] *Or* 47.19

hie   wæron cumen Leoniðan to fultume
they were   come   Leonidas as assistance

'they had come to help Leonidas'

[100] *GD(O)* 76.3

fela   þinga,   Petrus, beoð god gesegnu
many(INDECL) things(GEN PL NEUT) Peter   are   good seen

[101] *Bo* 33.14

Þonne . . . þa þeofas þe from gewiten wæron
when   . . . the thieves you from departed were

'When . . . the thieves had left you'

There is little participial inflection in the ME period.

12.6.3 Grammaticisation

As with the HAVE perfect there is room for disagreement over which stage
should mark grammaticisation and over what kind of examples would
demonstrate its achievement. Mitchell suggests that the following kinds of
participle are demonstrably adjectival in Old English, ruling them out as
instances of a grammaticised perfect (1985: §741):

(A) not corresponding to any finite verb, e.g. *ofhingrode* 'famished'
(B) translating a Latin adjective
(C) coordinated with an adjective, as in[14]

[102] *ÆCHom* I 31.456.20

næs   his reaf   horig ne tosigen
not-at-all his raiment filthy nor threadbare

'his clothing is not dirty or threadbare'

(D) modified by intensifiers like *swiþe* 'very'

But he cannot suggest tests which would demonstrate *non*-adjectival use and remains unsure whether the BE perfect ever was grammaticised (1985: §842). Mustanoja argues that when WESAN/BEON had moved from indicating a state to indicating the effect or result of an action, it had become a true auxiliary of the (plu)perfect, though it never lost its capacity to express a state (1960: 500). Rydén and Brorström find that the relevant point is not whether or when BE was grammaticised as a true perfect, but that it came to form a systematic aspectual opposition with HAVE (1987: 17 n.7, 26). See also the 'double perfect' discussed in §12.6.4 below.

The following quotations are suggestive of an event rather than a stative interpretation:

[103] c1180 *Orm.* 11551

  Affterr þatt he wass dæd forr uss & risenn upp off dæþe

  'after he had died for us and risen up from death'

[104] c1374 Chaucer, *Compl Mars* 71

  The grete joye that was betwix hem two | When they be mette, ther may no tunge telle.

  'The great joy there was between those two when they have met, no tongue may tell.'

[105] (c1395) Chaucer, *CT.Sum.* III.2190

  an odious meschief |This day bityd   is to myn ordre and me
  an odious mischief this day happened is to my order and me

  'Today a terrible misfortune has befallen my order and me.'

[106] c1489 Caxton, *Sonnes of Aymon* iii.86.33

  . . . theyr fayne aventure   that was happed   to theym
  . . . their good incident/adventure which had happened to them

  that daye.
  that day

[107] 1623(1605) Shakespeare, *Lr* V.iii.292

  Your eldest Daughters have fore-done themselues, | And desperately are dead

In example [107], treated as the perfect of DIE, the non-stative interpretation depends on the adverb *desperately*. By and large, however, the BE perfect is not found in the present tense with adverbials of definite past time, as it is in Modern French or German.

12.6.4   The paradigm of perfect BE

The paradigm of perfect BE developed in similar ways to that of perfect HAVE (§12.5.3 above). Finite forms were available from the start, and according to Visser (1963–73: §2153), infinitives collocated with modals from

early in the fourteenth century, though his earliest example, from c1300
SLeg(Hrl), is definitely erroneous, and his second can be analysed as a
passive (thus *MED* s.v. *flen* v. 1c 'put to flight'):

[108]   a1400(a1325) *Cursor* 1173

Sua ferr . . . I sel   be fled.
so   far . . . I shall be fled

'I shall have flown . . . so far/So far away . . . I shall be driven'

Fifteenth-century examples look better, but Mustanoja (1960: 502) and
others suggest that BE was less common than HAVE in the infinitive. These
observations on modal + perfect BE, plus Mitchell's (1985) silence, suggest
that it must have been at best very rare in Old English. Yet there is no
obvious reason why it should have been impossible, and indeed here are two
OE contenders:

[109]   *GD* 232.7

be þam ne dorste   us   nan wen   beon
by which not dared(SG) us(DAT) no   expectation(NOM) be

geðuht,   þæt hi   mihton beon dælnimende þæs heofonlican
seemed/thought that they might be   partaking   the heavenly

wuldres
glory(GEN)

'in consideration of which we should not dare think it likely that they
might partake in the glory of heaven'

[110]   *Nic(C)* 598.18

Mihte þiss eall beon soð geworden?
could this all be   true become

'Could all this have become true?'

(Example [109] has been discussed for different reasons in §11.3.1.1 above.)
    I have not found any statements as to the earliest appearance of infinitives
in other patterns, nor of *-ing* forms. Here are reasonably early examples of
each:[15]

[111]   1590–96 Spenser, *FQ* 2.i.1.4

Soone as the *Redcrosse* knight he vnderstands | To beene departed
out of *Eden* lands

[112]   1579 Lyly, *Euphues* I 201.9

Supper being ended, . . .

[113]   1660 Pepys, *Diary* I 141.25 (15 May)

. . . that I wondered from what time the King could look upon him to
be become his friend

[114]   1668 Pepys, *Diary* IX 55.7 (6 Feb)

and there, the girls being gone home, I to the office, where a while busy

There is actually an occasional HAVE perfect of the BE perfect (Visser 1963–73: §2162)! Rydén and Brorström find it obvious that 'this variant emerged to satisfy a need for stressing the resultative aspect more emphatically than the *be* + P[ast]P[articiple] construction was capable of at the time' (1987: 25):

[115]   a1400(a1325) *Cursor* 7074

Bot als þe tan   als be   þat toþer | Of al þis werld had
but as-if the one [*sc.* half] as against the other   of all this world had

risen bene
risen been

'but as if one half of this world "had been risen" against the other'

[116]   (modern) She's been gone a long time.

Visser suggests that the BE perfect 'gradually got the character of' copula BE + adjective, 'especially when the collocation was not accompanied by verbal adjuncts' (1946–56: §682). This would then have allowed the normal conjugation of (copula) BE to operate. Visser's suggested reanalysis is the exact converse of grammaticisation. It might be simpler to assume that the BE perfect never was fully grammaticised.

There is also an imperative:

[117]   1623(1597, rev. 1600–1) Shakespeare, *Wiv* III.iii.19

Be gone, and come when you are call'd.

12.6.5*   The BE perfect with transitives?

Mustanoja points to sporadic use of a BE perfect with transitive verbs throughout Middle English (1960: 500–1):

[118]   c1230(?a1200) *Ancr.* 45b.20

for ȝe   beoð iflohe þe [*MS. Nero*: þene] world
for you be   fled   the   world(OBJ)

'for you have fled the world'

[119]   c1350 *MPPsalter* 37.4

For myn wickednesse ben ouergon   myn heued
for my   sins   are gone-above my   head

'For my sins have risen above my head'

See also Visser (1963–73: §1902) on the verb PASS. Rydén and Brorström, giving further references, point out that the apparent object NPs in cases like [118]–[119] can be regarded as PPs with suppressed preposition, and the verb as intransitive (1987: 23). The BE perfect also occurs occasionally with reflexive verbs in late Middle English:

[120]   1375 Barbour, *Bruce* 13.100

That sum   . . . wer | Withdrawin thaim   in full gret   hy
that some . . . had withdrawn themselves in full great haste

'that some . . . had retired in very great haste'

Mustanoja accepts the possibility of French influence here (1960: 502–3).

12.7   Explanations

It seems best here to summarise the conventional wisdom, then to mention
several works which provide additional or alternative suggestions. Again we
take the HAVE perfect first. Brinton offers a useful survey of modern
opinions on the nature of its aspectual character (1988: Chapter 1).

12.7.1   The received view of the HAVE perfect

The traditional view of the HAVE perfect is that it started out as a breakaway
from one usage of HAVE 'possess' by the reanalysis sketched in §12.2 – a
syntactic reanalysis with concomitant changes in the meaning of HAVE and
the voice of the participle. Statements to this effect can be found in such
sources as Jespersen (1909–49: IV 29–30), Visser (1963–73: §§2001–3),
Mitchell (1985: §§724, 726–8), Traugott (1992: 192). Of the reanalysis
Traugott writes:

> It is likely to have occurred first in constructions with neuter accusative singular
> objects, since these had Ø inflection, and thus did not have overt morphology
> marking them as adjectives.

Similarly Mitchell, who regards the forms with zero-inflection as a possible
'analogical factor in the ultimate disappearance of the inflected forms' (1985:
§709). All scholars note the early appearance of the HAVE perfect, though as
we have seen there is some confusion as to exactly when in the Old English
period it became generalised beyond accusative-taking verbs. Harris sums
up its later progress like this (1984: 322):

> The rise of the modern [HAVE: D.D.] perfect can be traced as a gradual
> diffusion into more and more linguistic environments from which it has ousted the
> preterite, a present form, the old *be* resultative and the old split perfect . . .

12.7.2   The received view of the conclusive perfect

The traditional view of the conclusive HAVE perfect is that it is a direct
continuation of the 'possess' pattern (the assumed precursor of the ordinary
perfect) but without reanalysis. In the conclusive perfect the only change has
been a possible weakening of the 'possess' meaning of HAVE. This view
appears in Jespersen (1909–49: V 16), Kirchner (1952: 393–4, 401–9), Visser
(1963–73: §§2116–18), and others.

12.7.3 Brinton

Laurel J. Brinton (1988: §3.1.3) makes the following criticisms of the standard account:

(A) eOE HABBAN had developed meanings broader than 'possess' when not collocated with a past participle
(B) HABBAN 'possess' + past participle was at best rare in Old English
(C) evidence for stative meaning (inflection, word order) is not telling
(D) chronological evidence of a spread to actional meanings is weak, since perfect HABBAN occurred with intransitives and non-accusative-taking verbs from the earliest texts
(E) English HAVE perfects never became pure equivalents of the preterite, as did those of colloquial Modern French and German

Both D and E are, it seems to me, defensible without being certain.

Brinton's conclusion from these points is that any reanalysis occurred in prehistoric times, and that there was no semantic bleaching. What happened, she believes, is that there was a metonymic shift in the meaning of HAVE from 'hold' to 'have' (i.e. a relational meaning), probably in Common Germanic, and that a gradual spread of the perfect to more and more syntactic environments – which seems somewhat at variance with D – was a consequence of that semantic change.

However, A–D are not unique to Brinton. There is general acknowledgement in the handbooks that development of the perfect was largely a prehistoric change. Interestingly, Barbara Strang treats the conclusive perfect in Old English as a ninth-century *variant* of the ordinary perfect rather than as its putative *ancestor*. The reference is tantalisingly brief (1970: 311), but it almost seems to turn the reanalysis of [2] on its head.

Brinton (forthcoming) builds on observations by Kirchner (1952: 403–5) and Visser (1963–73: §§2001, 2116–17) to suggest that the conclusive perfect is *not* a survival of the older form of the perfect. (She had already anticipated this conclusion at her 1988: 101–2.) What she believes is that the modern conclusive perfect is best regarded as an innovation made possible when HAVE-PTCP-NP order became the only possible one for non-stative examples, leaving the HAVE-NP-PTCP pattern open to specialisation as a stative. This apportioning of functions, which she locates in the seventeenth and eighteenth centuries, should be related to the specialisation of the BE perfect as a stative (forthcoming: §4).

12.7.4 Visser

In looking at the opinions of Visser (1963–73: §§805, 2001–8) and Bauer I have found Robert W. McCoard's revised dissertation (1978), mainly a readable account of the semantics and pragmatics of the HAVE perfect in Present-day English, a helpful prompt.[16] Only the last, short chapter deals with history, with a somewhat schematic comparison of the conclusions reached by Visser and Bauer on the functions of the perfect and simple past. McCoard summarises Visser as arguing that the modern perfect ~ past opposition cannot have been a continuous development from the original

OE opposition between conclusive perfect and simple past, since the situation in Middle English was too chaotic: rather the modern opposition has developed independently since then. (I do not find Visser quite so categoric on this point as McCoard does.)

12.7.5 Bauer

By contrast, Gero Bauer's analysis (1970) of Chaucer and Gower leads him to the conclusion that the modern differentiation of present perfect and simple past had already been attained in large measure by the end of the fourteenth century, the main difference being that certain adverbs which now favour the perfect (*never*, *since*) seem to have favoured the simple past in Chaucer's English. As for the 'historical perfect' seen in [56], Bauer offers the possibility of French influence (1970: 104–6), which McCoard seizes on as a way of explaining the deviations from the expected distribution: deviations in favour of the perfect are perhaps due to French, (?)literary influence; deviations in favour of the simple past are due to conservatism in the face of the encroaching innovation of the perfect.

12.7.6 The received view of the BE perfect

It is widely assumed that the original form and meaning of the BE perfect was of stative BE + predicative adjective; thus Visser (1963–73: §1898) and others. It referred (normally) 'to a state as the result of a preceding action'. The contrast with the HAVE perfect, especially with verbs that permitted both, was one of state versus action/process.

One suggested eME impulse to the generalisation of HAVE is the increasing use of BE as auxiliary of the passive; thus Mustanoja (1960: 501), etc. Traugott argues that 'the generalization . . . is a very natural change' because 'nonmutative verbs outnumbered mutative ones and *have* + [past participle] was not heavily loaded with different functions' (1972: 145). In other words, explanatory weight is given to the heavy functional load on BE in collocation with past participles and the correspondingly light load on HAVE. Suggested explanations for the especially rapid retreat of the BE perfect in the eighteenth century (Visser 1963–73: §1898 and others) include the possible neutralisation of *is* and *has* in the clitic *'s*, and the attacks of prescriptive grammarians.

12.7.7 Fridén

Georg Fridén's monograph (1948) is a much-cited investigation of verb use, and particularly the choice between BE and HAVE, in Chaucer and other authors up the time of Shakespeare. Fridén takes over from a work on the Scandinavian perfect a number of factors which conduce to the use of HAVE with mutative verbs (1948: 44–57, summarised 116–17):

(A) repeated action or distributive meaning

(B) temporal adverbial
(C) resulting state no longer exists
(D) negatives and interrogatives
(E) adverbial of manner
(F) 'egressive' **Aktionsart** with verbs of motion where action emphasised[17]
(G) subjunctives and conditionals
(H) hypothetical comparatives, concessives, clauses after optatives, counter-
     factuals with *almost*
(I)   infinitives
(J)   coordination with a non-mutative

Each factor is illustrated with examples and counterexamples. Fridén then
goes on to a verb-by-verb survey.

12.7.8   Rydén and Brorström

Mats Rydén and Sverker Brorström are concerned with BE ~ HAVE
variation in late Modern English (1987; also summarised as Rydén 1991).
Their detailed study is an example of variation analysis. (For other work in
this 'tradition' see the volumes edited by Jacobson 1979, 1983, 1986.) They
examine a corpus dated 1700–1900 of private letters and comedies –
informal written prose thought most likely to approach the norms of
everyday speech. Division of the two-hundred-year span into four chronological periods is done on the basis of date of birth of the author (1987: 30).
Close attention to, and statistical testing of, the data are used to isolate as
far as possible the factors which determined the choice of auxiliary at
different times. A total of 6625 instances is counted in the tabulations, and
each lexical verb is discussed and tabulated separately. They show
(antedating *OED*) that *'s* was a shortening for *has* as well as for *is* almost
from the start of the eighteenth century, so they omit *'s* examples from their
statistics (1987: 32).
    An important component of the variationist approach is the removal of
'knock-out factors' in order to permit a more delicate assessment of the
factors relevant to cases where there is a genuine choice. Thus transitive
verbs, which have always formed their perfect with HAVE, are not
considered at all. No other factors are found to be 100 per cent knock-out
contexts, but some come close to enforcing the use of HAVE rather than BE
(1987: 184). Rydén and Brorström condense the eleven categories which
favour HAVE in the list of §12.7.7 to the following five (1987: 28):

(A) action as emphasised by modifiers (of place, manner, etc.)
(B) iteration/duration
(C) unreality (as manifest in, e.g., certain conditional and optative
     contexts)
(D) certain negated or questioned statements
(E) perfect infinitives

They go on to group A and B under the heading 'action' and C and D under
the heading 'unreality/uncertainty'. Iterative contexts and unreality are
factors which almost guarantee the use of HAVE (1987: 184, 186):

[121]   1714 *Wentworth* 383.3

   The letters have come so regularly of late that . . .

[122]   1717 *Verney* I 397.22

   if he had not come up as he did he would have had a Feaver or
   convultions

Remember too, as we have already noted (§12.5.6 above), that unreality
can also promote the use of the HAVE perfect instead of a simple tense.

   Category E, which belongs under neither main heading (though this is left
a little unclear), is a morphosyntactic context which has always favoured the
selection of HAVE (though here again notice the high proportion of infinitive
HAVE in the 'unreal' examples discussed in §12.5.6). Rydén and Brorström
later add to the list two more morphosyntactic contexts of limited
chronological validity (1987: 189–94):

(F)   past tense
(G)   *-ing* constructions

That is, near the end of the eighteenth century, when BE was still strong in
the present perfect, the *past* perfect began to show increasing use of HAVE.
The *-ing* form also showed a marked tendency to switch from BE to HAVE in
the nineteenth century. They write: 'The element of *prolonged* action easily
associated with the *ing*-construction . . . may have contributed to the
comparatively rapid proliferation of the *have* variant here' (1987: 193). I
confess myself unable to find much evidence of 'prolonged action' in the
large sample of quotations provided:

[123]   1815 *Bessborough* 244.9

   How happy I feel at having come.

   As far as overall development is concerned, Rydén and Brorström show
HAVE to have achieved predominance, at least in informal styles, by the
early decades of the nineteenth century, and almost complete takeover by
the end of the century (1987: 198); a chart of the average progression shows
a rather flattened S-curve (1987: 200).

12.8   Questions for discussion or further research

(a) Use the *Concordance* of Venezky and Healey (1980) to gather examples
    of OE HABBAN + past participle, confining attention to works which
    appear to be early Old English. (Gather, say, the first hundred examples
    which qualify.) What kinds of complementation do the lexical verbs in
    your examples show? And of those which take a simple accusative
    object, are there any which on semantic grounds would seem to rule out
    the [2](a)-type analysis with its 'possess' meaning for HABBAN? Do your
    results bear on the date at which the HAVE perfect was generalised (see
    §12.7.1 above)?
(b) It is claimed that most BE perfects in Old English involve mutative
    verbs. I suggested that BE + past participle of certain impersonal verbs,

as in [17], were probably BE perfects, but most impersonal verbs apart from the HAPPEN class are *state* verbs. Examine instances of this construction in context to see whether they can reasonably be given a mutative reading (e.g. *wæs geðuht* 'came to seem'). Do your findings help to resolve the syntactic analysis of examples like [17]?

(c) How would you explain the present perfect *haue doon* in the following example, which occurs in a clear past tense/past time context?

?c1425(?c1400) *Loll.Serm.* 1.240

and alle suche were vnbounden of   alle þe synnes þat þei haue doon.
and all such were released   from all the sins   that they have done

Investigate the history of the relationship between present perfect and past perfect (pluperfect).

(d) Explore the role of the HAVE passive (references in §12.3.3 above) as an alternative to the indirect passive (Chapter 6).

Notes

1. I shall ignore the two apparent examples in Old English of a periphrasis formed with the verb AGAN 'have, own' + past participle; see Mitchell (1985: §743).
2. Palmer defines **phase** as follows:

   > Phase is best seen as the marker of a complex set of time relations. Though there are several possibilities, all of them share the characteristic that what is involved is a period of time that began before, but continued right up to, a point of time which may itself be present or past according to the tense used. (1988: 46)

3. It is not relevant here to discuss such questions as whether any part of the VP is a small clause. One very obvious question concerns the precise categorial status of *has eaten* in [2](b), which depends on the theory in use. Indeed in some analyses it does not form a **constituent** in deep and/or surface structure.
4. Much the same development is supposed to have occurred independently in other Germanic languages, in Romance, and in Modern Greek (Traugott 1972: 92 n.11). However, Traugott (1992: 288 n.2), citing Benveniste (1968), says that Lat. HABERE followed a different path from English HAVE, since resultant states were mental states, not actions.
5. But note that Visser's first category of such verbs is '*Verbs not denoting motion, such as* be, abide, sit, rest, dwell, *etc.*' (1963–73: §1899). Admittedly some of his examples, e.g. those with LIE, could be taken as denoting motion after all.
6. But according to Matti Rissanen (in prep.), eighteenth-century grammarians referred to the BE perfect as a passive.
7. Mitchell (1985: §1129) cites a work which asserts that *ni* 'not' + *wertha* 'become'(INF) *did* contract in Old Frisian.
8. It may be relevant to [30] at least that invariable *fela* 'much, many' + genitive plural is usually but not invariably treated as plural in Ælfric; see Mitchell (1985: §430).
9. I reproduce Mitchell's footnote in full (1985: §713 n.165):

   > This example – which occurs again with variations at *CP* 409.16 and 409.22 – tests Khomiakov's assertion in *JEGP* 63 (1964), 675–6, that all the forms with the prefix *un-* must be considered as adjectives rather than participles.
   > Indeed it does. [43] bears also on the discussion of lexical passives in §7.6.2 above.

10. I discount the 'double perfect' of non-standard *If I'd've known . . .*, on which see §12.5.6 above, and the rare ME pattern exemplified by:

(a)   a1400(a1325) *Cursor* 13954

Fain þai wald   him þan had numen
fain they would him then had taken

'They would have liked to capture him.'

with *had* for the expected infinitive *have* found in the other MSS (see Visser 1963–73: §2168).

11. The context of [72] makes clear that a definite order for the wool had not yet been placed.

12. A curious exception is the following, where HAVE seems to be used to express not unreality but a wish – unless it implies that the supplicant is without serious hope of a favourable response!

(a)   a1474 *Stonor* 132 I 138.3

Besekyng yow as I schall be your pore Bedman to have ȝevyn me lysens
beseeching you as I shall be your poor servant to have given me licence

to have goyn hom to my cuntre   to have spokyn with my
to have gone home to my part-of-the-country to have spoken with my

ffader . . . . Besekyng yow to have grantt   me thys, and to have sende
father . . . . beseeching you to have granted me this and to have sent

sum mone   for my spendyng
some money for my spending

'As your humble servant I beseech you to give me leave to go home to speak with my father . . . I beseech you to grant me this and to send me some spending money.'

13. *Wezen* is a special infinitive form – differing from the normal infinitive *zijn* – used colloquially to replace the past participle *geweest* in this construction (Geerts et al. 1984: 578).

14. Since the passage containing [102] is generally in present tense, *næs* probably stands for *nalæs* 'not at all' rather than *ne wæs* 'not was'. On this assumption the example lacks explicit BE and so could hardly have been a regular BE perfect anyway.

15. Visser has an example of *being runne from his countrey* dated 1604 (1963–73: §1902), more likely to be perfect than passive, transitive RUN not being recorded in this sense by *OED* until 1727 (s.v. *run* v. B.44c).

16. One particular misconception of mine has gone, thanks to McCoard. I learn from his strictures (1978: 229) on Visser that *had gone* 'had disappeared' shows GO in a 'peculiar British sense'.

17. Conversely, BE is favoured if state is emphasised – the following presence of the referent of the subject in egressive Aktionsart, or its absence in ingressive Aktionsart.

Chapter 13

Progressive

13.1 The problem

I hesitantly retain the term **progressive** as the most familiar label applied by grammarians of Present-day English to *syntagms* of the form BE + V*ing*, as in

[1] Jim was singing the blues.

though without commitment to notional characterisations like 'ongoing action' or whatever. As in the previous chapter it will be convenient to use the one label for the whole period from Old English onwards, even at the risk of anachronism. (Visser, who prefers the slightly more neutral label 'expanded form', gives a long list of alternative terms, 1963–73: §1801.)

V*ing* is what is traditionally called a present participle. In Old English the present participle normally had the form V*ende*,[1] as in *feohtende* 'fighting', and syntagms of the form BEON/WESAN + V*ende* were in use at that time. Our main problems in this chapter are to decide

(A) where the OE usage came from
(B) whether the ModE progressive is descended directly from it

In tackling them we shall have to consider the meaning and distribution of the construction in Old English and the possibility of Latin influence.

In Middle English the picture is complicated by morphological changes whose end result was that present participle and verbal noun – plus an intermediate form, sometimes called a **gerund(ive)** – both had the same suffix, *-ing*. There is also the possibility of French or Celtic influence. The contribution of the prepositional construction

[2] He was on hunting.

must be assessed too. As we move towards the ModE period the **voice** of the progressive becomes an issue in the relation between 'passive' and 'active' meanings. This ties in with a topic deferred to §14.2.4.4: the use of the progressive *together with* the passive.

13.2 Progressives versus related constructions

13.2.1 VP, AP or NP?

It is frequently pointed out that two constructions can look very similar in form to a progressive. One involves the so-called **appositive** use of the present participle, as in

[3] Two students arrived later, looking rather ill.

The possibility of confusion arises when there is a BE in a neighbouring clause:

[4] Two students were there, looking rather ill.
[5] There were two students, looking rather ill.

In each of [3]–[5] the participle is verbal and head of its clause but does not form a *constituent* with another verb.

The second construction is the **adjectival** use seen in *a baffling mystery*, where the participial form is not verbal at all. However, an adjectival *-ing* form in predicative use after BE can show great formal resemblance to a progressive:

[6] This mystery is baffling.

A third source of indeterminacy, but only in Old English, is the resemblance of agent nouns (*nomina agentis*) in *-end* to present participles:

[7] (a) *Or* 137.28

  He wæs . . . ehtend   cristenra monna
  he was . . . persecutor Christian men(GEN PL)

  'He was . . . a persecutor of Christian men.'

  (b) He wæs ehtende   cristenra monna
  he was persecuting Christian men

When the verb in question governs a genitive, as does EHTAN 'persecute' in [7](b), the difference between analyses may depend solely on whether the *-end(e)* form is inflected.

Progressives are VPs whose head is a present participle modified by BE.[2] By contrast an appositive participle is head of a VP which does not contain BE, while an adjectival participle is head of an AP, and an agent noun is head of an NP. Separating 'true progressives' from these three lookalikes is not always easy, especially in early English. Many tests have been suggested, of which a selection is given below:

(A) modifiers of V*ende*/V*ing*
(B) complementation of V*ende*/V*ing*
(C) substitution for BE + V*ende*/V*ing*
(D) semantics and pragmatics
(E) inflection on V*end(e)*
(F) coordination
(G) metre

Let us take them in turn. Note the generous selection of examples in Visser's useful section on potentially indeterminate syntagms (1963–73: §§1813–15).

13.2.2 (A) Modifiers of V*ende*/V*ing*

According to Nickel (1966), modifiers like *hu* 'how', *swa* 'so', *to* 'too' indicate that an OE participle is adjectival, not verbal – but not *swiþe* 'much, very', which can modify verbs as well as adjectives. Visser adds degrees of comparison and prefixation by *un-* or *forth-*[3] to the list of adjectival criteria (1963–73: §1815(a),(f)). Some examples of adjectival participles follow:

[8]   *CP* 299.9

hu gewitende ða   ðing sint ðe hie gietsiað
how transitory those things are that they desire

[9]   a1225(?a1200) *Trin.Hom.* 125.17

his woreldes make was teames   atold. and unberinde
his world's   mate was childbearing past   and barren

'his worldly partner was barren and past childbearing age'

[10]   a1400(a1325) *Cursor* 4460

sir, we are þe droupander | For   tua sueuens we sagh in sight
sire we are the more-drooping because-of two visions we saw in sight

[11]   c1430(c1380) Chaucer, *PF* 548

Me   wolde thynke how that the worthieste |Of knyghthod . . .
me(OBL) would seem how that the worthiest of knighthood . . .

Were   sittyngest   for hire
would-be most-suitable for her

13.2.3 (B) Complementation of V*ende*/V*ing*

Constituent analysis can indicate a progressive:

[12]   *Or* 42.15

Þa   wæron simbel binnan Romebyrg wuniende
those [senators] were   always within Rome   dwelling

Example [12] cannot be appositive, argues Nickel, because WUNIAN 'dwell' is a verb which requires a locative complement: *binnan Romebyrg* therefore goes with *wuniende*, and *wæs* can only be an auxiliary (1966: 53–4). A variant of test B is to try omitting the participle:

[13]   hi wæron . . . on soþre lufe *(weallende)
they were . . . in true   love boiling

Had the syntagm remaining been self-sufficient, the participle could have been analysed as appositive. Since *weallende* is *not* omissible, it cannot be appositive. (What Nickel does not point out is that the missing portion of his extract is an AP coordinated with the participle:

[13′]   *HyGl* 2(Stevenson) 94.5

þæt hi   wæron genihtsume &   on soþre lufe weallende
that they were   contented   and in true   love boiling

See F below, §13.2.7.)

A progressive of a transitive verb should have a direct object. Mossé offers some ME and ModE examples with *to*-phrases instead (1938b: §314), and Visser has some ModE ones (1963–73: §1815(e)), while Jespersen gives some examples with zero complementation (1909–49: IV 230; quoted by Visser 1963–73: §1815). All are therefore APs:

[14]   c1400 *PPl.B* 13.16

And how louynge he is to ech   lif[*most MSS*: bestes] on londe
and   how loving   he is to each living-thing   on land

and on watre
and on water

[15]   1725 Wodrow, *Corr.*(1843) III.232 (*OED*)

It's satisfying to me to find him so warm and earnest . . .

[16]   1920 Kaye-Smith, *Green Apple Harvest* I.xxxvi.125.39

she was irritating at times

The presence of a direct object, on the other hand, suggests that a syntagm has VP status. Since this point is of particular interest when the verb form ends in *-ing*, I give a number of examples in the first century or so of the use of *-ing* as participle:

[17]   a1400(c1303) Mannyng, *HS* 5014

Ely sette   hym   at þe temple dore |yn a chayre, and was
Ely placed himself at the temple door in a chair   and was

herkenyng | Fro þe batayle sum tydyng
listening-for from the battle   some news

'Ely placed himself in a chair at the temple door and was listening for some news of the battle'

[18]   a1425(c1395) *WBible(2)* Acts Apost. 13.11

and thou schalt be blynde, and not seynge the sunne in to a tyme.
and you shall be blind   and not seeing the sun   for   a time

[19]   a1425(c1395) *WBible(2)* Luke 19.17 (sim. *Wycl.Serm.* II 78.59)

thou shalt be hauynge power on ten citees
you shall be having   power in ten cities

[20]   ?a1425(c1400) *Mandev.(1)* 122.9

all is envyronynge the roundnesse of the erthe &   of the see
all is encircling   the roundness of the earth and of the sea

[21]   ?a1425(c1400) *Mandev.(1)* 148.23

whan the enemyes weren ferr pursuynge the chace
when the enemies were far pursuing   the chase

[22]   a1425 *Wycl.Serm.* I 42.2

Þe story telluþ how Iesu was castyng owt a feend of   a man
the story tells how Jesus was casting out a devil from a man

[23]   (a1438) *MKempe* 47.15

On a   day as þis creatur was heryng hir Messe
on one day as this creature was hearing her mass

'One day when this creature was hearing her Mass'

[24]   c1454 Pecock, *Fol.* 22.12

. . . þat þo   bodies . . . schulen be distroiyng þe bodies to hem
. . . that those bodies . . . shall   be destroying the bodies to them

neiȝyng.
neighbouring

'. . . that those bodies . . . will be destructive to nearby bodies'

[25]   c1450 *Spec.Chr.(2)*(Hrl) 194.32

Beeȝ   not ȝe   ȝeldynge euyl for euyl
be(IMP PL) not you(SUBJ) returning evil for evil

'Do not do harm in return for harm.'

[26]   a1500 *Mirror Salv.* 5022

Whare I his delicable face be   euermore behaldyng;
where I his delightful face may-be evermore looking-at

[27]   (a1470) Malory, *Wks.* 100.7

. . . but allwey he woll be shotynge, or castynge dartes, and glad for to
se batayles . . .

' . . . but always he will be shooting or throwing spears and glad to see
battles . . .'

[28]   (1473) *Paston* 361.29

As I was wryghtyng þis bylle
as I was writing   this note

[29]   c1475(c1420) Page *SRouen*(Eg) 28.19

When they com unto Chartryte | The kyng hyryng masse
when they came to   the-Charterhouse[?] the king hearing mass

was he.
was he

[30]   a1475 Russell, *Bk.Nurt.*(Hrl) 301

Good soñ, þy tethe be not pikynge, grisynge, ne gnastynge;

'Good son, do not be picking your teeth, grinding them, or gnashing'

[31]   (1478) *Stonor* 229 II 69.17

. . . and he is ffast ryggynge hym þer ffore

'. . . and he is busily fitting himself out[?] for it' [antedates *OED* s.v.
rig v.[1]]

[32]   c1489 Caxton, *Blanch.* 129.12 (sim. ibid. 96.32)

The sayd kynge Alymodes is alwaye kepynge   his siege before her
the said King Alymodes is still   keeping-up his siege of   her

cyte of Tourmaday;
city of Tourmaday

[33]   a1500 *Partenay* 2917

Dolour or anguish be ye ought feling?

'Are you feeling any grief or anguish?'

[34]   a1500 *Partenay* 5528

behold what gift will be hauyng

'Look what gift will (you) be having?'

[35]   ?1514 *Let.* in Ellis *Orig.Let.ser.2* 69 1.236.14

he . . . is devysing new collers and goodly gere   for hur.
he . . . is devising new collars and fine   apparel for her

[36]   1694 *Hatton Corresp.* II 202.26

and Laws, who was making his escape in a hackney coach, was
pursued . . . and seized

also example [39] below. (Note that the continuation of Mossé's example
[27] has the participle coordinated with an AP.) A direct object is by no
means the only test of verbal status; **collocation** with certain adverbs is also
relevant, though I have not collected examples.

13.2.4 (C) Substitution

Consider the DO-clauses which follow these examples of the progressive:

[37]   *HomS* 8(*BlHom* 2) 23.8

þonne beo   we sittende be þæm wege,   swa se   blinda
then   should-be we sitting   at that way-side as   that blind-man

dyde
did

'then we should be sitting at the way-side, as that blind man did'

[38] *ÆLS* I 1.14.49

Đa gesceafta þe þæs   an scyppend gesceop synden mænig-fealde
the creatures that this[?] one creator   created are   manifold

. . . Sume syndan creopende on eorðan mid eallum lichoman, swa swa
. . . some are   crawling on earth with whole body   just as

wurmas doð. Sume gað on twam fotum . . .
worms do   some walk on two   legs . . .'

[39] ?a1425(c1400) *Mandev.(1)* 167.31

þei trowen þat after hire deth þei schull ben etynge &   drynkynge
they believe that after their death they shall be eating and drinking

in þat   oþer world & solacynge hem   with hire wifes as
in that/the other world and solacing themselves with their wives as

þei diden here.
they did   here

Example [37] has been discussed by at least two scholars. Traugott (1992:
188–9) tentatively suggests that the substitute *dyde* rather than *wæs* implies
that *beo . . . sittende* in the first clause is verbal, not adjectival – which is not
necessarily incompatible with Visser's implication that DO is used 'catachres-
tically' (i.e. wrongly) there (1963–73: §188); cf. §10.2.7.

13.2.5 (D) Semantics and pragmatics

Here we are concerned with the (rather unsafe) equations verb = action,
adjective = state. These equations are made use of, often implicitly, to
distinguish progressives from adjectival participles. Traugott (1992: 189)
suggests that an action interpretation is much more natural than a state
reading for the second *-ende* form of [40], *fremmende wæs*:

[40] *Or* 22.20

. . . hio ðyrstende wæs on symbel mannes   blodes,   ac
. . . she thirsting was in eternity man's(GEN) blood(GEN) but

eac   swelce mid ungemetlicre wrænnesse manigfeald
moreover also with immense   wantonness many-kinds-of

geligre   fremmende wæs
fornication performing was

' . . . she was continually thirsting for a man's blood but yet also was
performing many kinds of acts of illicit intercourse with immense
licentiousness'

In this instance the complementation by an object NP is decisive for interpretation as a progressive.

13.2.6 (E) Inflection

Tests E to G are weaker. Test E may help to distinguish between agent nouns and progressives. Historically the noun had NOM SG -Ø, NOM PL -Ø/-e, while the participial adjective had MASC NOM SG -e and MASC NOM PL -e, so the difference could be obliterated in the plural. Visser gives a number of examples which for him are decisively noun forms, followed by a collection of indeterminate examples (1963–73: §§1813–14). But the paradigms even got confused in the masculine singular; see Nickel (1966: 293), Mitchell (1976a: 481 and n.2; 1985: §974) and references.

13.2.7 (F) Coordination

This test relies on examples like:

[41]   *Bede* 4 7.280.25

se wæs timbrend &   abbud þæs mynstres
he was builder   and abbot the abbey(GEN)

[42]   *BlHom* 65.15

þæt wuldor þysses middangeardes is sceort &   gewitende
the glory   this   earth(GEN)   is brief and transitory

'The glory of this earth is short and transitory'

where a participle is coordinated with a noun or adjective. To their credit Nickel (1966: 51) and Visser (1963–73: §1815(d)) point out the unreliability of coordinations of adjective and participle as a test even in Present-day English:

[43]   One man was unconscious and groaning.

(See also Warner 1985:20.) Consider also these ModE examples, though it is arguable that they predate the grammaticisation of the progressive (§14.3.7 below):

[44]   1816 Austen, *Mansfield Park* III.xvii[xlviii].462.6

She was humble and wishing to be forgiven

[45]   1816 Austen, *Mansfield Park* III.xvii[xlviii].462.25

He became what he ought to be, useful to his father, steady and quiet, and not living merely for himself.

For Old English Nickel cites

[46]   *Or* 62.29

þæt ealle godas him   irre   wæren &   wiðwinnende
that all   gods him(DAT) angry were   and opposing

'that all gods were angry and contending with him'

apparently wishing to take *wiðwinnende* as verbal despite its coordination with an adjective. The converse is the coordination – in [47] **asyndetic** (without conjunction) – of a progressive and a finite verb:

[47] *Beo* 159

> ac se æglæca ehtende   wæs, | deorc deaþscua,   duguþe
> but the monster persecuting was   dark death-shadow old-retainers
>
> ond geogoþe, | seomade ond syrede
> and young-retainers remained and conspired

> 'Rather the monster, dark death-shadow, pursued warriors experienced and young, hovered in ambush'

There are also elliptical examples like the following, where the *-ing* form can be inferred:

[48] 1667 Pepys, *Diary* VIII 104.29 (9 Mar)

> for I perceive by his threats and inquiries he is and will endeavour to find out something against me or mine.

13.2.8 (G) Metre

For test G Nickel offers (1966: 54):

[49] *ChristA, B, C* 236

> Sylfa   sette   þæt þu sunu wære | efeneardigende   mid þinne
> self(NOM) ordained that you son   were   together-dwelling with your
>
> engan frean
> sole lord

> 'He Himself ordained that you should be the Son, dwelling together with your sole Lord.'

suggesting that *efeneardigende* is likely to be appositive, since he finds it rhythmically unnatural to read *wære efeneardigende* as a syntagm separated by enjambement.

In Middle English Mossé (1938b: §81) gives examples like:

[50] c1400(?c1390) *Gawain* 1894

> 3et is þe lorde on þe launde   ledande his gomnes.
> still is the lord in the countryside pursuing his games

> 'The lord is still out in the fields pursuing his sport.'

[51] c1400 *PPl.B* 5.130

> Amonges Burgeises haue I be,   biggyng [*many MSS*: dwellyng] at
> among   citizens   have I been living   in
>
> Londoun
> London

suggesting that the caesura falls just before the participle, making them appositive – but that in [51] there would be an easy transition to the progressive if the caesura was suppressed.

13.3   The data

13.3.1   BE + V*ende*/V*ing*

13.3.1.1   Old English

In Old English the progressive is unevenly distributed, its overall frequency low but in certain texts (notably *Orosius*) remarkably high. Here is a cross-section of prose examples, including some which are syntactically ambiguous in the ways discussed in §13.2:

[52]   *ChronA* 66.8 (855)

& þy ilcan geare ferde   to Rome mid micelre weorþnesse, &
and that same year travelled to Rome with great   honour   and

þær was .xii. monaþ wuniende
there was 12   months dwelling

'and that same year he travelled to Rome with great honour and stayed there for twelve months'

[53]   *CP* 58.5

. . . ðæs modes storm, se   symle   bið cnyssende ðæt scip
. . . the mind's storm which continually is battering the ship (of)

ðære heortan mid ðara geðohta ystum
the   heart   with the thoughts' tempests

[54]   *Bo* 93.6

Swa eac ure gast bið swiðe wide   farende urum
so   also our spirit is very widely travelling our

unwillum . . .
unwillingness (DAT PL) . . .

'So also our spirit travels very widely against our will . . .'

[55]   *Or* 36.1

hit God siþþan   longsumlice   wrecende wæs, ærest on him
it God afterwards for-a-long-time avenging was first on him

selfum   & siþþan   on his bearnum . . .
himself [Adam] and subsequently on his children . . .

'God avenged it for a long time afterwards, first on him himself and subsequently on his children . . .'

[56]   *Or* 100.20

þætte se consul wæs wenende þæt eall þæt folc   wære gind
so-that the consul was thinking that all the army was throughout

þæt lond   tobræd,   &   þiderweard farende wæs . . .
the country scattered and to-there   going   was . . .

'so that the consul assumed wrongly that the army was all scattered
throughout the country, and he was heading there . . .'

[57]   *Or* 123.2

Hit wæs þa   swiþe   oþþyncende þam oþrum consulum
it   was then very/greatly displeasing the other consuls(DAT)

'Then it displeased the other consuls greatly'

[58]   *LawAfEl* 1.0 26

DRIHTEN WÆS SPRECENde ðas   word to Moyse &   þus cwæð
God   was   speaking   these words to Moses and thus said

[59]   *HomU* 34(Nap 42) 25.15

eall middangeard bið þonne on dæg byrnende
all   middle-earth is   then   by day burning

'the whole earth will then be burning by day'

The progressive is relatively infrequent in poetry, on Nickel's figures 0.07
per cent of finite verbs (1966: 92):

[60]   *Beo* 3028

Swa se   secg hwata secggende wæs | laðra   spella;   he ne leag
thus the man brave saying   was   hateful stories(GEN) he not lied

fela | wyrda   ne worda.
much fates(GEN) or words(GEN PL)

'Thus the brave youth was a teller of grievous tales; nor was he much
amiss in facts or words.'

[61]   *And* 947

Him   sceal bot   hraðe | weorþan in worulde ond in wuldre
him(DAT) shall relief quickly happen in world   and in glory

lean, | swa ic him sylfum ær   secgende wæs.
recompense as I him self   earlier saying   was

'Relief in this world and recompense in glory will come to him quickly,
as I had told him previously'

Visser notes that the (uninverted) progressive 'does not easily fit into the
alliterative line' (1963–73: §1853).
   There is disagreement among modern scholars as to the precise
function(s) and meaning(s) of the OE progressive. Some examples
correspond well to modern usage, but often the progressive is used in Old
English where it could not now be used, and conversely; see for example
Mitchell (1976a). The writers discussed in §13.4 provide between them
numerous examples. Wülfing too has some examples from Alfredian prose
(1894–1901: §§398–402).

The progressive was often used in Old English to translate perfect (i.e. past) **deponent**[4] verbs in Latin texts (Wülfing 1894–1901: §399, etc):

[62] *Bede* 1 4.32.7

and hraðe þa   gefremednesse ðære arfæstan bene   wæs
and quickly then/the fulfilment   the   pious   prayer(GEN) was

fylgende
following

Lat. . . . consecutus est . . .

'and fulfilment of the pious prayer followed rapidly'

This has often been taken as evidence that the progressive was a Latin-influenced construction. Jespersen makes the plausible suggestion, however, that 'the translator wanted to render a Latin expression consisting of two words (an auxiliary and a verbal form) by means of a similar collocation' (1909–49: IV 166), and Visser adds that it 'happened strikingly frequently in interlinear versions where the glossator had two spaces to fill up underneath the Latin two-word cluster' (1963–73: §1854). For statistics which show that the progressive was much more frequent in translating a periphrastic form of a deponent verb in *Mt* than a simple form see Ide (1984: 60). A similar usage of the progressive was as a translation equivalent of the Latin ESSE + future participle.

13.3.1.2 Middle and Modern English

Here are some ME examples of the progressive:

[63] a1225(?a1200) Lay.*Brut* 3782

þat heo wolden . . . | faren into Flandre. and beo þer wuniende; |
that they would . . . go   into Flanders and be   there dwelling

a þat he iseȝen his time. þat he   mihten æft cumen liðen
until he saw   his time that they might back come   travel

'that they would . . . go to Flanders and stay there until he saw the right time for them to come back'

[64] a1450(?c1343) Rolle, *EDormio* (Cmb) 62.44

For if þow stabil   þi   lufe, and be byrnande whils þou lyfes
for if you establish-firmly your love and be burning   while you live

here
here

[65] c1425 *Glo.Chron.A* (Hrl) I 142.15 (= Clg. 2999)

þo   Octa hit onderstod, þat heo comyng were
when Octa it understood that they coming were

'when Octa learned that they were coming'

[66] a1425(c1395) *WBible(2)* Luke 19.47

And he was techynge euerydai in the temple.

Mustanoja has a survey of the ME dialectal distribution of the progressive (1960: 585–6). He suggests that it was not common in the early part of the period except in the north, in Kent, and in Worcestershire. By the fourteenth century it had become current in the central and east midlands and in London, and during the fifteenth century it reached the remaining parts of the country.

13.3.1.3 The paradigm of progressive BE

The paradigm of progressive BEON/WESAN was limited in Old English. Present and past tense forms were both possible, as well as infinitives after the modals SCEAL (commonest), WILL and MÆG – see Visser (1963–73: §2143), Mitchell (1985: §683):

[67] *ByrM* 242.28

> . . . he sceal beon cwylmigende mid deofle aa   butan ende
> . . . he shall be suffering   with devil always without end

> '. . . he shall be tortured along with the devil for ever and ever'

(Further examples are given in Wülfing 1894–1901: §401.) In close translations from Latin an infinitive of the progressive was possible in the VOSI construction:

[68] *Bede* 5 8.406.21

> Ðone seolfan riim   wintra   hiene   hæbbende beon,
> that very   number winters(GEN PL) him(ACC) having   be(INF)

> he oft   ær   his monnum   foresægde . . .
> he often earlier his men(DAT PL) predicted . . .

> Lat. quem se numerum annorum fuissse habiturum . . . suis praedicere solebat

> 'He had often predicted to his men that he would attain that very age . . . .'

[69] *Bede* 3 11.190.30

> oðþo ne getreowe   me   onfoende beon
> or   not believe(1 SG) me(ACC) receiving be(INF)

> Lat. me accepturum esse confidam

> 'nor do I trust to receive it [*sc.* a respite to live]'

The progressive did not combine with the perfect or the passive in Old English (Mitchell 1985: §684). There was an imperative:

[70] *Mt(WSCp)* 5.25

> Beo þu onbugende þinum wiðerwinnan   hraðe
> be you submitting your adversary(DAT) quickly

> Lat. esto protinus consentiens aduersario tuo

> 'Agree with your adversary quickly'

See Mossé (1938a: §248), Mitchell (1985: §§683, 881).

The paradigm showed some expansion in Middle English. From fairly early in the period the *to*-infinitive of progressive BE began to occur sporadically:

[71]   c1230(?a1200) *Ancr.* 39b.3

EAhte þinges nomeliche   leaðieð
eight   things in-particular/especially urge

us to wakien   . . . &   beo wurchinde.
us to be-watchful. . . and be   working

'Eight things in particular urge us to be watchful . . . and working.'

Mustanoja implies that the plain infinitive found in northern texts after modals like SHALL and WILL was a ME innovation (1960: 591), but in fact there are OE examples such as [67] above. Here is a ME example:

[72]   a1425(c1395) *WBible(2)* Luke 17.35

twei wymmen schulen be gryndynge togidir
two women   shall   be grinding   together

Lat. Duæ erunt molentes in unum

Example [19] is another. As a first example of plain infinitive after LETEN he cites

[73]   a1425(c1385) Chaucer, *TC* 3.1139

lat now no hevy thought | Ben hangyng in the hertes of yow tweye

'Don't allow any heavy thought now to be hanging over you two.'

A perfect of progressive BE is first recorded in Middle English:

[74]   a1400(a1325) *Cursor* 26292

if þi   parischen | In sin lang has ligand bene
if your parishioner in sin long has lying   been

'if your parishioner has long been lying in sin'

See Mossé (1938b: §§216–30), Mustanoja (1960: 590–2), corrected and supplemented by Visser (1963–73: §§2143–8). Within a short time the sequence modal + perfect + progressive turns up, though I have only one ME example (from Visser 1946–56: §712):

[75]   ?a1425 *Mandev.(2)*(Eg) 5.15

for þai   trowed   þat he schuld hafe bene hingand apon þat crosse
for they believed that he should have been hanging on   that cross

as lang as þat crosse myght last.
as long as that cross   might last

[76]   1722 Defoe, *Plague* (1756) 186 (*OED* s.v. *have* v. B.26)

Multitudes . . . wou'd ha' been continually running up and down the Streets.

On the 'double progressive' *being doing* see §13.3.8.1 below.

13.3.2   WEORÐAN + V*ende*

In Old English the verb WEORÐAN 'become' shows a limited ability to
commute with WESAN/BEON in this as in other constructions (cf. §§12.4.2
above, 14.2.2.2 below). Some examples:

[77]   *CP* 413.21

Ðinra synna   ne weorð ic gemunende, ac gemun   ðu
your   sins(GEN PL) not become I remembering but remember you

hiora.
them(GEN)

Lat. peccatorum tuorum memor non ero, tu autem memor esto

'I will not remember thy sins, but do thou remember them.'

[78]   *ÆCHom* I 26.374.5

Petrus wearð   æfterweard þus cweðende . . .
Peter became afterwards thus saying . . .

'Afterwards Peter spoke thus . . .'

There is brief mention in Wülfing (1894–1902: §402), Mossé (1938a:
§§263–6), Visser (1963–73: §§ 1798–9), Mitchell (1985: §683). Visser attaches
great importance to it, but Mitchell is dismissive: not only is the construction
even less clearly verbal than WESAN/BEON + *-ende*, but it is rare. Mossé's
figures (1938a: §263) imply that WESAN/BEON + present participle – itself
not all that frequent – is maybe a hundredfold commoner. Traugott suggests
that the infrequency of WEORÐAN as auxiliary of the progressive was
because its association with inception and change was inappropriate to
simultaneous action (1972: 90).

13.3.3   Other verbs + V*ende*/V*ing*

Many verbs other than BE and WEORÐAN have been collocated with an
-ing form. The collocations which come closest to the progressive are those
involving intransitive verbs. In Old English the usage is common with
intransitive verbs of movement and the SIT/LIE/STAND group:

[79]   *ÆCHom* II 2.15.124

þa earman bearn   . . . ferdon worigende
the poor   children . . . went   wandering

[80]   *BlHom* 17.30

Rihtlic þæt wæs þæt se blinda   be ðæm wege sæte wædliende
right   it was that the blind-man by the   way sat begging

'It was right that the blind man should have sat begging at the
roadside.'

See Mossé (1938a: §§267–75), Visser (1963–73: §§1793–5). For other verbs which Visser considers to show 'slight subordination' relative to the *-ing* verb see his (1963–73: §§1790–2, 1796):

[81] Hawthorne *Fr. & It. Jrnls.* I.124 (*OED*)

Niagara . . . keeps pouring on forever and ever.

Another pattern which is sometimes brought into consideration in the history of the progressive is the use of *-ing* forms in collocation with transitive verbs of perception or (rarer) causation:

[82] *Bo* 22.31

mænegum men   is leofre   þæt he ær   self
many   man(DAT SG) is preferable that he earlier himself

swelte   ær   he gesio his wif and his bearn   sweltende
die(SUBJ) before he see   his wife and his child(ren) dying

'many a man would prefer to die himself rather than see his wife and child(ren) dying'

[83] *Mart* 5 196.8

Þær   hy   gedydon þæt cild sprecende þæt ne was anre niht
there/where they had   the child speaking that not was one night
eald.
old

'There they made the child speak that was but one day old.'

[84] (a1393) Gower, *CA* 3.1468

This Piramus, which hiere I se |Bledende, what hath he deserved?
this Piramus whom here I see bleeding   what has   he deserved

'This Piramus, whom I see bleeding here, what has he done to deserve this?'

[85] c1522 More, *Wks.* I [99 B13]

[glotony] disfigureth the face, . . . it maketh . . . the nose droppyng, the mouth spetting, . . . the breth stinkyng, the hands trimbling, the hed hanging, and the feete totteryng

For further examples see Visser (1963–73: §§2084–5).

13.3.4 Present participle and verbal noun

In Modern English the same ending, *-ing*, is used both for the verb form which appears in the progressive and for a certain kind of abstract nominalisation, as in *the writing of books*. (The nominalisation may undergo semantic change towards a concrete meaning: *the binding (of the book)*.) Some grammarians use the term **gerund** or **gerundive** for certain partially verb-like uses of the nominalisation, as in

[86] Bill's carelessly throwing stones over the wall was bound to cause trouble.

Others give one of those labels to the *to*-infinitive, while others avoid the terms altogether.

The history of the forms is complex. In Old English the form of the present participle was V*ende*, with adjectival inflection. The verbal noun was formed with *-ung* or *-ing* and was clearly distinct. In the course of the ME period both forms underwent changes, the upshot of which was the modern coalescence. There are full expositions of the phonological, morphological and syntactic details in Mossé (1938b: §§129–75) and Visser (1963–73: §§1001–38). The *MED* prints a simple map showing a ME *isogloss* between *-ing* and *-nd* present participle endings ('Plan and Bibliography', p. 9, map 4), and far more detailed dot maps (numbers 345–51) and item maps (number 57) can be found in McIntosh et al. (1986: I 391–2, II 237–42).

13.3.5   BE + preposition + V*ing*

There are constructions with a preposition before an *-ing/-ung* form which are similar to the progressive in form and function. I give a few examples below; for fuller lists see Mossé (1938b: §§178–91), Visser (1963–73: §§1865–71). (Occasionally an *-ende* form – more typical of present participles – appears instead of the expected\verbal noun.)

13.3.5.1   Old English

The construction is not particularly common in Old English, to the extent that Åkerlund (1914: 323 n.4) suspected that it was a merely conjectural 'ghost-phrase'. But there *are* examples, usually with the preposition *on*:

[87]   *ÆColl* 68

ac gyrstandæg ic wæs on huntunge.
but yesterday   I was at hunting

[88]   *ByrM* 138.18

& na þænne his leoht beo ærest on weaxunge . . ., ac þonne he beo full

'and not when its [*sc.* the moon's] light has first begun to increase . . ., but when it is full'

Visser finds one example each with *an* and *in*.

13.3.5.2   Middle English

Examples with *on* are surprisingly rare, except in the idiom BE *on hunting* and similar expressions, while *an* and *a* are rare too before the end of the period. *At* is used sometimes – note that Visser's example [90] of *at* V*ing*, *at wenynge* 'in expectation'[?], is interpreted by Morris as an error for *a-*V*ing*, *a twenynge* 'in doubt' – but it is the preposition *in* which is dominant in Middle English:

[89]   a1325(c1250) *Gen. & Ex.* 2908

ðog woren he   get in strong murning
yet were   they still in deep   mourning

[90]   a1300 *I-hereþ ny one*(Jes-O) 595

heo . . . weren at wenynge. | Of vre louerdes aryste.
they . . . were   in expectation/in doubt of our Lord's   resurrection

[91]   c1450(?a1400) *Destr.Troy* 11735

While this gode   was in gederyng   the grettes   among, |
while this wealth was in gathering   the persons-of-rank among

Antenor to the temple trayturly   yode.
Antenor to the temple treacherously   went

'While this wealth was being collected among the nobility, Antenor treacherously went to the temple.'

[92]   (a1470) Malory, *Wks.* 80.26

and there mette with a knyght that had bene an-hontynge [*Caxton*: on huntynge].
and there met   with a knight who had been a-hunting

Visser speculates that the *in* type may have spread under the influence of the French pattern *en chantant* 'in/while singing' (1963–73: §1859).

13.3.5.3   Modern English

Several of the constructions continued into the ModE period. Of those still in use today, some are dialectally restricted (*What've you been a-doing?*), others no longer productive (BE *in hiding*).

13.3.6   V*ing* + *of* + NP

Visser records instances from late Middle English where the *-ing* form of a transitive verb is followed by an *of*-phrase (1963–73: §§1869–71):

[93]   (c1396) *Doc.* in *Bk.Lond.E.* 234.19

þe ȝomen of Schordych, þat þere were in amendyng of here
the yeomen of Shoreditch that there were in repairing   of their

berseles
archery-butts

'the yeomen of Shoreditch who were repairing their archery targets there'

[94]   a1400 *Wycl.MPl.* 45.35

thanne thei ben not scornynge of God but worschipyng.
then   they are not scorning of God but worshipping

[95]   (1482) *Let.Cely* 148.9

Now whyll I am a whryttyng of thys letter, Wylliam Mydwyttyrs mane
now while I am a-writing   of this letter William Midwinter's man

ys com to fet   mony
has come to collect money

I have given the earliest valid instances from his three sets of examples: with *in* before the -*ing*, with no preposition, and with *a*-, respectively.

13.3.7   Passival BE + V*ing* (= 'with passive sense')

Until the progressive passive

[96]   The house is being built.

entered the language in the late ModE period (on which see §14.2.4.4 below), it was necessary either to do without explicit progressive marking, as in [97] and the last clause of [98]:

[97]   1662 Pepys, *Diary* III 51.25 (24 Mar)

I went to see if any play was acted[5]

[98]   1838–9 Dickens, *Nickleby* v.52.14

he found that the coach had sunk greatly on one side, though it was still dragged forward by the horses;

or to do without explicit passive marking, as in the curious construction of [99]:

[99]   The house is building.

This is not formally a passive (there is no BE + past participle), but the subject NP is the argument which would be subject in a true passive and object in a normal active, which is why Strang (1982: 441) calls [99] a 'covert passive' and Visser calls it **passival**[6] (1963–73: §§1872–81). Passival [99] seems to have fulfilled the function of the missing [96].

13.3.7.1   Old and Middle English

Visser discusses in detail a number of possible OE and ME examples of passival progressives and accepts that early ones are doubtful (1963–73: §§1875–7). Raith (1951: 100–1) and more firmly Mitchell (1976b) reject all OE examples. The only ones worth considering are [100] and several of the type represented by [101]:

[100]   *LS* 23(MaryofEgypt) 109

Nu ic wille æfter þysum areccan hu   þæs mynstres gesetnysse
now I wish after this   tell   how that minster's ordinance(ACC)

healdende wæs
keeping   was

'Now I wish to tell after this how that minster's ordinance was held.'

[101]   *PsGlA* 118.52

& frofrende ic   eam
and comforting I(NOM) am

Lat. et consolatus sum

'and.I am comforted'

For [100] Mitchell postulates either the loss of *man* 'one' after *hu* or – if the final *-e* can be explained away and *gesetnysse* taken as nominative – the attested intransitive HEALDAN 'continue' (an **ergative** use of the verb, on which see also §13.3.7.3 below). For [101] and the like Visser suggests that a Latin passive has been mistaken for a deponent, and Mitchell points out that other OE Psalters have a true passive here. The rest seem to be isolated oddities or scribal errors, or to involve ergative uses of a verb.

Many of the eME examples involve the *-ing* form of verbs like WANT 'lack' which may well have had intransitive ergative uses, or forms like *vntelland* 'uncountable' which do not correspond to a verb *UNTELL. Some of the more convincing of Visser's ME examples are the following:[7]

[102]   a1400(a1325) *Cursor* 26812

Þat þere er dedis doand neu, | Þat þai agh   sare   wit resun
that there are deeds doing anew that they ought sorely with reason

reu.
rue

'that deeds are being done there again that they ought with reason to regret grievously'

[103]   a1500(a1450) *Gener.(2)* 5486

hym   thought som   tresone was ymagenyng
him(OBL) thought some treason was being-dreamt-up

[104]   a1500 *Partenay* 417

I beleue noght that terrene boody . . . | Of lusty   beute
I believe not   that earthly body . . . of attractive beauty

may haue such richesse, | So moche of swetnesse, so moche of
may   such riches   so much of sweetness so much of

connyng | As in your gentil body is beryng.
wisdom/erudition as in your noble body is being-carried

13.3.7.2 Modern English

More of the ModE examples of passival progressives in Visser (1963–73: §1878) are satisfactory, but there remains the problem that most of the verbs represented – OPEN (of doors), FILL *up* (of a room), SELL (of books), SHOW (of origins), etc. – have ergative uses which are not confined to the progressive, so that the boundaries between this 'passival' construction of a transitive verb and an ergative use of the same verb are blurred. (Some of the others could be adjectival.) In any event the 'passival' active is always used with an inanimate subject, or at least one that could not be mistaken as Agentive. Here are some strong examples containing verbs which do not as far as I know have an ergative use in non-progressive forms in Present-day English at least:

[105]   1660 Pepys, *Diary* I 113.26 (22 Apr)

Also, they told us for certain that the King's statue is making by the

Mercers Company (who are bound to do it) to set up in the Exchange.

[106] 1684 Bunyan, *Pilgrim's Progress* 259.22

and while Supper is making ready . . .

[107] 1759–67 Sterne, *Tristram Shandy* IV.0.199.1

At the very time that this dispute was maintaining by the centinel and the drummer – was the same point debating betwixt a trumpeter and a trumpeter's wife

[108] 1763 Woodforde, *Diary* I 25.6 (23 May)

. . . before whom I was examined for deacon's Orders, ... I was quite half an hour examining.

[109] 1784 Woodforde, *Diary* II 118.3 (8 Feb)

Whilst the Anthem was singing I was conducted by the Virger to the Pulpit . . .

[110] 1842 Dickens, *American Notes* vii.99.12

so that like many other great undertakings in America, even this is rather going to be done one of these days, than doing now.

[111] 1854 J. S. C. Abbott, *Napoleon* (1855) I.xxxvii.577 (*OED*)

A code is preparing for the regulation of commerce.

[112] 1900 Conrad, *Lord Jim* xliii.349.2

his canoe, which was towing behind the long-boat.

[113] 1957 Parkinson, *Law* vi.61.20

Bramante's palace was still building until 1565, the great church not consecrated until 1626, . . .

[114] 1983 *The Guardian* 22 Mar p.19

Inside the . . . room more than a dozen television cameras were setting up on an elevated stand to the left of the chamber.

Example [110] is interesting in its toleration of *is going to be done* before the apparent avoidance of *is . . . being done*. Note also [140]–[143] below.

Visser suggests that the retreat of this construction in the face of the advancing progressive passive did not begin until the twentieth century, which is likely enough in view of the slow spread of the progressive passive in the nineteenth.

13.3.7.3 Related constructions

Several other constructions also have an underlying object appearing as subject. I shall discuss them in turn.

The prepositional type could always be passival:

[115] The house is on building/a-building/in building.

It is very tempting to see the contribution of the [115] patterns as even more crucial to the passival than the prepositional [2] patterns were to other progressives, cf. the parallel or conjoined constructions in [116]–[117]:

[116]   1660 Pepys, *Diary* I 199.5 (13 Jul)

and while it was doing in one room, I was forced to keep Sir G. Carteret . . . in talk while it was a-doing.

[117]   1661 Pepys, *Diary* II 70.1 (10 April)

Then to Rochester and there saw the Cathedrall, which is now fitting for use, and the Organ then a-tuning.

See further §13.6 below. The type [115] with preposition has effectively died out of productive syntax, so that a sentence like

[118]   The athletes were in training.

is no longer perceived as related to an active syntagm *train the athletes*.

There was also support for [99] from ergative verbs which corresponded to homophonous transitive verbs. There are many such pairs, e.g. BREAK used with the thing broken either as subject (ergative) or as object (transitive). I give two eModE illustrations which juxtapose both members of such a pair. Example [119] has transitive WEAR in the first clause and ergative WEAR (no longer possible) in the last, while [120] has ergative LOCK (×2), CLOSE and OPEN as well as transitive CLOSE:

[119]   1623(1602–3) Shakespeare, *AWW* I.i.156

Virginitie like an olde Courtier, weares her cap out of fashion, richly suted, but vnsuteable, iust like the brooch & the toothpick, which were ['wear', i.e. 'are worn'] not now:

[120]   1590–96 Spenser, *FQ* 2.ix.23.6

Doubly disparted, it [*sc.* a gate] did locke and close, | That when it locked, none might thorough pas, | And when it opened, no man might it close

Furthermore, as Strang observes, there would be no ambiguity in the use of the passival BE + *-ing* at a time when the ordinary progressive virtually required a human subject (1982: 443). On the relationship between passivals and ergatives in Present-day English see §13.3.7.4 below.

As for the **medio-passive** [121], which can be regarded as a special case of ergative use:

[121]   These houses sell very well.

this resembles the passival in requiring its subject NP to be non-agentive, but differs from it in perhaps implying that the subject makes a major contribution to the course or outcome of the action (Kilby 1984: 46), in the virtual requirement for certain manner adverbials, and of course in normally occurring in the *non*-progressive. The examples in Visser which seem to correspond to the medio-passive (1963–73: §§168–9) include only three prior to 1600 – most are nineteenth and twentieth century – so that the medio-passive is unlikely to have fostered the passival progressive; thus also Mossé (1938b: §247). However, Lightfoot calls the medio-passive 'very productive' in early Modern English (1979: 28 n.1) and refers to Jespersen (1909–49: III 347–52).

13.3.7.4* Passival ~ ergative

In Present-day English the relationship between ergative and passival usages is a complex one. Arguably the passival construction is obsolete, or at least no longer productive:

[122] ?*A very strange house is building on Cross Street.

though, cf. the recent examples [113]–[114]. Incidentally, one reason that BUILD is so often chosen to illustrate the passival in earlier stages of Modern English, apart from its commonness in genuine attestations, is that BUILD (at least of houses) is one verb that is not normally used ergatively, so that

[123] *The house built/didn't build last year.
[124] *The house has built recently.

do not occur.
   However, if [122] is bad, other examples seem much better:

[125] The movie is filming in Vancouver.

(example due to Laurel Brinton, p.c. 6 June 1990). Given the awkwardness of

[126] *The movie filmed last year.
[127] *The movie has filmed recently.

which imply that FILM does not have an ergative use, [125] looks as if it is passival and that the construction therefore has at least limited productivity.
   I would suggest that most commonly-used passival sentences are gradually being interpreted as ergatives. The originally passival

[128] Supper's cooking.

is probably now perceived as an ergative (cf. [119]–[120]), given that [129] is possible:

[129] (Jim laid the table) while the beans cooked quietly in the oven.

However, the progressive remains more common than the non-progressive. Boundaries are fluid, and a prototype analysis is appealing here. In my conception of syntax there is no need to assume unique, black-and-white analyses everywhere. A recently dominant but now less salient analysis can still play a part in the behaviour of a construction, and not only in non-productive relics. The example of [128] seems to me a case in point. The earlier, passival analysis still affects the distribution of what is now (mostly) an ergative sentence.

13.3.8 Special cases of BE + V*ing*

I shall mention just two. A third special case, BE *going to*, the progressive of GO used as a semi-auxiliary of the future, receives a lot of attention in the handbooks but will not be considered further here.

13.3.8.1 *Being* + *Ving*

The syntagm *being* + *Ving* should occur when a finite progressive is turned into a gerundial or present participial construction, as in:

[130]   1660 Pepys, *Diary* I 302.21 (26 Nov)

     . . . I being now making my new door into the entry, . . .

[131]   1661 Pepys, *Diary* II 129.1 (30 June)

     . . . he being now going to end all with the Queene . . .

[132]   a1781 Watson, *Philip III* III.(1793) I.273 (*OED*[2] s.v. *rest* v[2] 1a)

     Considerable arrears being now resting to the soldiers.

[133]   1790 Woodforde, *Diary* III 218.4 (28 Sep) (sim. ibid. 1785 II 202.10 (25 Jul))

     Nancy did not make her Appearance being dressing.

[134]   1796 Woodforde, *Diary* IV 275.20 (6 May) (*being going* also ibid. 1785 II 221.1 (19 Dec); 1791 III 315.13 (5 Dec); 1793 IV 39.22 (28 Jun), 1794 IV 112.32 (31 May))

     Gave my Boy, Tim Tooley, being going to Norwich to Morrow to get some Cloaths 0. 5. 0. [5 shillings]

[135]   1816 Austen, *Emma* I.xviii.145.1

     . . . and exclaimed quite as much as was necessary, (or, being acting a part, perhaps rather more,) at the conduct of the Churchills

The *being* + *Ving* pattern had some currency at least from the mid-sixteenth century to the early nineteenth. Modern grammars claim it to be impossible in Present-day English.[8] The gap is an odd one. Consider the following pairs, where a finite clause in the (a) sentence is turned into a non-finite clause in (b) by altering the first verb to an *-ing*:

[136]   (a)   Jim teaches/taught five new courses.
        (b)   Teaching five new courses makes it easier.
[137]   (a)   Jim has/had taught these courses before.
        (b)   Having taught these courses before makes it easier.
[138]   (a)   Jim has/had been teaching these courses for some time.
        (b)   Having been teaching these courses for some time makes it easier.
[139]   (a)   Jim is/was teaching five new courses.
        (b)   *Being teaching five new courses makes it easier.

There is now a systemic gap at [139](b), a gap, furthermore, which has actually opened up where previously the paradigm was complete.[9]

   There are some glorious examples which combine *being* + *Ving* with passival usage, some of them scattered in the handbooks (*OED* s.v. *be* v. B.15b; Mossé 1938b: §§227, 237; Visser 1963–73: §§1834 n., 1878, 1879; *being committing* in c1680 Lady Fanshawe *Memoirs* appears to be a false reading):

[140] 1676 Prideaux, *Letters* 50.4

a great deal of mony beeing now expendeing on S^t. Mary's . . .

[141] 1685 R. Burton, *Eng. Emp. Amer.* ii 28 (*OED*)

Strong preparations being making for wars.

[142] 1751 Harris, *Hermes* 1.viii.155n.

But those things which, being not now doing, or having not yet been done, have a natural aptitude to exist hereafter, may be properly said to appertain to THE FUTURE.

[143] 1774 Woodforde, *Diary* I 125.12 (13 Mar)

I talked with him pretty home ['directly'] about matters being so long doing –.

13.3.8.2 Progressive of BE

The construction BE + *being* is interesting for the light it throws on the relation between the progressive and stative verbs – here the archetypal stative verb, BE itself. It may also be relevant to the history of the progressive passive, a syntagm which begins with an identical sequence of verb forms (§§14.3.4, 14.3.7.1 below).

WESAN is mentioned casually in a list in Nickel (1966: 200) as occurring once in Wulfstan in the progressive. The example, traced via Venezky and Healey (1980) is:

[144] *HomS* 8(*BlHom* 2) 19.25

He bið a   wesende, &   æghwær   ondweard, &   ælce
he is always being   and everywhere present   and each

stowe   he gefylþ &   ufan   oferwryhþ, &   a   biþ
place(ACC) he fills   and from-above covers   and always is

ece.
eternally

'He always exists, and is present everywhere, and he fills and covers each place, and always is eternally.'

It is doubtful how far this use of *wesende* is verbal. (A similar theological usage is cited by *OED*^{2} for 1656 s.v. *intemporally* adv.)

For later periods Visser has the details in his (1963–73: §§1834–5). He gives two examples of BE + *being* + AP from one fifteenth-century text and a dubious example – [147], more likely appositive – from another. After that there are none quoted till the late eighteenth century:

[145] a1500 *Partenay* 5393

With tendre youth was he hote being
with tender youth was he hot being

'he was hot with the tenderness of youth'

[146] a1500 *Partenay* 6248

. . . Sche vnto the pore ful gret good doing; | So gentile, suete,
. . . she unto the poor full great good doing   so noble   sweet

fre   in hert   was being;
generous in heart was being

'. . . she, doing very great good for the poor, was being so noble,
sweet, generous at heart'

[147]   c1490 *Lancelot of the Laik* 57

Thar was the flour, thar was the quen   alphest, | Rycht wering
there was the flower there was the queen Alceste   right weary(?)

being of the nychtis rest
being of the night's rest

'There was the flower, there was Queen Alceste, very weary from the
night's rest.'

[148]   1761 Johnston, *Chrysal* II 1.x.65.32

but this is being wicked, for wickedness sake.

Even then, Visser (likewise Mossé 1938b: §266) ignores the fact that [148]
and examples from Fanny Burney and Jane Austen over the next sixty
years[10] do not appear to contain a progressive verbal group *is being* at all:
rather the verb is just equative *is*, which links an inanimate pronoun subject
(*it, this, there*) to a gerundial phrase *being* AP. The surface subject is not an
argument of the AP. The pattern may have helped prepare the ground for
the introduction of a progressive of BE, but it is difficult to think of a
sentence like [148] which could actually have been reanalysed as a true
progressive, since the function of the subject NP would have to change so
radically. The first modern-looking example in Visser's collection is
Jespersen's first (1909–49: IV 225):

[149]   1819 Keats, *Letters* 137 357.4 (11 Jul)

You will be glad to hear . . . how diligent I have been, and am being.

Here *I* is underlyingly an argument of *being diligent*. Visser explicitly – but,
I would say, wrongly – accuses Jespersen of getting the date of introduction
too late (1963–73: 2426 n.1).

   For examples with NP rather than AP as complement, the one late-
seventeenth-century example, [150], is better analysed as a *non*-progressive,
just like [148]. For good examples we must wait until late in the nineteenth:

[150]   1697 Vanbrugh, *Provok'd Wife* III.i.198

That's being a spunger, sir, which is scarce honest:

[151]   1871 Meredith, *Harry Richmond* xxx.323.5

One who studies is not being a fool:

Note also this apparent example with PP as adjunct or complement:

[152]   c1515 Rastell, *Interlude* 376

Yet the eclyps generally is alwaye | In the hole worlde as [*sc.* at] one
tyme beynge;

13.4 Explanations of the origins of the OE progressive

All workers acknowledge the influence of Latin on the OE progressive. Some take Latin influence as central (Mossé, Raith), while others regard Latin as a secondary influence in translated texts on what was essentially a native development (Nickel, Visser, Scheffer, Mitchell). Scheler sits on the fence.

13.4.1 Mitchell

Bruce Mitchell's masterly survey of the OE data and of the explanations on offer (1985: §§682–701) leaves little to be added; the reader is recommended to start there. See also Mitchell (1976a).

As for the paradigm of progressive BE, Mitchell appears to give a morphological explanation for the absence of the perfect progressive from Old English: 'the late appearance of . . . "been" ' (1985: §684), which appears for the first time (1985: §1099), as a main verb, in

[153]   *ChronE* 232.19 (1096)

> . . . he heafde gebeon on þes cynges swicdome
> . . . he had   been   in the king's betrayal

'. . . he had been involved in treachery against the king'

But according to Visser (1963–73: §2148) the perfect progressive is not recorded until the fourteenth century; he gives a complete list of fourteenth-to-seventeenth-century instances. The morphological gap was closed, therefore, some two hundred years before the syntactic gap was filled.

13.4.2 Mossé

Fernand Mossé published his elegant monograph on the history of the progressive in two parts, each with its own page- and section-numbering (1938a,b, in French). The first part deals with the period up to the beginning of Middle English, except that an essay on prefixation in Old English as an *aspectual* device and its OE/ME weakening is found at the beginning of the *second* part (1938b: §§1–42).

Mossé suggests that by virtue of the meanings of the Indo-European present participle and of BE, the potential for a progressive to be formed was always latent in Indo-European languages. He concludes, however, that whenever a progressive appeared in any early Germanic language, Old English included, the event can safely be ascribed to direct influence from Greek or Latin.

His scenario for Old English is that the progressive arose as an expedient in interlinear glossing for dealing with various Latin forms which had no real equivalent in Old English:

(A) perfect tense of deponent verb
(B) ESSE 'be' + future participle
(C) appositive present participle of verbal meaning
(D) ESSE + present participle

These somewhat mechanical uses became a feature of learned translation style which lasted till the twelfth century.

The progressive entered as a more natural English usage through the influence of the Vulgate, whose frequent use of ESSE + present participle led to a parallel use of the progressive in the *West-Saxon Gospels* as a ***calque*** of the Latin construction. (Nickel 1966: 13 finds these two routes of entry inconsistent with each other.) Virtual absence from poetry confirms Mossé in his hypothesis. Mustanoja (1960: 584–5) seems to follow Mossé's account for Old English. As for the OE functions of the progressive, Mossé identifies eleven particular values plus two stylistic usages. This elaborate scheme is not convincing (Raith 1951: 97; Mitchell 1976a: 490).

13.4.3 Raith

Josef Raith's monograph (1951, in German) falls somewhere between Mossé (1938a) and Nickel (1966) in date, style and – what matters – conclusions, which I move to straight away, passing over his textual analyses. His research was done independently of Mossé, but on the origins of the construction they are in broad agreement (1951: 108–9).

For Raith the progressive had just three main functions: descriptive, durative, and intensive (1951: 98, 103, 105–6). In the durative function its use was not obligatory, so that it was not a grammatical category in Old English, though the ModE imperfective aspect could perhaps develop out of it. (The post-Old English development is deferred to a (?)never-published second part.) He points to the commonness of the progressive with SPRECAN/CWEÐAN 'speak' and SMEAGAN 'think', WINNAN/FEOHTAN 'fight' and WUNIAN 'dwell', noting that the last-mentioned is also common in the progressive in Middle English (1951: 101–2).

13.4.4 Scheler

Manfred Scheler's dissertation on syntactic Latinisms in Old English (1961, in German) first sets up a sensible set of criteria for identifying Latin influence, then moves on to a number of specific constructions, of which the progressive is the first. He lists half a dozen facts which to his satisfaction prove Latin influence on the OE progressive, but then adds four reasons for doubting that Latin was the sole source (1961: 66–7). The more significant of the points themselves are discussed elsewhere in this section.

13.4.5 Nickel, Visser

Gerhard Nickel's solid monograph (1966, in German; English summary, pp. 389–92) largely supersedes Mossé (1938a) and Raith (1951).

Nickel starts off with a structural analysis of participial constructions germane to the progressive, framed in an elementary TG account of Present-day English which serves the purpose adequately and is then hardly taken up again. Despite the tests mentioned in §13.2 above, many examples remain syntactically indeterminate between progressive and a collocation of BEON/WESAN with adjective or appositive participle or agent noun. These three kinds of indeterminacy are for Nickel both a descriptive problem for the modern analyst and the seeds of an explanation for the origin of the progressive.

Nickel also brings to bear a discussion of aspect and Aktionsart, a pedantic use of statistics (but the counting is not to Mitchell's satisfaction 1985: §690 n.152), and an attempt to classify text-types into poetry, prose relatively little influenced by Latin, and prose greatly influenced by Latin. Appendixes record occurrences in some (but not all) of his chosen texts.

Nickel's main conclusions are as follows. No branch of Old English lacked the progressive altogether. Infrequency in poetry is no proof that the progressive was a Latinate introduction, since the frequency of progressives has remained low in poetry even into modern times, and OE verse texts with a similar provenance to a prose work – occasional verses in the *Chronicle*, the *Metres of Boethius* – show far lower incidence of progressives than their prose counterparts (1966: 91–3). When Latin influence was felt, the use of the OE progressive remained independent of particular Latin forms. This is true even of the OE translator of *Orosius*, regarded by Mossé as an indiscriminate user of the progressive. Further evidence against unconstrained use in *Or* is that the progressive is never used with certain verbs (those prefixed by *a-*, *be-*, *for-*, *ge-*,[11] *ofer-*, *of-*, *on-*, *to-*) and that it almost always occurs with 'imperfective' verbs and with temporal, spatial or modal modification. But Nickel does concede that the high proportion of progressives in *Orosius*, not to be exceeded until the twentieth century, gives the lie to claims that the progressive was very rare before the late ME period (1966: 114–15). In the *Anglo-Saxon Chronicle* he finds further that verbs in the progressive very rarely govern an accusative object, and this seems to be true of Old English as a whole (1966: 135, 173). Looking at the more heavily Latin-influenced prose works, he decides that the influence of glosses and interlinear translations on the use of the progressive has been greatly exaggerated (1966: 205).

As for functions, Nickel attributes several identified by previous workers (ingressive, iterative, emphatic) to the context rather than to the progressive itself. The ones he himself recognises are temporariness (present tense only), backgrounding, framing-time, descriptive/characterising (1966: 233–67).

Having dismissed Latin as a source, Nickel traces the origins of the progressive to various similar constructions with which it can be confused (1966: 274–98; and summarised and developed in English, 1967):[12]

(A) predicative adjectives
(B) appositive participles
(C) the type *he sæt lærende* 'he sat teaching'
(D) agent nouns

It is D which Nickel gives greatest weight to. His strongest points are that some verbs which can take either an accusative or a genitive object always take an accusative in the simple form and a genitive in the progressive, something which can be explained if the progressives derive (in part) from agent nouns in *-end*, which would have had to have a genitive NP following. Corroboration is found in the greater frequency of *-end* agent nouns in Old English than in cognate languages, and in the subsequent replacement of *-end* by *-ere* as agent-noun suffix.

Visser's account of the OE origins of the progressive (1963–73: §§1853–8) is clearly set out and generously provided with examples. In its conclusions, however, it relies on Nickel (1966).

13.4.6   Scheffer

Johannes Scheffer (1975) offers a great deal of data in his monograph on the progressive. The first half of the work is an efficient, corpus-based[13] study of the uses and meanings of the progressive in Present-day English. The history of the form is dealt with at length too (1975: 131–273), starting with a full survey of progressives in the different kinds of surviving OE text. Scheffer's conclusion here is that rarity in poetry and commonness in translation from Latin do not prove Latin origin, since there is an appreciable frequency of ' "progressive-inducing" Latin forms' *not* translated by an OE progressive and of OE progressives used independently of the Latin original. The progressive was an 'autochthonous' (indigenous) construction greatly reinforced in written Old English by Latin influence. Clearly there is considerable overlap with Nickel's work.

As for meaning, Scheffer writes:

> It appears that in Old English the progressive has the same overall basic function of emphasizing contextually-defined temporal reference as in Modern English. For all the secondary meanings that have been noted in Modern English instances have been found in Old English, too. (1975: 213)

Scheffer offers a full study of progressives in Wærferth's translation of *Gregory's Dialogues* – a text not analysed by Nickel (1966) – and a comparison with the later version. One conclusion, from their relative incompatibility with the progressive, is that prefixed verbs are often perfective; cf. Nickel's similar observation, §13.4.5 above.

13.5   Explanations for the ME and ModE progressive

This too is a much worked-on topic, and there is a great deal of overlap between accounts. Brinton again gives a useful survey of opinions on the present-day functions of the progressive from the point of view of verbal aspect (1988: Chapter 1). As for history, Middle English had a multiplicity of competing forms. Some scholars regard the eventual winner, BE + V*ing*, as a direct descendant of OE BEON + V*ende* (van der Gaaf, Mossé, Mitchell, Nickel, Scheffer), others as a development mainly of OE BEON + *on* V*ung*/V*ing* (the early Jespersen, Dal, Braaten), others again as a hybrid formation (Jespersen, Visser). In part the disagreement reflects differing decisions as to whether *-ing* can be regarded as a straight morphological substitution for *-end(e)*. Most recent work has emphasised the continuity of the progressive from Old English to the present day. Some scholars give an important place to Celtic influence (Preusler, Dal, Braaten); several assign at least a minor role to French (van der Gaaf, Mossé, Braaten).

13.5.1 Jespersen

Otto Jespersen changed his view over the years; I take all the following quoted remarks from his (1909–49: IV 168–9). In 1905 he had asserted that the ModE progressive 'seems to have little, if anything to do with the OE *he wæs feohtende*' but is rather 'aphetic for *I am a-reading*, where *a* represents the preposition *on*, and the form in *-ing* is not the participle, but the noun'. A later formulation, in 1931, is that the ModE progressive is 'in some vague way a continuation' of the OE progressive, but that once the participle ending had become *-ing* there was an 'amalgamation' of the progressive and the prepositional construction with *on* (later *a*) and the verbal noun.[14] This blending is claimed to account for

(A) greatly increased frequency
(B) much greater precision of use
(C) frequency of *of* before the object

For examples of the progressive with *of* before what would otherwise be a direct object, see Visser (1963–73: §§1869–71), a much fuller collection than Jespersen's (1909–49: IV 176–7):

[154] (1470) *Paston* 338.18

> and ther   was he kepyng   of a coort
> and there was he holding   of a court-session

> 'and there he was holding a court-session'

The hypothesis of formal blending and the significance attributed to points A and C are attacked by Nehls; see §13.5.5 below.

13.5.2 Dal, Braaten, Keller, Preusler

Ingerid Dal's substantial article (1952, in German) offers a variant of Jespersen's earlier hypothesis. She suggests that Old English had two parallel sets of structures: literary ones involving the present participle in *-ende*, and popular ones involving *on* + verbal noun in *-ing/-ung* (1952: 58, 101–2). The structures concerned are as follows:

(A) appositive (1952: 52–7)
(B) with an intransitive verb of rest or movement (1952: 76–88)
(C) qualifying the NP object of a transitive verb of causation or perception (1952: 88–91)
(D) with BEON/WESAN (1952: 91–101)

Thus present participle and verbal noun were already functionally similar in several contexts. She claims that the 'literary' progressive in *-end(e)* died out in Middle English, to be replaced by a progressive derived mainly from the 'popular' form in *-ing*. Furthermore the popular forms were greatly influenced by Celtic (1952: 107–16). The evidence is largely circumstantial –

compare Poussa's work on periphrastic DO (§10.3.6 above) – and much of the argument is speculative; see the review by Keller (1956). Braaten (1967) adopts and reworks in convenient form some of Dal's material, finding that the English progressive has all sorts of foreigners under its bed:

(E) Celtic substratal influence in Old English
(F) acceptance of former colloqialisms after Norman suppression of English literary tradition
(G) possible French influence from the *en chantant* pattern
(H) possible earlier origin of *en chantant* in Celtic *yn canu* 'in singing'

Detailed discussion of the possible Celtic contribution to the OE progressive goes back to Keller (1925: 61–6), reported in Preusler (1956). That English, alone of the Germanic languages, should have picked on the verbal noun rather than the infinitive in the prepositional construction is, they argue, because it was a verbal noun that was used in the Celtic substratum in a closely analogous prepositional construction – and Celtic verbs lacked an infinitive. Preusler is convinced that the ME construction seen in

[155=93]   (c1396) *Doc.* in *Bk.Lond.E.* 234.19

þe ȝomen of Schordych, þat þere were in amendyng of here
the yeomen of Shoreditch that there were in repairing   of their

berseles
archery-butts

'the yeomen of Shoreditch who were repairing their archery targets there'

must have been a direct calque from Celtic and in turn a major contributor to the spread of the progressive in Middle English (1956: 334). A plausible explanation is offered for the delayed appearance in writing of the alleged Celtic substratal influence and of the virtual absence of loan words (1956: 348–9).

13.5.3 Mossé, van der Gaaf

13.5.3.1 Provenance

Having given a detailed frequency breakdown of the ME progressive by text and dialect area, Fernand Mossé argues that it must have been inherited from Old English, though it seemed to die out for a time in the south-west (1938b: §60). W. van der Gaaf too argues strongly for continuity: 'Why, then, should all sorts of juggling tricks be resorted to, in order to account for the occurrence of this construction, which I consider to be English "pure and undefiled", in thirteenth century and later texts?' (1930b: 205). Mossé does suggest, though, that it was supported by analogy with, and by transitions from, several other structures – roughly the participial versions of those listed as A to C in §13.5.2 above (1938b: §§78–89).

He then moves on to the possibility of foreign influence. French influence was very weak but may have sustained the English progressive in the period 1200–1340 (1938b: §§90–99; similarly van deɟ Gaaf 1930b: 213–15). The resemblance of certain Celtic structures to the prepositional pattern [2] in Middle English is coincidental (1938b: §100–12), though Mossé recognises substratal Celtic influence in *modern* dialects of English. Latin, he thinks, exercised some influence on translators, and more particularly it fostered an increasing predilection for present participles in various functions in late Middle and early Modern English (§§113–23).

Mossé then tackles the problem of the origin of the *-ing* ending (§§129–75), showing on the one hand how phonetic factors encouraged the merger of *-end/-ind* with *-ing* in the midlands and south. Nehls prefers to take Mossé's copious documentation of interchange of *-ng*, *-nd* and *-n* forms not as evidence of phonetic instability but of purely graphemic fluctuation, suggesting that all the relevant endings probably had the same phoneme /ŋ/ in speech (1974: 165). On the other hand Mossé shows that the functional merger of participle and verbal noun went ahead equally in the north, where *-and* and *-ing* remained phonetically distinct. Labov (1989: 87–8) quotes some sociolinguistic data on the [ɪn] ~ [ɪŋ] *variable* in PDE dialects which suggests that the historical difference between participle and verbal noun may not have entirely disappeared.

By the end of the twelfth century the verbal noun (at first 'disguised' with *-end*, later *-ing*) was being found with its own direct object (§§172, 174):

[156] a1225(?a1200) *Trin.Hom.* 55.16

on etinge to   michel. on estmetes   þe   bredeð sinnes
in eating too much   in dainty-foods that breeds sins

'in eating too much of dainty food, which breeds sins'

[157] a1225(?a1200) *Trin.Hom.* 65.24

þe þridde is menende his   synnes bifore gode
the third   is bewailing one's sins   before God

13.5.3.2*   The verbal noun

Here we may make a small excursus on the gerund or verbal noun. Tajima dismisses [156]–[157] as irrelevant: [156] because the fuller citation – Mossé had truncated it at *michel* – suggests that *etinge* is intransitive and has adverbial modification, [157] because *menende* may stand for the inflected infinitive *menenne* rather than the gerund (1985: 87 n.47; 73). In the latter case Tajima is following Visser (1963–73: §1018), but the absence of *to* before *menende* makes the dismissal insecure and means that Mossé may have been right as far as [157] is concerned. For Tajima gerund + object is first found from the end of the thirteenth century:

[158] c1330(?a1300) *Arth.& M.*(Auch) 1301

Þe messanger made anon   asking | Whi he made   swiche leiȝeing
the messenger put   at-once question why he produced such   lying

'The messenger immediately asked why he was telling such lies'

Note here Morton Donner's important observations on these matters (1986), based on the 15000 citations illustrating *-ing* nouns in *MED* in the letters *A–O*. He comes to the conclusion that when *nouns* in *-ing* occur with an NP functioning as their (semantic) direct object, over 90 per cent of the c2500 instances have the NP in an *of*-phrase. Of those instances where the NP is a true object, he suggests that most can be accounted for as follows:

(A) the *-ing* is itself dependent on a preposition, so that the otherwise normal use of *of* would have produced two consecutive PPs
(B) rhetorical patterning
(C) translationese or other stylistic idiosyncrasy
(D) in Pecock's works

and he finds just 16 clear instances of modification by a manner adverb out of nearly 6600 instances where an *-ing* noun is modified by an adjective and/or determiner. He rejects such examples as

[159] (1463) *Will Bury* in *Camd.49* 35.1

and at the brekyng vp . . .
and at the breaking-up [*sc.* of a household] . . .

on the plausible grounds that we have here a nominalisation of the phrasal verb BREAK *up* rather than an adverbial modification by *up* of a gerund *brekyng*; see also Denison (1981: 132–3). Overall, then, if his corpus is representative, we may have to accept Donner's conclusion that the gerund is sporadic and unsystematic and *not* established usage in Middle English. The frequency of Donner's category A – dependence of the gerund on a preposition – is confirmed independently by Osamu Koma (1987: 315): it is the *only* type of gerund use in the *Paston Letters*.

13.5.3.3 The prepositional pattern

Returning to Mossé's book, we then find a whole chapter devoted to the pattern *he is a-doing*, that is, the possible influence of the prepositional pattern on the progressive (§§176–215). Mossé's conclusion, which follows that of van der Gaaf (1930b: 202), is that the chronology does not support a derivation BE + *on* V*ing* > BE + *a*-V*ing* > BE + V*ing*, since the prepositional pattern came too late and was too infrequent to be more than a tributary to an already existent river; see §13.3.5.2 above. Furthermore, the preposition *in* was far more common than *on* in the ME period and yet cannot be the direct source of reduced *a*-. The final piece of evidence is that the prepositional patterns show a higher proportion of intransitive uses, which is consonant with *-ing* in *those* patterns being perceived as a verbal noun rather than a participle.

The remainder of the book is devoted to the extension of the paradigm and to the various functions of the progressive.

13.5.4 Visser

Visser's account of the history of the progressive from Middle English onwards assumes a 'polygenetic origin' for the ME BE + *-ing* progressive (1963–73: §§1859–71). The possible sources are the OE BEON/WESAN + *-ende* progressive and the prepositional *he is on huntunge* form; there are also a handful of dubious OE BE + -ing instances. Essentially, then, we are to envisage two concurrent, long-drawn-out, and in the end convergent processes:

(A) the replacement of -end(e)/-ind(e) forms by -ing, starting in the south and spreading northwards, both in the progressive and in other constructions
(B) a mainly phonetic change *he is on hunting > he is a(n) hunting > he is hunting*, followed by the syntactic acquisition by the originally nominal -ing form of verb-type complementation

We shall take up two points with reference to B. First, even though Visser describes prepositional forms as 'extremely frequent throughout the whole Middle English period', the number is actually not great, as Mossé had observed (§13.5.3 above), and the number where the preposition is *an* or *a* – the presumed intermediate stages in the elision of the preposition – is very small indeed; see §13.3.5 above. Second, Visser seems to assert that the -ing progressive was slow to develop verbal complementation, direct objects not becoming normal until the beginning of the ModE period[15] (1963–73: §1860), which would provide indirect support for route B. However, a cross-reference to his §1123 is not entirely to the point, since that section does not concern progressive syntagms but merely gerundial -ing (in which connection see also his §1035 and Tajima 1985). Neither Mossé nor Visser provides the materials to check the relative frequency of direct objects after -ing progressives, Mossé merely remarking that the progressive is 'very frequently' found with an object (1938b: §214). I have found some pre-sixteenth-century examples scattered among their illustrations of various functions of the progressive; see §13.2.3 above. In Scheffer's list of progressives in the Wyclifite New Testament (1975: Appendix VII) – which does not include [18] – just three out of thirty-three examples have a direct object, though of course that is a text which follows the Latin quite closely. It would be worth doing more work on the complementation of early -ing progressives: see Exercise (a) in §13.7.

As for the meaning or function of the progressive, Visser takes a ruthless line against those who find a multiplicity of functions. He prefers to offer a central function which will account for most or all of its uses (1963–73: §1806):

> The Expanded Form is that colligation [see Glossary: D.D.] *of a form of* to be with an -ing *which is used when the speaker chooses to focalize the listener's attention on the POST-INCEPTION PHASE of what is, was or will be going on at a point in time in the present, past or future.*

Other alleged meanings are contextual, or due to adverbials, or inherent in the semantics of the lexical verb. He claims (1963–73: §1830) that his formula covers even the use of the progressive with future meaning, as in:

[160]   1958 Greene, *Havana* V.ii(3).204.7

We are opening an agency in Cuba soon.

However, he suggests that the futural meaning is a leftover from those OE

examples which had a form of BEON/WESAN with the IE *bheu-* root, an
example of which would be:

[161]   *BlHom* 63.26

on domes dæg hi   beoþ   from Gode þysne cwide   geherende
on doom's day they will-be from God   this   message hearing

(For a discussion of possible differences between OE *bið/beoð* and *is/sind*
'is, are' see §14.2.2 below.)

13.5.5   Nehls

The dissertation of Dietrich Nehls (1974) offers a functional analysis of the
progressive in Present-day English from the point of view of aspect. The last
sixty pages give a diachronic account of the progressive from Old English
onwards, again concentrating on possible contrasts within the tense and
aspect system. On the OE origins he follows his supervisor, Nickel. Most of
his discussion is concerned with the *functions* of the progressive at the
various stages and will not concern us further. Where he contributes to the
history of the *form* is in his reassessment of the role of the prepositional
patterns. (A suggestion of his on the *-ende > -ing* change was mentioned in
§13.5.3 above.)

Nehls unpicks the logic of Jespersen's position (1974: 166–72). He
observes that four competing syntactic patterns were to be found in the
seventeenth century:

[162]   He was writing a letter.
[163]   He was a writing of a letter.
[164]   He was writing of a letter.
[165]   He was a writing a letter.

Type [162] was the progressive, [163] the prepositional pattern. These were
the 'pure' types. For Nehls types [164]–[165] are obvious symptoms of false
analogy, given the general functional equivalence of progressive and
prepositional patterns. Now Jespersen had used the existence of type [164]
as indirect evidence that *a* could be lost from [163], and hence that the
prepositional pattern could merge formally with the progressive. Nehls
accuses him of concealing the other 'mixed' type, [165], as found in:

[166]   1623(1605) Shakespeare, *Lr* V.iii.275

I kill'd the slave that was ahanging thee.

[167]   1684 Bunyan, *Pilgrim's Progress* II 182.14

I was a dreamed [*first edn*: dreaming] last night that I saw him.

(For many more examples see Visser 1963–73: §1866.) The existence of
[165] – and the survival in modern southern dialects of [164] – suggests to
Nehls that *a* was not in fact lost from type [163]. He also attacks Jespersen's
point A (recall §13.5.1 above) by observing that Lowlands Scots uses the
progressive even more frequently than Standard English and yet without the

-in(g) inflection of the verbal noun having merged formally with the *-an(d)* of the present participle (1974: 170). The Scots evidence is also mentioned by Scheffer (1975) among others, though cf. Visser (1963–73: §1861). The main source is Murray (1870–72: 210–11).

Nehls inclines to the view that the mutual substitutability of the [162] and [163] types as expressions of imperfective aspect led to the disappearance of 'intensive' functions of the progressive with stative verbs and in the imperative, which the prepositional type lacked anyway (1974: 171); to that extent he accepts Jespersen's point B. He does not accept that there was any *formal* blending. As supporting evidence for the functional influence of the gerundial form he notes that the progressive has not been similarly restricted in function in Scots. He suggests that periphrastic DO took over some of the discarded functions in standard English. Scheffer (1975) also discounts the contribution of the prepositional/gerundial construction to the progressive.

13.5.6   Bauer, Strang, Brinton, Denison

Here are gathered some brief observations on grammaticisation of the progressive. Gero Bauer (1970: 150) merely states that the grammaticisation of the progressive had not even started at the time of Chaucer and Gower (late fourteenth century).

In a stimulating article Barbara Strang (1982) explores the use of the progressive in literary narrative in the eighteenth and nineteenth centuries. Strang locates the grammaticisation of the form in the seventeenth century: 'unsystematic use' before 1600, 'systematic or grammatically required use' after 1700 (1982: 429). Her focus, however, falls on a slightly later period. She points out that in narrative prose of the first half of the eighteenth century the progressive was largely restricted to subordinate clauses, and that the general rise in frequency of the progressive during the second half of the eighteenth and the nineteenth centuries conceals a huge increase in main-clause use. She also suggests that an earlier predominance of animate subject NPs and of activity verbs gave way around 1800 to less restricted choice of subject and lexical verb. (All of these comments apply only to past-tense narrative prose and not, for example, to dialogue in the novels she examines.)

The history of the progressive comes up in Brinton's monograph only insofar as it touches on the themes of aspect and auxiliation. Her summary brings out well its similarities to the history of the perfect (1988: 109):

> Reanalysis of the combination of *be* and participle as a unified periphrasis undoubtedly involves steps parallel to those in the development of the perfect: loss of case ending on the participle, coalescence of *be* and the *-ing* form, weakening of the verbal meaning of *be*, foregrounding of the actional meaning of the *-ing* form, and generalization of the construction to include different classes of verbs.

In Denison (1990c) I argued that the progressive might have become grammaticised as late as the end of the eighteenth century. Some of the evidence for this view comes from passival progressives and *being* + V*ing* (§§13.3.7, 13.3.8.1 above), but since the crucial evidence involves the progressive passive, I defer the matter to §14.3.7, in the chapter dealing with the passive.

13.6 Explanations for the 'passival' progressive

This is the construction discussed in §13.3.7 and exemplified by

[168=99]   The house is building.

There are two main putative sources: the prepositional/gerundial construction and the ordinary progressive. Jespersen and Dal go for the former, Murray, Mossé, Nehls, Scheffer for the latter. Åkerlund and Visser support a mixed origin, with each source contributing to the passival progressive of different groups of verbs. If the former source, the passival progressive got its *meaning* from the original voice-neutrality of the verbal noun and its *form* by the weakening and disappearance of the prepositions *on* or *in* or *a*. If the latter, the usage might either derive from an ergative or medio-passive use of the lexical verb, or perhaps by ellipsis of the reflexive pronoun from a construction like

[169]   The house is building itself.

or merely from fundamental voice-neutrality of the present participle.

13.6.1 Reduction of the passival prepositional/gerundial construction

Jespersen attributes the passival use of the progressive entirely to an alleged origin of the progressive as a whole in phonetic reduction of the prepositional construction, ignoring his more judicious hypothesis of blending (§13.5.1 above). Since the verbal noun in *-ing* is neutral as to voice, he writes, '*is on (a) building* therefore may mean both "is engaged in the act of building" (active) and "is being built", as we say now (passive)' (1909–49: IV 205; cf. also III 351–2).

Note here Schibsbye's observation (1972–7: II §7.4.8) that the prepositional element in the gerundial construction was commonly reduced to *a* around 1400 when the meaning was passive, about a century before that reduction became common in syntagms of active meaning; Visser's material does not contradict this dating, though Schibsbye's 'common(ly)' places a heavy burden on Visser's mere handful of relevant examples (1963–73: §§1884, 1870). In any event Schibsbye makes no claim in this connection of further reduction to Ø. Dal, however, does make such a claim, suggesting that loss of the preposition can even be seen in an OE example (one of the five cited tentatively by Visser 1963–73: §1859):

[170]   (a)   *MkGl(Ru)* 5.26

&   wæs monigu ðrowunga
and was great   suffering

Lat. et fuerat multa perpesa

[170]   (b)   *MkGl(Li)* 5.26

&   wæs menigo   . . . ðrowungo   &
and was multitude . . . suffering(N) and

ðrouenda
suffering-ones(PTCP GEN PL)

She regards the gerundial construction as a colloquialism poorly represented
in written records. By the same token she argues (Dal 1952: 99–100) that
Mossé has understated the frequency of the *be a-doing* pattern in early
Modern English.

13.6.2   Development from the active progressive

Murray (1870–72: 225) states that in Scots at least the [168] type cannot
derive from the OE gerundial form, since the form used there is *buildan'*,
which is unequivocally present participle rather than verbal noun. He asserts
that the origin is the reflexive [169] pattern. His work is cited by Mossé
(1938b: §247), Nehls (1974: 153 n.135), Scheffer (1975: 254) and others as
evidence for English as a whole. Dal, however, dismisses Scots *the hoose is
buildan'* as evidence for the origin of the passival, seeing it instead as an
imitation of the English construction with *-ing*, where the *-ing* form has been
identified with the present participle (1952: 98).

Mossé discusses in detail the passival use both of prepositional/gerundial
constructions and of the progressive in historical English (1938b: §§202–15,
232–57). He denies that the former can have spawned the latter, on grounds
of chronology, of phonetics (once again it is the preposition *in* rather than
on which predominates in Middle English), and of modern Scots evidence –
the same arguments as came up in connection with the normal, active use
(§13.5.3 above) – though he grants the likelihood of mutual influence in the
sixteenth and seventeenth centuries and the eighteenth. For him the
essential fact is the voice-neutrality of the present participle. He also
observes that the passival progressive is associated particularly with one
semantic group of verbs, which he characterises as those meaning 'make,
do, build, prepare, cook'.

Scheffer, who follows Mossé here (though exaggerating the antiquity of
the passival progressive), points out a parallel between the two participles as
complement of BE in early Modern English (1975: 390–1), which we may
express as follows:

[171]

	BE + PRES PTCP	BE + PA PTCP
intransitive verb	active (progressive)	*active (perfect)
transitive verb	*passival	passive

Both starred entries have become virtually obsolete over the same period of
time, which Scheffer implies is part of the same sorting-out process.

13.6.3   Mixed explanations

Åkerlund (1914: 322–4) cites much previous work on the subject and
concludes that, Scots apart, both sources made a contribution: the

prepositional/gerundial for verbs like DO, MAKE, BUILD, and the inter-change between transitive and intransitive usage for many other verbs. Visser also cedes the possibility of a dual source, though in his case it must be said that the prepositional/gerundial gets more favourable attention (1963–73: §1874 and p.2019).

13.7 Questions for discussion or further research

(a) Take a sample of an early text with substantial numbers of BE + -ing progressives and see whether the progressives show a higher proportion of intransitive complementation than the non-progressives. (As a control you should try the same exercise (i) with a text that uses the -end or -and form, (ii) with a more recent text.) If the early use of the -ing progressive shows a greater tendency to disfavour transitive complemen-tation than the -end/-and progressive or the -ing progressive in later centuries, would this support the claim of derivation from the prepositional structure with verbal noun? Conversely, would little or no change in this regard support the idea that the BE + -ing progressive is a mere continuation of the earlier BE + -ende form? See §13.5.4 above.

(b) To what extent can the history of the present participle form be detached from the development of the progressive?

Notes

1. With certain weak verbs the form was V*iende*.
2. I would regard the lexical verb – i.e. the present participle if we exclude progressive passives – as head of the VP, but there are analyses even of apparently simple clauses containing auxiliary verbs which treat them as a stack of VPs or of clauses, each headed by one verb. (For discussion see e.g., Huddleston 1976.) In such an analysis the sentence *She was writing a novel* would be analysed with progressive BE as highest verb and head of its VP, and with complement consisting of *writing a novel*. Then we would have to characterise progressives as structures where the phrase headed by a present participle was sister to BE.
3. Visser's earliest example of prefixal *forth-* is dated 1816, implicitly acknow-ledging that in Old and early Middle English (and later still in poetry), *forth* could appear in pre*verbal* position. On the position of adverbial particles see Denison (1981: 111–45) and – though specifically on idiomatic *up* – Denison (1985b: 55–6).
4. A deponent verb is one which is passive in form but active in sense. The passive is mostly formed inflectionally in Latin, but the perfect passive is formed periphrastically by means of the auxiliary verb ESSE 'be' and the past participle of the lexical verb. Therefore the perfect passive *amatus est* 'he was loved' and the perfect deponent *secutus est* 'he followed' are identical in form. 'Perfect' here is used in the sense conventional for Latin grammar, not English.
5. The sense of [97] is 'if any play was being acted (later that evening)/was to be acted', so that it would not be a substitute for the central sense of the progressive.
6. I leave the reader to decide whether to pronounce **passival** with the stress pattern of *Parzifal/possible* or of *Poseidon/perspiring*.

7. Note that the MS reading in [103] is *ymagenyd*, emended by the nineteenth-century editor to *ymagenyng*. I have retained this example, which is made plausible by a rhyme with *ring*, but I have dropped what seemed a clear example, printed by Visser as *it is werkande*:

(a)   1394–5 in Salzman's *Building in Engl.* 471.14

. . . gratht   that pertenys to that werk quhil is werkande.
. . . equipment that pertains to that work while is working

since the missing subject could perhaps be *he* (as in ibid. 471.7).

8. Visser's collection (1963–73: 1955 and note) – which Strang (1982: 472 n.9) seems to have been unaware of – can be supplemented by a dubious late ME example given by Mossé (1938b: §227) and another similar one:

(a)   (1447) *Shillingford* 3 6.21

he at that tyme beyng right bysy goynge yn to his closet
he at that time being very busy going   in to his closet

(b)   1539–40 *Let.* in Ellis, *Orig.Let.ser.2* 139 II.140.6

I beinge in my ware howsse . . . ther being bessy brosshing sowche clothys as I hade ther . . .

(where the -*ing* is probably dependent on *busy*); by an example of 1748 given by Phillipps (1970: 116); by examples [130]–[134] above; by passing references in English grammars from 1789 to the late nineteenth century (Denison 1985d: 158); and by *being exhibiting* within a highly artificial sentence cited elsewhere without comment by Visser himself (1963–73: §1038):

(c)   1851 Brown, *Grammar of English Grammars* 3.vii.20.635.7

. . . considering ranting criticising concerning adopting fitting wording being exhibiting transcending learning, . . .

'. . . supposing empty criticism about the adoption of proper phraseology to be a show of extraordinary erudition, . . .'

(The sentence from which (c) is extracted contrives to pack thirty-one -*ing* forms into thirty-four words.)

As for Present-day English, Bolinger (1979) invented some examples and Halliday (1980) attested a few more, as I have:

(d)   1991 Colman (14 January)

I'm fine, apart from being doing most of John's teaching.

9. The judgements remain the same if the subject NP *Jim* is retained in the non-finite versions.

A similar exercise with passive examples reveals the possibly unexpected absence of *being* + *being* + V*ing*:

(a)   The courses are/were being taught by the same tutor.
(b)   *Being being taught by the same tutor makes it easier.

This is of less interest, however, since here the (a) pattern is relatively new.

10. It is worth pointing out that the two examples from Jane Austen – Mossé cites *Pride and Prejudice* II.iii[xxvi].144.18 and Visser *Emma* II.xiv[xxxii].280.11 – are dialogue by Eliza Bennet and Mr Woodhouse, respectively. It is highly unlikely that Austen, even with her general predilection for the progressive, would have put such a novel construction into the mouths of 'careful' speakers, especially the fussy, old, prim Mr Woodhouse.

Phillipps (1970: 117) cites an example outside dialogue:

    (a)   1816 Austen, *Emma* III.xv[li].444.15

        She was so happy herself, that there was no being severe.

By such gerundial usage, he suggests, 'Jane Austen does approach the modern construction'. And OED^2 has an example from 1679 s.v. *idiotical* a. 1.

11. Two exceptions: GEMUNAN 'remember', GEÞAFIAN 'allow, approve' (Nickel 1966: 122). Note too that the OE *Bede* shows far less disinclination to use prefixed verbs in the progressive; see Nickel (1966: 172–3), Visser (1963–73: §1857).

12. I cannot find the significant difference between Nickel (1966) and Nickel (1967) – the latter is not taken account of by Visser – which would justify Mitchell's charge (1985: §701 n.158) that Visser's account is therefore out of date; the main additions in Nickel (1967) seem to be a fuller discussion of the necessary theoretical conditions for syntactic innovation and blending.

13. A perfunctory generative derivation (1975: 124–30) is the only excursion into formal linguistics.

14. Jespersen gradually downplayed the role of the prepositional construction, as Nehls (1974: 166) points out. In fact he omitted all mention of it in his last revision of the work first published in 1905, *Growth and Structure of the English Language* (1946, but completed in 1938), citing Mossé (1938b) as the authoritative history of the progressive. However, his former view, that the progressive 'originated (or to a great extent originated)' from the prepositional/gerundial pattern, sneaks back in at (1909–49: IV 205), and also at (1909–49: V 415, completed in 1940).

15. Dal too reckons it to be a late development, though she puts it in the late ME period (1952: 32–3); however, she does not appear to be differentiating *-ing* forms from *-and(e)/-end(e)*.

Chapter 14

Passive

14.1 The problem

14.1.1 What is 'passive'?

Let us define the passive provisionally as a construction involving the verb BE + past participle of a transitive lexical verb:

[1]   Duncan was murdered by Macbeth.

As we shall see, there are passives and passive-like structures which do not share every feature of the prototype. Prototypically the subject of the passive corresponds to the direct object of an active sentence with the same lexical verb. (Such an active makes manifest the fact that – or justifies the claim that – the lexical verb is transitive. There is real danger of circularity here.) The semantic role of the passive subject will tend to be something like Patient (a word etymologically related to *passive*) or Theme, but this cannot be criterial. Nor is the use of BE, which is neither necessary, because other auxiliaries have been used, nor sufficient, because of the existence of a BE perfect (Chapter 12) of similar form. Nor can one insist on there being a corresponding active involving a transitive verb and a direct object, because of such examples as [2]–[4], amongst others:

[2]   (a)   People expected George to arrive late.
      (b)   George was expected to arrive late.

[3]   George is said to be indecisive.

[4]   (a)   Fierce winds broke the mast.
      (b)   The mast broke in fierce winds.

Example [2](b) may well be related to an active like [2](a), but it is at least arguable that *George* in [2](a) is not in an object relation to EXPECT (see §8.2.1 above). Example [3] has no corresponding active at all. And [4](b) is not usually regarded as passive, even though its subject corresponds to the direct object of [4](a). What this amounts to is that 'passive' is not a simple syntactic type. For useful discussions see Granger (1983) and Kilby (1984).

14.1.2 Historical change

In the history of the passive there are six main areas in which we shall look for change:

(A) function and meaning of passive
(B) form and function of participle
(C) choice of auxiliary verb
(D) paradigm of the auxiliary
(E) range of active verb-object *syntagms* available for passivisation
(F) expression of agent

Let us expand on at least some of these. One area which I shall *not* cover here is the growth of the passive infinitive in contrast with the active infinitive (*house to be let* vs. *house to let*, for instance). For discussion and references see Fischer (1991).

14.1.2.1 (A)–(C) Form and function of simple passive

The main distinction usually pointed to under A, function and meaning of the passive, is one between **actional** and **statal** passives. This distinction can hardly be discussed apart from the questions of relation between auxiliary and participle and choice of auxiliary verb.

As for B, the form and function of the participle, in the OE period participles in passive constructions could either agree with the passive subject in case, gender and number, or not. It might be possible to correlate lack of agreement in participles with a possible reanalysis from copula BE + participial adjective to auxiliary BE + lexical verb. Alternatively the distinction might correspond to one sometimes drawn between adjectival and verbal passives (see §7.6.2 above).

A question which I shall not enter into here is that of the incidence and meaning of the prefix *ge-* with OE participles. I shall content myself with quoting Kilpiö's summary of his findings for the OE *Bede* (1989: 124):

> There is a tendency to omit *ge-* in
> – the present tense when the passive predicate is actional. It is often iterative or durative at the same time.
> – the preterite when the action expressed by the passive is durative or iterative. [. . .][1]
> There is a tendency to prefix the past participle with *ge-* in
> – the present tense when the passive is statal, expressing a state resulting from a completed action.
> – the preterite when the action expressed by the passive is not iterative or durative, but is viewed as a whole. [. . .]

For further information see Lindemann (1970) and the reviews by Samuels (1972b) and Stanley (1973).

As far as C, choice of auxiliary, is concerned, WEORÐAN 'become' was an alternative to BEON and WESAN in forming passives in Old English. If the WEORÐAN passive was essentially actional – was it? – did use of the other auxiliaries correlate with stativeness? By the end of the fourteenth century WEORÐAN had disappeared from the language. Why? In Modern English the verb GET started to be used as an apparent auxiliary of the passive. To the extent that GET can be a mutative intransitive and thus forces an actional reading on passives, it seems rather similar to OE WEORÐAN. We can also discuss under this heading the grammaticisation of the passive auxiliaries.

Passive participles may also occur after other verbs, although there are no (other) grounds for regarding those verbs as auxiliaries:

[5]   They felt left out.
[6]   Tom remains much sought-after.

14.1.2.2   (D)–(F) Syntactic form

The most significant change under D, the paradigm of the auxiliary, is the very late appearance of -ing forms of passive BE, notably in the progressive passive. In the nineteenth and early twentieth centuries the interaction of progressive and passive allowed for alternation between patterns which were formally active and passive. Thus we have the older passival form [7] (discussed in §13.3.7 above) and the non-progressive passive [8], gradually being supplanted by the newer progressive passive [9] (discussed in §§14.2.4.4 and 14.3.7 below):

[7]   1816 Austen, *Emma* II.vi[xxiv].200.14

and while the sleek, well-tied parcels . . . were bringing down and displaying on the counter

[8]   while the . . . parcels . . . were brought down
[9]   while the . . . parcels . . . were being brought down

Heading E, the verb-object syntagm, concerns the extension of the passive to syntactic environments which had lacked a passive (unless impersonal) in Old English: the indirect passive (Chapter 6), the prepositional passive (Chapter 7), the 'second passive' of the VOSI construction (Chapter 8). What they have in common is a change in the relationship between an active verb and its possible object NPs, resulting in additions to the list of main verbs eligible for passivisation.[2] As we have seen, some scholars attempt to integrate some or all of these developments within essentially a single account.

As for F, only a minority of passives in running text have an explicit agent argument (in the sense of an NP which might have been subject of the corresponding active – hence not necessarily a semantic Agent), probably for the obvious reason that passives tend to be used when the agent is unknown or irrelevant. When expressed, the agent is usually in the form of a prepositional phrase.[3] In Old English the main prepositions for marking agents were *mid*, *þurh* and *fram*. Other prepositions were used too. It was *fram* that served principally for direct, personal agency. Over the course of the ME period both Agentive and Instrumental agent-phrases came increasingly to be marked by *of* and then *by*, which is the only preposition used productively in the passive construction in Modern English. For a discussion of agent marking and examples see Visser (1963–73: §§1987–2000)

and references given there, plus (for Old English) Mitchell (1985: §§802–33).
See also Peitsara (forthcoming).

14.2   The data

Headings B–D from §14.1.2 above will serve as convenient labels for the
presentation of data on the passive. (I shall give no data to correspond to A,
E or F.)

14.2.1   (B) Agreement

It is unclear to what extent the behaviour of participles in the passive
mirrors that of central adjectives used predicatively. Mitchell (1985: §§33–8)
treats adjectives and past participles together, though most of his examples
involve participles. It would be interesting if it could be shown that
participles showed a lower frequency of agreement or an earlier incidence of
loss of agreement than central adjectives occurring as predicatives. Certainly
Kilpiö asserts that the ending of the past participle in passive constructions
was 'already simpler than that of the adjective in early OE' (1989: 135). A
complication is that participles were almost all di- or trisyllables, and
phonological factors may have been responsible for zero inflection in many
instances. For fuller discussion than I can offer see Mitchell (1985:
§§759–65).

14.2.1.1   Passives with agreement

Agreement of the past participle with the subject NP is illustrated in the
following examples:

[10]   *Or* 59.10

> . . . þonne wæron ealle þa   dura   betyneda
> . . . then   were   all   the doors(NOM PL FEM) closed

[11]   *ÆLS* I 20.113

> Pær   wæron gehælede þurh   ða halgan femnan fela   adlige
> there were   healed   through the blessed woman many sick
>
> menn(NOM PL MASC)
> men

Agreement is still shown in the eME *Poema Morale*, as Mustanoja observes
(1960: 440), though erratically:

[12]   a1225(?c1175) *PMor.*(Lamb) 103

> Hwet sculen ordlinghes don. þa swicen &   ta forsworene | hwi boð
> what must   fornicators do   the traitors and the perjured   why are
>
> fole iclepede. &   swa lut icorene. | wi   hwi weren ho   biзeten to
> many called   and so   few chosen   woe why were   they begotten for
>
> hwon weren ho   iborene. | þet sculen bon to deþe idemet.   &
> what were   they born   that shall   be   to death condemned and

eure ma   forlorene.
ever more lost

'What are the fornicators, the traitors and the perjured to do? Why
are many called and so few chosen? Woe! Why were they begotten,
what were they born for, who are to be condemned to death and to be
lost for ever?'

14.2.1.2   Passives without agreement

Absence of agreement where a non-zero ending might have been expected:

[13]   *CP* 41.21

oft   him   gebyreð ðæt hie   weorðað
often them(DAT) happens that they(NOM PL MASC) are

bereafod ðara giefa   ðe   him   God for monigra monna
deprived the   gifts(GEN) that them God for many   men's(GEN PL)

ðingum geaf, næs   for hiera anra
sakes   gave not-at-all for their own

'often it befalls them that they are deprived of the gifts that God gave
them for many men's sakes, not just their own'

[14]   *Bede(O)* 4 21.322.13

swa swa þy seolfan dæge hire þam clænum leomam
as as   the very   day her the clean   limbs(DAT)

hi   ymbseald wæron.
they(NOM PL FEM) [*sc.* sheets] surrounded were

'as if the cloths had that very day been put around her pure limbs'

As is frequently pointed out, the majority of OE examples are indeterminate as to agreement because the expected inflection would have been -Ø
anyway:

[15]   *Bede* 4 29.366.30

Ða   him ða   ðæt sæd   broht   wæs, . . .
when him then the seed(NOM SG NEUT) brought was . . .

'When the seed had been brought to him, . . .'

And during the ME period agreement disappeared altogether.

14.2.2   (C) Choice of auxiliary

The verb WEORÐAN as a full verb meant 'become' in Old English, and
this fact – plus the Modern German (and Dutch) distinction between
passives with WERDEN (Du. WORDEN) 'become' and SEIN (Du. ZIJN) 'be' –
has suggested to many that passives with WEORÐAN were actional in
meaning while those with BEON/WESAN were statal. Mitchell cites, and
sounds off against, the scholars in question (1985: §§786–801), showing
clearly – and avowedly largely following Klingebiel (1937) here – that it is

merely wishful thinking on their part to assume that BEON/WESAN passives were exclusively statal. Examples [16]–[17] demonstrate that BEON/WESAN and WEORÐAN could form equivalent actional passives:

[16=11]   *ÆLS* I 20.113

Þær wæron gehælede þurh   ða halgan femnan fela   adlige
there were   healed   through the blessed woman many sick

menn
men

[17]   *ÆLS* I 21.132

Þær wurdon   gehælede æt ðære halgan byrgene eahta
there were/became healed   at the   holy   tomb   eight

untrume menn
infirm   men

For more such pairs see Visser (1963–73: §1916 – all from the two versions of *GD*) and Mitchell (1985: §795). This is not to deny – and Mitchell does not deny it – that *some* OE works may show a tendency to reserve BEON/WESAN for statal passives. Kilpiö reckons that forms like *is* 'is', *earon* 'are' are mostly statal in *Bede* and *CP*, while the majority of passives with *bið* 'is', *wæs* 'was', *wæron* 'were' are in fact actional (1989: 92). Note therefore that BEON/WESAN cannot always be regarded as a single verb in the way that PDE BE can be.

14.2.2.1   BEON, WESAN

The verb BE has always been the principal auxiliary verb used in passives. Morphologically it is a *suppletive* verb made up of three different PIE roots (compare *am, be, was*), and in the Old English present indicative and subjunctive there was actually a choice of forms from different etymological roots, for example *he is, he bið* 'he is'. Roughly speaking the forms like *bið* tended to be used for expression of future time or general truth, especially in the present indicative, though Mitchell's discussion demonstrates the difficulties of pinning down any semantic difference (1985: §§652–64). As auxiliaries of the passive the different forms behaved differently too; see Kilpiö (1989). Preusler (1956: 323–4) follows Keller in ascribing the OE use of the *b*-forms and their functions to Celtic influence. In most dialects finite *b*-forms dropped out of use by late Middle English, though *be* 'are' survived till the sixteenth century in London Standard, and southern dialects have preserved several finite *b*-forms; see Mustanoja (1960: 583–4) and *OED* s.v. *be* v.

14.2.2.2   WEORÐAN

After Mitchell's demolition job on the alleged actional ~ statal distinction, it may be unclear what is left of the conventional standpoint that WEORÐAN passives at least were exclusively actional. Mitchell thinks 'even this "rule" too rigid and not borne out by the facts' (1985: §796). He does not produce many convincing counterexamples, however (1985: §798). The best of them are:

[18] *ÆLS* II 35.244

Þæt cweartern wearð   afylled mid fulum adelan. and butan
the prison   was/became filled with foul   mud   and without

ælcum leohte atelice stincende
any   light   horridly stinking

'The prison was filled with foul mud and began to stink horribly and be without any light.'

[19] *ÆCHom* I 28.402.33

and hi   wurdon   ða utan   ymbsette mid
and they were/became then from-outside besieged with/by

Romaniscum here swa lange þæt . . .
Roman   army so   long that . . .

'and they were then besieged by the Roman army for so long that . . .'

The remainder either have WEORÐAN without a past participle, or a past tense passive like *wearð beloren* 'where the sequence of events suggests reference to a state "had been deprived" rather than to an action "was deprived" '. Why is 'had been deprived' a state? I presume that Mitchell is taking it as a (past) state resulting from anterior action, i.e. as if it were *was having been deprived*.

Now Kilpiö's detailed research on *Bede* and *CP* confirms that WEORÐAN passives in those texts are – as in the conventional view – exclusively actional. He suggests that WEORÐAN often implies a sudden change and in the present tense may even carry 'a stylistic overtone indicating the negative effect of the action on the subject' (1989: 67 and cf. also pp. 64, 72, 85).

Tense must come into our discussion of the choice of auxiliary in Old English. Passives with WEORÐAN in the present tense often have a future connotation (Visser 1963–73: §1918; Mitchell 1985: §755; Kilpiö 1989: 61–2), though overall they are relatively uncommon outside Wulfstan (Mitchell 1985: §797; Kilpiö 1989: 13). In the past tense, however, things are somewhat different. According to Mitchell the WEORÐAN passive 'is much more frequent in the past' (1985: §798), though in Kilpiö's limited corpus it is *less* frequent, both absolutely and relatively (2.9 per cent of past tense passives as against 8.5 per cent of present tense passives).[4]

Fourquet states that WEORÐAN, like HABBAN, occupies an intermediate position between BEON/WESAN and full verbs as far as positional behaviour is concerned in the *Anglo-Saxon Chronicle* entries up to 891, a weight in keeping with being a word half reduced to a grammatical tool (1938: 88).

14.2.2.3 GET

Most authorities follow *OED* in giving the mid-seventeenth-century [20] as the first recorded passive with GET:

[20] 1652 Gaule, *Magastrom.* 361 (*OED* s.v. *get* v.34b)

A certain Spanish pretending Alchymist . . . got acquainted with foure rich Spanish merchants.

Strang cautiously – and rightly – describes *acquainted* as a 'predicative which could be taken as a participle' (1970: 150–1). There is then something of a gap. In Jespersen's collection (1909–49: IV 108–9) the next examples chronologically are:

[21] 1731 Fielding, *Letter Writers* II.ix.20

so you may not only save your life, but get rewarded for your roguery

[22] 1759 Sterne, *Tristram Shandy* III.ii.126.19

he should by no means have suffered his right hand to have got engaged

[23] 1766 Goldsmith, *Vicar* xvii.90.16

where they give good advice to young nymphs and swains to get married as fast as they can.

For some reason Visser's collection (1963–73: §1893) misses [21]–[23] and continues with *OED*'s next examples, [24] and [25], dated around 1800:

[24] 1793 Smeaton, *Edystone L.* §266 (*OED*)

We had got (as we thought) compleatly moored upon the 13th of May.

[25] 1814 D. H. O'Brien, *Captiv. & Escape* 113 (*OED*)

I got supplied with bread, cheese and a pint of wine.

[26] 1823 Lamb, *Elia* Ser. I. x.(1865) 83 (*OED* s.v. *entangle* v. 1c)

You get entangled in another man's mind, . . .

[27] 1826 J. Wilson, *Noct. Ambr.* Wks. 1885 I.103 (*OED* s.v. *fankle* v. '(en)tangle', a Scotticism)

My long spurs . . . never got fankled.

[28] 1836–48 B. D. Walsh *Aristoph., Knights* I.iii (*OED* s.v. *fairish* adv. B)

I . . . got laughed at pretty fairish.

Strang, too, seems to be unaware of [21] when she writes that 'unmistakably passive structures are not found till late in the 18c' (1970: 151).

Since then the GET passive has increased in frequency, Visser commenting on its 'enormous popularity' in the twentieth century (1963–73: §1893). Yet from a sample of spoken material dated 1961–75, taken from the adult, educated, British English of the Survey of English Usage, Granger concludes that GET passives remain 'extremely rare . . . and are restricted to colloquial style'. She does concede, however, that among younger speakers, in more popular styles, and in American English there is far greater (and increasing) use (1983: 234–5). She lists 53 GET + PA PTCP forms in her corpus, of which 9 can be called passive (1983: 193, 365–7).

It is generally agreed that the GET passive is not synonymous or interchangeable with the BE passive. Compare:

[29] Megan got fired by the boss.
[30] Megan was fired by the boss.

Visser's summing-up is that the GET passive 'shares the notion of passivity' with the BE passive,

> but for an additional connotation of the reaching of the specified state in consequence of some kind of exertion on the part of the speaker (e.g. 'I was successful: he got expelled from the Organisation') or of activities from outside by persons interested in the result, which exertions or activities are as a rule not mentioned in the agentive adjunct introduced by *by*. The outcome can therefore often be apprehended as a piece of good or bad luck: . . . (1963–73: §1893)

Use of GET is associated with a dynamic reading, rather like OE WEORÐAN, though the elements of volition or 'luck' in the meaning did not belong to the OE verb. Wekker (1985: 459) cites a thesis by Paul Waterval which finds the GET passive to be most frequent in colloquial spoken usage in Present-day English and apparently concludes that its GET is in no way different to other uses of GET; that it always expresses a dynamic situation and has resultative aspect, usually involves a human being as discourse topic, and may express varying degrees of causality; and that benefactive or adversative meaning depends on extra-linguistic factors.

With an intransitive past participle GET may have a non-passive reading:

[31]   1764 T. Brydges, *Homer Travest.* (1797) II.54 (*OED* s.v. fratch v. 2 'quarrel')

   While thus they fratch'd, the Greeks were getting Just finish'd as the sun was setting.

I wonder whether Visser is right to call this 'rare' (1963–73: §1893). And much as BE + PA PTCP can be ambiguous between perfect and passive, so there is potential ambiguity in GET + PA PTCP, as in the early [20] and more modern examples like:

[32]   1837 Dickens, *Pickwick* xl.625.9

   As soon as I get settled, I will write and let you know.

Compare the discussion of *I had got sat down* in §12.3.1 above.

Note too that other inchoative verbs can form a sort of passive with a past participle. Visser lists BECOME, BEGIN, COME, FALL, GO, GROW, WAX (1963–73: §1893).

14.2.2.4   No auxiliary: the inflectional passive

One verb in the recorded history of English, OE HATAN 'call, name', is often claimed to have had an inflectional passive (as opposed to one formed by means of an auxiliary verb). The evidence for this comes from verbal morphology,[5] comparison with Gothic, the possibility of translation by a ModE passive, and *commutation* in Old English between the alleged passive [33] and a BEON + past participle form [34]:

[33]   *ÆLS* II 32.3

   and se   munuc hatte   abbo
   and that monk was-called Abbo

[34]   *ÆCHom* I 1.10.22

>   he wæs gehaten Leohtberend
>   he was called   Lightbearing

Kilpiö (1989: 102) states that although the [34] pattern (whether with HATAN
or with other verbs of naming) was far more common than the [33] pattern,
there are nevertheless about 450 occurrences of *hatte/hatton* in Venezky and
Healey (1980). The reduplicative past *heht* took over the function of *hatte*
and survived as *hight* into the early ModE period, and as a literary archaism
later still. However, it seems to me that *heht/hight* was always active in
form, and *hatte* is so different from the prototypical English passive that I
will not discuss it further here.

14.2.3 Grammaticisation

It is not easy to pin down the date (or even the fact) of grammaticisation of
the passive auxiliaries. What sort of evidence could we use? Generalisation
to all lexical verbs – which we used with perfect HAVE – is unsatisfactory
because some verbs have *never* had a passive turn; if we confine attention to
transitive verbs and define transitivity by ability to passivise, then the
definition is circular.

   Another indication is the acquisition of the NICE properties: passive BE is
a 'NICE' verb (an **operator**), passive GET is not. But then, main verb BE
remains a NICE verb, and GET only began to be used to form passives after
the NICE properties had more-or-less been established (though there are
signs that new accretions to the list of NICE verbs are possible, e.g. BETTER
as in *We better hurry up, bettn't we?*).

   Passives are unlike any other potential auxiliary as far as transparency to
argument structure is concerned, since a passive turn inevitably alters the
argument structure by removing one argument (either entirely or to a
relatively peripheral PP) and by promoting another to subject function.
Once a passive of ditransitive verbs as well as monotransitives had come into
existence, it could be argued that something analogous to transparency was
being demonstrated, since the 'retained object' is clearly part of the
argument structure of the lexical verb rather than of the auxiliary. That
gives us a date around 1400. But we could go further and argue that
transparency is equally demonstrated by impersonal passives in Old English,
since the Benefactive argument in such a passive has the same case as in the
active, determined by the lexical verb and not by the auxiliary. In most
examples of the impersonal passive the auxiliary is BEON/WESAN, but there
are some with WEORÐAN:

[35]   *CP* 341.11

>   Swa wyrð eac gestiered ðæm gitsere   ðæs
>   thus is also restrained the covetous-man(DAT) the
>   reaflaces
>   extortion(GEN)

>   'So also the avaricious man can be cured of extortion.'

[36] *CP* 333.5

   . . . ðonne weorðað hie   bedælede ðæs ecean   eðles   ures
   . . . then   are   they deprived the eternal homeland(GEN) our

Fæder.
Father(GEN)

'. . . then they will be deprived of the eternal country of our Father.'

This is perhaps an indication of grammaticisation as a passive auxiliary. Compare the tests of auxiliaryhood in Warner (1990) (discussion §15.3.3 below), where it is argued that OE WEORÐAN does *not* undergo post-verbal ellipsis. (It does show transparency to impersonal constructions, but not – I believe – as an auxiliary of the passive, rather of the perfect: see §12.4.3 above.) However, transparency also applies to non-auxiliary Raising verbs like PDE SEEM.

When the paradigm of the passive permits other auxiliaries to precede the passive auxiliary, that might seem to be an indication of grammaticisation, but in itself it does not rule out an analysis in which the preceding item – modal or HAVE – is an auxiliary while BE remains a main verb. A tentative dating based on the *non*-occurrence of perfect BE with the passive is presented in §14.2.4.3 below. The occurrence of the progressive passive, however, does strongly suggest grammaticisation of the passive auxiliary, since main verb BE at that time resisted occurrence in the progressive. Unfortunately, the date in question is too late to be of much use as a *terminus ante quem*. With GET the progressive is semantically inconclusive.

Our best hope is meaning change. With the BE perfect it was argued that one measure of grammaticisation is when the participle can be shown *not* to be adjectival. Does the same go for the participle in the passive? We can argue that the BE passive has become truly grammaticised once we find examples where it encodes action rather than state, and that would date the grammaticisation to Old English at least for certain forms of BEON/WESAN (see §14.2.2 and example [16] above). Co-occurrence with certain adverbials is useful too, including the use of an agent-phrase, and the time-reference of the periphrasis. Mitchell has an important discussion of the actional ~ statal and adjectival ~ verbal issues (1985: §§762–76); cf. also Visser (1963–73: §§1908–12).

But for actional passives with WEORÐAN and GET there is no – or at least less of a – meaning change from main verb use, so the meaning test fails for them. Occurrence with agent-phrases is well documented, though even this is not conclusive, since it can be found also with non-auxiliaries:

[37] Jan felt neglected by everyone.

14.2.4   (D) The paradigm of the passive auxiliaries

14.2.4.1   BE/WEORÐAN as first auxiliary

See Mitchell (1985: §§751–3) for the OE paradigm, and Wülfing (1894–1901: §§403–8) for further examples. Mitchell tabulates the possibilities for both BEON/WESAN and WEORÐAN in Alfredian texts and in Ælfric. There was an imperative, and a plain infinitive in the VOSI construction. A *to*-infinitive is not apparently found. It first occurs in Middle English. Visser cites such examples as the following (1963–73: §§992–3, 995–6, 1921, 2150–1):

[38]   c1400(?a1300) *KAlex.*(Ld) 7552

her   was þe gylt | To ben forbarnd, to ben forswelt
here was the guilt to be burnt-up to be   destroyed

[39]   a1450(a1401) *Chastising GC* 212.14

Þis nediþ not to be expressid   to ʒou
this needs not to be expressed to you

'This does not need to be spelled out to you.'

[40]   c1180 *Orm.* 343

Þatt streon   þatt wass Allmahhtiʒ Godd . . . &   lac   to
that offspring that was Almighty   God . . . and sacrifice to

wurrþenn offredd her   O rodetreowwess allterr
become   offered here on cross's   altar

'that offspring that was Almighty God . . . and a sacrifice to be offered here on the altar of the cross'

[41]   a1325(c1250) *Gen. & Ex.* 2427

So was him lif   to wurðen leid | Quuor ali gast still   hadde
so was him desirous to be   laid   where holy ghost secretly had

seid | Him . . .
told   him . . .

'So he was desirous to be buried in the place that the Holy Ghost had secretly told him . . .'

[42]   a1325(c1250) *Gen. & Ex.* 2685

oc summe flen | Into saba to borgen   ben.
but some   flee(PRES) into Saba to saved(PTCP) be(INF)

'but some fled into Saba to save themselves.'

[43]   (1419) *Will Bury* 155 (*MED* s.v. *bodi* n. 4)

My body to be beryed in þe chercheʒerd of Seynt Edm'.
my body to be buried in the churchyard of St.   Edmund

14.2.4.2   Modal + passive BE/WEORÐAN

Modal + passive occurs from early Old English onwards. I give examples with passive BEON/WESAN:

[44]   *Beo* 3021

Forðon   sceall gar   wesan | monig . . . mundum   bewunden
therefore shall spear be   many . . . hands(DAT) grasped

'Therefore many a spear will be . . . grasped in hand'

[45] *ÆLS* I 270.142

> he ne mot na   beon eft   gefullod
> he not may not-at-all be   again baptised

'He may not be baptised again.'

[46] c1180 *Orm.* 1963

> Forr ȝiff mann mihhte wurrþenn warr   Þatt ȝho wiþþ childe wære, |
> for if   one   might become aware that she with child was
>
> . . . | ȝho munnde   affterr   þe laȝheboc To dæþe ben
> . . .   she would-have-to according-to the lawbook to death be
>
> istanedd.
> stoned

'For if it should become known that she was pregnant, . . . according
to the law she would have to be stoned to death.'

[47] c1300 *SLeg.Kenelm*(Ld) 352.243

> Þo þis bodi ne moste beo i-founde in Engelonde
> then this body not could be found in England

'then this body could not be found in England'

[48] (c1390) Chaucer, *CT.Mel.* VII.1081

> men wolden nat be conseilled so ofte
> men would not be advised   so often

And with WEORÐAN:

[49] *CP* 387.26

> ðæt hie wolden weorðan forlorene &   oferwunnene
> that they would be   destroyed and vanquished

[50] c1180 *Orm.* 6860

> . . . þatt Godess Sune Jesu Crist þær shollde borenn wurrþenn
> . . . that God's Son Jesus Christ there should born   be

'. . . that the Son of God, Jesus Christ, was to be born there'

For further examples see Wülfing (1894–1901: §408), Visser (1946–56:
§665a; 1963–73: §§2150, 2152).

14.2.4.3 (Modal +) perfect HAVE + passive BE/WURTHE

Visser claims that perfect + passive BE can be traced back to Old English
(1963–73: §2161), citing the following examples:

[51] *Lk(WSCp)* 12.50

> Ic hæbbe on fulluhte beon gefullod.
> I have in baptism been baptised

> Lat. baptisma autem habeo baptizari

[52]   a1225(?a1200) *Trin.Hom.* 59.14

feren it is þat we and ure heldrene habbæð ben turnd fro   him.
afar it is that we and our ancestors have   been turned from him

'It is long since that we and our ancestors have been turned away from
him.'

But Mitchell rejects [51] as containing infinitival, not participial, *beon*, and
[52] as being Middle English (1985: §753 n.188). And indeed Visser has a
respectable collection of examples from early Middle English onwards:

[53]   c1180 *Orm.* 18232

& forr ðatt Crist ær   haffde ben Fullhtnedd att teʒʒre maʒʒstre
and because Christ earlier had   been baptised   by their   master

[54]   c1230(?a1200) *Ancr.* 86b.28

. . . ʒef ich hefde ibeon akeast   wið strengðe.
. . . if   I   had   been overthrown by force

The perfect auxiliary is always HAVE, which is interesting. Three reasons
suggest themselves:

(A) the BE perfect was already recessive
(B) passive BE was not yet grammaticised
(C) some restriction on double BE

Of these, B seems most cogent for early Middle English. Main verb BE has
never formed a perfect with auxiliary BE, but rather – since very late Old
English – always with HAVE. A syntagm consisting of grammaticised passive
BE + past participle, on the other hand, would arguably have been a
mutative intransitive, precisely the sort of syntagm liable to form its perfect
with BE; cf. §12.6.1. So perhaps passive BE was still an ungrammaticised
main verb. By the time it *was* grammaticised, perfect BE was obsolescent.

Instead of the non-occurring *BE + *been* + past participle, one often finds
BE + past participle:

[55]   (a1387) Trev.*Higd.* I 1.xxiv.235.20

And whan þe ymage was made, hem   semede þat þe legges
and when the image was made them(OBL) seemed that the legs

were to feble . . .
were too weak . . .

[56]   1623(1606) Shakespeare, *Mac* IV.iii.204

Your Castle is surpriz'd; your Wife, and Babes | Sauagely slaughter'd:

For discussion, references and further examples see Visser (1963–73: §1909).
    I have noticed one example of perfect + passive WURTHE, [57] – Visser
has some OE examples too in his §2166 – and here the perfect auxiliary is
indeed BE, as it is with all main-verb uses of WURTHE too, e.g. [58]–[59]:

[57] c1180 *Orm.* 19559

3æn himm, þatt wass att Sannt Johan Bapptisste wurrþenn
against him that was at Saint John Baptist become(PA PTCP)

fullhtnedd
baptised

'against him that had been baptised by John the Baptist'

[58] c1180 *Orm.* 3914

Annd Godess enngless wærenn þa Well swiþe glade
and God's angels were then well very glad

wurrþenn | Off þatt, tatt Godd wass wurrþenn mann
become(PA PTCP) concerning that that God was become man

'and the angels of God had then become very glad of the fact that God
had become man'

[59] c1180 *Orm.* 2272

Forr þatt nass næfrær wurrþenn, | Patt . . .
for that not-was never-before happened that . . .

'For it had never happened before that . . .'

There is one context in Present-day English, the 'strange existential'
mentioned by Lakoff (1987: 562–5), where the auxiliary before a passive
seems to hover between HAVE and BE:

[60] There's a man been shot.

In Lakoff's analysis *'s* in [60] is a contraction of perfect *has*, not *is*, but
cannot be used in uncontracted form – a 'rational property' which depends
on phonological identity with its 'ancestor' element, the *'s* = copula *is* of
normal existentials.

Visser records the participial form of HAVE + BE + PA PTCP from the
end of the sixteenth century (1963–73: §2163):

[61] 1590 Sidney, *Arcadia* 48.40

shee said, it might very well be, having bene many times taken one for
an other.

Strang was presumably misled into calling it a *nineteenth*-century innovation
(1970: 99) by the examples which Jespersen happened to cite (1909–49: V
57).

Visser states that modal + perfect + passive was 'already common in
Middle English' (1946–56: §710a). (No early examples are given in his
1963–73: §2181.) All ME examples apparently have a past-tense modal and
express an unrealised event:

[62] a1400(a1325) *Cursor* 14601

For wald he noght haf knaun bene
for would he not have known been

'for he did not want his identity to be revealed'

[63] a1500(c1340) Rolle *Psalter* 78.20

for thei wend   that he might noght hafe ben deluyered of   thaire
for they thought that he might not   have been delivered from their
hend
hands

[64] (1462) *Stonor* 65 I 58.20

. . . surmyttyng þat Jahne schulde furst hafe ben weddyd unto
. . . alleging   that Joan   should first have been wedded to
Amaryke Northlode
Amaric   Northlode

'. . . alleging that Joan was supposed to have been married first to
Amaric Northlode'

14.2.4.4 Progressive BE + passive BE

According to Mossé (1938b: §§263–4) and Visser (1963–73: §2158), finite
progressive passive constructions only began to be used in the eighteenth
century, with the first recorded case in the private, jokey letter of a young
man in 1795. The obvious alternatives were the 'passival' forms discussed in
§13.3.7 and the use of a non-progressive passive. Mossé and Visser show
that progressive passives were at first stigmatised in print and heavily
condemned. To Visser's 28 examples prior to 1872, including the earliest
known, [65] below, we can add a few more, all of them three-verb syntagms
of the type finite part of BE (+ . . .) + *being* + past participle:[6]

[65] 1795 Southey, *Life & Correspondence* I 249.24 (9 Oct)

like a fellow whose uttermost upper grinder is being torn out by the
roots by a mutton-fisted barber

[66] 1801 tr. *Gabrielli's Myst. Husb.* I.125 (*OED*[2] s.v. *make* v.[1] 91b)

'It [*sc.* a bill] is being made out, I am informed, Sir.'

[67] 1814 *Guernsey Star & Gaz.* in *New Age* (1919) 21 Aug. 278/2 (*OED*[2]
s.v. *profiteering* vbl. sb.)

The extortionate profiteering that is being practised by the tradesmen
in the public market.

[68] 1818 Keats, *Letters* 59 127.40 (8 Apr)

I am nearer myself to hear your Christ is ~~having~~ being tinted into
immortality – Believe me Haydon your picture is a part of myself –
. . .

[69] 1829 Landor, *Imag. Conv., Odysseus*, etc. (*OED*[2] s.v. *refreshment* 3b)

While the goats are being milked, and such other refreshments are
preparing for us as the place affords.

Since then the construction has become generally acceptable. Notice how it
coexists with the passival in [69].

14.2.4.5   Modal and/or HAVE + progressive BE + passive BE

Four- and five-verb syntagms with an additional modal and/or HAVE are found in prose only from the early twentieth century and remain infrequent (Jespersen 1909–49: IV 213; Visser 1963–73: §2182):

[70]   1915 Galsworthy, *Freelands* ix.95.25

She doesn't trust us. I shall always be being pushed away from him by her.

[71]   1918 Barrie, *Barbara's Wedding* 787.29

There's no wedding. Who could be being married?

[72]   1922 E. O'Neill, *Anna Christie* II.140 (*OED*^{2} s.v. *only* adv., conj. B.2)

And only for me, . . . we'd be being scoffed by the fishes this minute!

[73]   1929 Riddehough, *Can. Forum* 383.12

In view of the fact that the members of that class had been being educated for the previous four, five, or six winters by . . .

[74]   1977 French, *Women's Room* III.x.251.19

Because all these months you've been adoring him like a descended god, he's been being convinced he is.

Earlier instances that I know of are artificial. An early one, [75], is in a grammatical paradigm, 'avowedly being inserted by the author for the sake of theoretical completeness' (Visser 1963–73: 2427 n.2), while the mockery of [76] is directed at the three-verb *is being built* pattern and contains longer sequences evidently intended to sound ridiculous or even impossible:

[75]   1802 Skillern, *Grammar* [paradigm of passive voice] (Visser)

I can, may, or must be being conquered [etc]

[76]   1860(1858–9) Marsh, *Lectures* xxix.654.9

The reformers who object to the phrase I am defending [*the house is building*: D.D.], must, in consistency, employ the proposed substitute [*the house is being built*: D.D.] . . . in other tenses, as well as the present. They must say therefore: . . . the great Victoria bridge *has been being built* more than two years; when I reach London, the ship Leviathan *will be being* built; if my orders had been followed, the coat *would have been being made* yesterday; if the house had then *been being built*, the mortar would *have been being mixed*.

[77]   1871 White, *Words* xi.362.29

Could there be a more absurd affectation than, instead of, The tea has been drawing five minutes, to say, The tea has been being drawn five minutes? *Been being* – is that sense, or English? – except to children, who say that they have been being naughty, thereby saying only that they have been naughty.

A satirical dialogue on similar lines from 1883 is quoted widely in the handbooks, for example by Mossé (1938b: §280) and Visser (1963–73:

§2158), though that one does not push its luck beyond *will be being built* and *being only being built*. Visser's claim (1963–73: §2182) that 'in Sweet's *Elementarbuch* (1886) combinations like "I have been being seen" are registered as normal expressions' is highly misleading. What Sweet does is to give the full paradigm with sequences up to five verbs long, followed by the comment: 'Some of the longer forms – especially in the passive – seldom or never occur' (1898: §§2163–4, and similarly 1891: 50).

Presumably the patterns discussed in this section are not qualitatively new or different in the way that *is being built* was originally felt to be: they combine existing possibilities in a seemingly harmless way. What inhibited their acceptance is their sheer clumsiness, on grounds of length alone and possibly also the juxtaposition of *be/been* and *being* (cf. [77]). Mossé suggests (1938b: §271) that even authors who freely use the progressive passive in simple present or past tense revert to the passival when another tense (i.e. an extra auxiliary) is involved:

[78]   1843 Dickens, *Carol* iv.65.41

He sat down to the dinner that had been hoarding for him by the fire;

[79]   1855–7 Dickens, *Little Dorrit* 2.i.419.5

Baskets, troughs, and tubs of grapes, . . . had been carrying all day along the roads and lanes.

Elsewhere he has an example like [78]–[79] from Shakespeare (1938b: §240), and we can add some eighteenth-century citations from Visser and elsewhere (1963–73: §1879), for example:

[80]   1623(1612–13) Shakespeare, *H8* IV.i.56

God saue you Sir. Where haue you bin broiling?

[81]   1711 Addison, *Spect.* 29 I 121.12

But I have often seen our Audiences extreamly mistaken as to what has been doing upon the Stage

[82]   1740 Richardson, *Pamela* 145.12

This plot . . . has been too long hatching . . .

[83]   1795 Woodforde, *Diary* IV 216.3 (31 July)

The Pork had been boiling for them two Hours, . . .

[84]   1796 Woodforde, *Diary* IV 326.6 (31 Dec)

The Treaty on Peace, between England & France, which has been some time transacting, broke off very suddenly last Week by the French . . .

With a modal rather than perfect HAVE we can cite:

[85]   1740 Richardson, *Pamela* 195.13

Something must be hatching, I doubt!

And with both, though in a grammar:

[86]   1789 Pickbourn, *Dissertation* 78

The house will/shall have been building Domus ædificata fuerit [D.D.: *abstracted from a table*] . . . The tenses of the passive voice compounded with the participle in *ing* are never used but in the third person, and with relation to inanimate objects; or, at least, such as are incapable of the actions mentioned.

Poutsma (1926: 521) found no passival examples of WILL + BE + V*ing*, and I have seen no genuine examples like [86].

As for long sequences involving *active* progressives, it would be useful to trace the date of appearance and frequency of sequences like *may have been talking*, but I have no information on this point, only scattered examples like those quoted in §13.3.1.3. If we had statistics it might be possible to apportion the reason for the lateness and rarity of [70]–[74] between awkwardness on the one hand and lack of need on the other.

14.2.4.6   Precursors of progressive BE + passive BE

A precursor of the progressive + passive construction involved the participial or gerundial phrase *being* + past participle used absolutely[7] or separated from a finite BE. The gerundial pattern appeared in the fifteenth century; Mossé cites:

[87]   1417 *Let.* in Ellis, *Orig.Let.ser.2* 19 1.59.22

but now your sayd leiges, both their & els where, may suffer their goods and cattels to remayne in the feilds day & night wthout being stolen

'but now your said subjects, both there and elsewhere, may allow their goods and valuable-animals to remain in the fields day and night without being stolen'

[88]   c1454 Pecock, *Fol.* 126.26

and þe instrument is not wircher of þe same actyue deede principali
and the instrument is not doer   of the same active deed principally

and þoruȝ   his owen strengþ in beyng restid, but in
and through its own strength in being rested but by-virtue-of

strengþ of an oþir, and in beyng movid.
strength of another and in being moved

Mossé records the participial pattern from around the same time (1938b: §260); Visser has two other fifteenth-century citations in different sections of his work (1963–73: §§1920, 2158) and borrows from Åkerlund (1914: 334) some later examples from *OED* s.v. *be* v. 15c; and I add two. Here is a selection of such examples:

[89]   1422 *Let.* in Ellis, *Orig.Let.ser.2* 1.96.4

by meane whereof he being sore   febeled   and debrused, now
by means of-which he being sorely enfeebled and crushed   now

falle to greet age and poverty.
fallen to great age and poverty

[90]   ?a1475(?a1425) *Higd.(2)*(Hrl) VII 6.xviii.113.32

they dawncede, beynge drownede in snawe unto the myddes of theire
they danced   being   covered   in snow up-to the middle of their

body;
body

[91]   (1447–8) *Shillingford* 31 91.24

wyn by his officers ofte tymes   being ther   y put to sale yn retaill
wine by his officers often(times) being there put   on sale at retail

y-solde durer than hit aughte to be solde . . .
sold   dearer than it   ought to be sold . . .

[92]   (1456) *Paston* 562.4

. . . we being enformed þat the matiere is pitevous   praie you
. . . we being informed that the affair   is lamentable pray you

hertly   þat ye wul . . .
earnestly that you will . . .

[93]   1596 *Of Ghostes and Spirits* 14 (*OED*)

The noyse of a leafe being mooved so affrighteth him.

[94]   1653 H. More, *Antid. Ath.* 26 (*OED*)

Acting and being acted upon by others.

[95]   1754 Richardson, *Grandison* III.vii.32.9

. . . that Miss Jervois loves to sit up late, either reading, or being read
to, by Anne;

[96]   1769 Mrs. Harris in *Lett. 1st Ld. Malmesbury* (1870) I.180 (*OED*)

There is a good opera of Pugniani's now being acted.

[97]   1779 J. Harris, ibid. I.410 (*OED*)

Sir Guy Carlton was four hours being examined.

[98]   1798 Woodforde, *Diary* V 137.19 (14 Sep)

. . . that the French . . . had been defeated, and that the Irish were in
a fair Way, of being made quiet.

Sentences like [96] cannot be confidently separated from the progressive
passive, given that [96] looks like a normal *there*-transform of

[96']   A good opera of Pugniani's is now being acted.

with only a light adverb interrupting the verbal syntagm. I have found a
seventeenth-century example which looks exactly like the progressive
passive:

[99]   1667 Pepys, *Diary* VIII 249.28 (3 Jun)

. . . thinking to see some cockfighting, but it was just being done; and
therefore back again . . .

I believe, however, that [99] probably belongs with [89]–[98] above as another kind of *precursor* of the progressive passive, because *being done* seems to mean 'just finished' or 'becoming finished' for Pepys, like the non-finite [100]:

[100]   1667 Pepys, *Diary* VIII 250.30 (4 Jun)

and that being done, . . .

In the same way *being* seems to mean 'becoming' in:

[101]   1667 Pepys, *Diary* VIII 313.3 (1 Jul)

After being ready, we took coach;

[102]   1667 Pepys, *Diary* VIII 483.5 (17 Oct)

and there she found fault with my not seeing her since her being a widow;

[103]   1667 Pepys, *Diary* VIII 431.7 (10 Sep)

. . . the first time he hath been at the office since his being the Duke of York's Secretary.

There are also prepositional patterns which seem to resemble the progressive passive in the same way that BE + P + V*ing* resembles the ordinary progressive:

[104]   1669 Pepys, *Diary* IX 475.1 (8 Mar)

He tells me that Mr. Sheply is upon being turned away from my Lord's family, and another sent down

14.2.4.7   GET as passive auxiliary

Early finite uses of passive GET are discussed in §14.2.2.3 above. Many of the possible early examples of the GET passive involve the idiom GET *rid of* and other participial forms which might be adjectival rather than true passives:

[105]   1665 Boyle *Occas. Refl.* Ded. Let. (*OED* s.v. *rid* v. 3d)

The chief use . . . is to devise wayes to get ridd of the Later ['latter'].

[106]   ?1676 in *12th Rep. Hist. MSS. Comm.* App.V.33 (*OED* s.v. *rid* v. 3d)

I cannot get rid of my horrible cold heere.

[107]   1725 G. Rochfort, *Let. to Swift* in *S.'s Wks.* (1841) II.577 (*OED* s.v. *jaunt* sb.[1] 2)

If you have not got rid of your cold, . . .

[108]   1741 Chesterf., *Lett.* (1792) I.208 (*OED* s.v. *quit* a. 1b)

Aukwardnesses, which many people contract . . . and cannot get quit of them.

[109]   1753 H. Walpole, *Lett. H. Mann* (1833) III.40(D.) (*OED* s.v. *blood-guilty* a.)

I am glad you have got rid of your duel blood-guiltless.

[110]   1769 Bp. Warburton, *Lett.* (1809) 445 (*OED* s.v. *congratulate* v. 4)
        To congratulate him in having got well rid of [them].

[111]   1807 Wilkinson in Pike, *Sources Mississ.* (1810) II. App. 29 (*OED*
        s.v. *frosted* ppl.a. 1)
        Two more of my men got badly frosted ['frost-bitten'].

[112]   1859 Reeve, *Brittany* 236 (*OED* s.v. *exfoliate* v., *exfoliated* ppl.adj.)
        The columns were getting rusty and exfoliated.

[113]   1879 H. Grubb in *Proc. R. Dubl. Soc.* 184 (*OED* s.v. *diverge* v. 2)
        The makers [of stereoscopes] have got so accustomed to diverging
        their eyes, that . . .

Note the intensifiers *well* in [110] and *so* in [113]: the latter particularly
implies an AP rather than a passive verb.
    An early use of the imperative (though involving the problematic GET *rid
of*) is:

[114]   1786 Tooke, *Purley* (1798) I.111 (*OED* s.v. *approbative* a.)
        Get rid of that farrago of useless distinctions . . .

A *to*-infinitive is also found fairly early, e.g.

[115] 1759 Sterne, *Tristram Shandy* II.iii.72.27
        . . . the souls of connoisseurs . . . have the happiness . . . to get all
        be-virtu'd, – be-pictur'd, – be-butterflied, and befiddled.

14.2.4.8   Modal and/or HAVE/BE + passive GET

Soon after passive GET entered the language it began to occur with
preceding auxiliary verbs, including modals and DO, as in [21] and:

[116]   1816 'Quiz,' *Grand Master* viii.213 (*OED* s.v. *bamboo* v. 'cane')
        Or else they wou'd Get most confoundedly bamboo'd.

[117]   1819 Southey, *Lett.* (1856) III.150 (*OED* s.v. *bespatter* v. 3)
        I shall get plentifully bespattered with abuse.

[118]   1901 Shaw, *Cæsar and Cleopatra* II 272b.14
        CÆSAR. No man goes to battle to be killed. – CLEOPATRA. But
        they do get killed.

[119]   1989 Gurganus, *Confederate Widow* III.i.2 328
        If I do get killed, I'll only be dead.

When preceded by HAVE it seems reasonable to speak of perfect HAVE +
passive GET, as in [22], [24] and:

[120]   1832 Carlyle in *Fraser's Mag.* V.258 (*OED* s.v. *besmutch* v.)
        Her siren finery has got all besmutched.

[121]   1860 *All Y. Round* No.49. 545 (*OED* s.v. *be-* prefix 6b)

Have taken to drinking, and have got blotchy and bepimpled in consequence.

[122]   1872 Black, *Adv. Phaeton* xxiii.317 (*OED* s.v. *bank* v.[1] 8)

The clouds had got banked up in great billows of vapour.

[123]   1950– *SEU* N2

If they don't offer it this time, I won't drag it away once somebody mentioned it but it hasn't got mentioned very much.

[124]   1989 Gurganus, *Confederate Widow* II.i.2 164

. . . he settled near his company's bonfire. It'd got built one mile from the meadow where ..

Note also the dubious examples in [106]–[113].

When preceded by BE, there is room for doubt as to whether perfect or passive BE is concerned:

[125]   1837 Carlyle, *Fr. Rev.* I VII.x.281

the first sky-lambent blaze of Insurrection is got damped down;

[126]   1837 Carlyle, *Fr. Rev.* I III.ii.69.9

An expedient . . . has been propounded; and . . . has been got adopted

[127]   1870 Alford in *Life* (1873) 457 (*OED* s.v. *bedtime*)

I only hope the Master's work may be got done by bedtime.

[128]   1662 J. Davies, *Olearius' Voy. Ambass.* 220 (*OED* s.v. *get* v. 33)

They were both gotten sufficiently Drunk.

[129]   1701 W. Wotton, *Hist. Rome, Alexander*, iii. 510 (*OED* s.v. *get* v. 31)

Maximus was got as far as Ravenna.

[130]   1736 Butler, *Anal.* 1. iii (*OED* s.v. *rid* v. 3d)

These hopes and fears . . . cannot be got rid of by great part of the world.

[131]   1810 Syd. Smith, *Wks.* (1850) 183 (*OED* s.v. *rid* v. 3d)

Nor is this conceit very easily and speedily gotten rid of.

[132]   1888 *Berksh. Gloss.* s.v. *Veatish* (*OED* s.v. *featish* a. 'fairly well in health')

'I be got rid o' the doctor, an' be a-veelin' quite veatish like now.'

Examples [125]–[126], and [128]–[129] come from Haegeman (1985), discussed in §14.3.3 below. In my opinion it is highly doubtful whether any of [125]–[132] contain GET as passive auxiliary. If Carlyle is not to be charged with using a double perfect, BE in [126] should mark passive, not perfect, but in fact from a PDE point of view [125]–[127] look like passives of the pattern GET + NP + PA PTCP, and Jespersen seems to agree (1909–49: V 16, 36); he asserts that they correspond to the mainly American type (I give a later example):

[133]   1945 *Coast to Coast 1944* 103 (*OED*[2] s.v. *beat* v.[1] 10g)

Well, he's got me beat.

In that case the GET of [125]–[127] and [133] is no passive auxiliary. Nor is the GET of [128]–[129] either, since there is no lexical past participle. As for [130]–[131], the construction is still wholly grammatical. I assume that these apparent double passives were formed in the following steps:

[134]   A neat solution rids us of the problem.
[135]   (a) We are rid of the problem.
        (b) We get rid of the problem.
[136]   The problem is got rid of.

That is, although [135](a,b) were possible passives of [134], either of them could be interpreted as containing a statal AP *rid of the problem*, with BE/GET taken as ergative and the whole clause as active. (It is impossible to assign historical priority between active and passive readings.) Then [135](b) – which would also have had an overall dynamic meaning in the active reading – was open to reanalysis as containing a group-verb GET *rid of*. Only then could a new prepositional passive (cf. §7.5 above) be formed from it, in the same way as from TAKE *care of* or PUT *paid to*. In this way we can explain how [136] is possible but the double passives [137]–[139] are not:

[137]   *The problem is been rid of.   (⇐ [135](a))
[138]   *A ride is got taken for.   (⇐ He gets taken for a ride.)
[139]   *Free tickets were got given us.   (⇐ We got given free tickets.)

If this account is correct it suggests that the apparent GET passive [135](b) was *not* (exclusively) perceived as the passive turn of [134].[8] Compare the dual reading of *has been gone*, with BE as auxiliary or copula (§12.6.4 above). Finally we have the delightful dialect example [132]. Pleasing though it would be to come up with a *triple* passive, the obvious reading is as perfect BE + GET *rid of*.

For the sake of completeness we may note that the sequence Modal + HAVE + GET + PA PTCP is attested too, though my example is recent:

[140]   1950– *SEU* T1

If you, in fact, cleared that cupboard out to put offprints in it, it might have got cleared out then.

14.2.4.9   Progressive BE + passive GET

This is a predictable combination, though Visser, perhaps surprisingly, has no examples before the very end of the nineteenth century (1963–73: §2160):[9]

[141]   1819 Scott, *Let.* in *Lockhart* (1837) IV.viii.253 (*OED* s.v. *set-to* 2b)

My stomach is now getting confirmed, and I have great hopes the bout is over;

[142] 1837 Carlyle, *Fr. Rev.* I VII.viii.268.14

One learns also that the royal Carriages are getting yoked

[143] 1837 Dickens, *Pickwick* xxxii.479.34

Extraordinary place that city. We know a most astonishing number of men who always *are* getting disappointed there.

The gerundial use of passive GET is earlier still:[10]

[144] 1776 G. Semple, *Building in Water* 46 (*OED* s.v. *staunch* a. 1)

Our Coffer-dam . . . which we began to despair of ever getting made even tolerably stanch ['water-tight'].

However, at present I have no examples of progressive BE + passive GET preceded by another auxiliary, whether modal or perfect HAVE, though they are clearly grammatical in Present-day English. Examples like

[145] 1931 – *Big Money* xiii.309 (*OED*[2] s.v. *plaster* v., *plastered* ppl. a. b, and sim. 1958 s.v. *fed* pa.pple.)

. . . even if he had been getting steadily plastered ['drunk'] all the afternoon.

are not convincingly passive.

14.3 Explanations

Mitchell and Kilpiö discuss the OE passive forms. Mustanoja deals with the loss of WEORÐAN in the ME period, and Miller and Haegeman discuss the use of GET in Modern English. Mossé, Visser, Delancey and Denison consider the interaction of progressive and passive – and note also Kossuth (1982), dealt with in §15.3.2 below.

14.3.1 Mustanoja

Tauno F. Mustanoja summarises many previous views on the disappearance of WURTHE as auxiliary of the passive (and indeed altogether), for example the falling-together of present and past tenses of WURTHE and the influence of Latin, French or Scandinavian – none of them particularly convincing (1960: 615–19). Conceding that the disappearance was probably due to the convergence of many factors, he offers some additional factors, though his account seems just as ad hoc. He claims that the auxiliary in a passive is typically unemphatic and over time will become a mere structural sign: at that point 'one auxiliary is enough, two is one too many' (1960: 618). (So how come GET was adopted later on?) It was WURTHE that lost out because of its variety of other functions (but wasn't BE even more multi-functional?), and because BE was phonetically lighter, more suitable for the statal passive, and better supported by foreign models. But he then argues that use of WURTHE 'as a highly colourless auxiliary in passive periphrases probably weakened its position in the other functions' (1960: 618), leading to its replacement in the sense 'become' by BECOME, GROW, WAX, etc.

14.3.2 Miller

J. Miller's book on semantics and syntax devotes a chapter to GET, including a section on the GET passive which includes an account of its history (1985: §4.4.3). Miller is not a historical linguist – why did no one bring Visser (1963–73) to his attention? – and his dealings with Old English are prone to minor error, but he makes pertinent criticisms of some of the explanations for the demise of WEORÐAN found in Mustanoja (1960). Miller's own *localist* account suggests that the verbs used as auxiliaries in actional passives – WEORÐAN in Old and early Middle English, BECOME from late Middle English, TURN, FALL and GO in early Modern English, GET in Modern English – could only serve as such when their basic meaning incorporated the notion of **(concrete) movement**. The verbs which ceased – or like BECOME, virtually ceased – to serve as passive auxiliaries had lost the movement sense, and Miller speculates that GET could not take their place until it 'had become firmly established as a verb denoting the movement of people from one place to another' (1985: 190).

14.3.3 Haegeman

Liliane Haegeman (1985) tries to bring together several uses of GET in Present-day English, among them:

[146]   George got very wet.
[147]   The students got working on another topic.
[148]   His girlfriend got invited to all the meetings.

For her, GET in these constructions is an *ergative* verb, which means among other things that the surface subject is not thematically related to – is not an argument of – the verb, and that there is no Agent θ-role. It also explains why the perfect of this GET is formed with BE in 28 out of 51 *OED* citations (1985: 71), as in [128]–[129] above. Indeed she claims that GET in these constructions has not just a perfect but a passive (1985: 55–6), as in [125]–[126]. From a later discussion it appears that she is claiming that at least the eModE examples [128]–[129] are syntactically ambiguous between the passive of GET and the perfect of ergative GET (1985: 72–3), but cf. §14.2.4.8 above.

14.3.4 Mitchell

Bruce Mitchell is satisfied to attribute the absence from Old English of a progressive passive to the late appearance of a participle equivalent to *being* (1985: §§684, 753, 1099).[11] But there are still another eight centuries of non-occurrence to account for after that. Once he also points to the fact that the progressive was 'not established' in Old English (1985: §753). This explanation too – depending on what exactly it means – may not be valid much after the OE period.

14.3.5 Mossé, Visser

Fernand Mossé has an invaluable collection of material on the progressive passive (1938b: §§258–81), much of it taken over by Visser (1963–73: §§2158, 2182). Mossé argues that a precondition for its formation was the existence of participial and gerundive forms like *being printed*, which he dates to the fifteenth century (1938b: §259) – see §14.2.4.6 above. He gives a collection of different sorts of examples – they include [95]–[97] and [104] – which he says are very close to progressives, i.e. to progressive passives (1938b: §262). Visser prefers to see them as subsidiary causes, the main reason for the advent of the progressive passive being 'the urge, permanently inherent in English as an analytic language, to signal separately every separate shade of meaning, function or connotation' (1963–73: §2158).

Mossé shows that the earliest progressive passives followed on closely from the last of these precursors. He also notes that at first they occurred only in the private correspondence of young men in their twenties. He traces the ascent to respectability in the mid-nineteenth century, then makes the important point that the existence of the progressive passive remedies two separate ambiguities, since it permits an explicit contrast both with the active progressive (*he is shaving* ~ *he is being shaved*) and with the simple passive (*the house is built* ~ *the house is being built*) (1938b: §273). In §14.1.2.2 I discussed the period *before* the progressive passive [9] existed, when [7] and [8] had to act as substitutes for it. That was a mirror image of the same observation.

I find one of Mossé's alleged near-progressives, not as it happens repeated by Visser, particularly interesting:

[149]   1766 Goldsmith, *Vicar* xxv.141.22

> I . . . immediately complied with the demand, though the little money I had was very near being all exhausted.

The *all* confirms that semantically, [149] is no progressive. The analysis must be something like:

[150]   [$_{VP}$ was [$_{AP}$ [$_{DEG}$ very near] [$_{AP}$ being all exhausted]]]

Similar examples are:

[151]   1756 Toldervy, *Hist. 2 Orphans* III.111 (*OED*^{2} s.v. *scrag* v. 1a)

> Scragg'd, said she, is being hung in chains.

[152]   1780 Woodforde, *Diary* I 294.12 (12 Nov) (and similarly ibid. 1784 II 118.25 (8 Feb), 1791 III 244.22 (22 Jan))

> They [*sc.* two highwaymen] are both known and were very near being taken.

Compare my discussion of *is being wicked* in §13.3.8.2 above, where I recognised a non-progressive structure like [150] for some early examples.

Neither Mossé nor Visser distinguishes between older structures where BE and *being* are unrelated sentence elements, and newer structures where they are part of the same syntagm. Mossé merely observes that BE + *being* + AP/NP and BE + *being* + PA PTCP are analogous constructions which appeared at about the same time, but that the former remained rare until the end of the nineteenth century (1938b: §266). Visser, however, who claims a much earlier date, suggests that BE + *being* + AP may have been another subsidiary cause of the use of the progressive passive (1963–73: §§1834–5, 2158).

14.3.6 Delancey

Scott Delancey (1982) makes brief mention of the progressive passive in an article on aspect and viewpoint. His suggestion is as follows:

> The Modern English passive has never been clearly intrinsically perfective, but until well into the eighteenth century it was incompatible with the progressive construction (Mossé 1938). . . . If we consider the progressive construction to be a temporal analogue of *go* in that it specifies non-terminal viewpoint, then we can explain the cooccurrence restriction as a ban on conflicting viewpoint specifications: the terminal viewpoint specified by the passive construction is inconsistent with the explicitly non-terminal viewpoint specified by the progressive. (1982: 172)

This is an attractive way of redefining the problem, but it does not address the issue of how the ban came to be lifted. The implication is that the English passive has become less perfective over time.

14.3.7 Denison

It seems to me that the introduction of [65]–[74], the progressive passive patterns, is completely unmysterious from a present-day perspective. They provide useful meaning distinctions and – most important – fill a systemic gap in the patterning of English verbs, so that active and passive become symmetrical at every point in the extended paradigm. Why then did it take so long for them to appear? We can use their clumsiness – especially that of four- or five-verb syntagms with an initial modal or HAVE – as a partial explanation at least for their infrequency, but perhaps not for complete absence, nor for the torrent of abuse which their early use met with.

My contribution[12] is based on the familiar idea that all auxiliaries were once main verbs, and that the process of grammaticisation – which is a matter of both semantics and syntax – may have played a major part in this story. I suppose that the auxiliaries were grammaticised in the following order:

[153] auxiliary verb   grammaticisation

modals and ONGINNAN	already in OE
perfect HAVE	already in OE
passive BE	already in OE
	or fourteenth-eighteenth centuries?
periphrastic DO	fourteenth-fifteenth centuries
progressive BE	late eighteenth century?
passive GET	nineteenth-twentieth centuries?

In semantics grammaticisation probably involves generalisation and perhaps bleaching of meaning (but cf. Brinton 1988), while in syntax the (pre-) auxiliary changes from being head of its phrase to a modifier of the lexical head. (Here I shall ignore abstract formal analyses which treat PDE auxiliaries as *catenatives* and stack them in a nest of left-headed VPs or Ss.) For the various datings in [153] see Chapters 10–14.

The relevant conjecture concerns progressive BE. Of all the auxiliaries, this is the one where the semantic difference between a full-verb use and the auxiliary use is least perceptible, giving us wide latitude in dating the reanalysis. I hypothesise that it occurred comparatively late.

14.3.7.1 Progressive BE as main verb

If there has been a reanalysis of the progressive, what are the consequences of locating (the most rapid phase of) the changeover in the late ModE period? Consider these patterns:

[154] Being teaching made it easier.
[155] The house was being built.

In the earlier situation where BE was not an auxiliary but a copula followed by a predicative, [154] was unexceptionable. Compare:

[156] Being happy made it easier.

What about pattern [155], however? Had it existed it would have had the analysis main verb BE + *being built*. The phrase type *being built* did exist but tended to be resultative in meaning rather than durative, as illustrated in such examples as [157]–[158], repeated from earlier on:

[157=99] 1667 Pepys, *Diary* VIII 249.28 (3 Jun)

. . . thinking to see some cockfighting, but it was just being done; and therefore back again . . .

[158=149] 1766 Goldsmith, *Vicar* xxv.141.22

I . . . immediately complied with the demand, though the little money I had was very near being all exhausted.

See also the examples in Visser (1963–73: §1920 and cf. also §2175). So pattern [155] would probably have had an inappropriate meaning. However, some early *being Ved* examples *were* perhaps durative – I repeat one of the relevant examples [91]–[95] here – but presumably resisted acting as predicatives to BE because of the strangeness of sequences like *is being*, a problem less evident in *there*-sentences like [96], also repeated:[13]

[159=95] 1754 Richardson, *Grandison* III.vii.32.9

. . . that Miss Jervois loves to sit up late, either reading, or being read to, by Anne;

[160=96] 1769 Mrs. Harris in *Lett. 1st Ld. Malmesbury* (1870) I.180 (*OED*)

There is a good opera of Pugniani's now being acted.

Nor would a putative [155] have been supported by pattern [161], progressive BE + predicative adjective, which was not in use before the nineteenth century:

[161]   Jim was being stupid.

Here I follow Jespersen (1909–49: IV 225) and Strang (1970: 99) against Visser (1963–73: §2158); see §13.3.8.2 above. Hence the semantic and syntactic oddity of the progressive passive would explain the fierceness of some people's reactions to it.

The gap left by absence of [155] could be filled by the passival [162], whose origin was discussed in §13.3.7 above, and which looked superficially like [163]:

[162]   The house was building.
[163]   Jim was whispering.

Although [162] was theoretically ambiguous – passival or not? – it was usually possible to avoid its use where the subject was open to misinterpretation as an Agent, since the progressive was not yet grammaticised and was not generally as frequent as now. As already tabulated in §13.6.2 above, there was a partial analogy in the pair [164]–[165]:

[164]   The house was built.
[165]   Jim was arrived.

Just as with [162]–[163], a single surface pattern of BE + participle would be interpreted either as passive/ergative or as active according to the transitivity of the lexical verb and the potential agentiveness of the subject.

14.3.7.2   Progressive BE as auxiliary verb

After the reanalysis, the BE of *being* + V*ing* became merely an auxiliary verb. Although there was no overwhelming reason for [154] to become ungrammatical – and as mentioned it continues to reappear sporadically – it was now the only construction where the first auxiliary verb (the one which determines the syntax of the whole group) had the same morphology as the lexical verb. How big an anomaly that was or is, I'm not sure. With left-to-right processing it's hard to see a perceptual problem there, but all other instances have disappeared too: imperative DO + imperative V (if we assume that *keep* in *Do keep quiet* is an infinitive), infinitive DO/modal + infinitive V. It is tempting to relate the loss of the [154] pattern to the obsolescence of non-finite forms of modal BE after the time of Jane Austen (§11.3.9.3 above); see Question (d) in §14.4.

The progressive passive [155] now became possible, since it was the progressive not of passive BE but of the lexical verb. That meant that passival [162] was no longer needed to fill the gap and furthermore was now anomalous in being a one-auxiliary form that coded both aspect and passive voice (or alternatively, the only passive verbal group not ending in a past participle). Gradually it lost productivity, with those fixed phrases that survived increasingly interpreted as ergatives.

Why would the progressive have been reanalysed at that time? Well, it was roughly the time when regulation of DO went to completion, in negatives especially. What this meant was that there was now a glaring difference between verbs taking DO-Support and the 'NICE'-verbs. All *other* NICE-verbs complemented by another verb were already fully-fledged auxiliaries.[14] Perhaps this was the systemic pressure which brought progressive BE into line.[15]

14.3.7.3*   Jane Austen

Even more speculative, is it possible that Jane Austen's notorious idiosyncrasies in the progressive were for some reason *re*gressive chronologically – that is, that in her dialect BE followed by *-ing* was still a main verb? This in addition to questions of literary control and of differences between early and later novels, dialogue and narration, main clauses and various kinds of subordinate clause: see Strang (1982). Susan Wright tells me (p.c.) that the progressive is more common in her letters than her novels, in which case it would be difficult to claim that she maintained an 'old-fashioned' grammar purely for *literary* output. Warner cites another instance of Jane Austen being the last to use a particular BE construction, namely ellipsis of non-finite BE + complement after a finite antecedent (1986: 154).[16]

14.4   Questions for discussion or further research

(a) Can you find any explanation for the apparent absence from Old English of a *to*-infinitive of the passive auxiliary (§14.2.4 above)?

(b) What links can you find between the loss of the *being* + V*ing* construction and the loss of non-finite forms of modal BE (§§11.3.9.3 and 14.3.7.2 above)?

(c) (For aspiring literary detectives) Several early users of the progressive passive – among them Southey, Keats, the Shelleys, Lamb, De Quincey, Coleridge, Landor – had some literary connection with one another. Can *all* early examples be traced back to a single social network, or at least be localised regionally or socially? (Curiously enough, given examples [67] and [69] above, Landor was in the Channel Islands in 1814!)[17]

(d) Does the speculation advanced in §14.3.7.3 above – that in Jane Austen's grammar BE might have been a main verb rather than an auxiliary when followed by V*ing* – survive a careful examination of her usage? You may wish to refer to the data and explanations in Raybould (1957), Phillipps (1970), Page (1972), Strang (1982).

(e) Compare OE WEORÐAN and lModE GET as auxiliaries of the passive.

Notes

1. I have omitted two comments on the typical corresponding Latin tenses.

2. There is an oversimplification here. As we have noted, some passives do not correspond to any active form. However, prototypically there *is* correlation between passives and actives.

3. In Old English a dative or instrumental was sometimes used as an agent-phrase without a preposition, though it was usually an inanimate NP better

characterised as Instrument than Agent. See Mitchell (1985: §§1371–8), Kilpiö (1989: 153–8).

4. I have here collapsed a number of distinctions made by Kilpiö in his (1989: tables 1, 6, 7 and p.86) – indicative vs. subjunctive, *is* vs. *bið*, *sie* vs. *beo*, *Bede* vs. *CP* – to get figures of 983 BEON/WESAN to 91 WEORÐAN in the present, and 1261 to 38 in the past. A possible explanation of the difference between Kilpiö's findings and Mitchell's generalisation for Old English as a whole is that *CP*, not being a narrative work, has relatively few past tense forms, while *Bede* seems to disfavour WEORÐAN generally – which may perhaps be a Mercian dialect feature (Kilpiö 1989: 13, 98–101). For further figures Mitchell refers to Klingebiel (1937: 101–4), which I have not seen.

5. There were special forms 3 SG *hatte*, 3 PL *hatton*, used without tense variation to mean 'is/are called' and 'was/were called', respectively, which differed from the usual forms of HATAN 'call, command', namely 3 SG PRES *hæt(t)/hateð*, 3 PL *hatað*, and 3 SG PA *het/heht*, 3 PL *heton/hehton*.

6. Further examples up to c1830 in *OED*[2] (found by means of an early test release of the CD-ROM version) are dated 1826 s.v. *new* a. A.5b, a1834 s.v. *preconception*, 1828 s.v. *ring* v.[2] B.6a.

7. Non-finite *being* + passive participle should not be called 'progressive', since verbs like KNOW, OWN which resist the progressive have non-finite *-ing* forms.

   While Visser regards none of [91]–[97] as true progressive passives, Nehls (1974: 158 n.149) singles out [97] as the first certain example of the construction; see also my comment on [96].

8. It is perhaps not surprising that *OED* should be inconsistent in its analysis of what are surely parallel constructions, the idioms GET *quit of* and GET *rid of*, which provide many of the possible early examples of passive GET (to judge from a computer search of *OED* citations), such as [105]–[108]. It defines the former s.v. *quit, quite* a., therefore *not* as a GET passive, but the latter s.v. transitive *rid* v. 3d.

9. Note that his earliest examples of progressives of GET and BECOME + AP (GET *old*, BECOME *impolite*, etc.) are also from the turn of the twentieth century, though he has much older citations with the verbs GROW and WAX (1963–73: §1840). Earlier instances of progressive GET + AP, apart from the ambiguous examples of §14.2.4.7, include (a), (b) and (c) below and [112] above, while participial GET + AP is much older still, (d) below:

   (a) 1802 Woodforde, *Diary* V 403.19 (29 Aug)
        My Throat is daily getting better he says.

   (b) 1834 T. Medwin *Angler in Wales* I.21 (*OED* s.v. *genuine* a.[1] 2)
        The race of our bull-dogs is getting fast extinct, . . .

   (c) 1839 Dickens, *Ol. Twist* (1850) 60/1 (*OED* s.v. *afore* prep. B.2)
        'You're getting too proud to own me afore company, are you?'

   (d) 1624 Saunderson, *12 Serm.* (1637) 172 (*OED* s.v. *belly* v. 2)
        The Morter getting wet dissolveth . . .

10. Further examples in *OED* dated 1780 s.v. *sleep* v. B.9a, 1800 s.v. *ambs-ace*, 1827 s.v. *cram* v.

11. He cites Campbell (1959: §768) for the late West Saxon *wesende* and eleventh-century *beonde*. No present participle for WEORÐAN is recorded: the sole citation under *weorþend-* in Venezky and Healey (1980), at *GD(C)* 201.15, appears to be a manuscript error for *forweorðendan* 'vanishing'.

12. Some of the ideas in this section were first outlined in Denison (1990c).

13. Is it possible to reconcile this scenario with the typical analysis of PDE *there*-sentences in transformational grammars as derived from clauses without *there*? Would one argue that [96] derives from a pattern [96'] which was suppressed because of the unfortunate **collocation** *is . . . being*? Even Lakoff (1987: 560–1) in his discussion of PDE

    (a)   There was a man being shot.

argues that (a) 'is permitted because *A man was being shot* is permitted', because *there*-constructions have as their final phrase a syntagm which together with a finite form of BE (or GO or COME, if appropriate) can form a VP **constituent**. So on his analysis of (a), the pattern with *was* separated from *being shot* is **based on** a simple clause containing the syntagm *was being shot*.

14. I skate over modal uses of HAVE and BE.

15. Warner (1986: 164–5) also cites the regulation of DO as a factor in the reanalysis of constructions involving finite form of BE, giving 1700 and 1850 as extreme limits for the reanalysis. He further suggests that loss of *thou* and associated inflections was another causal factor, and that changes in the modals would have supported changes in BE. *All* uses of BE belong together in Warner's account.

16. From the evidence of Visser (1963–73: §1752), Sir Walter Scott is another late user of the ellipsis construction.

17. I am grateful to Grevel Lindop for his informed response to my speculations.

Chapter 15

Multiple Auxiliaries, Regulation of DO

15.1 The problems

So far we have dealt with co-occurrence of auxiliaries only to the extent that discussion of their individual paradigms has revealed what verbs, if any, could immediately precede them; see §§10.2.6.6, 11.3.6, 12.5.5, 12.6.4, 13.3.1.3, 14.2.4 above. In this chapter we review the co-occurrence possibilities as they have developed over the centuries, this time from the point of view of what verbs can *follow* a particular auxiliary. Having looked at possible pairings we can then consider longer sequences: here we must see whether these are wholly predictable from possible shorter sequences already identified. There are pros and cons in using grammatical labels like **perfect** rather than lexical items like HAVE. The former allow us to generalise across different possible exponents of the perfect (HAVE, BE, OE WEORÐAN), the latter to generalise across different uses of a particular verb (notably BE).

The virtual impossibility of periphrastic DO occurring in combination with any other auxiliary ties in with the so-called **regulation** of DO, whereby DO has come to serve as the default auxiliary in patterns where an *operator* is now obligatory. One such is in negatives, and this is the appropriate place for a brief survey of the history of negatives. And here too we may examine again (after Chapter 11) the coming into being of a grammatical category **auxiliary**.

15.2 The data

15.2.1 Combinations of auxiliaries

For the most part the verbs which we now call auxiliaries have always appeared in the same relative order as in Present-day English. The most common exceptions – and none of them are possible any longer in standard English – involve non-finite modal verbs appearing after another modal or perfect HAVE (§11.3.6.2). One can also find examples of perfect HAVE + DO (§10.2.6.6), perfect HAVE + HAVE (§12.5.6), and perfect HAVE + perfect

BE (§12.6.4). In what follows I shall make the simplifying assumption that all modal verbs can be treated together as a group – but cf. §11.4.6 above.

15.2.1.1   Two auxiliaries

A modal can be followed by an auxiliary of the perfect, the progressive or the passive, and this has been the case since Old English for all such pairs except perhaps modal + perfect BE, which is said to date from the fourteenth century but has a couple of possible OE examples (§§12.5.5, 12.6.4, 13.3.1.3, 14.2.4.2).

Perfect HAVE can be followed by an auxiliary of the progressive (from a1325) or the passive (c1180), and perfect BE by passive WURTHE (OE) (§§13.3.1.3, 14.2.4.3). For perfect HAVE + passive GET I have examples from 1832 (§14.2.4.8).

Progressive BE can be followed by an auxiliary of the passive. Finite progressive BE + passive BE is found from 1795 (§14.2.4.4), finite progressive BE + passive GET is found from 1819 (§14.2.4.9) – both rather earlier when the first verb is non-finite BE.

15.2.1.2   Three auxiliaries

If we treat BE as the only significant auxiliary of the progressive, the following four-verb combinations should be possible, with dates of their earliest occurrence where known:

(A) modal + perfect HAVE + progressive BE + V: ?a1425 (§13.3.1.3)
(B) modal + perfect HAVE + passive BE + V: a1325 (§14.2.4.3)
(C) perfect HAVE + progressive BE + passive BE + V: 1886/1929 (§14.2.4.5)
(D) modal + progressive BE + passive BE + V: 1915 (§14.2.4.5)

Patterns A to C require a past participle of BE. Patterns C and D combine progressive BE and passive BE in a single syntagm.

Including passive GET brings the following additional possibilities, all grammatical now, though data on first occurrences are not readily available:[1]

(E) modal + perfect HAVE + passive GET + V: 1950– (§14.2.4.8)
(F) modal + progressive BE + passive GET + V: PDE (§14.2.4.9)
(G) perfect HAVE + progressive BE + passive GET + V: PDE (§14.2.4.9)

The following table arranges the information given above so that dates of first occurrence of three-auxiliary (four-verb) patterns can be compared with the dates of first occurrence of each adjacent pair of auxiliaries they contain:

[1] pattern	first pair	second pair	three auxiliaries
A	OE	a1325	?a1425
B	OE	c1180	a1325
C	a1325	1795	1886/1929
D	OE	1795	1915
E	OE	1832	1950–
F	OE	1819	PDE
G	a1325	1819	PDE

Interestingly, it is always the first pairing which occurs earliest, then the second pairing, and finally the three-auxiliary pattern. However, the evidence for some of the dates is too skimpy to justify any weighty conclusions. (I have not discussed or tabulated the maximal, four-auxiliary – five-verb – sequences, on the assumption that nothing of great significance will be lost by the omission.)

15.2.2 Negation and other non-assertive forms

Negative sentences in Modern English sort the lexical sheep from the operator goats. In earlier English the distinction was of little or no significance – all verbs behaved alike – but then the form of negation was different too. In this section I give a brief survey of the changes.

Of course negation is only one of the NICE properties. I shall say the bare minimum about inversion here and nothing about code (i.e. post-verbal ellipsis) or emphasis. One other context which plays an important but idiosyncratic part in the history of auxiliaries and operators has not even been mentioned yet: the **imperative**. That too I shall neglect.

A brief excursus on inversion. Inversion of finite verb and subject can serve various purposes:

(A) to maintain V-2 (though as we saw in Chapter 4 above, **inversion** is then rather a misnomer for the syntactic processes involved)
(B) as an alternative to an *if*-clause (*Had I known who she was, I wouldn't have been so polite*)
(C) as a sign of interrogative structure

For C we can say without simplifying too grossly that throughout the recorded history of English, the principal means of forming interrogatives has been by inverting subject and finite verb. Unlike negation, the surface appearance of interrogatives has not changed much. Nowadays the only finite verbs permitted to invert are operators, but until the eModE period there was no such restriction.

In *wh*-questions a *wh*-word or -phrase appears in initial position (cancelling out the inversion if it happens to be the subject), and in earlier English it was possible to have WHETHER (*hwæðer, whether, wher*, etc.) in initial position even for polar questions, normally without subject-verb inversion:

[2] 1588 A. King tr. *Canisius' Catech.* 67 (*OED* s.v. *whether* conj. B.II.2)

Quhat is Baptisme? and quhidder it be   necessare to all
what is baptism   and whether it is(SUBJ) necessary for all
mankynd?
mankind

'What is baptism, and is it necessary for all mankind?'

See Visser (1963–73: §1454) for more examples. That usage, never very common, is now confined to dependent questions.

But the only context I have space to discuss is the finite negative, and that is where we go next. An important reference is Otto Jespersen's history of negation (1917; 1909–49: V 426–67).

15.2.2.1 *Ne* + finite verb

From Old to late Middle English the unmarked form of sentence negation[2] was simply the positive form with **proclitic *ne*** added before the finite verb:

[3] *CP* 5.16

    ac we him   ne cunnon   æfterspyrigean
    but we them(DAT) not know-how-to after-follow

   'but we do not know how to follow in their footsteps'

[4] c1400 *PPl.B* 6.144

    And al is þoruȝ   suffraunce þat vengeaunce yow   ne taketh.
    and all is through sufferance that vengeance you(OBJ) not takes

   'And it is wholly on God's sufferance that punishment does not fall upon you.'

Ne normally lost its vowel and contracted with certain verbs that began with vowel, *h-* or *w-*, namely (appropriate forms of) BEON/WESAN 'be', HABBAN 'have', and the overlapping sets of preterite-presents and modals (thus including WITAN 'know', AGAN 'have', and WILE 'will'). Contraction did not occur with WEORÐAN 'become':

[5] *CP* 5.12

    forðæmðe hie næron   on hiora agen geðiode awritene.
    because   they not-were in their own language written

   'because they were not written in their own language'

[6] *CP* 267.9

    We lacnodon Babylon, &   hio   ðeah ne wearð gehæled.
    we treated   Babylon and it(FEM) yet   not became healed

   'We treated Babylon, and yet it did not get healed.'

Proclitic *ne* (in the form *n-*) was also usually added as well to indefinite adverbs and quantifiers in the clause (*æfre* 'ever' → *næfre* 'never', *ænig* 'any' → *nænig* 'none', etc.):

[7] *ChronA* 48.8 (755)

    &   hiera   nænig   hit geþicgean nolde
    and them(GEN PL) none(NOM SG) it accept   not-wished

   'and none of them would accept it'

In non-finite clauses the equivalent form of negation was to have *ne* before the infinitive, or at least the first one if there were several (Mitchell 1985: §1602).

There was no sense that multiple negation was wrong, or that an even number of negatives cancelled each other out:

[8]   c1180 *Orm.* 13930

> Ne chæs himm nohht te Laferrd Crist Till nan   off hise posstless
> not chose him   not   the Lord   Christ for none of his   apostles

> 'The Lord did not choose him as one of his apostles.'

A small proportion of OE negatives, usually negated by *na* or *nalles* 'not at all' or *næfre* 'never', lacked preverbal *ne* (Mitchell 1985: §§1627–30):

[9]   *Beo* 247

> Næfre ic maran   geseah | eorla   ofer eorþan
> never I greater(ACC) saw   noblemen(GEN PL) over earth

> 'I never saw a mightier nobleman in the world'

15.2.2.2   *Ne* + finite verb + NOT

Over the same period it became increasingly common to reinforce the verb negator *ne* with the adverb NOT:[3]

[10]   c1230(?a1200) *Ancr.* 94b.10

> he ne   edstont nawt as foles doð; ah . . .
> he not stops   not as fools do   but . . .

> 'He does not stop, as fools do, but . . .'

By the end of the ME period the use of NOT was virtually obligatory if there was no other negative element than *ne*.

15.2.2.3   Finite lexical verb + NOT

Sporadically from early Middle English and increasingly commonly from later Middle English onwards, *ne* was omitted in favour of NOT:

[11]   c1180 *Orm.* 224

> &   spacc he nohht wiþþ tunge
> and spoke he not   with tongue

> 'and he did not speak out loud'

[12]   ?c1425(?c1400) *Loll.Serm.* 1.243

> for it sufficeþ noȝt to be vnbounden, but if . . .
> for it suffices not to be unbound   unless . . .

> '. . . for it is not enough to be unbound, unless . . .'

[13]   1667 Pepys, *Diary* VIII 514.2 (1 Nov)

> but saw not Betty

The most common position for NOT was after the finite verb. The historical development *ne* > *ne* + NOT > NOT is frequently compared to French *ne* > *ne* + *pas* 'not a step' > *pas* (the *ne* is generally omitted in colloquial spoken French). It is usually said that there were no restrictions on the list of finite verbs which could be negated by NOT, but see §15.4.9 below.

By the seventeenth century it was becoming increasingly rare to find finite verb + NOT with anything other than operators. Other verbs which survived longest in the construction were SAY, KNOW, MISTAKE, MATTER and a few others (see the slightly different lists in Ellegård 1953: 199, Strang 1970: 151, Visser 1963–73: §1441, Barber 1976: 267, Rissanen in prep.):

[14]   1769 Woodforde, *Diary* I 95.8 (17 Dec)

What it means I know not.

[15]   1785 Woodforde, *Diary* II 171.18 (23 Jan)

I doubt not of her happiness in a future Life

Apart from biblical echoes and deliberately archaic usage, examples like [14]–[15] were uncommon after about 1800.

According to Jespersen, multiple negation was already 'comparatively rare' in Elizabethan English, and from the beginning of the seventeenth to the nineteenth centuries he has only an isolated example from Goldsmith; then it came to be a literary sign of substandard English (1909–49: V 451).

15.2.2.4   Operator + NOT

By the late seventeenth or early eighteenth century we must call patterns like the following, instances of operator + NOT:

[16]   1787 Woodforde, *Diary* II 301.30 (3 Feb)

. . . her breakfast would not stay on her Stomach also

The standard way of negating verbs other than operators was to insert an empty operator, the dummy auxiliary DO:

[17]   1664 Dryden, *Dedic.* to *Rival Ladies* VIII 96.13

for did I not consider you as my Patron, I have little reason to desire you for my Judge

[18]   1787 Woodforde, *Diary* II 296.5 (18 Jan)

Briton did not return till 4 this Afternoon . . .

This is part of the so-called **regulation of DO**. Notice that [17] is a conditional sentence, which Söderlind says has an obligatory operator in Dryden's works in an inverted *protasis* without *if* (1951–8: I 219).

15.2.2.5   NOT + finite verb

As we have seen, the rule for negation with NOT had earlier specified 'finite verb' and later '(finite) operator'. After the regulation of DO, NOT *preceded* all lexical verbs except perhaps BE and HAVE. Around the time of the changeover – Visser suggests c1500–c1700 (1963–73: §1440) – a sort of intermediate pattern became moderately common:

[19]   1623(1598–9) Shakespeare, *Ado* IV.i.173

she not denies it:

This kind of negation involved the finite verb (i.e. old system) but placed

NOT before the lexical verb (i.e. new system). Kroch observes that in Visser's data it never occurs with an auxiliary verb (1989: 235).[4]

15.2.3 Regulation of DO

This label describes the process by which DO came to be virtually obligatory in NOT-negatives, inversion patterns (especially interrogatives), and emphatic sentences. The S-curve model of linguistic change seems to be appropriate here: gradual onset, rapid carrying through into majority usage, gradual elimination of residue of older usage. It seems that the regulation of DO in negatives was completed later than in interrogatives and other inversion types and emphatic affirmatives.

15.3 Explanations of history of auxiliary category

We begin with two papers within the generative tradition which tackle problems to do with multiple auxiliaries. Koopman's paper sticks to Old English and combines exhaustive data collection with a formal analysis. Kossuth's is less formal, introduces no data of its own, and has most to say about the ModE period. But what exactly would it mean for a verb to be called an **auxiliary**? Warner reviews the evidence for such a category in Old English. (We have already looked at his more general overview of its development in the history of English (§11.4.5.2 above), and a book-length study is promised.)

Here may be the place to mention a comment made in passing by Olga Fischer while discussing the OE V+I pattern (1991: §2.3.3.1). In Old English, she suggests, it was easier for the unexpressed subject of the *lower* verb, PRO, to have arbitrary reference than in Present-day English, where PRO tends to be *controlled* by the *higher* ('matrix') subject:

> This preferential control pattern for PRO did not yet exist in Old English. The strong link between PRO and the matrix subject became established only in the Middle English period when this control pattern was reinforced by the emergence of a variety of periphrastic constructions (perfect *have*, progressive *be*, inchoative *ginnen*, etc.).

Her attempt to explain the demise of V+I is linked in this way to the emergence of a number of auxiliaries, which she locates in Middle English.

15.3.1 Koopman

15.3.1.1 Multiple auxiliaries in Old English

Willem Koopman (1990c) considers the various possible orderings of three-verb clusters in Old English. All contain a modal, an infinitive (BEON/ WESAN, WEORÐAN or HABBAN), and a lexical participle. Koopman's purpose is to investigate which of the six theoretically available permutations actually occurred, and to offer an explanation in GB terms.

His starting-point is the assumption that base order is verb-final in Old

English, that a V-2 process is responsible for typical main-clause order, and that a rule of Verb raising is necessary. One surface order is not found outside interlinear glosses: infinitive – participle – finite verb. Koopman decides to rule it out as ungrammatical. Two other orders are just frequent enough to justify treatment as marginal. Comparison between the possible outputs of his rules and the actually attested patterns prompts him to reject Verb raising to the left of the higher verb and to permit raising of a V or of (part of) a VP only to the right; cf. §4.7.1.2 above. Koopman seems to have vindicated the application of formal syntax to a dead language, as he can explain distributions which traditional grammar has little to say about. As a bonus he succeeds in restricting the power of the grammar.

Unfortunately, two new optional rules turn out to be necessary: Inversion to swap adjacent verbs if they are non-branching sister nodes, and Reanalysis of verbal clusters like *wolde beon genumen* 'would be taken' from [20](a) to (b):

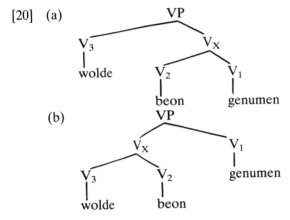

[20] (a)

(b)

Koopman does his best to motivate both of these rules with additional data. He treats Reanalysis as a marked rule in order to account for the low frequencies of the two surface orders which require its invocation. Does it, however, have any significance other than as a technical solution to a formal problem? Structurally it appears to imply the development of an auxiliary group in English, which would be interesting even outside GB formalism. Inversion too depends on the recognition that two verbs form a cluster, though Koopman's examples include both the inversion of two auxiliaries and the inversion of one auxiliary with the lexical participle, in one instance within the same derivation! It would be nice if the various structural clusterings posited by the analysis could be better motivated. Laurel Brinton, for example, identifies the possibility of treating potential auxiliary + lexical verb as a unit as an important factor in auxiliation. Writing of the modals she says:

> As with the development of the perfect, it is the collocation of preterite-present verb and infinitive, the possible analysis of this collocation as a single syntagm, and the semantic range of these preterite-present verbs which effect the reanalysis [of former main verbs as auxiliaries – D.D.]. (1988: 105)

Could Koopman's analysis be extended beyond Old English? – see Question (e) in §15.5 below.

15.3.1.2 Auxiliation

Koopman makes a brief case for treating perfect HABBAN and passive BEON/WESAN as main verbs in Old English, since they occurred in the same positions as modals (1990c: 287–8). He offers

[21] *ÆCHom* I 19.266.36

oðþæt ge habban ealle eowre gyltas geðrowade
until you have   all   your sins   atoned-for

'until you have atoned for all your sins'

as the kind of example most conveniently explained by a Verb-raising analysis. But this would be a main verb of auxiliary-like properties, for Koopman's analysis implies that

(A) in underlying structure HABBAN and BEON were main verbs
(B) in surface structure HABBAN/BEON + lexical verb had fused to form a single verbal group

Koopman's working assumption is that modals, perfect HABBAN, passive BEON/WESAN, and presumably progressive BEON/WESAN – all termed 'auxiliaries' – all behaved in essentially the same way in Old English.

15.3.2 Kossuth

Karen C. Kossuth (1982) offers a general account of combinations involving the principal auxiliaries. She assumes without detailed argument that BE was grammaticised as auxiliary of perfect, progressive and passive in Old English, and that perfect HAVE was grammaticised by Middle English. For modals she follows Lightfoot (1974). Periphrastic DO she dates conservatively to 'very late ME'. All these datings, necessarily based on indirect evidence, are of course open to challenge, though Kossuth rather takes them for granted. The focus of her interest, however, is the dating of auxiliary combinations, and here she is properly aware that individual 'first examples' are risky: they may be learned innovations which are uncharacteristically early, or alternatively the written record may be slow to record an innovation in the vernacular. I shall not present her timetables in detail, whether of grammaticisation of individual auxiliaries or of possibilities of combination, since I have already given my own versions at some length. (See her chart at 1982: 294.) Note, however, her theory 'that the order of appearance in co-occurrences parallels that of the original auxiliarization, but with a lag of a good century' (1982: 291). That last figure seems about right, to judge from my table in [1].

Kossuth works with two hypotheses:

(A) the Base Order Constraint
(B) the Once-per-Clause Constraint

Hypothesis A is the old TG assumption that optional *constituents* Modal,

Perfect and Progressive can be inserted only in that particular relative order in the base component of the grammar. Combined with the (now-abandoned) assumption that Passive can be added transformationally only at a position after all other auxiliaries, Kossuth gets the familiar order Modal – Perfect – Progressive – Passive essentially by stipulation (apparently both for Present-day English and as a historical invariant). B is more interesting. It states that each of these optional constituents can appear at most once, but the basis of the rule has undergone a significant change in the last two hundred years. Formerly it had to be stated in terms of lexical items like BE, latterly in terms of grammatical categories like Progressive.

Kossuth's attempts to corroborate this reformulation with some facts of auxiliary combination meet with mixed success. A brief discussion of double -*ing* patterns (with a rather loose use of the term **gerund**) leads to the claim that 'it is doubtful whether any such doubled gerunds could have found acceptance before the reformulation of the Once-per-Clause Constraint' (1982: 289): see §13.3.8.1 above for some eModE examples!

Then comes the following example:

[22]   a1225(?a1200) Lay.*Brut* 4152

> Twien þu hafuest i-beon   ouer-cummen
> twice you have   been(PA PTCP) overcome(PA PTCP)

'Twice you have been overcome'

wrongly described as a double perfect, when *i-beon* is clearly passive rather than perfect BE. Now there *are* valid ME examples of perfect HAVE + perfect BE (§12.6.4 above), but the pattern has remained possible to the present day, when the reformulated constraint ought to have ruled it out.

The next kind of doubling is double HAVE (discussed in §12.5.6 above). Kossuth argues that its failure to gain acceptance is in part due to the Once-per-Clause Constraint, but whereas the earlier, lexical form of the constraint should have been more pertinent to this construction than a later, grammatical one, the acceptability of double HAVE has gone the wrong way if Visser is correct in his belief that it was once fully standard (1963–73: §2157).

Kossuth's best evidence is the advent of the progressive passive, and here indeed the facts are with her – but then the reformulation was evidently thought up with this case in mind.

15.3.3 Warner

Anthony R. Warner (1992) examines two formal properties which might be thought distinctive of a potential word class 'auxiliary' in Old English:

(A) transparency to impersonal constructions
(B) post-verbal ellipsis, which includes pseudogapping

We shall take them in turn.

Property A, which for Warner comes second in order and significance, has been mentioned at several points already (§§9.3.5–6, 11.3.2.2, 11.3.9.6 above). The verbs which show it are: MÆG, SCEAL, ÞEARF, WILE, ?MOT,

BEON/WESAN, WEORÐAN, ONGINNAN/AGINNAN. The query over MOT is because there are no certain examples which are wholly subjectless. Warner argues that it is difficult to rule out a Subject-raising analysis of A in Old English, and that A correlates well with a semantic property, so that it does not provide strong support for analysing verbs as auxiliaries.

Now to B, mentioned briefly in the context of DO in §10.2.7 above. Pseudogapping is the construction seen in PDE examples like the following, where I have marked the ellipses with Δ:

[23] If you don't believe me, you will Δ the weatherman!
[24] – That carpet reminds me of the kind of thing you see in waiting rooms.
      – It doesn't Δ me Δ.

Warner argues (1992: 180–1) that the partial ellipsis in [23]–[24] is essentially the same as post-verbal (in Present-day English, post-*auxiliary*) ellipsis:

[25] Paul will bring Mary because he should Δ.

In both cases the gap must follow an auxiliary, so long as we include substitute DO in that category.[5]

After careful weeding out of cases where an apparent ellipsis can be reconstructed from the semantics of what is left (as in modal + adverbial of direction), or from the context of situation rather than the specific linguistic context, Warner finds the B constructions to be quite common in Old English and to function in a similar way to those of Present-day English. His list of verbs which exhibit one or both of the B constructions – I skip much careful discussion and several caveats – is as follows: MÆG, SCEAL, WILE, DEARR, MOT, ÞEARF, CANN, UTON, BEON/WESAN, DON, ?ONGINNAN/ ?AGINNAN (Warner 1992: 185–6 and Table 1, 200).[6] Some examples:

[26] *Bo* 25.27

forðy   is betere þæt feoh   þætte næfre losian ne mæg ðonne
therefore is better the property which never perish not can   than

þætte   mæg &   sceal.
that-which can and must

'therefore that property which can never perish is better than that which can and will Δ'

[27] *Bo* 19.15

þa   ðu wilnodest to   us þæs godes   ðe ðu to   him
when you desired   from us the good(GEN) that you from him

sceoldes.
should

'when you desired from us the good that you should Δ from him'

The query over ONGINNAN is because of neutralisation between post-verbal ellipsis and the intransitive use seen in

[28]   *ÆGram* 6.3

and þa   syx   ongynnaþ of   ðam stæfe *e* and
and those six [*sc.* letternames *flmnrs*] begin   with the letter 'e' and

geendjaþ on him sylfum. *x* ana   ongynð of   þam stæfe *i*
end   on themselves 'x' alone begins with the letter 'i'

æfter   uðwitena tæcinge.
according-to scholars' teaching

Similar worries about CANN, MÆG, ÞEARF and WILE are less pressing. There follows an intricate and cautious evaluation of the theoretical status of the B facts for Old English, with the interim conclusion that

> some Old English verbs (a potential auxiliary group, including pro-verbal *don*) shared a formal property distinguishing them from other verbs. (1992: 191)

Warner then tabulates the distributions of B – with pseudogapping and post-verbal ellipsis separately plotted – and of A among twelve verbs. The following verbs probably show both A and B: MÆG, MOT, SCEAL, ÞEARF, WILE, BEON/WESAN. A purely semantic explanation can be found for the absence of A with CANN, DEARR, UTON and perhaps DON. If this is accepted, A correlates very well with B, only WEORÐAN and ONGINNAN showing one property, A, but not the other. Warner's position on the notional significance of this grouping mirrors closely what he says about its syntactic/word-class significance:

> pigeonholing this group under the notional label 'auxiliary verb' would be an oversimplification. I prefer to conclude that the following view is plausible, where the term 'subordinate-level category' is used in Rosch's sense of a relatively poorly defined, less distinct level of categorization: Old English had a linguistically significant 'subordinate-level category' of verbs with some of the semantic characteristics of the notional class 'auxiliary verb'. (1992: 203)

15.4   Explanations of regulation of DO

This crucial topic in the history of English has been examined through all sorts of lenses, and only a sample can appear here.

Many workers give some sort of functional explanation for the rise and selective fall of DO. The spread of DO has been linked to a number of factors, while its regulation is often explained as a matter of pattern extension. Ellegård gives statistical backing to his account by careful counting of examples in a wide range of prose works. More recently his material has been given sophisticated statistical reinterpretation by Kroch and his fellow workers in what we might call the North American school of quantitative sociolinguistics. They are making increasing use of computer programs which manipulate numbers to infer causal relationships and to plot charts and graphs. A collection of frequencies which might be amenable to number-crunching is also available in Rankova's work, though her classification is fairly crude.

Stein downplays pure syntax but brings in many other kinds of factor, including phonetics and discourse marking functions. Penhallurick gives a semantic-pragmatic explanation. Salmon deals with both context of situation and purely intralinguistic factors in a very selective corpus. The Helsinki school – Rissanen and Nevalainen – work from well-constructed corpora and make a careful classification of data, and where they use computers it is mostly to store and search through the primary data. Nevalainen looks at liturgical language, Rissanen concentrates on speech-like writing, including early American material. Tieken also looks at informal writing and the distinction between speech and writing, concentrating on the seventeenth and eighteenth centuries. All of this work apart from Penhallurick's makes liberal use of tables and graphs, usually of simple frequencies without fancy statistical analysis. In a modest proposal made for the first time below – that the regulation of DO be seen as following on from a general trend in auxiliary usage, a proposal which bridges this section and §15.3 – I defend a tiny sample with elementary statistics.

F. Th. Visser is as always a treasury of examples and a useful survey of previous work (1963–73: §§1418–76), though some of his early examples are dubious or wrong (see §10.2.6 above).

15.4.1 Ellegård

Part II of Alvar Ellegård's dissertation (1953) offers statistical evidence from prose texts on the regulation of DO. Once again (cf. §10.3.4) Ellegård distils and refines some of the claims made by Engblom (1938) and other early workers.

Ellegård makes clear that negatives and interrogatives with DO have always been relatively more frequent than affirmatives, from the earliest times that the forms have been recorded at all. He tabulates over 9600 instances of periphrastic DO, divided into chronological periods of varying lengths, in five syntactic contexts. He sets each figure against an estimate of the potential maximum number of occurrences in his corpus (that is, the total number of finite verbs, apart from those which are auxiliaries other than DO). Questions, negatives and negative imperatives all moved towards categorical use of DO by 1700. Affirmative use reached a peak of 9.3 per cent in the 1550–75 period, then fell away again; negative patterns also showed a hiccup in their rise at this point. The table is also represented as a graph (1953: 162) which has been widely reproduced, among others by Mustanoja (1960: 608), Barber (1976: 266), Stein (1990: 15), Görlach (1991: 118), and in a more detailed variant by Kroch (1989: 223).

As far as sociolinguistic patterning is concerned, Ellegård suggests that the use of periphrastic DO in declaratives was mainly literary in the late fifteenth and early sixteenth centuries. By the middle of the sixteenth century, he thinks, the usage had spread downwards socially but was still something of an affectation. As regulation proceeded in the later sixteenth and seventeenth centuries, a mirror-image distribution developed, with 'unregulated' relic forms without DO becoming more a feature of literary than of popular language. In interrogatives, on the other hand, no social distinction or marking is perceptible (1953: 164–9).

Ellegård investigates earlier hypotheses that DO might facilitate the placing of an adverb before the lexical verb (1953: 180–7). His conclusion is that 'the less common anteposition was with an adverb, the more likely was the do-form to be used when anteposition was for some reason adopted' (1953: 186), but that the effect was not of great overall importance except with the adverb *but* and above all with *not*.

The discussion of negative sentences is . . . well, *negative* (1953: 192–201). It is difficult to extract a clear result, other than the early favouring of DO in this context, which Ellegård explains by the following sequence:

(A) lightly stressed adverbs came to stand before the verb
(B) NOT lost its stress after the demise of *ne*, but too late to join in A
(C) DO periphrasis allowed NOT to precede a lexical verb without losing its traditional disaffinity for the position before a finite verb

He offers conflicting messages on whether the use of DO was motivated by a desire to keep verb and object together in negative sentences (1953: 194–7), but he does conclude that the presence of a second adverb in a NOT-negative gave a significant advantage to the use of DO (1953: 198–9). The section closes with some discussion of verbs which resisted periphrasis with DO when negated: the familiar KNOW, DOUBT, and so on, but also surprises like COME.

Questions are of course next (1953: 201–7). By comparing direct and indirect questions, Ellegård immediately shows that it is the inversion which is significant for the use of DO. He continues:

> In declarative sentences with a transitive verb inversion was given up in favour of direct order. This way of avoiding inversion did not and could not easily be used in questions, since inversion had here the semantic function of indicating the interrogative nature of the statement. Simple direct order would have left this function to intonation only. Such might have become the development in England – as it has been to a large extent in France – but for the appearance of the do-form, which made inversion unobtrusive. (1953: 202).

Inversion questions favoured the use of DO from early on, especially polar = yes/no-questions. However, adverb-questions (= those where the *wh*-word is *when, where*, etc.) used DO slightly less frequently, and object-questions[7] less frequently still (relative to polar questions with transitive verbs). As for the polar questions (= 'v-questions' in Ellegård's terminology), substitute DO is suggested as a reinforcement:

> The striking advantage of the v-questions might perhaps also be explained as due to the fact that they – and only they – naturally suggest a (pro-verbal) do in the answer. Once the periphrasis had gained a firm foothold in the questions it might receive further strength from this additional anticipatory function. (1953: 205)

One of his examples:

[29]   1616 Jonson III, *Every Man in his Humour* I.ii.71

       or dost thou thinke vs all Iewes . . . If thou dost, come ouer

Negative questions show predictably greater use of DO than either negative declaratives or positive questions. The section concludes with some peculiarities of individual verbs, including the fact that in polar questions KNOW did not particularly resist DO but behaved like any other verb (1953: 207).

For inversion in sentences other than interrogatives Ellegård (1953: 187–92) reaches a similar conclusion to the one quoted above on anteposition of adverbs: 'when inversion was for some reason resorted to, it was more and more often achieved by means of the do-form' (1953: 190–1). It is with transitive verbs that this function of DO played a significant role. One kind of inversion is after a negative or restrictive (semi-negative) item:

[30] 1579 Lyly, *Euphues* I 205.9

   lyttle dost thou know the sodayne sorrow that . . .

[31] 1674 Dryden, *Morocco* XVII 84.8

   Never did I see such a confus'd heap of false Grammar, . . .

Ellegård confirms that this kind of inversion entered the language quite suddenly in the sixteenth century, and that for sentences without another auxiliary it was 'almost wholly achieved' by means of DO (1953: 192).[8] See also Jacobsson (1951).

Ellegård's overall explanation of the regulation of DO places central importance on two changes: movement of lightly stressed adverbs to a position between subject and main verb (point A above), and 'the virtual disappearance of inversion for other than auxiliaries and intransitive verbs' (1953: 209).

15.4.2 Rankova[9]

Maria Rankova's monograph (1964) is not without value, but her apparent lack of access to western research after about 1950 means that she often goes back over ground trodden by the earlier commentators. She treats the use of periphrastic DO in very late Middle English and early Modern English in considerable detail, using for the fifteenth century a corpus composed of drama, letters and a couple of prose texts, and for the period 1497–1642 a corpus of drama alone. Her approach is descriptive and interpretative, sensible but often impressionistic. Unlike Ellegård she does not give a full listing of examples, but she does quote rather more of them than he does. A tabular appendix on the later corpus of some 170 plays gives frequency of simple verb and DO periphrasis in the categories interrogative, negative,[10] imperative, and affirmative for each play and overall for each author, rather than grouping the material into chronological blocks by publication date.

15.4.3 Salmon

A paper by Vivian Salmon (1965) is worth noting here. She too takes her data from drama, but very selectively: only four of Shakespeare's *Henry* plays, only prose, and only those features of language which indicate one speaker's awareness of another, and his linguistic reactions to given situations, ... These are the structures which correspond in language to questions, commands and exclamations in the situation, as well as the 'incomplete'[11] . . . structures which are completed by some element in the situation, or which depend on some previous utterance' (1965: 106)

Her discussion of this choice of material as the best evidence for colloquial English of the time – better than letters, she argues – is interesting in its own right, as is her defence of (her, modern) native-speaker intuitions about the corpus, so long as there is contemporary evidence to support them, for example the testimony of grammarians of the time (1965: 109).

Her underlying assumption is that a choice of forms for a given function usually presupposes an opposition between marked and **unmarked** choices. We are concerned here with her comments on periphrastic DO, which naturally plays a large part in the discussion. A table of structures (1965: 115) offers rows corresponding to declaratives, interrogatives and imperatives and with either SV or VS order (and various subdivisions), and columns corresponding to simple verb, operator + infinitive, and operator alone (post-auxiliary ellipsis). Figures are given not in the table but in the discussion of individual cells. She discusses, for instance, the choice between simple verb and DO periphrasis in affirmatives, finding only 4 with DO from a possible total of 425 in *1 Henry IV*, and 41 in her whole corpus, so that DO must be the marked option. Various situational and linguistic reasons are offered for its use in those 41 examples (emphasis, intensity, formality, avoidance of consonant cluster, second adverb). She also reckons that DO is the marked option in negatives (25 out of a possible 99), but that the process of replacement of simple verb by DO was already in progress.

I have no room to discuss all of Salmon's material, which deserves a careful reading. Her deep knowledge of Elizabethan English guarantees that she has not merely leapt to conclusions (this small corpus cannot always give her real statistical backing), and she makes an interesting attempt to be explicit and definite about the reasons for the choice of a given structure.

15.4.4 Kroch et al.

Anthony Kroch, alone and in collaboration, has written a series of papers on the spread of periphrastic DO, two of which are discussed here.

15.4.4.1 Kroch, Myhill and Pintzuk

The paper by Anthony Kroch, J. Myhill and Susan Pintzuk (1982) uses Ellegård's sixteenth-century data[12] to investigate how DO became dominant in questions which lacked any other operator or auxiliary, tracing its use in a series of environments, and looking for a functional explanation for the order of adoption.

They say that 'transitive sentences with full noun phrase subjects are essentially categorical in their use of *do* from the earliest time that *do* in questions becomes noticeably frequent' (1982: 285) – 93 per cent of relevant cases in their sample. This is put down to the greater fixity of SVO word order, so that sentences like [32]–[33] became increasingly anomalous (though not ambiguous):

[32]   1503–5 *Val. & Orson*(W) 24.23

Alas wherfore lyghteth me the sonne . . . [?]

[33]   1509–21 Fisher, *English Works* 195.16

Of whome receyueth the sonne his course?

The subject, *the sonne* in both of these instances, is in [32] reversed in position with the object and in [33] 'in object position' – relative to an SVO norm. That DO served to discriminate subjects from objects is shown by the lag of intransitive sentences behind transitive ones in the use of DO.

Pronoun subjects reduced the rate of DO use because of their *enclitic* nature when following a verb, so that in an example like [34] the subject pronoun was more like an inflection than a separate word:

[34]   (a1470) Malory, *Wks.* 812.1

But for what cause slewyst thou thys nyght my modyrs squyar?

'But for what reason did you kill my mother's squire tonight?'

Hence [34] did not really have VSO order syntactically, unlike [33]. When the object was also a pronoun, however, the frequency of DO was higher, since two enclitic pronouns in sequence made for a phonologically awkward word, more so still if the clitic NOT was present as well – hence the rarity of the patterns [35]–[36]:

[35]   (a1470) Malory, *Wks.* 1174.6

Toke ye hym in the quenys chambir?

'Did you capture him in the queen's chamber?'

[36]   (a1470) Malory, *Wks.* 975.6

A, fayre sir . . . know ye me nat?

'Ah, good sir . . . do you not know me?'

Kroch et al. then give some evidence for the decliticisation of subject (but not object) pronouns in the course of the sixteenth century, and suggest that this went hand in hand with the gradual increase in frequency of DO. See Question (f) in §15.5 below.

15.4.4.2*   Logistic curve

Kroch (1989) uses the rise of DO as the most extensive of four historical changes intended to confirm his hypothesis that a linguistic change spreads at the same rate in all contexts. He first models the often-observed S-curve of linguistic change by a particular, and convenient, mathematical function, the **logistic curve**. A transform of this function – the natural logarithm of the ratio between the frequencies of advancing and recessive form – is a linear function of time. That is, when plotted on a graph against time it gives a straight line whose slope is a measure of the rate of replacement of the old form by the new. Figures for the use of DO for the period 1400–1575, again derived from Ellegård (1953), show a constant rate in all relevant environments distinguishable in Ellegård's data.

15.4.4.3   Kroch (1989)

The particular analysis for DO which Kroch develops in his (1989) is similar to that of Roberts (1985b) and van Kemenade (forthcoming) (§§11.4.3–4 above). The top-most verb in underlying structure moves from the V node in VP to an I(NFL) node outside the VP, so-called V-to-I raising. The significant historical change in English is that V-to-I raising came to be limited to auxiliary verbs only, culminating in the reanalysis of auxiliaries as underlying INFL elements and the demise of V-to-I raising. The reanalysis is dated c1575, since, in Kroch's view, Ellegård's data for negative declaratives and four categories of question show DO advancing in all these contexts along conventional S-curves until the end of the 1550–75 chronological block, where discontinuities occur. Plotting these five curves in the way outlined in §15.4.4.2 above allows him to claim that the rate of advance is the same in each context. An incidental but interesting finding is to suggest a starting-point for the process after 1300, perhaps around 1350 (1989: 224–5).[13] Kroch finds further support for his own argument – and for one of Ellegård's explanations – by calculating a very similar rate of change for the repositioning of unstressed adverbs, which for Kroch is another reflex of the loss of V-to-I raising.

(Unstressed) affirmative declaratives are different to the other, 'NICE' contexts for DO, however. Their rate of advance is lower (a tentative attempt is made to justify the difference between the figures). Kroch's syntactic explanation is that the use of DO here has nothing to do with V-to-I raising (1989: 229–32). And of course they decline in frequency after the late sixteenth century rather than going on to eventual categoriality.

Finally, after some discussion of unresolved issues, Kroch plots the rate of increase in various contexts after the late-sixteenth-century discontinuity. Now there appear to be three rather than two groups:

(A) affirmative declaratives
(B) negative declaratives
(C) questions

A tentative syntactic explanation is offered for each of the three. For group A the simple verb competed with the DO periphrasis and eventually won out. Groups B and C went their separate ways after the loss of V-to-I raising. For B Kroch proposes optional enclisis of NOT on the end of a tensed main verb (though no direct evidence is offered): this would have made the use of DO redundant and could therefore explain the temporary cessation in the rise of DO in negatives after 1575. In the middle of the seventeenth century there was a reanalysis of NOT from VP adjunct to head of its own phrase, which would have made DO obligatory in negatives, and the next couple of hundred years reflect the rivalry of the two analyses of NOT until the Negative Phrase analysis won out (1989: 234–6). For group C a new analysis with direct V-to-COMP movement is proposed as a rival –

eventually unsuccessful – to the use of DO in INFL (1989: 236–7). Many of the details here will no doubt change as the GB machine rolls on, but the attempt to relate syntactic change to variation analysis remains a very promising area of study.

15.4.5 Stein

Dieter Stein has elaborated his ideas on DO in a series of articles and a book (1985, in German), now superseded by another long monograph which has developed out of it (1990, in English), no less resistant to summary. Stein explicitly disavows monolithic explanations, especially purely syntactic ones. Almost every other kind is brought into his multi-factorial account, however.

Stein divides the history of periphrastic DO into four stages (1990: 13–16):

(I)   co-existence of causative and meaningless periphrastic DO: up to the fifteenth century
(II)   dramatic rise of DO occurrences in all syntactic contexts: end of fifteenth to end of sixteenth centuries
(III) beginning of regulation of DO, where frequency of DO co-varies with language-internal factors in a way not observed during stage II: last two decades of sixteenth and beginning of seventeenth centuries
(IV) completion of regulation apart from residual usages: seventeenth century and beyond

One of his theses is that the statistical discontinuity in use of DO around 1600 – shown as a dip in Ellegård's famous diagram – reflects a fundamental change in its meaning and in the factors which determined its distribution. (For Kroch, of course, it reflects a syntactic reanalysis; see §15.4.4 above.)

An important part is played by sociolinguistics and the distinction between 'change from above' (implicated in his stage II) and 'change from below' (implicated in stages I and III) (1990: 131). He discusses **phonotactic** factors (possible sound sequences), especially in the use of DO to avoid consonantal clusters like *disput(e)dst thou*. And he marshals evidence for the use of DO as a discourse marker, especially to mark discourse prominence or structural foregrounding, later subsumed under the heading of **intensity**.

15.4.6 The Helsinki school

15.4.6.1 Rissanen

Matti Rissanen (1985, 1991) offers an analysis of periphrastic DO in corpora of speech-like, seventeenth-century, AmE and BrE material. He explicitly contrasts his concentration on spoken usage with Ellegård's conclusion that DO was (at least early on, and in affirmatives) a literary and formal usage, suggesting that a largely literary corpus is partly responsible for Ellegård's judgement. Rissanen also emphasises that ' "spoken" is not synonymous with "colloquial", or "informal" ' (1991: 322), and he cites Nevalainen and Rissanen (1986) on PDE periphrastic DO in support of the claim that written texts – and indeed standard grammars – underestimate the extent to which unstressed affirmative DO has survived and so are unlikely to be good guides to historical usage either.

Rissanen finds that use of DO in affirmative statements reached a peak in the period 1570–1640, which he thinks may be a better dating than Ellegård's 1550–1575 (1991: 328 and n.15). Comparison is difficult, since the relevant parts of Rissanen's Helsinki Corpus are smaller than Ellegård's, have a coarser chronological mesh, but are more systematically constructed, and Rissanen counts DO per 10,000 words rather than as a proportion of possible instances, a procedure which is economical of time but which perhaps needs more defence than his (1991: 338–9 n.7).[14] Rissanen finds it 'obvious that *do*-periphrasis is a marked form even in spoken discourse' (1991: 328) and is able to give an explanation for the different patterns of usage in different text-types (sometimes, individual texts). I quote at length some particularly interesting observations on the period 1570–1640:

> It may seem astonishing . . . that the frequency of *do*-periphrasis drops sharply in trials . . ., while it increases in most other text types. But if we assume that the rapid increase in the use of the periphrasis in the 16th century began in spoken language and moved from there to writing, it is only natural that its equally rapid decrease in affirmative statements began at the spoken level. This decrease may have been, at least to some extent, due to the regularisation process of the periphrasis as an element in forming questions and *not*-negations, which undermined its "non-systematic" use as a discourse marker in affirmative statements. It is also worth pointing out that in the seventeenth century the periphrastic structure *be + -ing* was established, and this structure probably took over some of the functions which might otherwise have supported the retention of *do*-periphrasis in affirmative statements. (1991: 328–9)

After some discussion of the decline of DO in the period 1640–1710, Rissanen develops his case for differential use of DO according to medium to suggest – *à la* Tieken – an origin in OE speech (cf. §10.3.7 above). Rissanen (in prep.) includes some of the above points in a useful overview of the regulation of DO.

15.4.6.2 Nevalainen

Terttu Nevalainen (1991) virtually takes the other side of the coin: she concentrates on the *survival* of affirmative declarative DO in the seventeenth-century language of liturgy. Her data come from two eModE editions of *The Book of Common Prayer*, with comparative religious material from the Helsinki Corpus. Having evaluated various meanings for DO and found that no one of them accounts for enough of the data, she assumes that periphrastic DO in affirmative declaratives is meaningless (1991: 305–8). If the alternation with simple verbs is not semantically conditioned, what then are the conditioning factors? Nevalainen says that she selected the eight most promising candidates – (A) phonotactic, (B) syntactic, (C) stylistic, (D) textual – from an initial total of fifteen criteria:

(A1) second person singular
(A2) past tense
(B1) separation of subject from verb

(B2) preverbal adverbial
(C1) structural coordination, whether of V, VP, or clause
(C2) clause-final verb
(D1) translation
(D2) clausal subordination.

The phonotactic factors A1, A2 and textual factors D1, D2 turn out to 'yield a highly significant difference between the simple verb form and periphrastic *do*' (1991: 313). The syntactic factor B1 is **significant** in the 1662 edition and almost significant in 1552, but B2 is not. The stylistic factor C2 is significant, more so in 1662, while C1 is almost significant. In the comparative material factors A2, D2, C1 'have a relatively high incidence with *do*' (1991: 313), plus B1 in sermons.

A tabulation of the number of factors constraining use of DO in different samples shows *inter alia*

> that in the 1662 Prayer Book, *do* is only added to heavily marked contexts. This is of course what one would expect in a change-from-above situation: conscious change will emerge in the most salient linguistic environments (Naro–Lemle 1976 . . .) (Nevalainen 1991: 315).

Finally, after some discussion of the language of collects (i.e. short prayers), where the most potent factors converge, Nevalainen finds support for the idea of an established religious usage in the seventeenth century.

15.4.7 Tieken

Ingrid Tieken-Boon van Ostade mostly concentrates on the later history of DO. Her dissertation (1987) takes a purely syntactic approach to eighteenth-century data, drawing a collection of nearly 650 instances from major authors whose work extends over the different stylistic categories of informative prose, epistolary prose, and direct speech (i.e. dialogue). Her concern is with questions and negatives which lack DO in contexts where standard PDE usage would require it; the negatives predominate. Her tentative conclusion is that the eighteenth-century change, unlike the earlier stages of regulation, may well have been a change from above, and she considers the possibility that normative influence of the newly emergent grammatical tradition may have been partly responsible.

15.4.8 Penhallurick[15]

John M. Penhallurick (1985) approaches the semantics of PDE DO from the Bolingerian position that it is unlikely to be wholly empty of meaning. He suggests that it means 'occurrence questioned'. Thus DO is essentially modal in its semantics and is at least not inappropriate in NICE-contexts and in imperatives. A brief historical coda suggests that a meaningless auxiliary DO was created out of ME lexical DO to resolve a tension between historic inversion patterns and an increasing fixity of S-V order. Later the choice of

DO was interpreted as mean*ingful*, therefore modal, a semantic development which motivated the subsequent syntactic regulation.

15.4.9 Denison

I have two suggestions for future research (neither based on published work on the regulation of DO). One, already noted in §§4.8, 10.3.8 above, is that there might be a correlation between the rise of the DO periphrasis and the rise of idioms or semi-lexicalised units consisting of verb and other parts of the VP – items like TAKE *place*, TAKE *a swim*, LAUGH *at*, CLOSE *up*, CRY *out on*, PAY *heed to*, and so on. As far as I know this is one factor which has not been looked for in statistical work on DO.

The other is based on my longstanding impression that for centuries before the regulation of DO, quite a high proportion of clauses with NOT after the finite verb had (what is now) an *operator* as their finite verb. That is, the pattern *John saw not his father* seems to have been more uncommon compared to *John may not see his father, John has not seen his father, Max is not his father*, etc., than might have been expected given the frequencies of the corresponding affirmative sentences.

I have made a preliminary check by looking at a relatively colloquial text from the late fifteenth century, when periphrastic DO was in infrequent use and had by no means reached its peak, let alone been regulated. The distribution of tensed verbs and NOT in six of the *Paston Letters* is as follows, where +**op** stands for 'operator' (i.e. precursor of what in late Modern English would be an operator), -**op** for an ordinary lexical verb:[16]

[37]	+op	WIT, KNOW	−op	totals
+ NOT	23	3	3	29
− NOT	166	2	131	299
totals	189	5	134	328

We can apply the ***chi-square test*** to the **null hypothesis** that the apparent correlation between presence of NOT and presence of an 'operator' could have arisen purely by chance; for details of the statistics see for example Butler (1985). If we treat the verbs WIT and KNOW as ordinary verbs and thus conflate the middle and right-hand columns, $\chi^2 = 6.13$, or 5.19 with Yates's correction (Butler 1985: 122). Both these figures are **significant** at the 1.25 per cent level, suggesting that the correlation is much more likely to be real than an accident of sampling.

We could argue, on the other hand, that WIT and KNOW are really more like operators, since WIT always, and KNOW until quite late, tended to resist co-occurrence with DO. (There is a precedent for special treatment of WIT, KNOW – plus some other verbs – in Ellegård 1953: 199–200.) If we accordingly conflate the left-hand and middle columns, then $\chi^2 = 10.91$ with Yates's correction. At 0.05 per cent this is very highly significant.[17]

As far as I know, previous statistical work by Ellegård, Kroch, Rissanen and others has concentrated on presence vs. absence of DO in various contexts. The picture usually drawn is of a process in which DO is central,

first rising in frequency, then being regulated to ensure its presence in
'NICE-contexts' which lacked any other auxiliary. Here I have tried to look
at the behaviour of the incipient class of auxiliaries (or rather, operators) vs.
other verbs, and I suspect that the distinction may go back at least to Middle
English.

This idea is not entirely new. Ellegård (1953: 154) cites Bradley (1904:
71–2)[18] as having suggested that the regulation of DO could be explained by
the infrequency with which NOT, or the subject of a question, followed
anything but an auxiliary, though he himself dismisses the idea:

> This explanation need hardly be taken seriously. Is there any reason to suppose
> that auxiliaries were more frequent in negative sentences and questions than in
> other contexts? If not, why should it not become equally habitual to say, e.g., *I
> do seldom go there* as *I do not go there*? (Ellegård 1953: 155)

Bradley does not make clear whether his discussion extends to the period
before periphrastic DO became common. Ellegård himself suggests at least a
fifteenth-century beginning for the process of regulation (1953: 209–10).
Further support for my approach apparently comes from Henningsen's work
on inversion in Rolle's prose after an initial adverbial or object (1911). This
early fourteenth-century material shows 61 per cent inversion with an
auxiliary as against 40 per cent with a full verb (quoted by Ellegård 1953:
188), though I do not know how Henningsen defines **auxiliary**. Kroch too
embraces

> the argument that, from its first appearance, periphrastic *do* subcategorizes only
> for verbs that never function as auxiliaries and hence that the categorial
> distinction auxiliary/nonauxiliary must have been available from the beginning of
> the Middle English period, when the first instances of periphrastic *do* appear.
> (1989: 218)

If my finding is corroborated for larger samples spread over a wider range
of dates, and perhaps for interrogatives as well as negatives, it suggests that
the essence of the process now labelled as the 'regulation of DO' – namely
the tendency for negatives (and interrogatives?) to contain an operator –
had already begun long before DO itself was a statistically important element
in the language, possibly even before periphrastic DO first arose. See
Question (b) in §15.5 below.

15.5 Questions for discussion or further research

(a) Does multiple negation co-occur with the S-V-NOT pattern where V is
    not a precursor of an operator, or with the S-NOT-V pattern (see
    §§15.2.2.1, 15.2.2.3, 15.2.2.5 above)? Try to establish whether there is
    any correlation between multiple negation and the phonological weight
    of the main verb-negator. Does the prescriptive grammar tradition have
    any rôle in the decline of multiple negation?
(b) Extend the *Paston Letters* experiment noted in §15.4.9 above in
    whatever way(s) you think best: with more categories of verb and/or
    clause-type, with more sophisticated statistical testing, with a range of

texts from the thirteenth to the seventeenth centuries, with interrogatives as well as negatives. What are your findings? In particular, when does the correlation between negation with NOT and presence of an auxiliary or operator become significant?[19] If necessary refer to Butler (1985) for details of random sampling and the chi-square and other tests.

(c) Table [1] (§15.2.1.2 above) lists known 'first occurrences' irrespective of whether the individual verbs concerned can be said to be fully grammaticised auxiliaries. Modify the table so that only combinations of genuinely grammaticised auxiliaries are included. Which cells need to be post-dated? Do any combinations involving modals have to be subclassified according to the individual modal? Can any (different) conclusions be drawn from the modified table?

(d) What conclusions can you draw from the fact (§15.2.1.2 above) that auxiliaries 1 and 2 in three-auxiliary sequences are always found together as a pair earlier than auxiliaries 2 and 3?

(e) See whether Koopman's analysis of OE three-verb clusters (§15.3.1 above) can usefully be extended to (a dialect of) Middle English.

(f) Decliticisation of some pronouns is dated in the sixteenth century by Kroch et al. (1982). Decliticisation in the *fourteenth* century is discussed by van Kemenade (1987) and Stockwell and Minkova (1991); see §§15.4.4.1, 4.7.1.3, and 4.7.3, respectively. What kinds of evidence are offered for or against clitic status of pronouns? Is the same kind of cliticisation being envisaged? Attempt to clarify the issues.

15.6   Envoi

Here is a general question to end the whole book with. Among my criteria for inclusion of a topic were:

(A) interesting syntactic change during recorded history of English
(B) variety of published research
(C) scope for new research
(D) coherence of topic
(E) interrelationship with other topics covered

Identify a topic neglected in this book which satisfies A–E, and discuss it under those headings.

I would, of course, be disappointed to think of things really *ending* here. On the contrary, this book is meant to be an open-ended invitation to further exploration. Go ahead!

Notes

1. If we included passive WEORÐAN it would bring the additional possibility of modal + perfect HAVE/BE + passive WEORÐAN + V, but according to Mitchell this did not occur in Old English (1985: §§753, 1095), and I have not located any examples in Middle English. The theoretical combinations involving progressive BE + passive WEORÐAN did not apparently occur.

2. **Sentence negation**, as in (a) – at least under normal intonation – may be contrasted with **constituent negation**, as in (b, c):

    (a) James has not been taking his medicine.
    (b) James has been (ostentatiously) not taking his medicine.
    (c) James has been taking not medicine but exercise.

3. I use NOT to cover a huge range of etymologically related forms: OE *nawuht* 'no + thing', *nowiht*, OE/ME *naht*, *noht*, ME/eModE *nat*, ME/ModE *nought*, *naught*, *not*, ModE *n't*, and many further spelling variants.

4. But KNOW, CARE, and DOUBT, which were operator-like in their resistance to DO during the period of regulation, did occur in the NOT-V pattern.

5. Here, as Warner points out, there is room for disagreement as to whether ellipsis or substitution is the best analysis. The form of DO which can occur here is certainly substitute DO, which is unlike most auxiliaries in not having the NICE properties (i.e. not being an operator):

    (a) Probably drives him crazy to have her call him up all the time. It would do me.

6. Warner mentions without further discussion that in Middle English the verbs OUEN and perfect HAUEN were added to the list (1992: 190).

7. In an object-question the *wh*-phrase – an NP containing *what* or *which* or *who(m)* – is object of a transitive or prepositional verb, though in Ellegård's classification not necessarily of the topmost verb (1953: 204 nn.1 and 2).

8. Ellegård explicitly includes negative/restrictive **adverbials** and **objects** but leaves it unclear whether his discussion covers **conjunctions** as well.

    Stockwell (1984) treats this inversion pattern as a hangover from Old English, Visser (1963–73: §1436) as arising in the fourteenth century (though with very few early examples). As to the prevalence of DO, Söderlind (1951–8: I 220) points out that the only exceptions in Dryden and Defoe involve KNOW:

    (a) 1711 Dryden, *Rymer* XVII 191.9

    neither knew they the best common Place of Pity, which is love.

9. I am grateful to Anthony Warner for drawing my attention to Rankova (1964).

10. Rankova seems to ignore negation when dealing with interrogatives.

11. Explained in parentheses as 'non-finite verb', but this must be a slip, since the items in question are operators in the context of post-auxiliary ellipsis. And the paper is later described as 'concerned with finite-verb structures' (1965: 114).

12. Actually they give the dates 1490–1600. I am not sure whether the often-quoted *Works* of Malory, dated by Ellegård at c1480 and by *MED* as (a1470), are included in the statistics.

13. The dates come by testing Kroch's favoured hypothesis that periphrastic DO increased at a constant rate, against an alternative hypothesis that it started off with the same frequency in all contexts but increased at different rates. Setting a starting point at any time after 1300 gives statistically significant evidence against the alternative hypothesis; a date of 1350 gives a significance level of 2.5 per cent.

14. It is noticeable that in Rissanen's first extended example (1991: 324–5), given to show the infrequency of DO in quick exchanges between participants in trials, the first nine tensed verbs are operators and so not open to the use of DO anyway. Overall I count 31 finite verbs, of which 19 are operators (including NEED: see Visser 1963–73: §1347) and only 12 are full verbs (including WILL and KNOW ×2). So the score for DO in the extract is closer to 0/12 than 0/31, a kind of difference which *may* be important overall.

15. I adapt these comments from my brief review in *Year's Work in English Studies 1985* **66**, 97 (1988).
16. For this preliminary test I initially restricted myself to letters written by members of the Paston family from 1480 onwards: twenty-five letters by five writers. In the event there was sufficient material in the first batch I read, the relevant letters of William Paston III, born probably in 1459 (numbers 408–11, 413–14, omitting 412, a copy of a letter of King Henry VII). I counted all tensed, finite verbs – thus not imperatives – in the sample and classed as (precursors of) operators all auxiliary verbs, plus BE, HAVE and modals when used as sole verb. (N.B. I treated past tense forms like *wold(e)* as modal and hence +op, those like *wyllyd* as non-modal, –op.) Negation by means other than NOT was counted with the affirmatives.
17. I have treated these chi-square tests as directional, since my alternative hypothesis is that there is a positive correlation between presence of NOT and presence of an 'operator'. Even with the more common *non*-directional chi-square test (Butler 1985: 112), doubled significance levels of 2.5 per cent and 0.1 per cent would still be notable.
18. Curme (1931: 137) is also cited by Ellegård in this regard, though I cannot find such a remark there.
19. Different groups of students at Manchester have found the correlation to become significant either in Chaucer's time or soon after, but so far we have worked with small samples and with texts rather widely spaced in time.

PART VI
BIBLIOGRAPHY AND INDEXES

Glossary of technical terms

Brief explanations are given of the technical terms used in this book, including elsewhere in this glossary, which are printed in **bold italics** on their first occurrence in a chapter.

abduction   a term used by Andersen (1973) for the working out by language learners of an internalised grammar on the basis of utterances heard. A difference between the internalised grammars of successive generations may be caused by listeners making a different structural analysis of a given surface form from that in the system of the speakers.

Aktionsart   'an indication of the intrinsic temporal qualities of a situation' (Brinton 1988: 3), covering such possibilities as static vs. dynamic, punctual vs. durative, continuous or iterative.

anaphora   referring back (by means of an **anaphor**) to a constituent already mentioned, typically the use of a pronoun to refer back to a full NP. (Sometimes the term covers forward reference as well, otherwise that is called **cataphora**.) In **zero anaphora** there is no explicit anaphor. Zero anaphora in subject position is also known in the TG literature as Coordinate Subject Deletion.

apodosis   the consequent clause of a conditional, e.g. the main clause in:

(a) If you catch cold, (then) you'll be sorry.

(The *if*-clause is the **protasis**.)

argument   a referential constituent, usually an NP, which plays a part in the semantic structure of a verb in that it fulfils a semantic role which must be specified in the verb's lexical entry – what in traditional grammar would function as subject, direct object, indirect object, etc.

aspect   'a matter of the speaker's viewpoint or perspective on the situation' (Brinton 1988: 3), such as whether the situation is viewed as completed, ongoing, beginning, ending, or repeating.

calque   word-formation or syntactic combination using native elements to match a foreign pattern.

Case Filter   a condition in ***GB Theory*** which states that every NP must have exactly one abstract case, so that any derivation with a caseless NP or with case conflict on an NP is ill-formed.

cataphora   converse of ***anaphora***.

catenative   a lexical verb which has another verb in its complement, with or without an NP intervening. Examples are ENJOY, FORCE, FORGET in

(a)   Jim forced Tom to enjoy forgetting to eat.
(b)   Jim forgot to force Tom to enjoy eating.
(c)   Jim enjoyed forcing Tom to forget to eat.

They are so named from their ability to form chains of verbs. Unlike auxiliaries their order is not fixed.

chi-square test   a standard statistical test for comparing observed frequencies with the frequencies predicted by some hypothesis. Standard published tables give the critical values of the **chi-square sum**, often written 'χ^2', for, *inter alia*, different *significance levels*. There is a formula for computing χ^2 from a frequency table of one's data.

clitic   a syntactic word which is phonologically reduced to merger with another phonological word. It is **enclitic** if it follows the item to which it cliticises, as for example PDE *is* reduced to *'s* in *it's*. It is **proclitic** if it precedes, as with *'t* for *it* in eModE *'tis*.

colligation   systematic co-occurrence of two or more categories, e.g. of verb + *particle* to form an intransitive phrasal verb.

collocation, collocate   systematic co-occurrence of two or more *lexemes*.

commutation   two forms **commute** within a pattern if one can be substituted for the other. The working assumption is that the overall structure remains unchanged, which allows the structural analysis worked out for the simpler case to be carried over to the other one.

complementiser   a constituent, abbreviated as COMP, which is *sister* to a sentence and – when lexically filled – roughly equivalent to **subordinating conjunction** in traditional parts-of-speech terminology.

conspiracy   a series of rules (synchronic) or changes (diachronic) which produce similar results.

constituent   component of a larger *construction*.

construction   (A) used loosely to mean a syntactic type or pattern, or (B) used of a *syntagm* which dominates a complete set of *sisters* and nothing else, i.e. a syntagm which forms a branching constituent.

control   an *empty category* controlled by a preceding NP is co-indexed with it and takes its reference from it. A **control verb** is one which takes a non-finite clausal complement whose empty subject is controlled by one of the control verb's NP arguments.

deep structure, D-Structure   (most) abstract syntactic representation of a sentence, sometimes called **underlying** structure. Contrasted with *surface* or *S-structure*.

deixis   linguistic systems concerned with spatial or temporal relationship to the speaker, for instance in the contrast between ModE *this* (near) and *that* (far), or between *now* and *then*. The related adjective is **deictic** (the first syllable is pronounced [daɪk] like *dike*).

empty category   a node which is thought to be necessary in syntactic analysis but which – at some or all levels of structure – is not filled by any element with phonological realisation. See ***PRO***.

enclitic   see *clitic*.

ergative   intransitive usages like (a) in which the subject, usually having the semantic role of Theme, corresponds to the direct object of a transitive verb like that in (b):

(a) The ice melted.
(b) Sunshine melted the ice.

exceptional clause   a clause which unusually is not an *S'* but a plain S without a *complementiser* slot.

Extraposition   coined by Jespersen (1909–49: III 25) and used in transformational grammar to describe the rightward movement of certain constituents, especially *S'*s, as in (b) versus (a):

(a) That she will leave soon is quite likely.
(b) It is quite likely that she will leave soon.

Government-Binding (GB) Theory   a theory of language – the mainstream of transformational generative grammar – based on the interaction of largely independent modules. It is increasingly often called the **Principles and Parameters** (PP) model.

Heavy-NP Shift   the rule invoked in transformational grammars to explain examples like the following:

(a) John left a case on the train.
(b) ?*John left on the train a case.
(c) John left on the train a case stuffed with stolen diamonds.

The surface order of (a) reflects the presumed base order of Present-day English. Re-ordering of *a case* as in (b) is odd or even ungrammatical, but in (c) it becomes acceptable when the NP in question is in some (linguistic!) sense 'heavy'.

higher (clause, verb, etc.)   relative to the Ss of a complex sentence as represented in a conventional tree diagram. The highest S is the independent or **root** clause. Botanically this orientation is topsy-turvy, of course, but it at least corresponds to the super-/subordinate labelling of traditional grammar. A **lower** clause is always embedded, subordinate.

implicational hierarchy   a chain of statements of the form 'If a language (or dialect) has property X then it will also tend to acquire property Y.' 'If it has property Y then it will also tend to acquire property Z.' '. . .' Thus the implicational hierarchy just mentioned would predict that there could be languages with properties XYZ, or YZ, or just Z, but few or none with XZ or XY or just X or just Y. The properties are said to be **implicationally ordered**.

isogloss   the boundary between geographical areas which differ with respect to some linguistic *variable*. (Note that the etymology of *isogloss*, 'equal + tongue', is inappropriate: it does not join up points which are linguistically similar (cf. *isobar*).)

landing site   the *empty* slot to which a constituent is moved by a movement transformation.

lexeme   an abstraction which covers what is common to all the different inflectional forms in a *paradigm*. In this book I regularly use the notation of small capitals, indicating a lexeme, when discussing verbs, taking the infinitive, as a citation form unless (as with modals) infinitives are characteristically rare or lacking. Occasionally the concept is useful with nouns (NOM SG as citation form) and other inflected words, and even with non-inflected words that show wide variations of form.

localism   the hypothesis that spatial relationships underlie semantics, so that non-spatial meanings like time and possession are metaphorically based on location, and further that much syntactic form is determined by localist semantics.

lower (clause, verb, etc.)   converse of *higher*.

marked   converse of *unmarked*.

NP Movement   the main mechanism in **GB Theory** for the generation of several constructions. In passives an empty subject position, symbolised in derivations by a lower case 'np', is filled by an NP moved from a post-verbal ('object') position. The moved element leaves a *trace*, symbolised t and co-indexed with the moved NP.

null hypothesis   the hypothesis that some observed phenomenon could have arisen by pure chance, to be tested against some alternative (and usually more interesting) hypothesis.

operator   a class of verb from which the first verb must be drawn in any finite ModE clause showing negation, inversion, post-verbal ellipsis or emphatic polarity. For Present-day English the class of operators largely overlaps with the class of auxiliaries, but not entirely. In other linguistic contexts (an example occurs in §4.6.2.1) the term 'operator' is used with wholly different meanings. The usage defined here is non-standard but quite widespread in British linguistics.

paradigm   set of inflectional forms of a single *lexeme*.

particle   a cover term for adverbs, prepositions and prefixes of spatial meaning or derived historically from spatial meanings.

places   *argument* positions associated with a verb which are inherent in its semantics. Either only the VP arguments are counted or, as here, the subject (if not a dummy) is counted as well.

predicative   clear examples in Present-day English of **predicative comple-ments** are *nice* and *a teacher*, respectively, in:

(a)   Your hair looks nice.
(b)   Tim was a teacher.

and of **predicative adjuncts** *Chairman* and *furious* in:

(c)   They made him Chairman.
(d)   Injustice makes her furious.

They are typically NPs or APs which predicate some property of a coreferential NP.

primitive   a term in a theory which cannot be defined in terms of other terms of the theory.

PRO, pro   pronominal *empty categories* in **GB Theory**. Whereas PRO is **anaphoric** and does not *commute* with full referential NPs, pro is not anaphoric and occurs in positions otherwise occupied by full NPs.

proclitic   see *clitic*.

protasis   see *apodosis*.

Quantifier Floating   a transformation accounting for quantifiers which, instead of remaining within their NP as in (a), 'float off', as in (b):

(a) All the students will refuse to budge.
(b) The students will all refuse to budge.

Raising   a transformation which moves the subject of a lower clause into the next *higher* clause. A **raising verb** is one whose surface subject is underlyingly an argument of a verb in an embedded clause.

S', S̄   a *construction* in TG theory whose immediate constituents are COMP (*complementiser*) and S (sentence, i.e. clause excluding subordinator). In a simple declarative main clause the node COMP is underlyingly empty. To clarify the distinction between S' and S, here are two ModE examples of embedded clauses:

(a) (Tim knew) [$_{S'}$ [$_{COMP}$ that] [$_S$ his days were numbered]]
(b) [$_{S'}$ [$_{COMP}$ For] [$_S$ you to resign] (would be a mistake)

significant   statistically improbable that some result could have happened by pure chance. **Significance** at, say, the 5 per cent level means that the result has a probability of 5 or less in 100 of being due to chance, often written as 'p ≤ 0.05'. **Significance levels** of 1 per cent (p ≤ 0.01) or even 0.1 per cent (p ≤ 0.001) would naturally be more impressive still.

sisters   constituents which are immediate constituents ('daughters') of the same constituent.

small clause   sentential constituents in *GB Theory* which lack both C/COMP and I/INFL constituents.

strong   contrasts with **weak** in traditional Germanic philology to indicate types of inflectional behaviour. Strong adjective endings are those typically used when no determiner is present; like the various strong noun paradigms they show a large degree of person/number/case differentiation. The little-differentiated weak adjective endings typically co-occur with a determiner in the NP. In the NP **strong** and **weak** are of little relevance after the OE period. Strong verbs are those which differentiate present and past tenses by a change in stem vowel, while weak verbs mark past tense by addition of an alveolar suffix, one containing usually *-d-* or *-t-*.

subcategorisation frame   the syntactic structure into which a word can fit. The basic categories of words are N, V, A, etc., but V in particular has subcategories: for example 'intransitive', 'transitive', 'ditransitive', etc. More specific subcategories can be set up by specifying the case of the NP argument(s) associated with the verb, and if meanings are given too then the subcategorisation frame is essentially a lexical entry for the verb. A verb is said to **subcategorise for** particular arguments.

suppletive   a suppletive *paradigm* is one made up of etymologically unrelated roots, like ModE GO (*go, went*).

surface structure, S-Structure   in GB theory, a level of syntactic analysis closest to the actual form of a sentence. One significant terminological development in recent work is a distinction between **surface structure** (= output of the phonological rules, or in some formulations output of deletion rules) and the slightly deeper **S-structure** (= output of the syntax, or output of movement rules). cf. *deep structure*.

syncretism   identity between forms in the *paradigm* of a *lexeme*.

syntagm   a group of words which are syntactically related, often though not always forming a constituent. Also in Greek form **syntagma** (plural *syntagmata*).

thematic (θ) role   in *GB Theory*, a constituent which is a semantic *argument*. In the same sense **thematic** can also modify **dependent, grid, relation**.

Tough-Movement   a transformation posited to derive the (b) pattern from a structure more like (a):

(a)   It is tough to solve this problem
(b)   This problem is tough to solve

The (b) pattern is also known as the *easy-to-please* construction.

trace   the lexically empty constituent left behind when an item is moved by a transformation. Traces were invented mainly to allow semantic interpretation of a **surface structure**, but they may also play a part in syntactic and even phonological explanation. They are one instance of a more general phenomenon, the *empty category*. Marking by subscript i, j, etc. in a diagram – the usual notation for coreference – is without theoretical significance and serves merely to show which trace corresponds to which moved item.

unbounded   a relation or movement in *Government-Binding Theory* which crosses a 'bounding node' (NP or S).

unmarked   the term in a binary system which typically is morphologically simpler, more general in meaning, more frequent – in other words the default or 'unless' choice, opposed to **marked**. In recent generative linguistics **unmarked** means rather 'that given in Universal Grammar'.

variable   any linguistic item which shows variation at a given time within a population. An example of a syntactic variable in Present-day English might be the negation of *used to*, with choice of forms like *didn't use(d) to, never used to, usedn't to* conditioned by such factors as age, education, social status, and geographical location of speaker, and formality of situation.

verb conjunction   my (non-standard) term for the systematic combination of two clauses into one, with object(s) – and subject, if present – shared by two verbs. Early transformational grammars would have used the term **Conjunction reduction**.

verb phrase conjunction   the systematic combination of two clauses into one, with subject shared by two verb phrases.

weak   converse of *strong*.

X-bar theory   a syntactic theory which imposes severe constraints on the kinds of phrase structure (= underlying constituent structure) which are possible. All phrases have essentially the same internal structure, allowing generalisations across all the major lexical classes (N, V, A, P) and indeed clauses (S), and in recent work inflection and complementiser (I, C) too. A given category X is head of a phrasal projection $\overline{\text{X}}$ ('X-bar' – hence the name) and of the phrasal projection X-double-bar, which in recent work is usually the maximal projection. Primes are sometimes used instead of bars for convenience in printing, so that S′ is a mere notational variant of $\bar{S}$, likewise S″ for S-double-bar, etc. The older notation, NP, VP, etc., is very frequently retained for the highest bar-level of a given category.

Secondary sources (references)

ADAMSON, S., LAW, V. A., VINCENT, N. and WRIGHT, S. (eds) (1990) *Papers from the 5th International Conference on English Historical Linguistics: Cambridge, 6–9 April 1987.* (Current Issues in Linguistic Theory, 65.) John Benjamins, Amsterdam/ Philadelphia.

AHLQVIST, A. (ed.) (1982) *Papers from the 5th International Conference on Historical Linguistics.* (Current Issues in Linguistic Theory, 21.) John Benjamins, Amsterdam.

AIJMER, K. (1985) 'The semantic development of *will*.' In Fisiak (1985b) pp. 11–21. (p. 325)

AITCHISON, J. (1980) Review of Lightfoot (1979), *Linguistics* 18, 137–46. (p. 336)

AITCHISON, J. (1991) *Language Change: Progress or Decay?* 2nd edn. Cambridge University Press, Cambridge. (p. 14)

ÅKERLUND, A. (1914) 'A word on the passive definite tenses', *Englische Studien* 47, 321–37. (pp. 387, 409, 431)

ALLAN, W. S. (1987) 'Lightfoot noch einmal', *Diachronica* 4, 123–57. (pp. 330–1, 336–7)

ALLEN, C. L. (1975) 'Old English modals.' In Grimshaw (1975), pp. 91–100. (pp. 325–6.)

ALLEN, C. L. (1980a) *Topics in Diachronic English Syntax.* Garland Publishing, New York/London. (Revision of PhD dissertation, University of Massachusetts, 1977.) (pp. 6, 148–9)

ALLEN, C. (1980b) 'Movement and deletion in Old English', *Linguistic Inquiry* 11, 261–323. (pp. 133, 147–8, 161)

ALLEN, C. L. (1984) 'On the dating of raised empty subjects in English', *Linguistic Inquiry* 15, 461–5. (pp. 4, 170, 201, 220, 226)

ALLEN, C. L. (1986a) 'Reconsidering the history of *like*', *Journal of Linguistics* 22, 375–409. (pp. 75, 79, 81, 88–91, 96, 99–100, 102, 122, 236)

ALLEN, C. L. (1986b) 'Dummy subjects and the verb-second "target" in Old English', *English Studies* 67, 465–70. (p. 99)

ALLEN, C. L. (in prep.) *Case Marking, Reanalysis, and Grammatical Relations in English.* (pp. 112, 119, 121, 123)

ALLERTON, D., CARNEY, E. and HOLDCROFT, D. (eds) (1979) *Function and Context in Linguistic Analysis: a Festschrift for William Haas.* Cambridge University Press, Cambridge.

ANDERSEN, H. (1973) 'Abductive and deductive change', *Language* 49, 765–93. (p. 475)

ANDERSEN, H. and KOERNER, K. (eds) (1990) *Historical Linguistics 1987: Papers from the 8th International Conference on Historical Linguistics (8. ICHL) (Lille, 31*

August–4 September 1987). (Current Issues in Linguistic Theory, 66.) John Benjamins, Amsterdam/Philadelphia.

ANDERSON, J. (1971) *The Grammar of Case: Towards a Localistic Theory.* Cambridge University Press, Cambridge. (p. 23)

ANDERSON, J. M. (1977) *On Case Grammar: Prolegomena to a Theory of Grammatical Relations.* Croom Helm, London. (p. 23)

ANDERSON, J. (ed.) (1982) *Language Form and Linguistic Variation: Papers Dedicated to Angus McIntosh.* (Current Issues in Linguistic Theory, 15.) John Benjamins, Amsterdam.

ANDERSON, J. (1985) 'The case system of Old English: a case for non-modularity', *Studia Linguistica* **39**, 1–22 (p. 19)

ANDERSON, J. (1986) 'A note on Old English impersonals', *Journal of Linguistics* **22**, 167–77. (pp. 63–4, 83–4, 93, 101–2, 121)

ANDERSON, J. (1988) 'The type of Old English impersonals.' In Anderson and Macleod (1988), pp. 1–32. (pp. 19, 83–5, 98, 220)

ANDERSON, J. M. and JONES, C. (eds) (1974) *Historical Linguistics I: Syntax, Morphology, Internal and Comparative Reconstruction: Proceedings of the First International Conference on Historical Linguistics, Edinburgh 2nd–7th September 1973.* (North-Holland Linguistic Series, 12a.) North-Holland, Amsterdam/Oxford/American Elsevier, New York.

ANDERSON, J. M. and MacLEOD, N. (eds) (1988) *Edinburgh Studies in the English Language*, 1. John Donald, Edinburgh.

ARD, W. J. (1977) *Raising and Word Order in Diachronic Syntax.* (PhD dissertation, UCLA, 1975.) Indiana University Linguistics Club, Bloomington, IN. (pp. 197–9, 216, 248–9)

ARIMOTO, M. (1989) 'Against the raising analysis of *be*', *English Linguistics* **6**, 111–29. (p. 217)

BACQUET, P. (1962) *La structure de la phrase verbale à l'époque alfrédienne.* (Publications de la Faculté des Lettres de l'Université de Strasbourg, 145.) Les Belles Lettres, Paris. (p. 33)

BAILEY, C.-J. N. and SHUY, R. W. (eds) (1973) *New Ways of Analyzing Variation in English.* Georgetown UP, Washington D.C.

BAKER, C. L. and McCARTHY, J. J. (eds) (1981) *The Logical Problem of Language Acquisition.* MIT Press, Cambridge, MA/London.

BARBER, C. L. (1972) *The Story of Language.* Pan Books, London. (p. 14)

BARBER, C. (1976) *Early Modern English.* André Deutsch, London. (pp. 5, 451, 458)

BARBER, C. (forthcoming) *The English Language: a Historical Introduction.* Cambridge University Press, Cambridge. (p. 14)

BAUER, G. (1970) *Studien zum System und Gebrauch der 'Tempora' in der Sprache Chaucers und Gowers.* (Wiener Beiträge zur englischen Philologie, 73.) Wilhelm Braumüller, Vienna. (pp. 366, 407)

BAUGH, A. C. and CABLE, T. (1978) *A History of the English Language*, 3rd edn. Routledge & Kegan Paul, London. (pp. 11, 14)

BEAN, M. C. (1976) 'A study of the development of word order patterns in Old English in relation to theories of word order change.' PhD dissertation, UCLA. (p. 58)

BEAN, M. C. (1983) *The Development of Word Order Patterns in Old English.* Croom Helm, London/Barnes & Noble, Totowa, NJ. (pp. 42, 45, 47–8, 56)

BENNETT, J. A. W. and SMITHERS, G. V. (1968) (See *EMEVP* in List of primary sources.) (pp. 5, 338, 507)

BENNETT, P. A. (1979) 'Observations on the transparency principle', *Linguistics* **17**, 843–61. (p. 329)

BENNETT, P. A. (1980) 'English passives: a study in syntactic change and relational grammar', *Lingua* **51**, 101–14. (pp. 21–2, 156–7)

BENNIS, H. (1986) *Gaps and Dummies.* (Linguistic Models, 9.) Foris, Dordrecht. (p. 97)

BENVENISTE, E. (1968) 'Mutations of linguistic categories.' In Lehmann, W. and Malkiel, Y. (eds), *Directions for Historical Linguistics*. University of Texas Press, Austin, TX, pp. 85–94. (p. 369)

BEUKEMA, F. and COOPMANS, P. (1987) *Linguistics in the Netherlands 1987*. Foris, Dordrecht.

BIBER, D. and FINEGAN, E. (1986) 'An initial typology of English text types.' In Aarts, J. and Meijs, W. (eds) *Corpus Linguistics II: New Studies in the Analysis and Exploitation of Computer Corpora*. (Costerus new series, 57) Rodopi, Amsterdam, pp. 19–46. (p. 4)

BLAKE, N. F. (1973) *Caxton's Own Prose*. André Deutsch, London. (p. 505)

BLAKE, N. F. and JONES, C. (eds) (1984) *English Historical Linguistics: Studies in Development*. (CECTAL Conference Papers Series, 3.) The Centre for English Cultural Tradition and Language, University of Sheffield, Sheffield.

BOCK, H. (1931) 'Studien zum präpositionalen Infinitiv und Akkusativ mit dem *to*-Infinitiv', *Anglia* 55, 114–249. (pp. 176, 182, 185, 193, 199, 201–4, 209, 213, 216, 258)

BOLINGER, D. (1977a) 'Transitivity and spatiality: the passive of prepositional verbs.' In Makkai, A., Bekker-Makkai, V. and Heilmann, L. (eds) *Linguistics at the Crossroads*. (Revision of 1975, 'On the Passive in English'.) (Testi e studi, 4.) Liviana editrice, Padova/Jupiter Press, Lake Bluff, IL, pp. 57–78. (p. 144)

BOLINGER, D. (1977b) *Meaning and Form*. Longman, London. (p. 97)

BOLINGER, D. (1979) 'The jingle theory of double -*ing*.' In Allerton et al. (1979), pp. 41–56. (p. 411)

BORKIN, A. (1973) '*To be* and not *to be*', *Papers from the Ninth Regional Meeting of the Chicago Linguistic Society*, 44–56. (p. 240)

BRAATEN, B. (1967) 'Notes on continuous tenses in English', *Norsk Tidsskrift for Sprogvidenskap* 21, 167–80. (p. 402)

BRADLEY, H. (1904) *The Making of English*. Macmillan, London. (p. 468)

BRESNAN, J. and GRIMSHAW, J. (1978) 'The syntax of free relatives in English', *Linguistic Inquiry* 9, 331–91. (p. 147)

BRINTON, L. J. (1988) *The Development of English Aspectual Systems: Aspectualizers and Post-verbal Particles* (Cambridge Studies in Linguistics, 49.) Cambridge University Press, Cambridge. (pp. 219, 236, 364–5, 400, 407, 441, 453, 475)

BRINTON, L. J. (1991) 'The origin and development of quasimodal *have to*'. Paper presented at the Workshop on Verbal Periphrases, 10th ICHL, Amsterdam, August 1991. (p. 317)

BRINTON, L. J. (forthcoming) 'The differentiation of statives and perfects in early Modern English: the development of the conclusive perfect.' To appear in Stein, D. and Tieken, I. (eds) *Standardization in English in the Seventeenth and Eighteenth Centuries*. Mouton, Berlin. (pp. 341, 343, 348, 358, 365)

BROWN, K. and MILLAR, M. (1980) 'Auxiliary verbs in Edinburgh speech', *Transactions of the Philological Society*, 81–133. (p. 294)

BRUNNER, K. (1963) *An Outline of Middle English Grammar*. Johnston, G. (trans). Blackwell, Oxford. (p. 348)

BRUNNER, K. (1965) *Altenglische Grammatik: nach der angelsächsischen Grammatik von Eduard Sievers*, 3rd edn. Niemeyer, Tübingen. (p. 347)

BUNT, G. H. V., KOOPER, E. S., MACKENZIE, J. L. and WILKINSON, D. R. M. (eds) (1987) *One Hundred Years of English Studies in Dutch Universities: Seventeen Papers Read at the Centenary Conference, Groningen, 15–16 January 1986*. (Costerus new series, 64.) Rodopi, Amsterdam.

BURROW, J. A. and TURVILLE-PETRE, T. (1992) *A Book of Middle English*. Blackwell, Oxford/Cambridge, MA. (p. 5)

BUTLER, C. (1985) *Statistics in Linguistics*. Blackwell, Oxford/New York. (pp. 467, 469, 471)

BUTLER, M. C. (1977) 'Reanalysis of object as subject in Middle English impersonal constructions', *Glossa* 11, 155–70. (p. 79)

BUTTERS, R. R. (1973) 'Acceptability judgments for double modals in southern dialects.' In Bailey and Shuy (1973), pp. 276–86. (p. 294)

CALLAWAY, M. JR (1913) *The Infinitive in Anglo-Saxon*. (Carnegie Institution Publications, 169.) Carnegie Institution, Washington, D.C. (pp. 47, 184–6, 189, 193–4, 213, 217, 224, 227, 237, 243, 250, 322–3)

CAMPBELL, A. (1959) *Old English Grammar*. Clarendon, Oxford. (pp. 17, 444)

CANALE, [W.] M. (1976) 'Implicational hierarchies of word order relationships.' In Christie, W. M. jr (ed.) *Current Progress in Historical Linguistics: Proceedings of the Second International Conference on Historical Linguistics, Tucson, Arizona, 12–16 January 1976*. (North-Holland Linguistic Series, 31.) North-Holland, Amsterdam/New York/Oxford, pp. 39–65. (pp. 45–6)

CANALE, W. M. (1978) 'Word order change in Old English: base reanalysis in generative grammar.' Unpublished PhD dissertation, McGill University. (pp. 46–7, 58)

CARO, G. (1896) 'Zur Lehre vom altenglisch Perfectum', *Anglia* 18, 389–449. (p. 348)

CHEL = HOGG, R. M. (gen. ed.) (1992–) *The Cambridge History of the English Language* (6 vols, in progress). Cambridge University Press, Cambridge. (pp. 5, 14)

CHOMSKY, N. (1981) *Lectures on Government and Binding*. (Studies in Generative Grammar, 9.) Foris, Dordrecht. (p. 170)

CHOMSKY, N. and LASNIK, H. (1977) 'Filters and control', *Linguistic Inquiry* 8, 425–504. (pp. 145–6)

CLAHSEN, H. and MUYSKEN, P. (1986) 'The availability of universal grammar to adult and child learners – a study of the acquisition of German word order', *Second Language Research* 2, 93–119. (pp. 49–50, 56)

CLARK, C. (1970) (See *Peterb.Chron.* in List of primary sources.) (pp. 338, 513)

CLARK HALL, J. R. (1960) *A Concise Anglo-Saxon Dictionary*, 4th edn, with a supplement by H. D. Meritt. Cambridge University Press, Cambridge. (p. 6)

COLMAN, F. (1988) 'Heavy arguments in Old English.' In Anderson and Macleod (1988), pp. 33–89. (pp. 19, 53–4)

COLMAN, F. (ed.) (1992) *Evidence for Old English: Material and Theoretical Bases for Reconstruction*. (Edinburgh Studies in the English Language, 2.) John Donald, Edinburgh.

COUPER-KUHLEN, E. (1979) *The Prepositional Passive in English: a Semantic-Syntactic Analysis, with a Lexicon of Prepositional Verbs*. (Linguistische Arbeiten, 81.) Niemeyer, Tübingen. (pp. 140, 144, 160–1)

CULICOVER, P., WASOW, T. and AKMAJIAN, A. (eds) (1977) *Formal Syntax*. Academic Press, New York.

CURME, G. O. (1931) *A Grammar of the English Language*, III, *Syntax*. D. C. Heath, Boston, MA. (p. 471)

DAL, I. (1952) 'Zur Entstehung des englischen Participium Praesentis auf *-ing*', *Norsk Tidsskrift for Sprogvidenskap* 16, 5–116. (pp. 401–2, 408–9, 412)

DANCHEV, A. (1991) 'Language change typology and some aspects of the SVO development in English.' In Kastovsky (1991), pp. 103–24. (p. 50)

DAVENPORT, M., HANSEN, E. and NIELSEN, H. F. (eds) (1983) *Current Topics in English Historical Linguistics*. Odense University Press, Odense.

DAVIS, N. (1961) 'The earliest "do not" ', *Notes & Queries* 206, 48–9. (p. 265)

DEKEYSER, X. (1986) 'English contact clauses revisited: a diachronic approach', *Folia Linguistica Historica* 7, 107–20. (p. 132)

DE LA CRUZ FERNÁNDEZ, J. M. (1969) 'Origins and development of the phrasal verb to the end of the Middle English period.' Unpublished PhD dissertation, Queen's University of Belfast. (p. 160)

DE LA CRUZ, J. M. (1972) 'A syntactical complex of isogloses in the north-western end of Europe (English, North Germanic and Celtic)', *Indogermanische Forschungen* **77**, 171–80. (pp. 138–40, 155)

DE LA CRUZ, J. M. (1973) 'A late 13th century change in English structure', *Orbis* **22**, 161–76. (pp. 138–40, 155)

DELANCEY, S. (1982) 'Aspect, transitivity and viewpoint.' In Hopper (1982), pp. 167–83. (p. 440)

DENISON, D. (1981) 'Aspects of the history of English group-verbs: with particular attention to the syntax of the *Ormulum*.' Unpublished DPhil dissertation, University of Oxford. (pp. 57, 122, 138, 160, 404, 410)

DENISON, D. (1985a) 'Why Old English had no prepositional passive', *English Studies* **66**, 189–204. (pp. 122, 140–3, 153–4, 158, 160)

DENISON, D. (1985b) 'The origins of completive *up* in English', *Neuphilologische Mitteilungen* **86**, 37–61. (pp. 36, 410)

DENISON, D. (1985c) 'The origins of periphrastic DO: Ellegård and Visser reconsidered.' In Eaton et al. (1985), pp. 45–60. (pp. 260, 278–82, 287–8)

DENISON, D. (1985d) 'Some observations on *being teaching*', *Studia Neophilologica* **57**, 157–9. (p. 411)

DENISON, D. (1986) 'On word order in Old English', *Dutch Quarterly Review* **16**, 277–95; also in Bunt et al. (1987), pp. 139–55. (pp. 28, 34, 44, 48–9, 58)

DENISON, D. (1990a) 'The Old English impersonals revived.' In Adamson et al. (1990), pp. 111–40. (pp. 64, 70, 73, 92–6, 206, 241, 245, 345)

DENISON, D. (1990b) 'Auxiliary + impersonal in Old English', *Folia Linguistica Historica* **9.1**, 139–66. (pp. 87, 235, 239, 300, 330, 338, 345)

DENISON, D. (1990c) 'The passive in Modern English.' Paper read at the Sixth International Conference on English Historical Linguistics, Helsinki, 24 May 1990. (pp. 407–8, 444)

DENISON, D. (1992) 'Counterfactual *may have*.' In Gerritsen and Stein (1992), pp. 229–56. (pp. 336–8, 357)

DENISON, D. (forthcoming) 'The information present: present tense for communication in the past.' In Rissanen et al. (forthcoming), pp. 262–86. (p. 123)

DENISON, D. (in prep.) 'Syntax'. In *CHEL* IV, *1776–present day*. (p. 5)

DEUTSCHBEIN, M. (1917) *System der Neuenglischen Syntax*. O. Schulze, Cöthen. (p. 114)

DICKINS, B. (1926) 'The Peterborough annal for 1137', *Review of English Studies* **2**, 341–3. (p. 338)

DOE = CAMERON, A., AMOS, A. C., HEALEY, A. diP, BUTLER, S., HOLLAND, J., McDOUGALL, D. and McDOUGALL, I. (1986–) *Dictionary of Old English*, Fascicles *B–D*. Pontifical Institute for Mediaeval Studies (for The Dictionary of Old English project, Centre for Medieval Studies, University of Toronto). Microfiche. (p. 5)

DONNER, M. (1986) 'The gerund in Middle English', *English Studies* **67**, 394–400. (pp. 403–4)

DOST = CRAIGIE, W. A., AITKEN, A. J., STEVENSON, J. A. C., TEMPLETON, J. M. et al. (eds) (1937–) *Dictionary of the Older Scottish Tongue* (7 vols to date). Chicago University Press, Chicago/Oxford University Press, London; later Aberdeen University Press, Aberdeen. (p. 338)

DOWTY, D. (1979) *Word Meaning and Montague Grammar: the Semantics of Verbs and Times in Generative Semantics and in Montague's PTQ.* (Synthese Language Library, 7.) D. Reidel, Dordrecht. (p. 290)

DRYER, M. S. (1991) 'SVO languages and the OV : VO typology', *Journal of Linguistics* **27**, 443–82. (p. 27)

EATON, R., FISCHER, O., KOOPMAN, W. and VAN DER LEEK, F. (eds) (1985) *Papers from the 4th International Conference on English Historical Linguistics: Amsterdam,*

10–13 April 1985. (Current Issues in Linguistic Theory, 41.) John Benjamins, Amsterdam/Philadelphia.

ELLEGÅRD, A. (1953) *The Auxiliary 'do': the Establishment and Regulation of its Growth in English*. (Gothenburg Studies in English, 11.) Almqvist & Wiksell, Stockholm. (pp. 257–60, 264–71, 274–9, 284–5, 288, 451, 458–60, 467–8, 470)

ELMER, W. (1981) *Diachronic Grammar: the History of Old and Middle English Subjectless Constructions*. (Linguistische Arbeiten, 97.) Niemeyer, Tübingen. (pp. 66, 76–7, 93, 96, 98–9)

ELMER, W. (1983) 'Semantic-syntactic patterning: the lexical valency of *seem* in Middle English', *English Studies* **64**, 160–8. (pp. 77–8, 102)

ENGBLOM, V. (1938) *On the Origin and Early Development of the Auxiliary 'do'*. (Lund Studies in English, 6.) C. W. K. Gleerup, Lund/Williams & Norgate, London/Levin & Munksgaard, Copenhagen. (pp. 260, 267, 277–8, 458)

FAARLUND, J. T. (ed.) (1985) *Germanic Linguistics: Papers from a Symposium at the University of Chicago, April 24, 1985*. Indiana University Linguistics Club, Bloomington, IN.

FAARLUND, J. T. (1990) *Syntactic Change: Toward a Theory of Historical Syntax*. (Trends in Linguistics/Studies and Monographs, 50.) Mouton de Gruyter, Berlin/New York. (pp. 102, 123)

FILLMORE, C. J. (1968) 'The case for case.' In Bach, E. and Harms, R. T. (eds) *Universals in Linguistic Theory*. Holt, Rinehart & Winston, New York, pp. 1–88. (p. 23)

FISCHER, O. (1987) 'Some remarks on the analysis of perception verb complements in Middle English: a reply', *Kwartalnik Neofilologiczny* **34**, 57–67. (pp. 169, 208, 216)

FISCHER, O. (1988) 'The rise of the *for NP* to *V* construction: an explanation.' In Nixon and Honey (1988), pp. 67–88; also in Fischer (1990), pp. 22–52. (pp. 201, 219)

FISCHER, O. (1989) 'The origin and spread of the accusative and infinitive construction in English', *Folia Linguistica Historica* **8**, 143–217; also in Fischer (1990), pp. 53–150. (pp. 170, 176, 179–81, 183, 196, 199, 201, 207–12, 216)

FISCHER, O. (1990) *Syntactic Change and Causation: Developments in Infinitival Constructions in English*. (PhD dissertation, University of Amsterdam.) (Amsterdam Studies in Generative Grammar, 2.) No publisher, Amsterdam. (pp. 208, 217)

FISCHER, O. (1991) 'The rise of the passive infinitive in English.' In Kastovsky (1991), pp. 141–88; also in Fischer (1990), pp. 151–217, with paragraph numbering 1 higher. (pp. 172, 186, 208, 217, 219, 228, 414, 452)

FISCHER, O. (1992a) 'Syntax.' In *CHEL* II, *1066–1476*, pp. 207–408. (pp. 5, 281, 322)

FISCHER, O. (1992b) 'Syntactic change and borrowing: the case of the accusative and infinitive construction in English.' In Gerritsen and Stein (1992), pp. 17–88; also in Fischer (1990), pp. 218–309, with slightly different paragraph numbering. (pp. 14, 174, 176, 180, 182, 208, 210–12, 216, 319)

FISCHER, O. (forthcoming) 'Factors conditioning infinitive marking in late Middle English.' *Dutch Working Papers in English Language and Linguistics* **25**. (pp. 65, 208, 215)

FISCHER, O. C. M. and LEEK, F. C. VAN DER (1981) 'Optional vs radical re-analysis: mechanisms of syntactic change.' Review of Lightfoot (1979), *Lingua* **55**, 301–49. (pp. 86, 150–1, 221, 244–6, 276, 286)

FISCHER, O. C. M. and LEEK, F. C. VAN DER (1983) 'The demise of the Old English impersonal construction', *Journal of Linguistics* **19**, 337–68. (pp. 62–6, 73, 79–83, 89, 91, 93, 102, 220)

FISCHER, O. and LEEK, F. VAN DER (1985) Review of von Seefranz-Montag (1983), *Journal of Linguistics* **21**, 197–203. (pp. 86, 88)

FISCHER O. and LEEK, F. VAN DER (1987) 'A "case" for the Old English impersonal.' In Koopman et al. (1987), pp. 79–120. (pp. 18–20, 23, 84, 86–7, 102, 159, 161)

FISHER, J. H. (1977) 'Chancery and the emergence of standard written English in the fifteenth century.' *Speculum* **52**, 870–99. (p. 12)

FISIAK, J. (ed.) (1984) *Historical Syntax*. (Trends in Linguistics/Studies and Monographs, 23.) Mouton, Paris/The Hague.

FISIAK, J. (ed.) (1985a) *Papers from the Sixth International Conference on Historical Linguistics*. (Current Issues in Linguistic Theory, 34.) John Benjamins, Amsterdam.

FISIAK, J. (ed.) (1985b) *Historical Semantics. Historical Word-formation.* (Trends in Linguistics/Studies and Monographs, 29.) Mouton, Berlin.

FISIAK, J. (1987) *A Bibliography of Writings for the History of the English Language*, 2nd edn. Mouton de Gruyter, Berlin/New York/Amsterdam. (p. 6)

FLETCHER, P. (1979) 'The development of the verb phrase.' In Fletcher, P. and Garman, M. (eds) *Language Acquisition: Studies in First Language Development*. Cambridge University Press, Cambridge, pp. 261–84. (p. 284)

FOURQUET, J. (1938) *L'ordre des éléments de la phrase en germanique ancien: études de syntaxe de position.* (Publications de la Faculté des Lettres de l'Université de Strasbourg, 86.) Les Belles Lettres, Paris. (pp. 39, 58, 419)

FRIDÉN, G. (1948) *Studies on the tenses of the English verb from Chaucer to Shakespeare: with special reference to the late sixteenth century.* (Essays and Studies on English Language and Literature, 2.) Upsala University English Institute, Uppsala. (pp. 359, 366–7)

GAAF, W. VAN DER (1904) *The Transition from the Impersonal to the Personal Construction: in Middle English.* (Anglistische Forschungen, 14.) Carl Winter's Universitätsbuchhandlung, Heidelberg. (pp. 75–6, 92)

GAAF, W. VAN DER (1928) 'The post-adjectival passive infinitive', *English Studies* **10**, 129–38. (p. 230)

GAAF, W. VAN DER (1929) 'The conversion of the indirect personal object into the subject of a passive construction', *English Studies* **11**, 1–11, 58–67. (pp. 115–18)

GAAF, W. VAN DER (1930a) 'The passive of a verb accompanied by a preposition', *English Studies* **12**, 1–24. (pp. 129, 134–7)

GAAF, W. VAN DER (1930b) 'Some notes on the history of the progressive form', *Neophilologus* **15**, 201–15. (pp. 402–4)

GAAF, W. VAN DER (1931) '*Beon* and *habban* with inflected infinitive', *English Studies* **13**, 180–8. (p. 316)

GEERTS, G., HAESERYN, W., DE ROOIJ, J. and VAN DEN TOORN, M. C. (1984) *Algemene Nederlandse Spraakkunst.* Wolters-Noordhoff, Groningen. (pp. 357, 370)

GELLING, M. (1978) *Signposts to the Past: Place-names and the History of England.* Dent, London. (p. 281)

GERRITSEN, M. (1984) 'Divergent word order developments in Germanic languages: a description and a tentative explanation.' In Fisiak (1984), pp. 107–35. (pp. 49, 353)

GERRITSEN, M. and STEIN, D. (eds) (1992) *Internal and External Factors in Syntactic Change.* (Trends in Linguistics/Studies and Monographs, 61.) Mouton de Gruyter, Berlin.

GÖRLACH, M. (1978) *Einführung ins Frühneuenglische.* Quelle & Meyer, Heidelberg.

GÖRLACH, M. (1986) 'Middle English — a creole?' In Kastovsky and Szwedek (1986), vol I, pp. 329–44. (p. 11)

GÖRLACH, M. (1991) *Introduction to Early Modern English.* Cambridge University Press, Cambridge. (Translation of Görlach 1978.) (pp. 5, 458)

GOOSSENS, L. (1982) 'On the development of the modals and of the epistemic function in English.' In Ahlqvist (1982), pp. 74–84. (pp. 228, 298–9, 338)

GOOSSENS, L. (1984) 'The interplay of syntax and semantics in the development of the English modals.' In Blake and Jones (1984), pp. 149–59. (pp. 290, 329)

GOOSSENS, L. (1987) 'The auxiliarization of the English modals: a Functional Grammar view.' In Harris, M. and Ramat, P. (eds) *Historical Development of Auxiliaries*. (Trends in Linguistics/Studies and Monographs, 35.) Mouton, Berlin, pp. 111–43. (p. 330)

GORRELL, J. H. (1895) 'Indirect discourse in Anglo-Saxon', *Publications of the Modern Language Association of America* **10**, 342–485. (pp. 217, 339)

GRANGER, S. (1983) *The 'be + past participle' Construction in Spoken English: with Special Emphasis on the Passive*. (North-Holland Linguistic Series, 49.) North-Holland, Amsterdam/New York/Oxford. (pp. 413, 420, 514)

GREENBAUM, S., LEECH, G. and SVARTVIK, J. (eds) (1980) *Studies in English Linguistics: for Randolph Quirk*. Longman, London/New York.

GREENBERG, J. H. (1966) 'Some universals of grammar with particular reference to the order of meaningful elements.' In Greenberg, J. H. (ed.) *Universals of language*, 2nd edn. MIT Press, Cambridge, MA, pp. 73–113. (p. 27)

GRIMSHAW, J. (ed.) (1975) *Papers in the History and Structure of English*. (University of Massachusetts Occasional Papers, 1.) University of Massachusetts, Department of Linguistics, Amherst.

GRUBER, J. S. (1976) *Lexical Structures in Syntax and Semantics*. North-Holland, Amsterdam. (pp. 86, 216)

HAEGEMAN, L. (1985) 'The *get*-passive and Burzio's generalization', *Lingua* **66**, 53–77. (pp. 435, 438)

HALLIDAY, M. A. K. (1980) 'On being teaching.' In Greenbaum et al. (1980), pp. 61–4. (p. 411)

HARRIS, J. (1984) 'Syntactic variation and dialect divergence', *Journal of Linguistics* **20**, 303–27. (pp. 348, 364)

HARRIS, M. (1981) 'It's I, it's me: further reflections', *Studia Anglica Posnaniensia* **13**, 17–20. (p. 22)

HAUSMANN, R. B. (1974) 'The origin and development of Modern English periphrastic *do*.' In Anderson and Jones (1974), pp. 159–89. (pp. 283, 285–6)

HEALEY, A. diP. (1985) 'The Dictionary of Old English and the final design of its computer system', *Computers and the Humanities* **19**, 245–9. (p. 15)

HEALEY, A. diP. and VENEZKY, R. L. (1980) *A Microfiche Concordance to Old English: the List of Texts and Index of Editions*. (Repr. with corrections, 1985.) The Dictionary of Old English Project, Toronto. (pp. 15, 502)

HENNINGSEN, H. (1911) *Über die Wortstellung in den Prosaschriften Richard Rolles von Hampole*. Dissertation, Kiel. Junge, Erlangen. (p. 468)

HILTUNEN, R. (1983) *The Decline of the Prefixes and the Beginnings of the English Phrasal Verb: the Evidence from Some Old and Early Middle English Texts*. (Annales Universitatis Turkuensis, Series B, 160.) (Revision of unpublished DPhil dissertation, University of Oxford, 1981.) Turun Yliopisto (University of Turku, Finland), Turku. (p. 57)

HOFFMANN, G. (1934) *Die Entwicklung des umschriebenes Perfektums im Altenglischen und Frühmittelenglischen*. Dissertation, Breslau. (p. 348)

HOLTHAUSEN, F. (1934) *Altenglisches etymologisches Wörterbuch*. Carl Winter, Heidelberg. (p. 318)

HOPPER, P. J. (ed.) (1982) *Tense-Aspect: Between Semantics and Pragmatics. Containing the Contributions of a Symposium on Tense and Aspect, held at UCLA, May 1979*. (Typological studies in Language, 1.) John Benjamins, Amsterdam/Philadelphia.

HOPPER, P. J. and THOMPSON, S. A. (1980) 'Transitivity in grammar and discourse', *Language* **56**, 251–99. (p. 82)

HORGAN, D. M. (1981) 'The lexical and syntactic variants shared by two of the later manuscripts of King Alfred's translation of Gregory's *Cura Pastoralis*', *Anglo-Saxon England* **9**, 213–21. (p. 339)

HORNSTEIN, N. and WEINBERG, A. (1981) 'Case theory and preposition stranding', *Linguistic Inquiry* 12, 55–91. (pp. 151, 159, 161–2)

HUDDLESTON, R. D. (1976) 'Some theoretical issues in the description of the English verb', *Lingua* 40, 331–83. (pp. 255, 410)

HUDDLESTON, R. (1980) 'Criteria for auxiliaries and modals.' In Greenbaum et al. (1980), pp. 65–78. (pp. 268, 274, 292, 297)

HUDDLESTON, R. (1984) *Introduction to the Grammar of English.* (Cambridge Textbooks in Linguistics.) Cambridge University Press, Cambridge. (pp. 56, 229, 272, 292–3)

IDE, M. (1984) '*Beon/wesan gepuht(e)*', *Bulletin of Kanto Gakuin University* 39, 51–64. (pp. 345, 382)

IDE, M. (1985) 'The distribution of *beon/wesan gepuht(e)* in Old English texts', *Bulletin of Kanto Gakuin University* 43, 81–118. (p. 345)

IHALAINEN, O. (1982) 'On the notion "possible grammatical change": a look at a perfectly good change that did not quite make it', *Studia Anglica Posnaniensia* 15, 3–11. (pp. 284–5)

INADA, T. (1981) 'Problems of reanalyses and preposition stranding', *Studies in English Linguistics* (Tokyo) 9, 120–31. (p. 152)

JACOBSON, S. (ed.) (1979) *Papers from the Scandinavian Symposium on Syntactic Variation: Stockholm, May 18–19, 1979.* (Stockholm Studies in English, 52.) Almqvist & Wiksell International, Stockholm. (p. 367)

JACOBSON, S. (ed.) (1983) *Papers from the Second Scandinavian Symposium on Syntactic Variation: Stockholm, May 15–16, 1982.* (Stockholm Studies in English, 57.) Almqvist & Wiksell, Stockholm. (p. 367)

JACOBSON, S. (ed.) (1986) *Papers from the Third Scandinavian Symposium on Syntactic Variation: Stockholm, May 11–12, 1985.* (Stockholm Studies in English, 65.) Almqvist & Wiksell, Stockholm. (p. 367)

JACOBSSON, B. (1951) *Inversion in English with Special Reference to the Early Modern Period.* Almqvist & Wiksell, Uppsala. (p. 460)

JESPERSEN, O. (1909–49) *A Modern English Grammar on Historical Principles*, 7 vols. (Repr. London, 1961.) Carl Winters Universitätsbuchhandlung, Heidelberg/Ejnar Munksgaard, Copenhagen. (pp. 3, 74–5, 113–14, 121, 137, 196, 214–16, 243–4, 298, 309, 325, 346, 364, 374, 382, 393, 396, 401, 408, 412, 420, 427, 429, 436, 442, 449, 451, 477)

JESPERSEN, O. (1917) *Negation in English and Other Languages.* (Repr. 1962 in *Selected Writings of Otto Jespersen*, pp. 1–151.) Andr. Fred. Høst & Søn, Copenhagen. (pp. 309, 338, 449)

JESPERSEN, O. (1937) (repr. 1984) *Analytic Syntax.* University of Chicago Press, Chicago. (p. 219)

JESPERSEN, O. (1946) *Growth and Structure of the English Language*, 9th edn. Blackwell, Oxford. (p. 412)

JONES, C. (1972) *An Introduction to Middle English.* Holt, Rinehart & Winston, New York. (p. 290)

JONES, C. (1988) *Grammatical Gender in English: 950 to 1250.* Croom Helm, London. (p. 20)

JØRGENSEN, E. (1984) ' "Ought". Present or past tense?', *English Studies* 65, 550–4. (p. 315)

KAGEYAMA, T. (1975) 'Relational grammar and the history of subject raising', *Glossa* 9, 165–81. (pp. 197, 244–5, 247–8)

KASTOVSKY, D. (ed.) (1991) *Historical English Syntax.* (Topics in English Linguistics, 2.) Mouton de Gruyter, Berlin/New York.

KASTOVSKY, D. and BAUER, G. (eds) (1988) *Luick Revisited: Papers read at the Luick-Symposium at Schloß Liechtenstein, 15.–18.9.1985.* (In collaboration with J. Fisiak.) (Tübinger Beiträge zur Linguistik, 288.) Gunter Narr, Tübingen.

KASTOVSKY, D. and SZWEDEK, A. (eds) (1986) *Linguistics across Historical and Geographical Boundaries: in Honour of Jacek Fisiak on the Occasion of his Fiftieth Birthday*, 2 vols. (Trends in Linguistics/Studies and Monographs, 32.) Mouton de Gruyter, Berlin/New York/Amsterdam.

KATO, T. (1974) *A Concordance to the Works of Sir Thomas Malory*. University of Tokyo Press, Tokyo. (p. 511)

KELLER, R. (1956) Review of Dal (1952), *English Studies* 37, 75–8. (Chapter 13.)

KELLER, W. (1925) 'Keltisches im englischen Verbum.' In *Anglica: Untersuchungen zur Englischen Philologie, Alois Brandl zum Siebzigsten Geburtstage überreicht*, I, *Sprache und Kulturgeschichte*. (Palaestra, 147.) Mayer & Müller, Leipzig, pp. 55–66. (p. 402)

KEMENADE, A. VAN (1985) 'Old English infinitival complements and West-Germanic V-raising.' In Eaton et al. (1985), pp. 73–84. (pp. 52, 333)

KEMENADE, A. VAN (1987) *Syntactic Case and Morphological Case in the History of English*. (PhD dissertation, Utrecht.) Foris, Dordrecht. (pp. 12, 50–2, 57–8, 100, 145, 149–52, 161, 333, 337, 469)

KEMENADE, A. VAN (forthcoming) 'Structural factors in the history of English modals'. In Rissanen et al. (forthcoming), pp. 287–309. (pp. 240, 333–4, 338, 463)

KEMPSON, R. M. (1977) *Semantic Theory*. (Cambridge Textbooks in Linguistics.) Cambridge University Press, Cambridge. (p. 288)

KENNEDY, A. G. (1927) *A Bibliography of Writings on the English Language from the Beginning of Printing to the End of 1922*. Harvard University Press, Cambridge, MA/Yale University Press, New Haven, CT; Milford, London. (p. 6)

KENYON, J. (1909) *The Syntax of the Infinitive in Chaucer*. (Chaucer Society Publications, 2nd series, 44.) London/Oxford. (p. 214)

KEYSER, S. J. and O'NEIL, W. (1985) 'The simplification of the Old English strong nominal paradigms.' In Eaton et al. (1985), pp. 85–107. (p. 17)

KHOMIAKOV, V. A. (1964) 'A note on the so-called "passive participles with active meaning" in Old English', *Journal of English and Germanic Philology* 63, 675–8. (p. 369)

KILBY, D. (1984) *Descriptive Syntax and the English Verb*. Croom Helm, London/ Sydney/Dover, NH. (pp. 392, 413)

KILPIÖ, M. (1989) *Passive Constructions in Old English Translations from Latin: with Special Reference to the OE Bede and the 'Pastoral Care'*. (Mémoires de la Société Néophilologique de Helsinki, 49.) Société Néophilologique, Helsinki. (pp. 414, 416, 418–19, 422, 444)

KIRCHNER, G. (1952) *Die zehn Hauptverben des Englishchen: im Britischen und Amerikanischen*. Niemeyer, Halle (Saale). (pp. 364–5)

KJELLMER, G. (1986) ' "Us Anglos are a cut above the field": on objective pronouns in nominative contexts', *English Studies* 67, 445–9. (p. 22)

KLINGEBIEL, J. (1937) *Die Passivumschreibungen im Altenglischen*. Dissertation, Berlin. (pp. 417, 444)

KOHONEN, V. (1976/82) 'A note on factors affecting the position of accusative objects and complements in Ælfric's *Catholic Homilies* I.' In Enkvist, N. E. and Kohonen, V. (eds) *Approaches to Word Order*, 2nd edn (1st edn, 1976), pp. 175–96. (Publications of the Research Institute of the Åbo Akademi Foundation, 72 (1st edn, no. 8).) Åbo Akademi, Åbo. (p. 40)

KOHONEN, V. (1978) *On the Development of English Word Order in Religious Prose around 1000 and 1200 AD: a Quantitative Study of Word Order in Context*. (Publications of the Research Institute of the Åbo Akademi Foundation, 38.) Åbo Akademi, Åbo. (pp. 29, 40, 48–9, 58, 97, 240)

KOMA, O. (1981) 'Word order change and preposition stranding in ME', *Studies in English Linguistics* (Tokyo) 9, 132–44. (pp. 151–2)

KOMA, O. (1987) 'On the initial locus of syntactic change: verbal gerund and its historical development', *English Linguistics* 4, 311–24. (p. 404)

KOOPMAN, W. F. (1985) 'Verb and particle combinations in Old and Middle English.' In Eaton et al. (1985), pp. 109–21. (pp. 36–8)

KOOPMAN, W. (1990a) *Word Order in Old English: with Special Reference to the Verb Phrase.* (PhD dissertation, University of Amsterdam.) (Amsterdam Studies in Generative Grammar, 1.) No publisher, Amsterdam. (pp. 52, 57)

KOOPMAN, W. F. (1990b) 'The order of dative and accusative objects in Old English.' In Koopman (1990a), pp. 133–223. (pp. 36, 120, 122)

KOOPMAN, W. F. (1990c) 'Old English constructions with three verbs', *Folia Linguistica Historica* **9.**1, 271–300; also in Koopman (1990a), pp. 38–74. (pp. 36, 38, 52, 337–8, 452–4)

KOOPMAN, W. (1990d) 'The double object construction in Old English.' In Adamson et al. (1990), pp. 225–43. (pp. 31, 36–7, 122)

KOOPMAN, W. F. (1992) 'Old English clitic pronouns: some remarks.' In Colman (1992), pp. 44–87; also in Koopman (1990a), pp. 75–132. Earlier version in *Dutch Working Papers in English Language and Linguistics* **10** (1989). (pp. 36, 51, 100)

KOOPMAN, W. F., VAN DER LEEK, F., FISCHER, O. and EATON, R. (eds) (1987) *Explanation and Linguistic Change.* (Current Issues in Linguistic Theory, 45.) John Benjamins, Amsterdam.

KOPYTKO, R. (1985) 'Some observations on the possible interrelationship between synchronic and diachronic data in syntactic analysis.' *Kwartalnik Neofilologiczny* **32**, 27–32. (pp. 168–9)

KOSSUTH, K. C. (1982) 'Historical implications of the co-occurrence constraints on auxiliaries', *Lingua* **56**, 283–95. (pp. 454–5)

KOZIOL, H. (1936) 'Die Entstehung der Umschreibung mit *to do*', *Germanische-Romanische Monatschrift* **24**, 460–66. (p. 274)

KROCH, A. (1989(1990)) 'Reflexes of grammar in patterns of language change', *Language Variation and Change* **1**, 199–244. (pp. 452, 458, 462–4, 468)

KROCH, A., MYHILL, J. and PINTZUK, S. (1982) 'Understanding do', *Papers from the Chicago Linguistic Society* **18**, 282–94. (pp. 266, 290, 461–2, 469)

KRZYSZPIEŃ, J. (1984) 'On the impersonal-to-personal transition in English', *Studia Anglica Posnaniensia* **17**, 63–9. (p. 78)

KURYŁOWICZ, J. (1949) 'Le problème du classement des cas', *Biuletyn Polskie Towarzystwa Językoznawczego* **9**, 20–43. (Repr. in Kuryłowicz, J. (1960) *Esquisses Linguistiques.* Wrocław-Kraków, pp. 131–50.) (p. 86)

KURYŁOWICZ, J. (1964) *The Inflectional Categories of Indo-European.* Carl Winter, Heidelberg. (p. 86)

KYTÖ, M. (1987) '*Can (could)* vs. *may (might)* in Old and Middle English: testing a diachronic corpus.' In Kahlas-Tarkka, L. (ed.) *Neophilologica Fennica: Modern Language Society 100 years.* (Mémoires de la Société Néophilologique de Helsinki, 45.) Société Néophilologique, Helsinki, pp. 205–40. (p. 325)

KYTÖ, M. (1991) '*Can (could)* vs. *may (might)*: regional variation in Early Modern English?' In Kastovsky (1991), pp. 233–89. (p. 13)

LABOV, W. (1989) 'The child as linguistic historian', *Language Variation and Change* **1**, pp. 85–97. (p. 403)

LAGERQUIST, L. M. (1985) 'The impersonal verb in context: Old English.' In Eaton et al. (1985), pp. 123–36. (p. 98)

LAKOFF, G. (1970) 'A note on vagueness and ambiguity', *Linguistic Inquiry* **1**, 357–9. (p. 288)

LAKOFF, G. (1987) *Women, Fire, and Dangerous Things: What Categories Reveal About the Mind.* University of Chicago Press, Chicago/London. (pp. 96, 427, 445)

LANGENFELT, G. (1933) *Select Studies in Colloquial English of the Late Middle Ages.* Gleerupska Univ. Bokhandeln, Lund. (p. 275)

LENERZ, J. (1982) 'On the development of periphrastic *do* in the history of English.' In Welte, W. (ed.) *Sprachtheorie und angewandte Linguistik: Festschrift für Alfred Wollmann zum 60. Geburtstag.* Gunter Narr, Tübingen, pp. 211–20. (pp. 286–7)

LESLIE, M. (1990) 'The Hartlib Papers Project: text retrieval with large datasets', *Journal of the Association of Literary and Linguistic Computing* **5**(1), 50–60. (p. 13)

LIEBER, R. (1979) 'The English passive: an argument for historical rule stability', *Linguistic Inquiry* **10**, 667–88. (pp. 117, 155, 157–9)

LIGHTFOOT, D. (1974) 'The diachronic analysis of English modals.' In Anderson and Jones (1974), pp. 219–49. (pp. 327, 454)

LIGHTFOOT, D. (1976) 'The theoretical implications of subject raising.' Review article on Postal (1974), *Foundations of Language* **14**, 257–85. (p. 170)

LIGHTFOOT, D. W. (1979) *Principles of Diachronic Syntax.* (Cambridge Studies in Linguistics, 23.) Cambridge University Press, Cambridge. (pp. 6, 78–9, 90, 101, 122, 155–8, 245, 249, 286, 327–9, 337–8, 393)

LIGHTFOOT, D. (1981) 'The history of noun phrase movement.' In Baker and McCarthy (1981), pp. 86–119. (pp. 79–80, 90, 101, 158–9, 200, 249)

LIGHTFOOT, D. (1991) *How to Set Parameters: Arguments from Language Change.* MIT Press, Cambridge, MA. (p. 217)

LINDEMANN, J. W. R. (1970) *Old English Preverbal 'ge-': its Meaning.* University Press of Virginia, Charlottesville. (p. 414)

McCAWLEY, N. A. (1976) 'From OE/ME "impersonal" to "personal" constructions: what is a "subject-less" S?' In Steever et al. (1976), pp. 192–204. (pp. 83, 86)

McCOARD, R. W. (1978) *The English Perfect: Tense-choice and Pragmatic Inferences.* (North-Holland Linguistic Series, 38.) (Revision of PhD dissertation, UCLA, 1976.) North-Holland, Amsterdam/New York/Oxford. (pp. 343, 358, 365–6, 370)

McINTOSH, A., SAMUELS, M. L. and BENSKIN, M. (1986) *A Linguistic Atlas of Late Mediaeval English*, 4 vols, with the assistance of M. Laing and K. Williamson. Aberdeen University Press, Aberdeen. (pp. 12, 387)

MALING, J. M. (1978) 'An asymmetry with respect to *wh*-islands', *Linguistic Inquiry* **9**, 75–89. (pp. 145–6)

MANABE, K. (1989) *The Syntactic and Stylistic Development of the Infinitive in Middle English.* Kyushu University Press, Fukuoka. (pp. 180, 217)

MARCHAND, H. (1938–39) 'Syntaktische Homonymie: das umschreibende *Do*', *Englische Studien* **73**, 227–52. (p. 274)

MARCHAND, H. (1939) Review of Engblom (1938), *English Studies* **21**, 121–5. (pp. 274, 279)

MARCHAND, H. (1951) 'The syntactical change from inflectional to word order system and some effects of this change on the relation "verb/object" in English: a diachronic-synchronic interpretation', *Anglia* **70**, 70–89. (pp. 116–18, 155, 179)

MARKUS, M. (1988a) 'Reasons for the loss of gender in English.' In Kastovsky and Bauer (1988), pp. 241–58. (p. 20)

MARKUS, M. (ed.) (1988b) *Historical English: on the Occasion of Karl Brunner's 100th Birthday.* (Innsbrucker Beiträge zur Kulturwissenschaft, Anglistische Reihe, 1.) Institut für Anglistik, Universität Innsbruck.

MED = KURATH, H., KUHN, S. M., REIDY, J., LEWIS, R. E. et al. (eds) (1952–) *Middle English Dictionary.* University of Michigan Press, Ann Arbor. (pp. 5, 111, 122, 161, 267, 296, 315, 320–1, 387, 502)

MERITT, H. D. (1938) *The Construction ἀπὸ κοινοῦ in the Germanic Languages.* (Stanford University Publications, University Series, Language and Literature, vol. VI, no. 2.) Stanford University Press, Stanford/Oxford University Press, London, pp. 155–268. (p. 216)

MILLER, J. (1985) *Semantics and Syntax: Parallels and Connections.* Cambridge University Press, Cambridge. (p. 438)

MILROY, L. (1987) *Observing and Analysing Natural Language.* (Language in Society, 12.) Blackwell, Oxford. (p. 290)

MITCHELL, B. (1964) 'Syntax and word-order in *The Peterborough Chronicle*, 1122–1154', *Neuphilologische Mitteilungen* **65**, 113–44. (pp. 29, 33–5)

MITCHELL, B. (1969) 'Postscript on Bede's *mihi cantare habes*', *Neuphilologische Mitteilungen* 70, 369–80. (p. 315)

MITCHELL, B. (1976a) 'Some problems involving Old English periphrases with *beon/ wesan* and the present participle', *Neuphilologische Mitteilungen* 77, 478–91. (pp. 378, 381, 397–8)

MITCHELL, B. (1976b) 'No "house is building" in Old English', *English Studies* 57, 385–9. (pp. 389–90)

MITCHELL, B. (1978) 'Prepositions, adverbs, prepositional adverbs, postpositions, separable prefixes, or inseparable prefixes, in Old English?', *Neuphilologische Mitteilungen* 79, 240–57. (pp. 144, 161)

MITCHELL, B. (1979) 'F. Th. Visser, *An Historical Syntax of the English Language*: some caveats concerning Old English', *English Studies* 60, 537–42. (pp. 122, 158)

MITCHELL, B. (1985) *Old English Syntax*, 2 vols. Clarendon, Oxford. (pp. 5, 23, 34, 56, 65, 118–19, 161, 168, 172, 196–8, 258, 262, 295, 315, 322, 338–9, 346–50, 359, 364, 397, 416–19, 423, 438, 502, *et passim*)

MITCHELL, B. (1990) *A Critical Bibliography of Old English Syntax to the End of 1984 Including Addenda and Corrigenda to 'Old English Syntax'*. Blackwell, Oxford. (pp. 6, 338)

MITCHELL, B., BALL, C. and CAMERON, A. (1975, 1979) 'Short titles of Old English texts', *Anglo-Saxon England* 4, 207–21. 'Addenda and corrigenda', *Anglo-Saxon England* 8, 331–3. (p. 502)

MITCHELL, B. and ROBINSON, F. C. (1992) *A Guide to Old English*, 5th edn. Blackwell, Oxford. (pp. 5, 23)

MOSSÉ, F. (1938a) *Histoire de la forme périphrastique 'être + participe présent' en germanique*, I, *Introduction, ancien germanique, vieil-anglais*. (Collection Linguistique, La Société Linguistique de Paris, 42.) C. Klincksieck, Paris. (pp. 321, 384–6, 397–8)

MOSSÉ, F. (1938b) *Histoire de la forme périphrastique 'être + participe présent' en germanique*, II, *moyen-anglais et anglais moderne*. (Collection Linguistique, La Société Linguistique de Paris, 43.) C. Klincksieck, Paris. (pp. 374, 379, 387, 393–4, 396–7, 402–5, 409, 411–12, 428–31, 439–40)

MOSSÉ, F. (1952) *A Handbook of Middle English*. J. A. Walker (trans). Johns Hopkins University Press, Baltimore/London. (pp. 5, 20, 347)

MURRAY, J. A. H. (1870–72) 'The dialect of the southern counties of Scotland: its pronunciation, grammar, and historical relations', *Transactions of the Philological Society*, part II (1873) 1–248. (pp. 407, 409)

MUSTANOJA, T. F. (1960) *A Middle English Syntax*, I, *Parts of speech*. (Mémoires de la Société Néophilologique de Helsinki, 23.) Société Néophilologique, Helsinki. (pp. 5, 21, 116, 134, 169, 266–7, 322, 324, 344–5, 354, 361–4, 366, 383–4, 398, 416, 418, 437–8, 458)

NAGUCKA, R. (1985) 'Remarks on complementation in Old English.' In Eaton et al. (1985), pp. 195–205. (p. 207)

NARO, A. J. and LEMLE, M. (1976) 'Syntactic diffusion.' In Steever et al. (1976), pp. 221–40. (p. 466)

NEHLS, D. (1974) *Synchron-Diachrone Untersuchungen zur Expanded Form im Englischen: eine Struktural-Funktionale Analyse*. (Linguistische Reihe, 19.) Max Hueber Verlag, Munich. (pp. 403, 406–7, 409, 412, 444)

NEVALAINEN, T. (1991) 'Motivated archaism: the use of affirmative periphrastic *do* in Early Modern English liturgical prose'. In Kastovsky (1991), pp. 303–20. (pp. 465–6)

NEVALAINEN, T. and RAUMOLIN-BRUNBERG, H. (1989) 'A corpus of Early Modern Standard English in a socio-historical perspective', *Neuphilologische Mitteilungen* 90, 67–110. (p. 14)

NEVALAINEN, T. and RISSANEN, M. (1986) 'Do you support the *do*-support? Emphatic and non-emphatic DO in affirmative statements in present-day spoken English.' In Jacobson (1986), pp. 35–50. (p. 464)

NICKEL, G. (1966) *Die expanded Form im Altenglischen: Vorkommen, Funktion und Herkunft der Umschreibung 'beon/wesan' + Partizip präsens.* Karl Wachholtz Verlag, Neumünster. (pp. 373–4, 378–9, 381, 395, 398–400, 412)

NICKEL, G. (1967) 'An example of a syntactic blend in Old English', *Indogermanische Forschungen* **72**, 261–74. (pp. 399, 412)

NIXON, G. and HONEY, J. (eds) (1988) *An Historic Tongue: Studies in English Linguistics in Memory of Barbara Strang.* Routledge, London/New York.

OED = MURRAY, J. A. H., BRADLEY, H., CRAIGIE, W. A. and ONIONS, C. T. (eds) (1933) *The Oxford English Dictionary*, 12 vols and *Supplement*. Also 1989 CD-ROM version, also Burchfield, R. W. (ed.) (1972–86) *A Supplement to the Oxford English Dictionary*, 4 vols. Clarendon, Oxford. (pp. 3, 5, 102, 224, 228, 243, 256, 271, 296–7, 320–1, 338, 394, 418, 431, 444, 512

*OED*² = SIMPSON, J. A. and WEINER, E. S. C. (1989) *The Oxford English Dictionary*, 2nd edn, 20 vols. Also 1992 CD-ROM version. Clarendon, Oxford. (pp. 3, 7, 412, 444, 512)

OGAWA, H. (1989) *Old English Modal Verbs: a Syntactical Study.* (Anglistica, 26.) Rosenkilde and Bagger, Copenhagen. (p. 339)

OGURA, M. (1986) *Old English 'Impersonal' Verbs and Expressions.* (Anglistica, 24.) Rosenkilde and Bagger, Copenhagen. (pp. 64, 92–3, 96, 99–100, 231)

OGURA, M. (1991) '*Displese yow* and *Displeses yow*: OE and ME verbs used both "impersonally" and reflexively', *Poetica* (Tokyo) **34**, 75–87. (p. 236)

OHLANDER, U. (1941/42) 'A study on the use of the infinitive sign in Middle English', *Studia Neophilologica* **14**, 58–66. (p. 214)

ONO, S. (1989) *On Early English Syntax and Vocabulary.* Tokyo. (p. 338)

PAGE, N. (1972) *The Language of Jane Austen.* Blackwell, Oxford. (p. 443)

PALMER, F. R. (1979) *Modality and the English Modals.* Longman, London. (pp. 293, 295, 513)

PALMER, F. R. (1988) *The English Verb*, 2nd edn. Longman, London. (pp. 168, 292–3, 297–8, 320, 368)

PARKES, M. B. (1983) 'On the presumed date and possible origin of the manuscript of the *Orrmulum*: Oxford, Bodleian Library, MS Junius 1.' In Stanley and Gray (1983), pp. 115–27. (p. 512)

PARRY, D. (ed.) (1979) *The Survey of Anglo-Welsh Dialects*, II, *The South-west.* University College of Swansea. (p. 282)

PEITSARA, K. (forthcoming) 'On the development of the *by*-agent in English.' In Rissanen et al. (forthcoming), pp. 379–400. (p. 416)

PENHALLURICK, J. M. (1985) 'The semantics of auxiliary *do*', *Studies in Language* **9**, 311–33. (pp. 322, 466–7)

PHILLIPPS, K. C. (1970) *Jane Austen's English.* André Deutsch, London. (pp. 411, 443)

PINTZUK, S. and KROCH, A. S. (1985) 'Reconciling an exceptional feature of Old English clause structure.' In Faarlund (1985), pp. 87–111. (pp. 38–9, 57, 212–13)

PINTZUK, S. and KROCH, A. S. (1989) 'The rightward movement of complements and adjuncts in the Old English of *Beowulf*.' (Revision of Pintzuk and Kroch (1985).) *Language Variation and Change* **1**, 115–43. (pp. 38–9, 57–8, 212–13)

PLANK, F. (1981) 'Object cases in Old English: what do they encode? A contribution to a general theory of case and grammatical relations.' Unpublished MS, Englisches Seminar, Universität Hannover, pp. 1–67. (pp. 18–19, 23, 86)

PLANK, F. (1983) 'Coming into being among the Anglo-Saxons.' In Davenport et al. (1983), pp. 239–78. (pp. 18–19, 23, 86)

PLANK, F. (1984) 'The modals story retold', *Studies in Language* **8**, 305–64. (pp. 71, 101, 308, 311, 327, 329–30, 336)

PLATZACK, C. (1985) 'A survey of generative analyses of the verb second phenomenon in Germanic', *Nordic Journal of Linguistics* **8**, 49–73. (p. 36)

POSTAL, P. M. (1974) *On Raising: One Rule of English Grammar and its Theoretical Implications*. MIT Press, Cambridge, MA. (pp. 170, 197)

POUSSA, P. (1982) 'The evolution of early standard English: the creolization hypothesis', *Studia Anglica Posnaniensia* **14**, 69–85. (pp. 11, 15)

POUSSA, P. (1990) 'A contact-universals origin for periphrastic *do*, with special consideration of OE-Celtic contact.' In Adamson et al. (1990), pp. 407–34. (pp. 281–5, 287)

POUTSMA, H. (1926) *A Grammar of Late Modern English: for the Use of Continental, Especially Dutch, Students*. Part II, *The Parts of Speech*, Section II, *The Verb and the Particles*. Noordhoff, Groningen. (p. 431)

PREUSLER, W. (1956) 'Keltischer Einfluss im Englischen', *Revue des Langues Vivantes* **22**, 322–50. (Incorporates earlier articles with same title in *Indogermanische Forschungen* **56**, 178–91 (1938), *IF* **57**, 140–41 (1940), *Anglia* **66**, 121–8 (1942), *Taal en Leven* **7**, 90–91 (1944).) (pp. 275, 403, 418)

QUIRK, R. (1965) 'Descriptive statement and serial relationship', *Language* **41**, 205–17. (Repr. in Quirk, R. (1968) *Essays on the English Language, Medieval and Modern*, Longman, London, pp. 167–83.) (p. 92)

QUIRK, R., GREENBAUM, S., LEECH, G. and SVARTVIK, J. (1985) *A Comprehensive Grammar of the English Language*. (Index by D. Crystal.) Longman, London/ New York. (pp. 14, 56, 110, 219, 229, 255, 266, 268, 344)

QUIRK, R. and WRENN, C. L. (1957) *An Old English Grammar*, 2nd edn. Methuen, London. (pp. 5, 23)

RADFORD, A. (1988) *Transformational Grammar: a First Course*. (Cambridge Textbooks in Linguistics.) Cambridge University Press, Cambridge. (pp. 6, 170, 183, 220)

RAITH, J. (1951) *Untersuchungen zum englischen Aspekt*, I, *Grundsätzliches Altenglisch*. Max Hueber Verlag, Munich. (pp. 389, 398)

RANKOVA, M. (1964) 'On the development of the periphrastic auxiliary do in Modern English', *Annuaire de l'Université de Sofia* **58**, 509–605. (pp. 460, 470)

RAYBOULD, E. (1957) 'Of Jane Austen's use of expanded verbal forms: . . .'. In Korninger, S. (ed.) *Studies in English Language and Literature: Presented to Professor Dr. Karl Brunner on the Occasion of his Seventieth Birthday*. (Wiener Beiträge zur englischen Philologie, 65.) Wilhelm Braumüller, Vienna, pp. 175–90. (p. 443)

RESZKIEWICZ, A. (1966) *Ordering of Elements in Late Old English Prose: in terms of their Size and Structural Complexity*. Zakład im. Ossolińskich (Komitet Neo-filologiczny PAN), Wrocław. (p. 40)

RIEMSDIJK, H. C. VAN (1978) *A Case Study in Syntactic Markedness: the Binding Nature of Prepositional Phrases*. (Studies in Generative Grammar, 4.) Peter de Ridder, Lisse. (pp. 150–1)

RISSANEN, M. (1985) 'Periphrastic *do* in affirmative statements in early American English', *Journal of English Linguistics* **18**, 163–83. (pp. 274, 464)

RISSANEN, M. (1991) 'Spoken language and the history of *do*-periphrasis.' In Kastovsky (1991), pp. 321–42. (pp. 274–5, 464–5, 470)

RISSANEN, M. (in prep.) 'Syntax.' In *CHEL* III, *1476–1776*. (pp. 5, 369, 451, 465)

RISSANEN, M., IHALAINEN, O., NEVALAINEN, T. and TAAVITSAINEN, I. (eds) (forth-coming) *History of Englishes: New Methods and Interpretations in Historical Linguistics*. (Topics in English Linguistics, 10.) Mouton de Gruyter, Berlin.

ROBERTS, I. (1985a) 'Oblique case in the history of English', *Southern California Occasional Papers in Linguistics* **10**. (p. 159)

ROBERTS, I. G. (1985b) 'Agreement parameters and the development of English modal auxiliaries', *Natural Language and Linguistic Theory* 3, 21–58. (pp. 331–3, 339, 463)

ROBERTS, L. J. (1990) 'Finiteness in English and grammatical theory.' Unpublished BA dissertation, University of Manchester. (p. 336)

ROSCH, E. (1978) 'Principles of categorization.' In Rosch, E. and Lloyd, B. B. (eds) *Cognition and Categorization.* Lawrence Erlbaum Associates, Hillsdale, NJ, pp. 27–48. (p. 96)

ROYSTER, J. F. (1918) 'The causative use of *hātan*', *Journal of English and Germanic Philology* 17, 82–93. (pp. 194–5, 281)

ROYSTER, J. F. (1922) 'Old English causative verbs', *Studies in Philology* 19, 328–56. (pp. 195–6, 256–7, 279, 288)

RUSSOM, J. H. (1982) 'An examination of the evidence for OE indirect passives', *Linguistic Inquiry* 13, 677–80. (pp. 122, 158)

RYDÉN, M. (1979) *An Introduction to the Historical Study of English Syntax.* Almqvist and Wiksell, Stockholm. (p. 5)

RYDÉN, M. (1984) 'The study of eighteenth century English syntax.' In Fisiak (1984), pp. 509–20. (p. 5)

RYDÉN, M. (1991) 'The *be/have* variation with intransitives in its crucial phases.' In Kastovsky (1991), pp. 343–54. (p. 367)

RYDÉN, M. and BRORSTRÖM, S. (1987) *The 'be/have' Variation with Intransitives in English: with Special Reference to the Late Modern Period.* (Stockholm Studies in English, 70.) Almqvist and Wiksell International, Stockholm. (pp. 4, 49, 346, 359, 361, 363, 367–8)

RYNELL, A. (1964) 'On alleged constructions like "did wrote" ', *Studier i Modern Språkvetenskap* (*Stockholm Studies in Modern Philology*) n.s. 2, 132–47. (p. 260)

SALMON, V. (1965) 'Sentence structures in colloquial Shakespearian English', *Transactions of the Philological Society* 105–40. (pp. 460–1)

SAMUELS, M. L. (1972a) *Linguistic Evolution: with Special Reference to English.* (Cambridge Studies in Linguistics, 5.) Cambridge University Press, Cambridge. (pp. 6, 12, 14, 153, 274, 281, 283)

SAMUELS, M. L. (1972b) Review of Lindemann (1970), *Medium Ævum* 41, 289–92. (p. 414)

SCHEFFER, J. (1975) *The Progressive in English.* (North-Holland Linguistic Series, 15.) North-Holland, Amsterdam/Oxford/American Elsevier, New York. (pp. 400, 405, 407, 409, 412)

SCHELER, M. (1961) *Altenglische Lehnsyntax: die Syntaktischen Latinismen im Altenglischen.* PhD dissertation, Free University, Berlin. (pp. 194, 398)

SCHENDL, H. (1988) 'Semantic verb classes and the use of diagnostics in Old English.' In Markus (1988b), pp. 124–39. (pp. 273–4)

SCHEURWEGHS, G. and VORLAT, E. (1963–79) *Analytical Bibliography of Writings on Modern English Morphology and Syntax 1877–1960*, 5 vols. Nauwelaerts, Louvain. (p. 6)

SCHIBSBYE, K. (1972–7) *Origin and Development of the English language*, 3 vols. Nordisk Sprog- og Kulturforlag, Copenhagen. (pp. 5, 7, 408)

SCHMERLING, S. F. (1981) Comments on Lightfoot (1981). In Baker and McCarthy (1981), pp. 120–8. (pp. 79, 159, 200–1)

SCRAGG, D. G. (1974) *A History of English Spelling.* Manchester University Press, Manchester. (p. 14)

ŠČUR, G. S. (1968) 'On the non-finite forms of the verb CAN in Scottish', *Acta Linguistica Hafniensia* 11, 211–18. (p. 294)

SEEFRANZ-MONTAG, A. VON (1983) *Syntaktische Funktionen und Wortstellungsverän-derung: die Entwicklung 'subjektloser' Konstruktionen in einigen Sprachen.* Wilhelm Fink Verlag, Munich. (pp. 87–8, 236)

SEEFRANZ-MONTAG, A. VON (1984) ' "Subjectless" constructions and syntactic change.' In Fisiak (1984), pp. 521–53. (pp. 87–8)

SELLS, P. (1985) *Lectures on contemporary syntactic theories:* . . . . (CSLI Lecture Notes, 3.) Center for the Study of Language and Information, Stanford. (p. 6)

SERJEANTSON, M. S. (1935) *A History of Foreign Words in English.* K. Paul, Trench, Trubner, London. (p. 14)

SMITH, C. A. (1893) 'The order of words in Anglo-Saxon prose', *Publications of the Modern Language Association of America* **8**, 210–44. (pp. 29, 31–3, 122)

SÖDERLIND, J. (1951–8) *Verb Syntax in John Dryden's Prose,* 2 vols. (Essays and Studies on English Language and Literature [English Institute, Upsala University] 10, 19.) A–B Lundequistska Bokhandeln, Uppsala/Ejnar Munksgaard, Copenhagen/Harvard University Press, Cambridge, MA. (pp. 451, 470)

STANDOP, E. (1957) *Syntax und Semantik der modalen Hilfsverben im Altenglischen 'magan', 'motan', 'sculan', 'willan'.* (Beiträge zur Englischen Philologie, 38.) Pöppinghaus, Bochum-Langendreer. (p. 336)

STANLEY, E. G. (1968) 'The date of Laȝamon's *Brut*', *Notes & Queries* **213**, 85–8. (p. 510)

STANLEY, E. G. (1973) Review of Lindemann (1970), *Anglia* **91**, 493–4. (p. 414)

STANLEY, E. G. and GRAY, D. (eds) (1983) *Five Hundred Years of Words and Sounds: a Festschrift for Eric Dobson.* D. S. Brewer, Cambridge/Biblio, Totowa, NJ.

STEEVER, S. B., WALKER, C. A. and MUFWENE, S. S. (eds) (1976) *Papers from the Parasession on Diachronic Syntax.* Chicago Linguistic Society, Chicago.

STEIN, D. (1985) *Natürlicher syntaktischer Sprachwandel: Untersuchungen zur Entstehung der englischen 'do'-Periphrase in Fragen.* (Tuduv-Studien: Reihe Sprach- und Literaturwissenschaften, 19.) Tuduv, Munich. (pp. 15, 464)

STEIN, D. (1990) *The Semantics of Syntactic Change: Aspects of the Evolution of 'do' in English.* (Trends in linguistics/Studies and monographs, 47.) Mouton de Gruyter, Berlin/New York. (pp. 13, 15, 282, 287, 290, 458, 464)

STERN, [N.] G. (1931) *Meaning and Change of Meaning: with Special Reference to English.* Elanders boktryckeri, Gothenburg. (p. 289)

STOCKWELL, R. P. (1977) 'Motivations for exbraciation in Old English.' In Li, C. N. (ed.) *Mechanisms of Syntactic Change.* University of Texas Press, London/Austin, pp. 291–314. (pp. 43–5, 56, 58)

STOCKWELL, R. P. (1984) 'On the history of the verb-second rule in English.' In Fisiak (1984), pp. 575–92. (pp. 45, 470)

STOCKWELL, R. P. (1990) Review of van Kemenade (1987), *Lingua* **81**, 90–100. (p. 58)

STOCKWELL, R. P. and MINKOVA, D. (1990) 'Verb Phrase conjunction in Old English.' In Andersen and Koerner (1990), pp. 499–515. (p. 54)

STOCKWELL, R. P. and MINKOVA, D. (1991) 'Subordination and word order change in the history of English.' In Kastovsky (1991), pp. 367–408. (pp. 54–5, 58, 469)

STOCKWELL, R. P. and MINKOVA, D. (1992) 'Poetic influence on prose word order in Old English.' In Colman (1992), pp. 142–54. (pp. 54, 58)

STRANG, B. M. H. (1970) *A History of English.* Methuen, London. (pp. 13, 14, 23, 39–41, 53, 56, 354, 365, 420, 427, 451)

STRANG, B. M. H. (1982) 'Some aspects of the history of the *be* + *ing* construction.' In Anderson (1982), pp. 427–74. (pp. 389, 392, 407, 411, 443)

SUNDBY, B., BJØRGE, A. K. and HAUGLAND, K. E. (1991) *A Dictionary of English Normative Grammar 1700–1800.* (Studies in the History of the Language Sciences, 63.) John Benjamins, Amsterdam/Philadelphia. (p. 112)

SVARTVIK, J. and QUIRK, R. (1970) 'Types and uses of non-finite clause in Chaucer', *English Studies* **51**, 393–411. (pp. 213–14, 339)

SWEET, H. (1891) *Elementarbuch des gesprochenen Englisch:* . . ., 3rd edn. Clarendon, Oxford. (p. 430)

SWEET, H. (1897) *The Student's Dictionary of Anglo-Saxon.* Clarendon, Oxford. (p. 23)

SWEET, H. (1898) *A New English Grammar: Logical and Historical*, II, *Syntax*. Clarendon, Oxford. (pp. 277, 430)

SZALAI-SMITS, E. (1988) '(Non)Configurationality in Old English sentence structure', *Amsterdam Papers in English* 1, 43–65. (p. 120)

TAJIMA, M. (1985) *The Syntactic Development of the Gerund in Middle English*. Na'un-do, Tokyo. (pp. 403, 405)

TAJIMA, M. (1988) *Old and Middle English Language Studies: a Classified Bibliography 1923–1985*. (Library and Information Sources in Linguistics, 13.) John Benjamins, Amsterdam/Philadelphia. (p. 6)

TAYLOR, J. (1956) 'Notes on the rise of written English in the late Middle Ages', *Proceedings of the Leeds Philosophical and Literary Society (Literary and Historical Section)* 8, 128–36. (p. 15)

TELLIER, A. (1962) *Les verbes perfecto-présents et les auxiliaires de mode en anglais ancien: (VIIIᴱ S. – XVIᴱ S.)*. (Doctorat ès lettres dissertation, Paris.) C. Klincksieck, Paris. (p. 325)

TERASAWA, J. (1985) 'The historical development of the causative use of the verb *make* with an infinitive', *Studia Neophilologica* 57, 133–43. (p. 207)

THOMASON, S. G. and KAUFMAN, T. (1988) *Language Contact, Creolization, and Genetic Linguistics*. University of California Press, Berkeley/Los Angeles/London. (p. 11)

THORNBURG, L. (1985) 'The history of the prepositional passive in English', *Proceedings of the Annual Meeting of the Berkeley Linguistics Society* 11, 327–36. (pp. 143–4)

TIEKEN-BOON VAN OSTADE, I. (1987) *The Auxiliary 'do' in Eighteenth-century English: a Sociohistorical-linguistic Approach*. Foris, Dordrecht. (p. 466)

TIEKEN-BOON VAN OSTADE, I. (1988) 'The origin and development of periphrastic auxiliary *do*: a case of destigmatisation', *Dutch Working Papers in English Language and Linguistics*, 3. (pp. 283–4)

TOLLER, T. N. (1898) *An Anglo-Saxon Dictionary: Based on the Manuscript Collections of the Late Joseph Bosworth*, and (1921) *Supplement*. Also Campbell, A. (1972) *Enlarged Addenda and Corrigenda*. Clarendon, Oxford. (pp. 6, 228, 338)

TOTTIE, G. (1983) 'The missing link? Or, why is there twice as much negation in spoken English as in written English?' In Jacobson (1983), pp. 67–74. (p. 265)

TRAUGOTT, E. C. (1972) *A History of English Syntax: a Transformational Approach to the History of English Sentence Structure*. Holt, Rinehart and Winston, New York. (pp. 5, 246–7, 274, 303, 366, 369, 385)

TRAUGOTT, E. C. (1992) 'Syntax.' In *CHEL* I, *The beginnings to 1066*, pp. 168–289. (pp. 5, 23, 65, 299, 364, 369, 377)

TRNKA, B. (1930) *On the Syntax of the English Verb from Caxton to Dryden*. (Travaux du Cercle Linguistique de Prague, 3) Jednota Československých Matematikú a Fysikú, Prague. (p. 269)

VAINIKKA, A. and YOUNG-SCHOLTEN, M. (1991) 'Verb raising in second language acquisition: the early stages.' In *Universal Grammar in Second Language Acquisition*. (Theorie des Lexikons 4. Arbeiten des Sonderforschungsbereichs, 282.) The LEXLERN Project, Seminar für allgemeine Sprachwissenschaft, Universität Düsseldorf, pp. 1–47. (pp. 50, 56)

VAT, J. (pseud.) (1978) 'On footnote 2: evidence for the pronominal status of þær in Old English relatives', *Linguistic Inquiry* 9, 695–716. (pp. 145–7, 150)

VENDLER, Z. (1967) *Linguistics in Philosophy*. Cornell University Press, Ithaca, NY. (p. 290)

VENEZKY, R. L. and BUTLER, S. (1985) *A Microfiche Concordance to Old English: the High-Frequency Words*. (Publications of the Dictionary of Old English, 2.) Pontifical Institute for Mediaeval Studies, Toronto. (p. 7)

VENEZKY, R. L. and HEALEY, A. diP. (1980) *A Microfiche Concordance to Old English*. University of Delaware, Newark, DE. (pp. 3, 23, 80, 92, 96, 102, 119, 368, 395, 422, 444, 507)

VENNEMANN, T. (1974) 'Topics, subjects, and word order: from SXV to SVX via TVX.' In Anderson and Jones (1974), pp. 339–76. (pp. 41–2, 44, 49)

VENNEMANN, T. (1984) 'Verb-second, verb late, and the brace construction.' In Fisiak (1984), pp. 627–36. (pp. 29, 42–3)

VESTERGAARD, T. (1977) *Prepositional Phrases and Prepositional Verbs: a Study in Grammatical Function*. (Janua Linguarum series minor, 161.) Mouton, The Hague. (pp. 124, 140, 144)

VISSER, F. T. (1946–56) *A Syntax of the English Language of St. Thomas More*, 3 vols. (Materials for the Study of the Old English Drama, n.s. 19, 24, 26.) Librairie Universitaire, Louvain. (pp. 277, 313, 358, 363, 384, 425, 427)

VISSER, F. T. (1963–73) *An Historical Syntax of the English Language*, 3 parts; 4 vols. E. J. Brill, Leiden. (pp. 3, 5, 6, 118, 121–3, 137–8, 159–60, 165, 172, 196, 268, 276–8, 350–1, 353–4, 365–6, 373, 395–6, 404–6, 410, 421, 430, 439–42, 458, *et passim*)

WAGNER, H. (1959) *Das Verbum in den Sprachen der Britischen Inseln*. Niemeyer, Tübingen. (p. 290)

WAGNER, K. H. (1969) *Generative Grammatical Studies in the Old English Language*. (Wissenschaftliche Bibliothek, 11.) Dissertation, Kiel. Julius Groos Verlag, Heidelberg. (p. 325)

WAHLÉN, N. (1925) *The Old English Impersonalia*, Part I, *Impersonal Expressions Containing Verbs of Material Import in the Active Voice*. Elanders Boktryckeri, Gothenburg. (pp. 91–2, 97)

WALLMANNSBERGER, J. (1988) 'The "creole hypothesis" in the history of English.' In Markus (1988b), pp. 19–36. (p. 11)

WARNER, A. R. (1975) 'Infinitive marking in the Wyclifite sermons', *English Studies* **56**, 207–14. (p. 214)

WARNER, A. (1982) *Complementation in Middle English and the Methodology of Historical Syntax: a Study of the Wyclifite Sermons*. Croom Helm, London/ Canberra. (pp. 6, 159, 176, 184, 187, 204–7, 216, 250–1, 334, 339)

WARNER, A. R. (1983) Review article on Lightfoot (1979), *Journal of Linguistics* **19**, 187–209. (pp. 79, 90, 122, 329)

WARNER, A. R. (1985) *The Structuring of English Auxiliaries: a Phrase Structure Grammar*. Indiana University Linguistics Club, Bloomington, IN. (pp. 268, 272, 378)

WARNER, A. R. (1986) 'Ellipsis conditions and the status of the English copula', *York Papers in Linguistics* **12**, 153–72. (pp. 443, 445)

WARNER, A. R. (1990) 'Reworking the history of English auxiliaries.' In Adamson et al. (1990), pp. 537–58. (pp. 287, 335–6, 339, 423)

WARNER, A. R. (1992) 'Elliptical and impersonal constructions: evidence for auxiliaries in Old English?' In Colman (1992), pp. 178–210. (pp. 221, 224, 255, 271–2, 287, 336, 455–7, 470)

WASOW, T. (1977) 'Transformations and the lexicon.' In Culicover et al. (1977), pp. 327–60. (p. 155)

WEERMAN, F. (1989) *The V2 Conspiracy: a Synchronic and a Diachronic Analysis of Verbal Positions in Germanic Languages*. Foris, Providence, RI. (p. 58)

WEERMAN, F. (1991) 'The interplay between L1 and L2 in language change.' Paper read at Tenth International Conference on Historical Linguistics, Free University, Amsterdam. (p. 50)

WEKKER, H. C. (1985) 'Points of Modern English syntax LXVII', *English Studies* **66**, 456–9. (p. 421)

WEKKER, H. C. (1987) 'Points of Modern English syntax LXIX', *English Studies* **68**, 456–63. (p. 357)

WILDE, H.-O. (1939–40) 'Aufforderung, Wünsch und Möglichkeit: die englische Sprache und die Grundlage englischer Lebenshaltung', *Anglia* **63**, 209–391; **64**, 10–105. (pp. 324–5)

WILLIAMS, E. (1984) '*There*-insertion', *Linguistic Inquiry* **15**, 131–53. (p. 217).

WÜLFING, J. E. (1894–1901) *Die Syntax in den Werken Alfreds des Grossen*, 2 parts; 3 vols. P. Hanstein, Bonn. (pp. 180, 193, 227, 381–3, 385, 423, 425)

WURFF, W. VAN DER (1987) 'Adjective plus infinitive in Old English.' In Beukema and Coopmans (1987), pp. 233–42. (p. 219)

WURFF, W. VAN DER (1990) 'The *easy-to-please* construction in Old and Middle English.' In Adamson et al. (1990), pp. 519–36. (pp. 219–20)

WURFF, W. VAN DER (1992a) 'Another Old English impersonal: some data.' In Colman (1992), pp. 211–48. (p. 96)

WURFF, W. VAN DER (1992b) 'Syntactic variability, borrowing, and innovation', *Diachronica* **9**, 61–85. (Revision of 'Variability and syntactic change', *Dutch Working Papers in English Language and Linguistics* **23**.) (pp. 152–3, 219)

WYLD, H. C. (1936) *A History of Modern Colloquial English*, 3rd edn. Blackwell, Oxford. (p. 13)

ZEITLIN, J. (1908) *The Accusative with Infinitive and Some Kindred Constructions in English*. (PhD dissertation, Columbia University). New York. (pp. 172, 193, 196, 243)

ZWICKY, A. M. and PULLUM, G. K. (1983) 'Cliticization versus inflection: English *n't*', *Language* **59**, 502–13. (p. 293)

Primary sources (texts)

The editions cited in this book are listed here in order of abbreviated title of text. The abbreviations for Old English works follow the now-standard system of Mitchell, Ball and Cameron (1975, 1979) as used in Healey and Venezky (1980);[1] see also Mitchell's notes on the system (1985: I xxx–xxxv = II xl–xlv). Old English citations are therefore undated, whilst those for Middle English show manuscript and composition dates, normally following *MED Plan and Bibliography* (1954, 1984); where a revised dating is used the source of the reference is given. References are always to the line in which the first word of a citation appears. Unless otherwise indicated the form of citation is by volume/book, chapter, page, line, or act, scene, line, as appropriate.

Citations are unchanged apart from the following. 'Wynn' and <3> in the few OE editions which use them are replaced by <w, g>, likewise eModE 'long s' by <s>. Most abbreviations are silently expanded whatever the practice of the chosen edition, except that the ampersand <&> and Tironian nota <7> standing for AND (*and*, *ond*, *ant*) are retained in the form &. Scribal accents are omitted. The various editorial indications of emendation, insertion, and so on are not usually reproduced, nor are editorial markings of vowel length, nor metrical punctuation. The ME punctuation *punctus elevatus* is represented by a colon or semi-colon. The symbol <|> is used to indicate a line-end in poetic citations. Examples contained within quotations from other scholars are, if necessary, silently made to conform to the other citations in this book: errors are corrected; exact wording and line-reference are replaced by the equivalents from the edition used by me elsewhere, as long as the change does not affect the point under discussion. There are trivial changes in the typography of quotations taken from *DOE*, *MED* and *OED*.

The list is not a corpus of texts read, since only some of the works have been read all the way through, and even then in many cases before the final shape and contents of the book were decided. Rather it is a record of the editions in which citations may be found. Where verification was not possible, the fact is indicated below.

The following abbreviations are used in the list:

ASPR   *The Anglo-Saxon Poetic Records*: see below

d.o.b.   date of birth
EETS   Early English Text Society, Ordinary Series
EETS ES   Early English Text Society, Extra Series
EETS SS   Early English Text Society, Special Series
v.d.   various dates

1711–12 Addison, *Spect.* in Bond, D. F. (ed.) (1965) *The Spectator*, 5 vols. Clarendon, Oxford. By number, volume, page and line. d.o.b., 1672, 12.64, 14.81.

a1450 *Aelred Inst.(2)* (Bod) = Ayto, J. and Barratt, A. (eds) (1984) *Aelred of Rievaulx's De Institutione Inclusarum: Two English Versions* (EETS 287), 6.47.

c1450 *Alph.Tales* = Banks, M. M. (ed.) (1904–5) *An Alphabet of Tales: . . .* (EETS 126, 127), 9.161.

a1300 *A Mayde Cristes* (Jes-O), in Brown, *13 cent*, pp. 68–74, 11.65.

c1330(?c1300) *Amis* = Leach, M. (ed.) (1937) *Amis and Amiloun* (EETS 203), 8.155.

c1230(?a1200) *Ancr.* = Tolkien, J. R. R. (ed.) (1962) *The English Text of Ancrene Riwle, Ancrene Wisse* (EETS 249) By folio and line. *MED* cites as *Ancr.*(Corp-C), 5.33, 5.34, 5.53, 6.37, 6.42, 6.43, 7.35, 7.61, 7.73, 7.83, 7.84, 7.87–9, 7.91, 7.109, 7n11, 8.194, 10.41, 11.91, 11.111, 11.138, 12.65, 12.69, 12.118, 13.71, 14.54, 15.10.

c1230 *Ancr.*(Corp-C) in Tolkien (1962), passage not in Nero MS., 7.86.

a1250 *Ancr.*(Nero) = Day, M. (ed.) (1952) *The English Text of the Ancrene Riwle* (EETS 225), 7.38.

a1400 *Ancr.Recl.*(Pep) = Zettersten, A. (ed.) (1976) *The English Text of the Ancrene Riwle* (EETS 274), 10.13.

And = Andreas, in *ASPR* 2, 5.87, 8.54, 8.173, 11.74, 13.61.

c1330(?a1300) *Arth.& M.*(Auch) = Macrae-Gibson, O. D. (ed.) (1973) *Of Arthour and of Merlin* (EETS 268), 7.11, 13.158.

a1425 *Arth.& M.*(LinI) in Macrae-Gibson (1973), 8.118.

1545–68 Ascham, *Works* = Wright, W. A. (ed.) (1904) *Roger Ascham, English Works: . . . .* Cambridge University Press, Cambridge. d.o.b. 1515/16, 9.56.

ASPR = Krapp, G. P. and Dobbie, E. V. K. (eds) (1931–53) *The Anglo-Saxon Poetic Records: a Collective Edition*, 6 vols. Columbia University Press, New York and London.

1816 Austen, *Emma* = Chapman, R. W. (ed.) (1933–4) *The Novels of Jane Austen*, 3rd edn, 5 vols, vol. IV. Oxford University Press, London. Written 1814–15. d.o.b. 1775, 11.77, 11.78, 13.135, 13n10,10a, 14.7.

1816 Austen, *Mansfield Park* = Chapman (1933–4: III). Written 1811–13, 11.162, 13.44, 13.45.

1813 Austen, *Pride & Prejudice* = Chapman (1933–4: II). Perhaps first written 1796–7, 13n10.

(1375) *Award Blount* in *ORS 7* = Award of Dower by Sir Thomas Blount, etc., in Cooke, A. H. (ed.) (1925) *The Early History of Mapledurham*. (Oxfordshire Record Series, 7.) Oxfordshire Record Society, Oxford, pp. 204–6; also published by Oxford University Press, London, 6.44.

c1325 *A Wayle Whyt* (Hrl 9), in Brook, G. L. (ed.) 1964 *The Harley Lyrics: the Middle English Lyrics of MS Harley. 2253*, 3rd edn. Manchester University Press, Manchester, 10.69.

(1340) *Ayenb.* = Morris, R. and Gradon, P. (eds) (1965–79) *Dan Michel's Ayenbite of Inwyt*, corr. repr. (EETS 23, 278), 6.7, 10.111.

ÆCHom I = Thorpe, B. (ed.) (1844–6) *The Sermones Catholici or Homilies of Ælfric* I. Ælfric Society, London, 4.7, 4.9, 4.18, 5.3 = 5.73, 5.4 = 5.74, 5.20, 5n4a, 6.6, 6.11, 6.12, 6.29 = 12.18, 8.43, 8.61, 8.87, 8.92–4, 8.98, 8.110, 8.139, 8.141, 9.60, 9.96, 9.141–3, 11.34, 11.35, 11.136, 11.165, 11.166, 12.18, 12.19, 12.28–30, 12.37, 12.53, 12.54a, 12.54b, 12.96, 12.102, 13.78, 14.19, 14.34, 15.21.

ÆCHom II = Godden, M. (ed.) (1979) *Ælfric's Catholic Homilies: the Second Series* (EETS SS 5), 3.6, 4n11, 5.1, 5.37, 6.27, 6.28, 7.103, 8.88, 9.97, 9.98, 9.133, 12.17, 12.29, 12.38, 13.79.

ÆColl = Garmonsway, G. M. (ed.) (1947) *Ælfric's Colloquy*, 2nd edn. (Methuen Old English Library) Methuen, London, 8.64, 11.114, 13.87.

ÆGenPref = Preface to Genesis, in Crawford, S. J. (ed.) (1922) *The Old English Version of the Heptateuch* (EETS 160) (repr. with additions by N. R. Ker, 1969), 5.57.

ÆGram = Zupitza, J. (ed.) 1880 *Ælfrics Grammatik und Glossar*. (Sammlung englischer Denkmäler, 1.), Weidmann, Berlin, 15.28.

ÆHex = Crawford, S. J. (ed.) (1921) *Exameron Anglice or the Old English Hexameron*. (Bib. ags. Prosa, 10) Henri Grand, Hamburg (repr. Wissenschaftliche Buchgesellschaft, Darmstadt, 1968), 6.30.

ÆHom = Pope, J. C. (ed.) (1967–8) *Homilies of Ælfric: a Supplementary Collection* (EETS 259–60), 5.80, 10.88, 11.58, 11.167, 11.168, 11.197, 11.199, 11.200.

ÆIntSig = Maclean, G. E. (1884) 'Ælfric's version of *Alcuini interrogationes Sigeuulfi in Genesin*', *Anglia* 7, 1–59. By paragraph and line, 9.137 = 11.52.

ÆLet 2(Wulfstan 1) = First Old English Letter for Wulfstan, in Fehr, B. (ed.) (1914) *Die Hirtenbriefe Ælfrics:* . . . . (Bib. ags. Prosa, 9.) Henri Grand, Hamburg (repr. with supplement by P. Clemoes, Wissenschaftliche Buchgesellschaft, Darmstadt, 1966), pp. 68–145, [corrections] 269. By paragraph, page and line, 11.50.

ÆLet 7 = *De Sanguine* [an excerpt], in Kluge, F. (1885) 'Fragment eines Angelsächsischen Briefes', *Englische Studien* 8, 62–3, 5.8.

ÆLS = Skeat, W. W. (ed.) (1881–1900) *Ælfric's Lives of Saints* (EETS 76, 82, 94, 114) (repr. as 2 vols, 1966). By volume, life and line,[2] 5.5 = 5.75, 5.97, 6.70, 8.79, 8.105, 8.186, 9.47, 9.134, 11.81, 11.159, 12.61, 13.38, 13.100, 14.11 = 14.16, 14.17, 14.18, 14.33, 14.45.

1375 Barbour, *Bruce* = Skeat, W. W. (ed.) (1870–89) *The Bruce . . . Compiled by Master John Barbour* (EETS ES 11, 21, 29, 55), 6.35, 12.120.

1918 Barrie, *Barbara's Wedding*, in 1928 *The Plays of J. M. Barrie: in One Volume*. Hodder and Stoughton, London (repr. 1931). d.o.b. 1860, 14.71.

Bede = Miller, T. (ed.) (1890–98) *The Old English Version of Bede's Ecclesiastical History of the English People* (EETS 95–6, 110–11) (repr. 1959–63), 4.15, 6.31, 7.47 = 7.75, 7.98, 8.44, 8.59, 8.60, 8.77, 8.91, 8.120, 8.124 = 8.154, 8.128, 8.140, 8.160, 8.171, 8.185, 9.42, 9.44, 9.58, 9.89, 9.127–30, 9.168, 11.36, 11.79, 12.24, 12.34, 13.41, 13.62, 13.68, 13.69, 14.14, 14.15.

BenR = Schröer, A. (ed.) (1885–8) *Die angelsächsischen Prosabearbeitungen der Benediktinerregel*. (Bib. ags. Prosa, 2) Kassel (repr. with appendix by H. Gneuss, Wissenschaftliche Buchgesellschaft, Darmstadt, 1964), 3.5, 10.28.

Beo = *Beowulf*, in *ASPR* 4, 3.4, 4.17, 5.30, 5.70, 5.88, 6.24, 8.109, 8.153, 8.159, 8.172, 8.196, 9.20, 11.49, 12.26, 13.47, 13.60, 14.44, 15.9.

1523–5 Berners, *Froiss.* = John Bourchier, Lord Berners (trans), *Sir John Froissart's Chronicles:* . . . , repr. as 2 vols, Rivington et al., London, 1812. d.o.b. 1467, 6.34.

c1460(?c1400) *Beryn* = Furnivall, F. J. and Stone, W. G. (eds) (1909) *The Tale of Beryn* . . . (EETS ES 105), 10.49, 10.53.

1815 *Bessborough* = letter of Lady Caroline Lamb, in Bessborough, Earl of and Aspinall, A. (eds) (1941) *Lady Bessborough and Her Family Circle*. J. Murray, London. d.o.b. 1785, 12.123.

a1500(?c1300) *Bevis*(Cmb) = MS. Ff.2,38 in Univ. Library, Cambridge, in Kölbing, E. (ed.) (1885–94) *The Romance of Sir Beues of Hamtoun* (EETS ES 46, 48, 65), 11.64.

1611 Bible = Wright, W. A. (ed.) (1909) *The Authorised Version of the English Bible, 1611*, 5 vols. Cambridge University Press, Cambridge 12.21.

(v.d.) *Bk.Lond.E.* = Chambers, R. W. and Daunt, M. (eds) (1931) *A Book of*

London English. Clarendon, Oxford,[3] 6.46, 7.19, 7.76, 10.14, 10.24, 10.50, 10.58, 13.93 = 13.155.

1985 Blake *ES* = Blake, N. F., book review, in *English Studies* **66**, 170–1, 11.216.

BlHom = Morris, R. (ed.) (1874–80) *The Blickling Homilies* (EETS 58, 63, 73) (repr. in 1 vol. 1967).[4] By homily, page and line, 4n11, 5.2, 5.9, 5.12, 5.26, 5.27, 5.77, 5.89, 5n5, 8.62, 8.114, 9.59, 9.154, 11.38, 11.73, 11.137, 11.155, 11.185, 13.37, 13.42, 13.80, 13.144, 13.161.

Bo = Sedgefield, W. J. (ed.) (1899) *King Alfred's Old English Version of Boethius' De Consolatione Philosophiae*. Clarendon, Oxford. Latin text in Weinberger, G. [= W.] (ed.) (1934) *Anicii Manlii Severini Boethii Philosophiae Consolationis: Libri Quinque*. Hoelder-Pichler-Temsky, Vienna/Akademische Verlagsgesellschaft, Leipzig, 5.10, 5.24, 5.52, 5.91, 7.28, 7.29, 7.52, 8.78, 9.63, 9.132, 10.31 and 10n6, 10.113, 11.53, 11.54, 11.109, 12.101, 13.54, 13.82, 15.26, 15.27.

1849 Ch. Brontë, *Shirley* = Rosengarten, H. and Smith, M. (eds) (1979) Charlotte Brontë, *Shirley*. Clarendon, Oxford. d.o.b. 1816, 12.94.

Brown, *13 cent* = Brown, C. (ed.) (1932) *English lyrics of the XIIIth Century*. Clarendon, Oxford (repr. 1962), 11.65, 11.180.

1851 Brown, *Grammar of English Grammars* = Goold Brown, *The Grammar of English Grammars: . . . .* Wood, New York. (10th edn, 1869). d.o.b. 1791. By part, chapter, rule, page, line, 13n8c.

c1400 *Brut*-1333(Rwl B.171) = Brie, F. W. D. (ed.) (1906–8) *The Brut or the Chronicles of England* (EETS 131, 136), 10.20.

1678, 1684 Bunyan, *Pilgrim's Progress* = Wharey, J. B. and Sharrock, R. (eds) (1960) *The Pilgrim's Progress . . . by John Bunyan*, 2nd edn. Clarendon, Oxford. d.o.b. 1628, 11.182, 13.106, 13.167 and cf. 11.113.

ByrM = Crawford, S. J. (ed.) (1929) *Byrhtferth's Manual (A.D. 1011)* (EETS 177), 13.67, 13.88.

1965 Capote, *In Cold Blood* = Truman Capote, *In Cold Blood: a True Account of a Multiple Murder and its Consequences*. Random House, New York. d.o.b. 1924, 12.11.

1837 Carlyle, *Fr. Rev.* = Thomas Carlyle, *The French Revolution: a History*, 3 vols. (repr. Chapman and Hall, London, 1898.) d.o.b. 1795, 14.125, 14.126, 14.142.

1872 Carroll, *Looking-Glass* = *Through the Looking-Glass and What Alice Found There*, in Blackburn, P. C. and White, L. (eds) (1934) *Logical Nonsense: the Works of Lewis Carroll*. G. P. Putnam's Sons, New York. d.o.b. 1832, 11.106.

c1489 Caxton, *Blanch.* = Kellner, L. (ed.) (1890) *Caxton's Blanchardin and Eglantine: c.1489*. (EETS ES 58), d.o.b. 1422, 13.32.

c1483(?a1480) Caxton, *Dialogues* = Bradley, H. (ed.) (1900) *Dialogues in French and English by William Caxton: . . .* (EETS ES 79). Translation said to be 'much earlier' than printing, edn pp. v–viii, 11.121.

1490 Caxton, *Prol.Eneydos* = Crotch, W. J. B. (ed.) (1928) *The Prologues and Epilogues of William Caxton* (EETS 176). Also available in EETS ES 57 and in Blake (1973), 6n9a,b, 10.17.

c1489 Caxton, *Sonnes of Aymon* = Richardson, O. (ed.) (1885) *The Right Plesaunt and Goodly Historie of the Foure Sonnes of Aymon: Englisht from the French by William Caxton . . .* (EETS ES 44–5), 12.106.

Ch = Charter, in Harmer, F. E. (ed.) (1914) *Select English Historical Documents of the Ninth and Tenth Centuries*. Cambridge University Press, Cambridge, 12.49–52.

a1450(a1401) *Chastising GC* = Bazire, J. and Colledge, E. (eds) (1957) *The Chastising of God's Children: . . . .* Blackwell, Oxford, 14.39.

v.d.(1369–95) Chaucer = Benson, L. D. (ed.) (1988) *The Riverside Chaucer*, 3rd edn. Oxford University Press, Oxford. Citations from *RRose* are also taken from this edn. Abbreviations of works and dating as given in *MED*. d.o.b. c1343, 5.22,

5.35 = 5.62, 5.41, 5.51, 5.54, 6.10, 6.38, 7.17 = 7n1, 7n1, 7n9a, 8.50, 8.70–73, 8.86, 8.99, 8.100, 8.106, 8.107, 8.113, 8.117, 8.180, 8.195, 9.24–6, 9.34, 9.50, 9.67, 9.68, 9.91, 9.92, 9.138, 9.148, 9.149, 10.73, 10.112, 11.67, 11.69, 11.82, 11.132, 11.146, 11.173, 11.174, 12.31, 12.56, 12.91, 12.104, 12.105, 13.11, 13.73, 14.48.

ChristA,B,C = *Christ*, in *ASPR* 3, 9.116, 13.49.

ChronA = *The Parker Chronicle*, MS. Ā, in Plummer, C. (ed.) (1892–9) *Two of the Saxon Chronicles Parallel*, 2 vols. Clarendon, Oxford (reissued D. Whitelock, 1952), 4.16, 4.21, 4.23, 7.32, 7.33, 7.45, 11.152, 12.14 = 12.35, 12.27, 12.36, 13.52, 15.7.

ChronD = MS. D, in Classen, E. and Harmer, F. E. (eds) (1926) *An Anglo-Saxon chronicle: . . . .* Manchester University Press, Manchester, 7.90.

ChronE = MS. E, in Plummer (1892–9). See also *Peterb.Chron.*, 4.13, 4.22, 4n11, 5.45, 5.84, 5.99, 8.42, 8.82, 8.122, 8.161, 9.45, 11.202, 12.20, 12.22, 12.47, 13.153.

c1400(?c1380) *Cleanness* = Anderson, J. J. (ed.) (1977) *Cleanness*. Manchester University Press, Manchester/Barnes and Noble, New York, 7n15c.

a1425(?a1400) *Cloud* = Hodgson, P. (ed.) (1944) *The Cloud of Unknowing . . .* (EETS 218), 7.21, 9.146, 9.147.

1991 Colman = Fran Colman, phone conversation with author, 13n8d.

1900 Conrad, *Lord Jim* = Heilman, R. B. (ed.) (1957) Joseph Conrad, *Lord Jim*. Rinehart, New York. d.o.b. 1857, 13.112.

CP = Sweet, H. (ed.) (1871) *King Alfred's West-Saxon Version of Gregory's Pastoral Care* (EETS 45, 50) (repr. 1958). By chapter, page and line, 4n11, 5.11, 5.49, 5.69, 5.90, 6.5, 7.72, 7.97, 9.21, 9.95, 9.139, 10.27, 11.72, 11n18, 12.23, 12.33, 12.39, 12.43, 12.95, 12.98, 13.8, 13.53, 13.77, 14.13, 14.35, 14.36, 14.49, 15.3, 15.5, 15.6.

a1400(a1325) *Cursor* = MS. Cotton Vespasian A iii in British Library, London, in Morris, R. (ed.) (1874–8) *Cursor Mundi* (EETS 57, 59, 62, 66, 68), 5.58, 6.66a, 7.13 = 7n1, 7.58, 7.62, 7.63, 7.66, 7n1, 8.69, 8.89, 9.65, 9.66, 9.113, 10.72, 11.25, 11.44, 11.45, 11.66, 11.75, 12.55, 12.62, 12.67, 12.108, 12.115, 12n10a, 13.10, 13.74, 13.102, 14.62.

a1400 *Cursor* (Frf) = MS. Fairfax 14 in Bodleian Library, Oxford, in Morris (1874–8), 6.66b.

a1425 *Daily Work* = MS. Arundel 507, in Horstman, C. (ed.) (1895–6) *Yorkshire Writers: Richard Rolle of Hampole . . . and his followers*, 2 vols. Swan Sonnenschein, London. Vol. I, pp. 137–56, 11.70.

Dan = *Daniel*, in *ASPR* 1, 7.96.

1724 Defoe, *Roxana* = Jack, J. (ed.) (1964) Daniel Defoe, *Roxana: the Fortunate Mistress . . . .* Oxford University Press, London. d.o.b. 1660, 9.33, and cf. 13.76.

c1440 *Degrev.* = Casson, L. F. (ed.) (1949) *The Romance of Sir Degrevant* (EETS 221), 9.40.

c1450(?a1400) *Destr.Troy* = Panton, G. A. and Donaldson, D. (eds) (1869–74) *The 'Gest Hystoriale' of the Destruction of Troy* (EETS 39, 56), 5.17, 6.51, 9.101, 9.107, 9.162, 9.163, 13.91.

a1425 *Dial. Reason & A.* = Diekstra, F. N. M. (ed.) (1968) *A Dialogue Between Reason and Adversity: a Late Middle English Version of Petrarch's De Remediis*. Van Gorcum, Assen, 12.77.

1842 Dickens, *American Notes* = Charles Dickens, *American Notes and Pictures from Italy*. (The New Oxford Illustrated Dickens) Oxford University Press, London, 1957. d.o.b. 1812, 13.110, and cf. 14n9c.

1843 Dickens, *Carol* = *A Christmas Carol*, in Charles Dickens, *Christmas Books*. (The New Oxford Illustrated Dickens.) Oxford University Press, London, 1954, 14.78.

1848 Dickens, *Dombey* = Horsman, A. (ed.) (1974) Charles Dickens, *Dombey and Son*. Clarendon, Oxford, 11n10, 12.80.

1855–7 Dickens, *Little Dorrit* = Sucksmith, H. P. (1979) Charles Dickens, *Little Dorrit*. Clarendon, Oxford, 14.79.

1838–9 Dickens, *Nickleby* = Charles Dickens, *The Life and Adventures of Nicholas Nickleby*. (The Oxford Illustrated Dickens.) Oxford University Press, London, 1950, repr. 1982, 13.98.

1837 Dickens, *Pickwick* = Kinsley J, (ed.) (1986) Charles Dickens, *The Pickwick Papers*. Clarendon, Oxford, 11n10, 12.79, 14.32, 14.143.

(v.d.) *Doc.Brewer* in *Bk.Lond.E.* = Extracts from the Brewers' First Book, 10.50.

(c1396) *Doc.* in *Bk.Lond.E.* = Presentment by a Jury, 13.93 = 13.155.

DOE = citations taken from the concordance to *DOE* (Venezky and Healey, 1980) without further verification, 5n28a, 6n2b, 8.145, 9.109, 11.55.

v.d. Dryden = (various editors) (1956–) *The Works of John Dryden*, 19 vols, not all publ. University of California Press, Berkeley & Los Angeles. d.o.b. 1631, 15.17, 15.31, 15n8a.

v.d. (1500–20) Dunbar *Poems* = Kinsley, J. (ed.) (1979) *The Poems of William Dunbar*. Clarendon, Oxford. By poem and line. d.o.b. c1460, 10.78.

1387–1439 *EEWills* = Furnivall, F. J. (ed.) (1882) *The Fifty Earliest English Wills: in the Court of Probate, London* (EETS 78), 6.32.

EMEVP = Bennett, J. A. W. and Smithers, G. V. (eds) (1968) *Early Middle English Verse and Prose*, 2nd edn, glossary by N. Davis. Clarendon, Oxford.

Exhort = *An Exhortation to Christian Living*, in *ASPR* 6, 6.71.

Exod = Exodus, in Crawford, S. J. (ed.) (1922) *The Old English Version of the Heptateuch* (EETS 160) (repr. with additions by N. R. Ker, 1969), 8.143, 12.25, 12.45, 12.46.

1731 Fielding, *Letter Writers* = *The Letter Writers: Or, a New Way to Keep a Wife at Home*, in Stephen, L. (ed.) (1882) *The Works of Henry Fielding, Esq.*, 10 vols. Smith, Elder, London, VIII, pp. 407–53. d.o.b. 1707, 14.21.

c1380 *Firumb.(1)* (Ashm) = Herrtage, S. J. (ed.) (1879) *The English Charlemagne Romances, pt. 1, Sir Ferumbras* (EETS ES 34) (repr. 1903), 9.119, 9.120, 10.51.

1509–21 Fisher, *English Works* = Mayor, J. E. B. (ed.) (1876) *The English works of John Fisher . . .* (EETS ES 27). d.o.b. 1469, 15.33.

a1500(?c1400) *Florence* = Heffernan, C. F. (ed.) (1976) *Le Bone Florence of Rome*. Manchester University Press, Manchester, 8.53.

c1330 *Floris*(Auch) = extract beginning line 661 of *Floris and Blauncheflour*, in *EMEVP*, pp. 40–51, 11.116.

(a1399) *Form Cury* = Hieatt, C. B. and Butler, S. (eds) (1985) *Curye on Inglysch: English Culinary Manuscripts of the Fourteenth Century (Including the 'Forme of Cury')* (EETS SS 8). By part, recipe and line, 8.45, 8.197, 8.198.

?a1300 *Fox and W.* = *The Fox and the Wolf*, in *EMEVP*, pp. 65–76, 10.22, 10.93, 10n13a.

1977 French, *Women's Room* = Marilyn French, *The Women's Room*. Summit Books, New York. d.o.b. 1929, 14.74.

1915 Galsworthy, *Freelands* = John Galsworthy, *The Freelands*. Charles Scribner's Sons, New York, repr. 1928. d.o.b. 1867, 14.70.

c1400(?c1390) *Gawain* = Tolkien, J. R. R. and Gordon, E. V. (eds) (1967) *Sir Gawain and the Green Knight*, 2nd edn, rev. N. Davis. Clarendon, Oxford, 6.16, 9.160, 13.50.

GD = Hecht, H. (ed.) (1900–7) *Bischof Waerferths von Worcester Übersetzung der Dialoge Gregors des Grossen*, 2 vols. (Bib. ags. Prosa, 5.) Wigand, Leipzig (vol. I)/Henri Grand, Hamburg (vol. II), 5.25, 5.36, 5.48, 5.92, 5.98, 5n3a,c, 6.14, 6.26, 6n2a,c, 7.30, 8.40, 8.121, 8.129, 9.23, 9.43, 9.131, 9.151, 9n1a, 11.21, 11.186, 12.100, 12.109, 14n11.

Gen = Genesis, in Crawford (1922) (see under *Exod*), 4.11, 8.162, 9.167, 11.39, 12.44.

GenA,B = *Genesis*, in *ASPR* 1, 5.76, 8.115.

a1325(c1250) *Gen. and Ex.* = Morris, R. (ed.) (1865) *The Story of Genesis and Exodus* (EETS 7) (rev. 1873, repr. 1895), 7.57, 8.67, 13.89, 14.41, 14.42.

a1500(a1450) *Gener.(2)* (Trin-C) = Wright, W. A. (ed.) (1873–8) *Generydes* (EETS 55, 70), 13.103.

c1325(c1300) *Glo.Chron.A* (Clg) = Wright, W. A. (ed.) (1887) *The Metrical Chronicle of Robert of Gloucester* (Rolls Series, 86), 12.66.

c1425 *Glo.Chron.A* (Hrl) = Hearne, T. (ed.) (1724) *Robert of Gloucester's Chronicle*, Oxford (repr. as *The Works of Thomas Hearne, M.A.*, I–II, Bagster, London, 1810), 13.65.

1766 Goldsmith, *Vicar* = *The Vicar of Wakefield*, in Friedman, A. (ed.) (1966) *Collected Works of Oliver Goldsmith*, IV. Clarendon, Oxford. Probably written 1760–62. d.o.b. c1730, 14.23, 14.149 = 14.158.

(a1393) Gower, *CA* = Macaulay, G. C. (ed.) (1900–1) *Confessio Amantis*, in *The English Works of John Gower* (EETS ES 81–2), 5.21, 5.43, 5.47, 5.50, 8.102, 9.122, 11.68, 11.156, 11.175, 13.84.

1932 Greene, *Diary* = passage cited in Sherry, N. (1989) *The Life of Graham Greene*, I, *1904–1939*. Viking Penguin, New York. d.o.b. 1904, 11.29.

1958 Greene, *Havana* = Graham Greene, *Our Man in Havana: an Entertainment*. Heinemann, London, 13.160.

c1475 *Gregory's Chron.* = William Gregory's Chronicle of London, in Gairdner, J. (ed.) (1876) *The Historical Collections of a Citizen of London in the Fifteenth Century: . . .* (Camden Society, ns 17), pp. 55–239, 10.57.

(v.d.) *Grocer Lond.* in *Bk.Lond.E.* = Ordinances of the Grocers' Company, 10.14.

a1500(?a1450) *GRom.* (Hrl) = Herrtage, S. J. H. (ed.) (1879) *The Early English Versions of the Gesta Romanorum* (EETS ES 33), 6.48, 9.83.

1983 *The Guardian*, 13.114.

1989 Gurganus, *Confederate Widow* = Allan Gurganus, (1990) *Oldest Living Confederate Widow Tells All*. Faber & Faber, London. By book, story, chapter, and page. d.o.b. 1947, 11.30, 14.119, 14.124.

1751 Harris, *Hermes* = Alston, R. C. (ed.) (1968) James Harris,[5] *Hermes*. Scolar Press, Menston. d.o.b. 1746, 13.142.

1601–1704 *Hatton Corresp.* = Thompson, E. M. (ed.) (1878) *Correspondence of the Family of Hatton . . .* (Camden Society, ns 22–3), 13.36.

(c1300) *Havelok* = Smithers, G. V. (ed.) (1987) *Havelok*. Clarendon, Oxford, 7n15b, 8.48, 8.49, 9.37, 10.23, 10.71.

?a1475(?a1425) *Higd.(2)* = MS. Harl. 2261, in Babington, C. and Lumby, J. R. (eds) (1865–86) *Polychronicon Ranulphi Higden*, 9 vols. (Rolls Series, 41), 14.90.

c1390 Hilton *ML*(Vrn) = *An Epistle on Mixed Life*, in Horstman (1895–6) (see under *Daily Work*), I, pp. 264–9, 7.20 = 7n1.

?a1220 *HMaid* = Millett, B. (ed.) (1982) *Hali Meiðhad* (EETS 284). For date see edn pp. xvi–xvii, 5.56, 5.59, 7.92.

(?c1422) Hoccl. *ASM*(Dur-U) = *How to Learn to Die*, in Furnivall, F. J. (ed.) (1892) *Hoccleve's Works*, I, *The Minor Poems* (EETS ES 61), pp. 178–215. d.o.b. c1370, 11.92.

HomM 5 = Geheraŏ nu mæn ŏa leofestan . . ., in Willard, R. (1935) *Two Apocrypha in Old English Homilies*. (Beiträge zur englischen Philologie, 30) Tauchnitz, Leipzig, 11.56.

HomS 8(*BlHom* 2) = Quinquagesima Sunday, in *BlHom*, 13.37, 13.144.

HomS 26(*BlHom* 7) = Easter Day, in *BlHom*, 5.12.

HomU 14 = Holthausen, F. (1890) 'Angelsächsisches aus Kopenhagen', *Zeitschrift für Deutsches Alterthum* **34**, 228, corrected in Ker, N. R. (1957) *Catalogue of Manuscripts Containing Anglo-Saxon*. Clarendon, Oxford, p. 140, 11.59.

HomU 15 = Robinson, F. C. (1972) 'The devil's account of the next world', *Neuphilologische Mitteilungen* **73**, 362–71, 8.184.

HomU 18(*BlHom* 1) = Blickling Homily 1, in *BlHom*, 4n11.

HomU 20(*BlHom* 10) = Blickling Homily 10, in *BlHom*, 4n13a.

HomU 34 = De temporibus Anticristi, No. 42, in Napier, A. [S.] (ed.) (1883) *Wulfstan: . . .* (Sammlung englischer Denkmäler, 4) Weidmann, Berlin, 8.57, 8.111, 13.59.

HomU 35.2 = Sunnandæges spell, No. 44, in Napier (1883), 8.146, 11.189.

HomU 37 = Larspell, No. 46, in Napier (1883), 11.57.

HomU 46 = Sermo ad populum Dominicis diebus, No. 57, in Napier (1883), 11.151.

HomU 51 = De infantibus non baptizandis, in Napier, A. (1888) 'Ein altenglisches Leben des Heiligen Chad', *Anglia* **10**, 131–56, pp. 154–5, 9.90.

c1300(?c1225) *Horn* = MS.C, in Hall, J. (ed.) (1901) *King Horn: a Middle English Romance*. Clarendon, Oxford, 10.46, 11.187.

c1175(?OE) *HRood* = Napier, A. S. (1894) *History of the Holy Rood-tree* (EETS 103), 9.115.

HyGl 2 = Stevenson, J. (ed.) (1851) *The Latin Hymns of the Anglo-Saxon Church*. (Surtees Society, 23) Durham, 13.13'.

a1300 *I-hereþ ny one* (Jes-O), in *OEMisc*, pp. 37–57, 11.171, 13.90.

a1500 *Imit.Chr.* = Ingram, J. K. (ed.) (1893) *The Earliest English Translation of the First Three Books of the De Imitatione Christi* (EETS ES 63) (repr. 1908), 9.72, 9.86.

1394–5 in Salzman's *Building in Engl.*: see under Salzman.

c1450 *Jacob's W.* = Brandeis, A. (ed.) (1900) *Jacob's Well: . . .*, 1 (EETS 115) 11.149.

Jane Austen: see under Austen.

JnGl(Li) = John, The Lindisfarne Gospels, in Skeat, W. W. (ed.) (1871–87), *The Four Gospels in Anglo-Saxon, Northumbrian, and Old Mercian Versions*. Cambridge University Press, Cambridge, 5.28.

Jn(WSCp) = John, CCCC MS. 140, in Skeat (1871–87), 5.18, 7.51 = 7.104, 10.67.

1761–5 Johnston, *Chrysal* = 'An adept' [Charles Johnston], *Chrysal: Or, the Adventures of a Guinea*, 2nd edn, 4 vols. T. Becket and P. A. de Hondt, London. d.o.b. ?1719, 13.148.

v.d. Jonson = Herford, C. H., Simpson, P. and Simpson, E. (eds) (1925–52) *Ben Jonson*, 11 vols. Clarendon, Oxford. d.o.b. 1572/3, 8.4, 15.29.

Jud = Judith, in *ASPR* 4, 9.46.

Jul = Juliana, in *ASPR* 3, 8.66, 11.40.

c1400(?a1300) *KAlex.*(Ld) = Smithers, G. V. (ed.) (1952–7) *Kyng Alisaunder* (EETS 227, 237), 5.16, 10.10, 14.38.

1920 Kaye-Smith, *Green Apple Harvest* = Sheila Kaye-Smith, *Green Apple Harvest*. Cassell, London. d.o.b. 1887 13.16.

1816–20 Keats, *Letters* = Forman, M. B. (ed.) 1952 *The Letters of John Keats*, 4th edn. Oxford University Press, London. d.o.b. 1795, 13.149, 14.68.

c1275 *Ken.Serm.* = *Kentish Sermons*, in *EMEVP*, pp. 213–22, 10.18.

?c1450 *Knt.Tour-L.* = Wright, T. (ed.) (1906) *The Book of the Knight of La Tour-Landry . . .* rev. edn (EETS 33), 9.164, 10.44.

c1330 *KTars* (Auch) = *The King of Tars*, in Krause, F. (1888) 'Kleine publicationen aus der Auchinleck-Hs.', *Englische Studien* **11**, 1–62 [33–62], 10.19.

KtPs = Psalm 50, in *ASPR* 6, 5.100.

1175 *Lamb.Hom.* = Morris, R. (ed.) (1867–8) *Old English Homilies of the 12th and 13th Centuries*, ser. 1 (EETS 29, 34), 8.175, 11.60.

c1490 *Lancelot of the Laik* = Skeat, W. W. (ed.) (1870) *Lancelot of the Laik*, 2nd edn (EETS 6), 13.147.

a1400 *Lanfranc* = MS. Ashm., in Fleischhacker, R. von (1894) *Lanfrank's 'Science of Cirurgie'* (EETS 102), 9.104, 11.126.

1901 Lang, *Tennyson* = Andrew Lang, *Alfred Tennyson*, 2nd edn. Blackwood, Edinburgh/London. d.o.b. 1844, 11.141.

LawAfEl = *Laws Alfred-Ine* (Introduction to Alfred), in Liebermann, F. (ed.) (1903–16) *Die Gesetze der Angelsachsen*, 3 vols. Halle (repr. Scientia, Aalen, 1960), vol. I, pp. 26–46. By paragraph and page, 5.81, 13.58.

LawAf 1 = *Laws Alfred-Ine* (Alfred), in Liebermann (1903–16), I 46–88, 7.46.

LawGer = *Gerefa*, in Liebermann (1903–16), I 453–5, 11.51.

a1225(?a1200) Lay.*Brut* = MS. BL Cotton Caligula A. ix, in Brook, G. L. and Leslie, R. F. (eds) (1963–78) *Laȝamon: 'Brut'* (EETS 250, 277). On dating see Stanley (1968) in Secondary Sources list, 7.56 = 7n15a, 9.155, 10.36–40 and 10n7, 11.43, 11.170, 11.179, 13.63, 15.22.

c1425(c1400) *Ld.Troy* = Wülfing, J. E. (ed.) (1902–3) *The Laud Troy Book . . .* (EETS 121–2), 9.70.

1960 Lee, *Mockingbird* = Harper Lee, *To Kill a Mockingbird*. Lippincott, Philadelphia/New York. d.o.b. 1926, 12.5.

a1450(c1400–25) Legat *Serm.PD* = Hugo Legat, Sermon, In Passione Domine, in Grisdale (1929) (see under *Wor.Serm.*), pp. 1–21, 12.57.

(v.d.) *Let.Cely* = Hanham, A. (ed.) (1975) *The Cely Letters 1472–1488* (EETS 273), 7.42, 7.43, 10.7, 10.60, 10.96, 12.72, 13.95.

v.d.(v.d.) *Let.* in Ellis *Orig.Let.ser.2* = Ellis, H. (ed.) (1827) *Original Letters, Illustrative of English History, Series 2*, 4 vols. Harding & Lepard, London, 13.35, 13n8b, 14.87, 14.89.

(1415–24) *Let.War France* in *Bk.Lond.E.* = Correspondence . . . and proclamations relating to the war with France. By extract, page and line, 6.46, 10.58.

Lev = Leviticus, in Crawford (1922) (see under *Exod*), 8.125.

Lk(WSCp) = Luke, CCCC MS. 140, in Skeat (1871–87) (see under *Jn*) 6.25, 11.90, 14.51.

?c1425(?c1400) *Loll.Serm.* = BL Add. MS 41321, in Cigman, G. (ed.) (1989) *Lollard Sermons* (EETS 294), 5.23, 5.38, 8.51, 8.63, 8.84, 8.119, 8.200, 9.114, 10.74, 11.48, 11.76, 11.80, 11.112, 11.117, 11.153, 11.191, §12.8 Qc, 15.12.

(1389) *Lond.Gild Ret.* in *Bk.Lond.E.* = London Gild Returns, 7.19, 7.76.

a1450(c1410) Lovel.*Grail* = Furnivall, F. J. (ed.) (1874–1905) *The History of the Holy Grail by Herry* [*sc.* Henry] *Lovelich* (EETS ES 20, 24, 28, 30, 95), 6.33.

a1450(c1410) Lovel.*Merlin* = Kock, E. A. (ed.) (1904–32) *Merlin . . . by Herry Lovelich . . .* (EETS ES 93, 112, Ordinary Series 185), 8.108.

LS 10.1(Guth) = Gonser, P. (ed.) (1909) *Das angelsächsische Prosa-Leben des heiligen Guthlac*. (Anglistische Forschungen, 27), Carl Winter's Universitätsbuchhandlung, Heidelberg, 5.65.

LS 17.1 = *Life of St. Martin*, in *BlHom*, pp. 211–27, 5.9.

LS 20 = *Assumption of Mary the Virgin*, in *BlHom*, pp. 136–59, 5n5a, 11.185.

LS 23 = *Death of St Mary of Egypt*, in *ÆLS* II 3–53, 13.100.

LS 34 = *Seven Sleepers*, in *ÆLS* I 488–540, 9.134, 12.61.

LS 35 = *Vitas Patrum*, in Assmann, B. (ed.) (1889) *Angelsächsische Homilien und Heiligenleben*. (Bib. ags. Prosa, 3), Kassel (repr. with intro by P. Clemoes, Wissenschaftliche Buchgesellschaft, Darmstadt, 1964), pp. 195–207, 9.117 = 11.184.

?a1475 *Ludus C.* = Block, K. S. (ed.) (1922) *Ludus Coventriae or the Plaie called Corpus Christi* (EETS ES 120), 10.76.

(a1449) Lydg. *Epistle Sibille* = *An epistle to Sibille*, in MacCracken, H. N. (ed.) (1911) *The Minor Poems of John Lydgate*, I (EETS ES 107), pp. 14–18. d.o.b. ?1370, 8.47.

(?a1439) Lydg. *FP* = Bergen, H. (ed.) (1924) *Lydgate's Fall of Princes* (EETS ES 121–3), 9.82.

a1475(?a1430) Lydg. *Pilgr.* = Furnivall, F. J. (ed.) (1899–1904) *The Pilgrimage of the Life of Man* . . . (EETS ES 77, 83, 92), 11.177.

(a1420) Lydg. *TB* = Bergen, H. (ed.) (1906–10) *Lydgate's Troy Book* (EETS ES 97, 103, 106), 10.85.

1579 Lyly, *Euphues* = *Euphues – the Anatomy of Wit*, in Bond, R. W. (ed.) (1902) *The Complete Works of John Lyly*, 2 vols (repr. 1973). Clarendon, Oxford. d.o.b. ?1554, 12.112, 15.30.

Mald = *The Battle of Maldon*, in *ASPR* 6, 11.88.

(a1470) Malory, *Wks.* = Vinaver, E. (ed.) (1990) *The Works of Sir Thomas Malory*, 3rd edn, rev. P. J. C. Field, 3 vols. Clarendon, Oxford. Concorded by Kato (1974). d.o.b. ?c1410, 6.50, 7.67, 7.68, 8.189, 8.192, 9.93, 9.106, 11.83, 11.102, 13.27, 13.92 [and Caxton], 15.34–6, and cf. 11.181.

?a1425(c1400) *Mandev.(1)* = Hamelius, P. (ed.) (1919) *Mandeville's Travels* . . . (EETS 153), 7.23, 13.20, 13.21, 13.39.

?a1425 *Mandev.(2)*(Eg) = Warner, G. F. (ed.) (1889) *The Buke of John Maundeuill:* . . . . Roxburghe Club, London, 13.75.

a1450(a1338) Mannyng, *Chron.Pt.1* = Furnivall, F. J. (ed.) (1887) *The Story of England by Robert Manning of Brunne, AD 1338*, 2 vols. (Rolls Series, 87), 8.68, 8.156.

?a1400(a1338) Mannyng, *Chron.Pt.2* = Hearne, T. (ed.) (1725) *Peter Langtoft's Chronicle*, Oxford (repr. as *The Works of Thomas Hearne, M.A.*, III–IV, Bagster, London, 1810), 7nl, 10.102.

a1400(c1303) Mannyng, *HS* = MS. Harl. 1701, in Furnivall, F. J. (ed.) (1901–3) *Robert of Brunne's 'Handlyng synne'* (EETS 119, 123), 7.12, 8.199, 9.38, 9.48, 9.49, 9.103, 10.99, 11.143, 13.17.

1860(1858–9) Marsh, *Lectures* = George P. Marsh, *Lectures on the English Language*. Scribner, New York. d.o.b. 1801, 14.76.

Mart 3 = *Martyrology* fragment, in Sweet, H. (1885) *The Oldest English Texts* (EETS 83) (repr. 1966), 11.71.

Mart 5 = Herzfeld, G. (ed.) (1900) *An Old English Martyrology* (EETS 116). Corrections Binz, G. (1901) *Beiblatt zur Anglia* 12, 363–8, 13.83.

Mary Shelley: see under Shelley.

MCharm 9 = For theft of cattle, in *ASPR* 6, 11.89.

MCharm 11 = A journey charm, in *ASPR* 6, 7.60

MED = citations taken from *MED* without further verification, 9.27, 9.52, 9.53, 14.43.

Med3 = *Lacnunga*, in Grattan, J. H. G. and Singer, C. (1952) *Anglo-Saxon Magic and Medicine:* . . .. (Publications of the Wellcome Historical Medical Museum, n.s. 3), Oxford University Press, London, pp. 95–204. By paragraph, page and line, 11.85.

1871 Meredith, *Harry Richmond* = George Meredith, *The Adventures of Harry Richmond*. (Memorial Edition 9–10). Charles Scribner's Sons, New York, 1910. d.o.b. 1828, 13.151.

a1500(?c1450) *Merlin* = Wheatley, H. B. (ed.) (1865–99) *Merlin: or the Early History of King Arthur* . . . (EETS 10, 21, 36, 112), 5.39, 10.61.

Met = *The Meters of Boethius*, in *ASPR* 5, 11.130.

1667 Milton, *Paradise Lost*, in Darbishire, H. (ed.) (1952) *The Poetical Works of John Milton*, I. Clarendon, Oxford. d.o.b. 1608, 5.29, 9.80.

a1500(a1415) Mirk *Fest.* = Erbe, T. (ed.) (1905) *Mirk's Festial: a Collection of Homilies by Johannes Mirkus (John Mirk)* (EETS ES 96), 9.28, 9.81.

1530(c1450) *Mirror Our Lady* = Blunt, J. H. (ed.) (1873) *The Myroure of Oure Ladye:* . . . (EETS ES 19), 8.130, 9.159.

a1500 *Mirror Salv.* = Henry, A. (ed.) (1986) *The Mirour of Mans Saluacioun:* . . . . Scolar, Aldershot, 11.150, 13.26.

(a1438) *MKempe* = Meech, S. B. and Allen, H. E. (eds) (1940) *The Book of Margery Kempe* (EETS 212), 11.154, 13.23.

MkGl(Li) = Mark, *The Lindisfarne Gospels*, in Skeat (1871–87) (see under *Jn*), 13.170b.

MkGl(Ru) = Mark, *The Rushworth Gospels*, in Skeat (1871–87), 5.83, 13.170a.

Mk(WSCp) = Mark, CCCC MS. 140, in Skeat (1871–87), 8.81.

v.d. More, *Wks.* = (various editors) (1963–) *The Yale Edition of the Complete Works of St Thomas More*. Yale University Press, New Haven/London. References also given to 1557 edn by Rastell. d.o.b. 1477/78, 9.32 = 11.124, 9.75, 10.101, 11.103, 11.122, 11.124, 11.134, 11.135, 11.140, 12.68, 13.85 (1557 only).

c1350 *MPPsalter* = Bülbring, K. D. (ed.) (1891) *The Earliest Complete English Prose Psalter* . . . (EETS 97), 12.119.

MSol = *Solomon and Saturn*, in *ASPR* 6, 5.19, 5n3b, 8.58.

Mt(WSCp) = Matthew, CCCC MS. 140, in Skeat (1871–87) (see under *Jn*), 8.80, 8.142 = 10.83, 9.61, 9.62, 9.64, 11.158, 11.190, 13.70.

Nic(C) = *Gospel of Nicodemus Homily*, in Hulme, W. H. (ed.) (1904) 'The Old English Gospel of Nicodemus', *Modern Philology* 1, 579–614, 12.110.

1952–61 Norton, *Borrowers* . . . = Mary Norton, *The Complete Adventures of the Borrowers*. Harcourt, Brace & World, New York, 1967. Archaistic diction, d.o.b. 1903, 11.32, 11.107.

OED = citations taken from *OED* or *OED*[2] without further verification, 8.158, 9.55, 9.69, 9.73, 9.74, 9.76, 9.78, 9.79, 9.87, 9.88, 9.102, 9.123–5, 9.156, 11.26, 11.93–101, 11.105, 11.113, 11.123, 11.125, 11.129, 11.181, 12.85, 12.86, 12.92, 13.15, 13.76, 13.81, 13.111, 13.132, 13.141, 14.20, 14.24–8, 14.31, 14.66, 14.67, 14.69, 14.72, 14.93, 14.94, 14.96 = 14.160, 14.97, 14.105–14, 14.116, 14.117, 14.120–2, 14.127–33, 14.141, 14.144, 14.145, 14.151, 14n9b,c,d, 15.2.

OEMisc = Morris, R. (ed.) (1872) *An Old English Miscellany* (EETS 49) (repr. 1927).[6] 11.62, 11.63, 11.171, 13.90.

Or = Bately, J. (ed.) (1980) *The Old English Orosius* (EETS SS 6). Latin text in Zangemeister, C. [= K.] (ed.) (1882) *Pavli Orosii: Historiarvm Adversvm Paganos, Libri VII*. Geroldi Filium, Vienna, 4.6, 4.25, 5.13, 5.14, 5.44, 5.85, 6.20, 6.21, 6n13a, 7.40, 7.55, 7.99 = 7.101, 7.105, 8.97, 8.104, 8.138, 8.144, 9.126, 9.135, 9.140, 9.166, 11.42, 11.108, 11.110, 12.15, 12.40–2, 12.99, 13.7, 13.12, 13.40, 13.46, 13.55–7, 14.10.

c1330 *Orfeo* = Auchinleck MS., in Bliss, A. J. (ed.) (1986) *Sir Orfeo*, 2nd edn. Clarendon, Oxford, 9.112.

c1180 *Orm.* = Holt, R. (ed.) (1878) *The Ormulum: with the Notes and Glossary of Dr R. M. White*, 2 vols. Clarendon, Oxford. On date see Parkes (1983); *MED* has ?c1200. 'P' = Preface, 5.31, 6.15, 6n4a, 7.48–50, 7.85, 8.83, 9.99, 9.110, 9.121, 10.16, 10n8a, 11.86, 11.115, 12.103, 14.40, 14.46, 14.50, 14.53, 14.57–9, 15.8, 15.11.

OrW = *The Order of the World*, in *ASPR* 3, 9.136.

c1250 *Owl & N.* = Stanley, E. G. (ed.) (1960) *The Owl and the Nightingale*. Nelson, London & Edinburgh, 7.39, 10.92, 11.172, 12.16.

c1475(c1420) Page *SRouen* (Eg) = John Page's poem on the siege of Rouen, in Gairdner (1876) (see under *Gregory's Chron.*), pp. 1–46, 13.29.

1957 Parkinson, *Law* = C. Northcote Parkinson, *Parkinson's Law: and Other Studies in Administration*. Houghton Mifflin, Boston. d.o.b. 1909, 13.113.

c1450(?a1400) *Parl.3 Ages* = Offord, M. Y. (ed.) (1959) *The Parlement of the Thre Ages* (EETS 246), 11.148.

a1500 *Partenay* = Skeat, W. W. (ed.) (1899) *The Romans of Partenay, or of Lusignen:* . . . , rev. edn (EETS 22), 10.77, 13.33, 13.34, 13.104, 13.145, 13.146.

(v.d.) *Paston* = Davis, N. (ed.) (1971–6) *Paston Letters and Papers of the Fifteenth Century*, 2 vols. Clarendon, Oxford. By letter and line, 6.49, 6.52, 8.74, 8.191, 8.193, 9.71, 9.84, 9.85, 9.105, 10.11, 10.15, 10.21, 10.26, 10.59, 10.75, 10.95, 11.118, 11.120, 11.176, 12.70, 12.71, 12.78, 13.28, 13.154, 14.92.

1662 Patrick, *Latitude-Men* = Birrell, T. A. (ed.) (1963) Simon Patrick, *A Brief Account of the New Sect of Latitude-men*. (Augustan Reprint Society, 100) William Andrews Clark Memorial Library, UCLA. d.o.b. 1626, 7.128.

c1454 Pecock, *Fol.* = Hitchcock, E. V. (ed.) (1924) *The Folewer to the Donet by Reginald Pecock* (EETS 164). d.o.b. 1395, 11.128, 13.24, 14.88.

(c1449) Pecock, *Repr.* = Babington, C. (ed.) (1860) *The Repressor of Over Much Blaming of the Clergy, by Reginald Pecock*, 2 vols. (Rolls Series, 19), 8.133 = 8.179.

(c1443) Pecock, *Rule* = Greet, W. C. (ed.) (1927) *The Reule of Crysten Religioun: by Reginald Pecock* (EETS 171), 9.29, 11.127.

c1400 *Pep.Gosp.* = Coates, M. (ed.) (1922) *The Pepysian Gospel Harmony* (EETS 157), 7.22 = 7n1.

1660–69 Pepys, *Diary* = Latham, R. and Matthews, W. (eds) (1970–83) *The Diary of Samuel Pepys*, 11 vols. G. Bell (later Bell & Hyman), London. Text is deciphered from Pepys's shorthand, so spelling is modern except where his own preferred usage is known or he wrote something – typically proper names – in longhand. d.o.b. 1633, 5.82, 6.22, 6.36, 6.53, 6.54, 7.129, 8.41, 8.75, 8.76, 8.95, 8.96, 8.123, 8.131, 8.132, 8.136, 8.152, 8.201, 9.35, 9.108, 11.22, 11.87, 11.160, 11.161, 11.188, 11.194–6, 12.3, 12.10, 12.73–6, 12.113, 12.114, 13.48, 13.97, 13.105, 13.116, 13.117, 13.130, 13.131, 14.99 = 14.157, 14.100–4, 15.13.

(v.d.) *Peterb.Chron.* = The First and Final Continuations, in Clark, C. (ed.) (1970) *The Peterborough Chronicle 1070–1154*, 2nd edn. Clarendon, Oxford. By annal and line. See also *ChronE*, 4.10, 7.54, 10.5, 10.6, 10.9, 10.89, 10.90.

Phoen = *Phoenix*, in *ASPR* 3, 3.3, 12.90.

1789 Pickbourn, *Dissertation* = Alston, R. C. (ed.) (1968) James Pickbourn, *A Dissertation on the English Verb*. Scolar Press, Menston, 14.86.

c1450 *Pilgr.LM*(Cmb) = Henry, A. (ed.) (1985) *The Pilgrimage of the Lyfe of the Manhode*, I (EETS 288), 11.119.

c1440 *PLAlex.* = Westlake, J. S. (ed.) (1913) *The Prose Life of Alexander* (EETS 143), 7.125.

c1613(v.d.) *Plumpton Let.* = letter of John Townley, in Stapleton, T. (ed.) (1839) *Plumpton Correspondence* (Camden Society, 4). d.o.b. 1473, 7.127.

a1225(?c1175) *PMor.*(Lamb) = *Poema Morale*, in Hall, J. (ed.) (1920) *Selections from Early Middle English 1130–1250*, I. Clarendon, Oxford, pp. 30–53, 14.12.

c1400(a1376) *PPl.A(1)* = Kane, G. (ed.) (1988) *Piers Plowman: the A Version, Will's Visions of Piers Plowman and Do-Well*, rev. edn. Athlone Press, London/University of California Press, Berkeley. By passus and line, 7.15, 8.157.

c1400 *PPl.B* = Kane, G. and Donaldson, E. T. (eds) (1988) *Piers Plowman: the B Version . . .*, rev. edn. Athlone Press, London/University of California Press, Berkeley. By passus and line, 8.112, 10.42, 13.14, 13.51, 15.4.

c1400(?a1387) *PPl.C* = Pearsall, D. (ed.) (1978) *Piers Plowman by William Langland: an Edition of the C-text*. Edward Arnold, London, 7n1.

PPs = *The Paris Psalter*, in *ASPR* 5, 11.41, 11.164, 12.97.

1674–1722 Prideaux, *Letters* = Thompson, E. M. (ed.) (1875) *Letters of Humphrey Prideaux . . . to John Ellis . . .* (Camden Society, ns 15). d.o.b. 1648, 13.140.

Ps = Psalms 1–50, in Thorpe, B. (ed.) (1835) *Libri Psalmorum Versio Antiqua Latina; cum Paraphrasi Anglo-Saxonica*. Oxford University Press, Oxford, 5.93, 8.55, 8.56.

PsCaA 1 = Canticles of the Psalter (The Vespasian Hymns), in Kuhn, S. M. (ed.) (1965) *The Vespasian Psalter*. University of Michigan Press, Ann Arbor, pp. 146–60, 8.65.

PsGlA = Psalms, in Kuhn (1965), 13.101.

PsGlI = Psalms, in Lindelöf, U. (ed.) (1909–14) *Der Lambeth-Psalter*. (Acta societatis scientiarum Fennicæ 35, i and 43, iii) Finnische Literaturgesellschaft, Helsinki, 5.86.

c1977 att. by A. Radford = example quoted in Palmer (1979: 90), ultimately referred to personal attestation by Andrew Radford, 11.23.

c1515 Rastell, *Interlude* = John Rastell, *Interlude of the Four Elements*, in Pollard, A. W. (ed.) (1927) *English Miracle Plays Moralities and Interludes*, 8th edn. Clarendon, Oxford (repr. 1950) pp. 97–105. d.o.b. c1495, 13.152.

Rec 6.5(Whitelock) = Codex Aureus inscription, in Whitelock, D. (ed.) (1967) *Sweet's Anglo-Saxon Reader in Prose and Verse*, 15th edn. Clarendon, Oxford, pp. 205–6, 12.48.

1502-3 *Receyt Kateryne* = Kipling, G. (ed.) (1990) *The Receyt of the Ladie Kateryne* (EETS 296), 9.31.

a1450 *Rich.*(Cai) = Brunner, K. (ed.) (1913) *Der mittelenglische Versroman über Richard Löwenherz*. (Wiener Beiträge zur englischen Philologie, 42), W. Braumüller, Vienna/Liepzig. Composition date (?a1300), 6.65, 11.142.

1754 Richardson, *Grandison* = Harris, J. (ed.) (1972) Samuel Richardson, *The History of Sir Charles Grandison*, 3 vols. Oxford University Press, London. By original volume, letter, page, and line. d.o.b. 1689, 14.95 = 14.159.

1740 Richardson, *Pamela* = Sabor, P. (ed.) (1980) Samuel Richardson, *Pamela; or Virtue Rewarded*, Penguin, Harmondsworth, 14.82, 14.85.

Rid = Riddles, in *ASPR* 3, 8.174, 8n12a.

1929 Riddehough, *Can. Forum* = Geoffrey B. Riddehough, 'You Gotta Be Educated', *Canadian Forum* IX.107 (Aug.), 14.73.

v.d.(?c1343–a1349) Rolle *Bee/EDormio/FLiving*, in Allen, H. E. (ed.) (1931) *English Writings of Richard Rolle: Hermit of Hampole*. Clarendon, Oxford, 5.42, 7.53, 7.122, 10.94, 11.139, 11.144, 11.145, 13.64.

a1500(c1340) Rolle, *Psalter* (UC64) = Bramley, H. R. (ed.) (1884) *The Psalter . . . and Certain Canticles . . . in English by Richard Rolle*. Clarendon, Oxford, 14.63.

(1386) *RParl.FM* in *Bk.Lond.E.* = Petition of the Folk of Mercerye, 10.24.

a1425(?a1400) *RRose* = *Romaunt of the Rose*, in Benson (1988) (see under Chaucer), 8.101, 9.39, 11.147.

a1475 Russell, *Bk.Nurt.*(Hrl) = Furnivall, F. J. (ed.) (1868) *Early English Meals and Manners: John Russell's Boke of Nurture*, . . . (EETS 32) (repr. 1904), 13.30.

1394–5 in Salzman's *Building in Engl.* = Salzman, L. F. (1952) *Building in England: Down to 1540, a Documentary History*. (Corr. repr. 1967.) Clarendon, Oxford, 13n7a.

Sat = *Christ and Satan*, in *ASPR* 1, 10n21a, 11.37.

a1300 *Sayings St.Bede*(Jes-O), in *OEMisc*, pp. 72–83, 11.63.

Sea = *The Seafarer*, in *ASPR* 3, 5.15.

1950– *SEU* = *Survey of English Usage*, cited from Granger (1983) in Secondary sources list, 14.123, 14.140.

a1425(?a1350) 7 *Sages(2)* = Campbell, K. (ed.) (1907) *The Seven Sages of Rome*. Ginn, Boston/New York, 11.46.

1600–23 Shakespeare = Evans, G. B. (ed.) (1974) *The Riverside Shakespeare*, 2 vols. Houghton Mifflin, Boston; Booth, S. (ed.) (1977) *Shakespeare's Sonnets*. Yale University Press, New Haven/London; Hinman, C. (1968) *The First Folio of Shakespeare: The Norton Facsimile*. Norton, New York.[7] d.o.b. 1564, 9.77, 9.173, 11.84, 12.32, 12.93, 12.107, 12.117, 13.119, 13.166, 14.56, 14.80, 15.19.

v.d. Shaw = *The Complete Plays of Bernard Shaw*. Odhams, London, 1937. d.o.b. 1856, 11.31, 11.33, 14.118.

1817 Mary Shelley, *Six Weeks' Tour* = Mary Shelley, *History of a Six Weeks' Tour*, in Ingpen, R. and Peck, W. E. (1965) *The Complete Works of Percy Bysshe Shelley*, VI. Gordian Press, New York, pp. 83–143. d.o.b. 1797, 6.55.

(v.d.) *Shillingford* = Moore, S. A. (ed.) (1871) *Letters and Papers of John Shillingford, etc.* (Camden Society, ns 2), 9.30, 13n8a, 14.91.

1590 Sidney, *Arcadia* = Feuillerat, A. (ed.) (1912) Sir Philip Sidney, *The Countesse of Pembrokes Arcadia (The New Arcadia)*. Cambridge University Press, Cambridge (repr. 1962). d.o.b. 1554, 14.61.

a1400(?a1350) *Siege Troy(1)*(Suth) = Egerton MS. 2862, in Barnicle, M. E. (ed.) (1927) *The Seege or Batayle of Troye: . . .* (EETS 172), 10.82.

1802 Skillern, *Grammar* = Richard Solloway Skillern, *A New System of English Grammar: . . . .* R. Raikes, Gloucester, 14.75 (not verified).

a1500(?a1400) *SLChrist* = Foster, F. A. (ed.) (1926) *A Stanzaic Life of Christ* (EETS 166), 6n19a.

c1300 *SLeg* (Hrl) = D'Evelyn, C. and Mill, A. J. (eds) (1956) *The South English Legendary* (EETS 235–6), §12.6.4.

c1300 *SLeg.*(Ld) = Horstmann, C. (ed.) (1887) *The Early South-English Legendary . . .* (EETS 87), 10.47, 10.48, 10.79, 10.80, 14.47.

a1325(c1280) *SLeg.*(Pep) = Brown, B. D. (ed.) (1927) *The Southern Passion* (EETS 169), 10.81.

1795 Southey, *Life & Correspondence* = Southey, C. C. (ed.) (1849–50) *The Life and Correspondence of the late Robert Southey*, 6 vols (vol. I = 2nd edn). Longman, Brown, Green & Longmans, London. d.o.b. 1774, 14.65, and cf. 14.117.

c1450 *Spec.Chr.(2)* (Hrl) = Holmstedt, G. (ed.) (1933) *Speculum Christiani: . . .* (EETS 182), 13.25.

1590–96 Spenser, *FQ* = *The Faerie Qveene*, in Smith, J. C., de Selincourt, E. (eds) (1912) *The Poetical Works of Edmund Spenser*. Oxford University Press, London. By book, canto, stanza and line. d.o.b. c1552, 9.94, 12.111, 13.120.

1567 T. Stapleton, *Counterblast* = *A Counterblast to M. Hornes Vayne Blast . . . .* Louvain. d.o.b. 1535, 11.104 (not verified).

?c1450 *St.Cuth.* = Fowler, J. T. (ed.) (1891) *The Life of St. Cuthbert in English Verse, c. A.D. 1450.* (Surtees Society, 87) Andrews, Durham, 9.41.

1759–67 Sterne, *Tristram Shandy* = Ross, I. C. (ed.) (1983) Laurence Sterne, *The Life and Opinions of Tristram Shandy, Gentleman*. Clarendon, Oxford. d.o.b. 1713, 12.63, 13.107, 14.22, 14.115.

1768 Sterne, *Sentimental Journey* = Jack, I. (ed.) (1968) Laurence Sterne, *A Sentimental Journey Through France and Italy by Mr Yorick . . . .* Oxford University Press, London, 12.4.

c1225(?c1200) *St Juliana* (Bod) = MS. Bodley 34, in d'Ardenne, S. R. T. O. (ed.) (1960) *Þe Liflade ant te Passiun of Seinte Iuliene* (EETS 248), 6.8, 7.36, 8.147, 8.148, 10.68, 11.61.

c1225 *St Juliana* (Roy) = MS. BL Royal 17 A xxvii, in d'Ardenne (1960), 7.10 = 7n1, 7.37.

c1225(?c1200) *St Kath.(1)* = d'Ardenne, S. R. T. O. and Dobson, E. J. (eds) (1981) *Seinte Katerine* (EETS SS 7), 6.9.

a1450 *St Kath.(3)* = Gibbs, H. H. (Baron Aldenham) (ed.) (1884) *The Life and Martyrdom of Saint Katherine*. Roxburghe Club, London, 9.54.

c1225(?c1200) *St Marg.(1)* = MS. Bodley 34, in Mack, F. M. (ed.) (1934) *Seinte Marherete: þe Meiden ant Martyr* (EETS 193), 7.65, 8.149, 9.111, 9.118.

(v.d.) *Stonor* = Kingsford, C. L. (ed.) (1919) *The Stonor Letters and Papers, 1290–1483* (Royal Historical Society, ser. 3, 29–30). By letter, volume, page and line, 10.97, 11.47, 12n12a, 13.31, 14.64.

c1225(?c1200) *SWard* = *Sawles Warde*, in *EMEVP*, pp. 246–61, 5.32, 5.40, 7.59, 7.64, 8.85, 8.169, 9.144, 10.91.

1710–13 Swift, *Jnl. to Stella* = Williams, H. (ed.) (1974) Jonathan Swift, *Journal to Stella*, 2 vols. Blackwell, Oxford. d.o.b. 1667, 12.7.

1905 Synge, *Well* = *The Well of the Saints*, in Saddlemyer, A. (ed.) (1968) J. M. Synge, *Collected Works*, III, *Plays*, Book I. Oxford University Press, London, pp. 60–151. By act, page and line. d.o.b. 1871, 11.183.

c1250 *Þene latemeste dai* = in Brown, *13 cent*, pp. 46–9, 11.180.

a1300 *Þo ihu crist*, in *OEMisc*, pp. 84–6, 11.62.

1694(1671) Tillotson = 'The folly of scoffing at religion', in Simon, I. (ed.) (1976) *Three Restoration Divines: Barrow, South, Tillotson: Selected Sermons*, vol. II:ii, pp. 417–31. (Bibliothèque de la Faculté de Philosophie et Lettres de l'Université de Liège, 213) Société d'Éditions 'Les Belles Lettres', Paris. d.o.b. 1630, 11.133.

a1500(a1460) *Towneley Pl.* = England, G. and Pollard, A. W. (eds) (1897) *The Towneley Plays* (EETS ES 71), 8.52.

(a1387) *Trev.Higd.* = 'Trevisa', in Babington and Lumby (1865–86) (see under *Higd.(2)*). d.o.b. ?1340, 7.18, 9.51, 14.55, and cf. 9.52, 9.53.

a1225(?a1200)[8] *Trin.Hom.* = Morris, R. (ed.) (1873) *Old English Homilies . . .*, ser. 2 (EETS 53), 9.145, 10.30, 10.35 and 10n7, 11.169, 13.9, 13.156, 13.157, 14.52.

1883(1875–6) Trollope, *Autobiography* = Anthony Trollope, *An Autobiography*. Oxford University Press, London, 1950. d.o.b. 1815, 6.39.

a1500 *Tundale*(Adv) = MS. Edinburgh, Advocates' library 19.3.1, in critical apparatus of Mearns, R. (ed.) (1985) *The Vision of Tundale* (Middle English Texts, 18). Carl Winter, Heidelberg, 7.24.

?1528 Tyndale, *Obedience* = *The Obedience of a Christian Man*, in Walter, H. (ed.) (1848) *Doctrinal Treatises . . . by William Tyndale, Martyr, 1536*. (Parker Society) Cambridge University Press, Cambridge. d.o.b. c1495, 9.150.

a1400 *Usages Win.* = Engeroff, K. W. (ed.) (1914) *Untersuchung des Verwandt-schaftsverhältnisses der anglo-französischen und mittelenglischen Überlieferungen der 'Usages of Winchester', mit Paralleldruck der drei Texte* (Bonner Studien zur englischen Philologie, 12) P. Hanstein, Bonn. By paragraph, page and line, 10.25.

1503–5 *Val. & Orson* = Dickson, A. (ed.) (1937) *Valentine and Orson: translated from the French by Henry Watson* (EETS 204), 15.32.

1697 Vanbrugh, *Provok'd Wife* = Sir John Vanbrugh, *The Provok'd Wife*, in Gayley, C. M. and Thaler, A. (eds) (1936) *Representative English Comedies*, IV. Macmillan, New York, pp. 407–532. d.o.b. 1664, 3.10, 13.150.

1717 *Verney* = letter of Daniel Baker, in Verney, M. M., Lady (ed.) (1930) *Verney Letters of the Eighteenth Century . . .*, I. Ernest Benn, London, 12.122.

a1225(c1200) *Vices & V.(1)* = Holthausen, F. (ed.) (1888–1921) *Vices and Virtues: . . .* (EETS 89, 159), 5.46, 5.96, 8n9b, 10.12, 10.84, 10n4a.

c1450(c1400) *Vices & V.(2)* = Francis, W. N. (ed.) (1942) *The Book of Vices and Virtues: . . .* (EETS 217), 7.126 = 7n1.

(a1382–c1384) *WBible(1)* = *The Earlier Version*, in Forshall, J. and Madden, F. (eds) (1850) *The Holy Bible . . . made from the Latin Vulgate by John Wycliffe and his Followers*, 4 vols. Oxford University Press, Oxford, 6.23, 7.123, 8.18, 8.126, 11.192.

a1425(c1395) *WBible(2)* = *The Later Version*, in Forshall and Madden (1850), 7.82, 9.36, 11.193, 13.18, 13.19, 13.66, 13.72.

1714 *Wentworth* = letter of Lord William Berkeley of Stratton, in Cartwright, J. J. (ed.) (1883) *The Wentworth Papers 1705–1739: . . ..* Wyman & Sons, London, 12.121.

Whale = *The Whale*, in *ASPR* 3, 5.71.

1871 White, *Words* = Richard Grant White, *Words and their Uses, Past and Present: . . ..* Houghton Mifflin, New York (18th edn, 1889). d.o.b. 1821, 14.77.

WHom = Bethurum, D. (1957) *The Homilies of Wulfstan*. Clarendon, Oxford, 7.31, 7.34, 8.165, 10.29 = 10.70, 10.32, 11.131.

(v.d.) *Will Bury* in *Camd.49* = Tymms, S. (ed.) (1850) *Wills and Inventories from the Registers of the Commissary of Bury St Edmunds, etc.* (Camden Society, 49), pp. 15–51, 13.159.

c1450 Wimbledon *Serm.* (Hat) = Sundén, K. F. (ed.) (1925) *A Famous Middle English Sermon: . . . .* (Supplement to Göteborgs Högskolas Årsskrift, 31.) Elanders Boktryckeri, Gothenburg, 10.52'.

1635 Wimbledon *Serm.* = *A Sermon, No lesse fruitfull, then famous . . . Preached by R. Wimbleton, in . . . 1388 . . . .* Thos. Cotes, London, 10.52.

c1450(1352–c1370) *Winner & W.* = Trigg, S. (ed.) (1990) *Wynnere and Wastoure* (EETS 297). On dating see edn p. xxv, 7.14 = 7n1.

1987 Wolfe, *Bonfire* = Tom Wolfe, *The Bonfire of the Vanities*. Picador, London, 1988. d.o.b. 1931, 12.81.

1758–1802 Woodforde, *Diary* = Beresford, J. (ed.) (1924–31) (repr. 1981) *The Diary of a Country Parson: the Reverend James Woodforde*, 5 vols. Oxford University Press, Oxford. All citations may be found in World's Classics edn. d.o.b. 1740, 7.69, 13.108, 13.109, 13.133, 13.134, 13.143, 14.83, 14.84, 14.98, 14.152, 14n9a, 15.14–16, 15.18.

a1250 *Wooing Lord* (Tit) = Morris, R. (ed.) (1868) *Old English Homilies*, ser. 1, pt. 2 (EETS 34), (repr. 1905), pp. 269–87, 8.116.

a1450 *Wor.Serm.* = Grisdale, D. M. (ed.) (1929) *Three Middle English Sermons from the Worcester Chapter Manuscript F.10.* (Texts and Monographs, 5) School of English Language, University of Leeds, pp. 22–80, 10.100.

WPol = Jost, K. (ed.) (1959) *Die 'Institutes of Polity, Civil and Ecclesiastical': . . . .* Francke, Bern (Schweizer Anglistische Arbeiten, 47), 6.13, 10.33, 10.34.

v.d. *Wycl.* = Matthew, F. D. (ed.) (1880) *The English Works of Wyclif: hitherto unprinted* (EETS 74). d.o.b. c1320, 6.45, 7.16, 7.41, 7.124, 7n1, 8.90, 8.103, 8.168.

c1475(?c1400) *Wycl.Apol.* = Todd, J. H. (ed.) (1842) *An Apology for Lollard Doctrines, attributed to Wicliffe* (Camden Society, 20), 7.25.

?c1450(?a1400) *Wycl.Clergy HP* = *Clergy May Not Hold Property*, in Matthew (1880), pp. 362–404, 6.45, 7.124.

c1400(?c1384) *Wycl.50 HFriars* = *Fifty Heresies & Errors of Friars*, in Arnold, T. (ed.) (1869–71) *Select English Works of John Wyclif*, III. Clarendon, Oxford, pp. 366–401, 10.43.

?c1430(c1383) *Wycl.Leaven Pharisees*, in Matthew (1880), pp. 2–27, 7n1.

a1400 *Wycl.MPl.* = *Treatise of Miracle Plays*, in Wright, T. and Halliwell, J. O. (eds) (1841–3) *Reliquiæ Antiquæ: Scraps from Ancient Manuscripts . . . ,* II. Pickering, London/Asher, Berlin (repr. AMS Press, New York, 1966), pp. 42–57, 13.94.

a1500(?c1378) *Wycl.OPastor.* = *De Officio Pastorale*, in Matthew (1880), pp. 408–57, 7.16.

?c1430(c1400) *Wycl.Prelates*, in Matthew (1880), pp. 2–27, 8.103, 8.168.

c1475(a1400) *Wycl.Pseudo-F.*(Dub) = *De Pseudo-Freris*, in Matthew (1880), pp. 296–324, 7.41.

a1425 *Wycl.Serm.* = Hudson, A. (vols I, III), Gradon, P. (vol. II) (eds) (1983–90) *English Wycliffite Sermons*, 3 vols to date. Clarendon, Oxford. By volume, sermon (preceded by 'E' for Sermons on the Sunday Epistles), and line 7.26, 8.3, 8.46, 8.127, 8.134, 8.135, 8.137, 8.150, 8.151, 8.176, 8.177, 8.181, 8.182, 9.178, 11.214, 11.215, 13.19+, 13.22.

?c1430(c1400) *Wycl.Spec.Antichr.* = *Speculum de Antichristo*, in Matthew (1880), pp. 109–13, 8.90.

a1425 *Wycl.VOct.* = *Vae Octuplex*, in Gradon (1988) II, pp. 366–78, 8.183.

1463–77(a1450) *Yk.Pl.* = Beadle, R. (ed.) (1982) *The York Plays*. Edward Arnold, London, 10.45.

Notes

1. My numbering is sometimes simpler, however.
2. For convenience three *LS* citations found in Skeat (1881–90) are also listed here.
3. All citations from *Bk.Lond.E.* are gathered here as well as under the *MED* titles.
4. For convenience all references to *BlHom* are listed here, but they also appear under *HomS* or *HomU*, the forms used in the text, following *DOE*.
5. Harris was the father of the first Lord Malmesbury, cf. examples 14.96 = 14.160, 14.97.
6. For convenience all references to *OEMisc* are listed here, but they also appear under the *MED* title stencils used in the text.
7. Quotations and line-references follow the standard but modern-spelling Riverside edition, but for consistency with other citations the spelling (and punctuation) of examples is taken from facsimiles of early prints. As it happens there is only one substantive discrepancy (9.77, *Rom* I.v.135, where the First Folio is in error), and even then in a word not central to the syntactic point being illustrated. For the plays I give as printing date that of the First Folio, 1623, even though most were published earlier in Quarto, and in brackets the conjectural date of composition following vol. I, pp. 48–56.
8. *MED* gives two datings for *Trin.Hom.*: a1225(?OE) and a1225(?a1200). I have used the latter, since none of my citations are from homilies also found in *Lamb.Hom.*

Index of verbs in examples

This index of verbs is intended as an aid to tracing examples and discussions which centre on a particular verb. The crucial clause of each example is indexed by the relevant verb (plus *particle* and/or other group-verb elements, where appropriate). Neighbouring clauses cited as context are not indexed. *Catenative* and auxiliary verbs are ignored unless relevant to the discussion, as for example in Parts IV and V, where they often constitute its whole point – in which case the *lower* or lexical verb may be what is irrelevant. Quite often, however, there are index entries for both.

The citation forms used are mostly Modern English, even if the meaning has changed, with limited cross-referencing from older forms whose alphabetical positions are greatly different. There is also some limited cross-referencing of prefixal forms. The prefix *ge-* is ignored in the alphabetisation of OE forms. References are by chapter and example/note number.

ACCOUNT, COUNT 9.51–3, 9.55, 9.56
ACCUSTOM 14.113
ACKNOWLEDGE, KNOWLEDGE 8.74, 8.112
ACQUAINT 14.20
ACT 13.97, 13.135, 14.94, 14.96 = 14.160
ADON see DO
ADVENTURE 8.193, 9.101
AFANDIAN 'prove' 8.64
AFEALLAN see FALL
AFIERRAN 'remove' 6.14
AFYLLAN 'fill' 14.18
AGRISE, GRISEN 'feel terror/horror' 10.80, 11.61
AGYFAN see GIVE
AIL 5.65, 5.67, 5.68, 5.90
ALLOW 6.44, 6.49, 6.55
ALLUDE 9.123
AMEND 13.93 = 13.155
APPEAR 9.1, 9.32. 9.36, 9.173
ARREST 9.14, 12.6
ARRIVE 14.165
ASK 8.150, 12.10, 13.158

ASSIGN 6.46
ASTIGAN 'climb' 12.97
APREOTAN 'be irksome' 9.135, 9.136
AVOID 4.4
AWENDAN 'turn' 12.20
AWRITAN 'write out' 12.34
baffling PRES PTCP 13.6
GEBÆRAN *with* 'behave towards' 7.29
BE 4.1c, 4.21, 5.84, 5.85, 5.96, 7.51 = 7.104, 9.14, 9.132, 10.62, 10.65, 10.97, 10.101, 11.136, 11.141, 11.158–63, 11.192, 12.17–19, 12.21, 12.22, 12.47, 12.90–120, 13.1, 13.2, 13.4–7, 13.12, 13.13, 13.17–40, 13.43, 13.44, 13.46–76, 13.87–117, 13.122, 13.125, 13.128, 13.130–35, 13.138–55, 13.160–70, 13n7a, 13n8a,b,c,d, 13n9a,b, 13n10a, 14.1, 14.2b, 14.3, 14.7–12, 14.14–16, 14.30, 14.34, 14.38, 14.39, 14.42–48, 14.51–104, 14.112, 14.125–32, 14.135a, 14.136–9, 14.141–3, 14.145, 14.149, 14.151, 14.152, 14.154–65, 14n9a, b,c, 14n13a, 15.2, 15.5, 15.20, 15.22

BE *able/certain/(un)like(ly)*, etc 9.7, 9.57,
   9.65–88, 9.152, 9.153, 11.193, 11.195,
   11.196
BE *about* 7.64
BE *bound* 11.194
BE *busy* 13n8a,b
BE *difficult/easy/tough* 7.117, 7.118, 9.12
BE *dread of* 7.87
BE *good/better* 5.11, 9.10, 9.11
BE *nought of* 7.84
BE *time*, etc. 9.141, 9.142
BE *toward* 'be imminent' 9.58–64
BE *willing* 11.195
BE-equivalent in Dutch 12.84
BEAR, BE *born* 7.97, 13.104, 14.12
BEAT 14.133
BECOME 9.90, 12.93, 12.113
BEDÆLAN 'deprive' 6.71, 14.36
BEFALL see FALL
BEFON 'seize' 12.26
BEGET 14.12
BEGIN, GIN, ONGINNAN 5.77, 5n5a, 9.109,
   9.111, 9.113–20, 9.167, 9.168, 11.184–7,
   15.28
BEHOLD 13.26
BEHOVE 9.100, 9.145, 9.160
BELIEVE, (I)LEVE 8.16, 8.65, 8.129, 8.163,
   8.164, 8.183, 10n4a, 15.23
BELIEVE (LEVE) *on* 7.36
BELOVE 5.40
BEQUEATH 6.32
BEREAVE 6.14, 14.13
BEREOWEN see RUE
BESEECH *for* 7.59
BETIDE 'happen' 12.105
BETYNAN 'close' 14.10
BEWERIAN 'forbid' 8.128
BID (incl. BIDDAN, BEODAN, BEBEODAN)
   8.44, 8.54–6, 8.82–4, 8.88, 8.92, 8.109,
   8.123, 8.124, 8.148, 8.152, 8.154, 12.50
BIGGEN 'dwell' 13.51
BINEMNAN 'stipulate' 12.51
BIREN, GEBYRIAN 'ought' 9.98, 9.99
BLIN 'cease' *(of(f))* 7.85, 9.121
BOAST 8.69
BOIL 14.83
BOMB 10.103
BREAK *(up)* 13.159, 14.4
BRING 6.12, 6.34, 14.7–9, 14.15, 15.25
BRING *on* 7.88
BROIL 14.80
BRUSH 13n8b
BUILD 13.96, 13.99 = 13.168, 13.113,
   13.115, 13.122–4, 13.169, 14.76, 14.86,
   14.155, 14.162, 14.164

BURN 13.59, 13.64
CALL *on* 7n7b
CALL *up* 7n7a
CALL *upon (for)* 7.43
CAN 8.28, 11.1, 11.2, 11.4, 11.6–9, 11.19,
   11.20, 11.89, 11.96, 11.98, 11.114–18,
   11.120, 11.126, 11.127, 11.196, 11.201a,
   11.214, 14.71, 14.75, 14.106, 14.108,
   15.3
CARRY 14.79
CAST *(out)* 13.22, 13.27
CAUSE 8.47, 8.52
CHANCE 9.94, 9.102, 9.107, 9.156, 9.170
CHOOSE 14.12, 15.8
CLEPE 'call' 8.168, 14.12
CLOSE 13.120
CNYSSAN 'batter' 13.53
COME 4.5, 4n11, 6.15, 6n4a, 11.138, 12.99,
   13.65
COME *of* 7.65, 7.67, 7.83
COME *on* 7.55
COME *to* 7.21, 7.62
COMMAND 8.89, 8.90, 8.131, 8.189
COMMENCE 9.112
COMPEL 8.117
CONFIRM 14.141
CONQUER 14.75
CONSIDER 9.16, 15.17
CONSTRAIN 8.117
CONTINUE 9.122
CONVINCE 12.11–13, 14.74
COOK 13.128, 13.129
COSTIAN 'tempt' 11.137
COUNT see ACCOUNT
CREEP 13.38
CRY *out on* 7.128
CWEME see QUEME
CWEÐAN see QUETHE
CYÐAN 'make known' 6.13
GEDAFENIAN 'befit' 5.1, 5.69, 5.101, 5n28a,
   9.95, 9.97, 9.137, 11.52
DARE 11.21–3, 11.27–33, 11.129, 12.109
DEAL 12.38
DEAL *with* 7.115–17
DEBATE 13.107
DEBRUISE 'crush' 14.89
DEEM 6.6, 8.99, 8.113, 8.169, 14.12
DEFEAT 7.2
DENY 6.17, 8.76, 15.19
DEPART 12.111
DERIAN 'harm' 5.90
DESIRE 8.195
DESIST 9.125

DESTROY   13.24
DEVISE   13.35
DIE [BE *dead*]   12.103, 12.107
DINE   12.7
DISAPPOINT   14.143
DISPLAY   14.7
DO   4.2b, 6.42, 7.46, 8.43, 8.45, 8.57,
    8.118, 8.155, 10.1–82, 10.84, 10.88–102,
    10.111, 10.112, 10n5b,d, 10n8a, 10n13a,
    10n21a, 11.28, 11.29, 12.22, 12.29,
    13.37–9, 13.83, 13.102, 13.110, 13.116,
    13.142, 13.143, 13n8d, 14.81, 14.99 =
    14.157, 14.100, 14.118, 14.119, 15.17,
    15.18, 15.24, 15.29, 15.30, 15.31, 15n5a
DO *asseth for* 'make amends for'   7.123[?]
DO [ADO] *away*   4.15
DO *with*   7.24
DOUBT   15.15
DOUEN, DOW 'avail'   11.25, 11.26
DRAG   13.98
DRAW   14.77
DREAM   13.167
DRESS   13.133
DRINK   13.39
droupand PRES PTCP 'drooping'   13.10
DROWN   14.90
DUCK   10n5a,b
DWELL *in*   7.66
EAT   7.54, 12.44, 13.39, 13.156
EDSTONDEN 'stop, stand still'   15.10
EDUCATE   14.73
EFENEARDIGEAN 'dwell together'   13.49
GEEFENLÆCAN 'resemble, imitate'   3.5, 3.6
EGG *to*   7.49
EGLIAN   see AIL
EHTAN 'persecute'   13.7, 13.47
END   12.112
ENGAGE   14.22
ENTANGLE   14.26
ENVIRON 'encircle'   13.20
ESCAPE, SCAPE   7n15c, 12.91
EXAMINE   13.108, 14.97
EXFOLIATE   14.112
EXHAUST   14.149 = 14.158
EXHIBIT   13n8c
EXPECT   8.1a, 8.5, 8.6, 8.9, 8.15, 8.22–6,
    8.29, 14.2
EXPEND   13.140
FAIL   9.9, 9.26, 9.27[?]
FALL, BEFALL, AFEALLAN, OÐFEALLAN
    9.27[?], 9.103, 10.79, 10.81, 10.82, 11.66,
    12.15, 12.95, 12.98
FANKLE '(en)tangle'   14.27
FARE (*to*)   7.33, 12.16, 12.42, 13.54

FARE *with*   7.10, 7.18, 7.126
FAWN   5.91
FEEBLE 'enfeeble'   14.89
FEEL   13.33, 14.5, 14.37
FEIGN   8.68
FERAN 'go'   13.79
FIGHT *again(st)*   7.30
FIGHT *for*   7.68
FILM   13.125–7
FIND   8.167, 8.172, 12.2, 12.49
FIND *fault (with)*   6n9a,b, 7.130
FIND *out*   13.48
FINISH   14.31
FIRE   14.29, 14.30
FIT   13.117
FLEE, FLY   6.65, 12.108, 12.118
FOLLOW   3.3, 3.4, 13.62
FON *to*   7.32
FORBID   (incl. FORBEODAN)   6.45, 8.79,
    8.97, 8.125, 8.133 = 8.179, 8.186–8, 8.190
FOREKNOW 'have previous knowledge of'
    8.130
FORGIVE   6.66, 6.70, 6n2b
FORLÆTAN 'relinquish'   6.21, 8.114, 8.120
FORLOSE (PTCP *forlorn*)   14.12
FORÐFARAN 'pass away, die'   12.96
FORTUNE   9.105
FORWYRNAN 'deny, prevent'   6.30, 6.71
(GE)FREMMAN 'profit, perform'   4.17, 9.96,
    13.40
FROFRAN 'comfort'   13.101
FROST   14.111
FULHTNEN 'baptise'   14.57
GAIN   11.64
GAN   see BEGIN
GATHER, GEDER   13.91
GER 'cause'   8.48, 8.53
GET   7.118, 8.132, 10.104, 10.106–8,
    12.3–5, 14.20–29, 14.31, 14.32, 14.105–33,
    14.135b, 14.136, 14.138–48, 14n9a,b,c,d
GIVE, AGYFAN   4.2a, 6.1–4, 6.16, 6.23,
    6.24, 6.26, 6.33, 6.37–41, 6.47, 6.50, 6.62,
    6.65, 6n2c, 7.69, 12.8, 14.139
GO   12.114, 12.116, 12.117, 13.131, 13.134,
    13n8a
GO *through with*   7.129
GODIAN, GEGODIAN 'endow'   4.18
GRANT   8.71
GRIND   13.72
GRISEN   see AGRISEN
GROAN   13.43
GUESS   8.126
HAIL   5.14
HALLOW, HALGIAN   12.25 = 12.46

HANG 13.73, 13.75, 13.166, 14.151

HAP(PEN) 9.3–5, 9.8, 9.91–3, 9.104, 9.106,
  9.108, 9.159, 9.161–5, 9.174, 12.106

HATAN, HIGHT 'order, call, be called' 4.22,
  4.23, 8.44, 8.87, 8.91, 8.93, 8.105, 8.138,
  8.149, 8.153, 8.157, 8.159–62, 8.185,
  14.33, 14.34

HATCH 14.82, 14.85

HATE 11.16

HAVE 4.1a, 4.2c, 4.18, 10.87, 10.104,
  10.111, 11.20, 11.155–7, 11.190, 12.1,
  12.3–14, 12.23–57, 12.60–82, 12.85–9,
  12.115–16, 12.121–3, 12Qc, 12n10a,
  12n12a, 13.19, 13.34, 13.68, 13.74–6,
  13.153, 14.51–4, 14.60, 14.62–4, 14.73,
  14.74, 14.76, 14.78–84, 14.86, 14.107,
  14.109, 14.110, 14.113, 14.120–24, 14.140,
  14.145, 15.21, 15.22, 15n2a,b,c

HAVE better/lever 11.142, 11.143, 11.147,
  11.191

HAVE mercy of 7.63

HAVE-equivalents   in   German/French/
  Dutch 12.58, 12.59, 12.83

HEAL 12.37, 14.11 = 14.16, 14.17

HEAR 8.41, 8.60, 8.62, 8.139, 8.158, 12.28,
  12.30, 13.23, 13.29, 13.161

HEARKEN 13.17

HELP 6.5, 6.10, 8.31

HESITATE 9.172

HOARD 14.78

HOLD 8.156, 9.49, 13.100

HOLD to 7.37

HUNGER 11.58

HUNT 13.2, 13.87, 13.92

HUNT after 7.38

HWEORFAN 'change' 12.39

HYCGAN after 'think after, hanker for' 7.28

icorene PA PTCP see CHOOSE

ILIMP see (GE)LIMPAN

IMAGINE 13.103

INFORM 6.51, 6.52, 14.92

INSIST (on) 7.113, 7.114

INVITE 8.7, 14.148

irritating PRES PTCP 13.16

KEEP 7.112, 13.32, 13.81, 13.154

KILL 10n5c,d

KNOW 8.72, 8.191, 15.14, 15.30, 15.36,
  15n8a

KNOWLEDGE see ACKNOWLEDGE

LANGUISH 11.139

LAUGH at 7.1, 14.28

LEAD 13.50

LEARN 7.105

LEAVE 6.8, 8.80

LERE 'teach' 6n19a, 8.77

LET 'cause, allow, leave' 6.20, 8.32, 8.40,
  8.42, 8.50, 8.58, 8.94, 8.110, 8.111, 8.115,
  8.141–3, 8.147, 8.165, 8.184, 8.196,
  8n9a,b, 10.83, 11.172–83, 11n13a, 13.73

LET 'hinder' 8.134, 8.135

LET blood 6.31, 6.43, 10.22

LET by 'think of' 7.15

LET of 'think of' 7.14, 7.22, 7.73, 7.86,
  7.89–91

(GE)LIEFAN see BELIEVE

LIE 'tell untruth' 6.8

LIE 'recline' 13.74

LIE by 7.11, 7.23

LIGHT 15.32

LIKE 5.6, 5.29, 5.35 = 5.62, 5.44, 5.55 =
  5.66, 5.60, 5.61, 5.70, 5.80–83, 5.85, 5.93,
  5n3a, 8.104, 9.140, 11.54

(GE)LIMPAN 'happen' 5.9, 5.24, 5.25, 5.27,
  5.45, 5.53, 5.98–100, 9.89, 9.154, 11.59,
  12.19

LIST, LUST 5.31, 5.48, 5.71, 11.186

LIVE (for) 13.45

LIVE by 7.99 = 7.101

LIVE in 7.4–9, 7.58

LIVE near 7.108

LOATHE 5.59

LOCK 13.120

LONG, LANGIAN 5.19, 5.39, 5.51, 5.77,
  11.184

LOOK 9.33, 13.3–5

LOOK after 7.42

LOOK on 7.35

LOSE 15.26

LOVE 4.8

loving PRES PTCP 13.14

MAINTAIN 13.107

MAKE 5.54, 8.3, 8.4, 8.33, 8.46, 8.49, 8.51,
  8.95, 8.96, 8.107, 8.116, 8.166, 8.175,
  8.177, 8.180, 8.197, 8.198, 8.200, 8.201,
  10.84, 10.85, 13.36, 13.85, 13.105, 13.106,
  13.130, 13.141, 14.55, 14.76, 14.98,
  14.144

MAKE away with 7.127

MAKE mind of 7.125

MAKE out 14.66

GEMAN 'remember' 4.6, 13.77

MARRY 14.23, 14.71

MAY, MOW 4.25, 8.194, 9.13, 9.137 =
  11.52, 11.11–15, 11.17, 11.34–8, 11.42–50,
  11.53, 11.58, 11.60, 11.61, 11.66, 11.68,
  11.71, 11.72, 11.74, 11.76–8, 11.85–7,
  11.93, 11.104, 11.108, 11.109, 11.119,
  11.122–5, 11.130, 11.154, 11.200, 11.201b,
  11.204, 11.206, 11.208, 11.216, 12.110,
  14.63, 14.75, 14.140, 15.26

MÆLEN 'speak' *of* 7.48
MEET 8.173, 12.104
MEET *with* 7.60
MENE 'bewail' 13.157
METE 'dream' 5.54
MILK 14.69
MISBEFALL 5.21, 11.68
MISLIMPE 'go amiss' 11.60
MIX 14.76
MOOR 14.24
MOT see MUST
mourning N 13.89
MOVE 8.137, 14.88, 14.93
MUN (PA *munde*) 'must' 14.46
gemun- 'remember' see GEMAN
MURDER 14.1
MUST 5.41, 10n21a, 11.51, 11.55, 11.74, 11.81, 11.82, 11.132–4, 11.148, 11.149, 14.45, 14.47, 14.75, 14.85
MUST-equivalent in Dutch 12.83
NEED 11.27, 11.28, 11.150
NEGLECT 14.37
NIEDAN 'force' 8.81, 8.121
NIMAN 'take' 15.20
NOTIAN 'use up' 12.36
OFFER 6.11, 6.58, 6.59, 6.67, 6.68
OFHREOWAN see RUE
OFLICIAN, OFLIKE 'displease' 5.37
OFSEND see SEND
OFSLEAN, SLAY 'kill' 4.21, 7.47 = 7.75, 12.14 = 12.35, 15.34
OFTEON 'withhold' 6.27, 6.28
OFTHINK 'regret' 5.30, 10.84, 11.49, 13.57
ONBUGAN 'submit' 13.70
ONFON 'accept, receive' 4.16, 13.69
ONGIETAN 'understand, perceive' 9.44
ONGINNAN see BEGIN
OPEN 3.2, 13.120, 13.160
ORDAIN 8.130
OÐFEALLAN 'decline' see FALL
OUGHT, OWE, AGAN 5.42, 5.43, 11.18, 11.101, 11.106, 11.135, 11.144, 11.146, 11.151–4
OVERCOME 15.22
OVERGO 12.119
OWN 8.75
PACK 7.74, 7.111
PAINT 3.7, 10n12a,b,c
PAY 6.48
PAY *of* 7.53
PERMIT 6.60, 6.61
PERSUADE 6.63, 8.10, 8.15, 8.17, 8.136
PIPE *down* 4n7a
plastered 'drunk' 14.145

PLEASE 5.47, 5n17b
PRACTISE 14.67
PRAY 8.100, 8.106, 8.108, 8.151, 8.199
PREPARE 13.111, 14.69
PROMISE 6.69, 8.19–21
PROPHESY 9.150
PROVE 3.10, 8.73, 9.30
PULL 4n12a,b
PURSUE 13.21
PUSH 14.70
PUT (*in*) 7.44, 10.52, 14.91
QUELM 'torture' 13.67
QUEME 'please' 5.93, 5n3b,c, 6.7, 6.9, 12.25 = 12.46
QUETHE 'speak' 13.78
QUIT 14.108
RAIN 5.26, 5.86, 8.145, 8.146, 10.83, 10.85
READ 14.95 = 14.159
READ *of* 7.25
RECEIVE 15.33
RECKON 9.50
REMAIN 14.6
REMIND 15.24
REST 13.132, 14.88
RETURN 15.18
REWARD 14.21
RID 14.105–7, 14.109, 14.110, 14.114, 14.130–32, 14.134–7
RIG 'fit out'[?] 13.31
RIP 4n7b
GERISAN 'be fitting' 5.97
RISE 12.115
RISE *up*, UPRISE 12.92, 12.103
ROB 6.19
RUE 5.3–5 = 5.73–5, 5.7, 5.46, 5.50, 5.59, 5.76, 5n4a, 11.65
RUN 12.90, 13.76
satisfying PRES PTCP 13.15
SAY 4.7, 5.2, 6.25, 8.1b = 8.30, 8.16, 8.36, 8.101, 8.126, 8.127, 8.176, 9.149, 9.151, 10n8a, 11.15, 11.16, 12.40, 12.41, 13.60, 13.61, 14.3
SCOFF 14.72
SCORN 13.94
SCRAMBLE (*under*) 7.27
SEE 4.11, 8.11, 8.18, 8.59, 8.61, 8.63, 8.122, 8.144, 8.174, 8.192, 8n12a, 9.42, 9.43, 9.45, 9.54, 12.30, 12.48, 12.100, 13.18, 13.82, 13.84, 15.9, 15.13, 15.31
SEE *through* 7.109
SEEK *ymbe* 7.72
SEEM 5.23, 5.58, 5n17a, 9.2, 9.6, 9.17, 9.22, 9.24, 9.25, 9.28, 9.29, 9.31, 9.34, 9.35, 9.37–41, 9.148, 9.157, 9.158, 9.175, 9.178

SELL   6n2a, 6n13a, 13.121

SEND, ASEND   5.80, 6.22, 6.35, 8.140, 8.171

SEND, OFSEND *after*   7.13, 7.19, 7.40, 7.76

SEND *for*   7.77, 7.79

SET   12.23

SET *fire to*   7.119

SET *up*   13.114

SETTLE   14.32

SHALL   4.17, 4n13a, 9.132, 9.135, 9.136,
10.86, 11.18, 11.39, 11.40, 11.57, 11.59,
11.62–4, 11.73, 11.80, 11.88, 11.92,
11.102, 11.103, 11.105, 11.107, 11.131,
11.167, 11.178, 11.199, 11.202, 12.62,
12.63, 12.108, 13.67, 13.72, 13.75, 14.44,
14.50, 14.64, 14.70, 14.86, 14.117, 15.25,
15.26, 15.27

SHAME, (GE)SCEAMIAN   5.8, 5.49, 5.91,
5.92, 8.182, 10.88, 11.53, 11.56, 11.57

SHAPE   7.50

SHINE (*on*)   7.56 = 7n15a

SHOE   12.33

SHOOT   13.27, 14.60, 14n13a

SHOW   6.53, 6.56, 6.57

SIN   10.99, 12.45

SING   13.1, 13.109

SIT   12.4, 13.37, 13.80

SIT *by*   7.39

sitting PRES PTCP 'suitable'   13.11

SLAY   see OFSLEAN

SMART   11.63

SNOW   5.15, 5.16

SOLACE   13.39

SORROW *ymbe*   7.52

SPEAK, SPRECAN   4.9, 13.58, 15.11

SPEAK *of*   7.12, 7.61, 7.93–5, 7.122

SPEAK *with*   7.34, 7.81

SPEAK *ymbe*   7.45

SPIT *upon*   7.26

SPOIL   4.3, 4n5a

SPOWAN 'succeed'   11.59

STAND   7.98, 11.140

STARE to   7.96

STARVE   4.10

STAY   15.16

STEAL   6.18, 14.87

(GE)STIERAN, STEER 'restrain'   14.35

STOP   9.125

SUFFER   8.86, 8.119

SUFFICE   5.38, 15.12

SUPPLY   14.25

SUPPOSE   8.103

SURPRISE   14.56

SWEORCAN 'darken'   5.87, 5.88

TACNIAN 'betoken'   5.89, 9.46

TAKE   4.2b, 8.8, 9.110, 14.152, 15.4, 15.35,
15n2a,b,c

TAKE *advantage of*   7.120

TAKE *for*   14.138

TAKE *heed to*   7.124

TALA *við* (Icelandic) 'speak with'   7.80

TEACH   8.78, 13.66, 13.136–9, 13n9a,b,
14.154

TEAR *out*   14.65

TELL (*to*)   6.36, 6.54, 7n9a, 8.34, 9.48, 12.5

TELL *by*   7.16

TEND   9.123, 9.124

TEND *to*   7.20

(GE)TEON 'decree'   12.52

TEON 'draw' *forth/out*   4.13, 4n11

GEÞAFIAN 'grant'   8.98

ÞEARF, THAR   'need'   10.113,   11.56,
11.65, 11.67, 11.145, 11.168

THINK   5.13, 5.33, 5.34, 5.36, 5.52, 5.56,
5.57, 5.84, 8.181, 9.20, 9.21, 9.23, 9.47,
9.133, 9.134, 9.138, 9.139, 9.143, 9.144,
9.146, 9.147, 9.155, 9.166, 11.69, 12.17,
12.109, 15.29

THINK (*evil*) *of*   7.92

THINK *on*   7.41

THIRST   5.18, 5.22, 5.28, 5.48, 11.62, 13.40

ÞOLIEN 'suffer'   8.85

THROW   13.86

ÞROWIAN 'suffer'   7.103, 13.170, 15.21

THUNDER   5.17

GETIMIAN 'happen'   11.50

timbrend N 'builder'   13.41

TINT   14.68

(GE)TIÐIAN 'grant'   6.29 = 12.18

TOGGIN (?= TUG) 'struggle amorously'
with   7.35

TONIMAN 'divide'   12.27

TOSIGAN 'wear out'   12.102

TOW   13.112

TOWEORPAN 'destroy'   4.7, 4n11

TRAIN   13.118

TRANSACT   14.84

TRUST *on*   10.91

TRUST *to*   7n15b

TRY   11.201c

TUNE   13.117

TURN (*away*)   11.67, 12.21, 14.104

TWEO(GA)N 'doubt'   5.10,   5.20,   5n5a,
10.113, 11.185, 13.90[?]

unberinde PRES PTCP 'barren'   13.9

UNDERSTAND   8.192

ungefandod PA PTCP 'not tried'   12.43

USE, USED   11.188

UTAMÆRAN 'expel'   12.24

UTON 'let us' 10.92, 11.164–6, 11.170, 11.171

VANISH 12.94

VERZOEKEN (Dutch) 'request' 6.64

VOTE *against* 7.2

WADE *over* 7.82

WANT 5.32, 8.27, 11.203, 11.205, 11.207

WARN 'forbid' 8.133 = 8.179

WAX 'grow' 13.88

WEAR 13.119

WEEN 'think' 8.70, 8.101, 8.102, 13.56, 13.90[?]

WEEP 5.92

WELL 13.13

WHISPER 14.163

GEWIDERIAN 'be fine weather' 11.51

WILL 4.1b, 9.133, 9.134, 9.138, 11.3, 11.5, 11.10, 11.17, 11.19, 11.41, 11.54, 11.69, 11.70, 11.75, 11.77, 11.79, 11.83, 11.84, 11.90, 11.91, 11.95, 11.97, 11.99, 11.100, 11.110–13, 11.121, 11.128, 11.169, 11.197, 11.215, 11n13b, 12.61, 14.48, 14.49, 14.62, 14.72, 14.76, 14.86, 14.116, 15.7, 15.16, 15.20, 15.23

WILNIAN 'desire' 15.27

WIN 'contend' *again(st)* 7.31

WISH 13.44

WIT 'know' 8.66, 8.67, and cf. 10.16

GEWITAN 'depart' 12.101

gewitende PRES PTCP 'transitory' 13.8, 13.42

WITHDRAW 12.120

WIÐWINNAN 'oppose' 13.46

WITNESS 8.73

WLAT 'disgust' 11.70

WONDER *(up)on* 7.17, 7.57

WONT, GEWUNIAN 'be accustomed' 9.126–31, 9n1a

WORK 13.71, 13n7a, 14.147

WORSHIP 13.94

WRECAN 'avenge' 13.55

WRITE 13.28, 13.95, 13.162–5

WUNIAN 'dwell' 13.12, 13.52, 13.63

WURTHE, (GE)WEORÐAN 'become, happen' 5.12, 11.189, 12.15, 12.16, 12.20, 12.22, 12.110, 13.77, 13.78, 14.13, 14.17–19, 14.35, 14.36, 14.40, 14.41, 14.49, 14.50, 14.57–9, 15.6

YIELD 13.25

YMBSELLAN 'surround' 14.14

YMBSETTAN 'surround' 14.19

YOKE 14.142

General index

Index entries are intended to be helpful rather than exhaustive. (The references and texts are each separately indexed under Secondary and Primary sources, respectively.)

Page numbers in **_bold italics_** refer to definitions in the Glossary.

abduction 44, 54, **_475_**
accusative cum infinitive _see_ VOSI
actional 156, 281, 290, 361, 365, 377, 407, 414–15, 417–19, 421, 423, 438
adjacency 32, 55, 86, 150, 162, 212, 214, 269, 276, 285, 334, 341, 431
Agent, Agentive NP, agent-phrase 17, 83, 116, 140, 144, 161, 166, 169, 207, 217, 219, 234, 247, 343, 390, 392, 415, 423, 438, 442–4
agentive VP 273, 280, 342–3
Aktionsart 281, 288, 290, 367, 370, 399, **_475_**
ambiguity 42, 48, 75, 79, 88–9, 117, 121, 190, 210, 212, 217, 260, 288, 338, 342, 345, 392, 421, 438–9
analogy 45, 76, 96, 149, 199, 209, 213, 249, 281, 364, 402, 406
anaphora ~ cataphora 40, 52, 61, 75, 79, 88–90, 97, 115, 144, 167, 226, 256, 260–4, 271, 276–7, **_475_**
animacy 62, 80, 91, 100–1, 107, 113, 144, 147, 173–4, 208, 228, 233–4, 236–8, 244–6, 299, 390, 396, 407, 421
anticipative, cataphoric _see_ anaphora
apodosis ~ protasis 293, 297, 312–14, 355, 451, **_475_**
apposition 65, 101, 206, 260–2, 277, 372, 379
argument xi, 19–20, 53, 59, 61, 66, 86, 156, 163, 166–7, 180, 188, 216, 218, 233, 240, 243, 246, 248, 280, 331, 396, 422, **_475_**

aspect 281, 340, 399, 406–7, **_475_**
aspectual verb 219, 234–6, 238, 247–8, 339, 361, 397
auxiliary, auxiliation xi, 55, 102, 143, 195, 212, 215, 217, 219–20, 247, 253–471, 519

Benefactive 103–23, 140, 156, 158–9, 161, 422
blend 70, 76, 118, 138, 183, 224, 241, 281, 296, 322, 338, 342, 358, 401, 407, 412, 451–2

calque 10, 275, 398, 402, **_475_**
case 16–23, 46, 63, 104–6, 113–15, 118–19, 138, 179, 199, 213, 245–6, 258, 350, 399–400
Case Filter, Case Theory 101, 149, 158–9, 200, **_475_**
cataphora _see_ anaphora
catenative 163–251, 280, 354, **_476_**, 519
causative 114, 121, 172–5, 180, 193–7, 202–3, 207–11, 215, 217, 256–60, 271, 274, 278, 280, 283, 289–90, 342–3, 348, 386, 464
Cause 62–101, 160
CD-ROM _see_ computer
Celtic 139, 275–6, 281–3, 290, 401–3, 418
chi-square test 467, 471, **_476_**
child language _see_ language acquisition

CLAN-sentence 169, 206, 242
clitic 23, 33, 51–2, 55–6, 58, 100, 149, 160, 293, 309, 322–3, 335, 337, 345, 366, 449, 462–3, 469, 476
colligation 405, *476*
collocation 117, 124, 141, 290, 340, 376, 382, 385, 445, *476*
commutation 65, 167, 171, 188, 215, 314, 318, 320, 334, 352, 385, 421, *476*
COMP, complementiser 36–8, 50, 58, 144–5, 147, 149–50, 161, 200, 334, 463, *476*
compound verb 135–9, 160, 281, 399–400
computer 3, 5, 7, 13, 338, 444, 457
conclusive perfect 342–4, 348, 358, 364–6
conspiracy 248, 332, 335, *476*
constituent, constituency 124, 148, 183, 205, 325, 369, 372–4, 445, *476*
construction *476*
contiguity *see* adjacency
contraction 283, 309, 335, 357, 369, 449
control, control verb 52, 96, 114, 148, 163, 167, 171, 197, 212, 234, 240, 246–8, 290, 326, 333, 452, *476*, and *see* VOSI
coordination 34, 48, 89–90, 189, 214, 245, 267, 283, 346–7, 350, 360, 378–9, 392
creole *see* language contact

deep structure, D-Structure 18, 35, 79, 81, 103, 123, 329, *476*
deixis 20, *476*
deontic 293, 329–30, 333–4, 338–9
diachrony ix–x, 58, 120, 216
dialectal variation 9, 12, 105, 110, 264, 270, 275, 277–8, 281–3, 290, 294, 317, 342, 348, 383, 388, 403, 418
direct object 31, 156, 184, 276, 306–7, 327, 329, 331, 336, 340–1, 349, 374–6, 404–5, 413, 459, 461–2
discourse 4, 15, 49, 98, 322, 464
doubled auxiliary, verb 259, 294, 328, 337, 356–7, 363, 435–6, 446–7, 455
dummy auxiliary *see* periphrastic DO, GAN
dummy subject 61, 66, 79, 83, 96–100, 109, 167, 169–70, 197, 226, 232–3, 244, 427, 432, 445
Dutch 8, 28–9, 49, 52, 58, 114, 135, 146, 150, 282, 284, 320, 353
dynamic *see* actional
dynamic modality 293, 296, 325

easy construction *see* *Tough*-Movement
ellipsis 127–9, 141, 189–92, 272, 305, 338, 408

emphasis 266–8, 274, 278, 399
empty category 147, 149, 280, *476*
enclitic *see* clitic
epistemic 238, 293, 295, 298–303, 311, 327–30, 333–5, 339
Equi *see* control
ergative 390, 392–3, 408, 438, 442, *477*
error 118, 134, 224, 246, 265, 284, 323, 342, 377, 390
exbraciation *see* sentence brace
exceptional clause 170–1, 220, *477*
Experiencer 17, 62–102, 140, 144, 231–6, 239–40, 242–5, 295, 343
Extraposition 38–9, 45, 52, 109, 238, 328, 337, *477*

factitive DO 256, 276, 279
Floating 58
French 11, 49, 76, 87, 111, 115, 196, 203, 213, 249, 279, 353, 364, 366, 388, 402–3, 450
futurity 304, 405–6, 418–19

German 8, 28–9, 42, 49, 52, 87, 135, 213, 275, 282, 286, 353
Germanic 8, 10, 15, 39, 42, 194, 201, 283, 286, 365, 369, 397
gerund 386, 396, 403–4, 409
Goal 86, 106–7, 121, 140, 161, 166, 216
govern, government 81–2, 87, 150, 159, 171, 331–2
Government-Binding (GB) Theory 6, 18, 50–3, 80–2, 96, 215–17, 338, 452–3, 464, *477*
grammaticisation 330, 340, 352–4, 360–1, 363, 378, 407, 422–3, 426, 440–3, 454, 469
group-verb 108, 110, 117, 121–2, 155, 158, 519 and *see* phrasal verb

habitual 282–3, 288, 323
Halliday 56
Heavy-NP Shift 38–9, 52–3, 152, 212–13, *477*
Helsinki Corpus 3, 13–14, 465
higher ∼ lower clause, verb 65, 74, 165–218, 231, 303, 321, 452, *477*, 519
hypercorrection 117, 120, 321

Icelandic *see* Scandinavian
idiom 212, 318–19, 387, 433, 467
imperative 267–9, 274, 318–20, 363
impersonal 61–102, 104, 108–9, 114–15, 119, 140, 158, 184, 186–7, 219, 221, 223–4, 231–2, 235–6, 243, 248–9, 258, 261,

270–1, 285, 287, 303, 314–15, 317, 321–2, 331, 345, 368–9, 422–3, 455

implicational hierarchy   27, 45, 207, 283, *477*

inchoative   322, 370, 399, 421

indefinite pronoun, subject   116, 122, 136

indirect object   31, 41–2, 103–23, 156

indirect passive   103–23, 139–40, 289, 369, 415

Indo-European   8, 10, 41, 87, 150, 397

INFL, I   38, 50, 57–8, 200, 331–4, 463–4

inflection *see* morphology

Instrument   17, 161, 415, 444

interrogative   40, 45, 265–6, 367, 448, 459

inversion   32, 49, 255, 265, 293, 328–9, 448, 453, 459–60, 468

isogloss   387, *477*

knock-out factor   49, 367

Labov   xii

landing site   37–8, 144, 161, *477*

language acquisition   49–50, 283–5

language contact   10–11, 49–50, 281–3, 290, and *see* individual languages

language typology   27–8, 87, 138

Latin   9–11, 13, 96, 141, 175–6, 182, 185, 193–4, 199–204, 206–9, 211, 221–2, 225, 243, 257, 279, 283, 288, 369, 382, 397–400, 403

lexeme   5, 15, *477*

lexical diffusion   141, 159, 209, 330

lexical entry   80, 82, 90–1

Lexical-Functional Grammar (LFG)   6, 88–91, 112, 119–20

lexicalisation   117

lexical ~ transformational passive   155–6

localism   19, 86, 438, *478*

lower clause, verb *see* higher

marked *see* unmarked

meaning change *see* semantic change

medio-passive   392–3, 408

methodology   x, 3–4, 39, 80, 204, 207

modal   51, 212, 224, 236, 238–9, 270, 281, 286, 292–339, 357, 447, 449, 466–7

morphology
    nominal   16–23, 42, 73, 75, 82, 87–8, 104–6, 113, 136, 156, 341, 346–8, 359–60, 364, 416–17, 445
    verbal   10, 13, 113, 121, 275, 277, 289, 292–3, 296–7, 315–16, 327, 331–2, 334, 336–7, 357, 397, 421, 438

mutative   359, 366, 368–9, 415, 426

negation   14, 45, 48, 255, 265, 268–9, 293, 309, 323, 328–9, 367, 448–52, 458–9, 463, 470

neutralisation   17, 74, 82, 104, 277, 346, 366, 456

NICE properties *see* operator

nominalisation   386, 404

NP Movement, NP Preposing, Move NP   65, 81, 151–2, 158, 220, 236, 249–50, *478*

null hypothesis   467, *478*

Object raising   167, 169–70, 184, 197, 200–1, 205–6, 225

operator   41, 255, 268, 283, 285, 288, 293, 297, 309, 315, 317, 323–5, 343, 422, 443, 448, 451, 466–8, *478*

paradigm   20, 269–70, 281, 309–11, 317, 337, 354–5, 361–3, 383–4, 397, 423–37, *478*

particle   36–7, 42, 50, 57, 136, 138–9, 141, 153–5, 160, 410, *478*, 519

passival   389–93, 407–10, 415, 428, 430–1, 442

passive   92–3, 103–64, 342–6, 395, 413–45, 447, 454

Path   141

Patient   18, 102, 111, 140, 161, 343, 413

perception verb   51, 168–9, 175, 193–4, 196–9, 202, 207–9, 211, 215, 217, 242, 386

perfect   49, 93, 340–70, 407, 423, 425–8, 434–6, 446–7, 454–5

perfective   194–5, 280–2, 288, 290, 400, 407, 440

periphrastic DO   143, 195, 253–91, 297, 322–3, 329, 335–6, 407, 446, 451, 457–71

periphrastic GAN   322

phonological, phonotactic   42, 416, 427, 462, 464–6, 476, 479

phrasal verb   36, 55, 137–9, 143, 153–5, 160, 285, 404

pied piping   125, 133–4, 137, 144, 147

place, valency   63, 66–73, 80, 103, 113–15, 216 and 165–217 *passim*, 218, 244, 280, 321, 325, 327–8, 342, *478*

post-verbal ellipsis   255, 272, 287, 293, 307, 423, 455–7

Pred, predicative, predicative complement   45–6, 48, 183–4, 193, 198–9, 203, 206–7, 211, 215, 221, 223, 242, 420, 441–2, *478*

prefix   281, 285, 399–400, 412, 414

preposition   17, 57, 105, 115, 179, 387–9, 391–2, 401–2, 433

prepositional passive   124–62, 415, 436

prescriptive grammar *see* stigmatised form
preterite-present 296, 318, 327, 335, 338–9, 449
primitive 157, *478*
PRO, pro 149, 167, 171, 205, 212, 217, 234, 280, 290, 326, 328, 333, 452, *478*
proclitic *see* clitic
progressive 283, 311, 371–412, 415, 423, 428–33, 436–7, 440–3, 447, 465
pronominal, pronoun 10, 20, 22–3, 31, 33, 40, 47–9, 51–2, 54–6, 83, 117, 120, 122, 146–7, 462, 469
protasis *see* apodosis
Proto-Germanic *see* Germanic
prototype 96, 335, 393
pseudogapping 272, 287, 456–7

Quantifier Floating 90, 358, *479*, and *see* Floating
quasi-ellipsis 141–3

Raising, Subject raising 78, 87, 157, 187, 205, 218–51, 295, 327–8, 332, 423, 456, *479*
reanalysis 74–80, 87–8, 113, 115, 117, 119–20, 122, 124, 135, 140, 150–3, 162, 179, 243–6, 277, 281, 290, 332–3, 340, 363–5, 407, 414, 442, 453, 463
Recipient 83, 93, 102–3, 111, 166, 169, 171, 181, 216
reflexive 88, 167, 236, 321, 363–4, 408
register 3–4, 13, 112, 116–17, 120, 160, 203, 211, 215, 228, 274, 279, 281, 288–9, 323, 401, 411, 420–1, 428, 439, 458, 461, 464
regulation of DO 143, 442, 446, 448–52, 457–71
Relational Grammar 21–2, 155–7
relative clause, pronoun 45–6, 49, 130–3, 135, 139, 144–9, 161, 207
rhythm 39, 379
root clause 46, 57
root modality 293, 295, 303–4, 329, 332
Rosch 287, 335, 457

S, S' 161, 170, 220, 250–1, 339, 477, *479*
S-curve 330, 336, 368, 452, 462–3
S'-deletion 170, 200, 249
Scandinavian 8, 10–11, 42, 49, 58–9, 87, 102, 125, 140, 145, 159, 197, 215, 242
Scots 270, 275, 294, 309, 406–7, 409
second passive 167, 184, 187, 191–2, 194, 207, 215, 224–7, 242–3, 415
semantic change 75, 278–80, 289, 303–4,

315–16, 322, 330, 364–5, 386, 423, 438, 441
sentencé brace, *Satzklammer* 42–4, 48–9, 54, 58, 341, 348
Seppänen 241–2
sequence of tenses, backshifting 294, 338
serial relationship 92, 95–6
significant 466–7, 470–1, *479*
sisters 36, 86, 328, *479*
small clause 183, 220, 369, *479*
social network 152–3, 443
Source 62, 86–7, 166, 216
'Standard Average European' 125, 255, 293, 344
statal, stative 156, 281, 283, 290, 341, 343, 358, 361, 365–6, 395, 407, 414, 418–19, 437
statistics 28, 32, 40, 92, 96, 367, 399, 458, 464
stigmatised form 14, 110, 112, 120, 284, 286, 288, 356, 366, 391, 428, 451
Stimulus 140, 144, 160–1
stranding 124–5, 131–5, 138–9, 144–51
strong ~ weak 10, 12–13, 296, 337, *479*
subcategorisation (frame) 83, 89, 94–5, 179, 210, 332, *479*
subject 61, 74, 79, 84–5, 87–8, 90
subjectless 66, 81 and 61–102 *passim*, 190, 231, 241, 299–303, 338
Subject raising *see* Raising
subjunctive 10, 34, 181–2, 211, 313, 320, 324, 330–4, 338–9, 367
subordinate clause 27–58, 82, 99, 204, 216, 220, 325–7, 407, 443, 466
substitute DO 271–4, 278, 283, 286–7, 290–1, 376–7, 456, 470
substratum 275, 282, 290, 402
suppletive 324, 418, *479*
surface structure, S-Structure 18, 35, 79, 245, 331–2, *479*
synchrony ix–x, 58, 96, 120, 216
syncretism 20, 113, 117, 139, *480*
syntagm 110, 124, 317, 340–1, 371, 379, 394–5, 426, 439, 445, 453, *480*

tense 266, 278, 282–3, 294, 309, 312–15, 323, 327, 330, 337, 352–4, 365–6, 368, 406, 419
text type 3–4, 13, 96, 116, 160, 203, 209, 211, 264, 279–80, 282, 407, 428, 460–1, 464, 466
thematic (θ) dependent, grid, relation, role 18, 80–1, 83, 86, 149, 162, 170, 331–2, 438, *480*

theme, thematic structure   29, 40, 48–9,
    77–8, 99, 101, 120
Theme   63–5, 83–5, 100–1, 103–23, 166,
    216, 231–2, 242, 244, 295, 413, 477
To Be Deletion   221, 240
topic, Topicalisation   29–30, 41–5, 52, 56–7,
    79, 82, 88, 106, 113, 115–17, 119–20, 122,
    132–3, 147–8, 207, 212, 241, 284
Tough-Movement   149, 151–3, 187, 219,
    480
trace   79, 147, 152, 478, ***480***
Transformational Generative Grammar
    78–9, 103, 155–7, 225, 325–6
transitivity   63, 82, 93, 95, 105, 115, 119,
    138, 144, 211, 329, 340–1, 346, 350–1,
    363–4, 367, 410, 413, 422, 442, 461
Transparency Principle, transparency   79,
    101, 156, 328–9, 337
transparency to argument   235–6, 287, 331,
    335, 352, 422–3, 455
type (i)-(iii) impersonal   64–102, 219, 221,
    231, 235, 295, 321

unbounded   148, ***480***
underlying structure *see* deep structure
unmarked   22, 27–8, 30, 32–3, 39, 50, 212,
    449, 461, ***480***
unreality   293, 312–14, 336–7, 355–8, 367–8,
    427–8

V+I   165–217, 223, 257–8, 278–81, 452
vagueness   260, 279–80, 288

variable   4, 403, ***480***
variationist   3, 49, 367, 464
verb conjunction   94, 105, 124, 127–9, ***480***
verb final, verb late, V-F   29–30, 34, 36,
    39–40, 42, 50, 52, 54, 81, 135, 209–10,
    325, 452
verb first, V–1   28, 30, 32, 39, 43, 47–8, 51,
    100
verb second, V–2   28–58, 82, 97–100, 325,
    327, 334, 337, 448, 453
verb phrase conjunction   100, 119, 245, ***480***
Verb raising, V-raising   52, 208, 236,
    321–2, 333, 337, 453–4
verb third, V–3   28–30, 32, 35, 44, 47,
    54–5, 97, 143, 209–10, 461
voice-neutrality   295, 408–9
volitional   82–3, 85, 96, 421
VOSI   165–217, 224–5, 242–3, 256–8,
    279–81, 331, 383, and *see* control

weak *see* strong
weight   40–1, 48, 53–4, 56, 419, 468
Wh Fronting, Movement, pronoun   144,
    146, 148, 150, 152–3, 212, 241, 448
word order   11, 25–58, 75, 82, 87, 96, 110,
    115, 119–20, 122, 139, 143, 149, 208–10,
    212, 215, 239, 325–7, 341, 343, 348, 419,
    452–3
written language   9, 11–13, 15, 112, 265,
    269, 283, 288, 409

X-bar theory   339, ***480***